Biblical Commentary
on
the New Testament

By

Dr. Hermann Olshausen

Professor of Theology in the University of Erlangen.

Translated from the German
For Clark's Foreign and Theological Library.

First American Edition,
Revised After the Fourth German Edition,

by

A.C. Kendrick, D.D.,

Professor of Greek in the University of Rochester.

To Which is Prefixed Olshausen's
Proof of the Genuineness of the Writings of the New Testament
Translated by David Fosdick, Jr.

Volume I

Truth
Publications

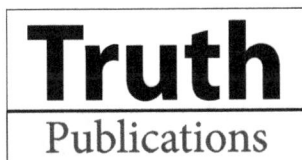

Taking His hand,
Helping each other home.
TM

ISBN 10: 1-58427-094-2

ISBN 13: 978-1-58427-094-2

Truth Publications, Inc.
CEI Bookstore
220 S. Marion St., Athens, AL 35611
855-492-6657
sales@truthpublications.com
www.truthbooks.com

TABLE OF CONTENTS.

FIRST PART.

OF THE BIRTH AND CHILDHOOD OF JESUS CHRIST.

MATTHEW i. ii.; LUKE i. ii.

FIRST SECTION.

MATTHEW'S ACCOUNT.—Chaps. i. ii.

SECOND SECTION.

LUKE'S ACCOUNT.—Chaps. i. ii.

SECOND PART.

OF JOHN THE BAPTIST.—CHRIST'S BAPTISM AND TEMPTATION.

MATTHEW iii. 1, iv. 12; MARK i. 2–13; LUKE iii. 1, iv. 13.

THIRD PART.

OF CHRIST'S WORKS AND DISCOURSES, PARTICULARLY IN GALILEE.

MATTHEW iv. 12, xviii. 35; COMPARED WITH MARK i. 14, ix. 50; AND LUKE iv. 14, ix. 50.

PART IV.

OF CHRIST'S LAST JOURNEY TO JERUSALEM, AND CERTAIN INCIDENTS
WHICH TOOK PLACE THERE.

LUKE ix. 51, xxi. 38; MATTHEW xix. 1, xxv. 46; MARK x. 1, xiii. 37.

ORDER OF THE SECTIONS OF THE GOSPELS IN VOLUME I.

ARRANGED AFTER EACH GOSPEL.

ST. MATTHEW.

ST. MARK.

ST. LUKE.

PREFACE

TO THE AMERICAN EDITION.

THE general character and merits of Olshausen's Commentary on the New Testament are too well known both abroad and at home to need being set forth in detail. In its combination of exact philological learning, careful tracing of the logical connexion and full unfolding of the thought, and hearty sympathy with the spirit of the sacred writings, it stands almost alone, having nothing fully corresponding to it in our own or any language. This union of rare and high excellences makes it almost equally valuable to the scholar, and the unlearned but intelligent student of the Scriptures. The latter finds the richest veins of thought opened, and Scripture truth unfolded in its depth and spirituality ; while the former finds the leading critical and philological points discussed, briefly indeed, but with a judgment and accuracy which furnish the best guarantee for the soundness of the rich doctrinal and practical teachings that are based upon them. A striking feature and excellence of the Commentary, is its clear and constant recognition of the organic unity of the entire Scriptures, and hence its constant illustration of the New Testament from the Old. Beyond, perhaps, the majority of commentators, Olshausen has traced the gradual unfolding of the divine revelation through its successive stages. He sees the New Testament rooted in the Old, the Old reaching its consummation in the New ; and he is eminently felicitous in employing the beautiful and blended lights which the two grand divisions of the sacred volume reciprocally cast upon each other.

His Commentary, in its English dress, has been for some years before the public, as part of the valuable series of works comprised in Clark's Foreign and Theological Library. It has been received with general and steadily-growing favor. The. present publishers, therefore, deemed that they might subserve the interests both of sacred learning and practical piety in making it, by an American edition, more accessible to the American public : and this the more, as the enterprise would enable them to add materially to the value of the English work. It was with great diffidence that the editor undertook the supervision of the work ; and he would have shrunk from it altogether had he foreseen the amount of labor which its execution would involve. It will be proper to specify briefly the improvements which have been attempted in the American edition.

1. Since the death of Olshausen, a new and thoroughly revised edition of his Commentary on the Gospels has been published by Dr. Ebrard, his pupil, friend, and successor in the theological chair at Erlangen. The general character of Ebrard's alterations is stated by himself in the accompanying preface. He has performed his work with judgment and fidelity. Without modifying the general character of Olshausen's work, he has greatly improved it by correcting errors, retrenching superfluities, striking out objectionable passages, and adding much valuable matter by way of illustration or correction. This (fourth German) edition has been adopted as the basis of the present edition, and been scrupulously followed throughout. The public has thus access to the latest and much improved German edition of the work.

2. Apart from these modifications, the translation itself has been subjected to a careful revision by a close and constant comparison with the original. Of the English work the editor would not speak in terms of unjust disparagement. It evinces fidelity and industry, and is in parts nearly unexceptionable. As a whole, however, it is marred by serious defects, sometimes mistaking, sometimes obscuring, and sometimes even directly reversing the sense of the original, and elsewhere injured by an awkward and unidiomatic style. The editor, therefore, has gone through the work sentence by sentence, correcting errors, clearing up obscurities, pruning redundancies, and, so far as might be, rendering the style more neat and idiomatic. He is aware that his work is but imperfectly accomplished ; but in regard to the more essential qualities of a version, viz., accuracy and clearness, he feels assured that the work will not be materially wanting. The nature and extent of his alterations will perhaps be best illustrated by a few examples. We present in parallel columns the two versions, confining our selections to the present volume.

EDINBURGH EDITION.

Vol. I. p. 4. The life of Jesus presented such a fulness of the most varied appearances, and his discourses breathed so rich a stream of life upon the circle of his disciples, that single individuals were incapable of adequately comprehending the exceeding grandeur of his character. In Him there was revealed something that surpassed the power of single human individuals to apprehend.

AMERICAN EDITION.

Page 137. The life of Jesus presented itself in so manifold a variety of aspects; his discourses poured upon his disciples so rich a stream of life, that any single individual was utterly incapable of apprehending the overwhelming fulness of his character. In him were disclosed elements which no single set of human faculties was adequate to grasp.

Vol. I. p. 12. As in the Saviour, the λόγος was manifested in a σῶμα, so in a comprehensive delineation of the life of Jesus, the popular and temporal element in his manifestation must appear vividly associated with the apprehension of its spiritual import.

Page 144. As in the Saviour, the λόγος, Word, was manifested in a σῶμα, body, so, in a comprehensive delineation of his life, along with the spiritual, the national and temporal elements of his character required to be livingly set forth.

Vol. II. Matt. xiv. 13, p. 163, note. De Wette thinks that Luke places this feeding in a different locality from Matthew and Mark; he knows nothing of a passage across the sea, and conceives Bethsaida to have been on the western shore.

Page 576, note. De Wette thinks that Luke places this feeding in a different locality from Matthew and Mark; that he knows nothing of a passage across the sea, and refers to the Bethsaida on the western shore

Vol. II. Matt. xii. 37, p 101. But the more that the word has reference to spiritual things, the more punishable becomes the abuse of it: yea, it is even the word, as the manifestation of what is in man, in which the whole nature of man is revealed.

Page 465. And the deeper the significance of speech, the more culpable its abuse; nay, in speech, as the expression of the soul, is man's entire character revealed.

Vol. II. Matt. xiv. 22, p. 169. For it is not so much an interposed influence brought to bear on nature, that is here spoken of (viz. in Christ's walking on the sea)—the special difficulty in this case consists in his withdrawing himself personally from the control of earthly natural laws.

Page 521. For we have here not so much an influence brought to bear on nature, as a personal withdrawal from the control of earthly natural laws, here, viz., that of gravity.

Vol. II. Mark xv. 7, p.178. In the next place, the καὶ οὐ introduces the supplementary remark—"and if any one says, Your property is consecrated to the temple, it is then unnecessary for him to honour his father and his mother."

Page 528. In the next place, the καὶ οὐ introduces the answering clause (the apodosis of the proposition):—" if any one says, What would have been yours is consecrated to the temple, he need not (οὐ μὴ, he shall not) honour father and mother."

EDINBURGH EDITION.

AMERICAN EDITION.

Vol. II. p. 194. Then although ζύμη is immediately explained at Matt. xvi. 12, as διδαχή, yet this is not to be looked on apart from the whole circumstances amidst which it stands; for, outwardly considered, there was much truth in the doctrine of the Pharisees.

Page 542. Since although ζύμη, *leaven*, is immediately explained at Matt. xvi. 12, as διδαχή, *doctrine*, yet this is not to be regarded separately from their entire moral condition; for, outwardly considered, there was much truth in the doctrine of the Pharisees.

Vol. II. p, 201. The representation thus given exhibits the earthly and the heavenly as united in the church. Inasmuch as heavenly powers are acting within the church, it is not dissevered by its perfected organs from the heavenly, rather has it its sanction in the heavenly.

Page 548. This representation exhibits an earthly and heavenly character and functions as united in the church. Controlled by heavenly powers, the acts of its earthly agents bear not merely human impress and authority, but have their sanction in heaven.

Vol. II. p. 209, Matt. xvii. 1. At the outset we summarily reject those views which reduce the fact itself to a dream, or an optical delusion, and we deal in the same way with the views as to thunder and lightning and passing mists which some would substitute for the voice of God, and the light-cloud.

Page 555. At the outset, we summarily reject those views which reduce the fact itself to a dream or an optical delusion; views in which thunder, lightning, and passing mists take the place of the voice of God and the cloud of light.

Vol. II. p. 236, ch. xviii. 5. The simplest explanation is that this description of it is occasioned by the preceding admonition (set forth clearly by Matt.) to enter into the kingdom of God.

Page 577. The simplest explanation is, that this form of description is occasioned by the preceding mention (made distinctly by Matt.) of entering into the kingdom of God.

Vol. III. p. 3, Luke xii. 50. He counsels therefore that they should without delay unite with their enemies.

He counsels therefore that they should in season become reconciled to their adversary.

These specimens have been taken almost at random, and they might be multiplied by hundreds, and in minor matters by thousands, even within the compass of the first two volumes. They will show the imperative need of a careful revision of the work.

3. It was the wish of the publishers to make the work more widely useful by a translation into English of the numerous Greek words and phrases scattered through the text. The Commentary of Olshausen is based on the original; its citations are made almost invariably from the original; and its criticisms and explanations are of course founded immediately upon the Greek text. The work is

thus designed primarily and almost exclusively for scholars. This its scholastic character the editor has felt it his duty fully to retain, and to make all his modifications in subserviency to this. He has, therefore, while translating the Greek words and phrases occurring in the text, retained the original, except in cases where it had been already once or twice given, or where nothing whatever was dependent on its retention. He has then (as, for example, where πίστις, δικαιοσύνη, ὁ υἱὸς τοῦ θεοῦ, etc., occurred with no peculiarity of meaning, and merely interrupting the flow of the English sentence) silently replaced them by their English equivalents. This process might, perhaps, have been advantageously carried much farther, but the editor preferred erring in this respect rather in deficiency than in excess. In the purely philological and critical remarks, which have value only for scholars, he has of course rarely added the translations. In his renderings he has generally adhered to the language of the common version. When this was inconvenient, he has unhesitatingly deviated from it.

4. The editor hardly ventures to add as another advantage of this edition the brief notes which he has himself here and there interspersed through the volume. Annotating the Commentary formed no part of his original purpose. But in proceeding he could scarcely resist the impulse here and there to express his dissent from the particular expositions of Olshausen, and especially in what he deems some serious errors of doctrine he has felt bound to do so. With a general soundness of judgment, and a warm sympathy with evangelical truth, Olshausen is yet not free from the characteristic faults of his countrymen. He speculates sometimes with a subtlety and sometimes with a mysticism characteristically German, and sometimes bends philology to the support of the favourite heresies of the German theologians. The editor has, therefore, both in minor and more important matters, occasionally added a note (signed K.) expressing his dissent. This he has generally done with the utmost brevity, choosing rather to suggest than elaborately argue the grounds of his opinion. The desire of brevity must be his apology for the dogmatical air which may occasionally characterize the notes. Of course it will not be understood that he has commented on all from which he dissented. He has introduced no modifications into the text, except that in two or three instances he has silently corrected an error in lexicography.

With these remarks the editor submits the present volume to the public. The remaining volumes will follow, it is hoped, at no long intervals. If they shall subserve the interests of evangelical truth, the deep love of which has evidently inspired their author, the highest aim of the editor and the publishers will have been attained.

A. C. KENDRICK.

ROCHESTER, August, 1856.

AUTHOR'S PREFACE.

THE plan and arrangement of this work, notwithstanding many alterations and additions in the details, remain essentially the same in this new edition of the Commentary, since I think I may take it for granted that, in these points, I have met the wants of our times. I regard it as my chief object to bring out the inward unity of the whole New Testament, and of the Scriptures generally, and, by the interpretation, to introduce the reader to the unity of life and spirit in the Sacred Books. To have been continually noticing interpretations which originate in entirely remote views, as well as to have been constantly opposing unchristian tendencies, would have rendered it impossible to enter into the spirit of the Bible, since in that way the flow of the spirit would necessarily have been interrupted. Exegetical lectures have to supply what is necessary in reference to the enumeration of different interpretations, to the refutation of errors, to grammar, archæology, and history.

Hence it naturally follows, that, in this third edition, such lately published works as Strauss' Life of Jesus, and De Wette's Commentary (who professes to agree with Strauss in the principles, but would prefer a less extensive application of them, which is, indeed, evidently inconsistent, as Strauss has very justly demonstrated in reply to him, see "*Berliner Jahrbücher*," 1837, No. 1, ff.), could not be noticed by me, so far as there is a difference of principles between their authors and myself. In those passages where that difference was not involved, I have not omitted to notice these works also, but have used them as well as treatises more congenial to my own mind, among which I mention particularly Tholuck's masterly exposition on the Sermon on the Mount, in order by strict impartiality to gather with ever-increasing purity the sense of the Word of God. Still it was very rarely that I gained any light from the works of Strauss and De Wette, even as to the externals of Scripture ; while I am greatly indebted to Tholuck's labours in every respect.

Still, as the notorious work of Strauss contains a continued series of attacks on my Commentary, I avail myself of this opportunity to explain my silence with reference to these attacks.

At first, I determined to write a special work on the subject ; but the composition of it was prevented by protracted illness. Meanwhile, such a flood of refutations is being poured forth, that I cannot even begin to write down my thoughts, because every moment brings some book or pamphlet, which has already discussed first this point and then the other on which I intended to enlarge. On the other hand, not a single work appeared in favour of Strauss ; and even in the few criticisms that were somewhat favourable, nothing new whatever was brought forward in confirmation of his view. All parties in the theological world are unanimous in the rejection of his work. This being the state of affairs, the danger to theology from Strauss' work may, we hope, be regarded as removed ; among the laity, indeed, it will do the more mischief. Of course science is not to expect thus to be freed from the conflict ; for even though the inapplicability of the mythical interpretation to the New Testament has been evidently demonstrated, yet heroes will soon arise to call our courageous and unprejudiced Strauss a cowardly poltroon, full of superstitious assumptions, because instead of venturing to speak out plainly, he only now and then gently hints that Christianity and the books of the New Testament are to him simply the product of unbounded fanaticism, or, to speak more decidedly, of a monstrous deception. As Dr. Paulus at first propounded his natural explanation of the miracles amid loud rejoicing, and now sees it turned to ridicule by Strauss, who stands upon his shoulders, a similar result awaits the latter, with his mythical explanation. And unless we are greatly mistaken in reading the signs of the times, Strauss will not need, like his predecessor, to live to be eighty years old, in order to hear with his own ears the derision of his more decided disciples. The history of the world advances with accelerated pace. The infant Antichrist struggles powerfully in the bosom of society, and hastens to its birth. May but the Church of Christ attain more and more to a knowledge of itself, so as to be able to separate itself from all antichristian elements ; and may Christian science vigorously guard itself against the dangerous error of supposing that such excrescences of unbelief, as the hypothesis of the mythical character of the New Testament, necessarily belong to its course of development ! Such phenomena, theology ought to treat purely apologetically—i. e., in that department which defends the domain of Christian science against attacks from without ; in its inward sanctuary such formations have no place whatever.

In an apologetic point of view, I still intend to contribute something towards a refutation of the mythical system, inasmuch as I propose to myself a renewed comprehensive investigation on the genuineness of the Gospels, to which Dr. Theile of Leipsic has kindly invited me in his work recently published against Strauss. If it be proved that our canonical Gospels are the productions of eye-witnesses of the facts, the applicability of the mythical interpretation of the life of Jesus vanishes most certainly and completely, according to Strauss' own confession. If God grant life and health, I shall proceed to this recasting of my earlier work on the genuineness of the Gospels, immediately after the completion of the printing of the third edition of the second volume.

    ❊   ❊   ❊   ❊   ❊   ❊   ❊   ❊

PREFACE

TO THE FOURTH GERMAN EDITION.

It was not without a degree of apprehension that I acceded to the request of the respected publisher, to subject to a revision the sainted Olshausen's Commentary on the Gospels. On the one hand, the Commentaries of Olshausen bear an impress of such marked peculiarity that the disturbing presence of a foreign hand would be immediately recognized; on the other, I was aware that I differed so widely from my lamented teacher, not only in the interpretation of many individual passages, but even in some more fundamental views, that it seemed to me difficult, if not impossible, to steer between the opposite extremes of depriving the public of Olshausen's expositions, and of proving false to my own convictions. Finally, veneration for my ever to be remembered teacher interposed additional obstacles to any thing that looked like correction. And still I could not conceal from myself that sacred learning had within the last fifteen years made such advancement, that this Commentary, if it was to perpetuate and extend its beneficent influence, stood assuredly in need of revision. I determined, therefore, upon the work, and proceed now to state to' the reader the mode of procedure by which the proposed end might be most nearly approximated.

I have frequently substituted the more for the less precise expression. (Comp. e. g. at Matt. ii. 23. Olshausen thus: " the Evangelist has reference to that use of language which employed *Nazarene* in the sense of despised." I thus : " the Evangelist has reference to the fact that the Nazarenes were despised by the nation.") Manifest inaccuracies (e. g. in the same place the derivation of the name Ναζαρέι from נֵצֶר) have been corrected. Polemical remarks which have no importance for the present time, have been erased ; and on the contrary, here and there more recent literary notices have been appended (as at Matt. ii. 21, on the death of Herod). I have some-times abridged widely extended discussions, removed repetitions, and in like manner thrown out occasional allusions to peculiar views of Olshausen (as e. g. on the *trichotomy*), which had been fully discussed elsewhere.

The corrections thus far mentioned are manifestly of a nature which involves no change in the coloring and spirit of the Commentary. But where I have dissented from Olshausen's view *in more important points*, I have allowed his explanations to stand, and subjoined my own with the utmost possible brevity in notes signed E. at the foot of the page, or incorporated them into the text en-closed in brackets, [ ]; here and there also I have added in the latter way mere *explanations* and *expansions* of the thought (as at Matt. vii. 15). It will of course be understood that I could not *always*, but only on more important questions, append my dissenting view, and hence I hold myself answerable only for that which I have thus actually added either in the foot-notes, or the bracketed remarks.

In the order of events I differ, as is well known, widely from Olshausen. I have allowed his remarks, with their proofs, to stand unchanged, and in appropriate places have merely made a reference to my *Kritik der Evang. Geschichte*, removing only *repetitions ;* as e. g. where Olshausen after once, at Luke ix. 51, having developed his view in relation to the narrative of Christ's journey to Jerusalem (Reisebericht), then at the beginning of every new section repeats the statement that this belongs to that narrative.

By many illustrative additions (e. g. at the parable of the field with its diversities of soil, of the unjust steward, etc.), I trust that I have added to the value of the book, and rendered to its readers a real service.

May this Commentary in its present form continue to impart the same rich blessings which it has hitherto dispensed.

DR. EBRARD.

ERLANGEN, Sept. 1, 1853.

PROOF OF THE GENUINENESS

OF THE

WRITINGS OF THE NEW TESTAMENT.

FOR

INTELLIGENT READERS OF ALL CLASSES.

TRANSLATED FROM THE GERMAN OF

DR. HERMANN OLSHAUSEN,

PROFESSOR OF THEOLOGY IN THE UNIVERSITY OF ERLANGEN.

WITH NOTES,

BY DAVID FOSDICK, JR.

CONTENTS.

PREFACE BY THE TRANSLATOR.

THE author of the following treatise is known to those conversant with the theological literature of Germany, as a writer of considerable celebrity. He was born in 1796 at Oldeslohe in the
Duchy of Holstein. He received his University education partly at
Kiel and partly at Berlin. In 1822 he became theological professor
at Königsberg, in the remotest north-eastern part of the Prussian
dominions, where he remained till, in 1835, he was called to occupy
the same chair at Erlangen in Bavaria. His fame has been derived
mostly from his Commentaries, as being his most extensive productions. They are characterized by an almost utter absence of philological display, although they are far from being deficient in learning and shrewdness. The author prefers to exhibit results rather
than the processes by which they were attained. His mode of exposition is altogether more suited to common minds than the erudite, cumbrous mode pursued by most German commentators. To
use the language of Professor Stuart, "the course of thought, and
things rather than words, are his chief objects."

The little work herewith given to the public in an English dress
(published in German in 1832), is an attempt to present concisely
and simply the present state of investigation concerning the genuineness of the New Testament. I do not know of a book upon the
subject, in any language, which combines so popular a cast with so
much comprehensiveness and justness of representation as are, in
my opinion, manifested in this. The unlearned but inquisitive
Christian may here find sources of reflection and conviction respecting the truth of the record on which he relies, that are not commonly accessible without the toil of severe study.

There will of course be found in the work a tone somewhat alien
from our English views and feelings. Reference is had to religious
circumstances differing in some important respects from our own.
This peculiarity of tone, however, does not, in my opinion, involve

anything of a clearly mischievous tendency. Its influence will, I think, be useful. It is well to enlarge our minds through an acquaintance with the sentiments entertained concerning religious things by men as fully imbued with the spirit of piety as ourselves, who have been nurtured in circumstances quite different from those by which we have been affected. By comparison and inference, in such a case, we may be much benefitted.

I would not be understood as assenting, without restriction, to all the views which this little work presents. They may be right, or they may be wrong. I feel content to launch them before the public, knowing that if right they will swim, and if wrong they will eventually sink. Of this, however, I am fully convinced (as may be judged from the present version) that the book is in the main a good one ; and I believe the public will endorse my opinion.

In proceeding with the business of translation, I have been guided by the sense rather than the letter. The grammatical construction of the original has been altered whenever it was thought advisable to alter it for the sake of rendering the sense more perspicuous and natural in English. I have in one or two instances ventured to qualify an expression which seemed to me too strong, but never in any case where the change was of much importance. For instance, I have altered *inconceivable* to *hardly conceivable*, etc. I have also, in a few cases, given biblical references in addition to those furnished by the author. Many of the figures in the original references were (typographically or otherwise) erroneous, and have been corrected. Biblical quotations are presented in conformity with our received English version, instead of being translated from the German.

The notes which I have subjoined are all designated by the letters TR.

D. F., JR.

AUTHOR'S PREFACE.

SEVEN years ago, when I published my history of the Gospels, it was my earnest desire to show the genuineness of all the books of the New Testament, in a small work, designed for intelligent readers generally. But, urgent as the necessity of such a work appeared to me even then, the execution of my plan has been postponed to the present time ; partly because I was hindered from entering upon it by multiplied avocations, and partly because I hoped some one would present himself who was more capable of such an undertaking than I felt myself to be. For I knew but too well how difficult it would be for me to write simply and plainly, so as to become even intelligible to those who are not conversant with investigations of such a description as must be noticed in this work. As, however, no one has yet appeared to present such a work to the Church of Christ, and the necessity of it has meanwhile much increased, nothing remained for me but to surmount my scruples, and execute the work as well as the Lord might permit.

The necessity of such a work will have been evident to every one who has observed how certain positions as to the pretended spuriousness, or at least suspicious character, of the writings of the New Testament (positions which were formerly current only within the circle of the clergy), are now entertained among the common laity. It is easy to imagine the injury which is effected by such foolish opinions. To the audacious opponents of Divine truth they afford a fine occasion for repelling every attempt to win their assent to it ; and well-meaning persons often find in them occasion of doubts and anxiety, which they might be spared, did they only at least receive the antidote at the same time with the poison. Such an antidote, to obviate, or at least lessen, the destructive consequences of the views of many theologians in regard to the biblical books (views which are diffused abroad sometimes indiscreetly, and sometimes with a bad intention), I wish this little work to be considered.

It will, at the same time, be my endeavour to correct the views of many not very clear-sighted, though well-meaning, persons, who appear to think that all critical investigations of the genuineness or spuriousness of the books of the Bible are, as such, wrong, and take their origin from unbelief. This idea is fundamentally erroneous, and not seldom arises from a religious conceit, to which there is a special liability on the part of persons who, conscious of their own internal religious life, dispense with all enlarged views of the connection of theology with the whole church of God on earth, and nevertheless are tempted to judge of things beyond the pale of their capacity. It would have been better, therefore, had all such investigations been confined within the circle of theologians ; but, as the doubts to which we have referred have been promulgated among the laity, their refutation must also find a place in general literature.

I should very readily have extended my investigations to the writings of the Old Testament; but have not, in the first place, because the results of researches in regard to the Old Testament are of a less stable character than in regard to the New ; and, moreover, because those who are not theologians by profession have far less need of such information in regard to the Old Testament as is here given concerning the New, inasmuch as to Christians the testimony of Christ and his apostles respecting the Old Testament, the canon of which was then completed, affords a much more certain evidence of its Divine origin (and thus of its genuineness), than any historical reasoning could exhibit, especially since, from the paucity of sources of information, the latter could not be so satisfactory as it is in relation to the New Testament. As to unbelievers, it is of much greater consequence to urge the claims of the New Testament upon them than those of the Old, because, so long as they are opposed to the former, they certainly will not admit the latter. In my closing remarks, however, I have endeavoured to designate briefly the right point of view in the determination of critical questions concerning the Old Testament.

To conclude, I pray that the Lord may be pleased graciously to accompany this my book with his blessing, and cause it to serve as an admonition to many a scoffer, and to console and set at ease the minds of such as have been perplexed with doubts.

OLSHAUSEN.

INTRODUCTION.

FOR fifteen hundred years the New Testament, as we now possess it, has been generally current in the Christian church, and constantly used, as well publicly in the churches as likewise in the
domestic circles of believers. This fact is admitted by the scholars
of modern times unanimously, since it can be' shown by the most
certain historical proofs. Hence all investigations concerning the
genuineness of the writings of the New Testament and the manner
of its formation relate only to the first few centuries after the ascension of our Saviour and the death of the Apostles. Indeed, it is
easily seen that in reality everything must depend on this primitive
period ; for after the New Testament was once made up and generally admitted in the church, it could not be lost. Even before the
invention of printing, it was spread abroad in all parts of the Christian world by a multitude of copies, it being more frequently tran-
scribed than all other books together. Hence, even supposing that
the New Testament, say by war or devastation, had utterly perished
in any country, it would immediately have been introduced again
from surrounding ones. Of this, however, there is no example.
Even such churches as entirely lost connection with the great
Catholic church, and on that account sank to a very low point, yet
faithfully preserved the sacred Scriptures, as is proved by the instance of the Ethiopian church, in which, on its discovery after the
lapse of centuries, the Bible was found still in use.

From the great importance of the New Testament to the church
and the whole civilized world, it was a very natural desire on
the part of scholars to know exactly how this momentous book
was formed. On entering upon this inquiry, however, in the
perusal of the earliest writers of the church, accounts were met with
which are somewhat difficult of adjustment. It was found that even
before the compilation of all' the writings of the New Testament into
one collection, many fathers of the church, perfectly well disposed
toward Christianity, had doubted the genuineness of particular books

of the New Testament. This circumstance naturally arrested attention, and the next inquiry was, what grounds such early fathers
might have had for scruples respecting these writings. In considering this question, one thought he had discovered this reason, and
another that ; and it often happened that these reasons were considered weighty enough to justify the ancient doubts as to the genuineness of the books. It was at the Reformation, particularly,
that this free investigation of the Bible began to extend widely ;
and among the Reformers, Luther himself was specially remarkable
for it. From these inquiries he became fully convinced of the genuineness of most of the writings of the New Testament ; but he
supposed it necessary to regard some of them, e. g., the Epistle of
James, and John's Revelation, as spurious. In this opinion he certainly erred, particularly, as is now acknowledged by nearly all
scholars, in his rejection of the Epistle of James ; but great as was,
and still is, his authority in the eyes of many millions of Christians,
his belief of the spuriousness of these two books has done no essential harm ; they have maintained their place in the New Testament
since as before, and the circumstance of his rejecting them has only
shown the church the truth of the old remark, that even God's
saints may err.

From this example may be clearly seen, however, the total groundlessness of the fear of those who imagine that such scrutinizing inquiries must be, in and of themselves, prejudicial to the church.
Such examinations of the origin of holy writ, and its individual
books, are not only *allowable*, but absolutely *indispensable;* and they
will injure the church no more than gold is injured by being carefully tried in the fire. The church, like the gold, will but become
purer for the test. In the Scriptures, both of the Old and New
Testament, the eternal revelation of God reposes in quiet security
and brightness. A wonderful Divine ordination has preserved it to
us without any essential injury, through a succession of dark ages.
It exerts at the present day, upon all minds receptive of its spirit,
the same blessed, sanctifying influence which the apostles claimed
for it eighteen centuries ago. How, then, can these sacred books
suffer from careful historical inquiry respecting their origin ? Investigation must rather serve to confirm and fully establish belief in
their purity and genuineness. That this is actually the effect of
really learned investigations is apparent, likewise, from the following
instance. When the very erudite and truly pious Professor Bengel
of Tubingen published his New Testament with all the various
readings which he had been able to discover, many minds were
filled with anxiety,' thinking that an entirely new Testament would
be the result in the end, if all the various readings were hunted up.
They thought it would be better to leave things as they were. But

mark—although 40,000 various readings were discovered in the ancient MSS., the New Testament was hardly at all altered thereby; for very few readings were of a nature to have any essential bearing upon a doctrine. Most of them consisted of unimportant transpositions, or permutations of synonymous words (such as in English *also* for *and*, etc.) ; and though some readings were more considerable (as, *e. g.*, the celebrated passage, 1 John v. 7 : "For there are three that bear witness in heaven, the Father, the Word, and the Holy Ghost, and these three are one," which must certainly be regarded as spurious), still they are really of no more consequence. For such is the nature of the Holy Scriptures, that there are always many proof-passages for any important doctrine ; and hence, although these words are withdrawn from the Bible, their purport is still eternally true, and the doctrine of the Holy Trinity remains at the present time, as before, the doctrine of the church. Now that all the MSS. have been read and accurately collated, there is no further occasion for fear that somewhere or other something new may be discovered, which will thrust the old-loved Bible aside. Moreover, the principles on which scholars determine the right one among different readings of the same passage are so skillfully devised, that it is almost impossible for a false reading to creep in ; and, should one individual err in this respect, another immediately steps in and corrects the error.

It certainly is not to be denied that pious persons, who valued God's word, might well for some time be anxious at heart ; for one biblical book after another was stricken from the list of those which were genuine, and at last we seemed to have none but spurious books in the Bible ; though, on the other hand, it remained inexplicable who could have taken pains either to forge so many spurious writings himself, or to make a collection of them after they were forged. And then, what could have been the character of the deceitful author or authors (for, at all events, the books must have been written by somebody), who could compose *such* writings—writings which for many centuries have consoled millions in calamity and death. It is now seen, however, that the reason why things were so for a time, was, not that men inquired and investigated (for no injury can ever accrue on that account), but that they did not prosecute the investigation with a *right spirit and disposition.* Every one can see that it is not a matter of indifference with what feelings we engage in investigations of this kind in regard to the sacred books. Suppose a man to see in the books of the New Testament only monuments of antiquity, of just as little or as much value as other ancient writings, to have felt nothing of the saving influence of God's word upon his heart, and on that account to be devoid of love for it ; yea, even to feel vexed that others should hold it so dear, and enviously and maliciously study how he might destroy their delight in this treasure—such a man, with his perverse disposition, would rake up any thing and every thing in order to undermine the foundation of the church. Whether such corrupt motives have really operated in the heart of any inquirer, no man can determine. It is always presumption to take it upon ourselves to judge respecting the internal position or intention of any heart. We may even suppose one who rejects the whole New Testament to possess honesty and sincerity, which want only the necessary light of conviction. But the *possibility* that such motives may affect these investigations, certainly cannot be denied ; and that is fully enough for our purpose. If, moreover, we look at the manner in which a Voltaire among the French, and a Bahrdt among the Germans, have treated the sacred books, we find cogent reason to *fear* that *they* did not keep themselves free from such corrupt motives, however heartily we wish that God's judgment may pronounce them pure. This consideration is of importance, however, because we may see from it how all depends on this interior state of mind with which a man commences his undertakings ; so that even the noblest enterprise may by an unholy intention lead to pernicious results. But, setting entirely aside the possibility that a man may undertake investigations respecting the Scriptures in a positively corrupt state of mind, he may also do much injury therein from *levity and frivolity*. If he is not sufficiently penetrated with a conviction of the great importance of investigations concerning the genuineness of the sacred Scriptures, if he does not treat the weaknesses of the church with sufficient tenderness (for she may feel herself wounded in her most sacred interests by the inconsiderate expression of doubts), it may easily happen that, at the first impulse, upon some supposed discovery, this discovery will immediately be blazoned before the world, without having been previously *tested* with soberness and care by all the means within reach. There is little reason to doubt that vanity is commonly at the bottom of this superficial haste ; for it is always delightful to what Paul calls the *old man* to be the author of any new and striking opinion. Had all inquirers been able properly to restrain this vain desire to shine, much offence would without doubt have been avoided, and many a heart would have escaped considerable suffering.

Still, in what department of life or knowledge have we not many errors to lament ? He who knows his own heart aright will therefore forgive learned men, if they have now and then been governed by vanity or other wrong motives. The misuse of a good thing should not abolish its use ; and it is still true that all investigations respecting the sacred books, their history and compilation, are in themselves very useful and necessary, as without them we must be entirely in the dark in regard to their true character. We will only wish that henceforth the God of truth and love may infuse truth and love into the hearts of all inquirers, and then it will not be of any consequence that many books have been *pronounced* spurious ; for, fortunately, they do not *become* spurious from the assertions of this or that man, and it is always allowable for another scholar to point out the errors of his predecessor. From this freedom of investigation the truth will certainly come to light by degrees.

If the thoughts here presented be duly considered, it will be readily seen, that he who has deep love for the word of God need not take it much to heart, that this or that scholar has rejected a particular book. After long investigation, and frequent assertions that most of the books of the New Testament are spurious, it is nevertheless now agreed among scholars generally, *that all the writings of the New Testament are genuine productions of the apostles.* As to several of them, it is true, precise certainty has not been attained, but it is to be hoped that uniformity will be exhibited soon in regard to these likewise ; and, moreover, the difference of opinion in this view concerning several of these books is not so dangerous as it may appear. Concerning the *Epistle to the Hebrews, e. g.,* there is not uniformity of sentiment as yet. Many very estimable divines, with whom I feel myself constrained to coincide in opinion on this point, think that the Epistle was not composed by the Apostle Paul, but by some other very worthy member of the apostolic church. It is clear, however, that even though Paul did not write the Epistle, we cannot on this ground regard it as spurious, inasmuch as its author is not mentioned in it. Hence the only question in relation to it is, *who* was its author ? and on that point it is hard to decide, from the obscurity of the accounts given by the ancient fathers of the church. All, however, regard this Epistle as genuine, *i. e.,* it is universally believed that its author composed it without any intention to palm it off as the production of somebody else, for instance the Apostle Paul. Had that been his purpose, he would have taken care that the Epistle should at once be recognised as Paul's production, by assigning his name to it, or in some other way. The case is certainly different as to *the second Epistle of Peter,* against the genuineness of which many doubts are prevalent. In relation to this Epistle, the first inquiry is not *who* was its author, for the apostle Peter is most clearly designated as such, but *whether* Peter was really and truly the author. If the conclusion be that the Epistle cannot be attributed to Peter, then it must be forged or spurious. It has been attacked with more plausibility than any other book of the New Testament ; and yet much may be said even in behalf of this Epistle, as we shall see hereafter. We may therefore assert, that by Divine Providence some good has already accrued from the rigorous sifting to which the books of the New Testament have been subjected in our day. True, it did at first seem as if the whole New Testament would in the course of time be declared spurious ; but when the first heat was over, and sober perspicacity returned, it was seen by inquirers that far the greater part of its books rested on a firmer historical foundation than most works of profane antiquity which all the world regard as genuine. Hence we may be of good courage in entering on the consideration of the individual books of the New Testament, for the result of critical investigation is by no means so much to be dreaded as is sometimes thought. First, however, we desire to premise something further respecting *the New Testament generally.*

CHAPTER I.

THE NEW TESTAMENT GENERALLY.

THE oldest traces of the existence of the whole New Testament as a settled collection, occur so late as three centuries after the time of the apostles. The particular reason why so long a period elapsed before this body of writings became definitely determined, was, that its individual books, which of course existed before the whole collection, were at first circulated in part singly and in part in smaller collections. For, so long as the apostles were upon earth, and the power of the Spirit from on high was in lively action in every member of the church, so long there was no sensible necessity of a book to serve as the norm or rule of faith and practice. Whenever any uncertainty arose in regard to either, application was made to one of the apostles, and his advice was taken. The Epistles of the Apostle Paul owe their origin to such inquiries. Now some of the apostles lived to a very great age. Peter and Paul, it is true, died under the emperor Nero (67 A. D.) suffering martyrdom at Rome ; but the Evangelist John, who outlived all the rest, was upwards of ninety years of age at his death, which did not happen till the time of the emperor Domitian, at the close of the first century. Hence, in the lifetime of the apostles, though their writings were highly valued, they were naturally not regarded as sacred writings, which were to be the rule of faith ; because there was a more immediate guarantee of truth in the living discourse of the apostles and their first companions, as also in the Holy Spirit, which was so powerfully exerting its influence upon the church. The apostolic writings, therefore, were indeed read in the public assemblies, but not alone, and not regularly. The book for regular public reading was still the

Old Testament ; and this is always to be understood in the New Testament when the Holy Scriptures are mentioned. Besides the apostolic writings, however, other profitable books were used for. the edification of the church. In particular, we have still some remains of the writings of immediate disciples of the apostles, commonly called *apostolic fathers*, which were publicly read in the ancient churches. These men all lived in the first century and some time in the second. Among them are Clement, bishop of Rome, Ignatius, bishop of Antioch, Polycarp, bishop of Smyrna, Hermas, who was probably presbyter at Rome, and the well-known Barnabas. The Epistles of Clement and Polycarp, as well as the Book of Hermas, were read with special assiduity in the ancient churches. On account of the great antiquity of these writings, the books of the New Testament are very seldom quoted in them, and much of what coincides with the contents of the New Testament, *e. g.*, Christ's sayings, may have been drawn by these apostolic fathers from oral tradition as well as from perusal of the Gospels. Indeed the former source is perhaps most probable, since Christians certainly did not then read the Gospels so assiduously as they were read in later times, when they could no longer listen to the living discourse of the apostles and their immediate companions. The reason why so few written remains of the immediate disciples of our Lord are now extant, is in part the long lapse of time, which has destroyed many books once current, but in part also that the ancient Christians laboured more than they wrote. The preaching of the gospel, and the regulation of infant churches, consumed so much of their time, that little remained to be employed in composition. Moreover, in the first century it was always as when Paul wrote the following declaration (1 Cor. i. 26) : "Not many wise men after the flesh, not many noble were called." For the most part only people of inferior standing joined the church of Christ ; and these had neither the capacity nor the inclination to labour with the pen. In these circumstances it is undoubtedly true that we find little information concerning the books of the New Testament in the first centuries. That they did, nevertheless, exist in the church we shall prove hereafter. But it might be expected, then, that although the most ancient Christians do not speak of their sacred writings, still the heathen writers of Greece and Rome must have done so, considering the multiplicity of their works on all subjects. The heathen writers, however, who were contemporary with the apostles and the apostolic church, make no mention of the apostolic writings, because they cared nothing at all about the Christian church. They considered the Christians as only a sect of the Jews, and despised them as much as they did the latter. They therefore credited the malicious reports which were circulated respecting the Christians, and treated them, accordingly, as the offscouring of humanity. Such is the procedure of Tacitus, a noble Roman, who relates the persecution of the Christians under Nero. Thus, of course, nothing could induce the Greeks and Romans to cultivate acquaintance with the writings of the Christians, particularly as they were distasteful on another account, from their not being clothed in the same elegant language as their productions. It was only when the number of the Christians became so great as to excite apprehension, that they began to pay attention to everything of importance concerning this new sect, and so at last to their sacred books. But it is not till after the middle of the second century that we find examples like that of Celsus, who, in order to confute the Christians, made himself acquainted with their sacred books.

The original condition of the primitive church, in which less stress was laid on the Scriptures than on the word of the apostles, was not indeed of long continuance. For the mighty outpouring of the Spirit, which, on the day of Pentecost, filled the disciples of our Saviour, had hardly been communicated to a considerable number of other minds, and lost its first power, ere erroneous schisms began to prevail in the churches. The germs of these may be discovered in the writings of the apostles. The first of these party divisions of the ancient church was that of the *Jewish Christians*. As early as in the Epistle to the Galatians, Paul speaks expressly of persons who desired to bring the Galatian Christians again under the yoke of the law. They wished faith in Christ and his redemption to be regarded as insufficient for salvation, unless circumcision and the observance of the law were added. The great preacher of the Gentiles, however, zealously opposes this restricted idea of Christianity, and shows that the soul must lose Christ, if it seeks to use any other means of salvation. It was the object of the law of Moses to lead by its injunctions to conviction of sin, and thus to a desire for salvation; by its prophecies and types of Christ it was a schoolmaster to guide us to him; but salvation itself could come only from Christ. Still, Paul was by no means of opinion that those who were Jews by birth must not observe the law when they became Christians; he rather favoured their doing so, if the pious customs of their fathers had become dear to them, or if their own weakness or that of the Jews around them would be offended by the contrary course. Hence, the apostles who remained in Jerusalem till its destruction, as did Matthew and James, observed the law invariably, and so did Paul likewise, when he was in Jerusalem. But the apostles, as well as their true disciples, were far from being desirous to impose this observance of the law upon the Gentiles also. The milder and really Christian view of the observance of the law was constantly entertained by many Jewish Christians in Palestine, who in later times were called *Nazareans*. Many on the contrary, took the wrong course, which the Apostle Paul reproved in certain individuals in Galatia, and these obtained the name of *Ebionites*. They, however, fell into other heresies besides their idea of the necessity of circumcision and observance of the law in order to salvation, particularly in regard to the person of Christ. They denied the real divinity of our Lord, and regarded him as a son of Joseph, thus seceding wholly from the true church of Christ.

In precise contrariety to this *Judaising* division of the church, others entirely discarded Judaism. The instructions of the Apostle Paul had taken deep hold of their minds, and given them a strong conviction that the gospel went far beyond the formalities of Jewish practice, and would bring all nations under its sway. But from this perfectly correct idea they wandered into an opposition to the Old Testament, which was never felt in the slightest degree by the Apostle Paul. They remarked rightly, that in the Old Testament, the Divine *justice* was most prominently exhibited, in the revelation of a rigorous law ; while the New most fully displayed the Divine *mercy* in the revelation of forgiving love. But this fact, which was necessary for the education of mankind, since the need of salvation will never be felt until the claims of justice are perceived, was employed by them for the purpose of wholly disuniting the Old Testament from the New, and referring it to a distinct author. This sect are termed *Marcionites*, from Marcion, the man who urged this view to the greatest extreme. In connection with their opposition to Judaism they also held Gnostic opinions (whence they are commonly ranked with the Gnostics), and these gave a hue to their absurd notion that the God of the Old Testament was different from that of the New. The Old Testament, they thought, presented to view a God of justice without love ; the New Testament one of love without justice ; while in reality the only true God possesses both attributes in perfection. It is easy to see that in these notions Paganism is mingled with Christianity. The sublime nature of the latter was admitted by the Marcionites ; but they could not look upon the other true form of religion, Judaism, as reconcilable with it. Hence, although they no longer revered the numberless gods of the heathen, they imagined the two attributes of God, justice and love, to center in two distinct divine beings. Besides this ungrounded violence against Judaism, the Marcionites maintained a silly error in regard to Christ's nature, which was the precise opposite of the opinion of the Jewish Christians. The latter denied his divinity, and the Marcionites asserted that he had no true humanity. The humanity of Christ, said they, was only apparent. In their opinion a purely heavenly vision was presented in the person of Jesus Christ ; his life and all his acts in life were merely in appearance, designed to exhibit him to men in a human manner.

This idea the Marcionites entertained in common with the *Gnostics*, properly so called, who did indeed judge more correctly than the former in regard to the mutual relation of Judaism and Christianity, but on other points maintained the most grievous errors. The seeds of their doctrine are referred to by the Apostle Paul, *e. g.*, in 2 Tim. ii. 17, 18, where he warns against the heresy of Hymeneus and Philetus, who maintained that the resurrection of the dead had already taken place. For, as they denied the true humanity of Christ, they could not, of course, admit the corporeal resurrection of all men ; and therefore understood it spiritually of the interior vivification of the heart by the spirit of Christ. Undoubtedly this perversion of doctrine on the part of the Gnostics is to be referred to their belief in another being besides God. While they regarded God as a pure spirit, the fulness of all good and beauty, they looked upon matter as another being, the source of everything corporeal and visible, as also of all evil. It was from a mixture of the spiritual and the material that this world originated, and particularly man, who at one time displays so much that is lovely and elevated, at another so much that is low and base. Thus the only way to purify and sanctify man was, that he should be gradually freed from everything material, and by the divine germs of life within him, be brought back to God. It is easy to imagine what a distorted view of all the doctrines of salvation must be produced by such an idea, since holy writ nowhere countenances the opinion that evil resides in *matter*, but rather expressly refers it to the *will* of the creature, who, by disobedience to the holy will of the Creator, has destroyed in himself and about him the harmony which originally prevailed in the whole universe.

In this condition of things, then, when Jewish Christians, Marcionites, and Gnostics, to say nothing of other insignificant sects, were disturbing the unity of the church, it was seen to be necessary that every effort should be exerted to uphold the purity of the apostolic doctrines. But as, at the time when these sects became very powerful, the apostles were no longer upon earth, no direct appeal could be made to their authority, whenever oral tradition was adduced against them, these heretics appealed themselves to pretended communications from the apostles. The Gnostics in particular, asserted that the deep wisdom which they taught in their schools was communicated by the apostles to only a few ; very simple Christian truth alone, they supposed was only for the multitude. What remained, therefore, since appeal to oral tradition from the apostles was of no avail, but reference to written authority ? This could not be altered and falsified like oral language ; it was better suited to be a fixed, unchangeable norm and rule of faith, and could therefore be employed with exceeding force and efficiency against all heretics. Thus the time was now come when a sifting and separation of the many professedly Christian writings scattered abroad in the church was necessary. Moreover, the different sects of heretics had all sorts of forged writings among them, in which their peculiar opinions were presented in the names of celebrated prophets and apostles. Against such writings explicit declaration must be made, in order to preserve the true apostolic doctrine from mixture with erroneous and confused notions. As of course, however, individual fathers of the church could have but little influence against the established sects of heretics, it was felt to be necessary that real Christians should be more closely and intimately united, and from the endeavour consequently made sprang the so-called *catholic*, i. e., *universal church.* The teachers of the church, as well as the laity, agreed together in the avowal of certain doctrines, which afterwards formed their creed, or the so-called *apostolic symbol*, because in them the true apostolic doctrines were stated in opposition to heretics. Thus it became practicable to set firm bounds to the tide of corruption ; and thus the various sects were gradually suppressed by the preponderant influence of the universal church. Still some of them lasted down to the fifth and sixth centuries.

This sifting of the various Christian writings demands a more careful consideration. It has been before remarked that certain edifying productions of estimable fathers, e. g., Clement of Rome, Hermas and others, were publicly read along with those of the apostles. Still, however profitable the perusal of these writings might be, the bishops of the Catholic church correctly felt that they could be of no service against heretics, as these would not allow them any weight. Since, however, they commonly acknowledged the writings of the apostles, these and these alone could be appealed to in confutation of them. All such writings, therefore, as were allowed to be the compositions of other authors were first separated from the rest. If this had not been done, it would have remained uncertain in all subsequent time what books were properly to be regarded as pure sources of apostolic doctrine ; and at the time of the Reformation it would not have been so easy to restore the true uncorrupted doctrine of Christ by means of the Scriptures, as it actually was, on account of the circumstance that the genuine Scriptures were possessed in a separate, fixed collection. Now, in the endeavour to gather the genuine apostolic writings together by themselves, some of them were very easily distinguished from the rest as the apostolic productions. These were called universally-admitted writings ; in Greek *homologoumena*. Among these were reckoned the four Gospels of Matthew, Mark, Luke, and John ; the Acts of

the Apostles ; the Epistles of the Apostle Paul to the Romans, Corinthians, Galatians, Ephesians, Philippians, Colossians, and Thessalonians, to Timothy, Titus, and Philemon ; and lastly, two Epistles of John and Peter, viz., only the first and largest of both
apostles. Among these writings, it is true, there appear two which
were not composed by apostles, i. e., by members of the first circle
of twelve men which our Lord Jesus gathered about him. [It is to
be observed that Paul ranked with these in authority, partly because
of his immediate call by the Lord (Acts ix.), and partly on account
of his extended and blessed labours in behalf of the church.] We
mean the Gospel of Mark and the work of Luke. We say the *work*
of Luke, for Luke's Gospel and his Acts of the Apostles do but
make two halves of the same work, as is plain from the commencement of the Acts. There was no scruple on the part of the Catholic church to class these two works of assistants of the apostles with
those really apostolic, because both wrote under the influence and
approval of apostles. According to the unanimous account of the
most ancient Christian Fathers, Mark wrote under the guidance of
Peter, and Luke under that of Paul, so that Mark's was regarded as
the Petrine, and Luke's as the Pauline Gospel.

These universally-received writings of the apostles were divided
into two collections. *First*, the four Gospels by themselves formed
a collection called *the Gospel*. For, although this collection contained four narratives of our Lord's life, they were not regarded as
different writings, but only as different aspects, or, so to speak, *sides*
of one and the same work. Hence an ancient Father of the church,
Irenaeus, bishop of Lyons in France, terms the four Gospels, the
one four-formed or four-sided Gospel. The other writings constituted a *second* collection, which was termed *the apostle*, or the
preaching of the apostle. Probably the name took its rise from the
fact, that at first the Epistles of Paul alone were collected together,
and he was called the apostle, by way of eminence, especially in
Europe, on account of his active labours. To this collection of
Pauline Epistles the Acts of the Apostles were added subsequently,
because it formed, as it were, an introduction to the Epistles, containing an account of Paul's travels and labours in the vineyard of
our Lord. Later still were also added the two larger Epistles of
John and Peter.

Besides these generally admitted writings, there were others,
which were indeed regarded by many as apostolic, but as to which
some estimable persons entertained doubts, viz., the Second and
Third Epistles of John, the Second Epistle of Peter, the Epistles
of James and Jude, the Epistle to the Hebrews, and John's Apocalypse. Hence these were termed *disputed writings*, in Greek,
Antilegomena. About the close of the second or the commence-

ment of the third century, most of the fathers of the Catholic church became united in believing the genuineness and apostolic origin of all these writings excepting the Epistles to the Hebrews and the Apocalypse. A *third* small collection was now formed of these epistles, and into it were transferred the two larger Epistles of John and Peter, which were at first contained in the *second* collection. Consequently, the third comprised *seven Epistles*, which were called the *seven Catholic, i. e., universally-admitted Epistles*, in contra-distinction from the various rejected writings. Out of these collections there now remained, therefore, only the *Epistle to the Hebrews*, and the *Revelation* of John. In regard to the Epistle, as has been already mentioned, no doubt was entertained of its genuineness ; the only controversy was, whether Paul was its author or not. At last, the opinion that it was Pauline prevailed, and it was introduced into the collection of Pauline Epistles ; though, as the collection was already made up, it was placed at the end, after the small Epistle to Philemon. In the Lutheran version of the Bible, however, the Epistle obtained another place, viz., between the Third Epistle of John and the Epistle of James, for reasons which will be stated hereafter. The whole question, therefore, in regard to the Epistle to the Hebrews was of little consequence; for, if Paul did not write it, it is certain that the author of it wrote under his guidance (as will be shown more at length in the sequel), and the case is the same with this Epistle as with the Gospels of Mark and Luke. It is otherwise, however, with the history of the *Apocalypse*, which also will be particularly related hereafter. Although it has the oldest and most trustworthy witnesses in its behalf, indeed beyond most of the writings of antiquity, it still early met with numerous assailants, on account of its contents. True, many did not exactly regard it as spurious ; they only maintained that it was written, not by John the Evangelist, but by another man of less note, bearing the same name. Others, however, felt such excessive dislike towards the book, that they declared it must have been composed by the worst of heretics. Yet here, too, truth fortunately obtained the victory, and the genuine apostolic character of this elevated production of prophetic inspiration was at last acknowledged. As the three smaller collections were already made up, nothing remained but to place it at the end of them all. This was precisely the position to which the Apocalypse belonged ; for, considering the Gospels to be, as it were, the root of the tree of life exhibited in the whole New Testament, and the Epistles as the branches and blossoms, the Apocalypse may be regarded as the fully ripened fruit. It contains a picture of the development of God's church down to the end of time, and therefore forms the conclusion of the Bible as properly as Genesis forms its commencement

In order that the various writings and small collections might be permanently united, the smaller divisions were entirely given up in the fourth century, and henceforward there was but one great collection, containing all the New Testament writings. A decisive decree on this point was issued by a council held in the year 393, at Hippo, now Bona, in Africa. In itself considered, this union of the smaller collections into a single large one is of no consequence, and hence, too, it is of none that it took place at so late a period; for, as early as during the third century and the commencement of the fourth, there was entire unanimity in regard to all essential questions concerning the books of the New Testament, as the following particular history of them will evince. Still there was this advantage arising from the union of the apostolic writings into one body, viz., that they were in a more safe and determinate form, and might now be placed with the Old Testament as a complete second part of holy writ.

CHAPTER II.

THE COLLECTION OF THE GOSPELS.

OF the three smaller collections of the writings of the New Testament, which, as we have before stated, were in use in the ancient church, none can be traced further back than that of the Gospels. We find so many and so weighty testimonies in its behalf, that it would seem as though Providence designed that this palladium of the church should be in a special manner secure against all attacks. Not only is it the case that some of the most ancient fathers testify to its existence, as, e. g., Tertullian, Clement of Alexandria, Irenaeus, Justin Martyr (all of whom lived in the second century after Christ, and were preceded only by the so-called apostolic fathers) ; but, moreover, the witnesses in its behalf belonged to all parts of the ancient church. Tertullian lived in Carthage ; Clement in Egypt ; Irenaeus was born in Asia Minor, and became bishop of Lyons in France ; Justin Martyr was born in Palestine (in Flavia Neapolis, otherwise called Sichem), but taught in Rome. Thus the testimonies in favour of the collection of the Gospels come from all the chief stations in the ancient church ; and this circumstance, of course, supposes its very general diffusion. The greatest number of testimonies, all proceeding from *one* province, would not be of so much weight as these coincident declarations from the most various parts of the world, as to the currency of the Gospels. A circumstance, however, still more important than these testimonies from different parts of the ancient church is, that not only the members of the Catholic orthodox church, but the heretics also, were familiar with our Gospels. If it be considered, what violent mutual animosity there was between the fathers of the Catholic church and the heretics ; that one party would not adopt or receive anything at all from the other, but was rather disposed to reject it, for the very reason that it came from so detested a quarter ; no one can help seeing in the circumstance that both the Catholic church and the heretics were familiar with the collection of our Gospels—an uncommonly cogent proof of its genuineness and great antiquity. For, had it been formed *after* the rise of these sects, either within the pale of the Catholic church, or in the midst of this or that party of heretics, it would be wholly inexplicable, how it could have been introduced into these sects, from the church, or, *vice versa*, into the church from these sects. Thus the collection of our Gospels must at all events have taken place *before* such sects arose ; for on no other ground can it be explained how these books, which were generally known and used before open rupture in the church, should have been admitted as genuine by both parties alike. Now the sects of the Gnostics and Marcionites originated as early as the beginning of the second century ; and from this circumstance we are entitled to regard the collection of the Gospels as in existence at a period very near the times of the apostles. Besides the heretics, moreover, we find pagans acquainted with the collection of the Gospels. We refer particularly to Celsus, a violent opponent to Christianity, against whose attacks it was defended by Origen. It is true this man did not live till about two hundred years after the birth of Christ (we do not know the precise period) ; but it is, notwithstanding, a decisive evidence of the general diffusion and acknowledgment of the Gospels throughout the church, that they are cited and assailed by pagan opponents as official sources of the Christian doctrines. For, had Celsus been aware that Christians themselves did not acknowledge these writings, it would have been an absurd undertaking to refute the Christians from the contents of the books.

Further, it is a wholly peculiar circumstance in the history of the Gospels, and one which goes a great way to sustain their genuineness, that we nowhere find, in any writer of any part of the ancient world any indication that only a single one of the four Gospels was in use, or even known to exist separately. *All possessed the entire collection of the Gospels.* It is true there is one writer, Papias, bishop of Hierapolis in Phrygia, concerning whom there is no express statement that he had all the four Gospels. But the manner in which Eusebius speaks respecting him in his Church History is such that there is nothing questionable in this silence. Eusebius

adduces from a work of Papias, now not extant, some notices of
Matthew and Mark. It is certainly true that nothing is said of
Luke and John; but this is undoubtedly because the ancient
bishop had not made any particular observations on these two
Gospels. His silence respecting them is the less an evidence that
he was not acquainted with them, as the theatre of the labours of
Papias was in the vicinity of Ephesus, where John lived so long,
and moreover wrote his Gospel. On this account Papias must
necessarily have been acquainted with it. Eusebius, moreover, remarks, in the same place, that Papias was acquainted with the first
Epistle of John. How much rather, then, with his Gospel? Thus
Eusebius says nothing concerning Luke and John, only because it
was a matter of course that Papias was familiar with them, and the
latter had not said anything special in regard to their origin. There
were, moreover, some heretics who made use of but *one* Gospel, *e. g.*,
Marcion used Luke, and the Ebionites Matthew; but they had
special reasons for doing so in their doctrinal opinions. They did
not, by any means, deny the three other Gospels to be genuine;
they only asserted that their authors were not true disciples of our
Lord. Marcion held the erroneous notion that all the disciples,
with the exception of Paul, still continued *half Jews.* The Jewish
Christians maintained that all the disciples, except Matthew, had
strayed away *too far from* Judaism, and on that account did not
receive their writings. In this state of the case there is clear evidence from their opinions also that the Gospels are genuine, and
were in that day generally diffused in the church. Now, as the collection of our four Gospels existed so very early and so universally,
the inquiry occurs, how it could have originated? Shall we say
that a particular individual or church may have formed it, and it
may then have spread itself everywhere abroad? This supposition
seems to be countenanced by the circumstance of the general uniformity as to the order of the four Gospels. A very few MSS. place
John next to Matthew, in order that the writings of the apostles
may be by themselves. Clearly, however, this transposition arose
from the fancy of some copyist, and has no historical foundation.
There is still, therefore, positive authority for the universally received
arrangement. The most weighty circumstance against the opinion
that the first collection of the Gospels was made in a particular
place, and diffused itself abroad from thence, is, that we have no
account respecting such a process, though we should expect one,
from the fact that John lived, and moreover wrote his Gospel, at so
late a period. For this reason had the Evangelist John himself, as
some suppose, or any other man of high authority in the church,
formed the collection of the Gospels, we should, one would think,
have had an account of its formation, as it could not have taken

place before the end of the first or commencement of the second century, which period borders very closely on that from which we derive so many accounts concerning the Gospels. But this same circumstance that we read nothing at all respecting a collector of the Gospels, that writers have been left to conjecture in regard to the manner in which the collection of them was made, leads to another view of its formation, which casts the clearest light on the genuineness of the books. It is in the highest degree probable that our Gospels all originated in capital cities of the Roman empire. Matthew probably wrote his in Jerusalem, the centre of Judaism, where also, as appears from the Acts of the Apostles, a large Christian church was early gathered. Mark and Luke undoubtedly wrote in Rome, the political centre of the empire, to which innumerable multitudes of men thronged from all quarters of the world for the transaction of business. In this city, too, a flourishing Christian church was early formed, as is seen from the Epistle of Paul to the Romans, which was written before Peter or Paul, or any apostle, had visited Rome. Lastly, John wrote at Ephesus, a large and thriving city of Asia Minor. It was the residence of many learned and ingenious heathen. The large church at Ephesus was, according to the Acts, founded by Paul. It was fostered by the labours of John. Now, let it be considered how many thousands must consequently have been most exactly aware who wrote the Gospels, and it will be perceived that these circumstances afford weighty evidence of their genuineness, particularly as *there is not to be found in a single ancient writer the faintest trace of any doubt in regard to it ;* for the heretics, who, as we have remarked, disputed the Gospels in part, did not deny their genuineness (they rather fully admitted it), but only their obligatory authority. Now, as very active intercourse was maintained among the Christians of the ancient church, partly by constant epistolary communications, and partly by frequent personal visits, nothing is more natural than the supposition that the Christians of Jerusalem very soon transmitted the Gospel of Matthew, which was composed in the midst of them, to Rome, Ephesus, Alexandria, and other places, and that, on the other hand, those of Rome and Ephesus also transmitted the writings composed among them to the other churches. In every church there were archives, in which were deposited important documents. Into these archives of the church the Gospels were put, and as only these four Gospels were composed or vouched for by apostles, the collection of Gospels took its rise not in this or that place, but in every quarter simultaneously. This statement of the matter is, in the first place, strictly in accordance with the circumstances known to us in regard to the ancient church, and also the only one capable of explaining satisfactorily the existence of the collection in everybody's hands, while no one knew how and whence it originated. As, further, we find *no other* Gospel but these in general use, it is clearly evident that only these four were of apostolic origin. It is true we find in circulation in individual churches Gospels which appear to have differed from our own, *e. g.*, the church at Rhossus in Cilicia, a province of Asia Minor, made use of a Gospel of Peter, and in Alexandria one called the Gospel of the Egyptians was current. It is possible, however, that these two writings were either the same or at least were very nearly allied, and also bore close affinity to our Mark ; and in that case their use is as easily accounted for as the use of Matthew and Luke by the Ebionite and Marcionite sects in Recensions somewhat altered from the original.

From this cursory view of the evidence in favour of the genuineness of the Gospels, it cannot but be admitted, that no work can be adduced, out of the whole range of ancient literature, which has so many and so decisive ancient testimonies in its behalf as they. It is therefore, in reality, a mere laboured effort to try to maintain and demonstrate the spuriousness of the Gospels. Since, however, this attempt is made, it may reasonably be inquired : *Whence is derived any occasion for doubt ? Is not everything, without exception, in favour of their genuineness ?* We cannot but say, that no thorough, serious-minded scholar, would ever have denied the genuineness of the Gospels, had not the question in regard to their genuineness been conjoined with another investigation of extreme difficulty and intricacy. In the ardent endeavour to get rid of this difficulty, scholars have been seduced into the invention of hypotheses irreconcilable with the genuineness of the Gospels. They should, on the contrary, have set out invariably with the admission of their genuineness, as an irrefragable fact, and then have employed only such modes of solving the difficulty above alluded to as were based on the supposition of their genuineness. The difficulty is this. On a close comparison of the first three Gospels we discover a very striking coincidence between them. This is exhibited, not merely in the facts and the style, but also in the order of narration, in the transitions from one narrative to another, and in the use of uncommon expressions, and other things of the same character. Further, the coincidence is interrupted by just as striking a dissimilarity, in such a manner that it is in the highest degree difficult to explain how this coincidence and this dissimilarity, as it is exhibited in the Gospels, can have originated. This is a purely learned investigation, which writers should have quietly prosecuted as such, without allowing it to influence the question respecting the genuineness of the Gospels. Such has been its influence, however, that some scholars suppose a so-called *Protevangelion*, or original Gospel, which the apostles, before they left Jerusalem, and scattered themselves abroad over the whole earth, prepared, in order to serve as a guide to them in their discourses. This writing is supposed to have contained the principal events of the life of our Lord. It was carried into all lands by the apostles. Now, in these different countries, it is said by the defenders of this hypothesis, additions were gradually made to this original Gospel. These were at first short, and thus arose the Gospels of the Jewish Christians, the Marcionites, and others ; afterwards they became longer, and in this way, at last, our Gospels were produced. Now, as it cannot be stated by whom these additions were made, this view is really equivalent to making our Gospels spurious, for, according to it, only the little portion of them which existed in the brief original Gospel is of apostolic authority. But, setting aside the fact that the hypothesis must be false, for this very reason, because it opposes the genuineness of the Gospels, which can be demonstrated by historical proof ; this theory has been, moreover, of late utterly discarded by learned men on other grounds. In the first place, no ancient Christian writer exhibits any acquaintance with such an original Gospel ; and is it conceivable that the knowledge of so remarkable a work should have been totally lost ? Then, too, the idea that a guide was composed by the apostles for themselves, in order to preserve unity in doctrine, is not at all suited to the apostolic period. At this period the Holy Spirit operated with its primeval freshness and power. This Spirit, which guided into all truth, was the means of preserving unity among the apostles. Not an individual of those witnesses to the truth needed any external written guide. Besides, this supposition solves the difficulty in question, respecting the coincidence of the Gospels, only in a very meagre and forced manner, while there is a much simpler way of reaching the same result far more satisfactorily. We must suppose more than one source of this characteristic of the first three Gospels. *Sometimes* one Evangelist was certainly made use of by another. This remark is applicable particularly to Mark, who undoubtedly was acquainted with and made use of both Matthew and Luke. *Moreover*, there existed short accounts of particular parts of the Gospel-history, such as narratives of particular cases of healing, relations of journeys, and the like. Now, when two Evangelists made use of the same brief account, there naturally resulted a resemblance in their history. Still, as each was independent in his use of these accounts, some variations also occurred. *Finally*, much of the similarity between them arose from oral narrations. It is easy to believe that certain portions of the evangelical history, e. g., particular cures, parables, and discourses of our Lord, were repeated constantly in the very same way, because the form of the narrative imprinted itself with very great exactness on every one's memory. In this manner the songs of

Homer and Ossian were long transmitted from mouth to mouth.
Uniformity in an oral mode of narration is not sufficient of itself
alone to explain the relation between the Gospels, because in prose
it is impossible (in poetry it is much easier) to imprint on the
memory minute traits and important forms of expression with so
much exactness as would be necessary to account for the mutual
affinity of the Gospels ; and, moreover, could their similarity be thus
explained, the variations between them would only stand out in
more troublesome relief. But that which cannot be effected by a
single hypothesis, can be by that in conjunction with others. And
here, perhaps, we may see the true solution of a problem which has
so long occupied the attention of theologians. But, whatever
opinion be entertained on this point, the investigation of it must always be kept aloof from the question of the genuineness of the Gospels, which should first be established or denied on historical
grounds. Thus will the collection of the Gospels be secure from
all danger.

CHAPTER III.

THE INDIVIDUAL GOSPELS AND THE ACTS OF THE APOSTLES.

OF the four Gospels, that of Matthew holds the first place in the
canon. The author of this first Gospel bore, besides the name of
Matthew, that of Levi also (Matth. ix. 9 ; Mark ii. 14), and was the
son of a certain Alpheus, of whom we have no further information.
Of the history of Matthew very little is known, in addition to the
accounts in the New Testament. After our Saviour called him
from his station as receiver of the customs, he followed him with
fidelity, and was one of the twelve whom Jesus sent forth to preach.
His labours as an apostle, however, seem to have been wholly confined to Palestine ; for, what is related of Matthew's travels in
foreign countries is very doubtful, resting only on the authority of
rather late ecclesiastical writings. But the information respecting
him which is of most importance to our purpose is given with perfect unanimity by the oldest ecclesiastical writers, who declare that
Matthew wrote a Gospel. It is true that they likewise subjoin,
equally without exception, that Matthew wrote in Hebrew, at Jerusalem, and for believing Jews ; and that this account must be correct, we know from the fact that the Jewish Christians in Palestine,
who spoke Hebrew, all made use of a Gospel which they referred to
Matthew. This Hebrew Gospel did, indeed, differ from our Greek
Gospel of Matthew, for it contained many things wanting in our

Gospel; but still it was in general so exactly like the latter, that a father of the fourth century, the celebrated Jerome, felt himself entitled to treat the Hebrew Gospel expressly as Matthew's. It is a singular circumstance, however, that, while all the fathers of the church declare Matthew to have written in Hebrew, they all, notwithstanding, make use of the Greek text as of genuine apostolic origin, without remarking what relation the Hebrew Matthew bore to our Greek Gospel; for that the oldest fathers of the church did not possess Matthew's Gospel in any other form than that in which we now have it, is fully settled. That we have no definite information on this point is undoubtedly owing to accidental causes; but, since it is so, that we have not any certain account, we can only resort to conjecture in regard to the mutual relation of the Greek and Hebrew Matthew. Existing statements and indications, however, enable us to form conjectures which, it is in the highest degree probable, are essentially correct. The idea that some unknown individual translated the Hebrew Gospel of Matthew, and that this translation is our canonical Gospel, is, in the first place, contradicted by the circumstance of the universal diffusion of this same Greek Gospel of Matthew, which makes it absolutely necessary to suppose that the translation was executed by some one of acknowledged influence in the church, indeed, of apostolic authority. In any other case, would not objections to this Gospel have been urged in some quarter or other, particularly in the country where Matthew himself laboured, and where his writings were familiarly known? There is not, however, the slightest trace of any such opposition to it. Besides, our Greek Gospel of Matthew is of such a peculiar character, that it is impossible for us to regard it as a mere version. Does a man, who is translating an important work from one language into another, allow himself to make alterations in the book which he is translating, to change the ideas it presents? Something of the kind must be supposed to have been done in the Greek Gospel of Matthew with regard to the Hebrew. This is beyond denial, if it be considered merely, how the quotations from the Old Testament are treated. These do not coincide either with the Hebrew text of the Old Testament, or with the version in common use at the time of the apostles, viz., the Septuagint (which was executed by some learned Jews at Alexandria, several centuries before the birth of Christ); but rather exhibit an independent text of their own. Now, as sometimes the argument is wholly based on this independent character of the text in the citations from the books of the Old Testament, and could not have accorded at all with the Hebrew Gospel of Matthew, it is clear that our Greek Gospel must be something else than a mere version. It is rather an independent work, though closely allied to the Hebrew Gospel of the apostle. Now, since this same work is universally regarded as an apostolic production, and as having been written by Matthew, there is no more simple and effectual mode of solving all the characteristics of the Gospel of Matthew, than to suppose *that Matthew himself, when he had composed the Hebrew Gospel, executed likewise a free translation or new composition of it in the Greek language.* It makes no essential difference, if we suppose that a friend of Matthew wrote the Greek work under his direction and authority ; but Matthew's authority must necessarily be supposed to have been the means of the diffusion of the Gospel, as otherwise it is inexplicable that there does not appear the faintest trace of any opposition to it.

No definite *objections* can be made against our supposition that Matthew wrote a Greek Gospel besides his Hebrew one. A single circumstance, however, may appear strange, viz., that Papias, the ancient bishop of Hierapolis in Phrygia, whom we have before mentioned, a man who was conversant with persons that had themselves seen and heard our Lord, informs us that every one endeavoured to translate the Hebrew Gospel of Matthew as well as he was able. Thus, according to this passage, our universally-received Greek transformation of the Hebrew Gospel was not commonly known in Phrygia, so that persons who did not very well understand Hebrew, made use, as well as they could, of the Hebrew Gospel. But the circumstance, that the Greek Gospel of Matthew was not yet current in the immediate vicinity of Papias, is no proof at all that it was not yet in existence. For, as Matthew's work was already diffused throughout the church in the Hebrew language, and the Greek Gospel of Matthew corresponded with the Hebrew in every essential point, it was very natural that the Greek Gospel should be circulated in a more dilatory manner ; and by some accident, it is probable, it was particularly tardy in reaching Phrygia. As, however, in the west generally, very few understood Hebrew, when the Greek Gospel of Matthew was once procured, that only was circulated there, and thus the Hebrew Gospel was completely lost in Europe. In Palestine alone, as the Hebrew was better understood, the Gospel in that language continued in use, though it was encumbered with divers foreign additions by the Jewish Christians.

Thus the genuineness of the Gospel of Matthew is fully confirmed on historical grounds, aside from its position in the collection of the Gospels. Recent investigators have raised doubts in regard to its genuineness from *internal* considerations. They say, in particular, that if the statements of Matthew, in the character of eye-witness (for he was one of the twelve apostles), be compared with the descriptions of Mark, who does not write as an eye-witness, it will be evident that the advantage is on the side of the latter. Everything which Mark narrates is represented in so graphic a manner that it is plain he derived his accounts from eye-witnesses; while the narrative of Matthew, whom we are to regard as himself an eye-witness in respect to most of his relations, is dry, and without the least vivacity. This remark is perfectly correct. Comparison of a few passages will at once show how much more minute and graphic are Mark's descriptions than those of Matthew. This is particularly the case as to the accounts of cures. In these Mark frequently describes the circumstances of the sick person before and after the cure in so lively a manner as to make us imagine the scene really before us; while Matthew, on the contrary, describes the occurrence only in very general terms. Let a comparison be made in this view between the following accounts which Matthew and Mark give of the same occurrences:

MATTH. viii. 28—34.	MARK v. 1—19.
"And when he was come to the other side, into the country of the Gergesenes, there met him two possessed with devils, coming out of the tombs, exceeding fierce, so that no man might pass by that way. And behold they cried out saying," &c.	"And they came over unto the other side of the sea, into the country of the Gadarenes. (This is another reading for Gergesenes.) And when he was come out of the ship, immediately there met him out of the tombs a man with an unclean spirit, who had his dwelling among the tombs; *and no man could bind him, no, not with chains, because that he had been often bound with fetters and chains, and the chains had been plucked asunder by him, and the fetters broken in pieces; neither could any man tame him. And always, night and day, he was in the mountains, and in the tombs, crying and cutting himself with stones. But when he saw Jesus afar off, he ran and worshipped him, and cried with a loud voice, and said," &c.*
Respecting their cure, Matthew merely says (ver. 32): "And he said unto them, Go. And when they were come out they went into the herd of swine, and behold the whole herd of swine," &c.	Respecting his cure, Mark says (ver. 13 and onward): "And forthwith Jesus gave them leave. And the unclean spirits went out and entered into the swine," &c. "And they (that were in the city and in the country) went out *to* see what it was that was done. And they come to Jesus, and see him that was possessed with the devil, and had the legion, *sitting, and clothed, and in his right mind:* and they were afraid."

ix. 18—26.	v. 21—43.
20. "And behold a woman which was diseased with an issue of blood twelve years, came behind him, and plucked the hem of his garment."	25. "And a certain woman which had an issue of blood twelve years, *and had suffered many things of many physicians, and had spent all that she had, and was nothing bettered, but rather grew worse,* when she had

heard of Jesus, came in the press behind, and touched his garment."
Moreover, the whole account contained in verses 29—33 is in Mark only.

xiv. 1—12.	vi. 14—20.
Account of the execution of John the Baptist by Herod.	The whole narrative is given in Mark with much more minuteness and vivacity.

Such a difference in the style of narration runs throughout Matthew and Mark; and it cannot well be denied that at first view there is something surprising in it. But careful examination of the object of the two Gospels plainly shows whence this different manner of narration in Matthew and Mark takes its rise, and thus does away with all the inferences which have been deduced therefrom in opposition to the apostolic origin of Matthew. The reason why Mark describes the outward relations of our Lord's life in so vivid and graphic a manner is, that it was his *special design* to portray *Christ's performance of the outward functions of his office.* Hence, all which related to that, he details very carefully ; while whatever did not pertain thereto, he either entirely omits, as, *e. g.,* the history of the childhood of Jesus, or communicates very briefly, as, *e. g.,* many of our Lord's larger discourses. Matthew, on the contrary, makes it *his* chief object to communicate our *Lord's discourses.* He commonly makes use of events only as points of support for the discourses ; to which he, like John, directs special attention. If it be considered, moreover, that the graphic nature of style is, in great part, owing to peculiar talent, such as is not bestowed alike on all men, and such as was by no means requisite in every one of the apostles, there remains not a shadow of reason, why the want of vivacity, which is certainly exhibited in Matthew's Gospel, should become a motive for denying its genuineness. In truth, moreover, there is no period at which a forgery of the Gospel in Matthew's name is even conceivable. For it is demonstrable from the book itself that it must have been composed a few years before the destruction of Jerusalem, and hence about sixty-six years after the birth of Christ. Now we find Matthew in use in the church before the close of the same century, at a time when John the Evangelist had but just died, and many disciples of the apostles were living and labouring in all parts of the world. How was it possible, in such circumstances, to introduce a work forged in the name of Matthew into so general currency, that not the very slightest opposition should ever have been raised against it ?

From what has been said it will have been inferred that the genuineness of Mark is not at all disputed. His graphic, lively manner has even been made to afford occasion for assailing the genuineness of Matthew. Nor, in truth, was there in ancient times the least opposition to Mark's Gospel. It was known to Papias of Hierapolis, *i. e.*, as early as the close of the first century, and there is an unbroken chain of evidence in its favour since that time. It is true, Mark's work was, in all probability, written at Rome, at that time the capital of the known world, and therefore a fixed and sure tradition as to the author of the work might be formed at once, and would easily diffuse itself everywhere abroad. Still, however, there is one thing which appears very remarkable in regard to the rapid diffusion and reception of Mark, viz., that it was a production whose author was not an apostle. John Mark, frequently called Mark only, was the son of a certain Mary who had a house in Jerusalem (Acts xii. 12). Mark himself, as we are told in the Acts (xii. 25 ; xiii. 5 ; xv. 36 *seq.*), at first accompanied the Apostle Paul in his travels for the dissemination of Christianity. He afterwards attached himself to his kinsman Barnabas. At a later period, however, we find him again in Paul's company (2 Tim. iv. 11). According to the fathers, he was also, for a considerable time, closely connected with Peter, and was interpreter to the latter when he preached among the Greeks. He invariably, however, occupied a dependent situation, and on this account it is impossible that his name alone should have procured his Gospel an introduction into the church. But, as has been already mentioned, Mark did not write without apostolic authority. *On the contrary, he was under the direction of the Apostle Peter.* This is stated by the entire series of church-fathers during the second and third centuries, with perfect unanimity in the main ; and the statement is corroborated by the case of Luke, which was exactly similar. On this account, the Gospel of Mark was considered as originating with Peter, and such individuals as were particularly attached to this apostle used Mark in preference to all others. Unfortunately, however, we have no minute accounts as to this matter, and hence do not know whether these individuals corrupted the Gospel of Mark, as the Jewish Christians did that of Matthew, or not. It is possible, however, that the so-called *Gospel of the Egyptians* was a corruption of Mark, though the fragments we have of it are not sufficient to enable us to form a certain opinion on this point.

As to *Luke*, we have more clear and certain evidence in this respect. We know that that sect which carried the sentiments of Paul to an erroneous extreme, the *Marcionites*, used only the Gospel of Luke, although Marcion was very well acquainted with the other Gospels, and regarded them as genuine. They had, however, altered Luke in conformity with their opinions, and thus formed, as it were, a new Gospel out of it, which, notwithstanding, still retained much resemblance to the original. The reason why the Marcionites selected Luke was, that this Gospel was written under the direction of the Apostle Paul, who alone, in their opinion, was a genuine apostle of our Lord. Luke, as we know from the Acts of the Apostles, had travelled about with the apostle Paul for a long time, and, in particular, had also accompanied him to Rome. This is clear from the final chapters of the Acts of the Apostles. Connecting this fact with the conclusion of the work, it is perfectly evident when the Evangelist finished it. According to the last chapter, Paul was two years in confinement at Rome. Here Luke breaks off, without mentioning the issue of his trial. Had this been concluded, should we not, of course, have had an account of the emperor's decision respecting the great apostle of the Gentiles ? It can be made very probable, by circumstances deduced from another quarter, that Paul was liberated from his first imprisonment at Rome, and did not suffer as a martyr till he had been a second time placed in bonds. Luke, however, abruptly breaks off in the midst of his narrative. Now, as the Acts of the Apostles are only the second part of Luke's work, the Gospel being the first (compare Luke i. 1 with Acts i. 1), the latter cannot have been written subsequently ; and probably, when Paul's death was apprehended, Luke wrote down the accounts he had received from him or through him, in order to secure them to posterity. Then the apostle, who was still living, attested the purity and accuracy of the work, and from Rome, the great central point of the religious, as well as the political world, it speedily made its way into the churches, in every province of the vast Roman empire. Thus, it was not Luke's name which procured for this Gospel its currency in the church, *but the authority of the Apostle Paul.* Without this, the work of Luke, with its two divisions, the Gospel and the Acts, would have been the less likely to obtain general credit, because it purports to be a mere private production, addressed to a certain *Theophilus.* It is, indeed, very probable, that this Theophilus was a man of note, who was either already a member of the church, or at least well-disposed towards it ; but still he was only a private man, whose name could have no weight with the whole church. He had, probably, already perused divers accounts concerning Christ, and the formation of the primitive churches, which, however, were not duly authentic and certain ; and for this reason, Luke determined to compose for his use an authoritative history of the important events in our Lord's life, and of the foundation of the churches. (Comp. Luke i. 1—4.) Under these circumstances, it is not astonishing that, in the primitive church, there was no opposition either to Luke's Gospel, or his Acts of the Apostles.[1] The many and close relations of the writer, together with the apos-

---

[1] So far as the Acts of the Apostles speaks of the circumstances of Paul, it has a perfect correspondence with Paul's Epistles, as the latter have with the former. See this fact more fully developed in the *fourth chapter* of this treatise.

tolic authority in his behalf, were such evidence in favour of the work, that not a single valid suspicion could arise respecting its genuineness.

Lastly, The circumstances in regard to the Gospel of John are particularly calculated to place its genuineness beyond dispute ; for John the Evangelist lived much longer than any of the other apostles. So far as we know, none of the others were alive after the destruction of Jerusalem by Titus, the Roman emperor, in the year 70 A.D. John, however, survived it nearly thirty years, dying about the close of the first century, under the reign of the emperor Domitian. Hence, many Christians who had heard of our Lord's farewell words to him (John xxi. 22, 23), believed that John would not die, an idea which the Evangelist himself declares erroneous. This beloved disciple of our Lord, during the latter part of his life, as we know from testimonies on which perfect reliance may be placed, lived at Ephesus, in Asia Minor, where the Apostle Paul had founded a flourishing church. The importance of this church, about the year 64 or 75 A.D., is evinced by Paul's Epistle to the Ephesians ; and subsequently it was very much enlarged. It was in this subsequent period that John wrote his Gospel. This is clear, *first*, from a comparison of the Gospel with the Revelation. This last work was written by John at an earlier period, before the destruction of Jerusalem. John's style in this prophetic composition is not so thoroughly easy as we find it at a later period in the Gospel, which he must have written after longer intercourse with native Greeks. *Again*, John plainly had the three other Gospels before him when he wrote ; for he omits all which they had described with sufficient minuteness, *e. g.*, the institution of the holy supper, and only relates that which was new respecting the life of his Lord and Master. Hence, these must have been already composed, and also so generally diffused, that John could presume them universally known in the church. *Moreover*, the persons to whom John's work has special reference, viz., certain Gnostics, did not attain importance till Jerusalem was destroyed, and most of the apostles had left this world. Now, if we duly consider all these circumstances, it will be even more incredible in regard to John's Gospel than any other, that it should have been forged in his name. From his being the sole surviving apostle, innumerable eyes were upon him and his movements. He lived and laboured in one of the chief cities of the known world, in which was a large church, and the vicinity of which was wholly peopled with Christians. We have an epistle of Pliny, a distinguished Roman officer of that region, written only a few years after the death of John the Evangelist, in which he describes the vast increase of the Christians in Asia Minor, and lays before the emperor Trajan (the successor of the emperor in whose reign John's death took place) measures for preventing the further extension of their tenets. Now, how was it possible that in this state of things a work could be forged in John's name ; or, supposing even that one might have been (though history says nothing of any such imposition under the name of John),[1] how is it conceivable that no opposition should have been made thereto, when many thousands were acquainted with John, and must have known exactly what he wrote, and what he did not ? *Of such opposition, however, there is nowhere the slightest trace.* Not merely all teachers of the orthodox church, in all parts of the wide Roman empire, but also all heretics of the most various sects, make use of the work as a sacred valuable legacy bequeathed to the church by the beloved disciple ; and the few heretics who make no use of it, as, *e. g.*, Marcion, still evince acquaintance with it, and regard it as a genuine work of John's, but are impudent enough to deny that John himself had a correct knowledge of the Gospel, because he was too much of a Jew. Whether, as was the case with the other Gospels, John's also was corrupted by the heretics, who felt that they were specially aimed at in it, is uncertain. The Gnostics, with the exception of Marcion (who, however, as has been already mentioned, is only improperly reckoned among the Gnostics), made most frequent use of John, as in their opinion specially favouring their spiritual ideas. We do not learn, however, that there existed in ancient times any Gospel of John corrupted by the Gnostics, as Luke's Gospel was mutilated by Marcion. In modern times, it is true, a Gospel of John thus disfigured has come to public knowledge ; but the alterations in it originated at a late period in the middle ages.

The doubts respecting the genuineness of John's Gospel which have, nevertheless, been proposed in recent times, took their rise, like those in regard to Matthew, solely from its *internal* character. When once doubts were thus occasioned, endeavours were made to sustain them on historical grounds likewise. These, however, are of little weight,[2] from the firmness of the foundation on which the Gospel rests. It was with John much as with Matthew, in regard to those characteristics which excited doubt of the genuineness of the book. It was correctly remarked, that John gives a different representation of our Lord from that presented by the first three Evangelists. In his Gospel, Christ's actions and discourses appear,

[1] There does exist in MS., it is true, a second apocalypse under John's name; but this production appears to belong to a much later period. There is also an apostolic history of older date, in which, however, John is only mentioned along with others; it is not ascribed to him.

[2] The most weighty opponent of the genuineness of John has given the excellent example of publicly acknowledging that he has become convinced of the genuineness of this jewel of the church, and retracts his doubts. May this example find numerous imitators!

as it were, transfigured and spiritualized, while in the other Evangelists they appear in a costume more or less Jewish and national. Now, as it is not conceivable, it is said, that the same person should be so differently represented, and John, the beloved disciple of our Lord, would certainly not have portrayed his Master as other than he really was, while the description of the actions of Jesus (who appeared as a Jew among Jews, and in behalf of Jews), given in the accounts of the first three Evangelists, is much more conformable to probability, the Gospel which bears John's name must be of later origin. But here, as in regard to Matthew, it may be observed, that from a perfectly correct remark false conclusions have been deduced. It is indeed true that John exhibits the Saviour in a far more spiritual and glorified character than the first three Evangelists ; but this proves nothing, except that John was the most spiritual of the Evangelists. The same individual may be regarded and described very differently by different persons. Of this truth we have a remarkable example in a great character of Grecian antiquity. Socrates is represented to our view in his actions and discourses by two of his confidential pupils, Xenophon and Plato. And how entirely different is the description given of him by these two writers ! In fact, these biographers may be said to sustain very much such a mutual relation as that of John and the first Evangelists. While Xenophon paid attention principally to the external acts of Socrates, Plato describes his spiritual characteristics. Now, if it was possible to represent a common human being of eminence in two very different lights, without doing violence to truth, how much rather might it be so in regard to one who was greater than Solomon, or than Socrates and his biographers. He who lived a purely heavenly life on earth, and spake words of eternal truth, could not but be very variously described, according to the characteristics of the human soul which received the rays of light proceeding from him. Each soul reflected his image according to its own profundity and compass, and yet each might be right. It was for this reason that more than one Gospel was included in the collection of the sacred writings, since only the presentation of different portraitures together could prevent a partial view of our Saviour's character. As it is only from connection of the accounts of Xenophon and Plato that we can obtain a complete picture of Socrates, so we cannot comprehend the life of our Lord, which affords so many different aspects, without uniting the peculiar traits scattered in all the four Gospels into one general portraiture. With all the difference of representation observable in the Evangelists, there are still resemblances and affinities enough to make it evident that they all had the same great personage in view. As John relates narratives of cures exactly like those in Matthew, Mark, and

Luke, so the Gospels of the latter contain passages which, in elevation, depth, and richness of thought, are not inferior to our Lord's
discourses in John, and indeed resemble them in phraseology.
Among these is the lofty and astonishingly beautiful passage,
Matth. xi. 25—30 :—" I thank thee, O Father, Lord of heaven and
earth, because thou hast hid these things from the wise and prudent, and hast revealed them unto babes. Even so, Father, for so
it seemed good in thy sight. All things are delivered unto me of
my Father ; and no man knoweth the Son but the Father ; neither
knoweth any man the Father save the Son, and he to whomsoever
the Son will reveal him. Come unto me, all ye that labour and are
heavy laden, and I will give you rest. Take my yoke upon you
and learn of me ; for I am meek and lowly in heart, and ye shall
find rest unto your souls. For my yoke is easy, and my burden is
light." He from whose mouth such language proceeded might certainly be represented in such an aspect as John has given to Jesus,
if the description were undertaken by one in some measure capable
of appreciating a character of this nature; and that John was thus
capable is sufficiently clear from his Epistles.

If, therefore, we look at the Gospels as a collection, or consider
each separately, we cannot but say that they are more strongly
accredited and sustained by external and internal proofs than any
other work of antiquity. *Few* writings have such ancient testimonies in their favour, reaching back to the time of the authors;
none have so many of them, so totally distinct, so corroborative of
each other. While, then, the chief argument in behalf of the Scriptures generally, and of the Gospels in particular, is the *witness of
the Holy Spirit*, perceived in his heart by every believer as he pe-
ruses the Scriptures (a point on which we shall enlarge at the close
of our treatise) ; still, the possibility of proving on historical
grounds the genuineness and primitive character of the Gospels is a
great additional cause of gratitude, inasmuch as it removes occasions of distrust, particularly from weak and doubting minds, and
affords motives for the confirmation of their faith.

CHAPTER IV.

THE PAULINE EPISTLES.

ALONG with the collection of the Gospels, there existed at an
early period of the church, as was related above,[1] a collection of
Paul's Epistles called the Apostle. In the lives of Irenaeus, Tertul-

[1] Comp. Chap i.

lian, and Clement of Alexandria, who were all acquainted with and
used it, this collection contained thirteen Epistles, viz. the Epistle
to the Romans, two to the Corinthians, those to the Galatians,
Ephesians, Philippians, and Colossians, two to the Thessalonians,
two to Timothy, and those to Titus and Philemon. The Epistle to
the Hebrews was not inserted in this collection, because opinions
were not united as to its origin. (See Chap. vi. below). Half a
century before the time of the fathers just mentioned, we find a collection of Pauline Epistles in the hands of Marcion. that extrava-
gant reverer of the Apostle Paul. He was born in Asia Minor,
where, as is well known, the Apostle Paul had long lived and
laboured, and was highly reverenced. Thence Marcion went to
Rome, carrying with him the collection of Pauline Epistles which he
had made use of in Asia. This, however, contained but ten
Epistles ; there were wanting the three commonly termed *pastoral*
letters, viz., the two to Timothy and that to Titus ; called *pastoral*
letters, because in them Paul gives directions to spiritual pastors in
regard to the suitable performance of their official duties. The
small Epistle to Philemon was known to him, because it stood in
close connexion with the Epistle to the Colossians ; but the three
pastoral letters seem to have been diffused but slowly, as independent private productions, and hence, also, not to have been inserted
in the original collection. How the collection of the Pauline
Epistles, in the form in which we now have it, originated, is unknown, and has not yet been satisfactorily accounted for by any
conjecture.[1] For the supposition that, like the collection of the
Gospels, it originated in different places at once, merely by the
gradual transmission thither of the Epistles of Paul as fast as they
were composed, is forbidden by the circumstance that, as can be
proved, they are not arranged in the order of their composition.
The collection cannot, however, have been accidentally formed ; for
it is clear that a certain plan has been followed. At the beginning
are placed the Epistles to the Romans and Corinthians, distinguished for their length and internal importance ; then follows a letter to
several churches in a whole province, the Epistle to the Galatians ;
then the smaller Epistles to churches in particular cities, to the
Ephesians, Philippians, Colossians, and Thessalonians ; lastly, come
the Epistles to private persons. Moreover, had the collection of
them been left to accident, sometimes one arrangement would have
been adopted and sometimes another, which is not the case, the
order having been the same that we now observe, as far back as the

---

[1] We find very few traces of a different arrangement of the Epistles of Paul: a different one, however, is followed in an old catalogue of the books of the New Testament,
probably pertaining to the church at Rome. It is called *Muratori's* Catalogue, from an
Italian abbot of that name who discovered the MSS. which contained it.

second century. As, therefore, the order of the Epistles was evidently the work of design, and its general reception throughout the church indicates that it proceeded from some authoritative source, the most reasonable supposition is, that the Apostle Paul himself made the collection. During the second imprisonment at Rome, to which, as we shall see hereafter, it is highly probable that the apostle was subjected, he may have collected together the ten Epistles, as being the principal ones of a doctrinal nature which he had as yet written, in order to bequeath them as a legacy to the church. It was in this original form that Marcion possessed the collection.[1] After the collection was made up, near the close of his life, Paul wrote the three pastoral letters, which were afterwards added to the original collection, and naturally placed last. By accident Marcion had not become acquainted with these ·letters, and therefore retained the most ancient form of the collection of Paul's Epistles. A very weighty testimony in favour of this view is presented in the second Epistle of the Apostle Peter, who, at near the conclusion of his letter, says : " And account that the long-suffering of our Lord is salvation ; even as our beloved brother Paul, also, according to the wisdom given unto him, *hath written unto you ; as also in all* (his) *Epistles, speaking in them of these things ;* in which are some things hard to be understood, which they that are unlearned and unstable wrest," &c. (2 Pet. iii. 15, 16). According to the first Epistle of Peter (i. 1, comp. 2 Pet. iii. 1), Peter wrote to the Christians in Pontus, Galatia, and other provinces of Asia Minor, to which also Paul's Epistles to the Galatians, Ephesians, and Colossians are directed. Peter, therefore, might presume that his readers were acquainted with these. The expression *all* (his) *Epistles*, however, clearly indicate a collection of Epistles. Otherwise, there is something of indefiniteness in it. Paul, no doubt, wrote more Epistles during his life than we now possess. But most of his Epistles were not exactly adapted for general diffusion. The expression, *all* (his) *Epistles*, must therefore have reference to a collection of the apostle's letters, which could be read through. If it be also considered that Peter was in Paul's company in Rome, and that consequently he would naturally have had acquaintance with the collection of his Epistles, it will be plain that this passage is hardly intelligible, except on the supposition that a collection of Paul's Epistles was already in existence.[2] It is true the genuine-

---

[1] According to the account of Epiphanius, it is true, the order of the ten Epistles in Marcion's Canon was different from that in ours, viz., Galatians, Corinthians, Romans, Thessalonians, Ephesians, Colossians, Philemon, and Philippians. If this statement be credited, it must be allowed that Marcion's collection originated independently of ours.

[2] Some may think that too much is inferred by the author from Peter's expression, and, indeed, it must be admitted, that to say that Peter's language is hardly intelligible, except on the supposition of an existing collection of Paul's Epistles, is somewhat ex-

ness of the second Epistle of Peter is now disputed, and certainly much that is of an imposing nature can be alleged against it. Still, however, all that can be said does not, I am convinced, demonstrate its spuriousness, while there is certainly much evidence of its genuineness. At any rate, this mention of a collection of Paul's Epistles should not be urged against the genuineness of the second Epistle of Peter, as all acknowledge that nothing certain is known in regard to the formation of this collection. But on these points we will speak more at large hereafter.

If it be admitted, however, that Paul himself made the collection of his Epistles, or at least, caused it to be made at Rome under his direction, we have then an explanation of the fact, that in regard to the genuineness of this collection, as in regard to that of the Gospels, *not the slightest doubt was ever expressed.* Members of the Catholic church in all parts of the world, as also of the various sects, make use of the collection and of the individual Epistles, without allowing themselves to intimate the smallest doubt in regard to them. Now, this undeniable fact is wholly irreconcilable with the supposition that all or any Epistles in the collection are spurious. Indeed, the first supposition, that all the Epistles of Paul are spurious, has never been maintained, and never can be, except in despite of all history. But even the idea that one or two spurious, forged Epistles may have obtained a place in the collection, is hardly to be reconciled with the universal acknowledgment of all the Epistles in the church of ancient times. Consider only, how universally Paul was known in the early church ! From Spain (which in all probability he visited), he had travelled about through Italy and all Greece to the remotest countries of Asia Minor, Syria, and Arabia ; he had resided for years in some of the large cities of the then known world, in Rome, Corinth, Thessalonica, Ephesus, Antioch, Cæsarea, Jerusalem ; he had everywhere founded numerous churches, and maintained the most active intercourse with them. How, then, when he was so well known, could a work be forged in his name, with any prospect of its being generally acknowledged ? The impossibility of this occurrence is the more evident, from the fact that all Paul's Epistles are addressed to important churches, or to persons living in well-known places. If those who received the Epistles were not always designated, then it might be supposed

travagant. Our English translation, by inserting the word *his* in the phraseology of Peter, has somewhat modified the sense of the original, and weakened the force of Olshausen's remarks. The Greek expression is, ἐν πάσαις ταῖς ἐπιστολαῖς, *i. e.*, perhaps, in all *the* Epistles. Now, though it would give an intelligible sense to these words to suppose that Peter meant to make his observation concerning Paul's Epistles generally, of which he presumed some might, and some might not, have come to the knowledge of those to whom he wrote ; still, it can hardly be disputed, that his phraseology becomes much more natural, if we suppose a current collection of the Epistles.—T.

that some spurious ones obtained general circulation. No one, perhaps, could then say with certainty, whether Paul wrote such a particular Epistle or not ; for it is not conceivable that Paul should at once have told every body he knew how many Epistles he had written ; and thus one might be personally acquainted with Paul, and still be deceived by an artfully-contrived Epistle. But take the case as it is. Were the Epistle to the Ephesians, against which, as we shall see, objections have been raised, really spurious, forged in Paul's name, we readily admit that it might have been received as genuine in the whole church beside, for it is as like Paul's Epistles as one egg is like another ; but could it have been acknowledged as genuine in Ephesus itself, and the Asiatic churches connected with the Ephesians ? Can we suppose that the Ephesians had so little regard for the great founder of their church, that they did not even know whether their beloved preacher had or had not written them a letter while in bonds ? And can they have been so totally wanting in sensibility to friendship and love, as not to preserve the apostle's communication, when every man, at all susceptible of emotions of friendship, is anxious to preserve what has been traced by a beloved hand ? It is hence plain, that a spurious Epistle to the Ephesians must have been known in Ephesus as what it really was, a forged production ; and it is impossible to suppose, that if the Epistle had been disputed by any considerable church, and particularly by the very one to which it purported to have been sent, the opposition should have been so completely suppressed. The declaration of the Ephesian church that they had received no such Epistle, that they had not the original in their archives, would have been sufficient to destroy its credit.

To this it is added, that all the Epistles of Paul go beyond general expressions, such as may be easily invented ; that they exhibit a definite concrete[1] purport, which has reference to the particular wants of each church, and its manifestations as to Christian life. Such representations of actual facts, in regard to the ancient churches, can have proceeded only from immediate contact with them, and consequently certify us of the genuineness of the Pauline Epistles. With all that is of a special nature, however, in each particular Epistle of Paul, there is observable, in all together, a uniformity of style, and a unity in doctrinal ideas, which wholly prevents suspicion respecting the genuineness of the epistolary collection. For the usual reason of forging writings in the name of another is, that the forger wishes to give currency to a favourite

---

[1] This term, in the sense in which it is here used, is borrowed from logic. In that science, it is known, abstract and concrete terms are contra-distinguished. An abstract term is one signifying some attribute, without reference to any particular subject; a concrete term designates both the attribute and the subject to which it belongs.—T.

idea under some celebrated name. In no Epistle, however, is there any prominent idea which is remote from the circle of Pauline doctrine, and seems to be a foreign idea clothed with the costume of Paul's style. We rather find every where the same main thoughts which actuated the life of Paul, running through the entire collection, and giving their stamp to the whole.

The principal evidence, however, of the genuineness of the Pauline Epistles, regarded in a historical light, is the circumstance, that we can assign to the Epistles their exact places in the life of the Apostle Paul by following the Acts of the Apostles. Thus are they most fully and firmly bound one to another, and all to the Acts of the Apostles. This arrangement of the individual Epistles in accordance with the thread of Paul's life, is effected in such a manner as to show in chronological order the occasions of their composition, and their strict relations to his known movements.

Paul, the great apostle of the Gentiles, who, as is well known, was at first named Saul, was a native Jew of the tribe of Benjamin, and was born in Tarsus in Cilicia. In order to perfect himself in the knowledge of the law of his native country, he early betook himself to Jerusalem, where he was taught by the celebrated Gamaliel. His zeal for the hereditary observances of his countrymen caused him to persecute the Christians, as soon as he had obtained knowledge of them, with all the vehemence of his fiery nature. At the death of *Stephen*, the first Christian martyr, he was busy keeping the clothes of his murderers while they stoned him. (Acts vii. 57 *seq.*) From Jerusalem Paul betook himself to Damascus, to stir up the Jews there also against the Christians; but the Lord Jesus appeared to him before the city in his divine glory, and showed him who it was that he persecuted. (Acts ix. 22—26). As Paul had not persecuted the Christians from intentional wickedness, or from carnal selfishness, contrary to his interior conviction, but rather with the honest idea that he was thereby doing God service, the divine light which enlightened his dark mind by this vision at once produced an entire change in his feelings. With the same ardent zeal for truth and right which he had manifested in persecuting the Gospel, he now defended it; though his zeal was indeed purified and made holier by the Spirit of the Lord. After a season of quiet reflection and repose, such as he needed to perceive the greatness of that internal change which he had undergone, and the depth of the new principle of life within him, Paul began to make known the conviction he had just obtained. It was in Antioch (about 44 A. D.) that Paul began formally to preach; and he taught in this city, along with Barnabas, a whole year. After a journey to Jerusalem, whither he carried money that had been collected for the poor in that city, the elders of the church at Antioch designated him as a messenger to the Gentiles ; and he with Barnabas set out on *the first missionary expedition,* about 45 A. D. It extended no farther than the neighbouring countries of Asia Minor. Paul travelled through Cyprus to Perga in Pamphylia, and Antioch in Pisidia, and returned through Lystra, Derbe, and Attalia by sea to Antioch. Consequently, on his first missionary enterprise, the apostle did not visit any of the cities or provinces to which he wrote Epistles. On his return to Antioch he found that some strict Jewish Christians had come thither from Jerusalem, and excited dissensions. Paul had begun to preach the Gospel to the Gentiles, and in such a way as to dispense with the observance of the Mosaic law as a necessary duty. Many Jewish Christians could not rise to the level of this evangelical freedom in regard to the external law. Even Peter at first adhered so strenuously to the forms of Jewish practice, that nothing but a vision could bring him to see, that under the New Testament, the Mosaic law, in regard to meats, had lost its external importance. (Acts x. 11 *seq.*) In order to come to a fixed decision on this important point, the church at Antioch determined that Paul and Barnabas, with several companions, should proceed to Jerusalem to present this question before the Apostles. They there declared what God had wrought by them among the Gentiles ; Peter testified the same in regard to his labours ; and James, the brother of our Lord, showed that it was foretold, in the prophecies of Scripture, that the Gentiles likewise should be called into the church of God. On these grounds the apostles, with the elders and all the church at Jerusalem, determined to send deputies to Antioch with Paul and Barnabas, and communicated their judgment in a letter carried by them to the church at Antioch. This important transaction at Jerusalem, which publicly announced the character of Christianity as an universal religion, is called the *council of the Apostles.* It was held about the year 52 A. D. The decision of this apostolic body was of the utmost consequence to the Apostle Paul, as in his subsequent labours he had to contend constantly with narrow-minded Jewish Christians, who wished to impose the Mosaic law upon the Gentiles also as essential to salvation. Against these Paul now advanced, not only his own personal influence, but the authority of all the apostles. This, at least, was effected thereby— that the supporters of the ceremonial law and its perpetual validity were compelled to secede from the universal apostolic church, and form themselves into a distinct sect. It is true, however, that their opposition to the Apostle Paul was continued with extreme obstinacy ; and we find in his Epistles numberless allusions to the persecutions which he encountered at their hand.

Soon after the apostolic council (53 A. D.) Paul undertook his *second* great journey. He separated from Barnabas, who united with his kinsman Mark in preaching the Gospel. Paul took Silas as his companion instead of Barnabas. He directed his course first to the churches founded on his previous journey ; and thence onward to *Galatia*, and to Troas, on the western coast of Asia Minor. Thence the Lord conducted him by a vision in a dream, into Macedonia, where he founded the church of *Philippi ;* and then went to Thessalonica. (Acts xvi. 10 *seq.* xvii. 1 *seq.*) Unfortunately, Paul could remain only about three weeks in the latter city, for, as he met with much success among the proselytes that had connected themselves with the Jewish synagogues, there arose an uproar against him among the Jews, who actually compelled him to leave the city, and flee to Berœa. (Acts xvii. 10.) As, however, the Jews in this place likewise vented their rage against the apostle of our Lord, Paul betook himself to Athens, where also some hearts were warmed by the fire of his preaching. He next proceeded onward to Corinth. Here, in one of the great cities of antiquity, where luxury and debauchery had reached their highest pitch, but where, on that very account, a strong desire for salvation was readily excited, Paul laboured with remarkable success for more than a year and a half. He found there a Jewish family from Rome, Aquila, and his wife Priscilla, celebrated in the history of the ancient church. As Aquila pursued the same craft with Paul, the latter lived and wrought with him, and besides discoursed in the house of a certain Justus. From hence Paul wrote the first Epistles among those still preserved to us, viz., the two Epistles to the Thessalonians. Now, if we compare the tenor of the Epistles with the situation of the apostle, and their relation to the church at Thessalonica, we shall find them throughout conformable to the circumstances. As Paul was unable to preach in Thessalonica more than three weeks, he must naturally have been very anxious respecting the fate of those who believed in that city ; he feared that they might again fall away on account of the persecutions which threatened them. Hence his apprehensions had already induced him, as soon as he arrived at Athens, to send Timothy from thence to Thessalonica, in order to learn what was really the condition of the church. Timothy rejoined him at Corinth ; and his mind being set at rest by the information which Timothy communicated, he wrote the first Epistle, for the purpose of confirming and establishing the Thessalonians in the faith to which they had so faithfully adhered. (Acts xvii. 15 ; xviii. 5 ; 1 Thess. iii. 2, 5, 6.) It is a circumstance entirely consonant with what we must suppose to have been the situation of the Christians in Thessalonica, that they did not rightly comprehend the doctrine of our Lord's resurrection. This would naturally be the case from the shortness of the period during which they enjoyed the apostle's instructions. (1 Thess. iv. 13 *seq.*) They feared that those believers who might die before the coming of our Lord, would be shut out from the joys attendant on the Messiah's reign upon earth. The apostle, however, sets them right in regard to their fear, showing them that there would be a twofold resurrection. Those who had fallen asleep in faith respecting the Saviour, would not rest till the general resurrection, but would be raised up at the coming of Christ, and would behold the Lord with those who were alive. The same subject also soon afterward caused the Apostle Paul to write the *second Epistle* to the Christians at Thessalonica, also from Corinth. The explanation of Paul had indeed quieted the apprehension of the believers of that city in regard to those of their number who met with an early death ; but some expressions used . by Paul in his first Epistle (particularly 1 Thess. iv. 17), together with false rumours respecting his view of the proximity of our Lord's coming, had led some susceptible minds to the idea that this important event not only *might,* but *must,* take place very soon. Thus they openly designated the period of our Lord's return, in total contrariety to Paul's meaning, who did indeed, with them, hope and ardently desire that our Lord might come in their time, and by no means stated expressly that he would not do so, since that would have been a negative determination of the point ; but maintained the *possibility* that he would, and founded thereon, after the example of Christ himself, an exhortation to constant watchfulness. In order, therefore, to moderate the excessive disposition of the Christians at Thessalonica to look upon this great event as *necessarily* about to take place in their own time, Paul presented to view certain things which must all take place before it. From the consideration of these points, it could not but be evident to the Thessalonians, that this event could not take place so suddenly as they anticipated, and thus their excited minds would probably be quieted. In these respects, as regards the state of things at that time, the two Epistles possess entire and undeniable historical keeping ; and we shall not err widely from the truth if we assign their composition to the years 54 and 55 of the Christian era.

From Corinth the Apostle Paul now returned to Antioch, whence he had been sent. (Acts xviii. 22.) Without, however, remaining long at rest, he in the following year (57 A. D.) entered upon his *third missionary tour,* going first to Galatia again, where he had preached on his second tour, and then to the wealthy and celebrated city of *Ephesus,* where he abode more than two years. From this city Paul wrote first to the *Galatians,* and subsequently to the *Co-rinthians.* The Epistle to the Galatians was occasioned by those same Jewish Christians, of whom we have before remarked, that they constantly strove to cast hindrances in the way of Paul's operations. The Galatian churches, which Paul, on his second visit to Galatia (Gal. iv. 13), had found walking in the true faith, had been misled by these men in regard to the requirements of religion. Through the idea that the observance of the Jewish ceremonial law was essential to salvation, the Galatian Christians were led to regard circumcision, the solemnization of the Sabbath and of the Jewish feasts, and other ordinances of the Old Testament, which the New Testament valued only from their spiritual signification, as of worth in an external view, and in this way suffered themselves to lose sight of the interior life of faith. The object of the apostle, therefore, in his Epistles, was to develope thoroughly to the Galatians the relation between the law and the Gospel, and to show that, in the spiritual freedom conferred by the latter, the external rites of the former might, indeed, be observed, but that they must be observed in a higher manner, *i. e.*, spiritually. Previously, however, he makes some remarks respecting himself personally. For, as the Jewish Christians presumed to dispute Paul's apostolic authority, he found himself compelled to vindicate it by a historical account of himself. He states (i. 12 *seq.*), that he did not receive his Gospel from man, but immediately from God ; that at first he had persecuted the church of God, but that God, who had called him from his mother's womb, had been pleased to reveal his Son in him, that he might preach him to the heathen, through the Gospel. This evidently refers to the event of our Lord's appearance to Paul near Damascus, on which occasion the Lord said to him, " I am Jesus, whom thou persecutest. But rise, and stand upon thy feet : for I have appeared unto thee for this purpose, to make thee a minister and a witness both of these things which thou hast seen, and of those things in the which I will appear unto thee ; delivering thee from the people and from the Gentiles, unto whom now I send thee, to open their eyes, and to turn them from darkness to light, and from the power of Satan unto God, that they may receive forgiveness of sins, and inheritance among them which are sanctified by faith that is in me." (Acts xxvi. 15—18.) This reference to so peculiar occurrences in Paul's life exhibits a sufficient security for the genuineness of this Epistle ; and, in connection with its entire contents, as also with its style, has sufficed to place it for ever beyond suspicion.

An occasion equally sad in respect to the apostle gave rise to the *first Epistle to the Corinthians*, which was likewise written from Ephesus. Before the first of the Epistles which are in our possession, Paul had written another to Corinth (1 Cor. v. 9), which, however, has perished. We have, indeed, *a pretended* Epistle of Paul to the Corinthians, which claims to be this lost Epistle, but a slight examination is sufficient to manifest its spuriousness. Moreover, this Epistle of Paul was regarded as lost by all Christian antiquity. This first Epistle, as is shown by 1 Cor. v. 1—9, was occasioned by the circumstance, that an individual in the Corinthian church had matrimonial intercourse with his mother-in-law, the wife of his deceased father. Paul pointed out to the church the necessity of excluding from among them him who sustained this incestuous relation, that he might be awakened to penitence. To this Epistle of Paul, the Corinthian Christians replied in such a way, as to show plainly that they misunderstood some parts of it, particularly what Paul had said respecting the avoidance of lasciviousness. These misapprehensions are corrected by Paul in the *first* of the two Epistles which have been preserved to us. He likewise speaks in this same letter of another important circumstance in regard to the Corinthian church, which presents considerable coincidence with the situation of the Christians in Galatia. It is that some of the Jewish Christians, who had excited dissensions among the believers there, had come to Corinth also. True, some had remained faithful to Paul; but others appealed, in contradiction of his authority, to Peter (Cephas), although he agreed perfectly with Paul in his views respecting the law. They probably objected to the Apostle Paul, as did the Jewish Christians in Galatia, that he had not, like Peter, known our Lord personally. Besides these two parties, Paul mentions two others (1 Cor. i. 12), the distinctive characteristics of which, however, are uncertain. There were, therefore, divisions in the Corinthian church, and from these had proceeded manifold disorders. Paul's first Epistle is occupied with the reconciliation of the former, and the removal of the latter.

Our first Epistle to the Corinthians comprises such an abundance of peculiar circumstances entirely conformable with the situation of the church in its earliest days, that we cannot for a moment suppose it possible that it is a forgery. Moreover, particular facts mentioned in it coincide most exactly with the events of Paul's life, as known from the Acts of the Apostles. Thus, according to Acts xix. 22, he sent away his two companions, Timothy and Erastus, from Ephesus, a short time before he himself left the city; and, according to 1 Cor. iv. 17, likewise, he had despatched Timothy to the Corinthians. According to the same passage in the Acts, Paul purposed soon to leave Ephesus, and travel through Achaia (this was the Greek province in which Corinth was situated) to Jerusalem, and the same thing is indicated by 1 Cor. xvi. 5. Thus, all circumstances unite to give a sure historical basis to the Epistle. As its composition must be placed a little before Paul's departure from Ephesus, it was probably written about 59 A.D., while the Epistle to the Galatians may have been written about the year 58 A.D.

Before the Apostle Paul left Ephesus, then, he sent Titus with a special commission to Corinth. He hoped to be able to wait for him in Ephesus, in order to receive an account of the troubled state of affairs in the Corinthian church, and of the reception which his Epistle encountered. But a sudden uproar created by Demetrius the silver-smith (Acts xix. 24 *seq.*), who was himself injured in respect to the gains which he derived from the sale of small silver models of the celebrated temple of Diana at Ephesus, compelled him to leave the city earlier than he wished. In Macedonia, however, whither Paul immediately betook himself, he again met with Titus, who then informed him particularly of the condition of the church at Corinth, and the impression which his Epistle had produced. This account induced the Apostle to write the *Second Epistle to the Corinthians*, from Macedonia. The contents of this other Epistle, which was written a few months after the first, bear so close a relation to the contents of the first, that the identity of the author is, thereby alone, made sufficiently evident. In the second chapter, *e. g.*, we find mention again of the incestuous person, whom Paul had enjoined it upon the church to exclude from communion with them. As he had now been excommunicated, Paul speaks in his behalf, that he might not sink into utter despondency (2 Cor. ii. 7). Of most importance, however, are the particular expressions in regard to those Jewish Christians who desolated the Corinthian church as well as others. Titus had informed the apostle with what an arrogant disposition they had received his letter. Against these, therefore, he expresses himself with the utmost severity, while he treats those who remained faithful to the truth, with suavity and great kindness. In rebuking the perversity of these Judaizers, he feels it necessary to speak of himself ; for these proud sectaries not only rejected the apostolic authority of Paul, but also sought by their calumnies to deprive him of the honour of being the most successful labourer in our Lord's vineyard. With noble plainness, therefore, Paul boasts of all that the Lord had done for him and through him ; and the further removed this plainness was from false humility, and the less he avoided giving ground for the imputation of *appearing* arrogant and self-conceited, the more likely was his account of himself to make an impression upon all his opponents. We do not know definitely what effect this Epistle produced upon the state of things at Corinth ; but, from the subsequent flourishing condition of the Corinthian church, we may with great probability infer that Paul's Epistle contributed essentially to the annihilation of divisions. At all events, the Epistle is so completely Pauline, and harmonises so exactly with all known historical circumstances, that its genuineness has never been contested either in ancient or modern times.

What was not effected by the Epistle of Paul to the church of

Corinth, was undoubtedly accomplished by the apostle's personal presence in this metropolis. For, from Macedonia Paul went to Achaia (Acts xx. 3), and abode there three months. The greater part of this time he certainly spent in Corinth, and from hence he wrote the *Epistle to the Romans*, shortly before his departure from Corinth for Jerusalem in order to carry a collection of alms for the poor of that city (Acts xxiv. 17 *seq.* Rom. xv. 25, 26). This important Epistle (viz., that to the Romans) bears the stamp of a genuine apostolic letter so completely in both thought and language, that neither ancient nor modern times have advanced a single doubt as to its origin. The particular doctrine which Paul presented to view more frequently and more prominently than any other apostle, viz., that man is saved by faith in him who was crucified and rose again, and not by the works of the law, either ceremonial or moral, forms the central topic of the Epistle to the Romans; and, moreover, all the historical allusions which occur in it are entirely suitable to the circumstances under which it was written. Paul, *e. g.*, according to this Epistle (Rom. i. 12, 15 ; Acts xxiii), had not yet been in Rome when he wrote it ; and this agrees exactly with the statement of the apostle in Acts xix. 21. The many persons whom he salutes at the end of the Epistle, he became acquainted with from his numerous travels in Asia Minor and Greece ; for, as there was a general conflux to Rome from all quarters, and also a general dispersion thence, it being the centre of the world, there was no city in which Romans did not reside, or of whose inhabitants many were not constrained by circumstances to journey to Rome, or to establish themselves there as residents. On account of this importance of the city of Rome, which must necessarily have been communicated to the church in that place, there is sufficient proof of the genuineness of this Epistle in the single circumstance that this church, in which Paul afterwards abode some years, never contradicted the universal opinion that Paul wrote this Epistle to them, but rather rejoiced in being honoured with such an apostolic communication.

Hitherto we have seen the celebrated apostle of the Gentiles constantly labouring with freedom and boldness ; but his departure from Corinth brought upon him a long and cruel imprisonment. For Paul immediately returned from Corinth to Macedonia, embarked there at Philippi (Acts xx. 3 *seq.*) and sailed along the coasts of Asia Minor. At Miletus he called to him the elders of the church of Ephesus (Acts xx. 17 *seq.*) and took pathetic leave of them ; for he was persuaded that he should never again see these beloved brethren (xx. 38). About the year 60 A. D. the apostle arrived at Jerusalem, having passed through Cæsarea ; but was there immediately arrested (Acts xxii.) and carried back to Cæsarea

(Acts xxiii. 31 *seq.*) Here he was indeed examined by the pro-consul Felix ; but as he could not pronounce sentence against him and hesitated to release him, Paul remained two years in captivity. At the end of that time there came another proconsul, Porcius Festus, to Cæsarea. He commenced the examination anew, but when the apostle, as a Roman citizen, appealed to Cæsar, he sent him to Rome. This was about 62 A. D. On the voyage thither, Paul, together with the Roman soldiers who accompanied him, suf-fered shipwreck, and they were compelled to pass the winter on the island of Malta. Paul did not, therefore, arrive at Rome before the commencment of the following year, and was there again kept as a prisoner for two years, *i. e.*, till 65 A. D., before his case was decided. Still his confinement at Rome was not so strict as that at Cæsarea. He was permitted to hire a dwelling in the city, to go about, speak, and write as he pleased ; only, he was always accompanied by a soldier. Luke alone details all these events in the last chapters of the Acts, with very great minuteness. From Paul's Epistles we learn nothing respecting this period ; for Paul seems not to have written at all from Cæsarea. Probably the strict durance in which he was held did not permit any communication by writing. In the providence of God, this long confinement may have served to ac-quaint Paul with himself, with the depths of his own interior being. For, the manner of life which Paul led and was obliged to lead, the perpetual bustle of travel, his constant efforts in regard to others, might have injured him by dissipation of his thoughts, and might, so to speak, have exhausted the fulness of his spirit, had he not possessed some quiet seasons in which, while his attention was turned wholly upon himself, he might be spiritually replenished and invigorated for future seasons of intense outward exertion.

But from the other of the two places where Paul was compelled to remain a prisoner for a long period, *i. e.*, Rome, he certainly wrote several Epistles, viz., *the Epistles to the Ephesians, Philip-pians, Colossians, and Philemon.* Still, although in these Epistles mention is made of some historical particulars, he supposes the oc-currences in regard to himself to be generally known among the Christians of the churches in Macedonia and Asia Minor, and there-fore does not enter into details respecting them. Unfortunately Luke closed his book of Acts at the point when Paul had lived two years as a prisoner at Rome ; and therefore, in further designating the historical connection of Paul's Epistles, we are not able to state the circumstances of time and place with so much precision and cer-tainty as hitherto. This circumstance, likewise, explains how, in such a state of things, the remaining Epistles of Paul afford more room to doubt of their genuineness than was the case in regard to those which, we see, well and easily fall into the history of Paul as

related in the Acts. We shall therefore devote separate consideration to these Epistles.

CHAPTER V.

CONTINUATION.—OF THE PAULINE EPISTLES COMPOSED DURING AND AFTER PAUL'S IMPRISONMENT AT ROME.

OF the Epistles composed by Paul during his imprisonment at
Rome, the Epistles to the *Philippians, Colossians* and *Philemon*,
can be easily shown with sufficient certainty to be genuine writings
of the apostle. First, as to the Epistle to the *Philippians*, Paul
clearly represents himself therein, not only as a prisoner, but also as
a prisoner at Rome ; for he speaks of the barracks occupied by the
imperial guards (the Praetorium : Luther translates the word by
Richt-haus, or hall of justice, Phil. i. 13), into which the fame of his
imprisonment had extended itself. Probably Paul had won over to
the gospel the soldiers set to guard him, to whom he was wont to
preach, and, through these, others in the camp may have been converted. Even the imperial palace itself is mentioned by Paul
(Phil. iv. 22), as having been already penetrated by the seeds of the
word of God. These clear allusions leave not the slightest doubt
that the Epistle was written from Rome. Nor can any doubt remain as to the question, whether it was really written to the inhabitants of the Macedonian city *Philippi*. For, according to Acts
xvi. 12 *seq.* the apostle's labours in this city had been particularly
blessed. The Lord at once opened the heart of Lydia, so that she
believed the preaching of Paul. An unfortunate occurrence respecting a damsel possessed with a spirit of divination, which the apostle
expelled, constrained him to leave the city. The church of Philippi,
however, always preserved a particular attachment to the Apostle
Paul, and his acknowledgement of this fact runs through the whole
of his letter to them. The apostle calls them his brethren dearly
beloved and longed for, his joy and crown (Phil. iv. 1), and thanks
the Philippian Christians that they so faithfully had respect to his
bodily necessities (Phil. iv. 15, 16). These characteristics are decisive in favour of the genuineness of the Epistles, which, moreover, has not been contested either in ancient or modern times.

The case is the same in regard to the *Epistle to the Colossians.*
This church was not founded by Paul in person ; as he himself indicates in Col. ii. 1. He had indeed been in Phrygia, but had not
visited the city of Colosse on his journey through this province of
Asia Minor. Paul nevertheless wrote to them, as also to the

Romans, in part from universal Christian love, which called upon him to acknowledge the members of every church of Christ as brethren, and in part from the special reason, that the Gospel had been carried to Colosse by disciples of his, particularly *Epaphras*. The immediate occasion of his Epistle, however, was, that heretics threatened to draw away the church from the true faith. These individuals were not of the ordinary Judaizing class ; along with much that was Jewish, they had some Gnostic characteristics. Now Phrygia is the precise spot where, from the earliest times downward, we find a prevalent tendency to fantastic apprehension of religion. Thus the circumstance that, according to Paul's representation, men of this stamp had gained influence in Colosse, suits perfectly well with what we know of that city. Nor is it otherwise than very natural, that few particular allusions occur in the Epistle, as he was not personally known to the church. He however mentions his imprisonment, and sends salutations also from some persons of their acquaintance who were in his vicinity, among others from Aristarchus (Col. iv. 10), who, as we learn from the Acts, had come to Rome with Paul and Luke (xxvii. 2). The latter companion of Paul likewise salutes the believers in Phrygia (iv. 14). Of individuals themselves resident in Colosse, he saluted especially *Archippus* (iv. 17), who occupied some ministry in the church. Concerning this man, as also concerning *Onesimus*, whom Paul mentions (Col. iv. 9), we gain more particular information from the Epistle to Philemon. In this Epistle to the Colossians, likewise, every thing harmonises so exactly with Paul's circumstances in general, and his relation to the church which he addressed in particular, that no one has ever been led to question its genuineness, either in ancient or modern days.

With the same entire unanimity has the genuineness of Paul's *Epistle to Philemon* likewise been always admitted. This delightful little Epistle so clearly exhibits all the characteristics of the great apostle, and is so utterly free from every thing which would make it probable that any person could have a motive in forging it, that no one would ever entertain the idea of denying that Paul was its author. Philemon, to whom the Epistle is addressed, probably lived in Colosse, for that Archippus, who held an office in the church at Colosse, appears here as his son, and Appia as his wife (Phil. v. 2). Probably Philemon was an opulent man ; for he had so spacious a house, that it accommodated the assemblies of believers. Paul wrote this Epistle, likewise, in confinement (v. 13), and sends salutations from all those who, according to the Acts and the Epistle to the Colossians, were in his vicinity (v. 23, 24). Onesimus, who had fled from the relation of bondage which he had sustained towards Philemon in Colosse, Paul sends back to his master, whom he informs that his slave had been led by him to obey the Gospel, so that Philemon is to receive back again as a brother him whom he had lost as a slave. The whole of this small Epistle comprises indeed no important doctrinal contents ; but it is an exhibition of interior, deep feeling, and delicate regard to circumstances on the part of the apostle, and as such has always been very dear and valuable to the church.

In regard to the *Epistle to the Ephesians*, however, the case is totally different from what it is in regard to the three other Epistles sent from Rome. There are so many remarkable circumstances in relation to this Epistle, that we can easily comprehend how its genuineness has been often brought in question. Still, all the doubts which may have been excited are completely removed on a closer examination, so that it can by no means be denied that the Epistle was written by the apostle, even if its actual destination to Ephesus cannot be established.

If it be considered that Paul, as we saw above in the historical account of the apostle's life, was twice in Ephesus, and that once he even resided there for about three years, it must certainly appear very strange that, in an Epistle to this church, of the elders of which Paul had taken leave in so pathetic a manner (Acts xx. 17), there should be found no salutations. In writing to the Romans, Paul, though he had never been at Rome, sent salutations to so many persons that their names fill an entire chapter, while in this Epistle not a single person is greeted. Moreover, there are no personal and confidential allusions in any part of the Epistle. Paul appears only in the general relation of a Christian teacher and a friend to his readers. There is certainly something extremely strange in this character of the Epistle, particularly, moreover, as that which we should especially expect to find in the Epistle, viz., allusion to heretics, against which Paul had so expressly warned the Ephesian elders, is entirely wanting (Acts xx. 29 *seq.*)

The difficulties are increased when we know what was the case originally concerning the address to the readers of the Epistle (Eph. i. 1). Instead of " Paul, an apostle of Jesus Christ, by the will of God, to the saints which are at *Ephesus*," as it stands in most copies, Marcion, in his MS., read : " to the saints at *Laodicea*." In other MSS. there was no name at all, neither Ephesus, nor Laodicea ; and in these the inscription of the Epistle ran thus : " Paul, an apostle of Jesus Christ, by the will of God, to the saints which dwell at ———." Instead of the name was a vacant space, which, however, was often neglected by the copyists, who thus perplexed the matter still further.

In addition to all this, if the Epistle to the Ephesians be compared with that to the Colossians, we shall find the same fundamental thought, and often even the same train of ideas, only the

first is more minute and expanded, while in the Epistle to the
Colossians the thoughts are more concisely and briefly presented.
On account of this relative character it has been declared that the
Epistle to the Ephesians is probably only an enlargement of the
Epistle to the Colossians, made with a special design by some other
hand. But though for a moment such a supposition might not appear altogether unfounded, its plausibility is completely dissipated
when the peculiar character of the Epistle is made apparent by a
right and thorough notion of its origin. The Epistle to the Ephesians is undoubtedly what is termed a circular letter, directed not
to a single church but to many at once. In such a letter, therefore,
there could be no personal allusions, because what might interest
one circle of readers might be unintelligible to another. In this
Epistle, therefore, Paul adheres exclusively to generalities, and
touches only on such topics as would be of interest to all members
of the churches for whom the Epistle was intended. Now, on the
supposition that Ephesus and Laodicea were of the number of those
churches for which the Epistle was intended, nothing is more easy
of explanation than the fact, that the name of the former was in the
inscription of some MSS., and the name of the latter in that of
others. The messenger who carried the apostolic letter may have
taken several copies with him, in which the space for the name of
the place was not filled out, and remained thus until they were delivered, when the name of the church which received any particular
one was added to it. The diffusion of the Epistle abroad was mainly
from the capital city of Ephesus ; and hence the name Ephesus got
into the inscription of most of the MSS. Marcion, however, came
into possession of a transcript from the copy which was delivered at
Laodicea, and for this reason he read Laodicea instead of Ephesus
in the inscription. In some copies there may have been a total
neglect to fill up the spaces left vacant for the names ; and in this
way some MSS. got into circulation in which no city was designated.

It is seen how satisfactorily and completely, on this single supposition, that the Epistle to the Ephesians was a circular letter, our
difficulties disappear at once. It is true the striking resemblance
of the Epistle to that to the Colossians still remains ; and in recent
times the greatest stress has been laid on this very point. Both
Epistles have essentially the same contents, only the Epistle to
the Ephesians is more full and minute, as has been already remarked. But let it be considered that the two Epistles were written not only about the same time, but under entirely similar circumstances. Is it then to be wondered at, that there is a striking
similarity in contents and arrangement ? What purpose could there
have been in forging or counterfeiting an Epistle, in which the
fraudulent author said the same things which were contained in a

genuine Epistle of the man to whom he wished that his production should be ascribed ? It is, therefore, clear that there is nothing in this resemblance of the Epistle to the Ephesians to that to the Colossians, which can justify us in inferring the spuriousness of either. For, whether we suppose that the longest (that to the Ephesians) was written first, and that Paul afterwards repeated the same thoughts in the shortest (that to the Colossians) ; or, *vice versa*, that he wrote the shortest first, and afterwards felt himself called upon to state the same ideas more at length in the other, there is not the least harm done by their similarity to each other, particularly as the Epistle to the Ephesians contains many ideas wholly peculiar to the Apostle Paul, which are wanting in the Epistle to the Colossians, and this too in his own phraseology and style.

It is to be observed, further, that Paul in his Epistle to the Colossians mentions a letter to the church at Laodicea, and charges the former to communicate their Epistle to the believers in Laodicea, and in return to request the Epistle addressed to them. Now, because, as we have seen, Marcion regarded the Epistle to the Ephesians as having been directed to the Laodiceans, it has been supposed that our Epistle to the Ephesians was the one meant by Paul. But, plausible as this may appear at first sight, it is still improbable, on a closer examination, that it is correct ; for, first, the great similarity between the two Epistles makes against it, as this must evidently have rendered their mutual transfer of less consequence. Then, too, it is not common to direct special salutations to be given to those to whom we write ourselves at the same time, which is done by Paul in relation to the Laodiceans in his letter to the Colossians (*passim*). Moreover, our Epistle to the Ephesians, as a circular letter, could not well be designated by the name, Epistle to the Laodiceans. Thus, it is far more probable that this letter was a separate one, which has been lost to us.

As early as the time of Jerome, there existed a separate Epistle to the Laodiceans, different from that to the Ephesians. But the father just mentioned remarks, that all without exception reject it. It is probable, therefore, that, on account of the passage, Col. iv. 15, 16, some one had forged an Epistle to the Laodiceans, just as was the case, as we have before stated, with the first Epistle to the Corinthians which was lost.

There remain, therefore, only the three Epistles of the apostle, which are usually comprehended under the title of *Pastoral Letters*, viz., the two to Timothy, and that to Titus. They are all three occupied with a consideration of the duties of a pastor of the church of Christ, and on account of this common purport are classed under the general designation which we have mentioned. In a close investigation of the contents and the historical allusions of these Epistles there arise very many difficulties, on which account they have become subject to doubt beyond all the other Pauline Epistles. Ancient tradition is certainly wholly in favour of their genuineness, as in relation to the Epistle to the Ephesians ; for the circumstance, that Marcion did not have them in his canon, is not regarded as important, even by opponents of the Epistles, who are at all impartial. It was undoubtedly only through accident that these Epistles remained unknown to him, and to his native city, Sinope, upon the Black Sea ; for had he possessed historical reasons against its reception, they could not have been so completely lost at a later period. We may here see, in fact, a very important evidence in behalf of the genuineness of these Epistles ; for Timothy lived when Paul wrote to him, not in a distant, unknown place, but in Ephesus, one of the chief cities frequented by the Christians of the ancient church. The scene of the labours of Titus was the isle of Crete, which also, on account of its vicinity to Corinth, and to other important churches, maintained lively intercourse with the churches generally. Now, how Epistles directed to persons labouring in places of so much note, and holding so high a rank, as being assistants of the apostle, could gain the reputation of being genuine throughout the whole ancient church, when they were really forged in the name of the apostle, is indeed difficult of comprehension, as so many must have been able to expose the deception. Supposing, therefore, that on a close investigation of the contents of the Epistle, there should appear much that is strange, it must be considered as losing a great deal of its influence in relation to the question of the genuineness of the Epistles, from the fact that this is so firmly established by the tradition of the church.

Another circumstance to be premised, which is very much in favour of their genuineness, is, that in all the three Epistles there occurs a multitude of personal and particular allusions. Now, it is clear that an impostor, who was palming off his own Epistles as another's (for such is the language which we must use concerning the author of these three compositions, if they are not the work of Paul himself, since he expressly names himself as the author, besides indicating the fact in a manner not to be mistaken), would avoid as much as possible all special circumstances, because he would be too likely to betray himself in touching upon them, since particulars cannot be very minutely known to a stranger. Moreover, a forgery generally wants that graphic exactness which is exhibited so manifestly in writings that spring out of actually existing circumstances. Hence every unprejudiced person would, in the outset, think it very unlikely that a writing was forged in which there occurred such special allusions as we find in 1 Tim. v. 23, where Paul says to Timothy, "Drink no longer water, but use a little wine for thy stomach's sake and thine often infirmities." Of the same nature, also, is a passage in the second Epistle to Timothy (2 Tim. iv. 13), in which the apostle complains that he had, through forgetfulness, left his cloak, some books, and parchments, with a friend, and desires Timothy to take care of them. Plainly, such things are not forged ; for to what end should any one give himself the useless trouble to invent such insignificant matters, if they did not actually happen, since they could not do either any harm or any good. In the same Epistle (2 Tim. iv. 20, 21), Paul sends salutations from many individuals, and gives various information respecting persons of their mutual acquaintance. "Erastus abode at Corinth," says Paul, "but Trophimus have I left at Melitus sick ;" and he invites Timothy himself to come to him before winter. If any person invented all this, we must at least call him extremely inconsiderate, for he ought not certainly to have mentioned such noted cities, since the Christians who dwelt in them could learn, without any great difficulty, whether any one of the name of Trophimus was ever at Miletus with the apostle, and was left there by him sick, and whether Erastus abode at Corinth. The same is true of the Epistle to Titus, as one may be convinced by examining Titus iii. 12.

Still, let us look at the reasons which are advanced *against* the genuineness of these Epistles. Certain investigators have thought that there was in all three of them something not only in the phraseology, but in the style altogether, which cannot but be regarded as unlike Paul. The weakness of such statements, however, may be clearly inferred from the fact that another investigator, of no less acuteness, supposes the second Epistle to Timothy and the one to Titus to be really genuine Epistles of Paul, while the first to Timothy is spurious, and imitated from the other two. This second investigator, therefore, founds his argument for the spuriousness of the first of the three Epistles on the genuineness of the two others, thus overthrowing, by his own reasoning, the position of the former investigators in regard to the necessity of supposing them all spurious. The historical difficulties, however, which are discerned on close examination of the Epistles, are of more consequence. It is from these, properly, that all attacks upon these pastoral letters have originated, and in these they find their excuse, only writers ought not to have so manifestly confounded *difficulties* with *positive arguments against the genuineness of a writing.*

As to the *First* Epistle to Timothy, the principal difficulty is, to point out a period in Paul's life exactly coinciding with the statement which the apostle makes at the outset (i. 3). He says that when he went to Macedonia he left Timothy at Ephesus, to protect the true faith and thwart heretics in that city. Now we know, indeed, that when Demetrius the silver-smith drove Paul from Ephesus, he went to Macedonia ; but it is impossible that he should then have left Timothy behind at Ephesus, since he sent him before himself to Macedonia with Erastus. Thus, when Paul wrote his Second Epistle to the Corinthians from Macedonia, Timothy was with him. (Comp. Acts xix. 22, 2 Cor. i. 1). Moreover, we are informed of no other journey of Paul from Ephesus to Macedonia, when he left Timothy behind in the city to watch over the church ; and hence arises a difficulty in assigning this Epistle its proper place in Paul's life.

There are similar circumstances respecting the *Second* Epistle. This Epistle, too, is directed to Timothy at Ephesus. Paul clearly writes from Rome. (Comp. 2 Tim. iv. 16, 17, with 2 Tim. i. 16, 18, iv. 19). He was in bonds (i. 16), and was expecting a new examination of his cause. Now, he invites Timothy to come to him, and requests him to make haste and come before winter (iv. 13, 21). But, according to Col. i. 1, Philemon ver. 1, and Phil. i. 1, Timothy, at the time of Paul's imprisonment at Rome, as related by Luke in the Acts, was in Paul's company ; and hence it seems impossible that Paul could have written to him at Ephesus. It is true Paul's imprisonment at Rome lasted two years, and it might be supposed that Timothy was for some time with him, and for some time away during his imprisonment ; but there are other circumstances which make it very improbable that the Second Epistle to Timothy was written during the same imprisonment in which the Epistles to the Ephesians, Colossians, and Philippians were composed. According to 2 Tim. iv. 13, Paul had left at Troas, a cloak, books, and parchments, which Timothy was to bring with him when he came to Paul (iv. 21). Now, before Paul's imprisonment at Rome, which lasted two years, he was also two years in Cæsarea. We should, therefore, be compelled to suppose that he had left these things behind at Troas, four years before. But certainly it is probable that Paul would have made some other disposition of them in the mean time, if they were of any consequence to him. But even if we may suppose that Paul would send for clothing and books which had laid at Troas for years, it is out of the question that he should say in relation to a journey made four years before : "Erastus abode at Corinth, but Trophimus, have I left at Miletus sick." (2 Tim. iv. 20). Miletus was in the vicinity of Ephesus, at a distance from Rome where Paul was writing. Now, if Paul had not been in Miletus for four years, it is wholly impossible that he should have mentioned the illness of one whom he had left behind at Miletus so long a time before, because his case must long since have been decided. Similar difficulties present themselves, likewise, on a close examination of the *Epistle to Titus.* For Paul writes in this Epistle (i. 4, 5, iii. 12), that he himself had been in the Island of Crete, and had left Titus there behind him for the same purpose which caused him to leave Timothy in Ephesus ; and states that he intended to spend the winter in Nicopolis, whither he directs Titus to come and meet him. Now, it is true, Paul, according to the Acts (xxvii. 8), was once in Crete, but it was as a prisoner, and on a voyage. In these circumstances, therefore, he could not accomplish much ; nor could he leave Titus behind, as on his voyage Titus was nowhere in his neighbourhood. Nothing is told us in any part of the New Testament history as to Paul's residence in Nicopolis, and it is the more difficult to come to any assurance respecting it from the fact, that there were so many cities of that name. Thus, this Epistle, likewise, cannot be assigned to its place in Paul's history, and therefore it is perfectly true, that there are difficulties incident to an examination of these pastoral letters ; but, as we have before observed, difficulties are not equivalent to positive arguments against their genuineness. It is true they would be, were we so exactly and minutely acquainted with the history of the Apostle Paul, that such a difficulty in assigning an epistle its place among the circumstances of his life would be the same as an impossibility. If, for example, we knew with certainty that the Apostle Paul never resided in any city by the name of Nicopolis, we should be obliged to consider the Epistle to Titus, which purports to have been written from some place called Nicopolis, as spurious and forged.

But this is so far from being the case, that in those Epistles of Paul which are admitted to be genuine, very many occurrences are noticed, of which we have no further information. A remarkable instance of this kind is the well-known passage, 2 Cor. xi. 23 *seq.*, in which Paul states, that he had five times received of the Jews forty stripes save one, thrice being beaten with rods, once stoned, thrice suffered shipwreck, etc., etc. Of very few of these sufferings of Paul do we know the particulars. How much, therefore, of what took place in his life, may remain unknown to us. It is to be remembered, too, that the brief general statements given by Luke in the Acts extend over long periods in the apostle's life. At Corinth, Ephesus, Cæsarea, and Rome, Paul abode for years. Now, as slight journeys abroad are, it is well known, commonly comprehended by historians in a residence at any particular place for a long period, may not this have been frequently the case in Luke's history ? Many have thought this probable, and have therefore supposed short journeys from this or that place, and in this way have attempted to find some situation in Paul's life, which should appear suitable for the composition of one or another of the pastoral letters. We will not trouble our readers, however, with an enumeration of these different views, which, nevertheless, show that it is not *impossible* to designate some situation in which Paul might have written these Epistles. We choose rather to confine ourselves to the development of an important supposition by which a suitable period of time is obtained for all the three Epistles together, and their relation to each other is determined. This supposition is, that Paul was set at liberty from the first imprisonment at Rome related by Luke (which had lasted two years when Luke finished his book of Acts), performed important missionary tours afterward, and was at last *imprisoned a second time at Rome*, and at this time died there a martyr's death. It is very evident that if we can in this way gain space of time for another journey to Asia and Crete, it will be easy to imagine the situations which gave rise to the first Epistle to Timothy and that to Titus. The second Epistle to Timothy must then have been written in Rome itself during the second imprisonment, and any remarkable expressions which it contains are then perfectly intelligible, if it be supposed that Paul wrote the Epistle after his arrival at Rome from Asia Minor. The only question is, whether this supposition, that Paul was a second time imprisoned at Rome, is a mere hypothesis, or can be sustained by any historical evidence. Were it a mere conjecture, it must be admitted, it would be of little importance.

There are not wanting, however, some historical facts of such a nature as to confirm the supposition. First, we find it current among the Fathers of the fourth century. It is true, they do not expressly present historical grounds for their opinion; they seem rather to have inferred a second imprisonment at Rome from the second Epistle to Timothy. But, that they at once assumed a second imprisonment, when they might have hit upon other modes of explanation, seems to indicate a tradition, however obscure, in regard to the fact of its having occurred. Moreover, we are told by a very ancient writer of the Roman church, the apostolic Father Clemens Romanus, that Paul went to the farthest west. This must mean Spain. In the Epistle to the Romans (chap. xv.) Paul expresses a strong desire to visit that country. This he cannot have done before his first imprisonment; it is not at all improbable, therefore, that he may afterwards have journeyed to this country, the most western region of the then known world.

Whatever may be thought of this supposition, so much is clear— the difficulties with which the attentive reader meets with in the Epistles, are no arguments against their genuineness. Indeed every thing essential is in their favour. The internal similarity of the Epistles, however, makes it probable that they were composed about the same time, and the idea that they were written during the second imprisonment, of which we have spoken, accords very well with this supposition.

CHAPTER VI.

OF THE EPISTLE TO THE HEBREWS

OF the investigations of learned men respecting the genuineness of the writings of the New Testament, we have hitherto been able to give a very favourable account ; but the case seems now to be different, in considering the investigations respecting the Epistle to the Hebrews. For, he who has been accustomed to reckon this epistle among those of Pauline origin (the Lutheran version, such as it now is, expressly attributing it to this apostle, although Luther himself, as will be shown presently, held a different opinion), may be surprised at hearing that the latest, extremely thorough and generally impartial, investigations respecting this important Epistle, determine that Paul was not its author.[1] We have before remarked, that the genuineness of the Epistle to the Hebrews is not at all in question : the only inquiry is, who was its author. For he has neither named nor designated himself throughout the Epistle. Thus, even though Paul should not be considered the author, it does not follow that the Epistle is a forged, spurious one.

Now, that the case of this Epistle must be peculiar, is clear from the fact, that it was not admitted into the midst of the other Pauline Epistles. In the Greek Testament it does indeed come directly after the Epistle to Philemon, and thus by the side of the collection of Paul's Epistles (though Luther has placed it after the Epistles of Peter and John) ; but it is clear that this large and important Epistle would have been placed among the other large Epistles of the same apostle to whole churches, perhaps after the Epistles to the Corinthians, had it been originally regarded as a production of the apostle to the Gentiles.[2] Consequently, its position after the Epistle of Philemon, the smallest and most inconsiderable of Paul's private letters, shows plainly, that it was not generally reckoned as one of the Pauline Epistles, until after the collection of them was completed. However, all this is, of course, of an incidental nature ; there are far more important reasons, which make it improbable that Paul was the author of the Epistle to the Hebrews ; and to the consideration of these we will now direct our attention.

[1] But see Professor Stuart's discussion of this point in his masterly Commentary upon the Epistle. See also an able discussion of it in a work published at London in 1830, entitled " Biblical Notes and Dissertations, &c.," written by Joseph John Gurney, an Englishman, member of the Society of Friends. Mr. Gurney's dissertation was republished in the Biblical Repository for July 1832 (Vol. II. p. 409).—TR.

[2] According to Epiphanius, a church-father of the fourth century, some MSS. placed the Epistle of the Hebrews *before the Epistles to Timothy ;* probably only because it seemed to some copyists improper that an Epistle to a whole church should stand after Epistles to private individuals.

The *form* of the Epistle is, it is seen, entirely different from that of Paul's letters. He opens each of his Epistles, not only with his name and the title of his sacred office, but also with an apostolic salutation ; " Grace be with you and peace from God our Father, and our Lord Jesus Christ." Nothing of this kind is to be seen at the commencement of the Epistle to the Hebrews. It begins like a treatise (which indeed many have been inclined to suppose it to be), without any reference to its readers : " God, who at sundry times and in divers manners spake in times past unto the fathers by the prophets, &c." The conclusion bears more resemblance to Paul's Epistles ; for it contains a salutation, such as those of the apostle, and announces a visit to the readers of the Epistle on the part of the author in company with Timothy. The writer sends a salutation on the part of the brethren *from* Italy ; from, whence it has been erroneously inferred that the Epistle was written in Italy, whereas the phraseology indicates exactly the contrary.[1] For the author would not have employed such an expression unless he was writing *out of* Italy in a place whither brethren had arrived *from* that country. The Epistle contains no particular salutations from one individual to another ; but this is not strange, as it is addressed to so many. For the *Hebrews*, to whom the Epistle was written, were the Jewish Christians who'lived in Palestine. Their benefit was intended by the entire contents of this profound Epistle. It analyzes thoroughly the relation of the Old Testament to the New.

Nevertheless, it may be said, no great stress ought to be laid upon the external *form* of the Epistle ; Paul might for once have deviated from his usual custom. But the *historical evidence* is very decisive in regard to this Epistle. For, in the western church, and particularly the Roman, the Epistle to the Hebrews was not at all acknowledged as Paul's production until some time in the fourth century. It was through Augustine's means, who died so late as 430 A.D., that it first became common to ascribe it to Paul ; and even this Father of the church sometimes speaks doubtfully of the Epistle, as do other Fathers after his time. Plainly this is very remarkable. For, if it be considered how well-known Paul was, and how deeply loved at Rome, and that he was twice imprisoned there for years, it will be evident that it must have been known in that city whether Paul was its author or not. Thus the testimony of this Roman church is of the highest importance in the question

---

[1] The original Greek reads, οἱ ἀπὸ τῆς Ἰταλίας, which is translated in our English version "they of Italy." Olshausen considers it necessary to translate ἀπό *from*, making the whole expression to mean, *those who had come from Italy to some place where Paul was writing.* Consultation of a good Greek lexicon will cause any one to doubt whether there is any such necessity as Olshausen supposes. See, for example, in Passow, under the word ἀπό, such expressions as, αἷμα ἀπὸ Τρώων, the blood of the Trojans, οἱ ἀπὸ Πλάτωνος, they of Plato's party, &c.—TR.

under examination. Now, it is observable, that Clement of Rome, an immediate disciple of Paul, makes very ample use of the Epistle to the Hebrews, and even introduces long passages of it into his own Epistle to the Corinthians. This is indeed a very decisive proof of the high antiquity of the Epistle ; but Clement does not mention the author of the writing from which he quoted, and therefore the use he has made of it has no further influence in regard to the question, who was its author. Still, he must certainly have liked the Epistle, and esteemed it very highly ; otherwise he would not have been induced to embellish his own Epistle with large passages from it, which are interwoven with his train of thought, as though they were original.

That in the West there was general uncertainty in regard to the author of the Epistle, is shown by the circumstance, that an African Father of the church, Tertullian, names Barnabas as its author. Others, especially some orientals, ascribe it to Luke, and some to the before-mentioned Clement, though unfortunately without good reason. There was no uniform tradition in the West in regard to its authorship ; it was, from conjecture alone, ascribed to various individuals.

The case was totally different with the Greek church in the East. The predominant opinion with this was that Paul was the author. It was the celebrated Fathers of the Alexandrian church especially, together with the Syrians, who made great use of the Epistle to the Hebrews, and referred it to the Apostle Paul. The old Syriac version contains it in its canon. This circumstance is not to be overlooked, particularly as the Epistle is directed to the Christians in Palestine, from whom of course it might very easily come into the hands of the neighbouring Syrians and Egyptians. Historical testimony, however, in favour of any Epistle, must be sought for mainly in the place where it was composed, and that to which it was addressed. One of these furnishes evidence against the Pauline origin of the Epistle, and the other in its favour ; a circumstance which, as we shall see hereafter, is of no slight consequence in an inquiry respecting the canonical authority of the Epistle.

Although the Greek, and especially the Alexandrian, Fathers were favourably disposed towards the Epistle to the Hebrews, the learned among them admitted the great difference between it and the other Epistles of Paul. They explained this difference by supposing that Paul wrote the Epistle in Hebrew, and Luke translated it into Greek. The Evangelist was fixed upon as the translator, because, as was thought, a resemblance was discovered between his style and that of the Epistle. The supposition, however, is not at all probable ; for the style of the Epistle to the Hebrews is so peculiarly Greek, that it cannot have been translated from the Hebrew.

We may see, merely from the conjecture thus presented, that inquiring minds, in perusing the Epistle, came to doubt whether it was really Pauline in its character, even where it was commonly considered as a Pauline production.

Hence it was that our Luther, when he studied the Scriptures in a critical manner, renewed the doubts respecting the Pauline origin of the Epistle to the Hebrews, after it had been regarded throughout the middle ages as the Apostle Paul's production. He writes on this point as follows : "As yet, we have mentioned only the principal, indubitably genuine books of the New Testament. The four following books, however,[1] have in times past held a different rank. And first, that the Epistle to the Hebrews is not St. Paul's, nor any apostle's, is proved by the tenor of v. 3 chap. ii. : 'How shall we escape if we neglect so great salvation, which at first began to be spoken by the Lord, and was confirmed unto us by them that heard him.' It is clear that he speaks of the apostles as though he were a disciple, to whom this salvation had come from the apostles, perhaps long after." (See Walch's Ed. Luther's Works, Th. xiv. p. 146.) The passage to which Luther refers is indeed remarkable, and has been employed by scholars of a more recent day to prove that Paul cannot have been the author of the Epistle. For we know that he always maintained strongly (particularly in the ouset to the Epistle to the Galatians), in opposition to his Jewish adversaries, who presumed to dispute his apostolic authority, that he was not a disciple of the apostles, but had received every thing from the immediate revelation of God. How then is it conceivable, that in Heb. ii. 3, he should have represented himself as a disciple of the apostles ; and this in an Epistle to Jewish Christians, before whom it was specially important for him to appear as a real apostle of our Lord ? This circumstance, moreover, that the Epistle to the Hebrews was written to Jewish Christians, deprives of all probability that interpretation of the passage according to which Paul speaks merely out of courtesy, as though he himself was a disciple of the apostles, which in reality was the case only with his readers. For then Paul would have expressed himself in a manner very liable to be misapprehended ; and that this should have happened when his relation to the Jewish Christians was so peculiar, is extremely improbable. Luther, with his free, bold disposition, which did indeed sometimes carry him beyond the limits of truth in his critical investigations, did not content himself with merely disputing the Pauline origin of the Epistle; he even ventured to institute conjectures respecting its author. He regarded the celebrated Apollos as its author; the same of whom mention is

---

[1] He means, besides the Epistle to the Hebrews, the Epistles of James and Jude, and the Revelation of John.

made in the Acts. In truth, this supposition possesses extreme probability, and has therefore, by all the hypotheses respecting the author of the Epistle, recommended itself most even to recent investigators. The book of Acts describes this man as having precisely that character of mind which the author of this Epistle must have had, to judge from its contents. He is stated (Acts xviii. 24) to have been by birth an Alexandrian, an eloquent man, and mighty in the Scriptures. Now, the author of the Epistle to the Hebrews shows himself to have been thoroughly acquainted with the Old Testament, and eloquently maintains the deep and sublime ideas which it presents. According to the same passage, he constantly overcame the Jews in conversation with them, and proved publicly, by means of the Scriptures, that Jesus was the Christ. Undoubtedly, in these disputes he made use of just such forcible expositions of the Old Testament, as those of which we find so many in the Epistle to the Hebrews, and which were very commonly employed by the Alexandrians in particular. The idea that Titus, or Luke, or Clement, might have been the author of the Epistle to the Hebrews is untenable, for this reason, if there were no other, that these men were Gentiles by birth, and the author declares himself a native Jew. There would be more reason for fixing upon Silas or Silvanus, who were, as we know, Paul's companions, or, likewise, upon Barnabas. For the last we have even one historical evidence, as we have already remarked. A Father of the church, Tertullian, expressly ascribes the Epistle to Barnabas. But, as we have an Epistle written by this assistant of the apostles, we are able to see from it with perfect certainty that he cannot be author of the Epistle to the Hebrews. His whole manner of writing and thinking is different from the course of ideas in this production. It is true there is nothing so decisive against Silas ; but, too, there is nothing definite *in his favour*. His peculiar character of mind is nowhere described, as the character of Apollos is in the Acts of the Apostles.

The idea, therefore, that Silas was the author of the Epistle, is a wholly unsupported conjecture. It is true, too, it is merely a conjecture, that Apollos wrote it ; but it is a conjecture more probable than could be required or wished in respect to opinions of any other nature than those in question.

But, though we could assign the name of the author, it would be of little consequence in our investigation. It is sufficient that we cannot suppose Paul to have been the author.

Here, however, arises the very difficult question, what we are to think of the *canonical authority* of the Epistle, if its author was not an apostle? for the primitive church would not receive the writings of any but these into the collection of sacred books; and those who rejected the Epistle to the Hebrews, *e. g.*, the Roman church, did it for the very reason, that they could not admit Paul to have been its author. *Must we then reject the Epistle to the Hebrews, or at least esteem it less highly than the other writings of the New Testament, because it was not written by Paul?* This inquiry merits the more careful consideration, because the contents of the Epistle are of a very profound and important nature to the church generally, and the evangelical church in particular. For the sacred doctrine of the high-priesthood of our Lord and Saviour Jesus Christ, is, in this very Epistle to the Hebrews, treated of more at length, and more thoroughly, than in any other book of the New Testament. Hence, the circumstance that the Epistle is not from the pen of the Apostle Paul might give rise to inferences against the validity of the doctrine which this Epistle in particular inculcates.

It must certainly be admitted that the ruling idea in the formation of the canon was to admit only apostolic productions. For although Mark and Luke, whose writings were acknowledged by the whole church, were not apostles, they were in intimate connection with Peter and Paul, and their works were therefore regarded as properly the productions of those apostles. And this principle was perfectly correct. Though it must be allowed that the Holy Spirit might exert its power on others besides the apostles, and might enable them to compose excellent productions, still it was wise in the ancient church to restrict the canon of the Holy Scriptures, which was to serve as the *norm* or *rule* of faith and practice, for the complete development of the kingdom of God, exclusively to apostolic writings. For the apostles, as most immediately connected with our Saviour, had received into their souls in the greatest abundance and purity the Spirit of truth which flowed forth from him. The more distant the relation which individuals sustained to our Lord, the feebler the influence of the Spirit from above upon them, and the more easily might their acts be affected by other influences. It was therefore necessary that the church should admit as the norm of faith, only such writings as sprang from the most lively and purest operation of the Holy Spirit, as it was manifested in the apostles. Otherwise there would have been ground for fear lest errors, perhaps indeed of a slight character, might have crept in, and then been continued from generation to generation in the Holy Scriptures, and propagated as of sacred authority. It was such thoughts undoubtedly which induced some learned men to distinguish the Epistle to the Hebrews and certain other books of the New Testament, which were not adopted with perfect unanimity by the primitive church, from those which were properly canonical and universally acknowledged, denominating the former *deutero-canonical.* They probably regarded it as possible that some error had crept into those books, notwithstanding the excellence of their contents generally ; and in order to obviate the influence of such errors they were desirous of introducing an external separation of these writings from those which were decidedly apostolical. But, with regard to the Epistle to the Hebrews, we must say, that this separation appears totally unfounded. Probable as it certainly is, that Paul did not compose the Epistle, it is still certain that its author wrote it under the influence of Paul, and an influence indeed which exhibits itself still more definitely than that of the same apostle over the writings of Luke, or of Peter over the Gospel of Mark. This position is sustained by history, as well as by the contents of the Epistle, in the most decisive manner.

On the score of history, in the first place, we cannot, except on the supposition that Paul had an essential share in the composition of the Epistle to the Hebrews, explain the remarkable circumstance that the entire oriental church attributed it to the apostle. This view continued to prevail in the East, even after it was very well known that the western churches, particularly that of Rome, held a different opinion. The tradition, that Paul was the author of the Epistle to the Hebrews, cannot have rested on mere conjecture, since there was in fact much in the Epistle itself which constrained learned men, who in the main shared the prevalent opinion respecting the author of the Epistle, to resort to expedients for the purpose of upholding the general idea that Paul wrote the Epistle, and at the same time of solving the difficulties which this supposition involved. Such an expedient, for example, was the idea, of which we have before spoken, that Paul might have written the Epistle in Hebrew, so that we have only a translation of it. Let it be considered, too, that this opinion of the Pauline origin of the Epistle prevailed in the very countries to which its original readers belonged ; and then no one will doubt that the only mode of explaining it is, to suppose Paul to have coöperated in the composition of the Epistle, and the first readers of it to have been aware of the fact, and on this account to have referred the Epistle to Paul himself.

To this is to be added, the character of the Epistle itself. For, although the ancient observation, that the style of the Epistle is not Pauline, is perfectly well founded, still the tenor of the ideas bears a resemblance, which is not to be mistaken, to the writings of the great apostle of the Gentiles. If we merely keep in mind, that the Epistle to the Hebrews was addressed to Jewish Christians, while the other Pauline Epistles were all of them[1] written to churches the majority of whose members were Gentiles, we shall not discover the least thing in the Epistle which could not have proceeded from the

---

[1] Though the expression is thus general in the original, of course only those Epistles which are directed to churches can be here referred to. The phraseology is exceptionable, as some of Paul's letters are not directed to churches at all. but to individuals.—Tr.

mind of Paul. Indeed, the main doctrine of the great apostle, that in the death of Jesus an offering of reconciliation was made for the whole world, that with and through it all the ceremonial observances of the Old Testament first obtained their fulfilment as types of what was to come, forms the central point of the Epistle to the Hebrews. If it be further considered, that there was always a certain distance of demeanor between the Apostle Paul and the Jewish Christians, even the best of them, it will be very easy to understand why Paul did not write to them himself; and still, it must have been his heart's desire to exhibit clearly and in suitable detail his views in regard to the law and its relation to Christianity, which were of a profound nature, and drawn directly from the genuine spirit of the Gospel. What more obvious mode of presenting these to the Hebrews, than through the medium of a disciple or faithful friend, who, like Apollos, had a correct apprehension of this relation between the old and new covenant.

Supposing this to have been the state of the case, all the circumstances in regard to the Epistle are explained. In the West it was known that Paul did not write the Epistle. On this account the western church denied that he was the author, without being able, however, to designate any other individual as the author. In the East, on the other hand, it was known that he had an influence in the composition of the Epistle; and moreover his spirit and his ideas were recognized in it. In the East, therefore, it was much used; in the West less. In our days we may impartially admit that Paul was not the writer of the Epistle, and still maintain its perfect canonical authority, since the apostle certainly exerted an essential influence over its composition.

Thus, though this Epistle belongs to the class of those which have not the unanimous voice of Christian antiquity in favour of their apostolic origin, still it can be shown that this want of agreement did not arise from any really suspicious state of things, but was occasioned merely by the peculiar circumstances under which it was composed.

CHAPTER VII.

OF THE CATHOLIC EPISTLES.

IT has already been observed, in the first chapter, that in early times the third collection of the writings of the New Testament was termed that of *the seven Catholic Epistles.* The Greek word *Catholic* means *general*, in oppostion to *particular*. Now, as the church general, in opposition to individual heretical parties, was termed

Catholic, so the same expression was used to denote those writings which, as universally acknowledged and used, it was designed to distinguish from those which were current only in particular circles. The fact that those writings, which, in addition to the collections called the Gospel and the Apostle, were acknowledged to be genuine and apostolical, were thus united into one separate collection, produced this advantage, that it became thus more difficult ever to confound them with the many apochryphal writings which were spread abroad in the ancient church. In regard to the origin of this third collection, however, there is an obscurity which can never be entirely dissipated. At the end of the third and commencement of the fourth century, the collection of the seven Catholic Epistles first appears in history ; but who formed it, and where it originated, we do not know. It is impossible, however, that it should have been *accidentally* formed, as the position of the Epistles is too peculiar for us to suppose this. The Epistle of James, which was by no means unanimously regarded as apostolic, holds the first place in the collection, while the first Epistle of Peter, and the first of John, which have always been regarded as of apostolic authority, come afterward. This very order of the seven Epistles, however, suggests to us, by the way, a probable supposition as to the place *where* the collection of these Catholic Epistles must have originated. James, the author of the Epistle of James in the canon, nowhere possessed a higher reputation than in Palestine and Syria ; for he was a cousin, *i. e.*, according to the Hebrew mode of speaking, a brother to our Lord, and at the same time bishop of the church at Jerusalem, and head of the Jewish Christians, as we shall presently show more at length. In the same countries, Peter was held in high estimation, as the one among our Lord's apostles to whom, in particular, was committed the preaching of the Gospel among the Jews. It is probable, therefore, that the collection of the Catholic Epistles originated in Palestine or Syria, and, out of veneration for the brother of our Lord, and the first bishop of Jerusalem, the author of the collection gave to the Epistle of James the first place, and put those of Peter next. The Epistles of John had less interest for him, on account of his Judaising sentiments, and the Epistle of Jude he placed at the very end. The supposition we have made finds confirmation in the fact, that a father of the Palestinian church, Eusebius, bishop of Cæsarea, gives us the first certain account of the existence of a collection of the seven Catholic Epistles.

From the various character of the writings classed together in the collection, we may see clearly its late origin ; for it has already been mentioned above (chap. i.), that the first Epistles of John and that of Peter were originally, as being very ancient and universally-admitted writings, connected with *the apostle*, so called, *i. e.*, the

collection of the Pauline Epistles. At a later period, in order to
leave these latter by themselves, the two Epistles were taken from
the collection of Pauline writings and classed with the five other
apostolic Epistles. These last, however, belonged to the number
of those which were universally admitted in primitive times, and
thus Antilegomena and Homologoumena were introduced into one
and the same collection. Still there arose from this procedure one
advantage, viz., that the Epistles of the same author were, as was
proper, brought together. Luther, with his excellent tact, correctly
felt that the collection of the Catholic Epistles unsuitably confounded writings which were universally admitted with those which were
not, and therefore placed the Epistles of Peter and John immediately after those of Paul, and then at the end, after the Epistle to
the Hebrews, the letters of James and Jude, and the Revelation of
John. Still, this did not wholly do away with the impropriety, as
the second Epistle of Peter also had been disputed with special zeal.
Had he, however, placed this Epistle likewise at the end of the
New Testament, along with the other Antilegomena, he must have
disturbed too much the old accustomed arrangement. He left it,
therefore, and also the two smaller Epistles of John, in connection
with the first and main Epistle of the two apostles. It is to be considered, too, that the bearing of the arrangement of the New Testament books upon our critical inquiries is of but secondary consideration ; the main point is their internal character, and in reference to
this no fault can be found with the original arrangement.

In regard, therefore, to the Catholic Epistles generally, little
further can be said. Of the Epistles individually, we will consider
first the *three Epistles of John.* As to the first, and main Epistle,
it, like the Gospel of John, was always regarded by the ancient
church as the production of the Evangelist of that name. In modern times, it is true, doubts have been started in relation to the
Gospel. But the principal writer by whom they have been suggested has himself since retracted them. Indeed, it was nothing but
the very striking similarity in style and ideas between the Gospel
and the first Epistle of John, which made it necessary, almost,
whether one would or no, to extend the opposition against the Gospel to the Epistle likewise ; for one cannot but suppose them both
to have had the same author, from their resemblance in every peculiar characteristic. If, therefore, the Epistle were admitted to have
been written by the Evangelist John, the Gospel also could not but
be attributed to him. But though there may have been a somewhat plausible reason for disputing the Gospel, in the idea that the
Saviour is represented by John very differently from the exhibition
of him in the other Gospels, in regard to the Epistle there is no
reason which possesses the slightest plausibility for disputing it. On

the supposition that it is spurious, the error of the whole ancient church in referring it, without contradiction, to the Evangelist John, would be completely inexplicable, especially if we carefully compare the history of the Epistle with that of the Evangelist. John, as we have before remarked, lived the longest of all the apostles, viz., till some time in the reign of Domitian, and he resided at Ephesus, in Asia Minor. From no country within the limits of the church, therefore, could we expect to receive more accurate accounts in regard to the writings of the beloved disciple of our Lord, than from those of Asia Minor. Now, it is from these very countries that we receive the most ancient testimonies in behalf of the existence and genuineness of the Epistle. Instead of mentioning all, I will name but two of these testimonies, which, however, are so decisive, that we can perfectly well dispense with all the rest. The first is presented by Papias, bishop of Hierapolis, in Phrygia, whom we have already mentioned. This man lived, as has been before said, at the end of the first century and beginning of the second, in the immediate vicinity of Ephesus, where the Evangelist John laboured so long and so successfully. He knew not only the Evangelist John, but other immediate disciples of our Lord, who were probably of the number of the seventy, particularly a certain Aristion, and another John, surnamed the Presbyter. Now, is it to be supposed that such a man, who had at his command so many means of arriving at certainty respecting John's writings, could possibly be deceived in regard to them ? We must, indeed, renounce all historical testimony, if we deny this witness the capacity to speak in behalf of the genuineness of the Epistle of John.

The second testimony, however, is of equal importance. One of the apostolic fathers, Polycarp, bishop of Smyrna, in Asia Minor, makes use of the first Epistle of John, in the same way as Papias, as though it was admitted to be a genuine production of the Evangelist. Now Polycarp lived till after the middle of the second century, and at the age of eighty-six died a martyr's death in the flames. He had not merely become acquainted with John in the neighbouring city of Ephesus, but had even heard him preach the way of salvation, and was his faithful disciple. The testimony of such a man, therefore, is likewise above all cavil, and is especially confirmed by the fact, that there never has been, in later times, any general opinion against its genuineness, either in the Catholic church, or among the adherents to any particular sect. Against this weight of historical evidence, therefore, nothing can be effected by the mere conjectures of modern times ; and at present all theologians are perfectly agreed in the acknowledgment of this precious relic of the beloved disciple of Jesus, his first Epistle.

If, in regard to the *second and third Epistles* of John, such per-

fect agreement of the ancient church in recognizing their genuineness cannot be asserted, the reason of this lies entirely in a circumstance, which also occasioned the tardy insertion of the pastoral
letters to Timothy and Titus in the collection of Pauline Epistles,
viz., that they are directed to private persons, and moreover are of
no very great extent or very important contents, and thus awakened
less interest in their diffusion.

The *second Epistle* of John is addressed to a Christian lady and
her family ; the *third* to a Christian friend named Gaius. Of the
private circumstances of these two persons we know nothing but
what is indicated in the letters. Now, although certainly these two
smaller Epistles afford no important information respecting the
Gospel, or the history of the ancient church, still, as estimable legacies of the disciple who lay in Jesus' bosom, they deserve a place
in the canon as much as Paul's Epistle to Philemon. The oldest
fathers of the church express no doubt in regard to the two Epistles.
Only at a later period do we find certain individuals entertaining
doubts whether these two Epistles were written by John the Evangelist. No one regarded them as forged in the name of the Evangelist, for we can by no means perceive for what purpose these
Epistles could, in such a case, have been written. They aim at no
particular object, but are merely expressive of the tenderest Christian love. Many, however, believed that another John, viz., *John
the Presbyter,* before mentioned, with whom Papias was acquainted,
was the author of the Epistles. This view appeared confirmed by
the fact that, in the salutations of both Epistles, John expressly
terms himself *Presbyter ;* and as, moreover, the other John likewise
lived in Ephesus, it is possible they might have been confounded.
But in modern times these doubts in regard to the apostolic character of the two small Epistles have been disregarded, because the
style and the sentiments of both Epistles are so entirely similar to
the style and course of thought in the Gospel and the first Epistle,
that the idea of a different author is totally untenable. Moreover,
we are able to show how John the Apostle and Evangelist might also
call himself Presbyter. This expression is nearly equivalent to the
Latin *Senior,* or the German *Ælteste.*[1] In the Jewish synagogues,
and also among the primitive Christians, it was applied to the principal persons in the church (comp. Acts xx. 17), and was at first
used in this sense as exactly synonymous with *Episcopos, i. e.,*
bishop. In Asia Minor, as we know from the writings of Papias,
there prevailed a peculiar custom of speaking, by which the apostles
were called, as it were by way of distinction, *elders.* Whether the
intention was thereby to denote the great age of the apostles, or
whether all the churches were regarded as forming one general

---

[1] Or the English *elder,* as it is translated in our version.—TR.

church, and the apostles as their presbyters, is doubtful. It is sufficient that the apostles were thus termed,[1] by way of eminence, for
in this fact is exhibited a sufficient explanation of the inscriptions
to the second and third Epistles of John. Thus the case is the
same with these two Epistles as with that to the Hebrews. The
primitive church adopted them, but not without opposition, and
therefore we must reckon them among the *Antilegomena ;* but still
the reasons which were addressed against their apostolic origin may
be so thoroughly refuted that not a shadow of uncertainty can
reasonably remain in regard to them.

The fourth of the seven Catholic Epistles is the first *Epistle of
the Apostle Peter.* As we have now come to the consideration of
the Petrine writings in the canon, the question forces itself upon us,
how is it to be explained that we have so few productions of Peter,
and so many of Paul, who was called latest to be an apostle.
When we consider what our Lord said to Peter : " Thou art Peter,
and upon this rock will I build my church, and the gates of hell
shall not prevail against it" (Matth. xvi. 18), and afterwards :
" Feed my lambs" (John xxi. 15 *seq.*), it must seem strange that
the powers of this rock of the church should have been exerted so
little in writings for posterity. It is true the Gospel of Mark is
properly Peter's Gospel, as we have seen ; but even this falls into
the back-ground by the side of Luke (the Pauline Gospel), and the
other Gospels, so that Peter according to the representation of himself in his writings, constantly appears insignificant compared with
Paul.

This fact finds a satisfactory explanation only in the relation of
the two apostles, Peter and Paul, to the propagation of the Gospel
in general. In reference to this, they had different destinations.
Peter, with the twelve, was called particularly to the dissemination
of the Gospel among the Jews. Had the Jewish nation acknowledged Jesus to be the Messiah, Peter would then have exhibited
himself in all his dignity and consequence. But that unhappy nation hardened itself against all the operations of the Spirit, and the
Gospel was carried to the Gentiles, because Israel rejected the grace
to which it was called. Paul was set apart for the express purpose
of preaching to the Gentiles (Acts xxvi. 17), and, as Christianity
first displayed itself in a flourishing condition among them, all the
other apostles, with the exception of John alone, fell into the back-
ground in comparison with Paul, both in oral discourse, as appears
from the Acts, and in these written efforts, as is shown by the New
Testament canon. It is, consequently, not at all strange that Peter
should be represented by two Epistles of so small a size, and that
the second of these is, moreover, the most disputed book in the

---

[1] Peter calls himself in his first Epistle, a *fellow-elder* (1 Pet. v. 1).

whole New Testament canon. His being thrown into the shade by Paul is rather in accordance with the facts respecting the extension of the church of Christ on earth in the times of the apostles. As to the *first Epistle of Peter*, we have before seen that it be- longs among the Homologoumena, along with the first Epistle of John. In all Christian antiquity there was no one who doubted the genunineness of the Epistle, or had heard of doubts respecting it. And yet the Epistle (1 Pet. i. 1) is addressed to the Christian churches in Asia Minor, where Christianity early gained great success, and where a lively intercourse was maintained between the individual churches. Here, of necessity, must have arisen soon an opposition to this Epistle, if it had not been known that Peter had sent a circular letter to the churches. Now, the oldest fathers of the church in Asia Minor, Papias and Polycarp, both made use of the Epistle of Peter, as well as that of John, as a genuine apostolic production. This Epistle of Peter does not seem to have made its way to Italy till a late period. At least it is wanting in the very ancient catalogue cited by Muratori, which probably exhibits the canon of the early Roman church. We can infer nothing, however, from this absence against the genuineness of the first Epistle of Peter, since there is not the slightest trace of its having been disputed in the first three centuries. Yet, in modern times, this decided declaration of Christian antiquity has been thought insufficient. An objection has been founded on the circumstance that Peter writes from Babylon (1 Pet. v. 13), while history does not relate that he was ever in Babylon ; as also upon the fact that he directs the attention of his readers to sufferings and persecutions which they should endure (1 Pet. i. 6 ; iii. 16 ; iv. 12 *seq.*; v. 10), referring, as is supposed, to Nero's persecutions, while he himself, it is said, died at Rome during this persecution, and therefore could not have addressed an Epistle from Babylon to those who suffered under it. Both these remarks, however, are easily obviated. As to the first, respecting the city of Babylon, we know too little of the history of Peter to be able to determine in what places he may have been, and in what not ; particularly as there were several cities of this name in the ancient world, and it is not specified which is meant in the Epistle. It is to be observed, too, that many of the fathers of the church understood the name Babylon to mean mystically the city of Rome, which showed itself the enemy of our Lord in the persecution of the faithful (Comp. Rev. xviii. 2). If this exposition be adopted, the second remark also is at once obviated ; for, in that case, the Epistle was written by Peter in Rome itself during the persecution, and he gave the believers in Asia Minor Christian exhortations in reference to such a grievous period among them. Yet, as this explanation cannot be *proved* to be correct, we set it aside, and merely observe, that in whatever Babylon Peter may have written his Epistle, his residence there can be easily reconciled with the exhortations which the Epistle contains. For, though these *may* be referred to the persecution of Nero, they may be understood with equal propriety as referring to any other persecution, since all individual characteristics, which could suit *only* this first cruel persecution of the church, are entirely wanting. Such general sufferings as these which Peter mentions must be supposed to have been endured by the church everywhere and at all times, as it is always comprehended in the very idea of a believer that he should excite opposition in those who are of a worldly inclination, and thus cause a combat. A more important objection than these two remarks is, that the style and ideas of the first Epistle of Peter exhibit a strong resemblance to the style and ideas of Paul. This cannot be denied, for it is too evident not to be observed ; but it does not serve its intended purpose, viz., to deprive Peter of the authorship of the Epistle. Notwithstanding all its similarity to Paul's manner, it still maintains enough independence and peculiarity to stamp it as the production of a man who thought for himself. As moreover, when Peter wrote this Epistle, he was connected (1 Pet. v. 12) with the old friend and companion of Paul, Sylvanus (or, as abbreviated, Silas), nothing is more easy than to suppose that Peter dictated to the latter, and in all probability in the Hebrew language, which alone seems to have been perfectly familiar to him. In translating into Greek, Sylvanus, who, from long intimacy with Paul, had become very much habituated to his diction, may have adopted many of its characteristics, and thus have been the occasion of the somewhat Pauline colouring which the Epistle possesses.

CHAPTER VIII.

OF THE SECOND EPISTLE OF PETER.

In regard to the second Epistle of Peter, its case is very different from that of the first. The former has always been so violently attacked, and suspected on such plausible grounds of not having been written by the Apostle Peter, that criticism is encompassed with as much difficulty in relation to it as in relation to any other book of the New Testament. And, moreover, such is the state of the matter, that the critical investigation of this Epistle is of particular importance. For, as we remarked in Chapter I., while, in regard to many writings of the New Testament (*e. g.*, the Epistle to the Hebrews, the second and third Epistles of John), the question

is, not so much whether they are genuine or spurious, as who was
their author, in regard to the second Epistle of Peter, the question
is, in truth, whether the Apostle Peter composed it, or some other
Peter, or somebody of another name, who meant no harm, but still
purposely endeavoured to deceive his readers into the belief that it
was written by Simon Peter, the Apostle of our Lord. In the first
place, the author of the Epistle not only expressly appropriates
Peter's name and title, " Simon Peter, a servant and apostle of
Jesus Christ" (2 Pet. i. 1), but he also states particulars respecting
his own life, which can have been true only of Peter. He says, for
instance, " For we have not followed cunningly-devised fables, when
we made known unto you the power and coming of our Lord Jesus
Christ, but were eye-witnesses of his majesty. For he received
from God the Father honour and glory, when there came such a
voice to him from the excellent glory, This is my beloved Son, in
whom I am well pleased. *And this voice, which came from heaven,
we heard, when we were with him in the holy mount,"* (2 Pet. i. 16
—18). These words, it is clear, refer to the transfiguration on the
mount (Matt. xvii. 1, *seq.*) But, besides James and John, the two
sons of Zebedee, no one was a spectator of this transfiguration except the Apostle Peter. If, therefore, the Apostle Peter was not
the author of this letter, the man who not only presumed to take
upon himself the name of an apostle, but designedly endeavoured to
make his readers think that he was the Apostle Peter, must have
been a downright shameless imposter ; and his production should by
no means retain its place in the canon, but it is necessary that it
should be at once thrust out of it.

It is for this very reason, viz., because the necessity of which we
have spoken has been sensibly felt, that the friends of the work have
so zealously prosecuted the investigation respecting it ; though certainly not always with due impartiality and coolness. It has been
forgotten that in truth very important objections may be urged
against the Petrine origin of this second Epistle, and it has been
attempted to establish its genuineness as firmly and incontrovertibly
as it is possible to establish that of other writings. The best
weapon, however, which can be used in defence of God's word, is
always truth ; and this compels us to admit that it is impossible to
attain so firm and certain proof of the genuineness of the second
Epistle of Peter, as of that of other books of the New Testament.
But certainly the opponents of the Epistle err greatly when they
assert that the spuriousness of the Epistle can be fully established.
Such an assertion cannot but be denied with all earnestness, even
though, as is often the case, it be connected with the opinion, that
the Epistle may notwithstanding retain its place in the canon as
hitherto, and be cited by preachers of the Gospel in their pulpit in-

structions. Such lax notions must be resisted with the utmost
moral sternness. For, would it not be participating in the fraud of
the author of the Epistle, were we to treat it as the genuine production of the Apostle Peter, while we consider it as spurious! If
it be really spurious, and can be proved to have gained its place in
the canon only through mistake, then let it be removed from the
collection of the sacred writings, which from its nature excludes
every fraudulent production. Christian truth would not at all suffer
by the removal of a single work of so slight extent.

We are convinced, however, that no such step is necessary.
The most prominent error in the critical investigation of this Epistle
has been, that writers have always striven to prove beyond objection either the genuineness or spuriousness of the production. It
has been forgotten that between these two positions there was a
medium, viz., an impossibility of satisfactorily *proving* either. It
cannot seem at all strange that this impossibility should exist in investigations respecting writings of the New Testament, if it be considered for a moment how difficult it often is to determine respecting the genuineness of a production even shortly after, or at the very
time of, its composition, if from any circumstance the decisive points
in the investigation have remained concealed. As in regard to the
author of the Epistle to the Hebrews it is entirely impossible to
come to any decided result, so it seems to me probable, that the deficiency of historical evidence makes it impossible to come to a fixed
conclusion in regard to the second Epistle of Peter. It is certain
there are several circumstances which give rise to reasonable doubts
respecting the origin of the Epistle ; still, so much may be adduced,
not only in refutation of them, but in the way of positive argument for the Epistle, that these doubts are neutralized. Only, the
favourable points do not amount to a complete, objectively valid
proof, and therefore a critical investigation of the Epistle does not
result exclusively to its advantage. Now this is certainly a very
unpleasant result, and one satisfactory to neither party, for men
commonly wish every thing to be decided in an absolute manner,
and therefore would have the Epistle declared positively either
genuine or spurious. But the main object should be the truth, and
not an agreeable result ; and faithful, impartial examination leads
us to the conclusion that in fact no perfect proof is to be obtained
in regard to the second Epistle of Peter. This conclusion affords us
the advantage, that we may with a good conscience leave the Epistle
in its place among the canonical books, since it cannot rightfully be
deprived of it until its spuriousness is *decisively proved.* Now,
whether it shall or shall not be used in doctrinal argument, must be
left to the judgment of each individual ; but at any rate no one can
prohibit its use so long as its spuriousness remains unproved.

It is time, however, to consider more closely all that can be urged against the genuineness of the Epistle, and to present therewith the counter considerations which either invalidate the former or argue the apostolic composition of the Epistle. Now the most important circumstance which presents itself against the genuineness of the book is, that it was to such a degree unknown in Christian antiquity. Not one of the fathers of the first two centuries mentions the second Epistle of Peter ; they all speak of but one Epistle from the hand of this apostle. Nor are there any passages in their writings which must of necessity be citations from it. Those passages which seem like parts of it may be explained either on the score of accidental coincidence or of mutual reference to the Old Testament. It was not till after Origen's time, in the third century, that the Epistle came into use, and even then doubts were always current in regard to its apostolic origin, and the learned father Jerome expressly remarks that *most* denied it such an origin. It is true, this statement cannot refer to all members of the church, but only to such as were capable of critical investigations ; for the same father of the church says further, that the reason why most denied it to be Peter's was, the difference in style which was observable on comparison with the first ; and clearly, uneducated persons were incapable of judging as to such difference in style. But still, it is extremely remarkable that even in the time of Jerome, *i.e.*, in the fifth century, there should be found in the church so many opponents of the Epistle.

It is, however, to be considered, in estimating the importance of this fact in relation to the genuineness of the Epistle, that no definite historical arguments are adduced against the Epistle from any quarter. Recourse is had, not to the testimony of individuals, nor to the declaration of entire churches, which denied the Epistle to be Peter's, but merely to internal reasons, deduced by the aid of criticism. This is the more strange, as it would appear that this second Epistle of Peter was addressed to the very same readers for whom the first was designed (Comp. 2 Pet. iii. 1), *i. e.*, to the Christians in several churches of Asia Minor. From these, one would think, there must have proceeded a testimony which could not be misunderstood against the Epistle, if Peter had not written to them a second time. Nor do the fathers say, that the Epistle contains heresies or any thing else totally unworthy of the apostle : indeed they do not make the slightest objection of this kind to the character of its contents. If, on the other hand, we look at their objections to other evidently fictitious writings, we find them asserting that they had an impious, detestable character, or that historical evidence was against their pretended apostolic origin. From the manner in which history represents the testimony of the fathers of the church, we may suppose that their opinion respecting the genuineness of the Epistle was founded in a great measure upon the fact that its diffusion was very much delayed. Since so many writings had been forged in Peter's name, the fathers of the church probably at once regarded an Epistle which came so late into circulation with some considerable suspicion, and then made use of the difference in language, or something of the kind, to confirm this suspicion. We must therefore say, that no decisive argument against the genuineness of the Epistle is to be drawn from historical considerations. Although it was but little known in the ancient church, this want of acquaintance with it may have been founded on reasons not at all connected with its spuriousness or genuineness. How many Epistles of Peter and other apostles may never have been much known? And still the circumstance that they have not been diffused abroad does not disprove their apostolic origin.

Thus, as the fathers of the church themselves had recourse to the internal character of the Epistle, it remains for us likewise to examine this, and as particular historical traditions respecting the Epistle were as inaccessible to these fathers as to us, and the art of criticism has not been carried to a high point of cultivation till recently, we may lay claim to greater probability, as to the result of our investigation, than they could.

Among the striking circumstances to which we are led by a careful investigation concerning the second Epistle of Peter, the first which presents itself, is the very ancient observation, that the *style* of this Epistle is quite different from that of the first. According to the most recent examinations, the case is really so. The style of the second Epistle is so different from that of the first, as to make it hardly conceivable that the same author should have written thus variously; particularly as the two Epistles must have been written at no great distance of time from each other, it being necessary to refer them both to the latter part of the apostle's life. But we have seen above, that Peter probably employed another person to write for him when he composed his first Epistle ; now, how natural to suppose, as Jerome has already suggested, that in writing the second Epistle Peter only made use of a different assistant from the one employed in writing the first, which supposition satisfactorily explains the difference in style. If it be insisted, however, that this supposition is a very violent one, we may then admit that the Epistles are in reality not apostolic, but are from Sylvanus, or some other writer. It is certainly true, that by this hypothesis we surrender the common opinion, that Peter either guided the pen himself, or at least dictated to the amanuensis word for word what he should write. But is it at all essential to admit that the writings of the apostles originated precisely in this way ? Is a prince's letter of less value, because his secretary wrote it, and the prince himself only signed it ? Do we esteem the writings of Mark and Luke any less because they were not apostles ? These last writings show best how the case is to be considered. Say that these two Epistles were written by Sylvanus or Mark ; is their importance to us in the least diminished, when Peter has given them the confirmation of his apostolic authority, as presenting his ideas, his mode of thinking ?

This hypothesis of Peter's having employed a writer in the composition of the second Epistle, explains, moreover, another remark which it has been usual to urge against its apostolic origin. If the Epistle of Jude be compared with the second chapter of this Epistle, there will appear a very striking similarity between them. This, as in the case of the Gospels, is so great that it is impossible it should have arisen accidentally. An impartial comparison of the two makes it extremely probable that Jude is the original, and was employed in the Epistle of Peter. Now this hardly seems suitable for the Apostle Peter, considering him as the author of the Epistle. He, the pillar of the church, should have been the original writer, though it would not have been strange that Jude, who held a far lower rank, should make use of his production. On the supposition, however, that Peter employed an individual to write for him, the latter might have made use of Jude's Epistle, and what would be totally unsuitable for an apostle, would not be at all strange in his assistant. If it be said that, as Peter must have known the use which was made of Jude, the circumstance still remains very strange, we may suppose that both, Peter (with his assistant) and Jude, conferred together in regard to combating the heretics, and agreed together in certain fundamental thoughts, and that thus coincidence in details was occasioned by their common written ground-work. Still, it may not be concealed, that, after all attempts to explain these appearances, there nevertheless remains in the mind something like suspicion ; and for this reason, although there are certainly not sufficient grounds for rejecting the Epistle, we cannot regard its genuineness as susceptible of proof.

There are other points of less moment, which are usually brought forward by the opponents of the Epistle. Among these is the passage 2 Peter iii. 2, in which the writer, it is said, is distinguished from the apostles, just as in Heb. ii. 3. But, in the first place, the reading in the former passage is not perfectly certain, since several ancient versions give it the same sense as Luther, who translates : "that ye may be mindful of the words which were spoken before by the holy prophets, and of the commandment of *us, the apostles of our Lord and Saviour.*"[1] But, even though we admit that to

---

[1] So, too, in the English version. The question alluded to in the text is, whether we should translate, *of us the apostles*, or, *of the apostles sent to us* (or *to you*, according to another reading)? See the original Greek.—TR.

be the correct reading, is one by which the author is distinguished from the apostles, we may explain the passage by supposing that the writer who was employed, instead of speaking in the name of the apostle, spoke in his own person. This was certainly an oversight, but not a very great one ; like that, *e. g.*, which occasioned the Evangelists to differ from each other in respect to the number of the blind men whom our Lord healed, and other points of the kind. The admission of such trifling oversight belongs properly to God's plan in regard to the Scriptures, since literal coincidence would, on the other hand, give rise to strong suspicion in regard to the veracity of the writers (as it would suggest the inference that there had been previous concert between them), and, on the other hand, there would be danger of confounding the letter with the spirit, to the disadvantage of the latter.

Of as little consequence is the reference made to 2 Pet. iii. 15, 16, where Peter says of his beloved brother Paul, whose wisdom he extols : "as also in all his Epistles, speaking in them of these things ; in which are some things hard to be understood, which they that are unlearned and unstable wrest, as they do also the other Scriptures, unto their own destruction." These words, it is said, clearly suppose a collection of Pauline Epistles to have been current in the church ; but one cannot have been made earlier than the commencement of the second century, and consequently the Epistle must be regarded as a work of later origin. But this assumption, that the collection of the Pauline Epistles was first made at so late a period, is by no means susceptible of proof. Indeed, in the fourth chapter we attempted to prove it not improbable that even Paul himself made a collection of his Epistles. At all events, no historical fact can be adduced against this hypothesis, and we must therefore consider thus much as certain, that the mention of a collection of Pauline Epistles ought not to induce us to conclude against the apostolic origin of the Epistle whose history we are investigating.

Thus is confirmed the position which we laid down above, that not one of the reasons usually adduced against the genuineness of the second Epistle of Peter is a decisive one. Notwithstanding, as has been already mentioned, impartiality enjoins it upon us to allow that, after considering these reasons, there remains a feeling in the mind which does not permit us to place this Epistle in the rank of those universally admitted. We find ourselves constrained to resort first to one expedient, then to another, in order to invalidate the arguments which make against the genuineness of the Epistle. Let us, however, cast a glance at the other side, and consider the arguments which may be adduced *in favour of* the authenticity of the Epistle. The impression made by the genuine apostolic manner, in the first and third chapters in particular, is so heart-stirring, the severe moral tone which prevails throughout them is so forcible, that very estimable scholars have found themselves induced to regard these two chapters, or at least the first, as truly Petrine, and the second or the last two as, perhaps, merely subsequent additions to the genuine Epistle. This hypothesis has indeed, at first view, this recommendation, that we can give proper weight to the reasons for doubt, without being obliged to regard the express statements respecting Peter personally as having been forged. But the close connection of all the chapters with each other, and the uniformity of the language and ideas throughout the Epistle is too much at variance with the supposition of an interpolation of the Epistle, to make it right that it should be admitted.

Still, we cannot but allow the great weight of the reason from which the hypothesis took its rise, viz., that it was an almost inconceivable piece of impudence for an impostor to assume the person of the Apostle Peter, so as even to speak of his presence at the transfiguration on Mount Tabor, and venture to invent prophecies of our Lord to him respecting his end. (Comp. 2 Pet. i. 14). It is true, appeal is made, on this point, to the practice of the ancients, according to which it was not so strange and censurable, it is said, to write under another's name, as it appears to us at the present day. And it is undoubtedly true, that in the primitive times of the church writings were much more frequently forged in the name of others than at the present time. But it is a question whether this is to be referred to the custom of the times, or does not rather arise from the fact, that in the less methodical book-transactions of the ancient world it was much easier to get fictitious writings into circulation than it is at present, on account of the great publicity which now attends such transactions. At any rate, we must say, that it was a very culpable practice, if it ever was common, to procure currency for one's literary productions by affixing a great name to them ; and every honourable man would have avoided it and written only in his own name. Suppose, however, it was less offensive than now to publish any thing under an assumed name, we must notwithstanding protest in the most earnest manner against the idea, that a man could permit himself fraudulently to appropriate such points from the life of him whose name he used as could be true only of the latter ; which must be the case in regard to this Epistle, if it was not written by Peter. Were this to be done in any case, the use of another's name would no longer be a mere form in writing, it would rather be a coarse piece of imposture, such as could not occur without a decidedly wrong intention ; and this leads us to a new and important point in the investigation of the origin of the second Epistle of Peter.

The alternative in which we are thus placed is as harsh as it could possibly be. Either the Epistle is genuine and apostolical, or it is not only spurious and forged, but was forged by a bold, shameless impostor, and such a person must have had an evil design in executing a forgery of the kind supposed. Now in the whole Epistle we do not find the slightest thing which can be regarded as erroneous or as morally bad. Its contents are entirely biblical, and truly evangelical. An elevated religious spirit animates the Epistle throughout. Is it conceivable, that a man actuated by this spirit can be chargeable with such a deception? Or is it supposed that this spirit is itself feigned? But this idea plainly contradicts itself, for he who is bad enough to forge writings cannot entertain the design of extending a good influence by his forgery. No forgery would be necessary for such a purpose. The design must have been to defend what was unholy in principle or practice under cover of a sacred name. The only probable purpose of the forgery of the Epistle is this; that the unknown author of the production wished to combat the heretics described in the second chapter, and in order that he might do this with some effect, he wrote in the name of the Apostle Peter, and made use of the Epistle of Jude in doing so. But if a man who was honest (in other respects) could have been induced to enter upon such a crooked path, would he not have contented himself with placing the apostle's name in front of his Epistle? Would his conscience have permitted him to appropriate falsely from the life of the apostle such particulars as are narrated in the Epistle? This is really hard to believe, and the efforts made to preserve the genuineness of the first chapter at least, which contains these very particulars, sufficiently prove how universal is the feeling that the statements it contains cannot have been forged.

It is true the case would stand otherwise, if it were a well-founded position, that the Epistle really contains erroneous tenets. But how truly impossible it is to establish this, is very evident from the nature of the points adduced as errors. In the first place, one is supposed to be contained in the passage, 2 Peter iii. 5, in which it is said, that the earth was formed out of water and in water by the word of God.[1] It is true, there are parallels to this view of the creation of the earth in several mythical cosmogonies; but is this circumstance a proof that the doctrine of the creation of the world out of water is false? Does the Mosaic account of the creation, or any other passage in the Bible, contain any thing which in the slightest degree impugns it? Or does the condition of the physical or geological sciences in our day prove that the earth certainly came into existence in a different manner? It will suffice, in regard to

[1] Our English version gives a somewhat different sense to this passage; but probably the translation above conveys nearly, if not exactly, its true signification.—TR.

this point, to remind our readers that the formation of the earth out of water was taught by the celebrated De Luc, not to mention many men of less note. At the most, then, it can only be said that in the passage referred to, there is something openly and definitely stated which is not found thus stated in any other book of the Bible ; though it is impossible to deny that the Mosaic account of the creation (" The Spirit of God moved upon the face of the waters") is susceptible of such an interpretation, as to convey the idea which is more plainly declared in 2 Pet. iii. 5. Thus there is no ground for talking about an error in this passage of the Epistle. The same remarks may be made respecting another position, that the doctrine (also presented in the third chapter of the second Epistle of Peter) concerning the destruction of the world by fire is erroneous. For it can by no means be shown in regard to this second idea, that it contradicts the common statement of the Bible, or contains any thing incorrect. Indeed, there are other passages, likewise, that contain an intimation, at least, of the same thing which is here openly stated. (Comp. Isaiah li. 6 ; Zeph. iii. 8). And so far are the similar mythical accounts in other religions from arguing any thing wrong in this idea, that we should rather consider the coincidence of the mythical accounts with the biblical doctrine as a confirmation of the real verity of the former.

If, therefore, we put together all which has been said of the second Epistle of Peter, thus much is certainly clear, that the circumstances which are calculated to excite suspicion respecting the Epistle, are by no means sufficient to constitute a formal proof of their spuriousness. True, the suspicious points cannot be so perfectly obviated, that every doubt will disappear. Some uncertainty will remain in the mind. Still the positive arguments in behalf of its genuineness so far allay these doubts that it is possible to obtain a satisfactory *subjective* conviction of the genuineness of the Epistle. But a proof of its genuineness which shall be of perfect validity and be generally acknowledged can no more be attained than such a proof of its spuriousness ; and, therefore, there will always be something dubious in the position of this Epistle. The ancient fathers of the church endeavoured to express this uncertainty by the term *Antilegomena*, and later teachers in the evangelical church by the designation *Deutero-canonical writings*, among which this Epistle is reckoned. Attempts to remove all the obscurity which envelopes the facts in regard to this Epistle will probably always prove vain, from the want of historical accounts respecting the use and diffusion of it in primitive times.

CHAPTER IX.

OF THE EPISTLES OF JAMES AND JUDE.

IN investigating the Epistles of James and Jude, the question is, as in the case of the Epistle to the Hebrews, not so much whether they are genuine or spurious, as who was their author. This may seem strange, inasmuch as the authors of both of them mention themselves in the salutations, which is not the case as to the Epistle to the Hebrews. Indeed, Jude, for the purpose of designating himself still more definitely, adds the circumstance that he was the brother of James. But, as both these names were very common among the Jews, and the relations between the persons of this name mentioned in the New Testament are quite involved, it is a very difficult inquiry, what James and what Jude were the authors of the Epistles which we are considering. Now, if it should be probable, on investigation, that the authors of the two Epistles were not apostles (*i. e.* among the number of the twelve disciples), then will arise a second inquiry, what we are to think of the canonical authority of the Epistles?

The first question is, how many persons of the name of *James* and *Jude* are mentioned in the Scriptures or by ancient Christian writers? From the catalogues of the twelve apostles (Matt. x. 2 *seq.;* Mark iii. 13 *seq.;* Luke vi. 12 *seq.;* Acts i. 13 *seq.*), we perceive that two individuals among them were named James. The first was the brother of the Evangelist John, a son of Zebedee and Salome ; this James is often mentioned in the evangelical history. His brother Peter, and himself, were of all the apostles the most intimate with our Lord. He was present at the transfiguration and at our Lord's agony in the garden of Gethsemane. According to Acts xii. 2, Herod killed him with the sword a few years after our Lord's ascension. As, therefore, this James disappeared from the scene of events very early, he does not cause much difficulty in the investigation. The second James is termed the son of Alphæus, and of this apostle we have so uncertain accounts, that it is difficult to determine much respecting him.

As there were two individuals of the name of James among the twelve, so there were two Judes. One, the betrayer of our Lord, of course is not concerned in this investigation. He cannot be confounded with any one else ; especially as he had the surname Iscariot from his birth-place Carioth. The second Jude, it would seem, bore many names ; for while Luke (in the Gospel as well as in the Acts) calls him Jude the son of James, Matthew and Mark call him sometimes Thaddeus, and sometimes Lebbeus. It was not at all uncommon among the Jews for one man to bear several names ; and, therefore, we may admit the validity of the prevalent opinion that Lebbeus or Thaddeus, and Jude, the son of James, are the same individuals. In John xiv. 22, a second Jude among the twelve is expressly distinguished from Jude (Judas) the traitor, who is termed Iscariot ; and hence the name Jude may have been the one by which the former was most commonly designated.

Now did we know with perfect certainty that the authors of the Epistles under consideration were of the number of the twelve, it would be easy to fix upon the individuals ; James, the son of Alphæus must have written the Epistle of James, and Jude, the son of James, that of Jude. But as Jude (v. 1) calls himself the brother of James, he must either mean another man of this name known to his readers, or we must suppose the term *brother* to signify step-brother or cousin, as indeed the word is often used in Hebrew. For the opinion of some, that in the catalogues of the apostles (see Luke's Gospel and his Acts of the Apostles), Jude is not called the son but the brother of James, must be totally rejected, because, though it is true that sometimes the word *brother* is to be supplied, for the genitive following a proper name, this is only the case when it is clear from the connection what is to be supplied. In the apostolic catalogue, however, *son* is everywhere else to be supplied for the genitive ; and hence it is incredible that in the case of Jude alone *brother* must be added.

But that the authors of these two Epistles of James and Jude were among the number of the twelve is very uncertain (indeed, as we shall show hereafter, improbable), and on that account we have still to determine the difficult question, what persons of these names wrote the Epistles? The following reasons show the uncertainty of the idea that the authors of the Epistles were apostles. In the first place, the fathers of the church speak of another James, the brother of our Lord, and first bishop of Jerusalem, and another Jude, likewise the brother of our Lord, as the authors of the Epistles ; and, moreover, these were disputed by many, and reckoned among the Antilegomena, clearly for this reason alone, that it was supposed perfectly correct to regard them as not apostolical. Thus, in the opinion of the fathers, there were beside the two Jameses and Judes among the twelve, two other persons of these names, called *brothers of our Lord*. These are mentioned in the passage Matt. xiii. 55, with two other brothers of our Lord, Simon and Joses, and with sisters of his whose names are not given. They are also mentioned in the later history of the apostolic age (Acts xv. 13 *seq.;* Gal. i. 19 ; ii. 9), particularly James, who is designated with Peter and John as a pillar of the church. According to the fathers of the church, he was the first bishop of Jerusalem, and the description which the New Testament gives of his position and operations perfectly accords with this statement. According to the account of the Jewish writer, *Josephus*, and a very ancient Christian historian, named *Hegesippus*, this James, the brother of our Lord, died a martyr's death at Jerusalem shortly before its destruction. He possessed such authority and such reputation for piety among the Jews, that, according to Josephus, the destruction of the city was a punishment from heaven for the execution of this just man. James was succeeded in the bishopric of Jerusalem by another brother of our Lord, viz., Simon (Matth. xiii. 55), who, as well as the third brother Jude, lived till the reign of the Emperor Trajan, *i. e.*, to the end of the first century after Christ. According to the account of Hegesippus, Simon also died a martyr's death, like his brother ; of the manner of Jude's end nothing definite is known. Although, however, we find these brethren of our Lord labouring with ardent Christian zeal after the resurrection of the Saviour, still, in the lifetime of our Lord they did not believe on him. This we are told by John· expressly (vii. 5), and therefore, we do not observe these brethren of Jesus among the disciples until *after* his resurrection from the dead (Acts i. 14). Probably the vision with which (according to 1 Cor. xv. 7), James was favoured, was the means of convincing them all of the Divine dignity of our Lord, which hitherto, perhaps on the very account of their close relationship to him by blood, they had been unable to credit. It is true the expression, *brothers of our Lord*, is not to be understood as meaning what the words strictly signify ; for Mary, the mother of our Lord, appears not to have had any other children. The passages Matth. i. 25, Luke ii. 7, in which Jesus is called the *first-born* son of Mary, prove nothing to the contrary, since, if no more children follow, the only son is also the first-born. If the statements of Scripture respecting these brethren of our Lord be put together, it cannot be doubted, that the children of the sister of Mary, the mother of Jesus, are intended by the expression. This sister of Mary was likewise named Mary, and was the wife of a certain Cleophas. She stood with the mother of Jesus beneath the cross of our Lord, as did also Mary Magdalene (John xix. 25). This same Mary is called in the parallel passage of Mark (xv. 40) the mother of James the Less and of Joses. Here, then, are named two of the persons who in Matth. xiii. 55, are termed brothers of our Lord. Nothing, therefore, is more natural, as it nowhere appears that Mary had any other children, than to suppose that these so-called brethren of our Lord were his cousins, the sons of his mother's sister. As it is probable that Joseph, the foster-father of Jesus, died at an early period (for he is not mentioned after the journey to Jerusalem in the twelfth year of

Jesus' age), Mary perhaps went to live with her sister, and thus Jesus grew up with the sons of the latter, which may have been the reason why it was so difficult for them to give credit to his Divine authority. It was very common in the Hebrew idiom to term cousins *brothers.* Hence in Gen. xiii. 8, Abraham and Lot, who were cousins, are termed brothers. If we were to take the word *brother* in its literal sense, and regard the four brothers of our Lord mentioned in Matth. xiii. 55 as own children of Mary, the mother of Jesus, we should have to suppose the extraordinary circumstance that the two mothers of the same name had also children named alike. Now, as we nowhere find mention, first of our Lord's brethren, and then of his cousins, but the same relations are always referred to, this supposition, cannot be admitted. The same may be said of another supposition, according to which two of these so-called brethren of our Lord, viz., Jude and James, were of the number of the twelve. For it is said that the Hebrew name which lies at the basis of the Greek one, Cleophas (abbreviated Klopas), viz., Chalpai, may also in Greek become Alphæus. Thus James the son of Alphæus would be equivalent to James the son of Cleophas. Now, it is true, that on the score of philology nothing can be reasonably objected against this supposition ; but, its validity is overthrown by the fact that one and the same writer (viz. Luke), presents both forms. Although the name could be differently expressed in Greek, at least the same writer would always have followed the same mode. Moreover, as we have already remarked, it is inadmissible to supply the word *brother*, instead of *son*, after the name Jude. Lastly, it is a decisive circumstance, that in John vii. 5 it is most expressly stated that the brethren of Jesus did not believe on him. It is, therefore, impossible that they should have been of the number of the twelve. Consequently, the New Testament mentions, besides the James, son of Zebedee, who was early executed, two other persons of this name, first the apostle, who was a son of Alphæus, and next, the brother of our Lord, the first bishop of Jerusalem. Thus, too, the New Testament mentions, besides the Apostle Jude, who was the son of a certain James, of whom we know nothing, another Jude who, likewise, was a brother of our Lord, and lived to a late period (till the time of Trajan), in Palestine. That these two brothers of our Lord, and not the apostles, were the authors of our Epistles, has been already intimated and will now be more fully shown.

Of great importance, and indeed almost decisive by itself, is the circumstance, that the fathers of the church refer the Epistle of James to the brother of our Lord of that name ; and, too, the fathers who lived in that very region which was the scene of the labours of this celebrated bishop of Jerusalem, viz., the east. Here they might and must have had the most exact accounts respecting this distinguished man, and information as to his writings must have spread itself very readily from Jerusalem to the neighbouring countries of Syria and Egypt. This historical testimony is confirmed very strongly by the great agreement which exists between the contents of the Epistle and the communications which are made by ancient fathers of the church, and particularly Hegesippus, in regard to the peculiar habits of James. According to the account of this writer, James distinguished himself by forms of piety which were very like those inculcated in the Old Testament. He fasted and prayed a great deal, so that, as Hegesippus relates, probably with some exaggeration, his knees had become callous. According to the New Testament, too (comp. Acts xv. with Gal. ii, 12), James, the brother of our Lord, appears to have been the head of the Jewish Christians. He, therefore, undoubtedly observed the Mosaic law, even after he became a Christian, and endeavoured to obtain the sanctity enjoined in the Old Testament. That, however, this endeavour[1] was not a narrow-minded one, as among the Ebionites, but a liberal one, as among the Nazarenes, is plainly shown by the narrative in the Acts, according to which he did not, along with the obstinate Judaizers, desire to impose the observance of the law upon the Gentiles, but only adhered to it himself, as a pious practice of his fathers. Still his whole disposition leaned somewhat to the side of the law, and this is clearly exhibited in the Epistle.

The same is true of Jude likewise. His very designation of himself as a *brother* of James can leave no doubt that he desired to represent himself as the brother of that James who was so celebrated, the first bishop of Jerusalem. He does not call himself an apostle, any more than James. Both term themselves merely servants of Jesus Christ, neglecting from modest humility to make any mention of their relationship by blood to our Lord. We have no statements on the part of the early fathers of the church in regard to the author of the Epistle of Jude. The later fathers, e. g., Jerome, call him an apostle, but they did not for that reason mean a different Jude ; only, as might very easily happen, considering the confused accounts we have of these men, they sometimes placed Jude the brother of our Lord among the number of the twelve, contrary to John vii. 5.

Another as important reason for believing that James the brother of our Lord, and not the Apostle James, was regarded as the author of the Epistle, is the circumstance that it was reckoned among the Antilegomena. Doubts did indeed arise, but not till a pretty late day. Clement of Rome, Hermas, and Irenaeus, make use of the Epistle

---

[1] The original reads *Schreiben*, which I take to be clearly a mistake for *Streben*, and translate accordingly.—TR.

without scruple. Origen first, then Eusebius, mention doubts. Now, as before the time of Jerome, there is no trace of the Epistle's having been regarded as forged in James' name, the ground of doubt can have been no other than that it was questionable whether an Epistle of any one not an apostle could claim admission into the canon. Jerome observes, that certain individuals believed the Epistle of James to have been forged by some one in his name. This opinion, however, is entirely devoid of probability, because in such case the author would not have neglected to ascribe the dignity of apostle to the James whom he wished to be regarded as the writer of the Epistle, that it might be more sure of admission into the canon. Those persons, therefore, of whom Jerome speaks, and who undoubtedly resided in the west, probably entertained doctrinal scruples respecting the Epistle. In the west, and particularly in Rome, the centre of the western churches, special regard was felt for Paul and his doctrines. Now, the second chapter of the Epistle of James was supposed to contain erroneous notions in contrariety to Paul, because as was thought, it inculcated justification by works instead of by faith. This passage even misled Luther into a rejection of the Epistle of James. In his preface to it he says, " This James does nothing but urge his readers to the law and to works, and his manner is so confused that I imagine he was some pious man who had gathered a few sayings from the disciples of the apostles, and put them down upon paper. . . . Hence the Epistle of James is but a *strawy* Epistle ; it has by no means an evangelical tone."

In more recent times, however, it has been proved, by very thorough and impartial investigations, that this harsh judgment of Luther is certainly unfounded, together with the apprehensions of the ancient fathers mentioned by Jerome.

James only opposed misconstructions and perversions of Paul's real doctrine, not the great apostle of the Gentiles himself. The two great teachers of the church are essentially one in sentiment ; only they had reference to different heresies, and thus their language wears a different aspect. In the Epistles to the Romans and Galatians, Paul presents the doctrine of faith, and justification thereby, in opposition to the reliance which the Jews placed on works. James, on the other hand, opposes a dead imaginary faith, which, without any renovating influence over the heart and mind, lulls a man into the sleep of sin, instead of making him active in works of love. If we thus consider the language of the two apostles with reference to the positions which they respectively opposed, we shall perceive the most perfect unity between these two teachers of the church, notwithstanding all their freedom and peculiarity of manner. Though they taught the same doctrines, their point of view was different. Paul had a predominant leaning towards faith, not meaning by any means, however, to deny that it must bear good works as its fruit ; James directed his attention more to the fruit, without, however, disparaging the root of faith from which alone they could spring.[1]

Thus, leaving wholly out of view the influence of doctrinal ideas, the discrepancy between the ancient fathers of the church was only whether the Epistle, as proceeding from the brother of our Lord, who was not an apostle, should or should not be admitted into the canon. The East, in general, maintained that it should, because James had exerted so much influence in that region ; the Christians of the West were less favourable to it. In reality, then, the question was not in regard to the genuineness of the Epistle, but in regard to the rank of James, whether or not he should be placed on a level with the apostles in respect to the abundance and power of the Spirit poured out upon him, so that a writing of his might be received into the canon as a norm of faith and practice for all future generations of Christians ; a question which we will soon consider further.

In regard to this second point, likewise, the case is the same with the Epistle of Jude as with that of James ; except that in the accounts concerning this Epistle given by ancient fathers we do not find the slightest evidence that the Epistle was ever regarded as the production of an impostor who forged it in Jude's name. Such a supposition respecting this Epistle is extremely improbable. In such case, would an impostor have contented himself with designating Jude as the " brother of James." Would he not at least have expressly called him an apostle of our Lord, in order to gain a place for the Epistle in the canon ? When we are told, therefore, of opposition to the Epistle, which caused it to be placed among the Antilegomena, we must refer it all to a refusal to accord to the author of the Epistle, who was not an apostle, sufficient consideration to procure its admission into the canon. Thus in regard to the Epistle of Jude, likewise, the point in question is, not the genuineness of the Epistle, but only the personal standing of the author, which by some of the fathers of the church was considered equal to that of an apostle, and by others inferior. The investigation of this question, then, what we are to think of the admission of two productions of writers who were not apostles into the canon of the New Testament, remains for the conclusion of this chapter.

Now, whether it be said, that the church has forsaken its principle of admitting no writing into the canon which was not either written by an apostle or composed under his supervision and authority, in admitting the Epistles of James and Jude ; or that they in-

<hr>

[1] See more complete discussions of the supposed discrepancy between Paul and James on the subject of faith and works, in the Biblical Repository, vol. iii., p. 189, and vol. iv., p. 683.—TR.

deed adhered to their principle, but erred in regarding James and Jude, the brethren of our Lord, to whom they correctly ascribed the Epistles, as apostles, and therefore admitting their Epistles into the canon—either way, it would seem as though we of the present day were entitled to charge antiquity with mistake respecting these Epistles. As to the Epistle of Jude the case certainly seems to be as we have here stated it. It was written by one who was not an apostle, by a man of whose acts and character we know nothing further ; a fact which appears to sustain the scruples of many of the ancients in regard to its being canonical. Moreover, it contains nothing which is not also found in the second Epistle of Peter, so that the church could dispense with it without suffering the slightest loss. We might therefore be disposed to consider this Epistle as a deutero-canonical production, which was received into the canon only at a late period on the ground that it was more advisable to preserve every writing of the days of the apostles than to reject any thing which might be of apostolic origin. It is not to be forgotten, however, that the use of Jude's Epistle in the second Epistle of Peter must be considered an apostolic confirmation of the former, if the latter be acknowledged genuine. Both productions, therefore, stand or fall together. The impossibility, however, of proving beyond doubt the genuineness of the second Epistle of Peter, will not permit the friends of these Epistles to entertain any thing more than a subjective conviction in regard to the authority of Jude.

The case is different, however, with the Epistle of James. For this remarkable man appears, both according to the New Testament and according to the fathers of the church, to have occupied a very influential position. It is true he was not of the number of the twelve ; but the fact that our Lord appeared to him separately, as he did to Peter (1 Cor. xv. 7), indicates his consequence ; as does also the circumstance that he was elected bishop of Jerusalem, and especially his relation to the Jewish Christians, of whom James seems to have been the real head. Hence in Gal. ii. 9, this man, with Peter and John, is called a pillar of the church, and Josephus represents the consideration in which he was held among the Jews to have been so great, that the destruction of Jerusalem by the Romans was looked upon as a judgment for his death. Although, therefore, James was no apostle, and moreover, no one of the twelve, so far as we know, afforded his confirmation to the Epistle, still the church might well have considered itself entitled to insert the production of so influential a man in the canon. It may be said, indeed, that James was in a precisely parallel situation to that of Paul (who too was not of the number of the twelve, and still enjoyed apostolic dignity) ; except that in regard to the appearance of our Lord which was vouchsafed to James, and the commissions

which were entrusted to him, we have not such particular information as is furnished us by the Acts respecting his appearance to
Paul. Yet passing by this, we cannot but declare, that an apostolic
confirmation of a particular book, such as we suppose in the case of
Mark and Luke, according to the testimony of history, is nothing
compared with the testimony which we have from Paul's own mouth
respecting James. He is designated, along with Peter and John, as
a pillar of the whole church of God upon earth, and thus, though
not one of the twelve, still placed entirely on a level with the proper apostles ; and hence no objection at all can be made to the reception of the Epistle by the church. She has not, in receiving it,
deviated at all from her principles ; indeed, she has thereby rather
applied them in their real spirit, not rigorously restricting the idea
of *apostolical* estimation to the number of the twelve, but referring
it to the fulness and power of the spirit exhibited in the life. This,
however, as appears from the Epistle itself, and from history, was
possessed in its utmost potency by James, as well as Paul, on which
account the Epistle of the former richly merits a place among the
canonical books.

CHAPTER X.

OF THE REVELATION OF JOHN.

THE sublime book which concludes the New Testament, the ·
Revelation of St. John, (ὁ θεολόγος,) with its wonderful images and
visions, has met with a more extraordinary fate than any other writing of the New Testament. The impressive and absorbing nature
of the contents of the book has seldom permitted any one to examine
it with cool impartiality, and while some have become the enthusiastic advocates of the book, others have appeared as its most violent opponents, not only rejecting the work as not apostolical, or as
forged, but even reviling it as the production of an heretical spirit.
Thus it has happened, that, while no production of the New Testament can exhibit more and stronger historical evidence of its genuineness and its apostolic authority than the Revelation, none has
met with more antagonists ; and, indeed, many of its antagonists
are men who have merited much gratitude from the church for their
struggles in behalf of the truth. Among these is Luther, who
shows himself a determined opponent of John's Revelation. He
says, in his preface to it :
    " There are various and abundant reasons why I regard this book
as neither apostolical nor prophetic. First and foremost ; the apos-

tles do not make use of visions, but prophesy in clear and plain
language (as do Peter, Paul, and Christ also, in the Gospel) ; for it
is becoming the apostolic office to speak plainly and without figure
or vision, respecting Christ and his acts.—Moreover, it seems to me
far too arrogant for him to enjoin it upon his readers to regard this
his own work as of more importance than any other sacred book,
and to threaten that if any one shall take aught away from it, God
will take away from him his part in the book of life (Rev. xxii. 19).
Besides, even were it a blessed thing to believe what is contained in
it, no man knows what that is. The book is believed in (and is
really just the same to us) as though we had it not ; and many
more valuable books exist for us to believe in. But let every man
think of it as his spirit prompts him. My spirit cannot adapt itself
to the production, and this is reason enough for me why I should
not esteem it very highly."

From this strong language of the great Reformer it is sufficiently
evident how repulsive the contents of the Revelation were to him.
As he termed the Epistle of James a *strawy* Epistle, because it
seemed to him to contradict Paul's doctrine in regard to faith, so he
rejected the Revelation, because the imagery of the book was unintelligible to him. This was obscure to him from the fact that he
could not thoroughly apprehend the doctrine of God's kingdom upon
earth, which is exhibited in the Revelation, and forms the proper
centre of every thing contained in it.

The same point has at all times in the church operated very
powerfully upon the judgments of learned men in regard to the
Revelation ; and therefore we must, before any particular examination of this production, make some general observations on the propriety of permitting doctrinal views generally, and the doctrine of
God's kingdom upon earth particularly, to have an influence on
criticism.

In recent times, critical investigations of the sacred books have
pretty generally proceeded on the principle, that the doctrinal views
ought not to exert any influence upon inquiries respecting the genuineness of the Scriptures. It has been easy to lay down this principle, because generally[1] the binding authority of Sacred Writ has been
denied, and writers have not felt it incumbent on them to admit as
an object of faith every thing that was stated in genuine apostolic
writings. Indeed, to many an investigator it has been very gratify-
ing, that in genuine writings of the apostles things should occur
which to him seemed evident errors ; since in such case it became more easy to prove that the apostles even had stated many
things erroneously, and that therefore what was true in their productions should be separated from what was false. With Luther,

[1] That is, in Germany.—TR.

however, and all the other old theologians the case was different. They acknowledged the Scriptures as binding on their faith, and therefore could by no means wholly exclude doctrinal considerations. For, were a book proved to be apostolical by all possible historical and internal arguments, and yet it plainly subverted the Gospel and preached a different Christ from the true historical Son of God and man, no faithful teacher of the church of Christ should receive and use any such production, notwithstanding all the evidence in its favour, any more than listen to an angel from heaven, who should bring another Gospel (Gal. i. 8). Such was Luther's position ; and in this view we may respect and honour his opposition to the Epistle of James and the Revelation of John. His only error in this, in itself commendable, endeavour boldly to distinguish what was anti-christian was, that he decided too rashly and hastily, and thus did not investigate with sufficient thoroughness, and, on the ground of appearances merely, pronounced that to be not biblical which in reality was so. That this was the case in regard to his judgment concerning the discrepancy between James and Paul, is at the present day universally admitted. In regard to the Revelation, however, many still think that he judged correctly, although, in my opinion, he erred here as much as in relation to the Epistle of James.

We cannot say, therefore, that doctrinal considerations are not of the least consequence in critical investigations ; though certainly we must not permit them to have an improper influence, so as to disturb the historical investigation, nor too hastily make an objective rule of our present subjective views, but endeavour to investigate more thoroughly what is at the moment obscure and inexplicable. Such an endeavour will often educe a modification of our views, and we may find that what seemed erroneous contains profound and sublime truth.

In particular, this would undoubtedly be the case with many, if they could determine to consider more closely the doctrine respecting God's kingdom upon earth, which has always been the greatest cause of offence in the Revelation. True, it is not to be denied, that the history of the fortune of this doctrine is by no means calculated to favour it ; for every thing which human ignorance and human malice have been able to devise, appears to have concentrated itself in the misapprehensions of this doctrine. If, however, pains be taken to separate these misapprehensions and perversions from the doctrine itself, and we are impartial enough to consider, that often very profound truths, which take a mighty hold of the human mind, are most exposed to abuse, and may become most dangerous, and that hardly any other religion has been misused to such abominable purposes as the Christian religion itself, and yet that it is not on that account the less true, or the less divine, he will easily attain the proper fundamental idea of the doctrine of God's kingdom upon earth ; which is so simple, that we cannot understand how its truth could ever be doubted, until we remember the farragos of non-sense which have been propounded under its sanction. This simple radical idea is merely, that as, in regard to an individual man, God, by the Saviour, redeems not merely a particular part of him, his spirit alone, his soul alone, or his body alone, but the *whole* man, his body, soul, and spirit, so the redeeming power of Christ has for its object the deliverance of the entire human race, and of the crea-tion in general, from the yoke of sin. As, therefore, the end of salvation for the individual is the glorification of his nature, the end of all things in the universe on the same principle is the glorifica-tion of the universe. Proceeding from this fundamental idea, the Revelation teaches in sublime imagery, agreeing perfectly with the statements of our Lord and the apostles (which are less formal, and rather take the doctrine for granted, and thus are more incidental), that a period will come in which not only, as has already been the case, the spirit of Jesus Christ should prevail in secret, and guide men's minds, but should also gain the victory externally, and found a kingdom of peace and righteousness upon earth. Now, that with the arrival of this reign of peace there will be connected on the one hand, the appearance of Jesus Christ, and a resurrection of many saints and pious men, and, on the other, a previous mighty struggle on the part of evil—does indeed follow very naturally from the fundamental idea, and the supposed development of good and evil ; but these points are only incidental. The principal idea is the perfect return of the supremacy of good, the restoration of the lost paradise to an earth which has been laid waste by sin. Millions desire this most earnestly, hope and pray for it even, without ever imagining that it is the very doctrine which they think themselves bound to oppose, or at least unable to admit, without deviating from correct belief. Even the excellent Reformers had but an im-perfect notion of this doctrine, though it is as simple as it is sub-lime ; and for this reason, in a great measure, that they saw around them senseless fanatics who dishonoured the Gospel, and caused un-speakable injury by the grossest misconstructions and perversions of this doctrine.

It would not have been worth while, with our present purpose, to say even the little we have said on this subject, were there not so many well-meaning men of real piety, who, notwithstanding the most striking historical proof, can never prevail upon themselves to admit the Revelation to be a genuine apostolic production, and therefore entitled to a place in the canon, and thus to become a rule of faith ; because they feel that then they must in consequence

admit the reign of God upon earth in their circle of belief, which
they suppose they neither can, nor ought to do. May such be led
to a thorough investigation of this idea, and of all the passages of
Scripture which relate thereto, that the acknowledgment of evangelical truth in this respect may be promoted, and its fulfilment be
rendered nearer at hand !

In passing now to the consideration of the historical evidence in
favour of the genuineness of the Revelation, we must again call to
mind the latter days of the life of John the Evangelist. He lived,
as we know with certainty, longer than any one of the other apostles, that is, as late as to the end of the first century. The scene
of his successful labours at the close of his life was the city of
Ephesus, in the vicinity of which were situated all those cities to
which were directed the seven Epistles contained in the first chapters of the Revelation. Ephesus, moreover, was one of the great
centres of business in the Roman empire, and was much frequented
by Christians from all countries.

It must, therefore, be admitted, that it was easy for the Ephesian church particularly, and indeed for the whole ancient church,
to arrive at the highest degree of certainty in regard to the writings
of John. In particular, there could be no uncertainty whether
John had composed so peculiar, so very remarkable a production as
the Revelation. We must therefore admit, that if among the fathers of the church in that region we met with even uncertainty in
regard to its author, it would be a very suspicious circumstance ;
and, on the other hand, unanimity in their conviction of the genuineness of the book must be a very decisive testimony in its favour.
Now we meet with this last to a surprising degree. First, we have
the testimony of Papias, bishop of Hierapolis in Phrygia, in behalf
of the book. This man was personally acquainted with several of
the apostles, and among them with the Evangelist John. His testimony is therefore of the greatest consequence. It is true an attempt has been made to invalidate it, on the ground that only a late
writer, named Andreas, attributes to Papias any knowledge of the
Revelation ; but careful consideration of the principal passage respecting Papias in Eusebius (Hist. Eccl., iii. 39), which certainly
ought to be thus examined, will show that Eusebius has given a
wrong representation concerning Papias in more than one respect,
and every thing is in favour of the supposition, that Papias was acquainted with all John's writings. Eusebius is one of those fathers
of the church who were very much prejudiced against the doctrine
concerning the millennium, and it is on this account that he so
strongly opposes Papias. Since this ancient bishop was a principal
supporter of that doctrine, his testimony may on that account appear partial ; and yet his close relation to John cannot have per-

mitted him, notwithstanding all his predilection for this doctrine, to attribute to that writer a production which was not his. Justin Martyr, too, along with Papias, testifies in favour of the apostolic origin of the Apocalypse. He was, indeed, born in Palestine, but he taught in Ephesus, and there had opportunity to learn how things really were. Now, this father expressly declares the Revelation to have been written by the Evangelist John, one of the twelve. So, too, Melito, bishop of Sardis, one of the cities to which the Epistles in the Revelation are addressed. We cannot but presume that such a man would know who was the author of a production which contained an Epistle to the church over which he presided.

The same is true of Polycarp, the celebrated bishop of Smyrna, to which church, likewise, an apocalyptic Epistle is addressed. This man was an immediate disciple of the Evangelist John. Polycarp's pupil, Irenæus, who removed from Asia Minor to the south of France, and, as has already been observed, became bishop of Lyons, gives us an account of Polycarp's relation to John, and makes use of the Revelation throughout his writings, without mentioning even the slightest opposition to it. It is also employed as really apostolical by the western fathers, Turtullian, Cyprian, Hippolytus, &c., without any mention of doubt as to its canonical authority. Still, it may be said, none of these were either learned or critical ; they found in the Revelation their favourite doctrine in regard to the kingdom of God upon earth, and therefore they readily received the book as a production of John's. In decided opposition to such remarks, we adduce the Alexandrian fathers, Clement and Origen. These were not only the most learned men of the day and the best skilled in criticism, but, in particular, were *opponents of the doctrine of the Millennium;* yet neither had any idea that the Revelation of John was not composed by the Evangelist of that name. They chose to get rid of the odious contents of the book by a forced interpretation, rather than by opposing the tradition of the whole church. A stronger combination of historical evidence in favour of the apostolic origin of the book is, in fact, hardly conceivable ! The weight of this evidence is augmented by what we know respecting those who doubted the genuineness of the book. Of this number was a presbyter of the Roman church, whose name was Gaius. This man made it a set purpose to oppose the doctrine of the millennium ; and because the defenders of it naturally appealed first of all to the Revelation, he declared it spurious, without, however, presenting any historical or critical reasons for doing so. In order to degrade the Revelation, it was even referred by him to a heretic, Cerinthus, who was said to have written it in John's name. But in this he clearly evinced that he was carried away by his feelings, for no one can by any means attribute the Revelation to an intentional deceiver, for this reason, that it would have been one object with such a man to denote with precision the person of the Evangelist, so as to cause the work to be regarded as his. This, however, has not been done, and thus we are not permitted to take any view in opposition to it, except it be that another John, and not the Evangelist, composed it. This opinion was first stated and defended in a formal manner by the learned Dionysius, bishop of Alexandria, a disciple of Origen. But, as this man lived at so late a period that authentic oral tradition was no longer within his reach, no more stress is to be laid upon his doubts than upon the learned objections of more modern days. We come therefore to this result : *All historical tradition is unanimous in behalf of John's composition of the Revelation.*

Now, in order to invalidate this decided testimony of antiquity, very striking arguments ought to be adduced ; but observe what are the reasons which prevail upon modern investigators to deny that the Evangelist John was the author of the Revelation, and then judge whether they are strong enough to countervail such testimony. In enumerating these reasons, I follow a distinguished scholar of the present day, whom I very much esteem and love as my former instructor, although I differ entirely from his views. I do indeed believe him to be in general very impartial and unprejudiced ; but nevertheless I think him to be influenced in his judgment of the Revelation by the force of prejudices which were largely imbibed by the church, and have been widely diffused.[1]

In the first place, it is urged by this learned man that John never mentions himself in the Gospel and Epistles as the author of these writings ; would he act differently then in the Apocalypse ? It is true, he says only that this circumstance is worthy of attention; but as it stands as one of his arguments, it seems to have been regarded as of considerable importance. Of what consequence, however, is such a difference in practice, since all we can say is, simply, that the author chose in this case to employ a different form from his usual one ? What writer is there who does not act as he pleases in regard to such points ?

In the second place, the variation from his other writings in point of language is adduced as an argument. The fact is indisputable. The language of the Gospel is pure Greek, smooth and accurate ; that of the Revelation, on the contrary, is harsh, rugged, full of inaccuracies of expression, and real grammatical mistakes. But it is not true that all difference in phraseology indicates different writers. Compare, *e. g.,* the earliest writings of Göethe, Schil-

[1] I mean Prof. De Wette, in his "Einleit. ins neue Testament" (Introd. to the N. Testament).

ler, Herder, with the latest productions of the same authors. Especially take an author who attempts to write in a foreign language ; must not his first essays be of a totally different character from his later ones ? He has not complete mastery of the language ; he struggles not only with the sense, but with the form ; and this must necessarily make the phraseology even of the most practised intellect somewhat cumbrous. This is exactly the case with John's Revelation. It was his earliest production in the Greek language, occasioned by the fearful occurrences during Nero's persecution. These cast the sympathizing mind of the beloved disciple of Jesus into deep meditation, during which the spirit of prophecy showed him the future fortunes of the church, and its final conquest over Judaism and heathenism. It was, therefore, composed some twenty years earlier than the Gospel and Epistles seem to have been written, and in a language which to John, a native of Palestine, must have been a foreign one. Now, the Revelation appears exactly like the production of a man who had not yet acquired the requisite skill in the Greek language, and as its internal characteristics, likewise, show that it was written in the early part of John's life, before Jerusalem was destroyed, it is in fact impossible to see how one can ascribe importance to this circumstance of the difference of style, in opposition to the tradition that the Evangelist John was the author of the production ; the rather as there is undeniably very much in the language which bears close affinity to those writings that are admitted to be John's.

The same may be said of the *third* observation, that the style of the Revelation is in the following respect very unlike that which we find in the Gospel and Epistles, viz., that the former exhibits a lively creative fancy, while, in the latter, quiet, deep feeling predominates. In regard to this remark, which likewise is correct, we are to consider, first, that the same individual in different stages of mental development will make use of different styles of expression. The earlier works of the same writer are accordingly more ardent, more imaginative than his later. Moreover, the imagery in the Revelation is not by any means to be regarded as the arbitrary production of a rich fancy, but rather as actual appearances to John's mind from the operation of the divine Spirit within him. I admit that John would not have been selected as the medium of these communications of the Spirit, had there not been in his whole organization a special adaptation for such impressions ; but still, susceptibility to them is not the same as positive productive fancy. Finally, it is not to be forgotten in this view, that John's other writings are of a more historical or else purely didactic nature ; while, on the other hand, the Revelation is a prophetic production. It would therefore be totally unnatural that the same style should be observable in the Apocalypse as in John's other writings.

The only remaining point alleged in confirmation of the difference between the Revelation and other writings of John is, that they exhibit a totally different *doctrinal aspect*. In particular, stress is laid on this circumstance, that in the Gospel nothing at all is found of what forms the main topic of the Apocalypse, viz., the expectation of a visible coming of our Lord, and the establishment of his kingdom upon earth. Moreover, all that is said in the Revelation respecting good and bad angels is of a more Jewish cast, we are told, than we should expect John's views to have been, from examining his other writings. It would appear that, if this be really so, it is a reason of some weight against the genuineness of the book ; for we cannot suppose the apostles to have altered their doctrinal views, and, plainly, difference in the character of the writings could not affect the doctrine, as both in historical and prophetical productions there must exist the same fundamental views on the part of the writer. Now, the remark is indisputably correct, but the true reason of the fact has been misapprehended. For, first, the same difference which is exhibited between the Gospel of John and the Apocalypse, also appears, on comparison, between the Gospel of John and the first three Gospels. These latter, like the Revelation, present many doctrines and views agreeable to the Jews, particularly the visible coming of our Lord to assume his kingdom upon earth ; while nothing of all this is touched upon by the Gospel of John, notwithstanding there was ample occasion for doing so. It does not thence follow, however, that either John or the others err in representing the discourses of Jesus Christ, since the same person *may* have spoken sometimes spiritually, as in John's discourses, and sometimes in a Judaizing manner, as according to the other Evangelists. The correct solution of this difficulty is to be sought solely in the *special purpose* of the Gospel of John, with which the first Epistle stands in such intimate connection that it is not strange it should partake of the same character. The two other Epistles are too short to be here taken into consideration. For above (in the third chapter in speaking of the Gospel of John), it was observed, that this Evangelist had a particular class of persons in view in his work, viz., men similar to the later Gnostics, and who in certain views coincided with them perfectly. In particular, they, like the Gnostics, speculated on Divine things in a peculiar manner, and sought to idealize the real facts in the history of Jesus, more than the true apostolic doctrine permitted. These men, among whom were many very sensible and well-meaning persons, were those whom John had particularly in view in the composition of his Gospel. With apostolic wisdom he avoided in this work every thing which could offend the prejudices of these persons. Many Jewish ideas, which had a very good and genuine foundation, and, according to the first Gospels, were expressed by the Saviour himself, he kept back, becoming in a manner a Gnostic to the Gnostics, without doing the least injury, however, to the cause of truth. He depicted Christianity, therefore, to their minds, just as they could most easily comprehend it, convinced that when once they had seized this idea, they would gradually learn to understand it thoroughly.

If, now, we adhere steadfastly to this point of view, it will appear perfectly intelligible, how the same John who wrote thus in the Gospel, should appear to express himself so differently in the Revelation, in the composition of which no such reference existed ; though still he was always governed by the same doctrinal views at every period of his life. And thus we must declare, that no one of these reasons is calculated to disturb us in regard to the correctness and truth of the tradition of the first centuries after Christ. If the repugnance which is felt towards the contents of the Apocalypse be only conquered, men will soon cease to rate so highly the reasons which are adduced against its apostolic origin, and to think so little of the importance of the unanimous tradition of antiquity. And that this may soon happen is the more to be wished, as the progressive development of the church makes the Revelation more and more important in testing what is now occurring among Christians, and what awaits them in the immediate future !

CONCLUSION.

HAVING thus passed through the entire series of the writings of the New Testament, taking notice of the critical questions in regard to them, we will now, for the sake of convenience, present a compendious view of the *results* at which we have arrived.

We find then most, and the most important, of the writings in the canon of the New Testament, so unanimously acknowledged in ancient times, and so universally made use of as apostolical in later days, that there cannot be the least doubt in regard to them. They are on this account denominated *Homologoumena*, universally-acknowledged writings, and form the main sources of the doctrine and history of the Christian church. Among these Homologoumena, as is stated by Eusebius so early as the commencement of the fourth century, were the four Gospels, the Acts of the Apostles, the thirteen Pauline Epistles, the first Epistle of Peter, and the first of John. If we attend only to the voice of Christian antiquity, as Eusebius correctly observes, the Apocalypse also does in reality belong among the Homologoumena. But the fortune of this book has been so peculiar, that some have not even been willing to class it among the Antilegomena, but have ranked it with the writings which are of a profane character, and are to be utterly rejected. Eusebius was therefore in great perplexity to what class he could properly assign the Revelation. As to the Epistle to the Hebrews, its author is unknown, merely ; its genuineness is not disputed. It belongs, therefore, to the class of the *Antilegomena* only so far as this, that its position in the canon was disputed ; the relation of the author to the Apostle Paul not being unanimously acknowledged in the church.

Properly, the class of the *Antilegomena* among the New Testament writings comprehends the two smaller Epistles of John, the Epistles of James and Jude, and the second Epistle of Peter. These five books were never universally acknowledged and used in the ancient church. More recent investigation has decided in favour of the first three. The two smaller Epistles of John are certainly apostolical, and from the author of the Gospel of John ; that of James was not, indeed, written by one of the twelve, but by a brother of our Lord, who held such a prominent rank in the ancient church as placed him, like Paul, fully on a level with the apostles. As to the two writings last in the list, however, it appears justly somewhat doubtful whether they are productions of the days of the apostles. The Epistle of Jude is, indeed, certainly genuine, but as certainly not apostolical ; and, as history attributes to this brother of our Lord no very prominent station or agency, the Epistle seems not properly to belong to the canon. It can be supported only by the second Epistle of Peter, which is not itself certainly of apostolical origin. For, in regard to the latter, a consideration of the circumstances makes it impossible to establish its genuineness objectively on valid grounds, although it may be made subjectively probable.

These results of the most careful critical investigation of the New Testament are very satisfactory. For, if we could wish that the genuineness and canonical character of the Antilegomena might be established by as valid arguments as we can adduce in behalf of the Homologoumena, still it must be admitted that those books upon which some suspicion rests, are the very books, of all the New Testament writings, with which we can most easily dispense. The chief and best of these writings are the very ones whose genuineness and apostolic authority are certified as strongly as possible.

If, now, we inquire into the relation between the *external* historical genuineness of the books of the New Testament, and their *internal* efficacy and determinate power over the faith and life of the individual, and of the whole community of Christians, it is certainly undeniable, that the former by itself decides nothing in favour of the latter; but still, on account of the circumstances of the church, demonstration of such genuineness is by no means unimportant or indifferent. It is clear that we may regard the writings of another religious system, the Zend-Avesta of the Parsees, or the Koran of the Mahometans, as genuine, and as having proceeded from the immediate circle of adherents which the founder of that system of religion possessed, without thereby attributing to it any internal efficacy and determining power over the heart and life. But it cannot be said that a conviction of the genuineness of the apostolical origin of the writings of the New Testament, likewise, is a matter of indifference. It is rather of great consequence in its connection with the church, *i. e.*, the great community founded by our Saviour, and actuated and sustained by his Spirit. You may prove the genuineness of the writings of the New Testament to him who is not within the pale of the church, or under its spiritual influence, and he may even acknowledge it upon incontestible historical grounds; but, as Christ, and his apostles themselves, are of no consequence in relation to his internal life, this proof has no more effect upon his faith or his life, than is produced upon those of the scholar who declares the Zend-Avesta to be a genuine work of Zoroaster. Far otherwise is it with him who lives in the bosom of the Christian church. Here he cannot completely withdraw himself from the influence of the Spirit of Christ, which operates upon his heart from his earliest youth; he feels himself spiritually affected, and in a manner constrained by it. It is true that sinful man very often strives against the influence of the Holy Spirit, it being troublesome to him, because it does not permit him to continue sinning so freely and peaceably as he could wish. In such case he seeks to obtain plausible grounds on which he may evade the force of the Spirit's influence. One such plausible ground is often presented by the supposition that the writings of the New Testament are spurious, whereby the extraordinary character of our Saviour, with the sublime impression he made on the hearts of men, is encompassed with doubt, and thus its effect is diminished. To members of the church of Christ, therefore, a firm conviction that the Scriptures are genuine, is of the highest consequence; the opposite opinion, yea, uncertainty merely, in regard to the character of the sacred writings, is ordinarily the natural concomitant of sin. Such a sentiment hinders the efficacy of the Holy Spirit, which manifests itself, in a manner not to be mistaken, to every simple, plain mind, on perusal of the Holy Scriptures, but exhibits its full strength only when the heart feels a quiet faith, undisturbed by any doubt. Hence the conversion of many has taken rise from their acknowledgment of the genuineness of the New Testament writings; and moreover, the apostacy of many from the truth has arisen out of the circumstance that they denied the authenticity of these books. We may therefore say, that the knowledge of the genuineness of the writings of the New Testament is of essential efficacy where the influence of the Spirit of God, and a susceptibility to its operations exist in any degree. To him who has already turned aside entirely from the truth, and who resists it with an unfriendly mind, a conviction of the genuineness of these books will be of little use, unless his opposition be first broken by the power of grace. To him who is converted, born again, the sure conviction of their genuineness will always be a pleasing concomitant of grace, and will excite his gratitude ; but, as he has experienced in his heart the divine power which dwells in the Scriptures, the testimony of the Holy Spirit will always be the proper foundation of his faith, which would support him even though he had no historical proofs in behalf of the sacred books. Persons, however, who have neither experienced a perfect change of heart and mind, nor are actuated by a positively hostile spirit, but ardently desire the former, though they are often assailed by doubts and uncertainties, will find in the firm historical foundation of Scripture something on which they may lean at first, and from which they may then be gradually led to the full knowledge of salvation. For, if it be only admitted that such a life as that which the Scriptures represent our Saviour's to have been was really spent, that such words as they communicate to us from him were really spoken, the obvious question is, Whence came such a phenomenon ? What is its import to the world ? to me ?

But, it may here be asked, if the case is thus, how happens it that God has permitted many plausible objections to exist against the writings of the New Testament, and that some cannot even be freed wholly from suspicion ? Would it not have been more consistent with the purpose of the Scriptures, had all the books been supported by so numerous and so completely incontestible testimonies, that not even a doubt concerning them could ever have entered any one's mind ? It may indeed seem so to short-sighted man. But his desires would not stop here, they would reach still further. He would wish to have a Bible without various readings, a biblical history free from the slightest variations, in short, Jehovah himself embodied in the letter of the word. The living God, who is eternal wisdom and love, has not thought any thing of this kind suitable for mankind ; otherwise he would undoubtedly have effected it for their benefit ; and the reasons why he has not we may at least conjecture, even with our weak powers. On the one hand, it would have become easier for man to confound the word and the Spirit dwelling in it with the letter ; for, even, as the case now is, this mistake has not been entirely avoided, from the want of spirituality in many men. On the other hand, the guilt of many persons would have been augmented, since they now have at least plausible reasons for their opposition to the truth, but in the other case would have had no such extenuation, and still would have retained their hostility to God's word. We may therefore declare, that the character of Scripture, in this respect likewise, corresponds most perfectly with the necessities of human nature, as well as with the designs of God, notwithstanding all its apparent imperfections and deficiencies.

The observations we have here made in conclusion are, moreover, such as are best suited to present the correct view concerning the peculiar character of the Old Testament in the light of criticism. For this portion of God's word has so few historical evidences in its favour, excepting those comprehended within its own compass, that it is impossible to frame such an argument for the genuineness of its books as we are able to exhibit in behalf of the New Testament. This want of evidence proceeds in part from the very great antiquity of the writings of the Old Testament, which were almost all composed before there existed any literature among the Greeks, and before the Romans were so much as known by name ; and in part, also, from the state of seclusion which the nations of the old world, generally, and particularly the Jews, always maintained. The Persians, Syrians, Egyptians, knew scarce any thing of the literature of the Hebrews ; and, had they even been acquainted with it, the circumstance would have been of little advantage to us, as we have but few writings of a date anterior to the time of Christ which originated with these nations. In these few, moreover, we find hardly any mention of the Jews and their productions. Hence, in investigating the earliest writings of the Old Testament, the critic has no other resource than a careful examination of the contents of the books themselves, and a comparison of them with each other. Were this examination and comparison invariably conducted with a believing and humble disposition, not the slightest objection could be made, and we might quietly await the results of such a procedure ; but, when the minds of investigators deviate from the proper spirit and disposition, it is very evident how easily such an inquiry, which is in its nature somewhat uncertain and precarious, may lead to pernicious results. Every one will, in such a case, determine the matter according to his subjective ideas and views, without obtaining any objective grounds of judgment from investigation. If we only look at the actual state of the matter, entirely aside from the holy character of the book, we shall be convinced that such a course of investigation could hardly afford any useful result, even with the best intentions. A book is presented to us, which contains the relics of a nation's literature during a period of 1200 years. We derive all that we can know of the history, the manners, the special circumstances of this people, excepting a few points, from this book alone. Thus it is at once the *object* and the *norm* of investigation. Since, moreover, in regard to many of the writings in it we have no statement as to their author and the time of their composition, the investigation of these writings cannot but have always a character of uncertainty. If we were only familiarly acquainted with the history of a single nation in close vicinity to the Jews, and found in its literature constant reference to the Jewish writings, we might then, by drawing a parallel, communicate more stability to the criticism of the Old Testament, but we have no such advantage, and must content ourselves with individual notices, which have come down to us from the most ancient times of the nations with which the Jews came in contact. It was not till the time of Alexander the Great, about 300 years B. C., that the Jews, with their literature, became known to the Greeks, through whom we have received much important information in regard to the Old Testament. For, as the Jews, after that period, when they fell under Greek dominion, made themselves acquainted with the Greek literature, and to some extent themselves wrote in Greek, as *e. g.*, the celebrated Jewish writers, *Josephus* and *Philo*, so, on the other hand, the Greeks began to take an interest in the Jews and their religious institutions. From this mixture of Hebrew and Greek life proceeded the celebrated *Greek Version of the Seventy.* This, according to the account of the ancients, was executed under the Egyptian monarch *Ptolemy Philadelphus*, at the instance of the learned *Demetrius Phalereus*, about the year 270 B. C. It is true, the Old Testament was not probably translated all at once, but, at any rate, even according to the most recent opinion, the Old Testament was entirely translated into Greek when Jesus Sirach was composed, *i. e.*, about the year 130 B. C. Consequently, it is placed beyond a doubt that the whole Old Testament, as we have it, existed in Palestine in the Hebrew language long before the time of Christ and his Apostles, and in a Greek version in the other countries of the Roman Empire, particularly in Egpyt, where there resided so large a number of Jews, and they possessed so great privileges, that they had even built a temple in the city of *Leontopolis* in close imitation of that at Jerusalem. In Egypt the collection of the Apocryphal books likewise, which were confessedly written in Greek, was inserted in the canon of the Old Testament, which was spread abroad by the version of the seventy interpreters, and from this version they were introduced into the Latin church-version (the so-called *Vulgate*), thus obtaining the same authority as the writings of the Old Testament, which authority they possess at the present day in the Catholic church. As, however, they are not *expressly* cited in the New Testament,[1] and are wholly wanting in the Hebrew canon of the Old Testament, Luther rightly separated them from the rest, but appended them to the books of the Old Testament, as " *Writings not to be equally esteemed with Holy Writ, but still profitable and excellent for perusal.*" The Reformed Church, however, has gone still farther, and dissevered them entirely from the collection of sacred books, in order to prevent them from being confounded with the inspired word. Hence arose this great evil, that the historical connection between the Old and New Testament, which is so well exhibited in the narrative writings of the Apocrypha, was totally sundered ; and this connection is by no means a matter of indifference to believers, because it is only through it that God's providence towards his people can be regarded in the light of an united whole. Hence it would seem best to retain the apocryphal writings along with the Sacred Scriptures, designating, indeed, the distinction between them and the canonical books.

Thus much, then, according to these statements, we know certainly from historical testimony, that the Old Testament, as we now have it, existed more than a century before Christ. It is true the learned would be gratified to know a great deal more respecting the formation of the canon of the Old Testament, respecting the authors of the individual writings, &c. But, in view merely of the relation of the Old Testament to the faith of the present day, the knowledge that the Old Testament was in a complete collected form before the time of Christ, is sufficient to afford us a firm conviction of the genuineness and importance of its books. Now, that the existing Old Testament was generally diffused and in use among the Jews, is attested by the Jewish writers of the apostolic times, who employed the Greek language in their writings. *Philo*, in Egypt, and *Josephus*, in Palestine, make use of the Old Testament throughout their works, thereby confirming the custom of the New Testament, which also everywhere refers to the Old Testament. The *manner* in which the Old Testament is cited by the New, and the definite declarations in regard to the former which are contained in the latter, are decisive as to the faith of Christians of the present day. These afford us more than the mere assurance that the books of the Old Testament are authentic ; this might be admitted, without the slightest acknowledgment of the value of the writings, since the most wretched and even hurtful productions may be perfectly genuine. They declare in the most precise manner the *Divine character* of these books, which of course presupposes their genuineness, for it is

[1] Allusions to them are pointed out by *Steir* in his " Andeutungen für Glaubwürdige Schrifterklärung" (or Hints towards the proper interpretation of the Scriptures), p. 486, *seq.*

very evident that no writings could be Divine which originated in deceit and imposture.

In the first place, we find in the New Testament citations from almost all the writings in the Old Testament.[1] The principal books, as, e. g., the Pentateuch, the Psalms, the Prophet Isaiah, are cited very often, and even those less important are referred to here and there in the New Testament. A very few are entirely neglected ;[2] of this number, in particular, is Solomon's Song, which is nowhere cited in all the New Testament. This circumstance is certainly not accidental. Perhaps it is not too much to conclude, that the books of the Old Testament which are not at all mentioned in the New, should be regarded very much as the so-called deutero-canonical books of the New Testament ; though the circumstance that they are not cited in the New Testament can be nowise objected against their genuineness, any more than the position of a New Testament book among the Antilegomena can be considered as a proof of its spuriousness. These non-cited books of the Old Testament, with the exception of the three minor prophets, probably present some-thing like a *transition* to the apocryphal books. At all events, the fact that these books are nowhere mentioned in the New Testament should inculcate upon us *caution in making use of them.*

Of more importance than the citations, are such passages of the New Testament as contain decisive declarations respecting the Old Testament as a whole. These occur particularly in the discourses of our Lord himslf. Jesus calls the law (Matth. v. 17 *seq.*) eternal, imperishable. Heaven and earth, he says, shall pass away, but not one jot or tittle of the law shall pass away till all be fulfilled. In a similar manner, in Luke xxiv. 44, prophecy concerning Christ is re-presented as something running through the law of Moses, the Prophets, and the Psalms, and as necessary to be fulfilled. In Luke xvi. 17, also, all created things (heaven and earth), it is said, will sooner and more easily pass away than the Law and the Prophets. Thus a lofty divine character is clearly claimed in behalf of the Old Testament. It may, indeed, be observed on the contrary, that, in the passages referred to, allusion is made, not to the whole Old Testament, but only to particular books, the Mosaic law, the Prophets, and the Psalms. But, first, it is to be noticed, that the expression, Law, or Law and Prophets, stands frequently for the whole Old Testament, just as Gospel stands for the whole New

[1] The Old Testament is expressly cited in the New more than four hundred times, and in a much larger number of places there are allusions to the Old Testament.

[2] The Books of Ezra, Nehemiah, Esther, Ecclesiastes, and Solomon's Song, as also the minor Prophets, Obadiah, Nahum, and Zephaniah. It is most proper, however, to consider the twelve Prophets as *one work;* and then the fact that these three are not cited loses its force. But in regard to other books of the Old Testament the circum-stance that they are not cited is not unimportant.

Testament. Moreover, the Law, the Prophets, and the Psalms, was the usual division of the books of the Old Testament among the Jews. The first part of the Hebrew Old Testament comprehends the five books of Moses, the second part falls into two sub-divisions, first the historical writings, the books of Joshua, Judges, Samuel, Kings, and, secondly, the three larger and 12 minor Prophets. In the third part (which in Luke xxiv. 44, is termed *Psalms*, from the principal book which it contains), belong moreover, besides the Psalms, the book of Job, the writings of Solomon, the book of Daniel, and some later historical books, and, lastly, the book of Chronicles. But entirely aside from this Jewish division of the Old Testament, the connection of these passages with the citations clearly shows, that they are intended to refer to the whole Old Testament. The citations in the New Testament from the Old are not adduced as mere confirmation, drawn from human productions of great value, but as irrefragable proofs from sacred books. This power of proof could have belonged to them only from the fact that they were not bare compositions of human wisdom, but those of men who were moved by the Holy Ghost. (Compare 2 Pet. i. 20, 21.) Now, as citations from all the principal writings of the Old Testament occur in the New, the general declarations we have mentioned must of course refer to all the writings of the Old Testament, so as to attribute to them *a common character*, viz., that of a divine origin.

To this it is to be added, that throughout Scripture there runs the doctrine of a deep, essential connection between the Old and New Testaments. As the Old Testament is always pointing onward to the New, so the latter is always pointing backward to the Old, as its necessary precedent. Consequently, both alike bear the character of a divine revelation ; only, this revelation manifests itself in a gradual development. In the Old Testament it appears in its commencement as the seed of the subsequent plant ; in the New Testament the living plant itself is exhibited. On account of this relation, there cannot be any thing in the Old Testament specifically different from what is to be found in the New Testament ; only, the form of presenting the same thing is at one time more or less plain and direct than at another.

These declarations of the New Testament in regard to the Old are, to Christians, not mere private assertions of wise, good, and pious men, such as many in our day are in the habit of supposing Jesus and his apostles to have been ; they exhibit, rather, authentic information respecting the real character of the Holy Scriptures of the Old Testament. Christ, as the Son of the living God, as absolute truth itself, who alone knew the Father, and, as the source of all real revelation from him, can have made such declarations con-

cerning the writings of the Old Testament, only with the strictest
sincerity (as is the case with every thing he did or said), and must
have designed that they should be a rule to his church, since his
whole life on earth had but one single aim, that of developing the
heavenly and eternal to the created world. Thus, had Jesus attributed the character of eternity to a production to which it by no
means belonged, he would have counteracted his own sole purpose.
The same is true of the apostles, who, in that respect to which our
attention is now directed, are to be considered as upon a level with
Christ himself ; they being pure organs of the mind of Christ ;
though, in themselves considered, they were but sinful men, and
desired to be so regarded. Under the influence of the Holy Spirit
they acknowledged the eternal character of the Old Testament, and
their declarations on this point are not (any more than those of our
Lord himself) mere subjective, private statements, they are rather
authentic accounts respecting the character of this part of Holy
Writ. In considering the force of the apostolic declarations concerning the authority of the sacred Scriptures of the Old Testament, we
are to regard, not merely the citations of individual passages from
it, or general statements respecting its authors, such as their being
at one time represented as moved by the Holy Ghost (2 Pet. i. 21),
and at another Holy Scripture being called instruction unto salvation (2 Tim. iii. 15), which, as the New Testament was not then
collected, can refer only to the Old ; but we are especially to observe the manner in which the citations are adduced from the Old
Testament. This is most remarkable in the Epistle to the Hebrews,
although similar passages also occur in the Gospels and other books
of the New Testament. In this remarkable Epistle, God or the
Holy Ghost is constantly named as the speaker, in the passages
which are adduced from the Old Testament ; and this not only in
regard to those which are accompanied in the Old Testament by the
expression, " God said," but also to those in which some man speaks,
for instance David, as author of a Psalm. Herein is clearly exhibited the view of the author in relation to the Old Testament and
the writers of it. He considered that God was, by his Holy Spirit,
the living agent and speaker in them all, so that, consequently, the
Holy Scriptures were to him *purely a work of God*, although
brought forward by men. That the genuineness of these writings
was equally certain to him, follows of course, because that which is
divine, as has been before remarked, can never appear in the form
of a forgery.

It is true, however, that such a proof in behalf of the Old Testament is valid only for him who has become convinced, by living experience, of the truth of God in Christ and the infallibility of the
Spirit which actuated his disciples. Where this truth and infalli-

bility are either flatly denied, or even merely doubted, the observations we have made may be of no weight. For such persons we cannot frame an argument in behalf of the Old Testament which shall be valid against all objections. As to us who live according to Christ, and to whom the power of his Spirit is accessible, every thing must radiate from the centre of the New Testament scenes, viz., the Saviour himself. The conviction of his eternal power and Godhead establishes the Old Testament retrospectively, and also establishes the New Testament prospectively, by the promise of his Spirit, which should bring all those things which he had said to his disciples to their remembrance. On this conviction the assurance of the genuineness and divinity of Scripture forever rests, and much more securely, than upon any external historical proofs ; for it wholly takes away the possibility of an attack in any quarter on the part of human sophistry, and leaves assurance safe in the unassailable sanctuary of our interior life.

INTRODUCTION.

§ 1. On the Origin of the Gospel-Collection.[*]

As the revelations of God to man assume two principal forms— viz., the Law and the Gospel ; so, the Scriptures are divided into two parts—of which the first relates to God's covenant with man in the *law ;* the second, to the covenant in *grace.* Since the living Word of God—the eternal cause of these ever-binding covenants— lives in those writings which refer to the covenants, the writings themselves have been denominated *Old and New Covenants* (בְּרִית= διαθήκη.[†] The Vulgate renders it Testamentum. Compare 2 Cor. iii. 14). It is to the writings of the New Testament that we here direct our attention ; these always, however, necessarily presuppose the Old Testament. The New Testament springs from the Old, as the tree from its root ; while the Old appears perfected in the New. (Matth. v. 17.) We do not find the New Testament, as a collected whole, till towards the end of the fourth century. In the course of this century three smaller collections were united into one —viz., the Gospels, the Pauline Epistles, and the general Epistles, together with some more isolated writings, which form the transi- tions and the conclusion—viz., the Acts of the Apostles, the Epistle to the Hebrews, and the Apocalypse.

The origin of the first of these smaller collections, the εὐαγγελι- κόν, chiefly claims our attention. The collecting of our four canoni- cal Gospels is lost in the remotest Christian antiquity. As far back as the historical records of the church extend, we find that collection *everywhere* in use : not only in every quarter of the world, but also in every division of the church, whether orthodox or schis-

---

* [*Evangeliensammlung* is the word in the original, which expresses a collection of the Gospels into one volume, forming a subdivision of the whole New Testament.]—*Tr.*

† The word διαθήκη occurs, however, in the New Testament (Acts iii. 25; Gal. iii. 15; Heb. ix. 16), also in the sense of "Testament," "leaving an inheritance to children."

matic, and even among heathen writers, as Celsus, it was known, used, and respected.* It is true, that many heretics, as Marcion, the Jewish Christians, and others, did not use the Gospel-collection, but only one or other of the Gospels ; the collection, however, was known to them, and they refrained from its use on the sole ground that, in accordance with their views, they did not believe themselves justified in regarding the writers as authorities in matters of faith.† This leads necessarily to the supposition of a very early origin of the Gospel-collection, of which, however, we have no definite information. Whether it was the work of an individual, or of a single church, or of a council, remains uncertain. The last supposition is the most unlikely, since we have no account whatever of church assemblies before the middle of the second century. But it is very possible that some eminent man, or an influential church, might have formed the collection. Yet there is no historical trace of such a fact extant ; and the *universal* dissemination of the collection, appearing, as it does, even in the first half of the second century, seems to point to another mode of formation. For, starting with the assumption, that the four Gospels are genuine, and with the further assumption (which we must do, since there is no credible account whatever of other apostolical Gospels), that these four *alone* are the work of *apostles*, or enjoy apostolical sanction, we do not then need to suppose a definite time, or a definite place, or any special occasion, in order to explain the origin of the collection of the Gospels ; but we may conceive that it was made in different places at the same time. The lively intercourse among the ancient Christian congregations led them to distribute, as quickly as possible, those Gospel histories which had apostolical authority in their favour, as precious gifts bequeathed to the church of Christ ; and, as only these four could shew credible evidence of being genuine apostolical writings, they were consequently united into one collection. Gradually, as they came into circulation in the church, they were deposited in the church archives, which must have been early formed by the presbyters and bishops, and were immediately multiplied by copying. If, then, we suppose likewise (and history supplies no ground of objection to the supposition), that the evangelists wrote in the order in which the Gospels are arranged in the canon, not only is their general dissemination accounted for, but also the circumstance, that we discover only slight traces of the existence of any arrangement different from the

---

* For a fuller discussion of this point, see the Author's work: Die Aechtheit der Evangelien, aus der Geschichte der zwei ersten Jahrhunderte erwiesen. Königsberg, 1823, 8vo, S. 267, ff.

† *E. g.*, Marcion, the Gnostic, believed St. Matthew, and even St. John, to be Judaizers. (See the Author's work, *ut supra*, S. 359, ff.)

present*—a circumstance which, apart from the above supposition might favour the opinion, that the collection had been arranged in this order by some particular individual or church ; since, otherwise, its contemporaneous formation in different places, would almost inevitably have produced variations in the arrangement, especially variations so natural as the placing of John and Matthew together.

§ 2. On the Character of the Gospel-Collection.

The ancient church justly regarded the Gospel-collection as a unity, on which account they call it simply εὐαγγέλιον [glad tidings], or εὐαγγελικόν,† as containing, in its portraiture of the life, labors, and passion of Jesus, the glad tidings of Him who had appeared as the Saviour of the world. See *Iren*. adv. hær. i. 17, 29, iii. 11. The uniting into a whole of these four authentic records of the Saviour's life, they regarded as not merely accidental. They recognised in their connexion, as in the general formation and arrangement of the Scriptures, a higher necessity. The number of the Gospels could have been no more changed than their position without disturbing the harmony of the whole. *Irenæus (ut sup.* iii. 11, p. 221, Ed. *Grabe*), therefore, very appropriately calls the Gospel-collection a εὐαγγέλιον τετράμορφον, *four-formed gospel*, and describes it as a picture, portraying the same sublime object from different aspects. The relation of the Gospels to each other, and to the remaining books of the New Testament, proves the correctness of this opinion. The Gospels supplement each other alike in their accounts of the Redeemer's life, and their mode of portraiture. The life of Jesus presented itself in so manifold a variety of aspects ; his discourses poured upon his disciples so rich a stream of life, that any single individual was utterly incapable of apprehending the overwhelming fulness of his character. In him were disclosed elements which no single set of human faculties

---

* Cod. D. and also the Gothic translation, place, for instance, the Gospel of St. John immediately after that of St. Matthew, evidently in order to separate the two apostolical works from those of the helpers of the apostles. See Hug. Introduction to the New Testament, p. 309 (Fosdick's Translation), and the Postscripts to the Gospels in Schulz' edition.

† The New Testament recognizes the proper signification only of the word εὐαγγέλιον = בְּשׂרָה chiefly in the special reference to the joyful tidings of the Messiah's actual appearance. A secondary signification, in conformity to which the writings that sketch the actions of the Messiah are called εὐαγγέλια, has been incorrectly given to the word in such passages as Rom. ii. 16; x. 16. The titles of our Gospels are of later origin; moreover, in them we should refer the term εὐαγγέλιον simply to the contents, not to the book. In classical use, εὐαγγέλιον signifies likewise a reward for a piece of good news, a present to one who brings good news. (See Liddell and Scott's Lex. s. v.)

was adequate to grasp ; hence there were needed several minds, which, as mirrors, caught the rays that proceeded from him, as from the Sun of the spiritual world, and reflected the same image in different directions. These varied conceptions of our Lord in his union of divine and human attributes, are contained in the Gospels, and must be *blended* together, to form a perfect delineation of Christ. But for God's providential arrangement, therefore, by which several persons, and those very different, narrated the life of Jesus, either his human and natural, or his divine and supernatural, conduct would be presented to us less carefully conceived, according as we were without the one or the other aspect of this grand fourfold picture.

But much as this view of the relation of the Gospels to each other must approve itself to every one who feels that he cannot ascribe the development of the church, and especially the formation of the Scriptures, to chance, it is yet difficult, in following out that view, to define accurately the character of each individual Gospel— a difficulty which certainly by no means leads to the rejection of the fundamental view, but rather invites to deeper research into the nature of the Gospels. That *Matthew* has rather seized the human, and John the divine element in the character of Jesus is too evident to be overlooked. In Matthew, we see the human element exalted to the divine ; in John, the descent of the divine to the human. It is more difficult to assign a definite position to *Mark* and *Luke*, since both stand as intermediate between the other two Gospels, as the extremes. The comparison of the Gospels with the prevalent tendencies in the ancient church, is our best guide. That is to say, as Matthew unquestionably represents the Judaistic, and St. John the Gnostic, or speculative and mystical element, so far as both are to some extent true, so Mark and Luke appear to represent the peculiar tendencies of the heathen Christians, the former perhaps more in the Roman, the latter more in the Greek, form. In Mark, however, the least of what is peculiar is discernible; yet, that it is not altogether wanting, is evident from the circumstance, that one party in the early church attached themselves specially to this Gospel. (On the party itself, however, rests an impenetrable obscurity. See the Author's Geschichte der Aechtheit der Evang. S. 96, ff). As, then, the Gospels, in the manner referred to, represent different tendencies of the early church, which, under other names and forms, belong to every period ; so they correspond to the progressive developments of the inner life, which can never proceed in its growth from the understanding of John downwards to Matthew, but, always upwards, from Matthew to John.

Further, if we consider the Gospel-collection in its relation to the entire New Testament, it appears plainly as the basis of the whole. In the Pauline Epistles, the Gospel is unfolded in its separate branches—in its doctrinal and practical bearing; the general epistles continue the development of what is contained in its germ in the Gospels, and finally in vital union with them as the root and branches, the fulness of New Testament life blossoms forth in the prophetic strains of the Apocalypse. The whole New Testament, therefore, like a living plant, has a complete and organic unity. The beginning and the end are the most difficult to understand, because there the thoughts appear in the most succinct form. Unless. inward experience be altogether wanting, it is best to begin the deeper study of the New Testament with the Epistle to the Romans, since that document purposely expounds at length the peculiar features of the Gospel. After an accurate investigation of this important epistle, much that is expressed more concisely and darkly in other portions of the New Testament, may be easily understood. But, as the whole New Testament is the subject of our labours, we follow the order of the books as there given, so as not to interfere with the wishes and views of any.

§ 3. ON THE AFFINITY OF THE FIRST THREE GOSPELS.

The *investigation* of the difficult problem of the striking affinity of the first three Gospels, which appears interrupted by variations just as striking, cannot, of course, be carried out in this place, any more than a history of the attempts to solve that problem: both belong to the Introduction to the Canonical Books of the New Testament, properly so called, where the subjects of the preceding paragraphs also meet with a more copious discussion. A commentator, however, owes to his readers an account of the way in which he looks upon this remarkable phenomenon, since the view taken of very many passages is determined by his opinion concerning the origin of the Gospels. I shall therefore endeavour here to give briefly the *results* of my inquiries.

The two Gospels of Matthew and Luke appear to me to have been composed quite independently—Matthew's principally from his own experience and oral tradition; Luke's principally from shorter written memoirs (diegeses)[*] which he edited. That which is found common to both Gospels may, in great part, be accounted for on the supposition of an affinity in the sources of information,[†] both oral and written, which the authors used independently

---

[*] [Διήγησις, Luke i. 1.]—*Tr.*

[†] The copious narrative of the journey, contained in Luke ix. 51—xviii. 14, which is peculiar to him, is probably to be regarded as a *diegesis* of that sort, edited by St. Luke. See on this subject, *Schleiermacher*, über die Schiften des Lucas, S. 158, ff.

of each other. In another respect, however, the supposition of their having used kindred sources of information, does not appear sufficient to account for the affinity subsisting between them. I do not indeed, by any means, discover a uniformity in the general structure of the two works, and especially not in the alleged fact, that the scene of Christ's history, up to his last journey, is confined to Galilee ; for in the general plan there are wide differences, and the above-mentioned limitation of our Saviour's ministry to Galilee, in the Gospels of Matthew and Luke, is totally destitute of proof, as it depends not on positive reasons, but merely on the omission of journeys to the feasts, and the want of chronological and topographical notices. Still, there is, in many places, so close a verbal coincidence between Matthew and Luke, that we can hardly maintain that both, in such places also, wrote altogether independently of each other, or only used kindred sources of information. Compare Matth. iii. 7–10, with Luke iii. 7–9 ; Matth. vii. 3–5, with Luke vi. 41, 42 ; Matth. vii. 7–11, with Luke xi. 9–13 ; Matth. viii. 9, with Luke vii. 8 ; Matth. viii. 19–22, with Luke ix. 57–60 ; Matth. ix. 5, 6, with Luke v. 23, 24 ; Matth. ix. 37, 38, with Luke x. 2 ; Matth. xi. 4–11, with Luke vii. 23–28 ; Matth. xii. 41–45, with Luke xi. 24–26, 31, 32. Yet the view, that the one made use of the *complete* work of the other, is beset with invincible difficulties, since, in that case, it remains inexplicable for what reason the one should not have either used or noticed the other's account of the Saviour's infancy. To solve this difficulty, I suppose that Matthew, who had written his Gospel in Hebrew, himself subsequently prepared* a Greek recension (no other than our canonical Matthew) ; and that for this work, he made use of smaller collections of those memoirs which Luke had used, particularly Luke iii. —ix., in which section the closest coincidence is found.

The affinity of Mark's Gospel with those of Matthew and Luke, must be differently explained.† Although he may have taken here and there a circumstance from tradition, or from shorter memoirs, yet, in the main (for there is very little in Mark that is peculiar to him ; with the exception of additional circumstances in various narratives, two cures, briefly narrated, are all that he alone has), he follows Matthew and Luke entirely ; where he leaves the one, he follows the other, but only to return from the latter to the former. It is impossible for so regular a coincidence to be accidental. Still I do not go so far as to maintain, that Mark had *both* the Gospels before him while composing. With respect to Matthew, this is not perhaps improbable ; but, with respect to Luke, it would suit

---

* This subject is handled more fully in § 4 of this Introduction.

† See *Saunier*, Ueber die Quellen des Marcus. Berlin, 1825. *A. Knobel* de origine evang. Marci. Wratislaviæ, 1831.

better to suppose that Mark also was acquainted only with the section, chaps. iii.—ix., where the closest agreement is found ; so that Mark may still have been finished earlier, and, consequently, received into the canon earlier, than the *complete* Gospel of Luke. For, had Mark had access to the whole Gospel of Luke, it would be inexplicable why he should not have incorporated much of the important narrative of the journey in Luke ix.—xviii.* Respecting the early chapters of Matthew and Luke, which contain the history of the childhood of Jesus, it might be said that Mark refrained from using them on the ground, that it was his purpose to describe only the *official labours* of Jesus.

§ 4. On the Gospel of St. Matthew.

Matthew, called Levi, the son of Alphæus (Matth. ix. 9 ; Mark ii. 14), is mentioned in the inscription as the author† of the first of our four canonical Gospels ; and tradition establishes the fact, that Matthew wrote a Gospel ; but the question about the genuineness of Matthew is so intimately connected with the inquiry into the *language* in which it was composed, that the one cannot, by possibility, be answered apart from the other. All accounts of the Fathers who give any information about the Gospel of Matthew (see the Author's Geschichte der Ev., S. 19 ff.), agree in this, that Matthew wrote his Gospel in the Syro-Chaldaic language. But on the relation in which our Greek Gospel by Matthew stands to the Aramaic, there rests an obscurity which previous investigations have not succeeded in penetrating. The readiest suggestion is, to pronounce the Greek Gospel a translation of the Aramaic. On closer consideration, however, difficulties arise in the way of this view. *First of all—Papias* (*Euseb.* H. E. iii. 39) might seem to speak against the existence of a translation, as he writes of the Hebrew Gospel of Matthew, ἡρμήνευσε δ' αὐτὰ, ὡς

---

* See, however, what is said concerning this in the remarks on Luke ix. 51.

† Although we are not, by any means, necessarily *compelled* to explain the inscriptions of the Gospels, as giving the author, yet they *may* be so taken grammatically ; it is the comparison of tradition that gives to this possible explanation its probability. The κατά might be taken = *secundum ;* so that the meaning of the formula would be—a Gospel of Jesus, after St. Matthew's mode of description, or St. Mark's, which explanation would admit the supposition of other authors of the Gospels. But universally-prevailing tradition, which cannot have arisen out of these superscriptions, because it is too widespread and too ancient, decides in favour of taking κατά as pointing out the author—a usage found also 2 Macc. ii. 13. This form of expression was chosen to convey the genitive relation, because the simple genitive could hardly stand here, since the Gospel is not that of the author, but of Jesus Christ. As εὐαγγέλιον Ἰησοῦ Χριστοῦ, *Gospel of Christ,* was in use, it was impossible to write εὐαγγέλιον Ματθαίου or Μάρκου, *Gospel of Matthew, or Mark.*

ἦν δυνατὸς ἕκαστος, *which each interpreted as he was able ;* which words are best taken to mean, that every one had to try to explain the Hebrew book as well as he could (either from his own knowledge, or from that of some one else), because there was no translation of it. However, we must not overlook the fact, that Papias says this, not of his own times, but of a time already past.* The passage cannot, accordingly, be adduced to show, that in the time of Papias, there was no Greek translation of Matthew in existence. *Next,* our Greek text of Matthew shews traces of originality, which render it extremely unlikely that we have in it a mere translation. In particular, the passages from the Old Testament are quoted in a way so free and independent, that no translator would have so treated them.† This character of the Greek text, taken in connexion with the universally current tradition, that Matthew wrote an Aramaic Gospel, and with the like universal reception of this very Greek text in the church, as the genuine Gospel, renders it probable to me, as before observed, that Matthew, after the composition of the Aramaic Gospel, himself prepared also a Greek edition of it, or, at least, had it done under his authority. This Greek edition may be regarded as another recension of the Gospel, whereby the difference that subsists between our Gospel according to Matthew and that of the Jewish Christians, which was a revision founded more on the Aramaic Gospel, is more easily accounted for. With the growing circulation of the Greek, the traces of the Aramaic Gospel were gradually lost, because to most it was inaccessible, by reason of the language, and its contents could be read as well in the Greek Gospel.

The view, just detailed, of the relation of the Greek Gospel to the Aramaic, agrees best with the *historical* data. But, very recently, an attempt has been made to disprove the apostolical character of our Greek Gospel, on *internal* grounds.‡ But, from the na-

* Sieffert (on the origin of the first canonical Gospel, p. 14, ff.) makes it probable that these are not the words of Papias, but of the elder presbyter John. According to this, even so early as John, must the time when each was obliged to translate for himself Matthew's Aramaic Gospel have been already past.—[E.

† True, this free mode of treatment may have sprung from the Aramaic original, since in this, of course, the citations from the O. T. must have been *translated* from Hebrew into Aramaic.—[E.

‡ Schleiermacher, Schulz, de Wette, Schulthess, were the first to utter these doubts. Heidenreich has endeavoured to refute them in Winer's Theol. Journ., Bd. III., H. 2. They were followed by Sieffert (Königsberg, 1832). Klener (Göttingen, 1832). Schneckenburger (Stuttgart, 1834). Consult Schleiermacher's Article on the Testimony of Papias (Stud. und Kritiken Jahrg. 1832, H. 4); and Strauss's Review in the Berl. Jahrbücher, 1834, No. 91, ff. Kern, Tübingen, 1834, defends the genuineness of Matthew against these attacks, still inclining to Sieffert's and Klener's views; he also supposes a re-touching of the original, together with spurious additions, only allowing but few such. I have given my opinion of these works and their arguments more at length in the Er-

ture of the case, such arguments have a very uncertain character ; much, if not every thing, depends on the feeling, and especially on the doctrinal views of the critic. Hence the opinions
of the learned differ greatly from each other ; where one sees a
proof *against* the apostolical authorship of Matthew, another sees a
testimony in its *favour*. We cannot, therefore, ascribe any importance to the results of internal criticism, as long as they are unsupported by historical proofs. (For further information on this subject consult the Programmes mentioned in the note.)

Lastly, in reference to the *place* and *time* of the composition of
the Gospel by Matthew, but little can be said. Doubtless it was
written in Palestine, and even in Jerusalem itself, since the tradition of Matthew's labours points thither. The circumstance, that
the Hebrew recension of the Gospel, under the title of εὐαγγέλιον
καθ᾽ Ἑβραίους [Gospel according to the Hebrews], was in use principally among the Jewish Christians in Palestine, also implies that
it was composed in that country, and for its inhabitants. The
Greek recension may certainly have had its origin in another
country ; yet there are no data to enable us to decide accurately
upon the point, and it is just as possible that Matthew, in
consequence of the very general use of the Greek tongue in Palestine, in the time of the apostles, may have prepared a Greek edition
of his Gospel for the benefit of the Hellenistic Jews who dwelt
there. The supposition of the Greek Gospel originating in any
other country is liable to this objection, that there are no remarks added illustrative of the localities and customs of Palestine,
such as we find in Mark and Luke, and which, in that case, would
have been equally necessary in Matthew. Respecting the *time* of
the composition we are totally destitute of express authority. The
statement of *Irenæus* (adv. hær. iii. 1), however, that it was written
while Peter and Paul were preaching at Rome, comes, probably,
very near the truth. According to Matth. xxiv., the Gospel was certainly written *before* the destruction of Jerusalem, since this event,
though near at hand, appears as still future. We can hardly, therefore, be wrong in placing the composition of Matthew somewhere
between A. D. 60–70.

And, in conclusion, to say something on the *distinctive character* of Matthew, it is clearly seen, as was before observed, to be this,
that Matthew labours to prove for Jewish readers that Jesus is the
Messiah foretold by the prophets. The special regard for Jewish
readers shows itself at the very commencement, in that the genealogy of Jesus is traced up to Abraham only ; it appears also in

langen Easter Programme for the year 1835, and the Christmas Programme for 1836.
On Sieffert's Work see the Author's Review in Tholuck's Liter. Anz. Jahrg. 1833. No.
14, ff.

various express explanations (Matth. x. 6 ; xv. 24) ; and lastly, in assuming the reader's familiarity with every thing relating to the Mosaic law, Jewish customs and localities. The distinctive character of Matthew is further evident in this, that he regards the outward features of the picture as entirely unessential and subordinate. He has conceived the life of Jesus from general points of view. At one time he pictures him as a new lawgiver ; at another, as a worker of miracles ; at another, as a teacher. The character of the Saviour he brings out specially by speeches, made up in part, apparently, of the elements of discourses delivered at different times.* These discourses, as chap. v.—vii., x., xxi., xiii., xviii., xxiii., xxiv., xxv., are connected by historical introductions, which to the Evangelist however seemed (much as in the case of John) in themselves of no significance, whence also he has elaborated them with much less care than the discourses. His work, regarded as a whole, exhibits its author unmistakably as absorbed by the majesty of the Saviour's character ; still he lacks the abundant susceptibility and refinement of spirit which we admire in John, while again he surpasses Mark in depth and spirituality. The Christ of Matthew is indeed not the Christ of the popular Jewish conceptions. Rather, he appears in direct conflict with what was false in the Jewish notion of the Messiah. Still the Son of God (whom Matthew, of course, in common with the other apostles, recognised in Jesus), presents himself, according to his portraiture, in a Jewish garb ; † while in John's, a robe of heavenly light floats around him ; so that the form in which the disciple of love introduces the Son of love, bears a spiritual glory corresponding to that of the Sacred Being whom it invests. As this cannot be said of Matthew, the ancients were not wrong in denominating the Gospel of Matthew, σωματικόν, *bodily*, that of John, πνευματικόν, *spiritual;* by which epithet it was not intended to mark that of Matthew as unapostolic ; but as in the Saviour the λόγος, *Word* was manifested in a σῶμα, *body*, so, in a comprehen-

---

* *Schlichthorst*, Ueber das Verhältniss der drei synoptischen Evangelien, und über den Charakter des Mt. insbesondere, Göttingen, 1835, attempts to substantiate too close a relationship between the separate parts of Matthew to each other. Various of his demonstrations are not without foundation ; but most of these references are undesigned, simply growing out of the spirit and harmony of the life of Jesus, not out of the reflection of the author.

† Matthew has committed to writing what constituted the substance of the oral preaching of the apostles to the Israelites; the proof that Jesus of Nazareth was the promised (Gen. xv.) *seed of Abraham,* and the promised (2 Samuel, vii.) *seed of David,* in a word, the Messiah. This must be satisfactorily shown to the Israelites before proceeding to the eternal deity of Christ. First his historical relation to prophecy ; then his essential relation to God, the universe, and the history of the world. Matthew in character and office belonged to the former of these periods. Hence we explain the prominence given by him to the *human* and *Israelitish* aspects of the Saviour's character. —[E.

sive delineation of his life, along with the spiritual, the national and temporal elements of his character required to be livingly set forth.

§ 5. ON THE GOSPEL OF MARK.

JOHN MARK, often called simply Mark, was the son of a certain Mary (Acts xii. 12), who had a house at Jerusalem, where the apostles often assembled. He is known from the New Testament as the companion of Paul. (Acts xii. 25 ; xiii. 5 ; xv. 36, ff.) Even during Paul's imprisonment at Rome, he is still associated with him (Col. iv. 10 ; Philem. 24) ; and whether we assume a second imprisonment of Paul at Rome or not, he, in any case, appears in connection with Paul till the close of the apostle's life. (2 Tim. iv. 11.) In this there seems to be some contradiction to the notices of the fathers, according to which Mark appears in company with Peter, of which only one trace is met with in the New Testament, and that has some uncertainty attaching to it. (1 Peter v. 13.) But the notices of the fathers may be reconciled with the statements of the New Testament, by supposing that after the contention between Paul, Barnabas, and Mark (Acts xv. 37, ff.), the last-named joined Peter *for a time.* On this point the New Testament is silent, because less is there said about Peter than about Paul ; but afterwards, when the old relation between Mark and Paul was restored, and Peter, moreover, was labouring in conjunction with Paul at Rome, Mark also appears again in connexion with Paul. But, together with the account of the connexion of Mark and Peter, an account too unvarying to be justly liable to question, the fathers tell us (see *Euseb.* H. E. iii. 39 ; v. 8 ; vi. 25. *Tertull.* adv. Marc. iv. 5) that Peter gave his sanction to the Gospel which Mark, as his interpreter, had written. That the fathers are not quite unanimous in their relation of subordinate circumstances, can be no reason for doubting the truth of the main fact ; because nothing else can render intelligible the fact, otherwise so astonishing, that the Gospel by Mark was acknowledged in the church without any contradiction. The authority of this companion of the apostles was surely too inconsiderable, and his previous relation to our Lord too uncertain, for them to have relied on his personal character in receiving his narrative of the life of Jesus into the canon. Had it been the product of a later period, some more celebrated name would certainly have been put at the head of the book ; so that, even if history did not supply any such account, we must have conjectured something of the kind from the fact of the reception of Mark into the canon. The authority of Peter, which this Gospel enjoyed, also alone explains how any persons in the ancient church could have thought of using this Gospel.

in preference to any other, as *Irenæus* (iii. 11, 17) tells us was the case. The character of the Gospel itself could not possibly lead to this, since it contains too little that is distinctive to gain a party to itself ; but it is easily conceivable, that partisans of Peter, on account of this very connexion, which, as they knew, subsisted between Mark and their leader, used this Gospel on the same principle that the partisans of Paul used that of Luke. But whether the Gospel by Mark suffered corruption in the hands of these. Christians of Peter's party, as that of Luke did among the ultras of Paul's (the Marcionites), and that of Matthew among the Jewish Christians, is uncertain. We know too little of the εὐαγγέλιον κατ' Αἰγυπτίους, *Gospel according to the Egyptians*, to be able to say any thing certain of its relationship to the Gospel of Peter.*

The *time* and *place* of the composition, can be determined with no more exactness than in the case of Matthew's Gospel. Here, also, we must rest content with one circumstance, that it was written *before* the destruction of Jerusalem. (Mark xiii. 14, ff.) From the relation it bears to Matthew, we may conclude, with much probability, that it was composed later than the Gospel of that apostle. We come nearest the truth in supposing that Mark wrote his Gospel in the period shortly before the overthrow of Jerusalem [according to tradition shortly after the death of Peter, in the summer of 64]. Respecting the *place* of its composition, tradition is divided between Alexandria and Rome. The Latin words which Mark has admitted into his book, favour the latter city ; and as, in any case, it had its origin in one of the centres of the early ecclesiastical life,† to which circumstance its rapid circulation must be partially ascribed ; and as nothing in the history of Mark is opposed to the idea that he wrote in Rome, the opinion that he did so seems to deserve the preference.

No definite *character* is displayed in the Gospel by Mark. We see, indeed, at once that he did *not* write for Jewish readers, because Jewish manners and customs are carefully explained by him (compare the remarks on Mark vii. 3, 4); but what particular tendency

---

* In my History of the Gospels (p. 97, ff.) I have too decidedly rejected the possibility of a connexion between the Gospel of the Egyptians and Peter, and that of Mark. According to the general analogy, it is very probable that the Gospel of Mark also suffered corrruptions; and it still remains possible that one of the writings belonging to the apocryphal books of Peter's partisans was a corrupted Gospel by Mark. *Schneckenburger*, Ueber das Evangelium der Aegyptier. Bern, 1834, takes it to be a work related to the εὐαγγέλιον καθ' Ἑβραίους, used by the Ebionites. From the Gospel of John, published by Münter (Copenhagen, 1828), we see that *it* also, though not till a late period, suffered corruption from the Gnostics. Consult Ullmann in the Studien und Kritiken, Jahrg. I., H. iv., S. 818, ff.

† Consult the Author's Gesch. der Evangelien, S. 440.

in the ancient church he had in view, does not clearly appear. The Latinisms found in his Gospel are not of themselves sufficient to stamp it with a Roman character. The evident pains bestowed on that vividness of narration which is characteristic of his Gospel, might be regarded as a more conclusive proof. The Roman national character, displays unquestionably an adaptedness to the outward and the practical, which is in some measure reflected in Mark. He depicts with graphic power the minuter features of an action, and transports his readers into the very scene. Compare particularly Mark v. 1–20, 22–43 ; vi. 17–29 ; ix. 14, ff., with the parallel passages ; also Mark vii. 32–37 ; viii. 22–26, which are peculiar to him. This picturesqueness manifests itself mainly in the narratives of cures, and most of all in the cures of certain demoniacs (Mark v. 1, ff.; ix. 14, ff.) In his exhibition of the Saviour's spiritual character, and especially of his discourses, he is strikingly inferior. We cannot, therefore, regard his mere vividness of portraiture as elevating him decidedly above Matthew. It would seem, also, that he aims only to give a vivid sketch of our Lord's official labours. His narrative therefore opens with the baptism.

§ 6. ON THE GOSPEL OF LUKE.

The person to whom tradition refers the third Gospel, is Luke, who is sufficiently known, from sacred history, as the companion of the Apostle Paul. His name is the shortened form of Lucanus—as Alexas of Alexander, Cleopas of Cleopatros. That he was a physician, is placed beyond doubt, by Col. iv. 14 ; and there is nothing improbable in the statement of the fathers, that he was a native of Antioch. He was a heathen by birth, as is satisfactorily proved by Col. iv. 14, compared with verse 11, and still more by the scope of his book. As Matthew evidently had in view the Jewish, so Luke the heathen Christians. He might be led to write for them, not only from national sympathy, but also by the example of the Apostle of the Gentiles, who controlled the direction of his labours. According to the tradition of the fathers (*Euseb.* H. E. iii. 4, v. 8, vi. 25 ; *Tertull.* adv. Marc. iv. 5), Paul is also said to have exercised a confirmatory influence on the Gospel of Luke, like that of Peter on Mark's ; which information is confirmed in a similar way by the rapid dissemination of the book, and its universal acknowledgment in the ancient church. But the internal structure of the Gospel shows more than all, that it sprang from the Pauline school, which it represents in the Gospel-collection.

The *universal character* of this Gospel manifests itself at once in its carrying the genealogy of Jesus up to Adam, while Matthew stops at Abraham, the ancestor of the Jews ; in the account of the sending forth of the seventy disciples as the representatives of all nations, while Matthew speaks only of the twelve apostles going forth as representatives of the twelve tribes ; and finally, in the omission of every circumstance which betrays any Jewish exclusiveness.* It may, therefore, be said, that as Matthew represents Jesus as the Messiah of the *Jews*, so Luke represents him as the Messiah of the *heathen*—*i. e.*, as he in whom all the higher aspirations of the heathen world were realized, and who made the heathen themselves the object of his labours. As respects the form of delineation, Luke has the peculiarity of exhibiting, with great vividness and truth (especially in the long journey narrated in ix. 51—xviii. 14), not so much the *discourses*, as the *conversations* of Jesus, with the occasions which gave rise to them, the remarks interposed by the bystanders, and the way in which they terminated ; so that each of the Evangelists teaches us, even in *his mode of delineation*, to view the Saviour from a different aspect. Accordingly it was founded in the nature of the relations, that the ultra partisans of Paul—and, as such, we must regard the Marcionites—used this Gospel, in which their tendency is most definitely embodied, in preference to the others, and only endeavoured to remove, as Jewish additions, so much as did not agree with their exaggerated or mistaken Pauline views of the law and the Gospel.†

In determining the *place* and *time* of the composition of Luke's Gospel, the person of Theophilus, to whom the Gospel is addressed, may, in some measure, guide us. He seems to have been a man of reputation (see note on Luke i. 3), and a resident of Italy. For we observe that the Evangelist, in treating of Oriental subjects, everywhere adds explanations, and particularly, exact designations of place, in regard even to the best known localities. In relation, on the contrary, to the most inconsiderable places of Italy, they are omitted, as with these he could assume a familiarity on the part of his reader. Rome is, therefore, in all probability, to be regarded as the place of composition for this Gospel also, whither, in particular, we are led, by the close of the Acts of the Apostles, the second

---

* Luke, alike in his active life, as companion of Paul, and in his writings, gives emphasis to all that which serves for proof of the truth that the Saviour came not for Israel as a people, but only for the believing Israelites, and not for the Israelites only, but also for the believing heathen.—[E.

† That the Gospel of Marcion is a mutilated Gospel by Luke, has been convincingly shown by *Hahn* in his well-known work, Das Evangelium Marcions in seiner ursprünglichen Gestalt, Königsberg, 1823. Consult the Author's work on the Gospels, p. 106, ff. The counter-assertions of *Schulz* in Ullmann's Studien (B. ii. H. 3) still remain unestablished.

part of the Evangelist's work. For, without a formal close, it breaks off with the second year of Paul's imprisonment at Rome ; and as Luke was in company with Paul during that imprisonment, we can assign the place of composition with much probability. Further, as nothing is added about the issue of Paul's affairs, there remains but little obscurity as to the *time* of the composition of the Gospel. It must have been written shortly before the Acts of the Apostles, during Paul's imprisonment at Rome, and about sixty-four years after the birth of Christ. For it is not likely that a great space of time elapsed between the composition of the Gospel and that of the Acts, as the two works are so closely connected. In all probability, also, Luke's acquaintance with Theophilus was the fruit of his stay in Rome. *De Wette* (Einleitung ins. N. T., S. 182) draws from such passages as Luke xxi. 17, ff., the conclusion, that this Gospel must have been written *after* the destruction of Jerusalem ; but our remarks on Matth. xxiv. 15, will show that this conclusion is untenable.

§ 7. On the Harmony of the Gospel-History.

The propensity to look everywhere for connexion and unity, is too deeply seated in human nature not to have sought its gratification in attempts to form a connected account of the Saviour's life out of the different Gospels. Such an undertaking meets a practical want, by rendering easier the survey of all the circumstances in his life ; so that it is not surprising that we hear, even at a very early period, of attempts to form the different accounts of the Evangelists into a connected whole, such as were made by *Tatian,** *Ammonius,* and *Eusebius.* But the narratives of the Evangelists do not admit of being reduced to a certain and strictly scientific unity. The difficulties in the construction of a Gospel harmony lie in this, that some of the Evangelists have conducted their narratives with no reference to the order of time. They begin their histories, indeed, with the Saviour's birth, and close them with his death, as it could hardly be otherwise in a biography ; but the main body of the Gospel-history—the exhibition of the official labours of Jesus—is so treated, that the intention of preserving a definite chronological order in the events narrated is

* *Tatian's* work I have called, in my History of the Gospels, p. 335, ff., a Harmony of the Gospels ; but the zeal with which Theodoret, in the fifth century, caused it to be destroyed, points to grave heretical corruptions which it contained. There is no doubt that Tatian made a compilation from the whole Gospel-collection, such as suited his purposes, and took the liberty of making considerable alterations in the text, which his adherents probably further increased. Concerning other harmonies, consult § 9 of this Introduction.

nowhere perceptible. In *Matthew*, first of all, there is found from the temptation (ch. iv.), down to the last journey to Jerusalem (xx. 17), no exact statement of time which might serve for the arrangement of the material. For the most part, the Evangelist passes from one point to another, without any thing to fix the time (iv. 12, 18, 23 ; viii. 5, 18, 23, 28 ; ix. 1, 9, 35 ;) or he uses an indefinite τότε, *then*, to connect them (iii. 13 ; iv. 1 ; ix. 14 ; xi. 20 ; xii. 22, 38 ; xv. 1); or he arranges the several histories, one after another, with the comprehensive formulas, ἐν ταῖς ἡμέραις ἐκείναις, *in those days* (iii. 1 ; xiii. 1), ἐν ἐκείνῳ τῷ καιρῷ, *in that time* (xiv. 1), ἐν ἐκείνῃ τῇ ὥρᾳ, *in that hour* (xviii. 1). Precise statements as to time (as Matth. xvii. 1, μεθ' ἡμέρας ἕξ, *after six days*) are extremely rare. The large collections of discourses in Matthew show that his prevailing aim was to portray the character of Jesus, apart from time and place, and, by a grouping together of kindred actions and discourses, to bring him before the reader's mind in his different spheres of labour. In the case of *Mark*, this neglect of time and place is still more striking : even these general data are for the most part wanting with him. He usually gives his narrative unaccompanied by remarks ; he aims merely at a vivid portrayal of the facts, without uniting them by any fixed principle of arrangement. *Luke's* chronology appears at first sight more exact ; so that we might expect to find in him events narrated in their natural succession. At the very commencement, in ch. i. 3, καθεξῆς, *in order* (see comment. on the passage), seems to point to a chronological arrangement ; then follows (iii. 1) a very important date for the chronology of the life of Jesus ; and (iii. 23) he remarks that the Saviour was thirty years of age at his entrance on his ministry. Yet, in the course of the Gospel, we find the same indefiniteness in his arrangement as in that of the others. For the most part, Luke, too, joins one narration to another, without statement of time (iv. 16, 31 ; v. 12, 33 ; vii. 18, 36 ; viii. 26 ; ix. 1, 18); sometimes the indefinite transitions μετὰ ταῦτα, *after this* (v. 27), ἐν μιᾷ τῶν ἡμερῶν, *on one of the days* (v. 17 ; viii. 22), and the like, are interchanged ; so that it often becomes doubtful whether, even in Luke, events are always arranged according to the succession of time ; but still, even if this be probable, a complete arrangement of the events in the Saviour's life cannot be accomplished by means of Luke, because no fixed points of connexion with the other Gospels can be laid down in the body of the narrative—that is, from the baptism of Jesus to his last journey to the feast (Matth. xx. 17 ; Mark x. 32 ; Luke xviii. 31); for, after this, there is less lack of chronological data. True, it might be thought, that such a point is to be found in the history of the transfiguration, since all the three Evangelists (Matth. xvii. 1 ; Mark ix. 2 ; Luke ix. 28) connect it with what precedes by μεθ' ἡμέρας ἕξ, *after six days.* (The ὀκτὼ ἡμέραι, in Luke are the same period, but differently reckoned). Yet if, commencing at this point, we make the attempt to arrange the events backwards and onwards, the thread is soon lost. But if, with the *events*, it appears impossible to connect the statements of the Evangelists into an orderly whole, it is still more so with the *discourses.* What appears in Matthew (v—vii., x., xiii., xxiii., and in several other places) as spoken in connexion, Luke gives broken up and widely scattered ; so that the very first attempt to restore the different parts of the discourses of Jesus to their chronological connexion, demonstrates the impossibility of so doing, at least if the compilation, instead of serving merely a practical purpose, is to claim scientific certainty.

Thus *John* alone remains, whose careful chronological arrangement strikes the eye, and who seems, therefore, to afford very important materials for the chronological arrangement of the chief events at least, in the first three Gospels. For though, now and then, an indefinite μετὰ ταῦτα, *after this,* occurs even in John (as iii. 22 ; vi. 1 ; vii. 1, and elsewhere), he usually states exactly, whether one day (i. 29, 35, 44 ; vi. 22 ; xii. 12), or two (iv. 40. 43), or three (ii. 1), or several days, intervened between the events recorded. The discourses, also, are in John so connected with the occurrences mentioned, and are so complete in themselves, that they acquire, in their full extent, a fixed chronological place. The chief point, however, is that John gives us great divisions in the life of our Lord, between which we can endeavour to arrange the separate events. Besides the last passover (xiii. 1), which is mentioned by the synoptical Evangelists also, he speaks *distinctly* of another passover, at which Jesus was present (ii. 13) ; and between these two fixed points at the beginning and end of the ministry of Jesus, John mentions further two feasts which the Saviour celebrated at Jerusalem—viz., the feast of the dedication of the temple (x. 22), and the feast of tabernacles (vii. 2). Besides these, mention is made (v. 1) of another feast ; but its character is left undetermined. If we possessed only the records of the first three Gospels, we should know nothing certain of these journeys of Jesus to the feasts ; we could only arrive at the probable conclusion, that he would certainly not have neglected the Old Testament command (Ex. xxiii. 17) to go up to Jerusalem at the three great feasts, since we find him so scrupulous in the observance of the law in other points. Yet there is no clear evidence, even from John, of the number of journeys to the feasts, which took place during the ministry of Jesus, and hence the relation of the occurrences to the chronology of Christ's active ministry still remains obscure. What John narrates, certainly occurred in the order in which he narrates it ; but it is uncertain how long a period is included—whether he details the events of one year, of two years, or of several. First of all, we cannot prove that John has left *no* journey of Jesus to the feasts unmentioned. Moreover, the indefiniteness of the passage (v. 1*) makes his whole chronology uncertain ; for although much may be said in favour of the opinion, that the festival there referred to was a passover,† yet this cannot be fully ascertained, particularly as we read so soon as vi. 4 of another nearly approaching passover ; for it is, after all, harsh to refer ἐγγύς, *near*, to the passover that was gone by, as *Dr. Paulus* does. (See the retrospect quoted in the note.) Whether, therefore, according to John's representation, Jesus celebrated three passovers or four at Jerusalem during his ministry, cannot be stated with certainty ;‡ and how difficult it must be to use the notices of John respecting the journeys of Jesus, for the purpose of arranging the historical materials of the other Gospels, appears sufficiently from the one circumstance, that, as he gives hardly any information about the life of Jesus but such as the other Evangelists had not given, no point of contact between them and him can be assigned. The history of the feeding of the five thousand (John vi. 1–15), with the walking on the sea immediately following it (vi. 16–21), is the only event which is parallel with Matthew (xiv. 13, ff.), Mark (vi. 30, ff.), and Luke (ix. 10, ff.); and the first two Evangelists, Matthew and Mark, like John, connect Christ's walking on the sea with the feeding of the five thousand. Yet as, on the one hand, the connexion of events cannot be pursued with certainty, and, on the other, the exact time of the miraculous feeding is uncertain, even in John, on account of the indefiniteness of v. 1 and vi. 4, so we reach nothing conclusive for the arrangement of the whole from this single point of contact.§ Whether any particular event belongs to the beginning or the close of the public ministry of Jesus, is sufficiently shewn, it is

---

* *Kaiser*, in his Synopsis (Nürnberg, 1828), regards it as a feast of tabernacles. Consult the commentary on the passage.

† Consult the chronological retrospect at the end of the first volume of Dr. *Paulus'* Commentary on the Gospels.

‡ In reference to the chronological difficulties in John's Gospel itself, we must further compare the passage (x. 22) in which John passes on to the feast of the dedication, in a way that leaves it altogether uncertain how the presence of Jesus at that feast stands related to his presence at the feast of tabernacles (vii. 2), since no mention is made either of his going away or remaining. It might even be thought to be the feast of dedication in another year, were it not that the following discourse (x. 27, 28) refers too plainly to the preceding context (x. 12, 13).

§ Just so *Lücke* observes in his *Commentar über den Johannes*, Th. i., S. 526 : "How that which John has mentioned out of the variety of events may be chronologically harmonized with what the first three Evangelists narrate in the above-mentioned (middle) period, is an insolvable problem of historical criticism." See the further remarks, S. 614, 615, of the same work.

true, partly by its position in the Gospels, partly by its internal character; but the character of the Evangelists' narrative, who commonly leave time and place undetermined, admits of our bringing neither all the separate incidents recorded of the Saviour, nor his discourses, into precise chronological connexion. We, therefore, take the Gospel-history as it is given to us, following the chronological order as far as the Evangelists enable us to discover it plainly, but nowhere bringing it out violently and artificially where it has not been given. According to the synopsis of *De Wette* and *Lücke*, which we take as the foundation of our exposition, we shall first treat of the history of the childhood of Jesus and his baptism; and, last, of the narrative of his sufferings, resurrection, and ascension (combining John's description of these latter circumstances); but with respect to the intermediate materials of the Gospel-history, we shall chiefly follow Matthew, incorporating with his narrative—where they appear to us most probably to belong—those portions contained only in Mark and Luke, or in either one of them. The editors of the synopsis have, indeed, treated this part in such a manner, as to give the whole matter three times over according to the order of Matthew, Mark, and Luke. A threefold exegetical discussion of this part would certainly have secured no small advantages; they had, however, to be sacrificed, as requiring too much space.

§ 8. ON THE CREDIBILITY OF THE GOSPEL-HISTORY.

The description given above of the origin of the Gospels from separate memoirs, whose authors are unknown, the character of the Gospel-history itself, through a large portion of which we can trace no chronological arrangement, and lastly, the distinct discrepancies discoverable in various events, particularly in the composition of the discourses—are all circumstances which seem to endanger the credibility of the Gospel-history, especially in such events as lay without the immediate knowledge of any one of the narrators, as, for instance, the childhood of Jesus. The Gospels seem in this way to acquire the appearance of an unarranged aggregate of separate and uncertain accounts, which neither agree precisely with each other, nor even, in each individual Gospel, stand in strict connexion. The older theology was apprehensive that, by a view such as modern criticism has established, the sacred character of the Gospel-history would be entirely taken away. Starting from the *literal* inspiration* of the sacred writers, they laboured to force a harmony,

---

* I distinguish *literal* inspiration from *verbal*, and maintain the *latter*, while I deny the *former*. The distinction between them does not lie, as I think, in the *essence* and the *form* (for the *form*, too, is necessary in one aspect), but in the *essential* and the *unessential form*. But the question, Where is the *essential* in the form separated from the *un*ₑₛ

and to reconcile all discrepancies in facts and words ; but, from the character of the Gospels, this procedure could not but lead to the most arbitrary treatment ;—that is to say, wherever there appeared a difference, whether in the events or in the discourses, the event or the discourse was always said to have been twice, and sometimes even thrice repeated. By setting up the principle, therefore, that the Gospel-history must agree in all things external and non-essential, they put weapons into the hands of the enemies of God's Word ; the evident non-agreement was used as an argument for denying the divine origin of the Scriptures. The true course, therefore, is, in this case, also, to adhere to the truth, plainly to acknowledge the evident fact of discrepancies in the Gospel-history, to seek for a reconciliation of these variations where it presents itself naturally, but to resort to nothing far-fetched or forced. An *external* agreement in the Gospel-history should not be absolutely required as proof of its divinity, any more than in the formations of nature ; as in them exact regularity is combined with the greatest freedom, so also, in the Gospel-history, perfect agreement in what is essential, is found with the freest treatment of what is unessential.* The credibility of the Gospel-history is securely based only on the identity of that vital principle which reigned in all the individual Evangelists, and in which the whole new communion, of which they were but members, shared. That vital principle was the Spirit who guides into all truth. But this Spirit, who inspired the Evangelists and the whole company of the apostles, neither relieved them from the use of the ordinary means of historical inquiry, as, for instance, the use of family memoirs or narratives of single events ; nor did he obliterate their peculiarities, and use them as passive organs ; he rather spiritualized their individual capacities and powers, gave them a sure faculty (*tact*) of separating every thing false in matters of faith and in the essentials of the narrative ; of recognizing what was genuine and appropriate, and of arranging it according to a profounder principle. Although,

---

sential ?—what is *word*, what is *letter ?*—will never admit of being answered as respects individual cases, so that *all* shall be satisfied, because the mind's subjective attitude exercises too much influence over our views on the point. In general, however, those who are one in the principles, will be able to unite in this canon : *The form of Scripture is to be regarded as essential, as far as it is connected with what is essential in the doctrine, and is, consequently, also to be ascribed to inspiration; it is only where there is no such connexion, that the form is to be regarded as unessential.* Consult, further, *Tholuck's* excellent dissertation on the contradictions in the Gospels, in his *Glaubwürdigkeit der Evangelischen Geschichte gegen Strauss*, Hamburg, 1837, S. 429, ff., which preserves just the right medium.

* Literal agreement in the Gospels, would have suggested to the enemies of the truth, the charge of a concert among the authors to deceive ; as Scripture now is, it appears at once divine and human. [A clear distinction must be drawn between *variations* and *contradictions*. The former may, of course, be assumed in the Evangelists. We must require the strongest evidence before admitting the latter.—[K.

therefore, the Evangelists sometimes threw the elements of our Lord's discourses into other than their original combinations, the import of those parts, although modified, is not altered. For, as the living Word, which the Lord himself was, wrought in the Evangelists also, and inspired them, it formed in each of them a new spiritual whole, in which the members of the separated whole appear harmoniously re-united.

This view of the Scripture—of its unity in essentials, and its diversity in non-essentials—equally leads away from the superstitious reverence of the *dead letter*, and prompts to the search for the *living Spirit;* yet it stands aloof from that hollow spirituality which fancies itself able to do without the external *word*, and thereby falls into the danger of taking its empty dreams for essential ideas of the truth. Although, therefore, Providence intended that external proofs of the genuineness of the Gospels should not be wanting, yet it has not permitted that the credibility of the events recorded in them should be incontrovertibly demonstrated. Occasions are left for doubt and suspicion ; and by these the Gospel history fulfils a part of its design, since Christ, in Scripture, as well as when personally labouring on earth, is set for the fall of many. (Luke ii. 34.) In every reader of the Gospel-history, therefore, is presupposed a readiness to receive the Spirit of truth. Where this exists, the Gospel-history, in its peculiar character, asserts its claims with overwhelming force. For, although the Gospel partakes of the general character of history and biography, yet, as its subject is itself incomparable, it is, in its treatment of the subject, not to be compared with any other work of the kind. The Evangelists write in a style of childlike artlessness and lofty simplicity, such as are found nowhere else thus united. Their individual views and feelings entirely disappear—they narrate without making reflections, without bursting into expressions of praise, or blame, or admiration, even in portraying the sublimest events. They appear, as it were, absorbed in the contemplation of the mighty picture displayed before them, and, forgetting themselves, reflect its features in their pure truth. The Gospel-history, therefore, bears witness to itself and its own credibility, in no other way than did our Lord himself ; He had no witness but himself and the Father, (John viii. 18) ; so the Gospel-history (like the Scripture in general) bears witness to itself only through the Divine Spirit, who reigns in it. He that is of the truth, hears his voice.

It is only where this Spirit has not yet displayed his power, that the conception could arise that the history of Christ is on a par with other biographies of great men ; and, that, therefore, what is miraculous in it, as well as in them, should be regarded as a myth. The want of personal experience of the regenerating power of Christ—the want of that testimony of the Holy Spirit, which alone assures us of the divine origin of the Scriptures, has always caused offence to be taken at the miraculous garb that invests the person of our Lord. In ancient times this offence simply took the form of a hostile attitude towards the church. It is reserved for very recent times, to see this offence pretending to be an advance in Christian science. It appeared first in the form of what was called the *natural* explanation, the very *unnaturalness* of which has, however, long since pronounced its condemnation; it needs, accordingly, no further refutation. Then, especially since the time of *Gabler*, it appeared in the form of the *mythical* explanation, which also has been pushed on to self-destruction through its very extreme application by Strauss. The inapplicability of the mythical exposition to the life of Jesus is incontrovertibly manifest: 1. *From the nearness, in point of time, of the documents which record it* —namely, the four canonical Gospels, the antiquity and genuineness of which are satisfactorily demonstrable on internal and external grounds. As long as the eye-witnesses of the miraculous events of the life of Jesus were living, there could be no such things as myths viz., formations of involuntary inventive rumour—but only productions of enthusiasm or deceit ; 2. *From the acknowledged genuineness of the Acts of the Apostles, and of the Pauline Epistles, as well as of the other principal writings of the New Testament.* Hitherto no one has ventured to pronounce the chief Epistles of Paul and John to be spurious,* and yet they contain precisely the same view of the person of Christ which lies at the basis of the four Gospels. This appears, consequently, to have been the early Christian view. If the mythical explanation is to be defended, nothing is left but to pronounce the Apostle Paul an enthusiast or a deceiver ; 3. *The rise of the Christian Church—the continuity of feeling in it—the purity of the Spirit that wrought in it, with especial power, in the first centuries*, do not allow us, in any way, to conceive of merely a beautiful romance as the ultimate foundation of these phenomena. That a church could be formed of Jews and heathen, who worshipped a crucified Son of God, is, according to the mythical view of the life of Jesus, a far greater miracle than all those which it is intended to dispense with. It is only from the records of the Evangelists, taken as history, that this fact becomes conceivable. Since, moreover, in this church, while gradually extending itself over the world, there was still a constant connexion of feeling, and a spirit of purity, never

---

* Since negative criticism has advanced to its extreme limit, it is no longer myths, but wilful fabrications which are discerned in the Gospels, the Acts of the Apostles, and the letters of John. In this, however, the theory has uttered its own sentence of death. See on this point, my Kritik der Ev. Geschichte, 2 te Aufl. (Critical view of the Gospel-history, 2d ed.) § 7 and § 123–147.—[E.

previously beheld, inspired it, especially in the very early times, we cannot perceive where we can find room for the pretended formation of myths. It can be found only on the unscientific assumption, that no existing records date from the first Christian century. The mythical scheme appears, accordingly, a partial, indecisive measure. The decided anti-Christian spirit will pronounce Christianity, together with the whole Scripture, the product of enthusiasm and deception.

[The theory which *Strauss*, in his famous " Life of Jesus," attempted to apply to the history of Christ's birth, life, sufferings, and death, needs to be known, as to its general features, before the remarks in the text above, and in many other parts of this work, can be understood. *Strauss* is a philosopher of the school of *Hegel* —an ultra-ideal school—and an avowed Pantheist. Entertaining such philosophical views, a miracle was, to him, impossible, and the history of Jesus could not, of course, be literally true ; and, to account for the form of our present Gospel-narratives, he adopted a theory something like the following :—Jesus was a Jew, who, by early training, had become enthusiastically desirous of seeing the fulfilment of the prophecies, and, at length, believed himself to be the Messiah. Filled with the loftiest ideas of purity, and of the high destiny of man, he gathered around him a band of devoted disciples, who were fired with something of his own enthusiasm. The leading idea enforced in his teaching, was the union attainable between the human mind and the divine. At length he died a violent death, from having incurred the hatred of the Pharisees. A mere skeleton is all that Strauss leaves of his life as historically true. It is not true, he says, that Christ was born of a virgin— that he wrought miracles—that he rose from the dead—and ascended to heaven. Then his disciples must have deceived us, we are ready to exclaim. No, says Strauss. The accounts of him contained in the Gospels were the product of their fervid imaginations ; and, without the slightest intention to deceive, there grew up among his followers a complete history, adorned with all that they thought could render their master's memory glorious. The Old Testament was the principal source of the additions thus made to the simple narrative of Christ's life. Whatever they found there of endowments from above, was at once ascribed to the Saviour, who, in their view, must possess all that Heaven had ever bestowed on man. And, in particular, they sought, to embody the main doctrine of their Master's teachings—viz., the union of our souls with God, as the aim of life, in his person, by uniting in that person the divine and human natures.

Taken alone, the theory seems too baseless to have been seriously proposed and applied in two considerable volumes ; but the history of religious opinion in Germany throws some light on its origin. What Kant and his followers denominated *moral interpretation*— that is, giving a moral and spiritual meaning to historical facts— had been exploded sometime previously, and had been succeeded by the *natural* interpretation adopted by the Rationalist school, with *Paulus* at their head. This scheme had, in its turn, been exposed as utterly hollow, because it was plain that the Evangelists *meant* to give a miraculous history; and it is dishonest to interpret their language otherwise. Driven from these two refuges, those who would not take the Gospel-history as a miraculous one, were bound to give some explanation of the fact of such a history, so attested, being in existence. And, as it has been the fashion in Germany, to assume a mythical period in the history of Greece and Rome, and many other nations, Strauss attempted to assign the history of Jesus to such a period. To attain his end, he is compelled to deny the genuineness of every one of the Gospels, and ascribes them all to a period subsequent to the first century of the Christian era. The theory hardly needs refutation. The work is a repository of all the difficulties that beset a harmony of the four Gospels ; and, as such, may cause uneasiness to readers who are not properly acquainted with the solutions of those difficulties, both in general and in particular instances ; but it could not satisfy any but a thoroughly infidel mind, glad to catch at any hypothesis that gives a semblance of ground for impugning the veracity of the witnesses of Christ's life].—*Tr.*

§ 9. Survey of the Literature.

As soon as the active labours of the apostles, who wrought chiefly with the living Word, ceased in the church, the people betook themselves to those written legacies which they had bequeathed to the church —in order, by the examination of the written Word, partly to establish themselves more thoroughly in the known truth, and partly by it to separate truth and falsehood. Since the second century, many distinguished men have devoted their powers to the interpretation of the Holy Scriptures, and of the New Testament in particular. Nevertheless, its contents are yet unexhausted. So great is the depth of the Word of God, that it meets the utmost wants of all times and all relations, of every degree of cultivation and development. It lies, however, in the nature of the church's progress, that by gradual advances she was enabled to penetrate with ever-increasing depth and thoroughness into the understanding of the Scriptures. Our own times, in particular, have made an immense advance in this point, that, in recognizing more and more the comprehensive sense of Scripture, we have learnt to regard the greater portions of previous expositions not so much as absolutely false, as rather embracing but a single phase of the thought. Hence we regard the labours of centuries to understand the Scriptures as connected, and supplemental to one another ; while, the view formerly prevalent, made it necessary to pronounce all the various expositions, except the *single* true one, a mass of errors. According to this, the church of earlier ages must, for the most part, have utterly failed to understand the Scriptures, which would be saying, in other words, that the spirit had not been in the church. We must rather say, that the church has always understood the Bible aright in essentials ; but that a still profounder understanding of it has been gradually attained.

In the first place, as respects the *general works* which embrace the whole New Testament, we do not possess a complete exposition of the whole New Testament by any of the teachers in the early church ; they used to apply themselves at first to single books. It is not till the ninth century, that the *Glossa Ordinaria*, by Walafrid Strabo, appears as a continuous commentary on the New Testament, if indeed, it deserves the name of a commentary at all. Subsequently to him, Nicolaus de Lyra and Alphonsus Tostatus, Bishop of Avilla, in Spain, wrote complete commentaries on the entire Scriptures—the latter in twenty-three folios. At the time of the Reformation, Calvin commented on the whole New Testament except the Revelation of St. John ; as well as Johann Brenz, among the Lutherans, seven folios of whose works are filled with expositions of almost all the books in the Bible. In the seventeenth century, several works appeared, embracing the whole New Testament. Besides Hugo Grotius (in his *Adnotationes in N. T.*, 2 vols. 4to), we may notice particularly the collection of expositions under the name *Critici Sacri* (London, 1660, 9 vols. fol.), of which Polus [Pool] prepared an abridgment ; and further, *Calovii Biblia Illustrata* (Francof. 1672, 4 vols. fol.), a work which was directed against Grotius, and includes the exegetical works of the author. These were followed by Pfaff's edition of the Bible, Tübingen, 1729 ; Wolfii Curæ Philologicæ et Criticæ, Hamburg, 1738, 4 vols. 4to ; Heumann's Erklärung des N. T., Hanover, 1750, 12 vols. 8vo ; Moldenhauer's Erklärung der Schriften des N. T., Leipzig, 1763, 4 vols. 4to ; J. D. Michaelis' Uebersetzung des N. T. mit Anmerkungen, Göttingen, 1789, 3 vols. 4to ; Bengelii Gnomon N. T., Tubingæ, 1773, 4to ; J. G. Rosenmülleri Scholia in N. T., Norimbergæ, 1777, 5 vols. 8vo. (The last edition [the sixth] appeared in 1825). Henneberg planned a complete commentary on the New Testament ; but only the first volume, containing Matthew, appeared, Gotha and Erfurt, 1829. The author died in 1831. H. A. W. Meyer has prepared a commentary on the New Testament. De Wette has also published an exposition of the New Testament. Among the general works on the New Testament, we must also reckon the well-known Observationen-Sammlungen, by Raphelius, (out of Xenophon, Hamb. 1720 ; out of Polybius and Arrian, Hamb. 1715 ; out of Herodotus, Lüneb. 1731), Alberti (Leiden, 1725), Kypke (Breslau, 1725), Elsner (Utrecht, 1728), Palairet (Leiden, 1752).

As regards the *Gospel-collection*,* the expositions of Theophylact and Euthymius Zigabenus have come down to us. The ancient exposition which Theophilus of Antioch is said to have composed on the four Gospels, is lost. Of the time of the Reformation, Mart. Chemnitzii Harmonia Quatuor Evangeliorum, continued by Polycarpus Lyser and Johann Gerhard (Hamb. 1704, 3 vols. fol.), is particularly distinguished. Clericus also composed a similar harmony (Amsterd. 1669, fol). Of more recent times, the following include all the four Gospels : Köcheri Analecta (Altenb. 1766, 4to), which are supplementary to Wolf's Curæ ; J. F. G. Schulz, Anmerkungen über die vier Evangelien, Halle, 1794, 4to ; Ch. Th. Kuinoel Commentarius in Libros N. T. Historicus, Lips. 1807, 4 vols. 8vo (including the Acts of the Apostles); Paulus, philologisch-kritischer Commentar über das N. T., Lübeck, 1800–1808, 5 vols.; also his Exegetisches Handbüch über die drei ersten Evangelien, Heidelberg, 1830, 1831, 2 vols. ; Fritzsche, evangelia quatuor cum Notis, Lips. 1825, 1830, 8vo. The first volume comprises Matthew, the second Mark.

Lastly as regards the *single* Gospels. Among the fathers we possess fragments of a commentary on Matthew by Origen. Chrysostom wrote ninety-one homilies on the Gospel by Matthew. Possin published a *catena* on this Evangelist, Tolosæ, 1646. In later times Salomo van Till, Frankf., 1708, and Jac. Elsner, Zwoll., 1769. 4to, wrote upon Matthew. Also, Götz, Erklärung des Matthäus aus dem Griechisch-Hebräischen und dem Hebräischen, Stuttgardt, 1785, 8vo ; Heddäus, Erklärung des Matthäus, Stuttgardt and Tübingen, 1792, 2 vols ; Der Bericht des Matthäus von Jesus dem Messias, by Bolten, Altona, 1792, 8vo ; Kleuker's Biblische Sympathien, Schleswig, 1820 ; Das Evangelium Matthäi, erklärt von Gratz (of Bonn), Tübingen, 1821, 2 vols. 8vo ; Pires, Commentarius in Evangelium Matthæi, Mogunt., 1825. Of special value is Tholuck's "Philologisch-theologische Auslegung der Bergpredigt Christi nach Matthæus" (Philological and Theol. Com. on Christ's Sermon on the Mount, as contained in Matthew.) Hamburg, 1833.

* For the complete literature of the Gospel harmonies, see Hase's Leben Jesu, S. 18, ff.

On the Gospel by Mark we have, likewise a *catena* edited by Possin, Rome, 1673. Jac. Elsner wrote a commentary upon Mark, Utrecht, 1773 ; and Bolten also, Altona, 1795, 8vo ; Matthäi published an Exposition of Mark, by Victor, a presbyter of Antioch, and other Greek fathers, Moscow, 1775, 2 vols. 8vo.

Lastly, in reference to Luke, we have a *catena* on it by Corderius, Antwerpen, 1628. This Gospel was separately commented on by Pape, Bremen, 1777, 1781, 2 vols. 8vo ; by Bolten, Altona, 1796, 8vo. We have also Morus, Prælectiones in Lucæ Evangelium, published by C. A. Donat. Leips. 1795, 8vo. The latest works on Luke, are Scholia in Lucam scripsit Bornemann, Lips., 1830 ; and Stein's Commentar über den Lucas. Halle, 1830.

SYNOPTICAL EXPOSITION

OF THE

FIRST THREE GOSPELS.

FIRST PART.

OF THE BIRTH AND CHILDHOOD OF JESUS CHRIST.

FIRST SECTION.—MATTHEW'S ACCOUNT.

CHAPTERS I. AND II.

---

§ 1. GENEALOGY OF JESUS.

(Matth. i. 1–17; Luke iii. 23–38.)

WHILE Mark at once, in the title of his Gospel (Mark i. 1), describes Christ as the Son of God, Matthew represents him as the Son of Man, since he first characterizes him as the promised descendant of the two great heads of the Old Testament economy— Abraham and David—and then introduces his entire genealogy. The character of Matthew's Gospel, as the σωματικόν, *corporeal*, in the nobler sense of the word, and its special adaptation to Jewish Christians, show themselves, in this form of beginning, too plainly to be mistaken. Since Jesus is introduced as υἱὸς 'Αβραάμ, *Son of Abraham*, he appears as the descendant of him whose family is blessed among the families of mankind ; but, as Son of David, he was more definitely assigned to a branch of the Abrahamic race— viz., the family of him who, even in the Old Testament, is described as the representative of the future head of the kingdom of God. Both expressions, therefore, point out Jesus as the promised Messiah. Yet this is still more definitely expressed in the name 'Ιησοῦς Χριστός, *Jesus Christ*. 'Ιησοῦς, * *Jesus*, as the proper name of the individual, refers immediately to the Saviour only as a historical

---

* The LXX. use 'Ιησοῦς for יְהוֹשֻׁעַ or יֵשׁוּעַ, which latter form is first found in writings, after the time of the captivity. The name marks our Lord's spiritual character, and was given to him by divine command (Matth. i. 21), to intimate his exalted calling. Just so the Old Testament names, Abraham, Israel, &c., denote the spiritual character which those persons were called to exhibit amongst mankind.

personage ; Χριστός, *Christ,* on the other hand, is the official name
for the expected deliverer of Israel. It corresponds to the Hebrew
מָשִׁיחַ, *Anointed,* which word is used in the Old Testament, sometimes of kings (1 Sam. xxiv. 6, 10 ; xxvi. 16, and elsewhere) ;
sometimes of high-priests (Lev. iv. 3, 5, 16, and elsewhere) ; sometimes of prophets (Psalm cv. 15) ; because all these persons were
consecrated to their office by the symbolical rite of anointing (on
the anointing of prophets see 1 Kings xix. 16), to intimate, that
for the due discharge of their office, they must be endowed with
spiritual powers. But the expression is rarely used in the Old Testament of the royal prophet and high-priest of the kingdom of God.
(Psalm ii. 2 ; Daniel ix. 25.) From these passages, with which
others were connected, in which the anointing was viewed spiritually (comp. Is. lxi. 1, with Luke iv. 18), arose the name Χριστός,
which, even at the time of Christ, had become the prevailing official
designation of the great desired one. In this view, the name
" Christ" expresses the union of the divine and human natures in
the person of the Saviour, since the humanity is the anointed—the
endowed ; the divine power is the anointing—the endowing.
Originally the Saviour was called either ὁ Ἰησοῦς, with reference to
his historical *individuality,* or ὁ Χριστός, with reference to his *dignity;* also, Ἰησοῦς ὁ λεγόμενος Χριστός (Matth. i. 16, on which consult
the commentary). It was only at a later period that the two terms
were united into the collective appellation Ἰησοῦς Χριστός, *Jesus
Christ.*

The first verse in Matthew does not, perhaps, form merely
a superscription for the subsequent genealogy. Βίβλος γενέσεως
(= סֵפֶר תּוֹלְדֹת Gen. v. 1) means primarily, " book of the descent,"
"genealogy," and forms in the Old Testament the general superscription to the genealogy in question, and to the accompanying
biographical sketches by which it is carried out and illustrated.
Matthew has doubtless employed the expression here in a similar
manner. His Gospel is the exposition of the genealogy ; the proof
that Jesus was the promised seed of Abraham and son of David.
The genealogy in Matthew, compared with that of Luke, shows
plainly the different character of the two Gospels. While Matthew
begins with Abraham, the ancestral father of the Jewish people,
Luke ascends to Adam, the first father of the whole human race—
heathen as well as Jews—and thus connects the Saviour with human
nature as such, apart from all national individuality. But in the
particulars we find that, from David downwards, the two genealogies
vary. Matthew traces the line of descent through Solomon, Luke
through another son of David—Nathan. Two names only—Salathiel and Zorobabel (see Luke iii. 27, compared with Matth. i. 12)
—are the same in both, the rest being entirely different ; but these

persons must be regarded as living at different times, since in
Matthew nine persons are enumerated between them and Jesus, and
in Luke eighteen.* The difficulty arising from the fact that
Matthew and Luke give quite different genealogies of Jesus, was
the subject of learned investigations, even in the earliest times of
the church ; *Julius Africanus*, in particular, gave his attention to
it (*Euseb.* H. E. i. 7.) Three hypotheses † for the solution of this
difficulty have been framed with great acuteness : 1. The supposition of a levirate marriage (Deut. xxv. 6) ; in which case, however, to explain all, we must farther suppose, that the two brothers,
who had successively the same wife, were not properly brothers, but
step-brothers, sons of the same mother by different fathers ; because, if they had been by one father, the genealogy would have
been the same. This hypothesis was first propounded by *Julius
Africanus* (*ut supra*). Agreeably to it, the descent would be as
follows :

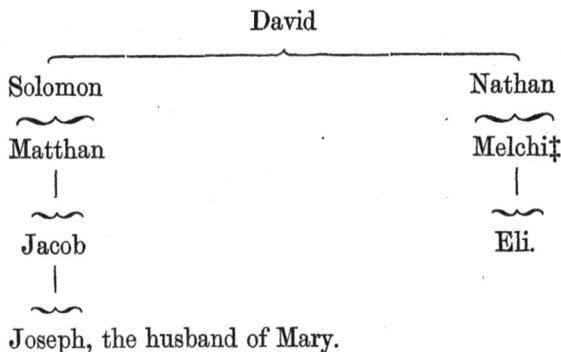

David

Solomon   Nathan

Matthan   Melchi‡

Jacob   Eli.

Joseph, the husband of Mary.

This hypothesis explains the difference ; yet, in the first place,
the supposition that Jacob and Eli had the same wife, one after the
other, and were, moreover, step-brothers, is somewhat harsh ; further, it cannot be demonstrated with certainty that it was the practice to take the *name* of the real father in the case of obligatory
marriages ; and lastly, both genealogies would be those of Joseph,
which appears unsuitable on this account, that Jesus, according to
the flesh, was descended from David and Abraham, not through
Joseph, but through Mary. That step-brothers, and still more distant relations, were also bound to fulfil the levirate marriage, is

* Luke has, on the other side, also between David and Salathiel twenty members;
Matthew only fourteen.—[E.
† Other attempts at explaining this difficulty are to be found in *Wolf's* Curæ, and
Köcher's Analecta, but they are futile. Consult also *Surenhusius'* βίβλος καταλλαγῆς,
page 322, *seqq.*
‡ *Julius Africanus* omits Matthan and Levi, and appears, therefore, to have had an-
other reading before him, or to have transposed the names. The name, however, makes
no difference in the hypothesis.

shewn by *J. D. Michaelis*, in his Commentaries on the Laws of
Moses (Smith's translation).   2. The assumption that Mary was
an heiress (ἐπίκληρος,) in which case she would be obliged to marry
within her own tribe. (Numb. xxxvi. 5–8). The husband of an
heiress was at the same time obliged to enter himself in the family
of his wife, and so came to have as it were two fathers. In this way
one of the genealogies would indeed be that of Mary ; but the latter
circumstance—viz., the being received into the wife's family, and
the taking the name of the father-in-law on the part of those who
married heiresses, which in this case is all-important, is precisely
what is uncertain ; at least Nehemiah vii. 63 is not sufficient to establish it.* This hypothesis, however, though it does not suffice for
solving the difficulty, is very suitable for explaining Mary's journey
to Bethlehem. (Luke ii. 4.) In general it seems well suited to the
course of development in David's family, that that line of it from
which the Messiah was to proceed, should close with an heiress, who
ended it in giving birth to the promised everlasting heir of the
throne of David. We may, therefore, combine the opinion, that
Mary was an heiress, with (3) the third hypothesis, according to
which the genealogy of Mary is given by Luke, that of Joseph by
Matthew. Thus Jesus is shewn, as well on the father's as the
mother's side, to be of the house of David. ' On the mother's side
the descent had a real significance, on the father's an ostensible one.
For, as Jesus passed in the eyes of the world for the son of Joseph
(see note on Matth. xiii. 55), the Jews acknowledged him in this
relation also as of the house of David ; and on this account not a
doubt of his descent from David is ever uttered by his enemies.
Agreeably to this hypothesis, Eli (Luke iii. 23) would be the father
of Mary (with which the Jewish tradition coincides, see *Lightfoot,
ad loc.*) ; and when Joseph is called his son, " *son*" (υἱός) is here to
be taken in the sense of " son-in-law," as Ruth i. 11, 12, and elsewhere. Genealogical tables are, indeed, unusual in the case of women, but for heiresses they *must* necessarily exist ; and at all events
the father of Mary had assuredly his genealogy. The actual descent
of Jesus from David through Mary, is, moreover, by no means to be
regarded as a merely external fact, intended to fulfil the prophecies.
The prophecy itself that the Messiah should descend from Abraham
and David, is rather to be viewed as having a deeper origin. The
appearance of the Messiah among mankind, presupposes conditions and preparations ; and these not merely *negative*, inasmuch as their need of salvation had to be awakened in the minds
of men, but *positive*, in so far as the Messiah, the bloom and flower
of humanity, must stand in relation to the root from which he
sprang. We must look upon the incarnation of Christ as a fact, for

---

* See *J. D. Michaelis*' Commentaries on the Laws of Moses (Smith's translation).

which preparation was made, by a vein of nobler life flowing through the whole line of our Lord's ancestors. The virgin chosen to be the mother of the Messiah could not spring suddenly from the bosom of a sinful race. Although not without sin, she was the purest of that race. And that she was such, was in consequence of her election by grace—her being born of the holiest family of mankind. As in the development of the human race we observe certain families growing in sin and wickedness, so we find families, also, in which the noblest germs of life are possessed and cherished from generation to generation. Of course, it is not to be understood that families which have been, through grace, specially shielded from the corruption of sin, had no need of salvation ;—(this is to be viewed as absolutely and equally necessary for all men)—but as more ready to receive salvation, since, as being of the truth, they more certainly hear God's call.

In the following enumeration of the links of the genealogy, Matthew omits several, e. g., ver. 8, between Joram and Josias. (See 1 Chron. iii. 11 ; 2 Chron. xxi. 17.) Luke, on the contrary, inserts Cainan in iii. 36, whom the Hebrew text does not mention. Doubtless, this name is derived from the LXX., which Luke, as a Hellenist, used for the most part. The LXX. translators may have received it from tradition. (Respecting such variations of the LXX. from the original Hebrew, as have been admitted into the New Testament, see the remarks on Luke iv. 18.)

Ver. 2.—Throughout the whole genealogical table, Luke appears in the character of a relater merely, while Matthew adds reflections ; he divides the list into classes, and adds special observations. Of Judah he remarks that he had brothers ; probably because the patriarchs of Israel—the twelve sons of Jacob—appeared to call for special notice. The same remark is made of Jechonias (ver. 11) ; in which passage, however, the term ἀδελφοί, brethren, must be taken in a wider sense, like אָח (Gen. xiii. 8) of father's brothers, as Jechonias had no actual brothers. (1 Chron. iii. 15, 16.)

Ver. 3.—It is also peculiar to the genealogy in Matthew, that it several times mentions women—a circumstance which did occur in Jewish genealogies, if any thing remarkable gave them special interest. (See Surenhusii, βιβλ. καταλλ. p. 110.) Tamar (Gen. xxxviii.), Rahab (Josh. ii.), Ruth, Bathsheba, are named by Matthew. Tamar, Rahab,* and Bathsheba, are liable to objection on account of their conduct ; Ruth, as a heathen (Moabitess). That they were nevertheless counted worthy to be among the ancestors of the Mes-

---

* Whether it is Rahab the harlot, that is meant, might seem uncertain, because of the chronology; she comes too near to Obed and Jesse, David's ancestors; yet the expression ἡ Ῥαχάβ (with the article) plainly points to the well-known Rahab mentioned in Josh. ii. Perhaps Matthew has omitted some links.

siah, must have imparted to them a very special and peculiar significance. Matthew makes this circumstance still more prominent by
the designation ἐκ τῆς τοῦ Οὐρίου, *from her who had belonged to
Uriah*, in order to point to the wondrous dealings of God's grace in
arranging the Messiah's lineage. As examples of the election of
grace, of renovation by faith and repentance, and of being received
out of heathen families among the people of God, the persons named
are noticed even by the Rabbins. (See *Wetstein's* New Test., on
ver. 3 compared with Heb. xi. 31.) But for Matthew's intention to
point out these leadings of the divine hand he would have mentioned
in preference the celebrated names of Sarah, Rebecca, Leah, in the
genealogy of the Messiah.

Ver. 6.—David, as a principal person, as it were a knot in the
genealogical tree of the Messiah, is called emphatically ὁ βασιλεύς,
the king, as the type of the Messianic king (Ezek. xxxvii. 24, and
elsewhere). A similar break is made afterwards (ver. 11), by the
μετοικεσία Βαβυλῶνος, *removal to Babylon*, = αἰχμαλωσία, *captivity.*
The LXX. use μετοικεσία for הָלֹה (Ezek. xxxiii. 21).

Ver. 16.—The term ἀνήρ, *man, husband*, in this verse, answers
to *sponsus* (v. 19); according to the Jewish law, the bridegroom
was already regarded as the possessor of the bride. (Gen. xxix. 21;
Deut. xxii. 23, 24.) Matthew expresses himself very carefully ; ἐξ
ἧς ἐγεννήθη Ἰησοῦς, *from whom was born Jesus*, in order to mark
the supernatural character of the generation of Christ ; γεννᾶν is
used as equivalent to τίκτειν (Luke i. 13). In the phrase Ἰησοῦς ὁ
λεγόμενος Χριστός, *Jesus who is called Christ*, Χριστός appears evidently as the official name. With the exception of this phrase,
Matthew almost always uses ὁ Ἰησοῦς, or ὁ Χριστός. It was only
gradually that, in the usage of the church, the name expressive of
the human character of the Saviour grew up into so close a connexion with his official name, that the two have formed a whole, as
is particularly the case in the Apostle Paul's writings. (See *Gersdorf's* Beiträge zur Sprachcharacteristik, S. 38, ff., 272, ff.) The
λέγεσθαι, in the phrase under remark, like καλεῖσθαι = נִקְרָא (on which
see comment. on Luke i. 32), has, in this place, the pregnant meaning, " to be called, and really to be." In the opposite sense, " to
be called, without being," the expression occurs in Ephes. ii. 11,
and Matth. xxvii. 17. It has frequently no emphasis, either the
one way or the other, as in Matth. xxvi. 14, Mark xv. 7.

Ver. 17—Matthew closes his genealogical account with a review
of the different divisions which may be made in the generations
from Abraham to Christ. He notices three of fourteen generations each,[*] which may, however, be reckoned in more than one

---

* Whether the number fourteen has a reference to the name David, the Hebrew letters of which, reckoned according to the Jewish custom, make up the number fourteen,

way. That reckoning appears the most convenient, according to which David and Josiah are reckoned twice,* (at the close of one and the beginning of another division), and Jesus omitted. If the person of Jesus is to be reckoned as forming the close of the third division, David only ought to be reckoned twice. The former plan appears to me, however, preferable. It is fitting not to include Jesus himself in the generations, as we ordinarily refrain from doing in reckoning a person's ancestry. Besides, since Matthew, as was remarked, has omitted some links, it cannot be his intention to lay stress on the number fourteen, nor ought this arrangement to be regarded as a mere help for the memory. Rather it is his purpose, by means of the equal number, to point out the inward symmetry and regularity of the historical development.† As the whole history of the world moves forward in its development by measured periods, and as, in general, every greater or lesser whole, in the wide creation of God, has its inward gradations ot progress, through which it advances to its completion, so there is a regularity in the development of that family also, as it were the inmost life-pulse of mankind, from which the Messiah was to come. *Bengel* recognized correctly this fundamental view (in his Gnomon on the passage) ; but the particulars which he adds, as well as his whole chronological system, which he brings into connexion with it, appear to me untenable. (Compare further remarks on this subject in the Commentary on the Revelation of John.)

We must notice too the extraordinary phenomenon of a family table of three times fourteen generations, and seventy-five ancestors extending through 2000 or 4000 years, with which the Evangelists open the life of Christ. The possibility of exhibiting such a genealogical table, always proceeding in the directest line of descent from father to son, and that, too, of a family long living in the deepest obscurity, would be inexplicable (since even the distin-

it might be difficult to decide. Such a supposition might, however, agree well enough with the complexion of Matthew's whole description. The number fourteen is moreover to be regarded as twice seven—a number which the Scriptures treat as a sacred one. The three times fourteen thus become six times seven, and the seventh seven opens with the person of Christ.

* Similar modes of reckoning are met with in other cases. A simple Nazarite vow lasted thirty days, a double one not sixty but only fifty-nine days, because the day in the middle was reckoned twice. The Germans call a week eight days, "acht Tage," but two weeks, fourteen days, "vierzehn Tage;" while the French call two weeks, "quinze jours."

† The omission of some links may be ascribed to the authors of the genealogy in Joseph's family. Matthew took it as he found it, without making any alteration in it, and, of course, his remarks upon it could only apply to its existing form. The want of some of the links can have no influence on the truth of the remarks themselves, inasmuch as the fundamental thought, that all things unfold themselves in God's world by measure and number, applies no less to the complete genealogy than to the shortened one.

guished families, whose genealogies attract the eyes of millions, cannot trace their pedigree a thousand years, and none of them, in a direct line), unless there had been constantly given to the members of this line a clue by which they were enabled to trace themselves out in the multitude of families, into which each stock and branch was subdivided, in order to hold fast *that* member which was destined to continue the succession. This clue was the hope, that the Messiah would be born in the family of Abraham and David. The desire of beholding him, and of participating in his grace and glory, suffered not the attention to weary through a thousand years.* By divine arrangement also, from time to time, as the member that continued the succession might become doubtful, it was again plainly marked out; so that the hope of the final fulfilment was anew excited and maintained in activity up to its realization. An excellent view of the miraculous element discoverable in the construction of these genealogies, is given by *Köppen* in his book: Die Bibel ein Werk der göttlichen Weisheit (Leipzig, 1798, 2 vols. 8vo., compare B. ii., S. 199, ff.);--a new edition of this work is being prepared by Scheibel.

§ 2. THE BIRTH OF JESUS.

(Matth. i. 18–25.)

Matthew's account of the birth of Jesus is characterized by the greatest simplicity and brevity. It contains not a single chronological or topographical reference. It assumes that the persons are, in general, already known to the readers. It barely sets forth in sober narrative, without embellishment, the great fact of the supernatural birth of Jesus, points to the fulfilment therein of Old Testament prediction; and, finally, recounts the providential guidance of Joseph, in this wondrous event. We readily pass by the want of circumstantial vividness, which this part of Matthew's narrative, in common with his whole Gospel, discovers, for the sake of that sober air of genuine historical narration, which is prominent throughout; a feature which his poetical effusions render less apparent in the narrative of Luke. Those scholars, therefore, are in error, who, while opposed to the general application of the mythical interpretation to the history of Jesus, have yet thought it necessary to admit a mythical element in the history of his birth and childhood. Here, in fact, the supposition appears most strikingly inadmissible, since, if the events did not take place

---

* That the Jews of later time also bestowed great care upon their family registers, is shown by *Julius Africanus*, as quoted by *Euseb.* i. 7. *Herod* had them all sought out and burnt, so that no one should be able to prove that his family was more ancient than the king's.

just as the Evangelists record them, gross conceptions about the origin of Jesus obtrude themselves upon us. For as Christ is undeniably a historical person, and must therefore have been begotten and born, to affirm the mythical character of the Gospel-history, can only favour a view that is destructive of the notion of a Saviour—viz., that Jesus came into existence in an impure manner, since Mary was *unmarried* at the time of his conception. The alternative resorted to that Jesus might have sprung from the marriage of Mary and Joseph, is self-refuted by its unhistorical character ; for if the circumstance, that Mary was with child *before* her marriage, is to be reckoned among the myths, the circumstances that she gave birth to Jesus, and even that Jesus lived at all, may equally well be reckoned among them.

Besides, it appears, on closer consideration, that what apparently most recommends the mythical interpretation of the history of the childhood of Jesus, is rather unfavourable to it. This holds good particularly of the appeal that is made to the traditions of the birth of great men from pure virgins (παρθενογενεῖς), as of Buddha, Zoroaster, Plato, and others. Such traditions are no more opposed to the Bible history, than are analogous longings for an expected deliverer. They rather attest the thoroughly correct feeling of the noblest men among different nations, that, in the way of *natural* generation, and thus from the bosom of humanity alone, nothing can proceed answering to the ideal existing in the human spirit. They witness to the general longing and desire for such a fact—to the truth of it in some one historical manifestation. Now, as we have so sober a historical account of the supernatural conception of Jesus in a pure virgin, as that of Matthew, which with even studied plainness repels every fanciful idea ; and, as all the phenomena in the life of Jesus confirm the opinion of his supernatural birth, since there is realized in him, that ideal of all ideals, which could never proceed from sinful humanity and the power inherent in it ; there is perfect historical foundation for the conviction, that this general longing is fulfilled in the person of Jesus. *In addition* to this, the narrative of the generation of Christ by the Holy Ghost, stands in necessary connexion with his whole destination to be the physician and the Saviour of diseased humanity, since it is impossible that any one who is himself descended from the fallen race of man could have any power to heal the hurt from which they suffer. It was necessary, indeed, that he should be most closely united with men, flesh of their flesh, bone of their bone (Ephes. v. 30), yet, at the same time, without sin. For this reason, he was not begotten by any man from sinful seed, but Mary, touched by divine fire from heaven, received into her bosom the only Begotten of the Father in his assumption of humanity. If, then, we recognise in Christ not a mere manifestation, however exalted, of humanity, but an actual incarnation of the Word of God (John i. 1, 14), then the narrative of his supernatural generation, so far from astonishing us, seems for the Saviour specially natural and befitting. A Saviour conceived in sin—sprung from the sinful race of man, is a self-contradictory notion; the very idea of a Saviour requires, that in him there should be manifested something higher, something heavenly, that cannot be derived from what exists in human nature itself.* But, *lastly*, the mythical view of the history of Christ's childhood must be seen to be untenable for this reason, that Mary, the mother of Jesus, lived considerable time after the ascension. Her statements were accessible to each of the apostles—any error could immediately have been set aside by her testimony.

With respect to *the appearances of angels*, the mention of which in Matthew's narrative might be regarded as the most important point in proof of its mythical character, we must, in interpreting, chiefly keep in view, that the historian *reports as facts* the appearances of angels in this, as well as in other places of his Gospel. Entirely after the manner of the Old Testament, Matthew incorporates angelic appearances into his records, as belonging to the actual economy of human affairs; without giving the slightest hint that he himself regards them as mythical expressions for psychological processes (mere illusions of fancy, the creation of passing circumstances), or as in any other way different from what they seem. The business of the expositor extends beyond the ascertaining of the author's view only in so far as he not merely expounds, but also vindicates the result of the exposition; a duty which, in the present position of science, cannot be neglected. The following observations may suffice to meet the requirements of the present case. On the testimony of the Scriptures, we are not to conceive of the angels as separated from men by an impassable gulf; but on the contrary, as actively employed around and in men—especially in the faithful. (Heb. i. 14.) Usually, however, their service is an invisible one. The possibility of their becoming visible lies in the nature of spirit itself, whose indwelling energy involves a capacity of making itself visible. This possibility, however, according to God's mode of dealing, becomes a reality only in those cases where it subserves men's good—that is, for the pur-

---

* The opinion that we might conceive, that, as the transfer of anything sinful from Mary to Jesus was prevented, *it could just as well have been prevented if Joseph had been his father in the ordinary way*, only shifts the miracle to a different quarter, without getting rid of it. If we actually suppose such an influence of the Holy Ghost to stay the transfer of what was sinful to Jesus, that is no less a miracle than his generation by the Holy Spirit. But wherefore should we make the miracles other than it has pleased the Spirit of God to present them to us?

pose of instruction and guidance. For the appearances of angels, like other σημεῖα, are intended to give to man the assurance of his being led by God, to save him from his tendencies to error. In this consists their importance in the divine economy ; but, compared with other forms of divine communication, they are manifestly subordinate. The agency of angels has reference principally to physical existence. They are the living supports and springs of motion to the world, for which the modern mechanical view of the world has substituted what are called powers of nature. The world of morals and religion is the scene of the divine Spirit's agency. Comp. Heb. i. 7-9, and 14. On this principle we can explain why to one, an angel appears (sometimes in a dream, sometimes waking), and to another, the Lord. Caprice is inconceivable in the case ; the different forms of revelation are adapted to the condition of those to whom they are granted. Communication by dream is manifestly the lowest grade of divine revelation ; it is, as it were, one that takes place in an unconscious state ; it is the kind made to Joseph, who discloses in the Gospel narrative, no decidedly spiritual character. From the appearances of angels seen in a waking state, the form of communication rises to a revelation received through the word within, which was the usual form of receiving the higher influences in the cases of Moses and all the prophets. The revelation of Jehovah himself, or of *the* Angel κατ᾽ ἐξοχήν, appears to be the highest grade, which was granted only to the princes among the saints—an Abraham, a Jacob, a Moses, and a Paul. The church of Christ needs no longer angelic appearances, as it possesses in the Holy Ghost given to it the very source of all truth. The *form* in which angels appeared (with wings, garments, and the like) should be regarded as quite accidental, determined solely by the conditions under which the phenomenon happens to take place. Yet in him who sees the angels, the unclosing of the inward eye is an invariable pre-requisite. Celestial manifestations cannot, like the objects of the outward world, be beheld by every one with the bodily eye. Even though other persons are present, he only for whom the visitation is designed sees the angel. Thus the angels were ascending and descending upon Jesus at the very moment that he was speaking the words in John i. 51 to the apostles ; but their inward eye was still closed to the transactions of the world of spirits. Every appearance of angels, accordingly, should be conceived not merely as an outward act, but also as an inward effect in the subject who sees it. (See Numb. xxii. 31.) Lastly, Christ, the Lord, *had* no revelation,* but *was*, not merely *a*, but *the* revelation of God in human

---

* It is in appearance only that such passages as Luke xxii. 43, which speaks of an angel appearing to Christ in Gethsemane, are opposed to this thought. For that angel

nature itself; on him the angels of God ascended and descended—
i. e., he is the centre and the medium of connexion between the visible and the invisible world ; so that the entire reciprocal action of these two portions of existence is conducted and ordered by him. (See note on John i. 51).

Ver. 18.—The first narrative after the genealogy is introduced with a special title, in which Ἰησοῦ is, in all probability, a spurious addition. (See *Gersdorf, ut sup.* p. 39.) Γένεσις, as the most Hebraizing reading, (= תולדות), is preferable to γέννησις. Μαρία, also Μαριάμ, corresponds to the Hebrew מרים. (Exod. xv. 20 ; Num. xii. 1.) The anxiety of the Evangelist to represent Mary as pure and innocent, cannot fail to be noticed. In addition to μνηστευθείσης γὰρ τῆς μητρὸς αὐτοῦ, *his mother being betrothed*, he says expressly, πρὶν ἢ συνελθεῖν αὐτούς, *before they came together.* Συνελθεῖν (parallel with παραλαβεῖν, ver. 20, 25) denotes living and dwelling together as husband and wife. Εὑρίσκεσθαι is not used absolutely for εἶναι, any more than נמצא is so used ; it rather expresses " being," with the additional idea of " being recognized as such." (On ἐκ πνεύματος ἁγίου, see note on Luke i. 35.)

Ver. 19.—Matthew's account leaves the impression, that Mary did not make known her condition to Joseph. (On this point, see further the remarks on Luke ii. 39.) When he noticed it himself, he sought to put her away without a stir (λάθρα—*i. e.*, without mentioning the cause in the writing of divorcement). Ἀπολύειν denotes the formal dismissal by a written declaration. (Deut. xxiv. 1.) According to Jewish custom, Joseph treated his betrothed just as his wife ;[*] but showed himself to be δίκαιος, *just, upright.* This term cannot here, as in Luke i. 6, signify one who diligently fulfils the precepts of the law ; for, according to them, he ought to have preferred an accusation against his betrothed. (Deut. xxii. 23, ff.) But he is called kind, mild. *Chrysostom :* χρηστός, ἐπιεικής. (Concerning the significations of δίκαιος and its derivatives, compare the remarks on Rom. iii. 21.) Παραδειγματίζειν, to make a παράδειγμα, *example*, contains the idea of φανερῶσαι, *make public*, but with the accessory idea of disgrace. (Heb. vi. 6.) Thus, therefore, the father left his only-begotten Son and his mother, just as he does his people in the church, to pass through evil and through good report ! That God permitted even the appearance of having committed sin to rest upon Mary (for her pregnancy must, in any case, have appeared premature), must be regarded, in reference to Mary, as a trial

revealed nothing to him, but was concerned only with his physical exhaustion;—he appeared to him merely for the purpose of strengthening him in body.

* *Maimonides* apud Buxt. de divort. pag. 76. Femina ex quo desponsata est, licet nondum a viro cognita, est uxor viri et, si sponsus eam velit repudiare, oportet ut id faciat libello repudii.

intended to perfect her faith; but in reference to Christ, as an additional trait in the character of his humiliation : he had to appear as sent in the likeness of sinful flesh. (Rom. viii. 3.)

Ver. 20.—That this purpose, to which he thought himself compelled, should have caused a great commotion in Joseph's soul, may be supposed probable. But, from these natural processes of mind, and from any dreams or illusions of fancy which they may perhaps have produced, there is distinguished a higher influence, which was imparted to him in a dream, and which determined him in his conduct towards Mary, as narrated ver. 24, 25. Nothing in the text requires us to assume, in this angelic visitation, any thing externally visible ; as Joseph saw it in a dream, the vision was probably internal. The same God, who most expressly warns against false dreams (Jer. xxiii. 32, xxix. 8), not unfrequently directs his people by true ones (Numb. xii. 6) ; since, for the sincere, who were really concerned for the truth, and for what was well-pleasing to God, he discloses infallible criteria by which to distinguish genuine visions from false ones. Yet as these are modified by individual disposition, they can be reduced to no objective rules ; all divine directions, whether by dreams or any other communications, are dependent upon earnestness and sincerity of heart ; the insincere man seeking to force, as it were, the intimations of the divine will, always hears and sees falsely. ('Ενθυμεῖσθαι is, to revolve in the θυμός, with the exercise of the affections. [See Matth. ix. 4; Acts x. 19.] Κατ' ὄναρ occurs only in Matth. ii. 12, 13, 19, 22 ; xxvii. 19. The phrase καθ' ὕπαρ is its opposite, but does not occur in the New Testament. 'Εν αὐτῇ = ἐν τῇ κοιλίᾳ αὐτῆς, the child unborn, yet reposing in the womb of its mother, but still already existing. The preposition ἐκ, denotes the Holy Spirit to be the creative cause of the child's existence.)

Ver. 21.—The indefinite neuter γεννηθέν, offspring, is more precisely characterized as son ; the name to be given him is mentioned, and the meaning of his name, in relation to his appointed work, is set forth. A significance in names is found throughout the Scriptures. A name, according to its proper intention, should not be arbitrary, but should express the nature of him who bears it. Sin annihilates this original significancy of names, by extinguishing the capacity of ascertaining the inward essence ; in the principal characters, however, who stand as the bearers of what is noble among our race, the Spirit from above supplied this deficiency. The last words of the verse declare the great and exalted destination of this divinely-begotten one ; he is described as the σωτήρ, Saviour, (יושׁיע) of his people. The expression λαός, people, = עם stands for the Jewish people, in opposition to the ἔθνη, Gentiles, = גוים, although ἔθνος also sometimes denotes the Jewish people. (John xi. 51.) That the angel, on this occasion, regards the appointment of the Messiah only in relation to the Jewish people is on the same principle upon which Jesus himself so represents it. (See note on Matth. x. 5, 6.) The Jews had, in fact, according to the whole divine economy and plan of salvation, the first call and appointment to the σωτηρία, *salvation,* This by no means excludes its relation to the heathen ; the Saviour's people (λαός) is, in a wider sense, the whole spiritual Israel—all minds desirous of righteousness and truth, among all people, tribes, and tongues. (John x. 16.) The addition of "from their sins," is significant of the character of the promised salvation. The moral import of the redemption to be looked for through the Messiah, which, at the time of Christ, was lost among the common mass, but not among the noble-minded of the people, is here prominent, and can be denied only by such as are blinded by partiality ; for it corresponds to the expression in the parallel passage (Luke i. 77), the ἄφεσις τῶν ἁμαρτιῶν, *forgiveness of sins.* Σώσει ἀπὸ τῶν ἁμαρτιῶν, *he shall save from their sins,* denotes, as it were, their removal—*i. e.,* their extinction. To refer ἁμαρτία, *sin,* to the punishment of sin (and, indeed, to the most external, the oppression of the Romans), is incorrect, for this reason, that ἁμαρτία never does, and never can, signify the punishment of sin *without* the sin, but only *together with* it.

Ver. 22, 23.—The following are evidently not the words of the angel, but of the Evangelist, who refers his Jewish readers to the Old Testament, in order to prove to them, that what was new in the Gospel, already existed in the sacred foundations on which their faith rested. The Lord himself appears as the effective cause (ὑπό *by,* like ἐκ, *out of,* above, is used of the source, the origin) ; the prophet appears only as the intermediate organ. (Διά, as distinguished from ὑπό, denotes the instrument, by means of which something is accomplished.) But, with respect to the formula : ἵνα or ὅπως πληρωθῇ, *that it might be fulfilled,* which appears to be a standing one, particularly with Matthew, it is evident, in the first place, that the New Testament writers themselves understood it, according to the natural meaning of the words ; that is to say, πληροῦσθαι, *to be fulfilled,* in the sense of something that was promised in time past, being realized at the present time ; so that πληροῦσθαι always supposes a previous promise. The conjunction ἵνα cannot be translated *so that,* denoting a *result* (ἐκβατικῶς), but always expresses an *intention* (τελικῶς), *to the end that, in order that.* In the whole formula it is evident, that the event being *intended,* is just what is meant to be brought into notice ; and πληροῦσθαι itself necessarily leads us to this idea. We may, therefore, supply ὑπὸ τοῦ κυρίου, *by the Lord,* after τοῦτο γέγονεν, *this took place,* since that which took place must not be regarded as accidental. The formula does receive its simple grammatical explanation in those cases where interpreters consider actual Old Testament prophecies referred to ; but when such are not found, a wider sense is wont to be given to the phrase in this way : ' The result is such, that the words of the Old Testament may be suitably applied to it.' This explanation is defended on the ground, that ἵνα, *that*, is used in the New Testament to express the event (ἐκβατικῶς ;)* but from the fact that ἵνα *may* be so used, it does not follow that it *must* be so taken in *some* of the passages which contain this phrase. This expression, which appears so constantly in the New Testament, can have but one and the same sense in *all* the places where it is used. To appeal to the custom universally prevalent among the Jews, of applying passages of the Old Testament in relations quite different from those involved in their original connexion, cannot in this case be allowed ; because, in the first place, it is inconceivable that the sacred writers should have accommodated themselves to a custom so unmeaning, and so much exposed to abuse ; and then, further, even if such were the case, the meaning of the phrase, ἵνα πληρωθῇ, *that it might be fulfilled*, would not be altered, since, if the New Testament writers did follow this habit, they must have held, in connexion with it, the principle out of which it arose—viz., that the Scriptures contain endless references, and can, therefore, be applied to all possible circumstances. The Rabbi imagines it really to be so with his quotations of Scripture (nonsensical as they may be) ; and agreeably to this view of the multifarious applicability of the contents of the sacred Scriptures, he believes that he finds a real fulfilment of the Bible language where he applies it. In my opinion, therefore, it is nothing but doctrinal prejudice which gave occasion to an interpretation varying from the

* The question of the use of ἵνα is of great importance doctrinally. It comes under special notice in the subject of predestination, as well as in that of the prophecies from the Old Testament. (See observations on Matth. xiii. 14, 15 ; John xii. 39, 40.) But it is worth noticing, that to assert that ἵνα is *very frequently* used ἐκβατικῶς, tends to take away the force of many passages, no less than is done by asserting that it is *never* so used. This is the case, for instance, with John xvii. 3, where the words αὕτη ἐστὶν ἡ αἰώνιος ζωή, ἵνα γινώσκωσι θεόν, are translated by some : " vita æterna in hoc cernitur studio, ut te cognoscant." Instead of the knowledge of God itself, nothing is left for us but a mere striving after it. It appears to me that in this case also, the truth lies midway between the two, and that John, in particular, certainly does use ἵνα of the event. This Evangelist has used ὥστε once only (John iii. 16) in all his writings ; and in that instance it is after a preceding οὕτως ; ὅπως, too, occurs only in John i. 57. But it is inconceivable that John should not sometimes have wished to express the notion of mere consequence without intention. Such passages as John iv. 34 ; ix. 2 ; xv. 13 ; xvi. 7 ; xvii. 3, shews that he employed ἵνα for this purpose. It appears to me, therefore, that *Winer* (Gr. of the N. T. Idioms, § 57) goes somewhat too far when he admits the less forcible meaning of ἵνα only after verbs expressing command, desire, request ; but denies altogether that ἵνα and ὥστε are interchanged.

simple grammatical explanation. Certain passages from the Old
Testament were quoted as prophecies in the New, which in
their original connexion, it was thought impossible to regard as
such ; then, in order that it might not seem as if the New Testament writers quoted passages from the Old which did not contain
prophecies, as if they did, ἵνα πληρωθῇ, with such quotations,
was translated in the manner above named. If this difficulty be removed, there remains no occasion for a departure from the literal -
sense of the words.

But the difficulty can be removed by our acknowledging in the
Old Testament prophecies a twofold reference to a present lower
subject, and to a future higher one. With this supposition, we can
everywhere adhere to the immediate, simple, grammatical sense of
the words, and still recognize the quotations of the New Testament
as prophecies in the full sense. And it belongs to the peculiar adjustment and arrangement of the Scripture, that the life and substance of the Old Testament were intended as a mirror of the New
Testament life, and that in the person of Christ particularly, as the
representative of the New Testament, all the rays of Old Testament
ideas and institutions are concentrated as in their focus.* (Consult
the Author's dissertation : *Ein Wort über tieferen Schriftsinn,*
Königsberg, 1824. On the opposite side : *Steudel* in Bengel's
Archiv, B. iii., St. 2. Lastly, *Kleinert's* observations in Tholuck's
Literarischer Anzeiger, year 1831, No. 28.) This general character
of the old Testament shews itself in the passage here quoted from
Isa. vii. 14. The immediate, grammatical sense of the words of the
passage, necessarily requires a reference to some thing present, since
the παρθένος, *virgin,* who was to bring forth Immanuel, is represented by the prophet as a sign of King Ahaz ;—a reference to the
Messiah, born of a virgin centuries after, appears to answer no end
whatever for the immediate circumstances. It is most natural to
suppose, that by παρθένος is meant the betrothed of the prophet,
called in Isa. viii. 3, נְבִיאָה, as being his wife. (Παρθένος, equivalent
to עַלְמָה, *unmarried woman,* is indeed in itself different from בְּתוּלָה,
which necessarily denotes pure virginity ; but the word עַלְמָה, too,
may, and *must,* in this case, be taken for a pure virgin.) The pas-

* See *Hamann,* in the history of his conversion (Werke Th. i., S. 211. ff.): "I found
the unity of the divine will in the redemption by Jesus Christ, inasmuch as all history, all
miracles, all God's commands and works, tended to this centre." In Hamann's works, a
spiritual exposition, like that which the writers of the New Testament employ, may be
seen in a modern author. *Bengel* also says very truly (Gnomon ad. h. 1), "Sæpe in N.
T. allegantur vaticinia, quorum contextum prophetarum tempore non dubium est, quin
auditores eorum *ex intentione divina* interpretari debuerint de rebus jam tum præsentibus.
Eadem vero *intentio divina, longius prospiciens, sic formavit orationem, ut magis proprie
deinceps ea conveniret in tempora Messiae,* et hanc, intentionem divinam apostoli nos do-
cent, *nosque dociles habere debent.*"

sage, then, affords the natural sense, that Isaiah gives Ahaz the sign, that she who is now his betrothed, and will soon be his wife, shall bear a son, named Immanuel ; and before this son shall have come to knowledge (that is, in two or three years), his prophecies shall be fulfilled. Thus the King Ahaz had given to him a sign (אות) close at hand, and intelligible ; but, at the same time, the birth of Immanuel had its higher reference to the Messiah, by whom the prophecy was fulfilled in a far higher sense, since he was born of a virgin, and as a sign (אות) for the unbelieving world, which Ahaz represents. This agrees well with the symbolizing manner in which Isaiah named his sons throughout. He represented a whole chain of ideas and facts, which were especially important to him, from the circumstances of the times, in the names of his children, one of whom was called Shear-Jashub (Isa. vii. 3) ; the second, Maher-shalal-hash-baz (viii. 3) ; and the third, Immanuel. Thus he formed with his family, as it were, an embodied and personified circle of ideas, in which his spirit moved. Such a form of teaching is quite in agreement with the prophetic agency ; and, at the same time, Matthew was perfectly justified in referring the event of the birth of Immanuel to the birth of Christ, because that parallel was intended by the Spirit of prophecy himself.* The words of Matthew, finally, do not follow the LXX. precisely, and differ from the original,

* I have not been convinced of the untenableness of the interpretation just given to the passage Isa. vii. 14, even by the able defence of the opposite view—viz., that no inferior subject is intended by the prophet's words—set up by Hengstenberg in his Christology, vol. i., p. 307, ff. It seems to me that he has not succeeded in solving the difficulty, how the reference to the Messiah could be a sign for Ahaz. Looking at it free from prejudice, one is necessarily led to expect that Ahaz must have had something given him, which he would live to witness. It is very forced to refer the period of two or three years spoken of to the coming of the Messiah, born centuries after. At any rate, the prophecy could not then have any meaning for Ahaz. The reasons brought forward against my view, seem to me unimportant; for when Hengstenberg reminds us, that there is no likeness between the birth of Immanuel in a natural manner, and that of the Messiah in a supernatural manner, it is certainly true that Matthew lays stress on the term παρθένος, which in the prophet has not the emphasis; but such a free use of prophecies is not uncommon in the New Testament, particularly in the Epistle to the Hebrews, and is quite safe when the passage so used is a real prophecy or a type, as in this instance. In this passage the unity of the reference lies in the *name Immanuel ;* Isaiah's son had the *name,* but Christ the *essence.* He *was* God manifested, whom the former merely represented. Besides, discordant features are necessarily found in every type or symbol, for otherwise it would not be a type, but the thing itself. All prophecies of Scripture have, therefore, points of similarity enough to be *understood* by him who needs them, and who because of his need, seeks for them ; but likewise dissimilarities enough to be *misunderstood* by him who will not perceive. In the main, I agree in my view of Isaiah vii. 14, with *Umbreit's* Observations in the Studien und Kritiken, year 1830, H. iii. S. 538, ff. The late Professor *Kleinert's* hypothesis in *Tholuck's* Anzeiger, year 1832, No. 25, ff., that we should conceive the facts respecting the virgin and Immanuel as a vision which God shewed to Ahaz by the prophet, would in fact explain several circumstances, if there were but one word in the text intimating that this was the account of a vision. Without such an intimation, however, the supposition of a vision remains purely gratuitous.

also, in translating קְרָאת (*thou shalt call*, 2d pers. sing. fem.) by καλέσουσι, *they shall call.*

Ver. 24, 25.—Joseph was in every thing obedient to the divine command, believed in the purity of his wife, took her to himself, and gave the child, after his birth, the appointed name. But the Evangelist adds a remark worthy of notice, in the words, οὐκ ἐγίνωσκεν αὐτήν, ἕως οὗ ἔτεκε τὸν υἱὸν αὐτῆς τὸν πρωτότοκον, *he knew her not until she bore,* &c. It is unnecessary to prove, that in these words γινώσκειν = יָדַע, *to know,* is used of connubial connexion ; the only question is, whether the meaning of the word is, that it did not take place in Joseph's marriage at all, or merely that it did not *previous* to the birth of Jesus ? The words suggest, *at first sight,* the latter, particularly ἕως οὗ, *until,* and πρωτότοκος, *first-born.* The former appears to suppose connubial intercourse *after* the birth of Jesus ; the latter seems to say that Mary had several children. As, however, it is not probable, from the Gospel-history, that Mary had other children (see note on Matth. xiii. 55, for a more particular account), no conclusion can be drawn from the word πρωτότοκος to compel us to suppose, that afterwards connubial intercourse between Joseph and Mary took place. The term is merely equivalent to בְּכוֹר or פֶּטֶר־רֶחֶם in Hebrew, which may signify either the *first* among others, or the *only* child. בְּכוֹר is the first son, preceding the birth of any daughter : for him the mother must offer the sacrifices for the first-born, while as yet entirely ignorant whether she would have other children. (It should be particularly noticed also, that the expression is πρωτότοκος α ὐ τ ῆ ς, HER *first-born.* The term has, of course, quite a different meaning in the phrases, πρωτότοκος ἐν πολλοῖς ἀδελφοῖς, *first-born among many brethren* (Rom. viii. 29), ἐκ τῶν νεκρῶν, *from the dead* (Rev. i. 5), πάσης κτίσεως, *of every creature* (Col. i. 15). So also in Heb. i. 6, where the term stands alone. (See the Commentary on these passages.) The formula ἕως οὗ, *until,* = עַד־כִּי does not necessarily assert, that what is said not to have taken place *before* a certain time, did happen *after* it. In the Old Testament, this is proved by such passages as Gen. viii. 7, 2 Sam. vi. 23. In the New Testament, indeed, none of the passages quoted in proof are quite conclusive—*e. g.,* Matth. xxii. 44 (compared with 1 Cor. xv. 28), Matth. v. 26, xviii. 30. But it is in the very nature of the particle, that it does not necessarily affirm that what had not taken place up to a certain point of time, has taken place since. All depends on the circumstances and relations. (If we were to say, we waited till midnight, but no one came, that does not imply, that after midnight some one came ; it means, no one came at all.)* We must say, therefore, that from this passage no conclusion

---

* But to say that no one came until midnight, would naturally imply that some one came after midnight. The *moral* consideration alleged against Mary's having other children than Jesus, viz., that it was *fitting* that the Messiah should terminate his line, cannot have much weight against positive grounds. On this principle, why did Mary marry at all? Why did Providence select a virgin who was actually betrothed?—[K.

can be drawn either for the one view or the other ; Matthew merely states as fact—" Till the birth of Jesus he knew not Mary." It is evident, however, that after what he had passed through, Joseph might justly think that *his marriage* with Mary had another purpose than that of begetting children. Perhaps the words of the Evangelist are framed purposely thus, to prevent any inference that might be drawn from these events against the sanctity of marriage ; yet it still seems consonant with the nature of things, that the last female descendant of David, in the family of which the Messiah was born, closed her family with this last and eternal scion. (The opposite view is defended by *Stier*, Andeutungen für gläubiges Schriftverständniss, Th. i. S. 404, ff.)

§ 3. ARRIVAL OF THE MAGI—FLIGHT INTO EGYPT—MURDER OF THE CHILDREN—RETURN TO GALILEE.

(Matth. ii. 1–23.)

Ver. 1.—It is only in passing, and as a supplementary remark, that Matthew states that Jesus was born at Bethlehem, in the time of Herod* (that is, the Great, the son of Antipater), while he says nothing definitely of the residence of Joseph and Mary : it is hence clearly seen, that the Evangelist, in his account of Christ's life, intentionally disregards the relations of place as well as of time—a fact not unimportant in the apparent contradictions between Matthew and Luke, which are presently to be noticed. (Βηθλεέμ, *Bethlehem*, = בֵּית־לֶחֶם lay two hours,† or six Roman miles south-west of Jerusalem. The town was originally named Ephrath. [Gen. xxxv. 19, xlviii. 7.] The addition, τῆς 'Ιουδαίας, *of Judea*, is to distinguish it from another Bethlehem in Galilee, in the tribe of Zebulun, mentioned in Joshua xix. 15. As being David's birthplace, it is called simply, " City of David." See Luke ii. 4, 11.)

The most important circumstance in Matthew's eyes is, that the new-born Messiah received at once the homage of the Magi. (Μάγοι, *Magi*, is well-known to have been originally the name of the learned class among the Parsees. In Jer. xxxix. 3, the term רַב־מָג is used of the head of the College of the Magi. The Greek explanation of the word, as given in Suidas, φιλόσοφοι, φιλόθεοι *sages, devout persons*, is less correct than that which explains

---

* As Matthew gives no more definite statement as to the person of Herod, several princes of which name reigned in Palestine (see the first chronological table before the Exposition of the Acts of the Apostles), it is clear that he supposes his readers to possess some knowledge of the circumstances, which accounts for several peculiarities in his narrative.

† [*Stunde*, *hour*, is used in Germany as a measure of distance. It is something less than three English miles.]—*Tr.*

it, *great*, *excellent*, from a Persian root. [In the Persian ar-
row-headed inscriptions appears the word Maghu, Magian. See
Theod. Benfey, die Pers. Keilinschriften, Leipz. 1847, p. 89.] In
later times, the name μάγος, *Magian*, like mathematicus, Chal-
dæus, was used of all who were attached to occult science—especially of astrologers. See Acts xiii. 6.) This narrative is most
simply explained, if we regard the Magi as adherents of the Zoroas-
trian worship of light, which, even before the time of Christ, was
widely spread through western Asia. Pompey found the worship of
Mithras, a branch of the Zend religion, among the Cilician pirates.
Cf. *Plut.* vit. Pomp. cap. 37. The expression ἀπὸ ἀνατολῶν,* *from
the east*, is hence best left in the indefinite generality proper to it ;
it applies, like מִקֶּדֶם, to all that is situated east of Palestine—to
adjacent Arabia, and even to the more distant Persia. Now the
hypothesis that these Magi were Parsees, is highly probable ; first,
because there are remarkable germs of truth in the Zend system
itself—*e. g.*, the idea of a Sosiosh—an expected Saviour ; and further, because an intermixture of Jewish ideas is more easily conceivable in their case than in that of any other nation. But such
an intermixture must on this occasion be supposed, since the Persians expected their Saviour from the family of Zoroaster ; but these
Magi come to seek for the King of the Jews (ver. 2).† The circumstance, too, that a star guided the Magi, points to the pursuit of
astronomy, which was not unknown among the Parsees. With respect to the statement that about the time of the birth of Christ,
the prophecy of the appearance of a great universal monarch in
the East was spread far and wide, even among the heathen (*Suet.*
Vesp. c. 4. *Tacit.* Hist. V. 13. *Joseph.* B. J. i. 5, 5 ; vii. 31)—a proof
how great events, affecting the whole of mankind, are ushered in by
a sort of presentiment—this vague expectation can scarcely be used
in explanation of the visit of the Magi. Their faith rested clearly
on firmer props than so indefinite a rumour could supply. They
recognized in the new-born one, whom they were seeking, not merely
a ruler, but the Saviour himself—their Sosiosh. But, substantially
correct as was their knowledge, we must still beware of ascribing
sharply defined doctrinal ideas to those believing strangers.‡ The

* Ἀνατολή, *rising*, *east*, used of a quarter of the world, appears like δυσμός *setting*
west, chiefly in the plural (see Matth. viii. 11, ἀπὸ ἀνατολῶν καὶ δυσμῶν), perhaps because of the daily return of the rising and setting sun.

† These Magi might also be thought to be Jews, perhaps of the dispersed ten tribes;
but the words, Βασιλεὺς τῶν Ἰουδαίων, evidently imply that they were not Jews.

‡ That this visit of the Magians was ordered by Divine Providence, had a special
significance, and was accompanied, perhaps, or followed by the germs of a sincere faith
in them, cannot be doubted. Yet it may well be doubted whether Olshausen does not press
the narrative quite too far. Did they not commence their journey because the appearance of an unwonted star led them to believe in the birth of some royal personage; and
come to Palestine because the star overhung that land, just as it subsequently guided

early church, moreover, looked upon these Magi as the representatives of the heathen world, which, in them, offered its homage to the Lord—a rational thought, full of deep truth! Agreeably to Old Testament hints of this fact (Ps. lxviii. 30, 32 ; lxxii. 10 ; Isa. xlix. 7 ; lx. 3, 6), the Magi were early taken to be kings, and, in the legend, bore the names of Caspar, Melchior, and Balthazar. It was an easy step for the advocates of myths in the New Testament, to view this occurrence of the appearance of the Magi, before the new-born Redeemer, as a philosophical myth, without any historical foundation whatever, by which tradition intended to express the idea awakened by the passages of the Old Testament just referred to, that the Messiah would exercise a universal influence, extending beyond the limits of the Jewish people.* But it is at variance with this view that Matthew is the Evangelist in whom this universal character of Christ's mission is least prominent. As related by contemporaries, this narrative if destitute of historical truth, could be nothing but gross deception.

Ver. 2.—The words which the family memoirs here employed by Matthew attribute to the Magi, indicate a knowledge of the special relation in which the new-born one stood to the Jewish people. The "King of the Jews" is not a king who rules over the Jews *alone*— the Magi represent their own subjection under his (spiritual) power by their symbolical action—but a King, who springs from the Jews, and from them, as a centre, extends his kingdom. Thus it expresses properly the true idea, "salvation is of the Jews" (John iv. 22). As the sure sign of his birth, they mention the sight of *his* star (εἴδομεν αὐτοῦ τὸν ἀστέρα). They knew, therefore, that a heavenly sign would stand connected with the earthly appearance of this (spiritual) king. That great events on earth had their corresponding appearances in the heavens, which shewed themselves principally in stars, was a very general opinion of antiquity (see, for instance, *Justin.* Hist. xxxvii. 2. *Sueton.* vit. Cæs. c. 88), and not without truth, though it commonly served the purposes of superstition.* In the life of the Saviour, the surmise expressed in this opinion attained to reality and truth. In what this ἀστὴρ Βασιλέως, *king's*

them to Bethlehem and the very house? The narrative implies surely no *spiritual* conception of the new-born king.—K.

* The advocates of the mythical view are quite arbitrary in using sometimes this and sometimes that circumstance, to defend their view, without regarding internal consistency. At one time, they make the apostles imagine that the mission of the Messiah was to be confined to the people of Israel; and yet, on the other hand, they make them invent myths, for the purpose of shewing his universal mission.

† In the tract, Yalkut Rubeni, it is said: "Qua hora natus est Abrahamus stetit sidus quoddam in oriente, et deglutivit quatuor astra, quæ erant in quatuor cœli plagis." (See *Bertholdti* Christol. Jud. page 55.) The words evidently describe a conjunction of planets, according to the sensible impression. Four stars united and formed a whole, so that one great star seemed to have swallowed the four little ones.

star, consisted, is hardly to be ascertained with certainty. The idea of a meteoric appearance is the most improbable ; it could not find any support but in ver. 9, where it is said, "the star *stood* over where the young child was." *Chalcidius*, the Platonist (Opp. Hippoliti eded. J. A. Fabricius, page 325), understood a comet to be meant by the star. The learned Bishop Münter, of Copenhagen, takes it to be a constellation, and refers to the conjunction of planets which took place in the year 1825. (See the Dissertations of the Academy of Sciences at Copenhagen, for the year 1820.) It is most probable to me that a particular star is intended,[*] because of the parallel between this passage and Matth. xxiv. 30, where, in like manner, a sign of the Son of Man in heaven is foretold, with reference to Christ's second coming ; just as in Numb. xxiv. 17, it is held up as a prophecy of the first coming of our Lord. (In order to apply this passage to himself, the well-known false Messiah, took the name of Barkochba—*i. e.*, son of the star.)

Ver. 3, 4.—This intelligence was a message of terror to the king and the city of Jerusalem (in its representatives—the ecclesiastical rulers of the Jews); partly, because in general what is great and mighty when it comes into our immediate neighbourhood, seizes us with a feeling akin to terror, (for we cannot suppose that all the chief priests and scribes would be terrified at the appearance of the Messiah, on account of their sins); partly, because conscience announced to Herod, now grown grey in sin, as well as to the priestly caste, from selfishness (at least in the majority) alive only to their own interest, that with the appearance of the King of Righteousness, their kingdom of iniquity was drawing near its end. From the external character which the expectations of a Messiah had acquired among the Jews, it is more than probable that, with most of those who heard of the appearance of a King of the Jews, political fears or hopes would be excited. Only we must not forget to notice, that the correct view of the spiritual character of the Messiah had main-

[*] *Ideler*, who follows the Abbot Sanclemente, so celebrated as a chronologer, has made me doubt whether the star ought not still to be regarded as a conjunction of planets. The above-mentioned scholars employ their view of it to fix the chronology of the year of Christ's birth, and shew that, six years before the Christian era, a most remarkable conjunction of all the chief planets in our system did take place. Now, as the planets, according to the latest and most exact calculations, were sometimes close together, at others, farther off from each other ; so that sometimes the star seemed to be there, and then, at others, to disappear—all which agrees well with Matthew's narrative—I am inclined to think this hypothesis very probable. In addition to this, according to Jewish tradition—*e. g.*, of Abarbanel (in his Commentary on Daniel), such conjunctions are said to have happened at the birth of Moses also, and of other men of note in the kingdom of God. See *Ideler's* Handbuch der Chronologie, Th. ii., S. 410, ff., and in the *Lehrbuch*, S. 428, where there is a new calculation by *Encke*. *Kepler* already held the same opinion, only, from his calculation not being quite correct, he fixed the date of conjunction somewhat too late. *Ignatius* (epist. ad Ephes. c. 19) describes the star as a remarkable one, surpassing all others in the splendour of its light.

tained itself in the small circles of true believers (see note on Luke
i. 76), and that by them outward changes were regarded but as the
consequence of his spiritual influence.

" By the ἀρχιερεῖς, *chief priests*, are here meant, not only the
high priests [כֹּהֵן הַגָּדוֹל] properly so called—that is, the one in office,
and those who had before passed through it, but also the heads of
the twenty-four classes (courses) of priests. [See note on Luke i. 5.]
Since these heads, as such, were members of the Sanhedrim, every member of the Sanhedrim was also called ἀρχιερεύς chief-priest, [John xii.
10]. The γραμματεῖς, = סֹפְרִים, *scribes*, include all who were skilled
in the law, like νομικός, *lawyer*, νομοδιδάσκαλος, *teacher*, *of the law* ;
so that every " chief-priest" was a " scribe," but not *vice versâ*.

Like the Magi (ver. 2), the king (ver. 4) inquires only for the
birth-*place* (ποῦ γεννᾶται) of the new king.   The birth itself appears
to all indubitably certain, which indicates a general expectation of
the Messiah.   The present (γεννᾶται, *is born*), does not require to be
taken as a future ; this tense is rather used in relation to the prophecies of Scripture, by which the scribes were to decide ; so that the
meaning is—Where is the king (of whom the prophets speak) to be
born ? which leaves it undecided whether he be already born, as the
Magi declared (ποῦ ἐστιν ὁ τεχθεὶς βασιλεύς, ver. 2), or is yet to be born.

Ver. 5, 6.—The learned Jews quite correctly assign Bethlehem
as the birthplace of the Messiah, according to Micah v. 2, in which
remarkable prophecy, acknowledged as such by most expositors, so
minute, and so literally fulfilled, the inconsiderable town (hence
called κώμη, *village*, in John vii. 42) is described as the birthplace of
the Messiah, and its spiritual glory is contrasted with its worldly lowliness.   In the quotation, the Evangelist follows neither the Hebrew
text nor the LXX. ; he quotes freely from memory.[*]   The *meiosis*,
which appears in the words οὐδαμῶς ἐλαχίστη εἶ, *art by no means
least*, is not contained either in the original or the translation of the
LXX.   Still the variation is purely formal.   Matthew gives merely
the thought of the prophet, which is simply this, that Bethlehem,
notwithstanding its mean exterior, is highly honoured.

(The words γῆ 'Ιούδα, *land of Judah*, added by Matthew himself, refer probably to the tribe of Judah, of which, according to Gen.
xlix. 10, the Messiah was to be born.   The γῆ, *land*, is put by *synecdoche* for πόλις, *city*, as *e. g.*, in Jerem. xxix. 7, עִיר is translated γῆ
by the LXX. [See Matth. x. 15 ; xi. 24 ; xiv. 34.]—Instead of
ἐν τοῖς ἡγεμόσιν, *among the rulers*, as in Matthew, the LXX. have
ἐν χιλιάσιν, *among the thousands*, after the Hebrew בְּאַלְפֵי.   The

---

[*] *Jerome* observes strangely on the passage: " Arbitror Matthæum volentem arguere
scribarum et sacerdotum negligentiam sic etiam posuisse (sc. verba prophetæ) uti ab eis dic-
tum est."—*i. e.*, "I think that Matthew, wishing to expose the carelessness of the priests
and scribes, gave the words of the prophet as used by them." But in that case Matthew
must, in other places, have laid himself open to the charge of the same " negligentia."

Jewish people were divided into families [אֲלָפִים, Judges vi. 15], over
which heads [שָׂרֵי אֲלָפִים, ἡγεμόνες, Ex. xviii, 21; Numb. i. 16] presided.
The heads of families are, therefore, in Matthew put for the families
themselves, and these again for the chief towns in which they were
settled.)

As the characteristic of him who was to be looked for from
Bethlehem (יָצָא, ἐξέρχεσθαι in the sense of "being born"), the Evangelist in his mode of applying the Old Testament quotation, marks
prominently his dominion over the people of Israel. The terms in
which that dominion is described appear chosen purposely to signify its mild and gracious character. ('Ηγούμενος, leader, = מוֹשֵׁל,
governor, expresses rather the idea of guiding to an object, than
of laying down law and restraining by force ; the additional clause
ποιμανεῖ τὸν λαόν μου, shall rule, be a shepherd to, my people,
which is wanting in the Hebrew text, is perhaps inserted from 2
Sam. v. 2, another prophetic passage. The ideas of governing and
tending are closely related, and are often interchanged ; yet ποιμαίνειν,
to tend as a shepherd, gives greater prominence to the ideal character of the true ruler, who has the good of his subjects at heart,
than βασιλεύειν, to reign. The special relation of this shepherd to
Israel (λαός = עַם, people, the opposite of גּוֹיִם nations), is to be regarded partly as again expressive of the view most readily suggested of the influence of the Messiah (see notes on Matth. i. 21 ; x. 6 ;
xv. 24), and partly as inclusive of its further extension to the whole
spiritual Israel, scattered among all nations. (See note on Matth.
viii. 11 ; Rom. ii. 28, 29.)

Ver. 7.—In order to smother all political excitement, the suspicious tyrant kept the arrival of the Magi, and the purpose of their
journey a secret—using them, as he imagined, for his own ends.
After having ascertained from his doctors the place of the birth, he
tried to discover the time likewise. This he connected with the appearance of the star (ἠκρίβωσε τὸν χρόνον τοῦ φαινομένου ἀστέρος), but
whether from the hints of the Magi or not, is uncertain. From ver.
16, therefore, we might conclude that the star had already been seen
some time—perhaps, since the time of the conception of Jesus.
('Ακριβόω, see ver. 16, = ἀκριβῶς ἐξετάζω, ver. 8.)

Ver. 8, 9.—By his outward smoothness Herod hoped the more
surely to deceive the simple men, and induce them to return to him;
but God preserved them and the young child from his malice.
(Πορεύεσθαι, to go, is used certainly according to the analogy of the
Hebrew הָלַךְ, but is not redundant, as the inquiry in this case involved a journey.) The relation of the travelling wise men to the
star, as stated in ver. 9, is not clear. First of all, with respect to
προῆγεν αὐτούς, preceded, led them on, it is not necessary to conclude thence that the star had disappeared, and then re-appeared.

The matter may be easily imagined thus—the star, which they had seen rise in the east (ἐν τῇ ἀνατολῇ, ver. 2) they discovered, having in its course changed its position, in the direction which they were to pursue from Jerusalem to Bethlehem. It continued, therefore, to precede them as a guiding star. (Προάγειν) is taken in its proper signification.*) But what follows is more difficult— ἐλθὼν ἔστη ἐπάνω οὗ (sc. τόπου) ἦν τὸ παιδίον, it came and stood over, etc., where mention is made of the star moving and arriving at a destined point. Now it is not easy to see how a star in the heavens, whether a comet or a constellation, could even apparently rest over a house. A fiery appearance in the air would more easily account for this, were it at all probable that any thing of that sort could be designated by the term ἀστήρ, star. The whole of Matthew's description evidently indicates a star that shone for a considerable time. It is simplest to take the expression, ἐλθὼν ἔστη, it came and stood, as the natural conception of their childlike feeling; so that the usual mode of inquiry after the child Jesus was not meant to be excluded, while the result, as well as the beginning, of the journey is still ascribed to the heavenly guide.†

Ver. 10, 11.—The remark again made, that the Magi saw the star (Ἰδόντες τὸν ἀστέρα), is not by any means to be referred to what precedes, so that Ἰδόντες, seeing, would be taken for a pluperfect. It is better to refer the expression to the ἔστη, stood, before men-tioned, so that the view of the star, so to speak, terminating its office, filled them with a peculiarly joyful surprise. (Ἐχάρησαν χαράν, rejoiced with joy, is a familiar Hebraism [see 1 Sam. iv. 5] ; some-thing analogous to which is found in all languages. The periphrasis of the superlative with σφόδρα, exceedingly, [מְאֹד], is also a well-known Hebraism.] In the description of the visit of the Magi, Mary only, the mother of the child, is mentioned. Joseph recedes quite into the back-ground throughout the whole Gospel-history, and pre-sents no perceptible spiritual character. (The reading εἶδον, saw, is every way preferable to the εὗρον, found, of the Textus Receptus.) Two things are distinctly noticed in the actions of the Magi ; first, the προσκυνεῖν, pay homage, worship, then the presenting of their gifts. We may imagine both included in one in this way, that they

---

* *Ideler* (*ut sup.*) explains this of the approach, or dispersion of the planets, which seemed, while in conjunction, to form one large star.

† If we take literally the preceding account, first that the star guided them to Pales-tine, and then to Bethlehem, what insuperable difficulty in supposing that it indicated the house? It was evidently an extraordinary, probably a miraculous phenomenon, and there seems no reason for receiving one part of the narrative, and staggering at another. The birth of Jesus as recorded both by Matthew and Luke is signalized by many miracles: and assuredly the *moral significance* of this transaction, as homage rendered by the Heathen world through its representatives to the new-born King of the world, forms quite as fitting an occasion for a miracle as the announcement to an humble company of Jewish shepherds.—K.

desired to testify their dependence in the presentation itself. The action was to be προσφορά, an *offering*, a solemn recognition of the superior character of the new-born one, as also the prophecy in Isaiah lx. 6, intimates. Προσκυνῆσαι, to *pay homage*, therefore, answering to the Hebrew הִשְׁתַּחֲוָה, is no proof, so far as the words go, of the view entertained by the Magi of the young child's dignity. The word often denotes nothing more than the well-known oriental form of political homage. Still the connexion of the narrative makes it certain, that the Magi ascribed a spiritual character to the child ; and their homage, combined with the ceremony of the προσφορά, *offering*, acquires a more spiritual meaning. Only we must not, as before observed, by any means ascribe to the Magi any doctrinal ideas of the divinity of Jesus ; but only a dim conception of the divine power *accompanying* and resting *on* him. We may say, they worshipped God, who had made this child for salvation to them also, but not the child.

Finally, as regards the gifts presented to the child (and his mother), we are not at liberty to conclude from the fact of their being Arabian products, that the Magi came from Arabia ; the articles were common throughout the east, as being necessary to their worship, for gold also was among the gifts usually presented to the gods. The idea of many expositors, that these valuable presents must needs be brought to Mary in her poverty, to aid her journey into Egypt (ver. 13), may not be altogether inadmissible ; the Gospel-history shows that, in after life also, the Saviour committed himself in reference to his bodily support, to the love of his friends. (See note on Luke viii. 3.) (The term θησαυρός *treasure*, signifies, like אוֹצָר, Deut. xxviii. 12, " vessel," " place of keeping ;" the idea of " what is kept"—" costly" is the derived one. Λίβανος = לְבֹנָה, signifies " incense," the produce of a balsamic plant of Arabia. In the Old Testament the term is found very frequently, because incense is so often mentioned in connexion with the sacrifices ; in the New it occurs only once more—viz., in Rev. xviii. 13. Σμύρνα = מֹר, *myrrh*, is a similar product, obtained from a tree like the acacia. [Ex. xxx. 23 ; Psalm xlv. 8.] Incense and myrrh were also used medicinally by the ancients ; but such a use of the presents is here totally inadmissible. On the history of the Magi in general see *Kleuker's* Bibl. Sympathieen, S. 36, ff.; and *Hamann's* Kreuzzüge des Philologen, Werke, Th. ii., S. 135, ff.)

Ver. 12.—As above, so here also, we should observe that the thoughts of the Magi, produced within them by natural reflection on the circumstances, must not be confounded with the higher impulse, which induced their determination not to return to Herod. (Χρηματίζειν signifies, in profane authors, " to manage public affairs"—" to give answers and commands ;" χρηματίζεσθαι, " to receive commands."

In the Hellenistic Greek, the term appears in the same signification, but with reference to divine transactions ; χρηματίζειν, "to give divine commands," Heb. xii. 25 ; χρηματίζεσθαι, "to receive divine commands." So in the New Testament, ver. 22 of this chapter, and elsewhere ; and in the Old, in Jer. xxvi. 2 ; xxix. 18. Lastly, it means, also, merely "to call" [Acts xi. 26 ; Rom. vii. 3], a meaning quite common in profane writers.)

Ver. 13, 14.—As the Saviour, after he had attained to the full consciousness of divinity (Gottesbewusstseyn), did and said nothing of himself, but always at the instance of the Father (John viii. 28), so the divine agency prevailed among the circle that surrounded him during his infancy, and before this consciousness was yet fully developed. The history of Jesus, even the child Jesus, is a divine history. By divine impulse, therefore, Joseph brings the holy child with his mother to Egypt.* (On the appearance of the angel "in a dream," [κατ' ὄναρ,] see i. 20. Ver. 13, ἴσθι, be, is imperative from εἰμί, and not to be confounded with a similar form from οἶδα. Εἶναι is to be taken here, as הָיָה is also used, in the sense of "being continuously"—i. e., "remaining." "Till I shall tell thee" intimates another appearance to be looked for. The whole narrative of the flight indicates haste and secrecy [νυκτός, by night, ver. 14] in their removal. The expression, τὸ παιδίον καὶ τὴν μητέρα αὐτοῦ, the child and its mother, delicately intimates that Joseph was only in the place of a father.) Tradition names Matarea as the place where Jesus is said to have remained with Mary in Egypt. The temple of Onias (at Leontopolis) stood in the neighbourhood—a circumstance which made many Jews resort thither.

Ver. 15.—The observation, that Jesus remained with his mother in Egypt till the death of Herod, is, as a chronological date, not unimportant, since the death of Herod, and the beginning of Archelaus's reign (ver. 22), can be accurately determined. True, the date is not void of uncertainty from the circumstance, that the Evangelist does not remark, either how old the child Jesus was at the time his mother fled with him into Egypt, or how long he was there ; nor do the passages, Luke iii. 1, 23, remove the uncertainty. Yet thus much is certain from this passage, that Jesus must have been born before the death of Herod ; and agreeably to this fact, the vulgar Christian era is at least three years too late. (See Paulus in his Commentary on the passage.) The investigations of Sanclemente and Ideler, as was observed, place the birth of Christ as long as six years before our era.—But with respect to the flight into Egypt, the Evangelist refers to an Old Testament prophecy—viz., Hosea xi. 1. The Greek words in Matthew differ from the text of

* On the flight into Egypt, see Schleiermacher's excellent sermon in the Magazine edited by him, Rhör and Schuderoff, vol. vi., Madgeburg, 1829, S. 301, ff.

the LXX. in a remarkable manner; the latter reads, ἐξ Αἰγύπτου μετεκάλεσα τὰ τέκνα αὐτοῦ sc. τοῦ Ἰσραήλ, *out of Egypt I called his sons.* In this form, the passage was wholly useless for the purpose of the quotation ; Matthew, therefore, follows the Hebrew text, which has the singular (לִבְנִי קָרָאתִי.) We see, hence, that in the Greek text of this Gospel, Matthew treats the quotation with an independence which we should not look for in an ordinary translator. (See Introd. § 4.) In its connexion in the prophecy, the passage evidently refers to the recall of the people out of Egypt by Moses ; the people being regarded as one man, are called God's son—God's first-born. (Ex iv. 22 ; Jer. xxxi. 9.) This passage, however, the Evangelist regards in so far a prophecy, as Israel after the flesh is spiritually represented in the person of Christ. The fortunes of the earthly Israel are a type of the fortunes of the Messiah, in whom Israel is first found in his true essence. (See 1 Cor. x. 1, ff. ; Gal. iii. 28.) If, on the principle that every author is to be explained by himself, we view this idea as one that was familiar to the New Testament writers, quite apart from its intrinsic and eternal truth, we obtain at least the advantage of being able to proceed more simply and naturally in the exposition.

Ver. 16.—The lengthened absence of the Magi now rouses the wrath of the tyrant Herod. He sees that he is deceived, and hopes, by means of a revolting barbarity, to destroy the dangerous child. To be certain of not missing his aim, he causes all the children in Bethlehem under two years of age to be killed.

(Ἐμπαίζειν means, first, "to deride," "to jeer at;" then, to "deceive," "to beguile," since deceiving often involves derision. Θυμοῦσθαι = חָרָה, *to burn with rage,* does not occur elsewhere. The immediate neighbourhood of the town, the "borders" [ὅρια = גְּבוּלִים, *suburbs, precincts*], were included in Herod's cruel order.)

The relation in which this note of time stands to the account of the Magi (ver. 7), makes it probable that the star appeared before the birth of Jesus, and that the Magi did not arrive immediately after his birth (see note on Luke ii. 40); in which case Herod might think it necessary, in order to be sure, to extend the limit to within a little of two years. (Διετής, *bimus, two-year old; ἀπὸ διετοῦς* stands for διετῶν, from the two-year old children downwards.) The fact of the murder of the children at Bethlehem has been doubted, because neither Josephus nor any other historian makes mention of it ;[*] and further, because it is a cruelty scarcely conceivable even for a Herod, and that too with no sufficient motive, as simpler means for accomplishing the removal of the child would have suggested themselves to

---

[*] *Macrobius* (Saturn, ii. 4) mentions the occurrence, but mixes it up with the murder of Herod's own son—a confusion which might easily occur, as no other royal offspring could be thought of, who could have been the object of Herod's persecutions.

him. But, in the *first place*, as respects the silence of the historians on an event so unimportant in a political point of view (the only view taken by all ancient historians), as the death of some children in a small Jewish town must have seemed to them; it is the less surprising, because, according to verse 7, the whole matter was kept secret as to its real connexion. *Then*, too, the murder of a few children was lost among the atrocities of a Herod, as a drop is lost in the sea. The number of those slaughtered on this occasion has been erroneously thought to be great, and the deed itself a horrible massacre; whereas, in the nature of things, there could be but a few children under two years in a little town like Bethlehem, and these might be put out of the way without any stir. *Lastly*, the remark that the affair is without adequate motive, since Herod could easily have sent secret messengers to accompany the Magi, appears indeed to be not altogether unfounded. Yet we must consider, that we are not to transfer modern police arrangements to antiquity; and, again, that, according to the king's intention, the birth of the King of the Jews was to be kept a secret, and he thought he might repose full confidence in the Magi; and, lastly, that in the history of all times there occur unaccountable oversights, which shew that a higher hand overrules history.

Ver. 17, 18.—The Evangelist finds in this event also the fulfilment of a prophecy, Jer. xxxi. 15. The prophet's language refers, in its connexion, to the carrying away of the Israelites by way of Rama, to Babylon, by Nebuzaradan (Jer. xl. 1); and Rachel, Jacob's beloved wife, the progenitrix of Israel, is represented as weeping over this misfortune. This circumstance of the mother bewailing her unhappy children, was regarded by the Evangelist as repeated in the murder of the children at Bethlehem, and, indeed, with increased force, because it was the Messiah, in whose neighbourhood, and on whose account, this affliction happened. While, in general, the forefather of the people is mentioned, the mother is here brought forward as bewailing those who were sacrificed to save the life of the Messiah, because sympathizing sorrow for the pains of her tender charge, shews itself more naturally in the mother. The words of the quotation deviate again from the translation of the LXX., yet not so as to discover an independent construction of the original; the passage is quoted from memory.

(Φωνή, *voice*, =בּ֫קֹל is here *lamentation, cry of sorrow*. The town Rama, in the tribe of Benjamin, lay scarcely a-half day's journey from Bethlehem (Jud. xix. 2, 9, 13). It might, therefore, be put for Bethlehem itself, as, in specifying this place, it was only intended to designate the land of Palestine in general. Besides which, Rachel was buried in the neighbourhood (Gen. xxxv. 19; xlviii. 7); so that it seemed as if the ancestral mother of the nation was disturbed in her peaceful grave by the cruelty of Herod.)

Ver. 19, 20.—The return from Eygpt is again instigated by special divine admonition ; and the death of the tyrant is assigned as the determining circumstance. The words τεθνήκασι γὰρ κ. τ. λ., *for they are dead, &c.*, contain a reference to Exod. iv. 19, where nothing but the formula ἵνα πληρωθῇ, *that it might be fulfilled*, is wanting to make it completely parallel with the previous references to Old Testament passages. What was there said of Moses and his flight from Pharaoh, Matthew interprets in reference to Jesus ; so that Moses appears here as a type of him. The plural οἱ ζητοῦντες, *they that sought*, applies to Herod as the representative of all God's enemies in general. (The expression "land of Israel"—not "land of Judah"—readily suggests Galilee, which, according to verse 22, the parents of Jesus chose for their dwelling. Ζητεῖν τὴν ψυχήν, *to seek the life*, corresponds to אֶת־נֶפֶשׁ בִּקֵּשׁ.)

Ver. 21.—The time of the return of Jesus from Egypt is not indeed stated ; but, as it was an event consequent on Herod's death,* his residence there cannot have been of long continuance. This circumstance of itself, therefore, is sufficient to overthrow the hypothesis that Jesus obtained his knowledge from Egyptian philosophers, which stands, too, in absolute contradiction to the idea of a Saviour. It must have been in very early childhood that Jesus returned to Palestine, at which period the depths of Egyptian wisdom cannot have been accessible to him.

Ver. 22.—On their return, report represented Archelaus to the holy family as not less cruel than his father Herod. They chose Galilee, therefore, for their residence, where Antipas reigned. Augustus, who confirmed the testament of Herod, appointed Archelaus Ethnarch of Judea, Idumea, and Samaria ; Philip obtained Batanea and Auranitis ; Antipas, Galilee and Perea.† Archelaus held his dominion only nine years. At the expiration of that period, Augustus deposed him, banished him to Vienna (in Gaul), and made Judea a Roman province. (*Josephus*, Ant. xvii. 10, 12 ; xviii. 1.)

(Γαλιλαία = גָּלִיל, גְּלִילָה signifies, like כִּכָּר, *circuit, district*. The name in full is גְּלִיל הַגּוֹיִם, γαλιλαία ἀλλοφύλων, or γ. τῶν ἐθνῶν, *Galilee of the Gentiles*. [1 Macc. v. 15 ; Matth. iv. 15 ; Isa. ix. 1.] As in this district heathenism was much mixed with Judaism, the strict exclusive character of the Jewish people appeared in a milder form ; but for this very reason the inhabitants of Galilee were despised among the rest of the Jews. [Matth. xxvi. 69 ; John i. 46 ; vii. 52.) According to *Josephus* [de Bell. Jud. iii. 2], the district was divided

---

* On the death of Herod, see *Euseb.* H. E. i. 6, 8 ; and, in respect of the chronology, the detailed discussion in *Dr. Paulus'* Exegetisches Handbuch, i., H. i., S. 227, ff.

† On this point, see the first chronological table to the Acts of the Apostles.

into Upper and Lower Galilee ; the former bordered on Tyre and
Sidon, the latter on the Jordan and the Lake of Gennesaret.
Tiberias first, and afterwards Sephoris, was the capital of Galilee.
'Εκεῖ, *there,* is put for ἐκεῖσε, *thither,* like םָשׁ for הָמָּֽשׁ. So, often, in
the New Testament.)

Ver. 23.—In Galilee, the parents of Jesus took up their residence
in the town of Nazareth. (The preposition εἰς is to be connected with
ἐλθών, and not, therefore, to be confounded with ἐν. When ἐν is
joined with words of motion, or εἰς with words denoting rest, we are
not to suppose an interchange of particles, but rather that the idea
of previous or subsequent rest or motion is to be supplied, according
as the case requires. See *Winer's* Grammar of the New Testament,
translated by *Agnew* and *Ebbeke,* § 51.) This little town of Galilee, of which neither the Old Testament nor Josephus makes mention,
was situated in the tribe of Zebulun, not far from Capernaum, on a hill
(Luke iv. 29) some miles distance from Tabor. The derivation of the
name from נֵצֶר, *bush, shrub* (Hengstenberg Christol. vol. ii., 1, ff.) is
incorrect, since (comp. Matth. 1, and Luke 3), the ζ corresponds to צ.
Bengel derives it from נֶזֶר, *a crown.* In this choice of the town of
Nazareth as the residence for the mother and child, the Evangelist sees also the fulfilment of the Old Testament predictions ;
he connects this with the name Ναζωραῖος, *Nazarene,* which was
given to the Saviour from his residence at Nazareth. But as there
is no passage in the Old Testament where the Messiah is so called,
the meaning of this reference is obscure. Some have supposed
the Nazarite vow to be intended, and have imagined in this place
a *paronomasia* between the name of the town and the word נָזִיר
(Numb. vi. 1). But, in the *first place,* it does not agree with the
Saviour's character to compare him with a Jewish Nazarite,
because his life was not, like that of John the Baptist, marked by a
rigid adherence to legal ceremonies ; and *then* the Nazarene is called
in Greek Ναζιραῖος, less frequently Ναζαραῖος, or Ναζηραῖος, while
the inhabitant of Nazareth is called Ναζαρηνός, or Ναζωραῖος. (See
Schleusner in his Lexicon to the LXX.) It is quite as untenable to refer to the term נֵצֶר, *shoot, branch,* by which the Messiah, as a descendant of David, is frequently denominated*—
e. g., Isa. xi. 1. Had the Evangelist so intended it, he would
have quoted a distinct passage from the prophets, where this term
occurs, as he did in the former quotations from the Old Testament.
But he could not, in that case, have employed the formula " that it
might be fulfilled," for there is no connexion between the name נֵצֶר,
shoot, and the dwelling in Nazareth. In our view of this passage
we must, therefore, be guided by the expression ῥηθὲν διὰ ~ῶν προφητῶν

* It was in this way that the learned Nazarene Jewish Christians explained the quotation to Jerome. See *Hieronymi* comm. ad loc. Jes. xi. 1.

spoken by the prophets. (The reading διὰ τοῦ προφήτου is obviously a mere correction without critical authority.) The *plural* indicates that the Evangelist had not any single quotation in view, but meant only to adduce a collective citation ; and the article indicating a reference to all the prophets, or some in particular, whom Matthew supposed to be known. Accordingly, the view becomes most probable, that the Evangelist had regard to the fact, that the Nazarenes were despised by the nation. In that case he would have those passages in view in which the Messiah is portrayed in his humiliation—as, *e. g.,* Ps. xxii. ; Isa. liii. [The *general* prediction that the Messiah should appear, not as a celebrated ruler, but as a despised, humble man, Matthew reproduces in this concrete form : "The prophets have predicted that he should be a genuine Nazarene (a despised one) ;—that he should be what the Nazarenes in fact are, and what he, as Nazarene, has really been."] An etymological allusion to נָצַר, *the despised one* (from נָצַר,) may be combined with this view, and is not improbable, particularly on the supposition of a Hebrew original of the Gospel. The endeavour of Matthew to represent Jesus as the Messiah, according to the Old Testament predictions, is most plainly evidenced even in these first chapters.[*] As he wrote for Jews, it was his chief aim to prove the connexion of the various events at the birth of Jesus with the important testimonies of the Old Testament. (On καλεῖσθαι, see note on Luke i. 32.)

If now, at the close of the first two chapters of Matthew, we glance at the objections which have been raised against their genuineness, we may take it for granted that, in our day, they may be regarded as set aside. No external reasons can be adduced for the opinion, that these chapters did not form part of the original Gospel, since it is proved that the "Gospel καθ᾿ Ἑβραίους, *according to the Hebrews,*" contained the history of the childhood of Jesus. (See the Author's History of the Gospels, p. 73, 76.) The Ebionites, indeed, had not the first chapters in their edition of that apocryphal Gospel ; but the fact of their having omitted them confirms their genuineness. (See *Epiph.* hær. xxx. 13.) And with respect to the internal evidences, *Gersdorf* (Sprachcharacteristik, S. 38, ff.) has shewn convincingly the affinity of the style which prevails in the first chapters with that of the following parts ; although it must be admitted that *Fritzsche* (Excursus iii. in Matth.) has here and there refuted *Gersdorf's* remarks. There is nothing left, then, to give any colour to these doubts, except the doctrinal objections taken against the contents ; but this reason will never be urged by judicious critics against the genuineness of the first

---

[*] *De Wette* is wrong in assuming, contrary to his other declarations, a double sense ; —the reference, according to him, is first to the town of Nazareth, and the residence there ; and then, further, to the word נֵצֶר.

two chapters, as, at most, it could only be brought against the credibility of the events narrated, not against the genuineness of this part of the work, since the Evangelist, in the subsequent parts, exhibits the same fundamental views which have given tone and character to the first chapters. Moreover, as reference is subsequently made (see iii. 1 ; iv. 23), to the preceding part, the first chapters are manifestly seen to be an integral part of the Gospel.* Precisely the same observations apply to the arguments urged against the genuineness of the first chapters of Luke. (For the Literature on the subject, see *Kuinoelii* comm. in Luc., vol. ii., p. 232.) Here, also, all external evidence is wanting ; since the character of the Marcionite Gospel is a testimony, not against, but for their genuineness, because Marcion omitted the early chapters, which he found in the canonical Gospel of Luke. (*Tertull.* adv. Marc. iv. 7.) No internal reason can be adduced, except the miraculous character of the events which they record—a character which agrees perfectly with that of the whole. We shall presently treat particularly of the contradictions which appear to exist between the accounts of Matthew and Luke, in the history of the childhood of Jesus ; but on the ground occupied by our opponents, even in case they were irreconcileable, they would furnish ground of argument, not against the *genuineness* of the early chapters, but only against the *credibility* of the history.

SECOND SECTION.—LUKE'S ACCOUNT.

CHAPTERS I. AND II.

---

§ 1. PRÖEMIUM.

(Luke i. 1–4.)

THE four verses with which Luke opens his work (consisting of two parts, see Acts i. 1), are worthy of notice in more than one respect. As regards the style, we perceive that the Evangelist's own style, which is pure Greek, as the first period shews, differs from the Hebraising style apparent in the subsequent part, where Luke communicates documents, whether unaltered or worked up, with which tradition had supplied him. His words next inform us, that, previous to his work, other records of the Gospel-history were in existence, which, however, were of questionable accuracy (ἀσφάλεια, i. 4) ; lastly, he indicates the sources from which

* Compare the Dissertation of *J. G. Müller* (Trier. 1830), which defends the genuineness of these chapters.

he drew, the principles which he had followed in the composition of his work, and the special object which he had in view. The construction of the Pröemium exhibits a certain indefiniteness, which gives the more room for diverse explanations, as they are influenced by the various views entertained of the origin of the Gospels. The sense of the whole passage depends on where the *apodosis* is made to begin ; it may begin either with καθὼς παρέδοσαν, *as they delivered them*, or with ἔδοξε κᾀμοί, *it seemed good also to me*. According to the latter division, the words " *as they delivered,*" etc., are connected with ἐπειδήπερ πολλοί, *forasmuch as many*, etc., and contain an observation on•the *quality* of the earlier Gospel records ; for to refer them to the mere *existence* of those records, as if Luke had not personally known these older works, but had only heard of them by παράδοσις, is evidently forbidden by the expression " eye-witnesses from the beginning," which necessarily implies a tradition respecting the history of Jesus.* Luke's opinion of the character of those older writings would, in that case, be a favourable one, since he claims the same sources of information for himself (καθὼς παρέδοσαν ἡμῖν) ; a supposition which would very well agree with an hypothesis, according to which these many Gospels were shorter, and our Gospels more lengthened, editions of the same original Gospel. But as (ver. 4) blame is plainly imputed to the πολλοί, since Luke leads Theophilus to expect historical certainty nowhere but in his Gospel, which could not therefore be found in the accounts of the early narrators,† it might be thought necessary to prefer that division of the sentence which places the beginning of the *apodosis* at καθὼς παρέδοσαν ἡμῖν κ. τ. λ. In that way, the tradition of the eye-witnesses would refer only to Luke's narrative ; and his narrative would stand distinguished from the earlier ones. But here, again, we are met, first, by the circumstance that, grammatically, the *apodosis* is more definitely pointed out in ἔδοξε κᾀμοί, than at καθώς, since κᾀμοί appears evidently in contrast with the πολλοί ; besides, too, the change from ἡμεῖς to ἐγώ is remarkable. It is, therefore, undoubtedly most correct to begin the *apodosis* with ἔδοξε ; but to join the clause, καθὼς παρέδοσαν κ. τ. λ., not to ἀνατάξασθαι—so that it would contain the description of the quality of the sources used by the πολλοί—but to πράγματα ἐν ἡμῖν πεπληροφορημένα. In accordance with this construction, the ἡμῖν after παρέδοσαν would be quite parallel with ἐν ἡμῖν πεπληροφορημένα, and the meaning would be, " since many have un-

---

* *Hug* (Introd. p. 387, ff., Fosdick's Translation) interprets καθὼς παρέδοσαν " as the eye-witnesses put them—*i. e.*, the writings of the 'many' into our hands;" an interpretation which stands or falls with the opinion of this learned author, that the writings of the "many" are works of the apostles.

† Thus *Origen* explains it correctly in Luc. Hom. 1. Quod ait " *conati sunt*" latentem habet accusationem eorum, qui absque gratia spiritus sancti ad scribenda evangelia prosilierunt.

dertaken to put forth a narrative of the events which are regarded
among us (members of the Christian church) as historically established, just as the eye-witnesses have reported them to us (to
myself and all members of that communion) ; so I also have determined," etc. Thus, therefore, the *events* only appear perfectly ascertained by the tradition of the church. The quality of the narratives is left at first undetermined ; but is afterwards represented as
suspicious by the contrast exhibited between Luke and the "many,"
and particularly by ver. 4.* This view agrees best with the opinion
which we endeavoured to establish in the Introduction—viz., that the
apostolical tradition concerning the character and history of Jesus
was concentrated in our four canonical Gospels, and that all older
writings of that sort bore more or less of an apocryphal character.

Ver. 1.—The words πολλοὶ ἐπεχείρησαν διήγησιν ἀνατάξασθαι, *many
have undertaken to set forth a narrative,* can hardly be understood
of single documents relating to single portions of the Gospel-history
(which from this passage are usually, though not very appropriately,
called *diegeses*), since the use of the singular suggests only connected
narratives (whether more or less full) of the entire Gospel-history.†
Indeed ἀνατάξασθαι, *to arrange, set forth in order,* leads to the supposition, that the "many" themselves composed their memoirs from
shorter records. But to what writings Luke refers can not be determined ; for, as he most probably was not acquainted with our
canonical Gospels (see Introd. § 3), we are left to imagine the works
of the "many" to have been apocryphal attempts to delineate the
life of Jesus, which, however, for want of historical information, cannot be more accurately characterized. The πράγματα ἐν ἡμῖν πεπληροφορημένα, *things fully believed among us,* are mentioned as the subject of the writings of the "many." As this Pröemium must be
viewed as introductory to Luke's whole work (the Acts of the Apostles being regarded as a second part of the Gospel), the expression
applies to more than the period of our Lord's earthly sojourn—it
embraces also the progress of the church up to the time when Luke

* Since the words "as they delivered," etc., depend on the words "undertook to set
forth in order" (ἐπεχείρησαν ἀνατάξασθαι), they seem to me by no means to contain the
positive praise which Olshausen finds in them, and which he regards as apparently inconsistent with the lurking censure of the concluding words. They seem to me rather to describe the *way* in which those narratives were produced: and thus the necessity of connecting the καθώς *as*, with πεπληροφορημένα instead of with παρέδοσαν, disappears. Many
(Christians of the class for whom Luke wrote) had made the attempt to record the Gospel histories, as they had heard them orally, and after the departure of the eye-witnesses,
who had been their informants. Luke, far from blaming them for this, recognizes the
need of writing to give definiteness and permanence to the Gospel narratives. He finds
these scattered sketches from memory *imperfect:* they furnish—precisely because they *are*
scattered and fragmentary—no certainty ; and hence, he, having examined every thing
carefully from its beginning, has determined to compose a connected history of the events.
(See more fully in my Kritik der ev. Geschichte 2te Aufl. § 135.)—[F
† But see above, note: διήγησις means simply "narrative."—[E.

wrote. But when the Evangelist immediately adds, in the words πεπληροφορημένα ἐν ἡμῖν, *surely believed, established, etc.*, a remark on the *credibility* of the events (those in the life of Jesus, as well as those which happened afterwards in the early church), it is probably because their character is such, that their miraculous form appears at first sight to contradict their credibility.

(The signification "happen," "take place," cannot be assigned either to πληροφορεῖσθαι, or to נִמְלָא, which some have thought to resemble it. Πληροφορέω has, in the first instance, the same meaning as πληρόω; then, as transferred to what is spiritual, "to afford conviction, certainty."[*]   So it is found, particularly in the writings of Paul, who uses πληροφορία as parallel with πίστις, πεποίθησις, *belief, persuasion*. The participle πεπληροφορημένα is therefore equivalent to βέβαια, *established, certain*, and should be connected with ἐν ἡμῖν. Immediately after the notice of the firm conviction of the members of the church of the important events [which the πολλοί had made the subject of their writings], there follows appropriately the mention of the vouchers for them.)

Ver. 2.—As vouchers, Luke mentions the οἱ ἀπ' ἀρχῆς αὐτόπται, *the eye-witnesses from the beginning*, and the ὑπηρέται λόγου, *ministers of the word*. As the Evangelist begins with the birth of John the Baptist and Jesus, we ought not to limit the "from the beginning" to the time of Christ's active ministry ; Luke meant to delineate the whole new phenomenon from its commencement.[†] The "eye-witnesses" in this place are doubtless Mary the mother of Jesus, and the other members of the families of whose private history the first chapters treat ; but, for the subsequent history of Jesus and of the church, the apostles also are eye-witnesses. Παρέδοσαν, *delivered*, is, accordingly, to be understood of oral as well as written tradition, since most probably the family information, as conveyed to us in the early chapters, is founded on written records. It is incorrect to take the "eye-witnesses" to mean the apostles, and the ὑπηρέται λόγου, *ministers of the word*, their assistants ; for though ὑπηρέτης, *minister*, is used, it is true, of apostolical assistants (see Acts xiii. 5, although the reading there is not quite certain), yet ὑπηρέτης λόγου, sc. Θεοῦ, *minister of the word*, sc. *of God*, is never so used. This name designates the apostles and all teachers in the church in common ; the expression does not therefore indicate a new class of witnesses, but only describes the same witnesses more fully. In reference to one portion of the events which Luke is about to describe, they were merely eye-witnesses ; but in reference to the

---

[*] *De Wette's* assertion, that πληροφορέω, in this sense, can be used of persons only, is indefensible.

[†] *De Wette* asserts boldly, that the narrative of the Gospel-history usually began with Christ's entrance on his official work. Why? Because Mark (i. 1) begins so!

other (later) portion, they were themselves the acting parties, so that there they bore witness of themselves.

Ver. 3.—Luke specifies three points, in which he explains, as it were, his historical method ; the terms ἄνωθεν, *from the beginning*, ἀκριβῶς, *exactly, accurately*, and καθεξῆς, *in order*, here come under notice. The first two words apply to his mode of dealing with the sources of information, the last to the narrative itself. (Παρακολουθεῖν, *follow along*, denotes the mind's action in following—living over again, as it were—the whole train of events, in connexion with a thorough examination and testing of the sources.) In the works of the " many," the opposites of all the three points are tacitly implied. In the first place, as to ἄνωθεν, *from the beginning*, it refers to ἀπ' ἀρχῆς, ver. 2 ; Luke meant to bring out to view, and fully unfold the earliest germs of this new phenomenon ; of course, the πάντα, *all things*, are only to be understood as implying all that appeared to Luke to belong to the description of the whole ; in the selection of facts, each writer naturally displayed his individual characteristics. But by no means ought πᾶσι to be referred to αὐτόπται ; it belongs to the πράγματα, on account of which alone the persons are mentioned. Ἀκριβῶς, *exactly, accurately*, characterizes the historical investigation as an intelligent and careful process—opposed to the uncritical method of the apocryphal writings. Lastly, καθεξῆς, *in order*, can apply only to the chronology, as in Acts xi.* (In Acts xviii. 23, it is used of local contiguity.) The plan of the book shows that Luke *intended* to observe that order in the main ; but this intention, it must be confessed, does not extend to the very minute chronological details, since in them he seems to have deviated from the order of time. (See Introd. § 7, and the commentary on Luke ix. 51.)

Ver. 4.—The laying down of these historical principles was intended to give historical certainty and warrant (ἀσφάλεια) to Theophilus, who, as being acquainted with classical literature, probably made stricter demands than the uncritical apocryphal writings could satisfy. In the first place, Luke wrote from the reports of eyewitnesses, and, next, with a discriminating use of those reports. Doubtless, he laid much stress on the character of the persons with whom these reports originated ; and the credibility of the whole Gospel-history rests, therefore, upon the Spirit, who animates a series of persons linked together by his living communication.†

* Comp., on the contrary, my Kritik der Ev. Geschichte, § 30.—[E.

† Justly does *Osiander* exclaim in his *Apologie des Lebens Jesu*, Tübingen, 1837, S. 63 : " What shall be said when *Strauss*, instead of refuting the strong anti-mythical argument afforded by Luke's preface, imagines it invalidated by the empty assertion. ' that Luke certainly might speak so, if he had no idea that he was narrating myths,' and degrades a historian, who begins so discreetly, to a thoughtless collector of unconsciously framed myths ?"

Facts such as the agency of the Holy Ghost in the birth of Jesus, could be attested only by Mary herself; but he who was moved by the same Spirit that enabled her to give such testimony, received her witness, and needed no other; he who was a stranger to that Spirit, found no other testimonies, and accordingly left the matter uncredited. The acknowledgment of the certainty of the Gospel-history always presupposes, therefore, faith in the Spirit of truth; and as in human life truth and falsehood appear side by side indeed, but yet are at the same time opposed, being distinguished as the kingdom of God and the World—*to him who is conversant with the world and its sprit, which every where suspects falsehood and deceit, because it carries them about in itself—to him, as such, the Gospel-history can not and will not be accredited.* But Luke's narrative afforded complete assurance to Theophilus, because he was not out of this sphere of the Spirit of truth, but lived within it. He was a member of the church (and the early church possessed the Spirit of truth fully), as indicated by the words περὶ ὧν κατηχήθης λόγων, *the things wherein thou wast instructed,* and the Spirit of the eye-witnesses was therefore in him also. (Κατηχεῖσθαι is the usual term for attending on instruction in religion. See Acts xviii. 25; 1 Cor. xiv. 19; Gal. vi. 6.) Only we must not conceive of the κατήχησις in the earliest times of the church to have consisted of a communication of doctrines; it was founded on history only (λόγοι—*histories, narrations.*) Reflection was not yet developed in the church, and doctrines had not yet been deduced from God's mighty acts by logical process. The apostles were content with bearing witness to the great facts of the life of Jesus; on this foundation of fact the Church was reared. Mere opinions, doctrines, dogmas, could never have given rise to a phenomenon such as the Christian Church presents. But after its formation, there could not fail to arise within it systematizing doctrinal activity, because the Spirit of Christ is destined to pervade all the powers of human nature. But though the instruction of the ancient church was historical, it was not confined merely to narration; rather, the testimony of the first ministers of the word was accompanied by a power which attracted those hearts that received it into the new sphere of life opened by the Saviour; and, by the agency of that Spirit, those who had received the testimony of the truth, became themselves, in turn, witnesses of those same great facts, which were not merely outwardly known to them as things past and over, but exerted a living power within, through the agency of the living Spirit. The church was thus built up purely from within itself; nothing foreign could intrude within its pale: first, the testimony to the truth had to be received and embraced with the accompanying power of the Spirit; then followed incorporation into this new sphere of life, and faith in its decisions. Even so the church is built• up at this day, and will be till the end of time ; it needs, therefore, no further warrant for the truth of the Gospel-history than the reports of eye-witnesses, which are open to us, and which are still accompanied by the same power of the Spirit of truth, as their oral narrations formerly were, causing in those hearts which give it admission, the same assurance as was produced by the words of the witnesses of Jesus in the apostolic age.

Who and what Theophilus was (compare Acts i. 1), cannot be determined further, than that the character of Luke's work leads us to conjecture it to have been addressed to one who was familiar with Rome and Italy, and, consequently, in all probability resident there.* The opinion that the Theophilus to whom Luke wrote, is the high-priest Theophilus spoken of by Josephus (Antiq. xviii. 6, 3 ; xix. 6, 4), is therefore to be rejected, since we cannot imagine him to have been so intimately acquainted with Italy. Besides, the title κράτιστος, *most excellent,* like the Latin *splendidus,* intimates considerable dignity, with which this Theophilus was invested. It was granted to proconsuls in the provinces (Acts xxiii. 26 ; xxiv. 3 ; xxvi. 25); at a later period, however, inferior officials also enjoyed it. (See *Hug's* Introd., p. 395, Fosdick's translation.) Although, therefore, the Gospel of Luke, as well as the Acts of the Apostles, were, in the first instance, addressed to a distinguished private person, yet the church has justly received them into the canon, like the Epistles to Timothy, Titus, and Philemon ; because the individuals for whom they were immediately intended, shared, as members of the church, its general wants ; and, therefore, what was adapted to them might be given to all.

§ 2. ANNUNCIATION OF THE BIRTH OF JOHN THE BAPTIST.

(Luke i. 5–25.)

Luke carries his "from the beginning" (ἄνωθεν), in verse 3, so far back, that he begins the history of Christ, and of the formation of the church, as early as the birth of John the Baptist. This view results from the nature of the phenomenon which he was historically to set forth. For after the spirit of prophecy became silent from the time of the building of the second temple, and seemed entirely to have vanished from among the people, there first reappeared, in the person of John the Baptist, a prophet like those of the Old Testament. His history, therefore, must be embraced in the narrative, since it formed an integral part of the Gospel-history.

* The opinion that Theophilus should be taken as an appellation = Friend of God, and as including all believing readers, may be regarded as antiquated.

—There is a striking change of style in passing from the preface to the narrative which follows; while in the former, pure Greek prevails, in the latter, appear the strongest Hebraisms. This is most naturally accounted for on the supposition, that Luke drew his historical details from written sources, and incorporated them into his work, often quite unchanged, or but slightly amended. The character of the narratives, moreover, particularly in the first two chapters, renders this conjecture extremely probable; for they record events which took place in the bosom of two families, and which must have been preserved in them as a sacred treasure, till the hopes expressed of the two scions of the families had been made good by the result. But afterwards, when the Saviour's great work was accomplished, and Mary, the mother of our Lord, was numbered among the first disciples (Acts i. 14), nothing was more natural than that she should impart to the community the wonders that clustered round the birth of him whom she herself now adored as her Saviour. The holy family had, as it were, expanded; and, in connexion with it, the sacred histories also, of which it had been the scene, could be more widely diffused.

Ver. 5.—Luke begins with a general designation of time (see note on Matth. ii. 1), by setting out from the reign of Herod the Great; he then describes the family which is to be the immediate subject of his narrative. His object did not allow him, like Matthew, to assume much as already known. He describes with exactness all the characters; Zacharias and Elizabeth were both of a priestly family (as Joseph and Mary were both of the lineage of David), which gave lustre to their offspring.* Of Zacharias we are further told, that, as priest he belonged to the course or the class of Abia. This was the eighth of the twenty-four classes of priests appointed by David. (See 1 Chron. xxiv. 10.) Each of these classes took the service in the temple for a week. (In *Josephus* [Antiq. vii. 15, 7], they are called πατρίαι, with reference to the relationship which existed among them. The name ἐφημερία, *course,* which does not occur elsewhere in the New Testament, is chosen with reference to their duty in the temple.) The use which *Scaliger* (opus de emendatione temporum) and *Bengel* (ordo temporum) have attempted to make of the definite succession of the twenty-four classes of priests in the temple service, as a chronological datum, cannot afford any results to be at all depended upon, because the *terminus a quo* of the rotation cannot be definitely fixed.

Ver. 6.—The account of their family relations is followed by that of their personal character. Both were δίκαιοι, *just, righteous,* and not merely outwardly before men, but before God. The idea of

---

* Josephus (vit. c. 1) remarks, Παρ' ἡμῖν ἡ τῆς ἱερωσύνης μετουσία τεκμήριόν ἐστι γένους λαμπρότητος.

δικαιοσύνη, *righteousness,* used of persons under the law (as it is in Luke ii. 25, of Simeon, and 2 Peter ii. 7, of Lot), can of course be understood of legal righteousness only, as is shewn by the explanatory clause, πορευόμενοι ἐν πάσαις ταῖς ἐντολαῖς καὶ δικαιώμασι τοῦ Κυρίου ἄμεμπτοι, *walking in all the commands,* etc. The ἐντολαί and the δικαιώματα, *commands and ordinances,* are the individual declarations and statutes of the law, which they had striven to follow with upright mind, and without pharisaical hypocrisy. But when, in this and other passages (Matth. x. 41 ; Luke xv. 7), righteousness (δικαιοσύνη) is ascribed to certain persons, there is no contradiction to Rom. iii. 20, according to which passage the law causes knowledge of sin. The δικαιοσύνη τοῦ νόμου, *righteousness of the law,* never is an absolute righteousness (Gal. iii. 20); but relatively, it always implies, in those who strive for its attainment, repentance and faith ; and hence a longing for the Finisher of that which is wanting to them. Thus, on account of their righteousness, the desire for a Saviour was lively in Zacharias and Elizabeth. (On δικαιοσύνη, and all cognate words, see the complete exposition in the note on Rom. iii. 21.)

Ver. 7.—But the want of a blessing in respect of offspring formed a contrast with their righteousness, as in the case of Sarah. Elizabeth was barren (στεῖρα, see Luke xxiii. 29 ; Gal. iv. 27), and both were no longer young.* The age of Zacharias must be considered relatively only—viz., with respect to his office. According to Numb. viii. 25, no one was permitted to perform the functions of a priest beyond the fiftieth year of his age. If we take into account also the oriental custom of marrying early, Zacharias and Elizabeth might well have given up the hope of offspring on account of their long childless marriage, notwithstanding that the age of Zacharias, considered in itself, was not so great.

(Καθότι is found only in the writings of Luke, sometimes with the meaning *siquidem,* as in this passage and xix. 9 ; Acts ii. 24 ; sometimes meaning "according as," "as far as," Acts ii. 45 ; iv. 35. The phrase προβεβηκὼς ἐν ταῖς ἡμέραις = בָּא בַּיָּמִים, Gen. xviii. 11, and frequently elsewhere.)

Ver. 8, 9, 10.—After these prefatory observations, which inform the reader of the circumstances of the family whose history is about to be told, there follows, introduced by an ἐγένετο δέ = וַיְהִי, *and it came to pass,* the special narration of the events connected with the birth of John. According to the arrangement of the Jewish service, incense was offered twice daily—at the morning and

---

* It was the same with the mothers of Isaac and Samuel. The *Evangelium de nativitate Mariæ* (Thilo. vol. i., p. 322), remarks appropriately on this point : Deus cum alicujus uterum claudit, ad hoc facit, ut mirabilius denuo aperiat, et non libidinis esse quod nascitur, sed divini muneris cognoscatur.

evening sacrifice. (Ex. xxx 7, 8.) The ministering priest carried the censer with incense (θυμίαμα) into the holy place (ναός =בֵּיכָל, the temple properly speaking, while ἱερόν includes the courts also ; see Matth. xii. 5 ; John ii. 14), in front of which the courts extended, where the multitude assembled for prayer stood, awaiting the return of the priest. The twenty-four classes of the priests alternated according to a determinate cycle ; but the priest who was to minister for the day was chosen by lot (ἔλαχε τοῦ θυμιᾶσαι) from among the priests who constituted each class. This had become the established custom of the priest's office. (Ἱεράτεια differs from ἱεράτευμα, *priesthood*, 1 Peter ii. 5, and ἱερωσύνη, *priestly service*, Heb. vii. 11, 12, 14.) Once upon a time, then, as the turn (τάξις) came to his class, it fell to Zacharias, by lot, to fill this office. (In verse 8 ἔναντι is preferable to the more common form ἐναντίον. It is found in the New Testament only in this passage, and corresponds with ἔναντα used by Homer. In the Old Testament the LXX. has ἔναντι in the passage Job xvi. 21.)

Ver. 11.—It is possible that the lot brought Zacharias into the temple for the first time, and the quiet sanctuary around powerfully affected him. These possibilities cannot make a sober expositor doubt that the narrator intends the appearance of the angel to be regarded as a fact ; nor can they lead a believing critic of this narrative to require the commonness of every-day life in the most eventful moments of the life of our race. At the time when the eternal Word descended to become flesh (John i. 1, 14), there appeared in the world of men phenomena from the world of spirit, such as were not needed in seasons of less powerful excitement. (See note on Matth. i. 18 ; ii. 8.) From a vivid conception, those minute features are given, which confirm the historical fact, and are unfavourable to the mythical view. The angel appeared by the altar, on the right side of it. (The θυσιαστήριον τοῦ θυμιάματος, *altar of incense*, is described Ex. xxx. 1, ff. ; it stood in the holy place, and must be carefully distinguished from the great altar of burnt-offerings in the court, Heb. vii. 13.)

Ver. 12–14.—Although the vision was to be a blessing to Zacharias, yet fear seized him when he saw it, as frequently in similar circumstances. (Compare Luke i. 29 ; Rev. i. 17 ; Dan. x. 7, 12.) *In one aspect*, this fear, at the immediate view of phenomena from the unseen world, is an expression of the feeling of sinfulness. But for sin, man would see in what is divine something akin to himself ; and instead of fear, he would experience ravishing delight. *In another aspect*, however, this fear is expressive of a sensibility to this contrast between what is pure and what is unholy; and in this consists its nobler character. Hence, such fear of God is never considered as blameworthy, but as the beginning (Psalm cxi.

10) and the end (Isaiah xi. 2) of all wisdom. This fear of God, which is consistent with love (see Rev. i. 17, where the disciple of love falls to the earth with fear at the sight of him whom he loves), must not, therefore, be confounded with the fear engendered by the spirit of bondage (πνεῦμα δουλείας). The latter implies being afraid of God (vor Gott), which is absolutely culpable; the former might be called fear of ourselves, or fear for God (für Gott). (See note on Rom. viii. 15.) The heavenly messenger quiets this holy fear, and then communicates his message of joy. (The δέησις, prayer, indicates that Zacharias had not altogether given up the hope of offspring. Γεννᾷν is here equivalent to τίκτειν, bear, as Gal. iv. 24.) At the same time a name is given, as Matth.·i. 21, to the promised son, and a name expressive of his spiritual importance. (Ἰωάννης = יְחֹהָנָן, bestowed of Jehovah.) Thereby he will bring joy not only to the parents by his natural birth, but also to all the pious by his spiritual character and office, which are here, by anticipation, connected with his birth. (Ἀγαλλίασις, exultation, is a stronger term than χαρά, joy. In this passage, as in Matth. i. 18, the reading γενέσει is preferable to the common one γεννήσει.)

Ver. 15.—In the following verses the words of the angel describe, first, the character of this promised one ; next, his labours; and lastly, his relation to the Messiah, in whom all the hopes and expectations of believing Israelites centred. In reference to his character, it is first observed in general, that a spiritual significancy would attach to him. (Μέγας = גָּדוֹל, great, in respect of influence, as Hosea i. 11. The additional clause " before the Lord" sets aside the idea of worldly importance ; he bears a purely spiritual character.) Then the type of his piety is more precisely described by the circumstance, that he will live the life of a Nazarite. (See more particularly the note on Matth. ix. 14. Σίκερα = שֵׁכָר is used of all intoxicating drinks ; the passage has reference to Numb. vi. 3, ff.) In the life of a Nazarite there appears concentrated the strict legal character which John, the close and crowning-stone, as it were, of the old dispensation, was called to exhibit. This form of piety is not, therefore, to be regarded as the highest, because a heavenly messenger ascribes it to John as an excellence ; it is rather assigned to him as a duty, as being specially suited to his whole calling and destination. The wisdom of God embraces every variety of individual character and of circumstances, and neither requires every thing from, nor gives every thing to, each. The negative characteristic " not drinking" (οὐ πιεῖν) is followed by the positive one, "filled with the holy Spirit" (πλησθῆναι πνεύματος ἁγίου). That this does not imply furnishing with natural capacities, is sufficiently plain from πνεῦμα ἅγιον, Holy Spirit, which always denotes a superior, heavenly life-power, that does not belong to fallen man as such. To suppose this power at work in John (as in all Old Testament prophets), would be attended with no further difficulty; but the phrase ἔτι ἐκ κοιλίας μητρός, *even from his mother's womb*, is obscure. ('Εκ κοιλίας μητρός = אָבִי מִמְעֵי, Psalm lxxi. 6. 'Ετι, *still*, is not precisely equivalent to ἤδη, *already, immediately;* it is rather to be taken in its proper sense, as the writer conceives the agency of the Holy Spirit continuing from the mother's womb down to a later period.) Considered in itself, the expression ἐκ κοιλίας μητρός might indeed mean merely " from early youth onward ;" but, in connexion with ver. 44, we must allow, that, without doubt, the writer intends us to conceive of an active influence in the Baptist *before* his birth. But this thought becomes perfectly intelligible if we consider, *first*, that the πνεῦμα ἅγιον in this passage, is not to be taken as identical with the Holy Spirit, whose outpouring is connected with the completion of the work of Jesus. (See note on John vii. 39.) The expression denotes here the divine power, in so far as it is a holy power, as Psalm li. 13; Isaiah lxiii. 10. And *further*, as the Divine Spirit influences even the κτίσις, *creation* (Rom. viii. 19), we can have no hesitation in admitting his influence in the elect *before* birth. In like manner we must conceive of the influence of baptism on unconscious children; but not that it should be thought identical with regeneration.

Ver. 16.—The immediate agency of this prophet promised anew, after so long a silence of the prophetic spirit, is now described as limited to the people of Israel, warning of destruction, and awakening to repentance. ('Επιστρέφειν = הֵשִׁיב refers to μετάνοια, which forms the central point of John's labours, Matth. iii. 2.) A new and higher principle of life John could not impart, nor was that his destination; but the " Spirit" in him was intended to awaken the sense of the higher end of life—to point men back to God. His ministry was confined to Israel, like that of the Saviour (Matth. xv. 24), not that the other nations were to be excluded from the favours of God, but because what was wrought among the central people of mankind was for the benefit of all. There a hearth had first to be prepared for the holy fire, and for that reason the influence of God's messengers was concentrated on that spot. That it was not, however, the whole nation, but only certain members of it, that would be gained, is expressed plainly in the words: πολλοὺς τῶν υἱῶν τοῦ Ἰσραὴλ ἐπιστρέψει, *many of the children of Israel shall he turn, etc.* Just so when God is called " their God," as in the Old Testament, " The God of Abraham, Isaac, and Jacob"—this does not imply at all the exclusion of other nations (Luke ii. 31) from the blessing of the true God, nor a limitation of it to Israel, but the fact that God no more sustains a uniform relation to different nations than to different individuals. The Bible knows of no national God of the Hebrews ; it teaches only, that it hath pleased the one true God, the maker of heaven and earth, to bring Israel into special relation with himself (Lev. xx. 26 ; Sirach xxiv. 13), and in Israel again, certain individuals. The angel speaks here, certainly, in a *human* and Jewish manner—*i. e.*, so as men and Jews could understand ; but, at the same time, in a *divine* manner, since it is purely divine determinations to which his words refer, and with which are connected new divine ordinances.

Ver. 17.—*Lastly,* The appearance of the new prophet is shewn to be connected with the Messiah, as prophesied by Malachi (iv. 5, 6); according to which passage, Elijah was to precede the Messiah, exercising a preparatory influence (Matth. iii. 3, ff.—Προέρχεσθαι, *go before,* involves preparation.) But the expression : ἐν πνεύματι καὶ δυνάμει Ἠλίου, *in the spirit and power of Elijah,* gives this passage an explanatory character. John was not to be Elijah raised from the dead, but his antitype ; being of a like spiritual nature, he was to exercise a kindred influence. While "spirit" (πνεῦμα) has a more general application, indicating his general characteristics, as controlled by the quickening principle from on high—"power" (δύναμις) denotes rather what is special and extraordinary. In Elijah, the idea of divine *power,* and that in its sterner features, is, as it were, personified ; the same is the spiritual character of John. (Comp. more particularly in note on Matth. xi. 14.) The angel's referring to the language of Scripture, is parallel with the quotation from Scripture in Christ's temptation, on the part of the devil. (Matth. iv. 6.) Passages like these are erroneously employed for the purpose of assailing the historical reality of angelic appearances. The true conception is not that the angels formally quote the Scriptures ; but that the language of the Scriptures themselves originates in the counsels of that heavenly world to which these spiritual personages belong. The attaching of the thought to the words of Scripture, is to be viewed as merely clothing them in the form familiar and intelligible among men. Angels do not, therefore, quote the words of Scripture, because they wish to derive from the Bible a proof or an illustration of what they say ; but the thoughts expressed by them are in the Bible, because they contain a truth, which stands good, as well in heaven as in earth.* This verse is, further, of the highest importance on account of the expression, ἐνώπιον αὐτοῦ, *before him,* which refers grammatically to Κύριον τὸν Θεὸν αὐτῶν, *the Lord their God,* ver. 16, so that God him-

---

* It is difficult to see why an angel, in holding communication with men, should not quote Scripture in the same direct and formal way, and for the same purposes of "proof or illustration" as did the Saviour, or the Holy Spirit speaking through those whom he inspired. That angels do not avail themselves of the Scriptures as one·means of "looking into" the gracious dispensations of God (see 1 Peter i. 12), can be neither proved nor rendered probable.—K.

self is conceived as appearing in the Messiah. Were this thought foreign or contradictory to the doctrine of Scripture, a less natural explanation might be attempted (as, *e. g.*, that αὐτός = אוה denoted the Messiah, that well-known, that desired one); but as even the Old Testament (Isa. xl. 3, 5; Jer. xxiii. 6; Joel iii. 21; Mal. iii. 1) intimates the same truth, and the New Testament (John i. 14) expresses it clearly in doctrinal form, the interpreter must abide by the simple construction of the words. It was the exalted destination of the Baptist to lead the hearts of men, alienated by sin from what is divine, to the Lord of all lords, who revealed himself in Christ visibly and near. The concluding words of ver. 17 are a free quotation from Mal. iv. 5, 6. The LXX., which substantially follows the Hebrew text, translates ὃς ἀποκαταστήσει καρδίαν πατρὸς πρὸς υἱὸν, καὶ καρδίαν ἀνθρώπου πρὸς τὸν πλησίον αὐτοῦ, *who shall restore the heart of the father to the son, and the heart of a man to his neighbour.* In this way the words affirm only that he will remove the alienation of men's spirit, and restore love and peace. But, according to the words in Luke, the second half of the sentence, ἐπιστρέψαι ἀπειθεῖς ἐν φρονήσει δικαίων, *to turn the disobedient into the wisdom of the just,* acquires, apparently, a different meaning. But if we look on ἀπειθεῖς, *disobedient,* as corresponding to "the children," and the δίκαιοι, *just,* as corresponding to the "fathers," the thought remains essentially the same; he will produce a great moral effect on the people, restraining the fierce outbreakings of sin; he will awaken a salutary endeavour after righteousness, and thus call forth a λαὸς κατεσκευασμένος, *prepared people,* whose character consists in the sense of a need of salvation. (Φρόνησις is here nearly related to σοφία, [חָכְמָה], although not identical with it; it is בִּינָה in the noblest sense; so that ungodliness appears as the true folly, godliness as the true wisdom. [Matth. x. 16.] Ἐν φρονήσει in construction with ἐπιστρέψαι· must be viewed as another case, where a verb of motion is joined immediately with a preposition of rest.)

Ver. 18.—The angel's promise of a son was not to exclude natural generation; Christ's birth happened differently from John's. Parallel with this is Isaac's birth in the Old Testament; but the unbelief of Zacharias forms a striking contrast to Abraham's faith. Of Abraham it is said, "he considered not his own body already dead" (οὐ κατενόησε τὸ ἑαυτοῦ σῶμα ἤδη νενεκρωμένον), Rom. iv. 19. Zacharias looked at his age and his long unfruitful marriage in a doubting spirit. It is not, therefore, the forethought exercised by the father that is blamed, but his unbelief;* he was certainly con-

---

* Such an expression of unbelief at such an instant, is not so much to be conceived as proceeding from reflection and intention, but should be viewed rather as an involuntary utterance of the soul. In such moments, the inmost being of the soul becomes manifest; it is seen whether faith or unbelief occupies the heart's core. The event had, therefore, for Zacharias himself, a perfecting effect on his spiritual life.

vinced that the vision in the temple beside the altar, which filled his heart with holy fear, was a heavenly one, but, nevertheless, he allowed unbelief a place in his heart. The wrong lay not in the words of the question, but in the disposition from which it pro- ceeded. (Mary's question [Luke i. 34] *sounds* like one that pro- ceeded from doubt, and yet she exercised a childlike trust.) The asking for a sign (אות, σημεῖον) in confirmation of the promise, is never disapproved (see Gen. xv. 8, where Abraham asks בַּמָּה אֵדַע = κατὰ τί γνώσομαι τοῦτο); on the contrary, under certain circum- stances, not to ask for one is rebuked. (Isa. vii. 13.) Zacharias' re- quest for a sign is therefore granted; but, for his unbelief, he re- ceives a sign that is a punishment.

Ver. 19.—To accredit himself, as it were (and to correct the un- believing Zacharias), the heavenly messenger makes himself known in his high dignity; he calls himself Gabriel (גַּבְרִיאֵל, Dan. viii. 16; ix. 21—*i. e.*, *man of God*), representing the creative power of God. That the angel applies a Hebrew name to himself, ceases to surprise us, if we view rightly the meaning of names. A name is nothing else than the term which corresponds to the inmost essence of the object named. In so far, therefore, as the beings of the spiritual world possess definite characters, they have their names; whether those names assume a Hebrew form or any other form of human speech, depends on circumstances. Here we have, at the same time, an explanation of the fact, that the names of the angels are not met with till the later periods of the Jewish state; for it would be much easier to form a general idea of a world of spiritual beings, than to individualize sharply their separate characters, and not till then could names be framed to denote such individualities. By the adjunct : παρεστηκὼς ἐνώπιον τοῦ Θεοῦ, *standing in the presence of God*, the in- dividual that appeared is further associated with a certain class of angels. (See more fully in note on Matth. xviii. 10.) The grada- tion of existences everywhere prevailing throughout creation, men with perfect consistency conceive as existing also in the world of spirits. Hence in the doctrines of Zendavesta, there appear, in like manner, degrees among the angels; the seven Amshaspands are imagined to be nearest the throne of God.* That there is truth in this mode of conceiving the matter is proved by the Scriptures, which, long before the Jews had any connexion with the Persians, represent angels in the more immediate presence of God. (Isa. vi.

---

* Agreeably with this, we find in the Persian constitution, which was intended as a copy of the heavenly order, *seven* princes of the kingdom (or chamberlains), who stood first round the king's throne. (Esther i. 10, 14.) The supposition that the Jews derived their doctrines about angels from the Parsees, is discountenanced by the fact, that the Hebrews had only *four* throne-angels, as well as by general reasons. (See note on Matth. viii. 28. Compare also *Buxt. lex talm.*, p. 46.) It must be confessed, however, that they had the number seven as well as four. (See more fully in note on Rev. iv 5, 6.)

1, ff.) The descriptions in Dan. vii. 9, ff. and Rev. iv. 1, ff., also evidently convey the idea of the existences of the spiritual world standing at various degrees of distance from God, and of corresponding grades of dignity.

Ver. 20.—Zacharias, for his unbelieving language, has inflicted upon him the punishment of dumbness ; but, at the same time, the period of healing is foretold as an alleviation, and for a sign of the promise given.

(Μὴ δυνάμενος λαλῆσαι is merely an explanatory clause of σιωπῶν for κωφός, which term is used, ver. 22. 'Ανθ' ὧν [Luke xii. 3 ; xix. 44] answers both to אֲשֶׁר תַּחַת, Deut. xxviii. 47, and to עַל־אֲשֶׁר, Jer. xxii. 9. Εἰς τὸν καιρὸν αὐτῶν is to be taken " according to the succession of the several incidents ;" first the birth of the child must take place, and then he would show himself to be the promised one.)

Ver. 21, 22.—According to the later tradition, the priests would seem not to have remained long at prayer in the temple, in order not to excite the fear of some misfortune having happened to them in the temple, which, as the officiating priest was regarded as the representative of the nation, would have been viewed as a national calamity. Hence the continued stay of Zacharias in the temple, though not in itself long, was already beginning to excite surprise. The observation that they perceived he had seen a vision (ὀπτασία = מַרְאָה.) does not refer to his silence, but probably to his whole appearance, in which violent excitement may have been expressed, which, from his coming out of the temple, was immediately referred to a spiritual cause. Zacharias confirmed the opinion thus expressed, by signs (αὐτὸς ἦν διανεύων αὐτοῖς).

Ver. 23, 24.—After the completion of the week, during which the class of the priests to which Zacharias belonged had fulfilled their service, he returned to his house, and his wife became with child. During the first period of her pregnancy, however, she kept herself retired, that all uncertainty might be removed.

(In the New Testament λειτουργία, from λεῖτος = δημόσιος, public, never means political service ; yet it is used of external service, as Phil. ii. 30 ; 2 Cor. ix. 12. The term commonly denotes holy service, as Heb. ix. 21, and is applied also to purely spiritual relations, as Phil. ii. 17, λειτουργία τῆς πίστεως.)

Ver. 25.—The happy mother acknowledges, with gratitude, the divine blessing in her pregnancy. According to the Old Testament notion, to be without children was a reproach, (Isa. iv. 1 ; Hos. ix. 11, 12) ; and in this the prevailing tendency to what is external is plainly expressed. The more spiritual character of the New Testament, renders temporal blessings entirely subordinate.

(῞Οτι, introducing the direct sentence, often appears in the New Testament according to the analogy of the Hebrew כִּי. [See Exod. iv.

25 ; xviii. 15.] רָאָה and פָּנָּה are often used, like ἐπείδω, in the sense of " to direct the countenance to any thing as a token of favour." In the opposite signification—which פָּנָה also often has —ἐπείδω occurs in Acts iv. 29.)

§ 3. ANNUNCIATION OF THE BIRTH OF JESUS—MARY'S VISIT TO ELIZABETH.

Luke i. 26-56.

Luke's record is here more specific as to time and place than Matthew's. We can, therefore, by his help, render Matthew's account more full and circumstantial. The words " in the sixth month," which refer to verse 24, furnish a datum of some importance for the age of Jesus in relation to John ; and the observation, that the annunciation took place at Nazareth, explains to us Matth. ii. 23. Doubtless Mary (or Joseph) had property in Nazareth as well as in Bethlehem ; on which account Nazareth is called, in Luke ii. 39, πόλις αὐτῶν, their city. (On Nazareth and Galilee, see note on Matth. ii. 22, 23. Μνηστεύεσθαι = אָרַשׂ, see Deut. xxii. 23.)

Ver. 28, 29.—The description which follows, of a secret transaction of the most delicate character, is conceived with a simplicity and tenderness, and, at the same time, with a freedom from any uncalled for intermixture of reflection, which confirm the fact to every mind open to truth ; and it is only by force that it can be perverted to any impure associations. With a heavenly salutation the messenger of the higher world introduces himself to the humble, child-like Mary—Χαῖρε κεχαριτωμένη, hail, thou highly favoured. (Χαριτόω, to MAKE pleasant, agreeable, is found in Ephes. i. 6, besides in this place. It is in use also among the later authors— e. g., Libanius.) The expression does not imply any self-produced holiness and excellence in Mary, but only her election by grace. The Lord had chosen her, even in the line of her ancestors, to be the mother of the Saviour. With child-like innocence she dreamed not of her high destination, and thought herself not worthy of this happiness—the highest that a daughter of Abraham could imagine. While, therefore, κεχαριτωμένη, highly favoured, applies to her whole spiritual state, the subsequent expression, εὐλογημένη ἐν γυναιξίν, blessed among women, refers to her special destination ; so that ἐγενήθης, thou art become, may be supplied.* Mary fell into meditation on the meaning of this salutation (ποταπός denotes as much the quantity as the quality, Matth. viii. 27 ; 1 John iii. 1); and on

* Εὐλογεῖν, like בָּרַךְ, has a double sense, according as it is used of the relation of superior to inferior, or of inferior to superior. In the former relation it means " to bless;" in the latter, " to praise," " to thank," which presupposes our having been blessed.

the appearance of the heavenly messenger (on διεταράχθη, *was dis-turbed*, see note on i. 12), she did not know how to apply it to her-self. (On διαλογισμός, διαλογίζεσθαι from λόγος = νοῦς, see note on ii. 35.)

Ver. 30, 31.—The further execution of the commission begins with a quieting μὴ φοβοῦ, *fear not* (see i. 13), and an assurance of the favour of God. The idea of "favour" (χάρις = חֵן, εὑρίσκειν χάριν = מָצָא חֵן) involves here the free exercise of divine love, which does not appear determined by any thing existing out of or in her. It is consequently an expression of the pure choice of grace, which leaves the creature no possibility of personal merit. The an-nouncement, that Mary was to become a mother, is accompanied, as in Matth. i. 21, with the mention of the name which the child was to receive.

Ver. 32, 33.—The character of this expected child of God is now described by infinitely more exalted traits than was that of John above, ch. i. 16, 17.[*] He comes as υἱὸς ὑψίστου, *son of the highest* (John as δοῦλος, *servant*), and as ruler over the house of Jacob, to which John himself belonged.

(On μέγας, *great*, see note on verse 15 ; and on υἱὸς ὑψίστου, fur-ther remarks in note on i. 35. The term ὕψιστος, *highest*, corre-sponds to the Hebrew עֶלְיוֹן, Gen. xiv. 18. Καλεῖσθαι, *to be called*, is sometimes used of false, empty speaking ; and then the essence, as being something superior, is opposed to it ; but, sometimes, of being named, in as far as it is a correct denomination of the essence ; and in this latter meaning it is (like מָרָא) synonymous with εἶναι, *to be*, but with the accessory idea of being recognized to be such. This meaning, which is connected with the use of ὄνομα, *name*, (שֵׁם) is often found ; e. g., immediately after in verse 35, 76 ; Matth. v. 9, 19 ; and frequently. The former meaning appears verse 36, and frequently.)

With respect to the dominion assured to the promised offspring, it is, in the first place, connected with the person of David. The principal passage which establishes this connexion is 2 Sam. vii. 13, ff. In its immediate literal sense, it applies to Solomon, who, how-ever, is, at the same time, viewed as a type of the true Prince of Peace. The passage is so treated even by the prophets (Psalm lxxxix. 4 ; Isaiah ix. 7 ; Jer. xxxiii. 15, ff.) Next, the dominion of the expected King is described as an everlasting one. The indefinite phrase εἰς τοὺς αἰῶνας, *for ever* (LXX. have εἰς τὸν αἰῶνα in 2 Sam. vii. 13, 16) is defined more accurately by οὐκ ἔσται τέλος, *there shall be no end;* so that the dominion of Jesus is here described as an everlasting, endless one, in its proper sense. This thought leads to

---

[*] See *Theremin's* incomparable Sermon on the words, "He shall be great," in his *Kreuz Christi*, Th. i., Sermon 2.

the right view of the limitation here made of the Messiah's kingdom to the house of Jacob. A dominion that extends beyond all time, cannot, at the same time, be conceived as limited by political boundaries. The special reference to the house of Jacob is to be viewed here in the same manner as in Luke i. 16; and, at the same time, the people of Israel is regarded (as in Matth. ii. 6) as a type of the sanctified portion of mankind brought together in the kingdom of the Messiah. (John xi. 52.)

Ver. 34.—With child-like innocence Mary expresses her doubts at this wonderful language; she does not live in marriage connexion with any one (γινώσκω = יָדַע,) and cannot, therefore, be a mother. According to the entire form of the answer, it *might* have proceeded from unbelief; at least the words are not expressive of faith. The connexion, however, implies that Mary believed, but wished to know *how* this promise could be accomplished. Believing inquiry, directed in a child-like spirit, is therefore not blamed.

Ver. 35.—In answer to this question, the angel discloses to her, that the Son of God, whom she was to bear, would be conceived in a pure and chaste manner in her virgin womb. In words of deep import the heavenly messenger declares to her this sublime mystery. In the first thought, πνεῦμα ἅγιον ἐπελεύσεται ἐπί σε, the Holy Spirit shall come upon thee, the πνεῦμα ἅγιον, Holy Spirit, is, as in i. 15, the divine essence in general, which, in its nature, is holy. As the *physical* generation of Jesus, is here spoken of, we cannot refer the creative agency to the Holy Spirit in the narrow sense, who, according to the fundamental view of the Trinity, makes the world of conscious moral agents the sphere of his agency.* The absence of the article favours this view; πνεῦμα ἅγιον, Holy Spirit, has indeed acquired the nature of a proper name, but δύναμις ὑψίστου, power of the highest, could not have been without the article, if the third person of the Godhead had been intended. In ἐπελεύσεται ἐπί σε, shall come upon thee, there is also, most probably, an allusion to the description of the creation of the world (Gen. i. 2, where the LXX. translate מְרַחֶפֶת, ἐπεφέρετο ἐπάνω τοῦ ὕδατος), of which the creation of that miniature world, the first man was a copy, which has its antitype in regeneration. (John iii. 5, 8.) The latter half of the verse explains the former more particularly. "Power of the highest" here corresponds to "Holy Spirit," and indicates the correct notion of it as the creative power of God. (רוּחַ אֱלֹהִים, Gen. i. 2.) Ἐπισκιάσει σοι, shall overshadow thee,

---

* If we were to hold this to refer literally to the third person of the Godhead, it would, moreover, follow that the Holy Ghost was the Father of Jesus Christ; a mode of speaking very rightly never sanctioned by the Church, since the Holy Ghost does indeed proceed from the Son, but the Son has not his origin from the Spirit. God the Father is the Father of Jesus in his divine and human nature.

stands as explanatory of ἐπελεύσεται ἐπί σε, *shall come upon thee.*
'Ἐπισκιάζειν, *overshadow,* does not at all involve the idea of "protecting, screening" (according to the analogy of the Hebrew סָכַךְ);
the connexion leads evidently to the idea of generation. It is best,
therefore, to compare it with the Hebrew פָּרַשׂ כְּנָפַיִם (Ruth iii. 9 ;
Ezek. xvi. 8) in the signification of spreading out the wings (=
skirts of a garment), consequently "to surround," "to overshadow,"*
which is an euphemistic expression for connubial intercourse. Perhaps the term contains also a remote allusion to מְרַחֶפֶת in Gen. i. 2.
The word רָחַף is well known to have the meaning "to hover over ;"
and in Deut. xxxii. 11, it is placed in parallelism with פָּרַשׂ כְּנָפַיִם.
The whole thought of the remarkable verse is, therefore, no other
than this, that Mary, without the intervention of a man, would become a mother—the pure and chaste power of the creative Divine
Spirit would be the generator.† Consequently, the appearance of
the Saviour among mankind is represented as a new, immediate,
and divine act of creation, and thus the transmission of sinfulness
from the sinful race to him is excluded. But inasmuch as this act
of creation did not altogether exclude the substance of human
nature, in consequence of Mary's relation to Jesus, the Saviour,
though free from sinfulness in the principle of life, yet partook
in common with men of the ἀσθένεια τῆς σαρκός, *weakness of the
flesh* (2 Cor. xiii. 4.) On this depended his capacity of suffering,
which again was a necessary condition of his whole work as the
Saviour.‡ In *his* human nature he glorified human nature *in general.* The fact of the promised offspring being referred for his origin
to the "Holy Spirit," necessarily shews him to be holy himself,
and as such he is called Son of God.§ (The words ἐκ σοῦ were pro-

---

* The cherubim also spreading their wings over the ark of the covenant, denote the
active presence of God. Exod. xl. 34; Numb. ix. 18, 22. See also *Suiceri Thes.,* vol.
i., p. 1175.

† The ἐπισκιάζειν, *overshadow,* hardly implies *creation.* Of Christ's being generated
Scripture nowhere speaks, and how could the Son, who existed before the world
(John xvii. 5), be *generated?* Evidently he could only *enter* a new form of existence, passing, viz., from an eternal, absolute, omniscient existence, to the limitations that belong to
the soul of a child. Having *become* a human soul, he entered the bosom of a virgin (was
conceived), and there formed to himself a body. For this the existing material was *to be
prepared and sanctified* by that overshadowing of the Holy Ghost, precisely as, Gen. i. 2,
the elements of chaos were prepared, by the overshadowing of the Holy Ghost, to receive
the influences of the Word of God.—(E.)

‡ If Jesus had come into the world by ordinary generation, he would have shared
in the *necessitas* moriendi, together with general depravity; if he had not been born of a
human mother, the *impossibilitas* moriendi would have belonged to him; accordingly,
only the narrative presented in the Gospels fulfils all that is required in the idea of a
Saviour. Being born as a man, the Saviour passed a really human life; but, like that of
Adam *before* the fall, with a *possibilitas* tentationis et mortis, which then, by his victory
became an *impossibilitas.* (See further note on Matth. iv. 1, ff.)

§ *Son of God,* υἱὸς Θεοῦ, is here no designation of the eternal, pre-existent Son of
God, *as pre-existent;* it designates primarily the assuming of humanity, the man Jesus, as

bably subjoined to γεννώμενον by the transcribers, to whom the thought appeared imperfect ; no tangible reason can be given for their having been intentionally omitted.)

The name Son of God, like Son of the Highest in ver. 32, has here undeniably a reference to the *human* nature of Christ. He is called Son of God, because he was born, *corporeally*, of Mary, from the overshadowing of the Holy Spirit. That the same *physical* meaning of the word υἱός, *son*, is to be assumed in ver. 32, is shewn partly by the connexion with ver. 31, and partly by David's being denominated πατήρ, *father*. Passages like Mark xiii. 32 ; Heb. v. 8, (in which, however, υἱός, stands alone), appear likewise to come under this head. Jesus is therefore here called Son of God in the same sense as Adam in Luke iii. 38, inasmuch as he received his being immediately from God's hand ;—the first and second Adam are parallel in this respect also. Both form a contrast to the sons of men, who, as descendants of fallen Adam, bear in themselves the image of the fallen one (Gen. v. 3.) When, on the contrary, Jesus is called ὁ υἱὸς τοῦ ἀνθρώπου, *the son of man* (with the article, which is very rarely omitted, as it is in John v. 27), this name is very nearly allied to the physical meaning of the name Son of God, mentioned above. It refers also to the human nature of our Lord, but to this nature as conceived in its *ideal* character. The term has its origin in the Old Testament, which, in several remarkable passages (forming the basis of the rabbinical dogma of *Adam Kadmon*), transports the human nature in its *ideal* into the divine essence itself. (Compare 2 Sam. vii. 19 ; 1 Chron. xviii. 17 ; Ezek. i. 26 ; Dan. vii. 13, 10, 16, with 1 Cor. xv. 45, ff.) Hence an intimate oneness with the Father and the heavenly world is ascribed to the son of man (John iii, 13), and all power and glory, without reference to the humiliation, is ascribed to him (John v. 27 ; Matth. xxvi. 64 ; Acts vii. 55.) Yet, as the apostles *never* use this name of him (out of the Gospels it occurs *only* in Acts vii. 55, and that with a special reference to the *bodily* appearance of our Lord), and Jesus, on the contrary, chiefly uses it when speaking of himself ; it is probable that he desired in that way to bring himself near to man, and intended, at the same time, to set before their eyes the *ideal* of human perfection. In recent times, some would allow the name " the son of man" to be nothing more than a customary name of the Messiah ; but this view is very improbable—for the reason, that then the people would sometimes have given Jesus that name,* or

the boon of heaven to the human *race*. But although Christ is not *in form* designated as the Son of God from his eternal, but from his earthly and phenomenal existence, still, as *matter of fact* (in opposition to *Hofmann*, Scripture-proof, I. p. 114), the church doctrine is by no means thus done away—that Christ was not a Son of God by Mary, but the Son of God from eternity, and became the son of Mary by conception and birth.—(E.)

* In the Apocryphal book of Enoch, the name does indeed occur; but undoubtedly

a false Messiah would have assumed it. It is probable, that only a very few of the enlightened among the people understood the name בַּר אֱנָשׁ, *son of man,* in the true sense of those prophetic passages, in which it embodies the idea of an original man—an *ideal* of humanity. The name for the Messiah most usual among the people at the time of Jesus, was ὁ υἱὸς Δαβίδ, *the son of David.* By this name our Lord was commonly addressed by those who implored his help, and who thus acknowledged his power to help ; and the Saviour himself presupposes this name, as so well known and familiar, that he argues upon it, and proves thence the superior dignity of the Messiah. (See Matth. ix. 27 ; xii. 23 ; xv. 22 ; xx. 30, 31 ; xxi. 9, 15 ; xxii. 42, 45.) That this name became so familiar as a designation of the Messiah, is partly because the prophecies of the Old Testament declared very fully and distinctly, that the Messiah was to come of David's descendants ; on which account the prophets often use the name of David for that of the Messiah (Isa. xi. 1, 10 ; Jer. xxiii. 5 ; xxxiii. 15, 21 ; Ezek. xxxiv. 23, 24 ; xxxvii. 24, 25 ; Psalm lxxxix. 4, 21) ; and partly, because David was to the Jews the splendid *ideal* of a ruler over his people, under whom their dominion was most widely extended. The use of this name, therefore, was connected with that range of secular conceptions of the Messiah, which was prevalent among the Jews. In order, therefore, not to countenance these, our Lord in speaking of himself, avoided the use of that name altogether, and endeavoured rather, by the use of the more obscure expression, "son of man," to give to the inquiry in relation to the character of the Messiah another direction ; for although the name was not a familiar one, he might yet assume it as understood among the better portion, from those prophetic passages in which it occurs. But the phrase υἱὸς Θεοῦ, *Son of God,* is commonly used in the New Testament in a sense very different from the *physical* one, in which it occurs in Luke i. 32, 35 ; and then the article is wanting. The phrase usually denotes, in a *metaphysical* sense, the eternal existence of Christ, which he has with the father —his relation as God to God, as the manifestation of the unseen God. In the Old Testament, the name ὁ υἱὸς τοῦ Θεοῦ, *the Son of God,* does not occur to express this idea ; for in passages like Psalm ii. 7 ;* 2 Sam. vii. 14, the prevailing reference is to earthly forms of manifestation. But although the *name* is wanting (as is the case with the idea of the βασιλεία τοῦ Θεοῦ, *kingdom of God*), yet the idea itself is widely diffused in the Old Testament. It appears as early as Genesis (see *Steinwender* diss. Christus Deus, in V. T. Regiom. it is only through Christian influence that the name has been put there. John xii. 34, shews that the name was quite strange to the Jews.

* The words בְּנִי אַתָּה (Psalm ii. 7) do not, as ver. 6 shews, refers to the eternal generation of the Son by the Father, but to the appointment of the Son to universal dominion in the world.

1829, where the passages from the historical books are collected),
and often subsequently in the prophetic writings, Isa. ix. 6, 7 ; xi. 1,
2; Micah v. 1 ; Jer. xxiii. 6 ; xxxiii. 16, and often. In the Apocrypha, see Wisdom vii. 25, ff. ; viii. 3 ; Sirach xxiv. 4, ff. In the
formation of the name " Son of God," passages like Psalm ii.
7, probably exercised important influence at a later period, since
the different relations in which the phrase might be employed,
were not sufficiently discriminated. Moreover, we find it in many
passages in the New Testament ; and, indeed, while Jesus himself
prefers to call himself " son of man," the apostles, for the most
part, use the name " Son of God." The Saviour, as son of man,
brings himself near to men. Men elevate him, as Son of God,
above themselves. Yet our Lord (in John's Gospel) often calls
himself *Son of God*, or *Son*, with a pregnant meaning. But that
the name *Son of God*, was merely a name for the Messiah common among the Jews, and without a deeper meaning—they will
hardly be convinced, who consider, *first*, that the ordinary popular opinion among the Jews regarded the Messiah as merely a distinguished man, who, on account of his excellencies, was chosen by
God κατ' ἐκλογήν, for the office. (*Justin Martyr* dial. c. Tryph., p.
266, sq.) According to this view, names, such as Χριστός, βασιλεὺς
τῶν 'Ιουδαίων, υἱὸς τοῦ Δαβίδ, *Christ, King of the Jews, son of David*,
and others would be more readily suggested. *Again*, if the name
had been so familiar, there would not have been such astonishment
at Jesus so calling himself. (John v. 18, ff. ; x. 33, ff.) *Lastly*, too,
we never find any false Messiah calling himself " Son of God." The
passages John x. 33, ff. ; xix. 7, ff., rather shew that the people regarded it as presumption even on the part of the Messiah. The
only plausible support to this low view of the phrase is, that υἱὸς
τοῦ Θεοῦ, *Son of God*, is found in some few places in the Gospels,
joined to Χριστός, *Christ ;* but, on closer inspection, it is plain that
no one of them warrants the conclusion that, at the time of Christ,
this name was in common use, as synonymous with that of the
Messiah ; and that, therefore, the same ideas were attached to it
which were usually associated with the name of the Messiah. With
respect to the passages in which *Son of God* is joined with *Christ*,
we should *first* distinguish carefully between those in which *Christ*
precedes, and those in which it follows. In the former (*e. g.*,
Matth. xvi. 16 ; John vi. 69 [according to the Textus Receptus,
Griesbach reads ὁ ἅγιος τοῦ θεοῦ] ; xi. 27 ; xx. 31), the phrase " Son
of God" contains only the more precise determination of the idea of
the Christ. The disciples thought Jesus to be the Christ immediately after they united themselves to him (John i. 41) ; but it was
not till after prolonged intercourse that the idea of the *Son of God*,
who had appeared in Christ, was unfolded to them, through the

revelation of the Father. (Matth. xvi. 16.) *Again*, when the High
Priest asks (Matth. xxvi. 63 ; Mark xiv. 61) whether he is the
Christ, the *Son of God*, this question had reference, not to the conceptions prevalent among the people, but to what Christ affirmed
of himself ; and because of these declarations the people cried out,
"If thou be the Son of God, come down from the cross," Matth.
xxvii. 40. The words of the centurion (Matth. xxvii. 54, and the
parallel passages) refer to the heathen mythology. We grant indeed
an apparent difference in the case of those passages, in which *Son of
God* stands first, which, however, are very few, as John i. 50 ; ix. 35,
compared with ix. 17. But that, even from these passages, it can
not be concluded that *Son of God* was only a common name for
the Messiah, is shown in the particular exposition of them in their
connexion. (See Commentary on those places.) Thus there remain only the passages, Matth. iv. 3, 6 ; viii. 29, and the parallel
passages in which Jesus is addressed as *Son of God*, as in other cases
he is called *son of David*. But these passages occur only in the
history of the temptation, or in reference to demoniacs ; we may
therefore with the utmost probability infer from them that only
the superhuman demoniacal power recognized Jesus in his divine
nature and dignity. We must, therefore, say, that υἱὸς τοῦ Θεοῦ,
Son of God, does, indeed designate the Messiah ;* but *so far
only* as he was born of the essence of the Father ; that, therefore,
whoever so called him, either acknowledged him as such, or blamed
him for declaring himself to be such. *Lastly*, with respect to the
relation of the name *Son of God*, in as far as it is applied to
Christ, and the same name as applicable to man, we have to
observe, that υἱοὶ Θεοῦ, *sons of God*, or τέκνα Θεοῦ,† *children of
God*, are used in a twofold reference, corresponding to the two
meanings, which belong to the phrase, as applied to the Saviour.
On the one hand, it has reference to the physical existence of
men. They are called sons of God, inasmuch as God (indirectly) is their Creator. This meaning, however, is very rare ; but

---

* On this construction *Schleiermacher's* opinion, too, is set aside, who says in the
Glaubenslehre, Th. ii., S. 707 : "Son of God" denotes probably not the divine nature *alone*,
but the *whole* Christ, in his divine and human nature. Passages, such as 1 John i. 7, certainly shew that the physical and metaphysical meanings were conjoined, as, indeed, the
Scriptures in general are far from any Nestorian separation of the natures. Still, *Son of
God* denotes the whole Christ, inasmuch as he was born from eternity of the essence of
the Father. *Son of Man*, on the other hand, denotes the whole Christ, inasmuch as he
represents the *ideal* of humanity.

† Τέκνον is not used of the person of Christ, though παῖς is. (Matth. xii. 18 ; Acts iii.
13, 26 ; iv. 27, 30.) This term does not, however, so much correspond to υἱός, as to the
Hebrew יְהֹוָה עֶבֶד, which is so often applied to the Messiah, especially in the second part
of the book of Isaiah. (See note on Acts iii. 13.) Τέκνον could not be used of Christ, for
this reason, that the notion of something undeveloped predominates in the word, while
υἱός denotes what has manly force and energy.

Ephes. iii. 15, John xi. 52, and Mal. ii. 10, come under this head. Otherwise, even in passages of the Old Testament, as Isa. lxiii. 16, Deut. xiv. 1, the reference to salvation predominates. In the latter sense it appears also in very many passages of the New Testament (1 John iii. 1, 2 ; v. 2 ; Rom. viii. 14, 16, 17 ; ix. 8 ; Gal. iii. 26, etc.), and denotes the regeneration which, as a new act of creation, restores to the condition of children those who were estranged from God by sin. This reference corresponds to the deeper signification of the name " Son of God," as applied to the Saviour. In regeneration there is the likeness of his eternal generation from the essence of the Father ; and in reference to the spiritual children of the one Father, our Lord calls himself also the first-born among many brethren. (Rom. viii. 29 ; Heb. ii. 11.) He who from eternity was Son of God, lived as Son of Man on earth in time, in order to raise the children of men from earth to heaven, that, as children of God, they might be like him, and become partakers of the divine nature. (2 Peter i. 4 ; 1 John iii. 2.)

Ver. 36–38.—Mary, too, receives a sign (σημεῖον, אוֹת), like Zacharias (i. 20) ; but it is a favourable one. As what had happened to Elisabeth is here made known to Mary from above, so also what had happened to Mary was made known to Elisabeth (ver. 41). Such dispensations were necessary under such extraordinary circumstances; and, just for that reason, we may assume similar facts for the solution of difficulties in those instances where they are not expressly noticed. (See note on Luke ii. 39.) The address concludes with the general truth, that the Divine Omnipotence accomplishes its plans notwithstanding all apparent impossibilities. The words are from Gen. xviii. 14, where they are used of Sarah in similar circumstances. The truth thus expressed, in its widest generality, should also be conceived as so far limited, that every thing true (ῥῆμα= דָּבָר) is also capable of expression ; for what is contradictory is, as such, not a ῥῆμα, word, thing, and, consequently, impossible with God, precisely because he is God. Mary, believing with childlike humility, submits herself to God ; she acquiesces in her destination for the fulfilment of the divine purposes. The birth of the Saviour became thus an act of her faith also. Mary's faith repaired Eve's unbelief. (In ver. 36, for the common reading γήρᾳ, which form stands for γήραϊ, and that again for γήρατι, from nominative γῆρας, Griesbach reads γήρει for γήρεϊ, from γῆρος. [See Winer's Grammar of the New Testament, translated by Agnew and Ebbeke, p. 59.]—Ver. 37. The expression οὐκ—πᾶν ῥῆμα is a pure Hebraism ; it corresponds with לֹא כָל־דָּבָר.)

Ver. 39.—In consequence of the suggestion of the angel, (verse 36), Mary visits Elisabeth, to whom, as a relative, she was, probably, already known. Zacharias' place of abode, which was left undetermined in verse 23, is now stated more precisely. He lived in the hill country of Judah (ὀρεινή scil. χώρα), in a Levitical city called Juda, more correctly spelt 'Ιούθα or 'Ιούττα. In the Old Testament it is called יֻטָּה (Josh. xv. 55 ; xxi. 16), for which the LXX. write 'Ιτάν in the first passage. The reading 'Ιουδαίας is at all events a correction ; if we retain the form 'Ιούδα, the name of the city must be supplied. In that case, Josh. xxi. 11 affords an appropriate parallel, where it is said of Hebron, Χεβρὼν ἐν τῷ ὄρει 'Ιούδα. (Μετὰ σπουδῆς corresponds with the more common expression σπουδαίως. It is found in the LXX. also, Exod. xii. 11 ; Ezra iv. 23 ; Dan. vi. 19.)

Ver. 40, 41.—The narrative evidently implies that there was no previous communication between the two women about what had happened. As Mary knew nothing of the circumstances of Elisabeth before she was informed by the angel (verse 36), so Elisabeth also was ignorant of Mary's fortunes. Both were led and taught by the Spirit. Nor was there time for such communications, according to the dates given us. As Mary received the visit of the angel in the sixth month of Elisabeth's pregnancy (verse 26, 36), and stayed three months with her (verse 56), she must have repaired to Elisabeth immediately after the annunciation. Joseph was then, undoubtedly, altogether ignorant of the circumstances, and did not become acquainted with them till Mary was advanced in pregnancy. (See more fully on this point in note on Luke ii. 39.) Being espoused, she might, therefore, without exciting attention, spend some months with a distant relative, by permission of her intended husband. The sacred emotions of soul experienced by the mother, are shared by the child yet unborn, and the Spirit from above filled the happy mother, who saw the most ardent hope of her soul realized. Like Hannah, the mother of Samuel, she, doubtless, often devoted her earnestly-desired child to God. (1 Sam. i. 11.) Respecting the πνεῦμα ἅγιον, see note on i. 15.

(Σκιρτάω = κινεῖσθαι is used particularly of the leaping motion, to which joy incites. The LXX. translate Mal. iv. 2 : σκιρτήσετε ὡς μοσχάρια. In Gen. xxv. 22, it is used also of the motions of children in the womb.)

Ver. 42, 43.—Elisabeth, as the elder, here blesses Mary and her child (καρπὸς κοιλίας = פְּרִי בֶּטֶן), as afterwards John the Baptist, though the inferior, had to baptize our Lord. Elisabeth, though she blesses, still makes herself inferior to Mary, when she says, καὶ πόθεν μοι τοῦτο κ. τ. λ.,* and whence is this ? etc. (Καί in questions, is emphatic ; see Mark x. 26.) Elisabeth's words, ἡ μήτηρ τοῦ κυρίου μου,

---

* The words ἵνα ἔλθῃ, involve the idea of some previous instigation or command, and might be paraphrased, " Who arranged that the mother of my Lord must come to me?" She regards it as a fresh proof of the favour of her God.

the mother of my Lord, are very remarkable. Turn them as we may, it cannot appear appropriate to call an unborn child κύριος,* *lord,* except upon the supposition, that Elisabeth, by the illumination of the Holy Spirit, like the ancient prophets, recognized the divine nature of the Messiah, as the mother of whom she greeted Mary. The passage is therefore parallel with verse 17, where, in the address of the angel, the same idea of the incarnation of God in the Messiah was hinted at, and κύριος, *lord,* is emphatic—equivalent to the Hebrew אֲדֹנָי or יְהֹוָה.

Ver. 44, 45.—Elisabeth's language passes, towards the close, into the third person. She speaks in prayer *of* Mary, and extols her *faith.* By the Holy Spirit, she probably recognized this as the fundamental disposition of Mary's heart, and as the condition of her happiness. The τελείωσις, *fulfilment,* has reference to the fulfilment of all that had been promised of her son in verses 32, 33. But with respect to the nature of her *faith,* it is clear, that this word does not here mean faith in any doctrinal proposition, but describes only the spirit of submission to the divine will, in which Mary was found at the announcement of the heavenly message. Faith is susceptibility to the operations of divine grace and their reception into the heart.† (See further remarks in note on Matth. viii. 2.)

Ver. 46, 47.—If we imagine Mary as living in intimate communion with the Sacred Scriptures, whose promises had doubtless often affected her soul, and drawn forth the wish, that God would at last help his people, and send the Saviour, and even that she might become the blessed mother of the Messiah, there is then nothing surprising in the expression of enthusiastic joy which follows. Under the consciousness of having become partaker of the highest happiness, she gave thanks for the mercy she had experienced, and for the fulfilment of God's promises, which she viewed as already performed ; expressing her thanks with prophetic intuition, and in words of Scripture familiar to her, particularly after the pattern of Hannah's song of praise, uttered under similar circumstances. (1 Sam. ii. 1–10.) Thus viewed, these poetical effusions lose all that

---

* *Dr. Paulus* is of opinion, that κύριος, *lord,* stands simply for βασιλεύς, *king;* and that Elisabeth merely expresses her faith that Mary will give birth to the Messiah. But as not even Augustus and Tiberius ventured to use the name κύριος of themselves, it is plain that this mode of designating kings was then very uncommon. Least of all, then, can it be believed, that pious Jews, who called God alone "the Lord," should have so applied the term. Certainly, if we do not regard these accounts of the history of the childhood of Jesus as family documents, the hypothesis is feasible, that, from a later and more matured conviction of the dignity of Jesus, such an expression was put into Elisabeth's mouth. But her divine illumination is sufficient evidence of her knowledge.

† [It is scarcely necessary to point out the defective view of faith expressed in the text. It does not agree with the definition in Heb. xi. 1, nor with the Calvinistic view of the nature of faith. Faith necessarily implies truth or facts as its object, and whatever else is included, this reference cannot be excluded.]—*Tr.*

strangeness which at first sight appears to attach to them. Even
Schleiermacher made use of them to support the opinion, that the
history of the childhood of Jesus had been cast into a mythical
form. Were the poetical effusions independent poems, they
would be calculated to awaken some suspicion; but as they are
merely reminiscences from the Old Testament, which we must
suppose to have been quite familiar to the parties concerned, their
introduction here is no way inconceivable or even inappropriate.
The following song of praise (verses 46–55) is usually called *Mag-
nificat*, from the first word in the Vulgate; we have an excellent
practical exposition of it by Luther. (Μεγαλύνω = הִגְדִּיל, Acts x.
46; xix. 17; Phil. i. 20.) The combination of πνεῦμα, *spirit*, and ψυχή,
soul, the distinction between which will be found at length in note
on 1 Thess. v. 23, denotes the whole internal being; the powers of
the soul, both high and low, were moved with joy. (See Psalm
ciii. 1, נַפְשִׁי and כָּל־קְרָבַי.) In ἐπὶ Θεῷ τῷ σωτῆρί μου, *in God my Saviour*,
the reference to an external salvation should not be altogether excluded (see verse 52); doubtless Mary looked forward to the
exaltation of David's family. But the deep religious fervor expressed in the song, does not leave us at liberty to regard this
reference as predominant, or to conceive of it at all under a coarse
and sensual aspect, particularly as we must certainly suppose
Mary to have been illuminated by the Holy Spirit, agreeably to
verse 41. The entire fulness of blessings, consummated by the
appearance of the Messiah, lay spread out before her, and she applied the general salvation (spiritual as well as external) to herself
also. God was in Christ her Saviour also; and as she was now
about to give birth to the Son of Man, so she was afterwards to receive the Son of God also into her heart. (See note on Luke ii. 35.)

Ver. 48–50.—With our spiritual conception of the passage, the
mention of the humiliation does not refer *primarily* to Mary's
outward political lowliness, since she was of David's family; it is
rather the expression of conscious inward poverty, which could
discover no pre-eminence in herself, because of which such happiness should have fallen to *her* lot. (Ταπεινός = עָנָו, אֶבְיוֹן [see note
on Matth. xi. 29], is closely related to πτωχός, Matth. v. 3.) We
ought not, however, entirely to exclude a reference to what is external; as a *result* of the mercy of God bestowed upon her, Mary
probably pictured external splendour to herself. But those who
have found in this fact a key to the Saviour's training, and show what
Messianic hopes he imbibed with his mother's milk, in fact but
enhance his glory in giving to the doctrine of the Messiah a character
so completely spiritual.* But again it is no false notion that

* [The views referred to above may not be familiar to some English readers. It has
been the great aim of the schools of theology opposed to the Gospel truth, to account for

the Messiah was to exercise a mighty influence on the outward affairs of this world. The error in the popular conception consisted in their desire for the external *without* the internal. If the people of Israel had been brought to a thorough change of heart, they would have acquired a powerful influence externally also. Though Mary, therefore, as she was not sinless, may, for single moments have been tempted by vanity, yet her views of the Messiah were entirely Scriptural. The Old Testament, as well as the New, deduces from the Messiah's sway over the spiritual world, the entire transformation of the external also. Christ is the king of all kings ; the highest earthly power is made his footstool. In the first instance, Mary brings into notice only the idea of the after-glory which would be her portion as the mother of the Messiah—a prediction which has been fulfilled in a more extensive sense than she could have wished. (Γενεά = ᴅᵒᴿ, *generation*, those who are living contemporaneously ; πᾶσαι γενεαί, the whole succession of future generations.) In the light of the Spirit she duly estimated the importance of the Messiah's birth for all times and circumstances. (Μεγαλεῖα = ᴺᴵᴰᴸᵀ, as in Psalm lxxi. 19 ; ὁ δυνατός = ᴿᴵᴮᴳ.) From the specific reference to herself, her language, in the last words from verse 49, καὶ ἅγιον τὸ ὄνομα αὐτοῦ, *and holy is his name*, becomes more general ; but the succeeding thoughts are still to be conceived as specially applicable to the present case. (Φοβούμενοι τὸν Θεόν, believers, in opposition to the unbelieving world, are the constant objects of his care, notwithstanding all appearance to the contrary. Ὄνομα, *name*, as the designation of the essential character in general, is more accurately defined by the special term ἔλεος, *mercy*.)

Ver. 51, 52.—With God's grace in blessing the *humble* (ταπεινοί,= φοβούμενοι—whence the choice of the term *mercy*, ἔλεος), is contrasted his rigour in the punishment of the *proud*, ὑπερήφανοι. Mary, in the Spirit, views both—the blessing for the humble as well as the curse for the proud—as connected with the birth of the Messiah. The words καθαιρεῖν δυνάστας ἀπὸ θρόνων, *to cast down potentates from their thrones*, compared with ver. 32, 33, render it not improbable that Mary contemplated external dominion also for her son. Like the prophets, she connected, in perspective, the future manifestation of the kingdom of Christ with its first appearance. But though she did conceive of an external dominion of Christ, an idea which

the extraordinary character of Jesus on merely human grounds. One of these explanations is alluded to above. Jesus Christ is supposed to have been trained by a mother full of ardent hopes and aspiring ambition to conceive of himself as the Messiah. But, as our author observes, the explanation, so far from accounting for the most extraordinary parts of the Saviour's character—the spiritual views of his kingdom—renders these more inexplicable.]—*Tr.*

has a true foundation in the Bible (see note on Matth. xxiv.), still her conception of it was doubtless different from the coarse material views of the great mass of the Jewish people. (With respect to the phrase ὑπερήφανοι διανοίᾳ καρδίας— καρδία, *heart*, in the biblical anthropology, is the seat of life, and of the most general and immediate manifestations of life, and therefore of sensation, and of thoughts and wishes influenced by sensation ; while σπλάγχνα, *bowels*, denotes pure sympathetic emotion. Hence we can explain the frequent combination of διάνοια, *thought*, and its synonyms λογισμός διαλογισμός, νόημα, διανόημα, ἐπίνοια, with καρδία, *heart*. This does not imply that the διάνοιαι, *thoughts*, are actions of the heart—they are rather actions of the νοῦς or λόγος, *mind* or *reason*—but that the incitement to these actions of the mind proceeds from the heart. See the fuller remarks in note on Luke ii. 35 ; Matth. ix. 3.)

Ver. 53–55.—A kindred thought is expressed in several similar figures ; poverty and hunger, wealth and fulness, are kindred ideas. The satisfying of longing desires—the repelling of self-satisfied curiosity after divine things, are both included in the notion of the Messiah. Nowhere does Mary betray any thing false in her views of the Messiah ; for the relation which, at the close, she represents his manifestation to bear to Israel and the predictions of its prophets, is to be explained agreeably to i. 16. (Ἀντιλαμβάνεσθαι = βοηθεῖν ; see Acts xx. 35 ; Sirach ii. 6. Israel is viewed as παῖς Θεοῦ, *a child of God*, agreeably to Exod. iv. 22, if παῖς, *child*, does not here stand equivalent to עֶבֶד, *servant*. Ἕως αἰῶνος,* *forever*, is not to be connected with μνησθῆναι, *to remember*, but with σπέρμα, *seed*, to intimate that the blessing of the Messiah would have a future influence on the whole human race in its nobler members, which the seed of Abraham represents. The datives are to be viewed as *dativi commodi*. The construction μνησθῆναι τινὸς τινί is classical.)

Ver 56.—After three months Mary returned ; as she was probably unmarried at the time of her journey (see note on Luke ii. 39), the expression οἶκος αὐτῆς, *her house*, leads us to suppose that she resided at Nazareth.

§ 4. JOHN'S BIRTH AND CIRCUMCISION—PROPHECIES OF ZACHARIAS CONCERNING HIM AND CHRIST.

(Luke i. 57–80.)

Ver. 57–59.—Shortly after Mary's departure to Nazareth, Elisabeth gave birth to the promised son,† who, according to very ancient usage, was named at the time of circumcision. (Gen. xxi. 3, 4.)

* Some editions read εἰς τὸν αἰῶνα.—*Tr.*

† The ancient Alexandrian church celebrated John the Baptist's birthday on the 23d April (28th Pharmouti.) Subsequently, the Greek church, as well as the Latin, devoted

This took place, agreeably to the Mosaic law, on the eighth day. (Lev. xii. 3.) The happy mother's joy over this son of her old age was shared by her neighbours. (Μεγαλύνειν ἔλεος = הִגְדִּיל חֶסֶד, Gen. xix. 19.)

Ver. 60–62.—According to the wish of those present at the circumcision, a family name was to be given to the child; but the mother (from the command, ver. 13) insisted on his being named *John*. In this dilemma they apply to the father to decide. The word ἐννεύειν, *beckon*, does not warrant us in supposing him deaf; in the first place, the expression does not actually exclude accompanying words, and then again we easily get into the habit of treating dumb people as if they were deaf. ('Αποκρίνεσθαι = עָנָה, means not merely giving a reply to a previous question, but beginning to speak in general—a use of the word well-known, and of frequent occurrence in the Gospels. In ver. 61, instead of ἐν τῇ συγγενείᾳ, Codd. A.B.C.L. read ἐκ τῆς συγγενείας, which Lachmann has rightly preferred. In the question τὸ τί ἂν θέλοι κ. τ. λ., the τό stands as connecting with the verb the whole clause which contains the question. It is used similarly in Mark ix. 23.)

Ver. 63–65.—The father decides for the mother (ver. 60), and writes down the name John. (Λέγειν, in connexion with γράφειν, has only the general meaning, " to declare," " to make known one's mind," as in Luke iii. 4, and in the oft-recurring phrase, λέγει ἡ γραφή. Πινακίδιον = γραμματίδιον, *a little writing tablet*.

Agreeably to the prediction (ver. 20), the punishment of unbelief inflicted on Zacharias was removed after the birth of the child. He speaks, and immediately makes use of his tongue to proclaim the praises of God, who had so glorified himself in the fulfilment of his promises. (As ἀνεῴχθη did not seem to agree well with γλῶσσα, some Codd. of inferior value have added ἐλύθη, διηρθρώθη, which may properly enough be supplied.) As the sense of a higher superintendence in these events forced itself upon those present, they were seized with the holy awe, seen in those who fear God, when divine influence comes perceptibly near them. (See note on Luke i. 12.) What had happened in the family was spread by report through the whole neighbourhood. It was confined, however, to the hill country (ὀρεινή i. 39), without reaching Jerusalem, the theocratic centre. Undreamed of by the Pharisees and scribes, the mightiest events of the kingdom of God were preparing among the simple-minded. (Διαλαλεῖσθαι, *to be talked or spoken of up and down*, Luke vi. 11. 'Ρῆμα = πρᾶγμα, after the analogy of the Hebrew דָּבָר, see Luke i. 37.) He who does not agree with *Schleiermacher*, in regarding this nar-

the 24th June to that purpose, evidently from the datum supplied by the Bible, that Elisabeth was with child six months earlier than Mary. They reckoned six months backward from the 25th December.

rative as " a charming little invention by a Christian of the refined Judaizing school," will have no hesitation in taking the fact of the healing of Zacharias, as well as his dumbness, and the angelic appearances, as historically true. In the light of Scripture we see that all physical phenomena subserve moral and spiritual development ; and, if this event be thus viewed as discipline for Zacharias, any objection to its historical character must arise from a false view of the fundamental relation in which God stands to the world. If we do not conceive of God as an extra-mundane being, who leaves the phenomena of nature to roll on according to laws left to themselves, but as sustaining the world by his breath, and as the inherent cause of all physical phenomena, then the miracle lies not in the single external fact (which always has its connexion in laws higher or lower, known or unknown ; for the Spirit of God itself is the law), but in the harmonious agreement of the individual phenomenon with the highest interests of the whole. Without this agreement the miracle would be on a level with a magical trick. (See more fully on this subject the note on Matth. viii. 1.) The supposition, that we have here not a fact, but a myth (apart from the general reasons already mentioned, which forbid the supposition of myths in the sacred Scriptures at all), is further discountenanced by the circumstance, that such a fabrication as the infliction of dumbness for a punishment, is most improbable, since it is altogether destitute of analogy.* There is surely in the whole transaction no internal contradiction which forms an argument against its historical character. It is only the dogmatic prejudice of a school that boasts its freedom from prejudice, which in order *to get rid of the miracle,* declares the whole account mythical !

Ver. 66.—A passing reference is made to the impression produced in the neighbourhood by these events in the family of Zacharias. In this way, expectations of the importance of the infant were excited, which his progress fully justified.

(Χεὶρ κυρίου = יַד יְהוָֹה, *the hand of the Lord.* The hand, as the most general organ of action, is here viewed in the light of protecting and blessing. · That this hand of the Lord was with the child in his growth, is mentioned by anticipation, in order to intimate that men's expectations were realized. The phrase τιθέναι ἐν τῇ καρδίᾳ, *lay up in the heart* = שׂוּם, with the prepositions עַל, אֶל, בְּ, with לְב, includes, not merely retaining in the memory, but also turning over and considering the matter with interest.)

Ver. 67.—There is not, properly speaking, any break here, as

---

* *Strauss* does not hesitate, notwithstanding this decisive point, to hold to his opinion, even in the second edition of his work (B. i., S. 141), though the production of analogies is the only means which he has in order to give the semblance of support to his arbitrary views.

ver. 66 only anticipates certain thoughts. The following prophetic words of Zacharias are rather in immediate connexion with ver. 64. (On πνεῦμα ἅγιον, see note on ver. 15, 41.) It is only to such an elevated moment, in which heavenly power strengthened Zacharias, bodily and spiritually, and raised him above himself, that the following words are suited, in which he speaks prophetically of his son's relation to the Messiah, and of the fulfilment of all the hopes which the seers of the Old Testament had excited. Zacharias begins with the main subject (ver. 68–75), and then places John (ver. 76–79) as exercising a preparatory influence, in his proper relation to our Lord, in whom all the promises of the prophets are fulfilled. Although here, too, the work of the Messiah is referred immediately to the people of Israel, and the whole representation bears a national colouring, *it is yet free from any alloy of error ;* for which reason those special references, as they are based on a truly moral conception of the Messiah's kingdom (ver. 74, 75), admit the same general application, which we have already vindicated above (ver. 16, 54.) The language finally is so strongly tinctured with Hebraisms, that it may be re-translated, word for word, into Hebrew —a circumstance, which, as already hinted, makes it extremely probable that we have here presented to us family memoirs, which Luke adopted as he found them. As such, these precious narratives have a double value, because they throw light on the circle of ideas in which John grew up ; and there is no difficulty whatever in supposing that he was made familiar with these by conversation and positive instruction, as it is only in the case of the Saviour that we are compelled to suppose an absolutely free development from within.

Ver. 68, 69.—In true prophetic inspiration Zacharias contemplates, as completed, the work of salvation, which appeared now in its germ, in the birth of the forerunner of the Messiah (for which reason the Aorists are not to be confounded with the Futures).* His unbelief (ver. 20) appears, therefore, here transmuted into the most assured faith, which enabled him to behold unseen things as visibly present. (On ὁ Θεὸς τοῦ Ἰσραήλ, *the God of Israel,* see note on ver. 16. It expresses only the genuine limitations of Scripture, such as were recognized by the Saviour and the Apostles. The relation of the Israelites to the Lord was different from that of all other nations.) In the birth of his son—whom Zacharias, however, views only in connexion with the appearance of Christ—he sees a rich visitation of God's favour, after long waiting on the part of the pious. ('Επισκέπτεσθαι is used quite like פָּקַד in the Old Tes-

---

* This description ill accords with the supposition that the Gospels were fabricated in the second century, and falsely ascribed to the apostles; for at that time the Church had acquired so little external splendour, that no one could have been prompted to such descriptions by its condition. •

tament, which denotes a visitation for punishment, as well as for deliverance [here of course the latter]. Λύτρωσις, redemption = פְּדוּת, see more fully on the idea in note on Matth. xx. 28.—Ver. 75 plainly forbids our thinking of political deliverance merely ; but that Zacharias connected external blessings with the appearance of the Messiah, is more than probable, and, regarding the work of the Messiah as completed, not erroneously.) In sending the Messiah, divine grace was revealed as both saving and defending. (Κέρας σωτηρίας, horn of salvation = קֶרֶן יֵשׁוּעָה, Psalm xviii. 3, is used here with reference to passages like Psalm cxxxii. 17, where we read of the " horn of David." The point of comparison in the figure is the power, which is here conceived as protecting the godly, and punishing enemies.)

Ver. 70.—The whole matter is at once connected with the hallowed company of ancient seers, who had predicted the general fact (the redemption of the people), as well as the special one, that a descendant of David should accomplish it. (Καθὼς ἐλάλησε sc. ὁ Θεός, as God spake, etc., is to be referred to the whole previous sentence.) The prophets are conceived as stretching in a continuous succession through the history of the people of Israel, and of our entire race. The result of their prophecies appeared at last realized. (Ἀπ᾽ αἰῶνος, ἐκ τοῦ αἰῶνος, and similar forms of expression, are used with an indefiniteness which must be more precisely determined by the context. They always require, however, that the subject spoken of should be carried back to the beginning of the period [αἰών] to which it naturally belongs. [See Luke i. 2, ἀπ᾽ ἀρχῆς.] Here the context indicates a reference of ἀπ᾽ αἰῶνος to the origin of the Jewish nation—that is, to Abraham [ver. 73], unless it is preferable to go back to the beginning of the human race itself, since the earliest advocates of righteousness and of the fear of God are conceived as prophets. [2 Peter ii. 5 ; Jude, ver. 14.] See more fully on αἰών in note on Matth. xii. 31.)

Ver. 71.—After the intermediate thought, the idea of the salvation is again taken up from ver. 69, and is viewed, first of all, as deliverance from enemies (ἐχθροί, μισούμενοι). In these words the political view of the Messiah's influence appears to come out most definitely, and assuredly it is here not to be altogether rejected. Here, as in ver. 47, there combined itself with Zacharias' view of the appearance of the Messiah, the contemplation of his completed work, in which the outward corresponds to the inward, as will be the case in the kingdom of God. But that very glance at the distant future, shows that the idea of enemies is to be taken in a deeper sense, and includes all whose life was under the influence of hostile principles. Then, too, this salvation is only one aspect of the Messiah's work ; it has its completion in the serving in holiness and righteousness, λατρεύειν ἐν ὁσιότητι καὶ δικαιοσύνῃ (ver. 74), and thus also the σωτηρία ἐξ ἐχθρῶν, *salvation from enemies*, acquires a deeper meaning, since the mere freeing from the dominion of the Romans would fail to confer any true holiness and righteousness.

Ver. 72, 73.—The construction proceeds entirely after the Hebrew mode (the infinitives ποιῆσαι, μνησθῆναι, are put for the common form εἰς τὸ ποιῆσαι = חֶסֶד לַעֲשׂוֹת, see Winer's Grammar of New Testament Idioms, p. 256) ; ποιῆσαι ἔλεος, *to perform mercy*, etc., is evidently not added as something different from the σωτηρία (ver. 71) ; but merely unfolds it. In the words : ποιῆσαι ἔλεος κ. τ. λ., it is not the present that is spoken of, but the past. By the present salvation, mercy was to be shewn also to the fathers in the past. (Ποιεῖν ἔλεος μετά corresponds with the Hebrew עָשָׂה חֶסֶד עִם "to be gracious to any one"—" to shew favour." Gen. xxiv. 14.) This thought is peculiarly calculated to bring out the spirituality and depth of view expressed in Zacharias' conceptions of the Messiah. The work of the Messiah is viewed as a saving one to the whole body of their forefathers, since in him first they all *really received* salvation and forgiveness, which they had *believed in* up to the time of his manifestation. The deliverance from enemies appears here to be such as confers benefits on the dead also ; and this shews clearly enough, that the enmity*—salvation from which is celebrated—is to be viewed as essentially deeper in its character. (The reference to the covenant and oath sworn to Abraham is put, as a *part* only, for the whole of the revelations and promises of God to the forefathers. The idea of the divine oath [ὅρκος] implies something inviolable, and consequently, now fulfilled by the faithful God. It is best to construe ὅρκον also with μνησθῆναι [see Is. lxiii. 7 ; Wisd. of Sol. xviii. 22], so that it stands parallel with διαθήκης.)

Ver. 74, 75.—Zacharias, resuming the idea of the σωτηρία in the words : ἐκ χειρὸς τῶν ἐχθρῶν ἡμῶν ῥυσθέντας, *being delivered from the hand of our enemies*, now adds a second thought, expressive of a new effect of the appearance of the Messiah, which exhibits itself at the present time—(*i, e.*, according to the prophetic view of Zacharias, who beheld the kingdom of God already complete)—viz., ἀφόβως λατρεύειν θεῷ ἐν ὁσιότητι καὶ δικαιοσύνη, *to serve God without fear in holiness and righteousness*. In its connexion with the τοῦ δοῦναι ἡμῖν, *to give to us*, the clause marks the true worship of God, described in it, as an effect and a gift resulting from the coming of the Messiah. It is not a mere consequence of the withdrawal of enemies, requiring the emphasis to be laid on ἀφόβως, but something

* To apply it *merely* to political enemies, as the Romans, is inadmissible. They are not indeed, to be excluded altogether ; and Zacharias was not in error, in anticipating an altered political condition of his nation ; it was nothing but the sin of the Jews that had made them then subject to the Romans, as they had before been to the Chaldeans— true repentance would have made them free again.

newly bestowed—never before realized. The words are parallel
with all those passages of the prophets which connect the establishment of righteousness with the appearance of the Mesiash.
This view alone is in agreement with what follows in ver. 77, where
Zacharias first speaks of the gift of the knowledge of deliverance,
and of its connexion with the forgiveness of sins ; while John was
to awaken the feeling of need, the Saviour was appointed to provide the holiness and righteousness themselves, and the λατρεία,
service, which springs from them. Λατρεύειν ἐν ὁσιότητι καὶ δικαιοσύνῃ,
to serve in holiness, etc., may be appropriately compared with προσκυνεῖν ἐν πνεύματι καὶ ἀληθείᾳ, *worship in spirit and truth* (John iv.
23), which also stands connected with the appearing of the Messiah.
In Ephes. iv. 24, both terms (ὁσιότης and δικαιοσύνη) are used, just
as in this place, to mark the new man created after God. (See also
1 Thess. ii. 10 ; Tit. i. 8.) The two terms here include the whole
extent of true piety. Only, ὅσιος = חָסִיד, *holy*, applies rather
to the pious man's relation to God ; δίκαιος = צַדִּיק *righteous*, to his
relation to his fellows.* Δικαιοσύνη, *righteousness*, is here conceived
more after the manner of the Old Testament. (See more fully on
this point in note on Rom. iii. 21.) In the concluding words of
ver. 75, πάσας τὰς ἡμέρας ἡμῶν, *all our days*, a more earthly conception of Messiah's kingdom seems again to shew itself, since its glory
is limited to the duration of life. The words may, however, be
viewed as a simple expression of the indefinitely protracted enjoyment of the blessings of the Messiah, whose kingdom is most plainly
designated (in ver. 33) as a lasting one. (The words τῆς ζωῆς are
spurious ; they were added as explanatory of ἡμῶν.)

Ver. 76.—Zacharias now first speaks of his son, and of his relation to the Saviour as his prophet and forerunner. (Προφήτης
ὑψίστου, *prophet of the highest*, stands in contrast with υἱὸς ὑψίστου,
Son of the highest, verse 32. On καλεῖσθαι, see note on Luke i. 35.)
Προπορεύεσθαι, *go before*, and ἑτοιμάσαι ὁδούς, *prepare his ways*, describe John's work according to the terms of the Old Testament.
(See Isa. xl. 3, and note on Matth. iii. 3.) That work was to
awaken a sense of need, the satisfying of which was to be accomplished by the Saviour himself. The words : πρὸ προσώπου
κυρίου, *before the face of the Lord*, contain again, as in verse 43, an
intimation of the divine nature of the Messiah, to which we are
also led by the actions ascribed, and the epithets applied to him in
the following words. The extent and clearness of Zacharias' views
respecting the mystery of the manifestation of God to mankind,
cannot be further determined. Probably the stream of divine light

---

* See *Polybius* (xxiii. 10, 8), who thus characterizes these relations : τὰ μὲν πρὸς
τοὺς ἀνθρώπους δίκαια, τὰ δὲ πρὸς τοὺς θεοὺς ὅσια.

which poured through his soul at this sacred moment, bore him
beyond the bounds of his everyday knowledge.

Ver. 77.—Zacharias proceeds to describe the labours of John,
using the same construction as above, verse 74, ff. The γνῶσις
σωτηρίας, *knowledge of salvation*, is specified as the object of his
preparatory labours. The Lord himself gives the salvation (verse
71), John awakens the perception of its necessity. (The special
connexion of this γνῶσις with the λαὸς Θεοῦ, appears here as in verse
68.) There can be no doubt how the following clause : ἐν ἀφέσει
ἁμαρτιῶν, *in the remission of sins*, should be connected. The salvation itself consists in this, and, as a divine act (Psalm xlix. 8, 9),
it can proceed only from God. (The clause is best completed thus,
σωτηρίας ἐν ἀφέσει ἁμαρτιῶν οὔσης, *salvation consisting in the remission of sins*.) The forgiveness of sin appears here, consequently,
as the grand prerogative of the times of the Messiah, which was
lacking to the Old Testament economy. (Comp. Jer. xxxi. 33–34.)
The sacrifices of the Old Covenant could not effect an inward, essential remission, but merely καθαρότης τῆς σαρκός, *purifying of the
flesh* (Heb. ix. 13), inasmuch as they restored its interrupted relation to the Old Testament theocracy. Sin itself remained under
divine sufferance. (See note on Rom. iii. 25.) But in the New
Testament essential forgiveness was bestowed, on the one hand, by
the actual removal of the consequences of sin; on the other, by
the implanting in man of a new, higher life—that of holiness and
righteousness. The purity of Zacharias' views of the Messiah is
here strikingly evident ; and hence we must from this passage,
gather a more precise meaning for the previous indefinite expressions, if we wish to interpret the speaker by himself.

Ver. 78.—The sending of the sin-destroyer is now set forth as
the effluence of God's mercy (just as in John iii. 16), and thus
Zacharias is led back to the Saviour himself ; so that the view of
his son merges, as it were, in the wider, grander view of the work
of Christ, just as John himself modestly withdraws behind the
Saviour (John iii. 30), as the morning star fades before the rising
sun. (Σπλάγχνα = רַחֲמִים frequently in the LXX., thence σπλαγχνίζεσθαι. The term is derived from the lower organs below the
heart being regarded as the seat of the purely sympathetic emotions ; but especially the womb [רֶחֶם, *uterus*], which, as the
organ of maternity, was put for mother's love. In some respects,
therefore, the term appears to denote the lowest grade of love, as
if it were purely physical love. But, because this shews itself to
be, at the same time, the most immediate and the strongest, it is
used also to denote the love of God, in order to express its essential
and immediate nature, of which maternal love is but a faint image.
The addition of ἐλέους, *mercy*, defines the divine love more precisely

to be such as is directed towards the miserable—the unfortunate.) As the effect of the divine compassion, Zacharias now brings forward the appearance (see note on ἐπισκέπτεσθαι, verse 68) of the ἀνατολὴ ἐξ ὕψους, *day-spring from on high.* The terms ἐπιφᾶναι, *to give light,* and κατευθῦναι, *to guide,* used in the following verse, shew that the Messiah is called a day-spring as being the light of men, φῶς τῶν ἀνθρώπων. In itself, the term might be appropriately compared with the Hebrew צֶמַח, *shoot,* according to passages such as Isa. iv. 2 ; Jer. xxiii. 5 ; Zech. iii. 8 ; vi. 12 (where the LXX. translate it by ἀνατολή), but that the word ἐπιφᾶναι following it, seems to make the former view preferable. The rising, namely, is put for the rising sun itself (Mal. iv. 2), which gives light to the wanderers, and shews them the right way. The addition of ἐξ ὕψους, *from on high,* marks the phenomenon as a heavenly one, descending hither from a higher system. (῞Υψος = מָרוֹם.)

Ver. 79.—In these concluding words there is reference to passages in the Old Testament (particularly Isa. ix. 1 ; lx. 1), in which the Saviour is described as the light of a world shut up in the night of ignorance and alienation from God. (See Matth. iv. 16.) The expression : ἐν σκιᾷ θανάτου καθήμενοι, corresponds exactly to the Hebrew צַלְמָוֶת בְּאֶרֶץ יֹשְׁבֵי, Isa. ix. 1. (On צַלְמָוֶת, see note on Matth. iv. 16.) Lastly, restoration to the way of peace is described as the result of the enlightening of those who sit in darkness. (Ὁδὸς εἰρήνης, *way of peace,* denotes that walk, that course of life, which is carried on with inward peace, and leads thither as its final aim. This presupposes the absence of peace in those that sit in darkness.)

Ver. 80.—A concluding formula, which depicts, in its general features, the physical and spiritual growth of the Baptist, and speaks of his life up to the time of his public appearance, concludes the family history of Zacharias. A similar formula closes likewise the family history of Mary (ii. 40, 52), which may indicate, perhaps, that both memoirs are by the same author. The words : ἦν ἐν ταῖς ἐρήμοις, *he was in the deserts,* refer to i. 15, and denote the Nazarite character of the Baptist's life. (῎Ερημος = מִדְבָּר, does not mean strictly *a desert,* but still a comparatively uninhabited tract of country. The solitude of his early life seems intended to be contrasted with the ἀνάδειξις, *shewing,* as the formal opening of his official labours as a prophet. On ἀναδείκνυμι, see note on Luke x. 1.)

§ 5. BIRTH, CIRCUMCISION, AND PRESENTATION OF JESUS IN THE TEMPLE.

(Luke ii. 1–40.)

A few months after the birth of John, Jesus was also born. The Evangelist first narrates how, by the leading of Providence, an

external political circumstance was made the occasion of Mary's
journeying from Nazareth, her usual dwelling-place (Luke i. 56), to
Bethlehem, the original residence of her family, where, agreeably to
the prophecies, the Messiah was then born. (See note on Matth. ii.
6.) A decree of the heathen emperor Augustus brought the
mother of our Lord to the city of David, to shew that " the king's
heart is in the hand of the Lord as the rivers of water : he turneth
it whithersoever he will." (Prov. xxi. 1.)

Ver. 1.—The previous verse gave by anticipation, and only briefly,
some notices about the Baptist. The words ἐν ἐκείναις ἡμέραις, in
those days, refer, therefore, to the history of John's birth detailed
in the former chapter. The passage contains some not inconsiderable historical difficulties, which have been employed by the advocates of the mythical interpretation, to demonstrate the unhistorical
character of Luke's Gospel. However, Savigny's investigations into
the Roman taxation, contained in the Zeitschrift für geschichtliche
Rechtswissenschaft, B. vi., have shewn that Augustus did, in fact, contemplate the introduction of a uniform system of taxation throughout
the whole Roman empire—a fact which had long been doubted. (Liv.
epit. lib. 134 ; Dio. Cass., liii. 22 ; Isidor. orig., v. 36 ; Cassidor,
iii. 52 ; Suidas, s. v., ἀπογραφή.) That this undertaking was extended to Palestine, too, though not at that time a Roman province,
is divested of all that appears strange, if we take the ἀπογραφή to
mean the mere registering of the landed estates, and not an assessment of property—the proper term for which is ἀποτίμησις. The
emperor might well take the liberty of making such a register, considering the dependence of the Jewish kings on him, a dependence
so great that the Jews had, along with the oath of allegiance to
Herod, to take one to the emperor. (See Tholuck's Glaubwürdigkeit der evangelischen Geschichte, S. 191.)

Ver. 2.—The words of Ver. 2, which seem to fix the enrolment
with greater historical precision, are still more difficult, since the
most obvious meaning does not agree with the accounts of historians ;
for the Κυρήνιος* (Quirinus) here spoken of was proconsul of Syria
at a much later period, since, about the close of Herod's life, Sentius
Saturninus, after him, Quinctilius Varus, and not till after both of
them, Publius Sulpicius Quirinus, were respectively invested with
this dignity. (Joseph. Ant. xvi. 13 ; Tacit. annal., iii. 68.) If, therefore, the census were meant, which, according to Joseph. xviii. i. 1,
was made by Quirinus in Syria and Palestine, the birth of Jesus
would have to be placed ten years later—whereby the whole chrono-

---

* Josephus (Ant. xviii. 1, 1) says of him: Κυρήνιος δὲ, τῶν εἰς τὴν βουλὴν συναγομένων
ἀνήρ, τάς τε ἄλλας ἀρχὰς ἐπιτετελεκὼς, καὶ διὰ πασῶν ὁδεύσας ὡς καὶ ὕπατος γενέσθαι, τά
τε ἄλλα ἀξιώματι μέγας, σὺν ὀλίγοις ἐπὶ Συρίας παρῆν, ὑπὸ Καίσαρος δικαιοδότης τοῦ ἔθνους
ἀπεσταλμένος, καὶ τιμητὴς τῶν οὐσιῶν γενησόμενος.

logy would be thrown into confusion.* According to both Matthew (ii. 1, 19) and Luke (i. 5, compared with iii. 1, 23), the Saviour was born during the reign of Herod ; a census, consequently, under this monarch could have been carried into effect only by the proconsul Sentius Saturninus, to whom, indeed, Tertullian (adv. Marc. iv. 19) assigns it, without any historical confirmation, but probably by conjecture only. From this passage we cannot so much as conclude that there was a different reading in the MSS. used by Tertullian. But even if there were, it would have no value, since it must be regarded as a correction of the original text. As the common text has been so perfectly established by the critical authorities, none of the conjectures that have been hazarded can obtain any sanction. Some have wished to insert πρὸ τῆς between πρώτη and ἡγεμονεύοντος κ. τ. λ., so that the sense would be : " this taxing took place before that (well-known one) under the proconsul Quirinus." It would be better to read αὐτή instead of αὕτη, which would give this meaning : " the taxing itself (the taxation *proper*, the real carrying out of the assessment in contradistinction from the preparatory registration) did not take place till under the proconsulate of Quirinus." The change of an accent cannot be regarded as a change in the text, since the oldest MSS. are written without accents.† We may also take πρώτη for προτέρα (as John i. 30 ; xv. 18) in the sense, " this taxing took place before the proconsulate of Quirinus." Yet I do not deny, that the observations, by which *Tholuck*, in his Glaubwürdigkeit der evang. Gesch., S. 182, endeavours to defend this explanation, are not

---

* With respect to the time of Christ's birth, this passage, on account of its internal uncertainty, cannot well be used to determine the *year*. Besides the star (see note on Matth. ii. 2), *the death of Herod*, before the end of whose reign Christ was born, contributes to the determining of this date. He died according to *Josephus* (Ant. xvii. 9, 3), shortly after the insurrection of a certain Matthias. Herod had him and forty companions burnt on a night, in which there occurred a total eclipse of the moon, which was soon followed by the Passover. This eclipse took place in the night of the 12th and 13th March. A.U.C. 750; and as there were no eclipses visible in Palestine for some years either before or after, Christ must have been born before A.U.C. 750. His birth, then, falls in a time of universal peace, on which the fathers lay so much stress. In A.U.C. 746, the temple of Janus was shut on the return of Tiberius from Germany, and it was not opened again till A.U.C. 752, on occasion of the war with the Parthians. See *Jo. Kepleri*, liber de J. Chr. vera anno natalitio. Francf. 1606, 4; *Wurm's* astron. Beiträge zur Bestimmung des Geburtsjahres Jesu in *Bengel's* Archiv., B. ii. St. 1; and further, the dissertation on the year of the birth of Jesus in *Kleiber's* Stud., B. i., H. i., S. 50, ff. (Jesus cannot have been born later than the beginning of March, 4710 of the Julian period—*i. e.*, the year of Herod's death, A.U.C. 750), and the supplement, *ib.*, H. ii., S. 208, ff. With respect to the *day* of our Lord's birth, the ancient Alexandrine church, according to Clemens Alexandrinus, assigned it to the 20th May (25th Pachon); while in the Western church, the 25th of December was fixed for it.

† This is, perhaps, the most natural solution of the difficulty. Luke directs attention to the fact that the Saviour was born precisely at the moment when the first preparatory steps were taken to strip Israel of its independence, and make it tributary to the Romans.
—[E.

quite satisfactory to me ; (see *Winer's* Grammar of the New Testament Idioms, p. 193) ; in particular, it seems to me harsh to take πρώτη ἡγεμονεύοντος for πρὸ τοῦ ἡγεμονεύειν, although the LXX. have a kindred construction in Jer. xxix. 2. Be that as it may, Tholuck, in his masterly treatment of this passage, has clearly proved, in answer to Strauss, that, even supposing all the difficulties in it should not be solved, we can draw no conclusion thence against the credibility of Luke, who everywhere shows himself intimately acquainted with Jewish and Roman history, and, in particular, with that first complete census under Quirinus. (Compare Acts v. 37 with *Joseph.* Ant. xviii. 1, 1.) If, on the most accurate historical inquiry, Luke's main assertion, so long doubted, that a taxing of the whole Roman empire took place under Augustus, is confirmed, we may be sure that the minor circumstance he mentions will also prove correct.

Ver. 3.—That the families had to go to their *own cities*, either was the result of the state policy of the Romans, who accommodated themselves to the Jewish custom, or more strictly that the registering, though made in accordance with a Roman edict, was executed by the Jewish kings, according to Jewish forms. Mary's accompanying her husband was not from any legal necessity (the Roman law would indeed have required it : Dion. Halic. Ant. iv. 15) but, as shown by the words οὔσῃ ἐγκύῳ, because Joseph was unwilling to leave her in her pregnancy.

Ver. 4, 5.—The fact that Mary too went to Bethlehem, is explained also on the supposition of her being an heiress, and possessing landed property in Bethlehem. (See note on Matth. i. 1.) As in journeying to Jerusalem, so in the journey to Bethlehem, the term ἀναβαίνειν = עָלָה, *go up*, has the secondary signification, implying to go up to what is elevated in a moral and religious point of view. (See *Gesenius* in the Lexicon, s. v.) Mary's being called μεμνηστευμένη, ver. 5, is explained by Matth. i. 25.

Ver. 6, 7.—In Bethlehem, whither the taxing had brought them, Mary gave birth to the Saviour of the world—in the deepest seclusion. (Ἐπλήσθησαν αἱ ἡμέραι τοῦ τεκεῖν αὐτήν, corresponds to the Hebrew וַיִּמְלְאוּ יָמֶיהָ לָלֶדֶת. See Gen. xxv. 24 ; Luke ii. 21.) As there was no room in the inn (κατάλυμα = ξενοδοχεῖον), she laid the infant down in the φάτνη, *manger*. (See ver. 12, 16.) This indicates that it was a stable which the mother of our Lord was obliged to choose for her resting-place, as the house was occupied. Ancient tradition speaks of a σπήλαιον, *cave*, as the place where Jesus was born. They were frequently used, in mountainous districts, as folds for flocks. As it is mentioned as early as *Justin Martyr* (dial. c. Tryph. Jud., p. 304), and *Origen* (contra Cels. I., xi. 3), and is in no way improbable in itself, it may, perhaps, be looked upon as established. (On πρωτότοκος, see note on Matth. i. 25. Σπαργανόω, *to wrap in swaddling clothes*, occurs elsewhere only in ver. 12.)

Ver. 8, 9.—The communication of the news of what took place in the sacred night is again limited to the humble unknown circle of a few shepherd families—to whom this very cave, which our Lord chose for his first dwelling, might belong. The unostentatious character which adorns the whole history of Jesus, is manifest in this feature also. The shepherds were, doubtless, like Simeon, ver. 25, waiting for the consolation of Israel ; the angel announced to their desire the fulfilment of all God's promises in Christ. Although ideas of the Messiah were spread through the whole nation, yet the sacred Scriptures make a distinction between the rude, carnal expectations of the mass, and the hopes of the few nobler spirits, which were founded on a deep-felt religious and moral need. ('Αγραυλέω, *to remain in the open field*, particularly by night. In the words ἄγγελος ἐπέστη, the idea of something sudden and unexpected in the appearance is conveyed. Δόξα κυρίου = יְהֹוָה כְּבוֹד, the radiant light, which is imagined as floating round all heavenly appearances.

Ver. 10, 11.—We must explain the contents of the angel's announcement by the previous more definite passages. (See i. 17, 32, 33, 74, 75, 78.) As the idea of the remission of sins is involved in the σωτήρ, *Saviour* (ver. 78), so κύριος, *Lord*, implies the divine dignity of the Sin-destroyer. (On λαός, see note on Luke i. 68.)

Ver. 12.—The angel, of his own accord, gives to the believing shepherds a sign (σημεῖον, אוֹת), which is not in itself necessarily a miraculous one. Still we may lay the stress on εὑρήσετε, *ye shall find*, to which ἀνεῦρον, *they found*, answers in ver. 16. In that case we need seek no external circumstances by which the shepherds were guided to look for the child just where he was ; a secret spiritual influence guided them to the right place through the darkness of the night.

Ver. 13.—This representative of the heavenly world, who communicated the joyful intelligence, was suddenly joined (ἐξαίφνης ἐγένετο = ἐπέστη, ver. 9) by a heavenly host (στρατιὰ οὐράνιος, = הַשָּׁמַיִם צְבָא), transferring the employments of their higher existence to this poor earth, which so rarely echoes with the pure praise of God. In this appearance there is *prefigured* the full realization of the kingdom of God, which secures the perfect union of things heavenly and earthly.

Ver. 14.—It is from this import of the angel's appearance, and its relation to the birth of the Messiah, that the words of the angelic song of praise are to be explained. Since all that was desired was restored by the Messiah, and his work is contemplated as complete, it is more suitable to supply ἐστί, *is*, than ἔστω, *let there be*, which latter gives to the words the form of a wish. On this the division of the words depends. If we put a period after δόξα ἐν ὑψίστοις Θεῷ, glory to God in the highest, it would not be suitable to supply ἐστί, is, and ἔστω, let there be, would be preferable, which would make the words more evidently an expression of thankful joy ; but then, ἔστω must be supplied for the latter part also ; and thus the thought would assume the form of a kind wish to be fulfilled in the future, while it is infinitely more significant to take it as an enthusiastic announcement of what is present in the Messiah. Accordingly that division is undoubtedly preferable which places a period after γῆς, earth ; so that the thought is this : "God is now glorified, as in heaven (ἐν ὑψίστοις = בַּמְּרוֹמִים in contrast with ἐπὶ τῆς γῆς), so on earth." The words then prominently point out the characteristic feature of Christ's work ; He makes earth heaven, and transplants hither the essence of heaven, thus fulfilling his own prayer : "Thy will be done, as in heaven, so on earth." In the language of enthusiasm, the plant of God's kingdom is represented in its maturity. According to this division, εἰρήνη, peace, is connected with what follows, and we must necessarily read εὐδοκίας, so that the whole forms but two parts.* The thought of the second half thus connects itself very naturally with the subject of the first. As the true glory of God (which results from the recovery of the lost) is restored by the Messiah, so also is peace restored on this earth accustomed to war, both externally and internally, and the ἄνθρωποι ὀργῆς, men of wrath, are transformed into ἄνθρωποι εὐδοκίας, men of good will. The critical authorities are certainly much more in favour of the reading εὐδοκία (only Codd. A.D., some translations, and several fathers defend the reading εὐδοκίας) ; still an erroneous punctuation of the first half might so easily make an alteration appear necessary in the second, that the origin of the reading εὐδοκία is, in that way, very easy to be accounted for. If there existed a further misunderstanding of the import of the words as a lively announcement of the present, and ἔστω was supplied, then the tripartite division appeared the easier, inasmuch as it seemed incongruous for men to be called ἄνθρωποι εὐδοκίας before the Saviour had finished his work and exercised his influence. The song of praise is more spirited and profound, if we take it as consisting of two parts, and not as a wish, but as an announcement of grace bestowed. Besides, with the threefold division, it is difficult to avoid the tautology in ἐπὶ γῆς εἰρήνη, peace on earth, and ἐν ἀνθρώποις εὐδοκία, good will to men; in that case we must interpret εἰρήνη, very superficially, of external peace merely in the relations of men among one another ; εὐδοκία = רָצוֹן,of men's relation to God.†

---

* The preponderance of reasons still seems to me to be in favour of those who divide the angelic song into two parts. Men such as Beza, Mill, Bengel, Nösselt, Morus, likewise viewed the passage in this light.

† Against this twofold division is the unhebraistic omission of καί before εἰρήνη. The

Ver. 15–17.—The heavenly ones returned to their heavenly abode —the men went to Bethlehem, found what was foretold, and made known what they had witnessed to the circle of like-minded friends (ver. 18) ; for, that the angels' words did not belong to the multitude, was well understood by those to whom they were addressed. (On ῥῆμα, see note on Luke i. 37. Διαγνωρίζω = divulgo scil. τὰ περὶ τοῦ ῥήματος.)

Ver. 18–20.—Those who heard the glorious intelligence were amazed ; the shepherds praised God, like the angels (ver. 13), and with child-like faith viewed what they had seen as the fulfilment of that which was foretold, trusting to the accounts of the mother ; but Mary thankfully received this homage as a confirmation of her faith. (Συντηρεῖν implies rather active remembrance ; συμβάλλειν ἐν τῇ καρδίᾳ, denotes reflection with pleasurable emotion and interest. In ver. 51, ἐν τῇ καρδίᾳ is connected immediately with διετήρει ; and thus both the actions of the memory and of the heart are combined in one expression.)

Ver. 21.—Agreeably to the Mosaic law (Lev. xii. 3) the circumcision of the child was performed on the eighth day, and, at the same time the name of Jesus was given to him, as the angel had commanded (i. 31). The Son of God—the pure and the purifier— was in all things made under the law (Gal. iv. 4); and as he appeared even ἐν ὁμοιώματι σαρκὸς ἁμαρτίας, in the likeness of sinful flesh (Rom. viii. 3), the Father called him to undergo circumcision also, as the symbol of purification from the σὰρξ ἁμαρτίας, sinful flesh. In all respects (κατὰ πάντα, Heb. ii. 17) he was made like his brethren, yet without sin. (Heb. iv. 15.) This divine arrangement had, in the first place, a relation to the work of the Saviour. In order to save those that were under the law (Gal. iv. 5), he himself descended into all the depths of human misery, and with toil ascended the steps which the Father himself had appointed. It had a relation to his person also. Participation in the cleansing rites of the Old Testament was not, on the part of the Saviour, an unmeaning action for appearance' sake, but one of essential import. Holy, pure, and perfect in his divine nature, he shared in his human nature our common infirmity. He was θνητὸς σαρκί, mortal in respect to the flesh (1 Peter iii. 18), and the temple of his body was only gradually spiritualized to ἀφθαρσία, incorruptibleness, by the indwelling of the heavenly Spirit. (See note on Matth. xvii. 1, ff.) The circumcision, therefore, the participation in the purification (ver. 22), in the baptism of John, and in all the sacrifices in the temple, were proofs that the Saviour declared them to be divine

triple division is perhaps simpler. The angels thus rejoice, 1. That in heaven God is honored for the work of redemption begun; 2. That on earth a kingdom of peace is established destined to terminate strife; 3. That between heaven and earth such relations are re-established that God can look approvingly on men.—[E.

institutions, and by taking part in them, placed himself, in one element of his being, on an equality with his brethren. True, there was no absolute *necessity* of this method of bodily perfection to the Saviour (see note on Matth. iii. 15 πρέπον ἐστὶν ἡμῖν), as there was to the other members of the Jewish nation; in whose case the omission of circumcision would have occasioned their being cut off from among the people. But the harmony of God's scheme of salvation required just this form of development in his human life; agreeably to which, by means of this sacred act, which in all Israelites formed and strengthened the bond of the covenant with God, he was received as a member of the theocracy of the Old Testament, in order that, after he had attained to a full consciousness of his higher nature, he might raise the whole community, to which he was so variously related, to his own higher sphere of life.

Ver. 22.—The participation in the καθαρισμός, *purification*, is explained on a similar principle. The woman was obliged, according to the Jewish law (Lev. xii. 1), to remain at home as unclean for forty days after the birth of a boy, and for eighty after the birth of a girl, and then to purify herself by an offering. The period was much too long for sanatory purposes—the ordinance had a religious and moral import. It kept alive a consciousness of sin, which, from the first, displayed itself so prominently in the sexual relations (Gen. iii. 10, 16), and directed her view, through the offering that followed, to the coming deliverance from all impurity.

(The reading αὐτοῦ is remarkable; for although it is certain that αὐτῆς is an alteration, which arose from narrow doctrinal views, since καθαρισμός did not seem to be required for the σωτήρ; yet we cannot imagine that any one would have altered the text to αὐτοῦ. With the exception of Cod. D., it has only some Codd. of inferior authority in its favour; still it is a question, whether the reading αὐτοῦ is not preferable to the common one αὐτῶν.)

Ver. 23.—According to the law of the Old Testament (Exod. xiii. 2), every first-born (בְּכוֹר = רֶחֶם פֶּטֶר אֲשֶׁר = διανοῖγον μήτραν), if a male, was holy to the Lord (קָדוֹשׁ ἅγιος, *sacer*, signifies primarily only what is separated from that which is profane, and destined for sacred use.) But as according to Numb. iii. 12, 13, the Lord had taken the tribe of Levi for himself, instead of all the first-born, the first-born sons had indeed to be presented before the Lord (παραστῆσαι = הִקְרִיב), as a symbolical act of consecration, of surrendering for his service; but they could be redeemed for five shekels. (Num. xviii. 15, 16.) Jesus was thus redeemed, according to the forms of the law, from service in the earthly tabernacle, that he might build a greater, a more perfect tabernacle. (Heb. ix. 11.)

Ver. 24.—The offering had immediate reference to the woman (Lev. xii. 8), with whom, however, the child was regarded as one.

The circumstance that Mary offered doves, is a proof that she was poor—the rich presented a lamb. Nevertheless, she may have possessed some small plots of ground at Bethlehem and Nazareth ; for the regulation of bringing a lamb of the first year, as an offering, for purification, applied only to the rich, strictly so called. (Lev. xii. 6.)

Ver. 25.—The sojourn at Jerusalem gave occasion for a fresh confirmation of Mary's faith, from the circumstance, that a certain man, Simeon by name, uttered words prophetic of the child's importance. Simeon's personal history is not known ; for the conjecture that he was father to Gamaliel (Acts v. 34), and son of Hillel, is extremely improbable. The indefinite expression ἄνθρωπός τις, a certain man, indicates rather that he belonged to the lower ranks, in which the deeper religious life appears to have concentrated itself at the time of Christ. Simeon, like Zacharias and Elisabeth (i. 6), is called δίκαιος, righteous, which denotes the external legal aspect of his life ; while εὐλαβής, pious, akin to ὅσιος (i. 75), denotes rather the internal aspect, the disposition towards God ; but, of course, in relation to the Old Testament form of piety, since piety is equivalent to fear of God. His religious life is characterized most definitely by the words : προςδεχόμενος παράκλησιν τοῦ 'Ισραήλ,* waiting for the consolation of Israel, which are akin to the following phrase : προςδεχόμενος λύτρωσιν, awaiting redemption (verse 38). The latter expression regards the deliverance from sin and misery in the appearance of the Messiah ; while the former specifies the consolation afforded by it. Both are included in the phase, προςδέχεσθαι τὴν βασιλείαν τοῦ Θεοῦ, waiting for the kingdom of God.

(With respect to παράκλησις, it is only in this passage that it is used for the concrete παράκλητος. Παράκλητος = מְנַחֵם, in Rabbinical writers, though פְּרַקְלִיט or פְּרַקְלִיטָא is also found in them, occurs frequently, but in the New Testament principally of the Holy Ghost [John xiv. 16, 26 ; xv. 26 ; xvi. 7]; yet of Christ also in 1 John ii. 1, although in a modified sense. The term as here used of the Messiah, has a reference to the suffering state of the people, which is conceived to be removed by the appearance of the Messiah.) This pious man also, at that richly blessed season, when what earth ever witnessed of noblest was in silent preparation, had received the Holy Spirit (see note on Luke i. 15), and, in his power, prophesied of the Saviour. (The phrase ἦν ἐπ' αὐτόν [see ver. 40] is to be explained by supplying ἔρχεσθαι, which is involved in ἦν. " The Spirit came upon him, and consequently wrought in him.")

Ver. 26, 27.—Simeon, waiting for the consolation of Israel, had been assured by the Spirit, that he should not die before being honoured with a view of the Messiah. (On χρηματίζεσθαι, see note on Matth. ii. 12. As to the form of this χρηματισμός, whether it came

* The expression ἐλπὶς τοῦ 'Ισραήλ, in Acts xxviii. 20, is very similar.

to him when awake, or in a dream, the narrative is silent. Instead
of ἰδεῖν θάνατον, γεύσασθαι θανάτου [Matth. xvi. 28] is also used elsewhere, since perception by the senses is put for actual experience of
every kind.) The same Spirit who had given the promise, conducts
him also at the proper moment to its fulfilment. Such a guidance
by the Spirit, which stands in contrast with choice from reflection,
is seen in the life of all Scripture saints, from Abraham to Paul.
It is the prerogative of the true children of God, who possess innocence in the noblest sense of the word, that they know the voice of
truth (John x. 4), and are enabled to follow it without falling into
error, though they do not on that account neglect the use of natural
means, such as reflection and attention to circumstances. (See e. g.
Acts xvi. 6.)

Ver. 28, 29.—By the power of the same Spirit, Simeon, with
indubitable certainty, recognized the promised Saviour in the child,
without needing any information from Mary of what she had experienced. With fervour the old man immediately pours out his
grateful heart to God, who had fulfilled his promise to him. (The
words κατὰ τὸ ῥῆμά σου scil. πρὸς ἐμὲ ἐρχόμενον, refer to ver. 26.)
This sight of the desired One he regards likewise as the end of his
earthly existence, and, with a swan-like song concerning his glory,
he takes leave of life below. (In ἀπολύειν ἐν εἰρήνῃ, dismiss in peace,
there is an allusion to the service and the spiritual office of Simeon ;
he was a prophet in his day, and doubtless maintained a lively and
vigorous hope in the circle of those who looked for redemption.
[Ver. 38.] In εἰρήνη, peace, there is not merely a reference to the
fulfilment of the hope which inspired Simeon, of yet beholding the
Saviour ; the term denotes, with a profounder meaning, the peaceful consciousness in general, that the people of Israel, and himself
with them, had attained its everlasting goal in the now manifested
Messiah. Δεσπότης, Lord, is used several times of God [Acts iv.
24 ; Jude, verse 4 ; Rev. vi. 10]; once only of Christ. [2 Pet. ii. 1.]
The term differs from κύριος in this, that it denotes more precisely
the relation of a ruler with unlimited power ; while κύριος suggests
the milder idea of possession of property.)

Ver. 30, 31, 32.—Simeon, in prophetic rapture, follows up this
thanksgiving with a description of the influence of the Messiah,
whom he had seen bodily. (The expression οἱ ὀφθαλμοί μου, my eyes,
refers to bodily sight, for with the eye of the Spirit he had long
beheld the coming of the Saviour ; he longed for his appearance in
the flesh, John i. 14.) Although, therefore, above (ver. 25),
Simeon's hopes of the Messiah were conceived with a national
reference, in that the Saviour was called " the consolation of Israel,"
yet here there appears most distinctly a consciousness that this
desired One would, by God's appointment, exercise an influence

over *the whole human race.* In the light of this plain assertion, therefore, we may judge of the former passages in which such expectations were set forth. Their seeming limitation to Israel, and their reference to earthly relations, form but the one aspect of the idea of the Messiah, which we must complete by the other, even where it is not expressly mentioned. The Messiah's most immediate relation is certainly to Israel, but thence the vivifying influence of his Spirit extends to all nations ; and though his agency commences in the depth of the soul, yet it thence influences external relations also ; so that, in the most proper sense, the human race, as such, in all its members, and in all its external and internal relations, is the subject on which the Messiah exercises his saving and sanctifying power. As this relation of the Messiah's work to the entire human race, even to the most distant nations, is just the doctrine of the Old Testament also (see Gen. xii. 3 ; xviii. 18 ; xxviii. 14 ; xlix. 10 ; Psalm lxxxvii.; Isa. xi., xix., xlii., and other passages), we are the more obliged to presuppose this correct view in the pious at the time of Christ, in that *they* appear as living in the spirit of the Old Testament. That its connexion with their own nation, however, and their deliverance from bondage to the heathen, should occupy the foreground with them, is perfectly accounted for by their circumstances. The same form of representing the subject is sanctioned by the Old Testament, which never permits the Messiah's relation to the nation to degenerate into bigoted exclusiveness, nor its hopes of external good to be without a moral and religious foundation. But the contrary was the case with the conceptions of the gross and sensual multitude, who rejoiced in excluding all heathen, as such, from the blessings of the Messiah, and who, with their carnal dispositions, and without true change of heart, hoped to be allowed at once to follow the Messianic King, as their general, to a war of extermination against the heathen. That such gross conceptions are not to be confounded with the noble views which were preserved in the circles of the pious at that time, is shewn by ver. 38, where those who waited for redemption are spoken of as a special class. But the expectations of a Messiah were, as already intimated, a common property of the nation at the time of Christ ; if, therefore, those which were current among the multitude were acknowledged as the true ones, then the waiting for redemption could not have been used as characteristic of a certain class of men. (In verse 30, as in i. 71, the abstract is put for the concrete person, σωτήριον = σωτηρία for σωτήρ. It is called " God's salvation," both because it springs from God, and because it is agreeable to his nature ; and these two coincide, since only what is godlike comes from God. Ἐτοιμάζειν = προορίζειν [Rom. viii. 29, 30] marks the relation towards the heathen, as founded on God's gracious purpose, which Simeon correctly perceived in the prophecies of the Old Testament. In κατὰ πρόσωπον = ἐνώπιον = לִפְנֵי, *in the face of, before,* there is implied not only being known externally, but having also an inward efficacy, since everything beheld externally produces kindred internal effects. The expression reminds us of Isa. xi. 10, where the Messiah is called אֲשֶׁר עֹמֵד לְנֵס עַמִּים, since he stands before the people as a sign of gathering—as forming a spiritual centre. In like manner, in ver. 32, φῶς εἰς ἀποκάλυψιν ἐθνῶν, *a light to enlighten the Gentiles,* refers to passages, such as Isa. xlii. 6 ; [John i. 4;] Isa. xxv. 7. The being covered [פְּנֵי־הַלּוֹט, Isa. xxv. 7] is opposed to ἀποκάλυψις. But the blessing of the heathen is, on the other hand, a " glory" of Israel. Λαός and ἔθνος, are here interchanged, as Israel is also called ἔθνος, John xi. 48, ff. It is only when used in the plural that ἔθνη = גּוֹיִם has the meaning " heathen.")

Ver. 33, 34.—The parents of Jesus did not wonder, probably, so much at the thoughts uttered concerning their son's mission and influence, as that the Spirit uniformly testified from the most various quarters to his high spiritual dignity and importance. (The reading Ἰωσήφ for πατήρ is evidently the offspring of doctrinal scrupulousness. Copyists feared that the term might be misunderstood.) Simeon's being here represented to us as *blessing* the Saviour, must be explained on the principle stated at Luke ii. 21 and Matth. iii. 15. On the principle, " the less is blessed of the greater" (Heb. vii. 7), Simeon here appears exalted above the Saviour, just as do John who baptizes him (Luke ii. 46), and the Rabbins whom Jesus questions. In his human development, the Saviour takes his place among men according to the ordinary stages of human development ; as a child, therefore, he is *really* a child, and consequently in subordination (verse 51) to those in the more advanced stages of life. Yet in every period of his life, and in each stage of his gradual development, he unfolded himself sinlessly, and thus exhibited in each separate stage its own pure ideal of excellence. In the succeeding context, Simeon specifies more particularly Christ's work, which is viewed as discriminating and separating according to the qualities of men, and as causing ruin as well as blessing. A slight intimation of the path of sorrow by which the end must be attained, is then appended. (Luke xxiv. 26.) The figure employed, to which the expression refers, is that of a stone (Isa. xxviii. 16 ; Dan. ii. 34 ; Zech. iii. 9 ; Matth. xxi. 42); which becomes a πρόσκομμα, *stone of stumbling* (1 Pet. ii. 7, 8) to the proud, who stumble at it, but, to the humble, a means of elevation from their low condition. Ἀνάστασις is here simply the opposite of πτῶσις.) In these opposite departments of his work, the Saviour manifests himself according to divine intention and arrangement. (Κεῖσθαι, *to be set*, is by no means absolutely synonymous with εἶναι, *to be;* the term combined with εἰς, involves a reference to an intention—a purpose, Phil. i. 17.) And it is not merely at his first appearance, but also as his work extends through the whole of the world's history, that the Saviour manifests himself at all times and places, quite as much in the way of punitive justice, as in that of redeeming efficacy ; the two are the mutually supplementary parts of our Lord's work. (The remark that not *all*, but *many* individuals among the people, were affected by it, may be thus explained, that, so far as Christ's intention is concerned, all should be saved ; but unbelief prevents this result ; to many he is salvation, to many ruin.) In the concluding words, καὶ εἰς σημεῖον ἀντιλεγόμενον, *and for a sign spoken against*, there is an intimation of Christ's passion. Those who stumble at him are also those who speak against him (ἀντιλέγοντες.) ('Αντιλέγειν is taken as a general expression of hostile disposition, which involves the act also.) But even in this ἀντιλογία the Saviour appears as a sign, set before the world by the Father, and, that as much before the unbelieving as the believing world, though indeed in different relations. The expression is to be taken in the same way as Isa. viii. 18. God speaks to the world by the Saviour and his entire complex manifestation—by the Man with the cross and the crown of thorns, and the eternal Son of God, the Judge of the quick and the dead—in the mighty language of fact, and sets him up, in truth, as a miraculous sign for mankind, as Isaiah and his sons, with their symbolical names, were in their time. (See note on Matth. i. 23.)

Ver. 35.—At the mention of the opposition of the world to· the Anointed, the far-seeing prophet gives a glance at the development of the blessed mother's life. She who gave birth to the Son of God was still, as such, not born of God. She was, as all mankind are by nature, γεννητὴ γυναικός, *born of a woman* (see note on Matth. xi. 11), and therefore, like them, needed regeneration, which cannot be effected without affliction, Rev. vii. 14. But the words : τὴν ψυχὴν διελεύσεται ῥομφαία, *a sword shall pierce thy soul*, cannot contain the mere idea of suffering, without including that of consolation ; this would cast a shade over the joyful tone of the whole prophecy. The idea of the deepest, most exquisite agony of soul, rather includes here the idea of salvation and perfecting through it, just as the ἀντιλέγεσθαι (ver. 34) comprises the victory over every ἀντιλογία. Mary's distress, which was one with her Son's, appears at once killing and quickening. At the sight of him she must endure not only the struggle of a mother's love, but that of faith also, which appeared to die in her along with him, who had been bestowed from above.—The revealing of the secret depths of the hearts—of the good as well as the bad—is declared to be the end of this discriminating, judicial work. Christ appears here as Judge of the world, even during the progress of the human race ; wherever he appears, his pervading agency compels to a decision for or against. (The διαλογισμοί, *thoughts*, are here again, as was observed in note on Luke i. 51, connected with the *heart* (καρδία). So also the less usual terms, ἐπίνοια [Acts viii. 22], ὑπόνοια [1 Tim. vi. 4], νόημα [Baruch ii. 8.] All these expressions, as indeed the etymology intimates, denote actions of the νοῦς or λόγος, and correspond to the word " thoughts." *Heart* cannot therefore denote that power to which they belong. But the Sacred Scriptures, according to a view which is psychologically quite correct, never conceive of the active exercise of the thinking faculty apart from the inclinations, and the bent of a man's whole life ; they refer every rising thought to the latent inclination of the heart.* As the central point of personal life, the Bible regards the heart = לֵב [see Prov. iv. 23 ; כִּי מִמֶּנּוּ תּוֹצְאוֹת חַיִּים.] Hence ἐκ καρδιῶν, *out of the heart*, points out quite correctly the impulse given to the διαλογισμοί, *thoughts*, from the heart, though they themselves belong to the νοῦς, *mind*.

Ver. 36, 37.—One other individual is mentioned to us by name† out of the pious circle at Jerusalem—probably a very narrow one—Anna, who also had received the Spirit (Προφῆτις = πνεῦμα ἅγιον ἔχουσα, ver. 25.) It is remarked, as the distinction of this woman, otherwise unknown to us, that, although eighty-four years of age, she had been united with a husband only seven years, and spent her whole remaining life in widowhood. It is the tender fidelity with which she treasured the memory of her husband, that is here brought into notice. Her piety is conformed to the Old Testament model. Her religious life assumed an ascetic and Nazarite form. (See i. 15.)

Ver. 38.—She repaired to the temple at the same time, perhaps at the hour of prayer (ἐφιστάναι, *to appear suddenly*, see Luke ii. 9), and joined in the praise of God, when she received the intelligence that all her hopes were fulfilled in the appearance of the Messiah. (The term ἀνθομολογεῖσθαι means, in classic Greek, " to strike a bargain," " to agree," " to make mutual concessions." In the Hellenistic language it is used for הֹדָה, *to praise*, Psalm lxxix. 13. 'Εξομολογεῖσθαι is used in the same sense in Gen. xxix. 35, and the simple verb, in Job xl. 9. It is found nowhere else in the New Testament.) The aged woman imparts the joy of her heart to the like-minded

---

* Old *Michael Montaigne* has a very beautiful remark in the *Stimme der Wahrheit*, Th. i., S. 4: " In man," he says, " we may overlook the *head*, though it is always good not to do so, if it be in the right place, and gives birth to nothing wrong; but the *heart* is still the main thing. We need the head for *life* only, but the heart for *death* also."

† Even *Schleiermacher* has observed, that this mention of a second individual, who reiterates Simeon's testimony, is against the mythical character of the narrative. One event of that sort would have satisfied the tendency in the church to the formation of myths.

members composing the circle of the Messiah's friends in Jerusalem.
(On προσδέχεσθαι λύτρωσιν, see Luke i. 68 ; ii. 25.—Λύτρωσις is here
put for λυτρωτής.—Περὶ αὐτοῦ refers to the object of praise, not, indeed, expressly mentioned—viz., the Messiah who was come.

Ver. 39, 40.—After the completion of the ceremony of purification (ver. 22), the mother and child returned to Nazareth. The
mention of the final limit of the journey, from its being Mary's actual
place of constant abode, does not directly exclude other journeys,
(See the subsequent narrative of Jesus' childhood.) At this point
the memoirs evidently become more general, and ὑπέστρεψαν εἰς τὴν
Γαλιλαίαν, they returned into Galilee, is not so much a new fact intended to be recorded by the narrator, as a form of conclusion. The
more particular and accurate accounts were wanting here, and therefore he brings back the mother and the child to the place where he
knew they constantly resided (Πόλις αὐτῶν, see Luke i. 56.)—The
last verse, just as was related of John (i. 80), notices that purely
human development of our Lord, corporeal and spiritual, to which
even his life in its human aspect was subject.) The only peculiar
feature is that which is added in the words πληρούμενον σοφίας, filled
with wisdom. But that the idea of wisdom is to be taken relatively,
is shewn partly by ii. 52, which describes the wisdom of Jesus himself as still unfolding itself ; and partly by the idea of childhood, to
which the character of wisdom always belongs only relatively. But
this is precisely the idea of the Messiah in his human development,
that he presents each stage of life pure and unsullied by sin ;
yet so as never to obliterate the character of the stage itself ;
which would be the case on the supposition that the child Jesus
possessed perfect wisdom.* Χάρις ἦν ἐπ' αὐτό, grace was upon
him (see ii. 25), not merely expresses God's being well pleased in
Jesus, but intimates also the effective cause of the pure unspotted
development of the Saviour's life. Grace is nothing but love revealing itself—shewing itself actively ; and in every moment of the life
of Jesus the love of God shone forth in active exercise in him. He
was completely a child—completely a youth—completely a man ;
and thus hallowed all the stages of human development ; but nothing incongruous ever appeared in him, which would have been the
case if utterances of a riper age had escaped him in childhood.

Here, at the close of the history of Jesus' infancy, we must glance
at the relation of the narratives of Matthew and Luke, of which it
is maintained, that they do not supplement, but contradict each

---

* Schleiermacher observes very justly in the Glaubenslehre, Th. ii., S. 178—"If we
choose to deny the gradual development of the Saviour, we must either suppose, that his
whole childhood was a mere semblance, and that in his first year, for instance, he had
entire command of language ; or we must return to the solution of Cerinthus, and separate that in which Christ was similar to all men from that which was archetypal in him."

other; that they are the offspring of totally different traditions, and are, as it were, lines running parallel with each other. According to Luke, the parents of Jesus live at Nazareth, and his birth at Bethlehem seems the result of accidental circumstances; in Matthew, on the contrary, they would seem themselves to have lived at Bethlehem. Further, Luke's narrative of the annunciation appears irreconcileable with Joseph's being ignorant at first of the nature of Mary's pregnancy, and his being informed by the angel, as Matthew says; and again, the adoration of the Magi, Herod's slaughter of the children, and the flight into Egypt, as recorded by Matthew, appear irreconcileable with Luke's account of the journey to Jerusalem for the purification. On closer consideration, however, the first objection, that Matthew appears to follow a different tradition as to the residence of Jesus' parents, resolves itself into something purely negative. For Matthew evidently follows no tradition whatever concerning the residence of Jesus' parents, and gives no remarks at all as to time and place; he merely recounts the facts. The circumstance of his naming Bethlehem (ii. 1) as the birthplace of Jesus, happens, as the following verses shew, only in consequence of that place being so assigned in a prophecy of the Old Testament. Otherwise, Matthew would hardly have named the place of birth at all. Just so he would have been content with the general statement, εἰς τὰ μέρη τῆς Γαλιλαίας, *into the district of Galilee* (ii. 22), had not a reference to the prophecies induced him (ii. 23) further to mention Nazareth. Besides, the passage Matth. ii. 22, 23, does not oblige us, as *Sieffert* asserts, to suppose that Matthew was ignorant of Mary's having been at Nazareth before the birth of Jesus; we have only to suppose that, during the stay in Egypt, it had appeared desirable to Joseph to establish himself at Bethlehem, but from fear of Archelaus, he gave up the plan, and returned to Nazareth. Accordingly, we can only say of Matthew, that he passes over the particulars of place, and notices incidentally one or two points, which must be more precisely fixed by a reference to Luke, the more exact narrator.

Next, as regards the supposed contradictions in the details of the two narratives, no such thing as an impossibility of reconciling them can be talked of, if only in Luke ii. 39 the words ὑπέστρεψαν εἰς τὴν Γαλιλαίαν, *they returned into Galilee*, be understood with proper latitude. To regard this expression in its immediate connexion with ver. 40, as a form of conclusion, and, consequently, as intended only to point out the habitual abode of Jesus, where the development described in ver. 40 proceeded, is at least an available mode of escape, which no one, who feels himself called upon to avoid the quicksands of myths, will hesitate to adopt. There remains then, in fact, nothing in the two narratives necessarily contradictory; for no one will seriously urge the objection, which Schleiermacher brings against the supposition of a return from Jerusalem to Bethlehem, after the purification was accomplished—viz., that the return is improbable, because the mother would have found herself there in inconvenient circumstances ; for these circumstances' were evidently produced by the enrolment, which, in the nature of the case, increased for only a few days the population of the town. The relation of the accounts in the two Gospels is therefore such, that both may be very well reduced to a connected whole by supplying the little circumstances that are passed over in silence. And what historical narration, composed by different historians, who give their accounts independently of each other, and who follow different points of view in them, does not stand in need of such supplementing ?

It must be confessed, that the reconciliation of the two Gospels in reference to Joseph is more difficult. Yet the difficulty lies not so much in the reconciliation of their accounts, as in the obscurity of the recorded event, which can be cleared away only by a comparison of both. For it is left uncertain from Matth. i. 18, 19, how and when Joseph became aware of Mary's being with child. Εὑρέθη, *she was found*, however, appears to indicate, that Mary did not tell Joseph any thing of it ; and what we read in Luke i. 36, 39, 56, increases this probability to almost a certainty ; for, according to these passages, Mary went to Elisabeth when the latter was six months advanced in pregnancy, stayed there the next three months, and returned shortly before Elisabeth was delivered. Such a visit of three months, supposes that Mary was already married ;* Mary's pregnancy was thus already discovered before the journey, viz., by the *pronubis*, the שׁוֹשְׁבִין, who conceived suspicion and imparted their distrust to Joseph. Then followed the divine disclosure (Matth. i. 20, ff.) ; Joseph immediately took Mary as his wife, and she went to Elisabeth. Mary, therefore, never came into the position of herself making the disclosure to Joseph. This pain was spared her by the divine arrangements. How could it have been otherwise ? The events that had happened to her were of so extraordinary a kind, that she could not communicate them without having any other voucher than her word. The same childlike faith with which she said : " Behold the handmaid of the Lord ; be it unto me according to thy word," could not but inspire her with the confidence, that divine compassion would find ways and means to satisfy her intended husband that she was the pure bride of heaven.

* Virgins and brides were not allowed to journey. (Philo de leg., sec. II., p. 550 · Misch. Ketuboth, op. 7, sec. 6., Hug. Gutachten gegen Strauss S. 85.)—[E.

§ 6. JESUS CONVERSES WITH THE PRIESTS IN THE TEMPLE.

(Luke ii. 41–52.)

The import of this *apparently* insignificant occurrence—the only one told us of the life of Jesus up to the time of his public appearance—demands a few preliminary remarks.* Viewed in its connexion with his entire manifestation, it presents to us unquestionably the sacred moment, when the higher divine consciousness arose within him. As was partially noticed before, the Saviour, in his human manifestation, followed the general course of human development ; and though the child's consciousness in him was a pure, holy, and glorified one, yet it was a *child's*, and, consequently, not a divine one.† This latter gradually formed itself in the progress of his general development (Luke i. 80 ; ii. 40, 52), and on occasion of his being present for the first time in the holy city, to which the child's desire had probably long aspired, the thought then first presented itself distinctly to him, as glowing embers burst into a flame, that *he* was God's Son, and God *his* Father. The divine nature of Jesus, appears, therefore, a distinct thing from the knowledge of that nature. To the latter he attained gradually, as the result of the progress of his human development. The springing up of that consciousness bore him at that instant to his real home, of which the temple appeared to him the type, and, in spiritual rapture, he might forget the earthly representatives of his heavenly Father. But this forgetting was not in him an act of disobedience, but, in fact, of superior obedience. He followed faithfully the stronger attraction from above, and therefore he reunited himself to his parents with childlike submission, when they reminded him of the *rights* of parents, while they had forgotten the parental *duties*.‡ The mother had done wrong in having neglected her highest duty to God—the care of the divine child—a deep symbol of the relation of the human and the divine agencies in the work of regeneration, in which, after a similar manner, the new man, in his birth, is entrusted to his soul,

* That Strauss reckons even this occurrence among the mythical portions, proves undeniably the exaggerated, wanton rage for doubt that possesses him. A history, which might cast an imputation of disobedience on Jesus, or of a want of care on his mother, certainly would not have been fabricated in later times.

† If the *child's* consciousness precludes the element of divinity, why not equally the *man's* consciousness ? The distance of the two states from each other is lost in the infinite interval which separates both from Deity. It may well be questioned whether in fixing the moment when the divine consciousness first developed itself in Jesus, Olshausen is not venturing beyond his depth. Who shall say that Jesus was ever destitute of it ?—K.

‡ That the mother had committed any wrong does not appear in the narrative. Jesus rebukes only her undue anxiety regarding him, reminding her of his higher relations and duties.—K.

which has to fulfil the duties of a mother towards him! In that
exalted moment of the first kindling of this divine spiritual light,
and of its piercing through the human covering, this occurrence thus
opens to us one far reaching glance, but only again to let fall the veil.
But it is precisely in this historical purity that the divine character
of our Gospels shews itself, particularly when compared with the
apocryphal ones, which fill up this veiled period with absurd fables.
During this period the divine plant of righteousness was invisibly
unfolding within itself; and the reason that nothing is narrated of
this period doubtless is, that there was nothing special to narrate.
Jesus presented doubtless the *ideal* of a quiet, truly childlike child
and youth; and it was only in the depth of his soul that his nature
was unfolding, which, at most, may have been betrayed by his look
and bearing. The influences from the spiritual world, which he was
intended to manifest, gradually descended into him; and all surrounding circumstances, conversations, sights, and reading of the
Scriptures, must have become the occasions of one spring after another opening in him. For, to imagine that, according to the ordinary process of training, any formative power was exercised over
him, or direction given to his mind, through Egyptian, Essenaic, or
Rabbinical wisdom, is altogether at variance with our conception of
the Messiah, whom we are to regard as absolutely determining and
controlling all agencies. His development is, therefore, purely independent, and altogether internal—a continual outpouring from the
heavenly world into the earthly tabernacle, of which outward circumstances must be considered as merely the exciting cause.* It is
in this light that we are to view his position towards the priests in
the temple. The questions he put to the priests, and their answers,
were exciting, awakening incidents for his inner life. But the idea
that Jesus *taught* in the temple, must be rejected as monstrous. A
child teaching, demonstrating, would be a contradiction which it is
impossible the God of order could have designed. Ἀκούων and ἐπε-
ρωτῶν, *hearing*, and *asking* (ver. 46), point plainly enough to his
capacity for receiving impressions. The Scriptures and the lofty
hopes which they excite, formed probably the basis of his questions.
He inquired respecting himself; and we may say, the whole endeavour and desire of the child Jesus was nothing but a longing for a
revelation of himself. The miraculous union of the opposites in the
God-man, the conjoining of temporal and eternal, of individual
and universal, is here presented before the reader's mind in its
growth; and ruling and serving, unfettered dominion and child-like
submission, are here united to form an ineffable whole, which the

---

* The words οἱ γονεῖς αὐτοῦ, contain an intimation, that Joseph the father was yet
living; but from this time he does not re-appear in the Gospel-history. He died, probably before the public appearance of Jesus. See Matth. xiii. 55.

parents of Jesus, like unregenerate men in general, might indeed
wonder at (ver. 48), but were not able to understand.

Ver. 41–43.—According to the law of Moses (Ex. xxiii. 14, ff.;
xxxiv. 23), the males had to go up to Jerusalem three times yearly
to the principal feasts;* children accompanied them in these journeys from their twelfth year. They were called at that age בְּנֵי הַתּוֹרָה,
sons of the law, and were then under an obligation to keep the law.
This time of legal maturity coincides, therefore, very appropriately
with the first awakening of his spirit to a higher consciousness.—
The feast of the passover lasted seven days (to which τελειωσάντων
τὰς ἡμέρας, ver. 43, refers), the first and last of which were observed
as Sabbaths, Exod. xii. 14; Deut. xvi. 4.

Ver. 44–46.—The parents, accustomed to the thoughtful and
obedient habits of the child, commence their journey without him, supposing, doubtless, that he was among their kindred or acquaintances.
Συνοδία from συνοδεύω, signifies one of the festal caravans, which
were common among the pilgrims journeying to the feasts, to afford
each other more protection and convenience on the journey. (See
the charming description of such a pilgrimage in *Strauss'* beautiful
romance, "*Helon's Pilgrimage.*") It was not till after three days,
full of anxiety and trouble, that they found the holy child in the
holy place. The ἱερόν, *temple*, (to be distinguished from ναός, see note
on Luke i. 9), was an extensive structure, and had many halls and
separate rooms, in which judges pronounced their decisions, or
Rabbins taught their schools. In such a school (מִדְרָשׁ) we have to
imagine Jesus.

Ver. 47, 48.—In that company the child was an object of universal astonishment; and this again was a matter of wonder to his
parents. Though informed of the high destiny of their child, they
could not comprehend this phenomenon. (Σύνεσις generally stands
in the same relation to φρόνησις, that νοῦς does to σοφία and γνῶσις;
σύνεσις denotes " the understanding," = בִּינָה. Yet this term [Isa.
xi. 2] is often applied to divine things and the comprehension of
them—e. g., Col. i. 9; Eph. iii. 4; 2 Tim. ii. 7.) The mother's exclamation (τί = διατί = לָמָּה) contains a gentle reproof; but its force
is invalidated by the following words. The fault was the mother's,
who had forgotten the spiritual destination of her son.

* It is not meant in this to advocate any thing like the views of the Docetæ, but
only to bring forward to view the specific character of the Saviour's advanceing development. If his human nature, as sinless, was specifically different from fallen human nature, then the progress of his training must also have been so; and it must be conceived,
too, in the way indicated; because if put in any other form, Christ is rendered subject to
the sinful influences around him. In point of form only, we can conceive Christ as
receiving—that is, as purely passive, e. g., in learning language and letters. The substance of his knowledge is, however, to be conceived as active at every stage of develop
ment, because in that way alone it can be pure. *Tholuck's* remarks to the contrary in his
Glaubwürdigkeit der evangelischen Geschichte, S. 219, ff., do not appear to me decisive.

Ver. 49, 50.—Without its being intended, the words of Jesus convey censure upon Mary, because they exactly declare the truth. Had she borne perfectly in mind her son's spiritual character, she would herself have led him to those scenes, whither the higher Spirit now attracted him. (Ζητεῖν, in connexion with the following δεῖ εἶναί με, conveys the notion of uncertainty, indecision; this was what was wrong in Mary's state of mind; she might have known where alone Jesus would naturally be found.) Τὰ τοῦ πατρός refers certainly immediately to the temple, as the visible dwelling-place of the invisible God. But in the child's higher consciousness, which tended upwards, the meaning of the words goes further. This deeper sense of the words, which points to the oneness of the Son with the Father, was not understood by the parents, from their Old Testament point of view; for they could hardly fail to perceive, that he spoke with immediate reference to the temple. Still the mother felt a strong impression from the deep saying (ver. 51), and laid it up in her heart (ver. 19), where it revived at its time, so that she could tell of it.

Ver. 51.—The words : καὶ ἦν ὑποτασσόμενος αὐτοῖς, and he was subject to them, are evidently intended here to guard against the possible misunderstanding, that Jesus had manifested a will not subject to his parents ; not so much in the sense of ordinary disobedience, which is inconceivable in an offspring of the Spirit, as in a higher relation. It might be supposed, that the spirit of Jesus would now have assumed the appearance of ruling over the parents ; this the Evangelist contradicts by the express observation, that the Son of God still submitted himself always to the human will of his parents. The general idea of our Lord's voluntary humiliation (Phil. ii. 7, ff.) appears, therefore, here again, as already pointed out in the note on Luke ii. 21, 22.

Ver. 52.—The history of the childhood closes with a new mention (see Luke ii. 49) of the child's bodily and spiritual advancement. (Προκόπτειν, in the sense of " to advance," " to grow." [See Gal. i. 14 ; 2 Tim. ii. 16; iii. 9.] Ἡλικία is not to be taken in the sense of "greatness," " stature," as in Luke xix. 3 ; it is better to take it as " age," in which the whole physical part of life is included. Χάρις, favour, is to be taken in a different sense from that which it has in ii. 40. It is here represented as being in a state of development, which is not applicable to the divine love ; for towards the Son of God, that was always alike and the same. The reference to God and man shews that the idea of being pleased is prominent in χάρις, so that it may be taken = εὐδοκία, good-will. This might increase, in so far as, in the human life of Jesus, that glory unfolded itself more and more, which must secure the approval of God and of all the good.

SECOND PART.

OF JOHN THE BAPTIST—CHRIST'S BAPTISM AND TEMPTATION.

MATTH. iii. 1—iv. 12; MARK i. 2–13; LUKE iii. 1—iv. 13.

---

§ 1. JOHN'S TEACHING AND BAPTISM.

(Matth. iii. 1–12; Mark i. 2–8; Luke iii. 1–20.)

IN the second part of the Gospel-history, the reader is brought nearer to its great cardinal events. The Evangelists tell us, in the following paragraphs, how the public appearance of Jesus was prepared for. First, the Baptist visibly and outwardly prepared the way for our Lord ; then, inwardly and in the narrow circle of those who feared God, the outpouring of the Spirit, and the temptation of Jesus, completed the preparation.

John appears here quite in conformity with the angel's prediction in Luke i. 17, repeated by Zacharias in ver. 76, as a prophet in the spirit and power of Elias. In the whole of his labours he represents the law, which *demands* holiness and righteousness, but *supplies* no power. His outward appearance answers to his inward character; he presents himself austere and stern, separated from the world, and revealing to it the strictness of the Divine Judge. His preaching of repentance is a commentary on Rom. iii. 20 : " By the law is the knowledge of sin." John was appointed to awaken slumbering minds, to rouse to a sense of the need of salvation, that the Saviour might find hearts prepared to receive the fulness of blessings, which he came to bring ; whence, too, Jesus begins at once to invite to himself the poor and the hungry. Though John, therefore, stands in close contact with the New Testament economy, yet, in his character and work, there is no approach to the spirit of the Gospel ; he represents purely the law, and forms only the point of contact between the Old and the New Testaments, as the top-stone of the Old Testament edifice. (Here compare Matth. xi. 9, ff.) This close *proximity*, and yet undeniably wide *separation*, of Jesus and the Baptist, expresses very vividly the difference of the two economies ; the law and the Gospel are two separate spheres of life, which may not be blended ; faith alone, and the mysterious act of regeneration thence resulting, conduct us from the one to the other. John, therefore, as the crown and completion of the Old Testament economy, and perfectly expressing its character, stands exalted among those who are born of women ; but the least in the kingdom of God (as being born of God) is greater than he.* But the work of the Baptist was not confined to the "preaching of repentance ;" it included also an external rite—namely, baptism.† As regards this rite, we are here less concerned with its relation to proselyte-baptism, than to the Christian sacrament of baptism. With reference to the baptism of proselytes, it seems probable to me, that an actual baptism—*i. e.*, a lustration performed on the proselyte by another, did not take place *before* the baptism of John ; subsequently, it may have arisen out of the lustrations so long customary, which every one performed on himself.‡ Had such a baptism existed, the choice of this rite would have been less appropriate; for it was by no means John's intention to set up a new communion, into which he was to initiate by his baptism ; it was only that those who were living under the Old Testament economy should be thereby represented as provisionally cleansed, and consequently not unworthy to receive the Messiah. Just as little does it seem possible to prove that the view of the later Jews respecting the Messiah's baptism existed before the time of

* See Hengstenberg's Christol., B. iii., S. 460, ff., where this view is opposed, and a higher character claimed for John. But if the New Testament is not to relinquish all that is specific, regeneration and the real experience of the forgiveness of sins ought not to be anticipated. Under the Old Testament there was only faith in the forgiveness *to come;* sin itself remained, under divine forbearance, till the sacrifice was offered on Calvary. (Rom. iii. 25.) All that the Old Testament possessed and could give, the Baptist did possess; but the *essence* of the New Testament was not his, since he died before the completion of Christ's work. (See 1 Pet. i. 10, ff.; Heb. xi. 39, 40.) [Olshausen is surely wrong. The *essence* of the New Testament is precisely what John and the ancient saints *did* possess. In the outward *form*—in clearness of view, in the fulness and freedom of spiritual development—the New Economy is immeasurably superior.—[K.

† See a fuller discussion on John's baptism in note on Acts xix. 4, from which passage it is probable that John baptized with the formula: Βαπτίζω σε εἰς τὸν ἐρχόμενον, *I baptize thee into him who cometh.*

‡ The preponderance of arguments seems to me to be on the side of *Schneckenburger :* Ueber das Altar der Proselyten-Taufe, Berlin, 1828; the opposite opinion, that John adapted the custom already existing to his purpose, is defended by *Bengel*, in a book with the same title, Tübingen, 1814. As the Old Testament furnishes no *data* for the decision of the question, and all Rabbinical writings can be but uncertain testimonies on matters before the Christian era, it would be difficult to arrive at any well established conclusion as to the earliest customs at the receiving of proselytes. See also *Matthies* de Baptismate, Berol. 1831. 8vo.

Christ ; the very circumstance, that John baptized, seems opposed to this supposition ; for, if it had been generally regarded as the prerogative of the Messiah to baptize, John would not have assumed it himself. (See this point more fully treated in note on John i. 25.) No special historical incident is necessary to account for the origin of John's baptism. Since lustrations were common in the Jewish worship, it would readily occur to him to represent, by a symbolical rite, the repentance which he preached. True, this was not done by his own arbitrary will—the Divine Spirit who quickened him was his guide in this institution, as in all that he did ; he was *sent* to baptize with water, John i. 33. The question, how John's baptism, should be viewed in relation to Christian baptism, is of more importance. It is evident, that the baptism of John cannot be identical with the sacrament of baptism, which was not ordained till after the resurrection (Matth. xxviii. 19 ; Mark xvi. 16); the former was wanting in the essential power of the Spirit (John i. 26); it was a λουτρὸν μετανοίας, *a washing of repentance*, but not a λουτρὸν παλιγγενεσίας, *a washing of regeneration* (Luke iii. 3 ; Tit. iii. 5). Quite parallel with John's baptism of repentance was the baptism of the disciples *before* the perfecting of our Lord and the appointment of the sacrament, to which John refers particularly, John iv. 1, 2. Since the regenerating Spirit was yet wanting (John vii. 39), that baptism could only exercise a negative effect, just as the preaching of the disciples before the Saviour's glorification, had more of the character of John's. (Matth. x. 7, compared with iii. 1.) Notwithstanding the similarity in the form of the action,* the essence was very different. In Christian baptism, according to its ideal conception (Rom. vi. 4), the birth of the new higher being, which the Holy Spirit alone can impart, was to coincide with the extinction of the old life.† In the baptism of children, however, which the church, for wise reasons, introduced subsequently, the sacred action returned, as it were, again to the lower ground of John's baptism ;‡ for which reason a fresh act must be joined to it after the baptized attains to actual consciousness, in order to complete that which can take place only in a conscious individual. If, therefore, John's baptism was on

* John's baptism was most probably like the Christian, not only in this, that, in it, the baptizing party performed the immersion on the baptized (which was the specific difference between baptism and all other lustrations), but that a *formula* was used at the immersion, as remarked above.

† The distinction may be thus stated. In John's baptism it was virtually said ; "As thou art now immersed, so hast thou reserved to be destroyed in death; as thou now arisest, so *shouldest* thou arise as a new man." In the Christian baptism, on the contrary the language is : "As thou art now immersed, so art thou now buried into the vicarious death of Christ; as thou now emergest, so art thou born again to a new man."—[E.

‡ Perhaps not entirely! Grant that, as conscious conversion to conscious faith in Christ is impossible in the infant, a new man is not yet *born*, still he is, as it were, passively conceived.—[E.

a much inferior level to the Christian ordinance, yet it was not an empty rite; only, it could not impart more than he who administered it possessed. It accomplished the blessing of the law in those who received it, since it brought repentance to perfection; but then, indeed, it pointed to another baptism, which bestowed the Spirit— a sense of whose need that first baptism had excited.

Luke iii. 1, affords us an important chronological datum. John the Baptist began his ministry in the fifteenth year of Tiberius; as John was six months older than Jesus (Luke i. 36), the mention of this circumstance (compared with Luke iii. 23) is a hint as to the Saviour's age. True, it is only a hint. For, in the *first place*, the age of Jesus is not given exactly (Luke iii. 23, ἦν ὡσεὶ τριάκοντα ἐτῶν); then, too, the interval between the public appearance of John and of Jesus, is not definitely stated. In any case, the year of Christ's birth, as is evident from the previous remarks on that point, is placed too late in the chronology of Dionysius, as the fifteenth year of Tiberius begins with the 19th of August of the year 27 after Christ.* The mention of the different princes ruling in Palestine at that time, is another aid in determining the date of John's public appearance.

(The term ἡγεμονεύω, *govern*, like διέπω, is used for different gradations in the Roman provincial administration. Pilate was only procurator of Judea, which office he sustained ten years, and laid it down about the time of Tiberius' death, being deposed by Vitellius, at that time pro-consul of Syria. (Τετραρχέω, *to be tetrarch*, meant originally to govern the fourth part of a great territory, then in a wider sense to rule in general, but still in an inferior capacity. Thus Cicero calls Deiotarus a tetrarch [Cic. ad. div. i. 15.] Ethnarch was a higher title; it was borne by Archelaus, Herod the Great's eldest son. Luke comprises the two provinces of Batanea and Auranitis, under the name Ἰτουραία.)

The only remarkable circumstance in Luke's enumeration is, that in the words "Lysanias being Tetrarch of Abilene," he mentions even the governor of Abilene, the territory of the town Abela near Antilibanus, which lay beyond the boundaries of Palestine. Besides, no Lysanias is spoken of as governor of this region in the time of Tiberius; but thirty years earlier, a man of that name was governor, who was slain by Antony. If we consider, however, that the town, and the territory belonging to it, was so inconsiderable, that it could not possibly be expected that all its rulers should necessarily be

---

* In this way the years of his associated rule with Augustus are not included. It is according to this date that the calculation of the Abbot *Dionysius Exiguus* is made, with whom our era had its origin. *Hase*, in his Leben Jesu, S. 39, ff., whom *Meyer* follows in his commentary on this passage, is inclined, erroneously, to hold to this interpretation as the correct one, as he regards the rest of the information in the history of the childhood as mythical.

mentioned by the historians, the silence of authors about this prince is not at all surprising. To remove all doubt, we need only to suppose that Augustus restored a son or a descendant of that elder Lysanias. As Abilene was on the borders of Galilee, the scene of Christ's ministry, this might induce the Evangelist to mention the prince of this limited territory.* What Luke had designated so precisely, Matthew gives (iii. 1) in the indefinite formula "in those days." It is not impossible that the memoirs, which Matthew undoubtedly used in the first chapters, extended further, and that in them this formula would be in connexion with some nearer event. It has, however, like the Hebrew הָהֵם בַּיָּמִים, often a more extensive reference (see Exod. ii. 11.) After the chronological reference to the political rulers of that period, Luke subjoins a notice of the heads of the ecclesiastical government at that time. Two high priests are mentioned, Luke iii. 2—Annas and Caiaphas. The reading ἀρχιερέως is doubtless preferable to the plural. From the circumstance of two names following, the singular was changed, which, however, in the meaning of the Evangelist, referred to the proper high priest—the one actually in office. The latter was the officiating high priest; but his father-in-law Annas, who had held the office before, and was deposed, still possessed great influence. (See this point more fully discussed in the history of the passion in the note on Matth. xxvi. 57, ff.) At this time, then, John came forward publicly (παραγίνεται in Matth. iii. 1, = ἦλθεν in Luke iii. 3) and preached repentance. The wilderness (ἔρημος) is spoken of as the place where he preached, which is not to be understood, of course, as literally void of men, but rather as pasture ground (מִדְבָּר). But in the fact, that John preached in the wilderness, and not in towns, we discover the peculiar character of this witness to the truth. It belongs to John's character to *flee* from man (Luke i. 80), and to preach to those who seek him; while the Redeemer himself *seeks* men. (The wilderness of Judea [Matth. iii. 1] bordered on the Jordan and the Dead Sea. See *Joseph* de. bell. Judg. i. 3, 10. Luke [iii. 3] calls it therefore περί-χωρος τοῦ Ἰορδάνου = הַיַּרְדֵּן כִּכַּר, Gen. xiii. 10.) The subjoined clause, ἐγένετο ῥῆμα Θεοῦ ἐπὶ Ἰωάννην, the word of God came to John, is peculiar to Luke iii. 2. It corresponds to the phrase so common in the prophets עַל יְחֹיָה דְבַר הָיָה. This remark, in the first place, represents the public appearance of John, not as something originating from himself, but as determined by an influence from above. Moreover, according to it, the manner in which the higher world influenced the mind of John, was not different from its influence on the prophets of the Old Testament. While in the New Testament we find a more quiet, continually active influence of the Divine Spirit

* See *Tholuck*, Glaubwürdigkeit der ev. Gesch., S. 198, and *Schneckenburger's* article in the Studien und Kritiken, 1833, H. 4.

in the minds of believers, as peculiar to them (expressed by μένειν in John's language), it appears in the Old Testament rather as a sudden, momentary one, which is then succeeded by other dry, and, as it were, spiritless periods, such as appeared afterwards in the life of the Baptist. (See note on Matth. xiv. 1, ff.) For this reason the formula יַד־יְהֹוָה עַל, the hand of Jehovah upon one, is frequently applied to the inspired moments of the prophets, to denote the violent and sudden character of the influence. Such formulas are, of course, not used of Jesus, because divine things were not manifested to him at single moments of his life ; but he himself was the one eternal manifestation of the Divine—the Word. (On the relation of ῥῆμα and λόγος, which imply the same fundamental idea of the relation of λέγεσθαι and εἶναι, see note on John i. 1.)

The object of the Baptist's preaching, which is not specified in Matth. iii. 1, Luke describes more definitely, by designating it, in iii. 3, βάπτισμα μετανοίας, a baptism of repentance. (See Matth. iii. 11, where John says, βαπτίζω εἰς μετάνοιαν.) Μετάνοια, repentance, change of mind, denotes here the result of the law in its effect on the mind. By its form of inflexible requirement, it rouses to a sense of weakness, and to a longing for a power sufficient to satisfy it. It is therefore, in fact, a change of mind (νοῦς) in its deepest vital principle. Considered in itself, indeed, it is something merely negative, which stands in need of a positive element to complete it ; and this is the Spirit, whom Christ obtained, and whom men receive by faith. This is conveyed in the additional clause in Luke iii. 3, and Mark i. 4, εἰς ἄφεσιν ἁμαρτιῶν, for the remission of sins. John's preaching was not itself to effect the remission, but to prepare for that remission, which was to be accomplished by Christ. It is not inappropriate therefore to supply ἐρχομένην, coming, future. (On this point see note on Acts xix. 4, where Paul instructs the disciples of the Baptist in the import of their baptism.)

Matth. iii. 2.—The presence of the kingdom of God is put forward as a motive for repentance, since it excluded persons in their natural unchanged state of heart. (The perfect ἤγγικε, is to be taken in a present sense ; so that the meaning is, the kingdom of God is already present—that is, in the person of the Messiah, who represents it, and of whom John says : μέσος ὑμῶν ἔστηκεν, ὃν ὑμεῖς οὐκ οἴδατε, there standeth one among you, etc. John i. 26.)

The phrase βασιλεία τῶν οὐρανῶν, kingdom of heaven, does not occur except in Matthew. In 2 Tim. iv. 18, we find βασιλεία ἐπουράνιος, heavenly kingdom. The more common phrase is βασιλεία τοῦ Θεοῦ, τοῦ Χριστοῦ, kingdom of God, of Christ,* or simply βασιλεία,

---

* It is very seldom that the phrase βασιλεία τοῦ υἱοῦ τοῦ ἀνθρώπου is put for βασιλεία τοῦ Χριστοῦ, as in Matth. xiii. 41. In the passage Mark xi. 10, βασιλεία τοῦ Δαβίδ occurs, inasmuch as David is viewed as a type of Messiah the king.

Θεοῦ being left to be supplied (Luke xii. 32, and frequently). In the Old Testament, the expression מַלְכוּת הַשָּׁמַיִם, or מַלְכוּת אֱלֹהִים, does not occur, nor does it appear, except in the later Jewish writings. In the Apocrypha we meet with βασιλεία Θεοῦ as early as Wisdom x. 10. On the other hand, the *idea* of the kingdom of God pervades the whole of the books of the Old Testament, but appears in its most mature form in the prophets. See Isa. ii. 1–4 ; Micah iv. 3, ff. ; Isa. xi. 1, ff. ; Psalm lxxxv. 11, 12 ; Jer. xxiii. 5, ff. ; xxxi. 31, ff. ; xxxii. 37, ff. ; xxxiii. 14, ff. ; Ezek. xxxiv. 23, ff. ; xxxvii. 24, ff.) Daniel describes the expected holy state of things, which all the prophets regarded as future, expressly as a kingdom of everlasting duration. (Dan. ii. 44 ; vii. 14, 27.) Just as the Messiah also is often described as a king (in which respect David is especially regarded as his type, Dan. ix. 25 ; Psalm ii. 6 ; Zech. xiv. 9; Ezek. xxxvii. 24.) The fundamental idea of the anticipated kingdom of God, as presented in the Old Testament, does not differ from that of the New. The idea of a kingdom necessarily implies the distinction of the governor and the governed. But in the kingdom of God the divine will appears as ruling absolutely. In so far, therefore, as in the sinful world the will of God is conceived as being subordinated, the period of his absolute rule must yet be future. The kingdom of God, therefore, forms a contrast to the kingdom of sin, or of its representative, the ruler of this world, ἄρχων τοῦ κόσμου τούτου. The coming of the former kingdom involves the destruction of the latter : the prevalence of the latter limits the influence of the former. But as the Old Testament, in its prophecies does not usually develope the ideas, which are the subjects of its contemplation, and especially does not present them in their gradual unfolding in successive ages, but, as it were, concentrated in a single picture ; so also with its declarations respecting the kingdom of God. The prophetic communications contain lively delineations of it, agreeably to which the dominion of sin, both internal and external, is depicted as overthrown, and the dominion of God, and his will, established ; but as the external and internal are not kept perfectly distinct by them, but are blended together, succession of time is also particularly neglected ; the great outline of the world's spiritual progress is drawn at once in grand perspective, and events separated by wide intervals of time are brought into juxtaposition. What is included in the Old Testament as a germ, appears in the New in its free expansion, and thus first reveals in its fulness the fundamental idea which it includes. The kingdom of God appears, accordingly, as a kingdom always existing—established among fallen men contemporaneously with the first announcement of the Gospel—typically represented in the Mosaic theocracy—bestowed in Christ essentially complete in its conception—since then secretly advancing in the souls of men—destined to a final conquest over every thing, and to penetrate harmoniously all forms both of outward and inward life throughout creation. With respect to the manner in which the New Testament Scriptures unfold this idea of the kingdom of God, they distinguish, first, clearly between its external and internal character. In the *latter* relation, the kingdom of God appears according to the New Testament conception as actually present, not merely in the person of the Saviour himself, but also in his believing followers, who were translated into the spirit of his life. In the spirit's inner life and consciousness—*i. e.*, in faith, the absolute dominion of the divine is realized. We find it thus viewed as the kingdom of God in the soul, in Luke xvii. 21 : ἡ βασιλεία τοῦ Θεοῦ ἐντὸς ὑμῶν ἐστιν. (See Rom. xiv. 17.) But in its *external* relation, the kingdom of God appears in the New Testament also as yet future, and still an object of desire. The Spirit of Christ, as the principle which secures an immediate dominion in the depths of the inward life, strives for an unconditional supremacy over all its outward relations. But the extension of this divine dominion ·in Christ to external circumstances, is gradual, and hence even believers must hope only for its gradual realization. In its relation to external things, we find, however, a *twofold* modification of the idea in the New Testament. *First*, the sphere of life in which the Christian element prevails—that is, the church—is conceived in its visible form as an external communion. In this respect the kingdom of God itself is progressive—expanding gradually in this sinful world—still mixed, to a certain extent, with sinful elements. (See note on Matth. xiii. 47, ff.) For it was only in the person of the Saviour that the βασιλεία, *kingdom*, was exhibited as at once outwardly and inwardly complete. But *further*, its external condition also is conceived as made to harmonize with the internal, and as correspondingly penetrated by the sovereign will of God ; and in this view the kingdom appears absolutely complete, but future. That which was first to sway the souls of men, presents itself in the end as ruling likewise in the creation. (Rom. viii. 19, ff.) In this respect the βασιλεία might be called ἐπίγειος *earthly* (in contrast with ἐπουράνιος, 2 Tim. iv. 18) ; but for wise reasons this epithet is not applied to it ; the idea itself, however, is everywhere to be met with in the New Testament, in the promise, that at the coming of Christ the kingdom of God will become externally prevalent (see note on Matt. xx. 21 ; xxvi. 29 ; Luke xxi. 31 ; John xviii. 36.) In very many passages, however, its internal and external aspects are not strictly separated, but are blended with greater generality and indefiniteness, as in the Old Testament. The kingdom is then the *ideal* future world (see Luke xxiii. 42, the words of the thief), which, as being present in the souls of believers, but absent in its completeness, may be spoken of as at once near and distant.—There is another division in the idea of the kingdom of God in the New Testament, which is equally unknown to the Old—viz., its relation sometimes to the *individual*, at others to the *human race collectively*. According to these different relations, again, the kingdom is represented sometimes as already come, at others, as to come. For in so far as that spiritual element, which in Christ diffuses itself through mankind, and establishes among them the kingdom of God, has taken possession of an individual, to him the kingdom of God is present, and *he* is in that kingdom ; yet even for him it is still *to come*, not merely in so far as the higher principle of life obtains but a gradual control over his faculties, but also in so far as it is destined to quicken the entire race, and to meet his view as manifested among them. The relation of the whole human race—viewed as an individual—is similar ; for though the kingdom of God (in the church) exists in the race, and the race (in believers as its representatives) in the kingdom of God, yet, on the other hand, the kingdom is still to come with respect to the race also.

Thus the one idea of the kingdom of God appears in the New Testament alone, applied to different relations ; and from the various contrasts in which it is placed, sometimes one of these relations is more prominent, sometimes another. Among the great mass of the Jews held captive by the Pharisaical spirit, the idea of an external manifestation of the Messiah's kingdom prevailed. In opposition to this material view, the Saviour put forward its *ideal* character. Even in the apostolic times sprung up the germs of the Gnostic idealism, which in its doctrine of the βασιλεία, denied any future real and outward manifestation of the divine dominion. This point had therefore to be defended in opposition to that heresy. On the other hand, the Alexandrine school had, at a later period, to oppose the *ideal* aspect of the kingdom of God to the rude millennarian views of the ancient church ; and through its influence the view was again gradually forced into the back-ground—that it is in the nature of the divine to pursue its subduing and ruling course from within to without— from the individual to the universal. The pure *realism* of the Bible points out the medium between the two false paths of materialism and spiritualism in the doctrine of the βασιλεία. It is not *from* this world, but yet *in* the world (John xviii. 36) ; and as, in the individual, its renovating process is from the inmost fountain of life, on which it first seizes, to the purifying and glorification of the body ; so it proceeds gradually from the individuals, who at first represent the kingdom of God, to the whole, raises the earth to paradisaic purity, and finally perfects the universe, as a new heaven and a new earth. (2 Pet. iii. 13 ; Rev. xxi. 1.)

If now, in conclusion, we cast a glance on the passage under consideration (Matth. iii. 2), and ask, in what sense John the Baptist may have understood the "kingdom," it is most probable, that, in his relation to the law, he conceived of it with the generality and indeterminateness of the Old Testament, but without incorporating with the idea any thing false. We may concede a certain affinity between John's notions of the Messiah's kingdom, and those that prevailed among the people. Their belief in its appearance as an external one, was not in itself false ; for that is in fact its consummation. Their error consisted in desiring its external, without its internal and more essential features. Thus, as the carnal man makes his God for himself, so he makes his kingdom of God for himself. The spiritual man has a spiritual God, and a spiritual kingdom of God ; but as the true God became man, so the kingdom of God, or of heaven, comes down to earth, that heaven and earth may celebrate a perfect reconciliation.

Ver. 3.—The Evangelists establish the divinity of the Baptist's mission by passages from the Old Testament. All four Evangelists (see John i. 23) quote the passage Isa. xl. 3–5. Luke gives it most fully. In common with the other two, he follows the LXX. with slight variations. Mark introduces Mal. iii. 1 before it.* This passage, however, appears to have first occurred to him as parallel, while in the act of writing ; for, on the one hand, he cites it (from memory) with great variations, from the LXX., and, on the other, he has also applied the formula, ἐν 'Ησαΐα τῷ προφήτῃ to the passage from Malachi. The transcribers have indeed given ἐν τοῖς προφήταις, *in the prophets*, as a correction ; but that this reading is without value needs no proof. This passage of Mark is perhaps an unequivocal sign that he had documents before him, and made use of them. He took the formula of quotation from Matthew and Luke, but inserted from memory the words of Malachi, without changing the formula.† The whole prophetic passage is founded on the figure of the triumphal entry of a king, for whom the road is leveled. Since the king and his kingdom, are alike spiritual, the heights and depths are also to be taken spiritually, and are to be understood of those mental states of unbelief and despair, of pride and self-sufficiency, which stand in the way of the Saviour's work. Φωνή, *voice*, forms an interesting contrast with λόγος (John i. 1.) In the notion of " word," the idea is likewise included, which is conveyed by the articulate word. The " voice," as such, denotes simply that which

* On the passage, Mal. iii. 1, see further the observations on Matth. xi. 10 ; Luke vii. 27, where the same quotation is adduced with similar variations, evidently indicating the use of the same sources of information.

† Hengstenberg's supposition, in his Christology, vol. iii., p. 398, ff., 464, ff., that Mark quoted the passage out of Malachi as belonging to Isaiah, because the former borrowed it from the latter, and Malachi is therefore, only the *auctor secundarius*, appears to me to be forced. They are still the words of Malachi.

awakens, excites. John introduced no new idea among mankind. He claimed supremacy over no peculiar department of life, to which he could have introduced men. He was a mere organ for a powerful spiritual influence in the spiritual waste of humanity. He awakened the sense of need, which the Redeemer satisfied. (Φάραγξ, in Luke iii. 5, 6, = τάφρος, (?) *hollow place, valley.* This is the only place where it is found in the New Testament. The opposites to it are βουνός and ὄρος. The first of these words, βουνός, is found only in Luke xxiii. 30. The LXX. use it for נִבְעָה, *elevation, hill.* On σωτήριον τοῦ Θεοῦ, see Luke ii. 30 ; Acts xxviii. 28 : σωτηρία is used in the same way, Luke i. 69. In the concluding formula, ὄψεται πᾶσα σάρξ κ. τ. λ., the Evangelist follows the LXX., contrary to the Hebrew text, where the words σωτήριον τ. Θ. are wanting. On the other hand, the words ὀφθήσεται δόξα τοῦ κυρίου, which the LXX. have, agreeably to the original, are omitted by Luke. In the prophecy, the Saviour's work is represented, quite after the prevailing mode of Old Testament representation, at once in its completion.

Ver. 4–6.—The Baptist's dress and manner of life quite agree with the portrait of Elijah (2 Kings i. 8, compared with Zech. xiii. 4.) John lived and laboured in an austere and strictly ascetic manner. ('Ακρίς is the well-known large oriental locust, used as food by the poor ; Lev. xi. 22.) It was by means of this strict form of life, and the reproving severity of his character, that the prophet roused the slumberers ; a form from the past seemed to have entered the spiritless present. The voice of exclamation echoed loudly through the wilderness ; those who were awakened gathered round the prophet, to gain ease for their consciences. The βαπτισμός, *baptism,* and ἐξομολόγησις, *confession,* are specified as the forms which John's work assumed. Confession is to be viewed as the condition of baptism, since it was intended to be, as it were, a type of the coming forgiveness to be completed by the Messiah, which required genuine repentance, so that where confession was wanting, baptism also was refused. (See ver. 7, ff., the rejection of the Pharisees.) The confession, however, is not necessarily a special confession of individual facts (though that is not to be excluded in particular cases), but a genuine expression of a felt need, cognizable to John's searching, prophetic spirit.

Ver. 7.—Those whom Luke comprehends under the term ὄχλοι, *multitudes* (excluding the few sincere-minded), Matthew describes more definitely as Pharisees and Sadducees. These Jewish sects, so thoroughly known from the history of the church, appear in the New Testament as the representatives of hypocritical superstition and carnal unbelief. Phariseeism, however, had the deeper foundation ; it was based on the Divine Word, only that traditional precepts had been associated with it. Although, therefore, the Pharisees (taken collectively) are constantly opposed to the New Testament, and particularly in the Gospels, because, by confounding things external with things internal, they had sunk into hypocrisy, and pursued godliness as a trade ; yet there were individual believers among them. But Sadduceeism was utterly devoid of any deep foundation, or any high principle of life ; pure worldliness shews itself in it, though often, as it would seem, united with a certain kindness of disposition. This sect was hence inconsiderable, while Phariseeism, embodying, as it did, something positive, was both more dangerous in its corruption, and, in its nobler manifestation, more susceptible of a union with the Gospel. The New Testament does not speak of the *Essenes*, partly because they did not come in contact with the public life of the Jewish people—partly because their aim, though noble on the whole, was, still, deformed by subtle errors, too dangerous to render them proper objects of imitation. Besides, it is the nature of the Gospel to set up nothing for imitation but the Saviour himself, in whom the fulness of all that is desirable is included. There was no call for positive opposition to the Essenes, since their exclusiveness as a sect rendered them unknown, except in narrow circles, and because the best antidote to their errors lay in the principles of Christian truth itself.[*]

The Baptist's exhortation to the multitude, who were under Pharisaic or Sadduceean influence, and shared in the corruption of these sects, bears the stamp of the strict legal spirit which John represents. He contrasts, in the Spirit, the kingdom of the prince of this world with the kingdom of God, proclaimed by him, and takes the depraved minds, that hypocritically pretended to purity of heart, as types of this evil kingdom. (The language γεννήματα ἐχιδνῶν = צֶפַע צֶפַע, Isa. xiv. 29, *generation of vipers*, is certainly harsh ; but it is in the nature of love plainly to call evil evil, and, in accordance with the truth, to refer it to its origin. The serpent denotes what is satanic ; and that Jesus himself so intends it, is seen by a comparison of Matth. xii. 34 ; xxiii. 33, with John viii. 44 ; Rev. xx. 2.) But their subjection to the condemnation of God is not to be regarded as absolute (see note on Acts xiii. 10, 11); the

* A correct view of the Essenaic sect, which had all the faults common among Separatists, particularly secret arrogance and dependence on good works, is a sufficient refutation of the notion that Jesus had been brought up in their schools. That our Lord knew them, is beyond a doubt, since Galilee was their stronghold; that their existence may have had a stimulating effect on him, is likewise highly probable : only we must never forget that the development of the Saviour's character was purely internal, influenced only by spiritual streams from above; that therefore nothing can have been adopted by him from the Essenes. Christ brought down into the world a principle of spiritual life, different as heaven and earth from Essenism, and every other human form of religious life—a principle which invariably exercised a positive influence on what surrounded it.

exhortation which follows in ver. 8 shews clearly the wish, that they may cease to be what they are. But, as such, they necessarily come under the Divine condemnation. The passage, therefore, involves the doctrine of the possibility of the generation of vipers being transformed into children of God by repentance and faith. ('Οργὴ μέλλουσα, for which ὀργὴ ἐρχομένη is put in 1 Thess. i. 10, expresses the idea of God's punitive justice ; hence the ἀποκάλυψις τῆς ὀργῆς = κρίσις. See Rom. i. 18. In John's exhortation, agreeably to the Old Testament form of conception, the last judgment [ἐσχάτη κρίσις] is considered as concurrent with the appearance of the Messiah, as his first and second coming are not here separated. On ὀργὴ τ. Θ., see note on Matth. xviii. 34.

Ver. 8.—These words of reproof in John's discourse are followed by words of exhortation, which urge the necessity of the manifestation in actual life of genuine repentance. Luke iii. 11. ff., contains the comment on the works which the Baptist, from his point of view, demanded. (The phrase, καρπὸς τῆς μετανοίας ἄξιος, occurs once more, with some variation, in Acts xxvi. 20. The reading καρπούς in Matthew is spurious ; it was probably derived from the parallel passage in Luke.

Ver. 9.—John contrasts the boasting of external advantages with the practical evidencing of that sincerely repentant disposition required by him. (Μὴ δόξητε, think not, in Matthew is no more superfluous than μὴ ἄρξησθε, begin not, in Luke. The former is to be understood of the fancied right, which the Pharisees imagined they possessed, to boast of their descent from Abraham ; the latter, of their beginning with self-sufficiency and vanity to plume themselves on that right, both aloud in the presence of men, and in their own minds.) Being a child of Abraham, is spoken of as the substance of all the advantages belonging to the theocracy. In its true import, this descent was not so much an advantage in itself, as a stronger obligation to a godly life and walk. Where this obligation was left unfulfilled, the supposed advantage was turned to a disadvantage. (See Rom. ii. 28, 29 ; iv. 16, on the ideal conception of being a child of Abraham, and sharing in the advantages of the theocracy.) In order to teach them properly to estimate the value of natural descent, the Baptist refers to the free grace of God. As it was purely of grace to have been born in the bosom of the theocracy, so the Almighty can reject those who shew themselves unworthy of such grace, and call others who were far from his promises. ('Εγεῖραι, viewed in relation to those who were born children of Abraham, involves their rejection.) The words : δύναται ὁ Θεὸς ἐκ τῶν λίθων τούτων ἐγεῖραι τέκνα τῷ 'Αβραάμ, God is able, etc., do certainly admit of being understood figuratively of the heathen ; just as in the passage before us, the "trees" denote the Jews in that Pharisaical sect which was going onward to destruction. But the added τούτων, *these*, compels us, doubtless, to understand them of the stones lying on the banks of Jordan, in which case the parallel with the history of the creation must not be overlooked. As God formed man out of the dust of the earth, so he can even now form men out of stones.

Ver. 10.—To enforce the exhortation, the time is represented as a decisive one. In the Old Testament, the parallel is drawn between the moral world and the physical in the same way as here (Psalm i. 3; Isa. vi. 13); in the New Testament it is very frequent. (Matth. vii. 19; Rom. xi. 17.) The time of harvest is that of decision (κρίσις), when the chief question is of fruit. The fruit required here was outward righteousness (δικαιοσύνη), and genuine inward repentance (μετάνοια.) (Ἐκκόπτεσθαι, εἰς πῦρ βάλλεσθαι, are emblems of the ὀργή, ver. 7.) In Luke iii. 11–15, there follows an expansion of John's address peculiar to that Evangelist. It reveals plainly the Baptist's legal position. He recommends a faithful fulfilment of the law; "the voice of him who crieth in the wilderness" penetrates not the domain of faith and love. He directed to *doing* only, as those who asked for instruction put only the question, What shall we do?[*] (Πράσσειν in ver. 13, = בָּגַשׂ *exigere* scil. φόρον, *to exact tribute.*—Διασείω, *to frighten, to exact by terror.*—Συκοφαντέω denotes properly "to perform the part of a petty and false informer;" then "to be greedy," "avaricious," see Luke xix. 8.) As a peculiar trait in the character of the Baptist, appears his childlike humility, which is intimated in the following verses, but which John, in the early chapters of his Gospel, portrays carefully for special reasons. Even in John's lifetime, his disciples would have him to be the Christ; but he himself humbly acknowledged his inferiority, and pointed his followers to the Saviour. Against his own will, his later self-willed disciples (the Sabeans) made him the historical prop of their sect.

Ver. 11.—Disclaiming for himself the dignity of the Messiah, the Baptist points to him to whom it belongs. He calls him: ὀπίσω μου ἐρχόμενος, *one coming after me*, leaving the time of his appearance undetermined. The Evangelist John, who had special reason to be more circumstantial regarding the declarations of the Baptist as to his relation to the Saviour (see on this point notes on John i. 19, ff.; iii. 27, ff.), mentions facts, which prove that John had a deep and true knowledge of the Saviour and his work. Matthew notices particularly this point only in the Baptist's words, that Jesus possessed a greater spiritual power (ἰσχυρότερός μου ἐστίν.) He therefore represents John's relation to the Saviour as that of a servant to his master. (The ὑποδήματα λῦσαι, or βαστάζειν, *to loose or carry the sandals*, is put for menial service in general.) But the Baptist

[*] Compare the New Testament answer to the question, What shall we do? in Acts ii. 37.

marks especially the superiority of the Messiah, in reference to his baptism. (See note on John i. 25, ff.) He contrasts the baptism of water (ἐν ὕδατι βαπτίζειν) with that of the Holy Ghost and fire (βαπτίζειν ἐν πνεύματι ἁγίῳ καὶ πυρί.) We might feel tempted here to join πῦρ, fire, with πνεῦμα, spirit; so that either fire should appear as a concomitant (as if the baptism of the Spirit would be accompanied by fiery appearances, as on the day of Pentecost) ; or πνεῦμα, spirit, be taken as qualifying πῦρ, fire, (= πῦρ πνευματικόν, a spiritual fire), fire, as the more powerful element, being contrasted with water. But the passages, Matth. xx. 22 ; Luke xii. 50, appear to me to favour the ancient distinction of a threefold baptism (fluminis, flaminis, sanguinis.)* In this the Saviour appears as the type of believers, who, like himself, if not outwardly, yet inwardly, must all pass through the consummating baptism of blood. In the triple elements of baptism—viz., water, spirit, and fire, there is intimated a gradation in the development of the spiritual life, and in the element from which it results. While the lowest stage, baptism with water, implies external purification from sin, and repentance, the baptism of the Spirit refers to the inward cleansing in faith (the Holy Spirit being conceived of as the regenerating principle, John iii. 1, ff. ; Acts i. 5) ; and lastly, the baptism of fire expresses the consummation and complete triumph of the new and higher life in its peculiar nature.

Ver. 12.—The exhortation concludes, very appropriately, with a renewed admonition of the nearness of the κρίσις, judgment (ver. 10), the execution of which belonged to the Messiah's office. The act of judging is here represented under the figure of the winnowing of chaff and wheat. The same figure occurs in Jer. xv. 7 ; Luke xxii. 31. (Οὗ ἐν τῇ χειρὶ αὐτοῦ = בְּיָדוֹ אֲשֶׁר זֹרֶה. Πτύον = vannus, ventilabrum. Ἄχυρον = מֹץ, Psalm i. 4. On πῦρ ἄσβεστον, see note on Mark ix. 44.) In the concluding verses in Luke iii. 18–20, the Evangelist calls these addresses of the second Elijah a εὐαγγελίζεσθαι, bringing good news (ver. 18), inasmuch as they treated of the coming of the Mes-

---

* De Wette is altogether wrong in taking πῦρ to denote punishment, for the idea of baptism does not admit of any reference to punishment. It is always subservient to salvation. [May not fire and spirit point prophetically to Acts ii. ? When did the apostles receive the Christian baptism, as a symbol of regeneration, if not at the Pentecost ? (Acts i. 5.) Then came in place of the inward repentance the external spirit (as res sacramenti), and in place of water, fire (as signum sacramentale.) And by this spiritual baptism were they prepared to administer the ordinary Christian baptism (that of water and spirit.)*—[E.

* I think neither of the above explanations correct. John is discriminating Christ's office and work from his own as higher and more profoundly searching and spiritual. For this he makes use of the rite which formed so prominent a feature of his ministry. What spirit and fire are to water, that is Christ's baptism and general work to his. He is not, I think, speaking of the Saviour's baptism of believers particularly, but of the general searching, discriminating character of his work. This h̥ ⁔dicates by combining with spirit the subtle, purifying, powerful element, fire. De Wette's explanatio⌐ ₔmbraces a part of the truth, but not the whole of it.—[K.

siah, and even of his presence. (John i. 26.) Luke's incidental observations on the Baptist's imprisonment may, perhaps, have been occasioned by a document used by him, in which John's subsequent fortunes were narrated. Luke mentions, by anticipation, in this place, what occurred long after. (See note on Matth. xiv. 1, ff., for a fuller discussion.)

§ 2. The Baptism of Christ.

(Matth. iii. 13–17; Mark i. 9–11; Luke iii. 21–23; John i. 32–34.)

The fact of the baptism of Christ by John is somewhat surprising, as it is undeniable, that the less is blessed by the better (Heb. vii. 7); but here the reverse takes place. As before observed, that which specially distinguishes baptism from mere lustrations, is, that one party appears as the baptizer, the other as the baptized; and the baptizer, so to speak, elevates the baptized into his own element of life. Now, it is not clear how the weaker can raise the stronger to a higher stage of life.* John himself was penetrated with a sense of the inappropriateness of Christ's being baptized by him (ver. 14), and acknowledged that he rather stood in need of a higher baptism from Jesus. Objectively viewed, this was quite right; but by the divine dispensation, which assigns the limit to every thing, and thus also to each individual's course of life (without prejudice to liberty, which has its expansion within the assigned limits), John was not called for the New Testament; he formed the completion of the Old; and, like Simeon (Luke ii. 25, ff.,) beheld the Messiah without experiencing his regenerating efficacy in himself; he was saved, like the saints of the Old Testament, through faith in the coming Saviour. For though John beheld Christ, yet redemption was still future to him, since Christ's work was not completed till after the death of the Baptist. It was, therefore, part of John's humility, that, taking his stand purely and simply, he baptized Jesus; a formal refusal to baptize him would have been false humility—a want of obedience to the divine will, which had ordained this relation be-

---

* The essential feature of baptism should not, perhaps, be sought so much in the relation between the baptizer and the baptized, as between the latter and God, of whom the baptizer is but an instrument. It is not the raising of the baptized into the sphere of *the baptizer* which essentially characterizes baptism; but that he *before God buries himself into death as one laden with guilt*, in order to *arise again from death as a new, divinely born man*. The Jew who submitted to John's baptism, acknowledged: "I have deserved death; I need a new life." Christ in his baptism, declared: "I will, laden with the guilt of humanity, descend into death, and as a glorified conqueror will arise from it." Thus his baptism by John was a type and prophecy of the real baptism of death and resurrection, and for⁓ . the real connecting link between John's baptism and Christian baptism (Matth. xᴀviii. 19.) Such is the simplest explanation of Christ's baptism.—[E.

tween John and Christ. The words of Jesus : οὕτω πρέπον ἐστὶν ἡμῖν πληρῶσαι πᾶσαν δικαιοσύνην, *thus, it becometh us*, etc. (Matth. iii. 15), give the key to the understanding of it. The term δικαιοσύνη, *righteousness* (the meanings of which will be treated connectedly in note on Rom. iii. 21), denotes here δίκαιον, *what the law demands*. The words contain, therefore, the general principle on which the Saviour proceeded, and which John, too, had to follow on this occasion—viz., to observe all legal ordinances as divine institutions. This was not, indeed, the consequence of any internal necessity (for which reason πρέπον ἐστί is used, and not δεῖ or χρείαν ἔχω), but a propriety, and a ᛫propriety in the highest and noblest sense ; the opposite would have been a disturbing of the harmony of life. As, therefore, Jesus was in all things γενόμενος ὑπὸ νόμον, *subjected to law* (Gal. iv. 4), he must submit to John's baptism, thus establishing it as divine ; by God's will that was to be also the moment of his being anointed with the Spirit—his solemn inauguration as the Messiah King.* The baptism of Jesus stands, therefore, on a level with his undergoing circumcision and the purification. (See note on Luke ii. 21, 22.) The Mediator himself took part in the sacrifices and the other atoning rites ordained by God in the temple service, until, by his one sacrifice on the cross, he had made the repetition of all other sacrifices superfluous. According to God's promise (John i. 33), *the baptism with the Spirit* coincided with John's baptism with water, to which Jesus submitted ; the former, of course, could not come through the medium of John, it was rather a sign (σημεῖον, אות) for John himself, by which he might infallibly recognize the promised Messiah. By this anointing of the Spirit, the gradual development of the *human* consciousness in Jesus attained its height, and that fulness of power was imparted to him which was requisite for the fulfilment of his office as a teacher. Even the pure offspring of the Spirit needed the anointing of the Spirit ; it was not till his human nature (the ψυχή) was strengthened to bear the plenitude of the Spirit, that it was abidingly filled with power from above. The baptism, accordingly, was the sublime season, when the character of the Χριστός, מָשִׁיחַ, which was dormant (as it were, *potentiâ*) in the gradually developing child and youth, now (*actu*) came forth and expanded itself ; the baptism is the inauguration of the Messiah, primarily for himself and John.†

---

* The law required not that he should submit himself to John's baptism; but it did require that *an expiation should be* offered, and his willingness to offer this was expressed by Christ in the symbolical rite of baptism. The anointing of the Spirit, *attached itself* to this expression, but formed no part of it.—[E.

† Compare the remarkable words in *Justin, dial. cum Tryph. Jud.*, p. 226. Χριστὸς δὲ εἰ καὶ γεγέννηται καὶ ἐστί που, ἄγνωστός ἐστι καὶ οὐδὲ αὐτός πω ἑαυτὸν ἐπίσταται, οὐδὲ ἔχει δύναμίν τινα, μέχρις ἂν ἐλθὼν Ἡλίας χρίσῃ αὐτὸν καὶ φανερὸν πᾶσι ποιήσῃ. *Though the Messiah has been born and lives, he is unknown, and does not even know himself, nor has*

Ver. 13.—According to Mark's account (i. 9), our Saviour appears to have continued at Nazareth till the time of his public appearance. The inner life in him was, doubtless, silently and secretly unfolding itself. But when the hour was come, which the Spirit within gave him to know with indubitable certainty,* he came to John at the Jordan (on the locality, see note on John i. 28, 29), in order to be introduced by this messenger of God.   ‚

Ver. 14, 15.—The important conversation between Jesus and John, *before* the baptism, is narrated by Matthew only. It is of the highest importance for an understanding of John's relation to the Saviour ; and Matthew gives, even in this communication, a proof * of the importance and originality of his peculiar sources of information, particularly in the discourses.

Ver. 16, 17.—The process of John's baptism of Christ is not minutely detailed ; whether the Baptist uttered any words, or what words, over Jesus, is left unnoticed. We are told only what took place after the baptism was over—that is, *at* the emersion out of the water (ἀνέβη ἀπὸ τοῦ ὕδατος). That the outpouring of the Spirit did not take place *before* the submersion, perfectly accords with the symbolical character of the action (see Rom. vi. 1, ff.), which is not indeed in itself applicable to John's baptism, but which the Saviour, by his baptism, typically imparted to the action. The one part of the action —the submersion—represents its negative aspect—viz., the taking away of the old man (Rom. vi. 4); the other—the emersion—denotes its positive aspect—viz., the appearance of the new man ; the communication of the Holy Ghost would therefore be naturally connected with the latter. Luke adds (iii. 21), that Jesus prayed, which must be understood of being absorbed in inward devotion. After the emersion, these three circumstances constitute the progress of the action—the opening of the heavens, the descent of the Spirit, the utterance of the voice. But that all this did not pass as a spectacle before the assembled multitude, but was seen by Christ and John alone, is clearly implied in Matth. iii. 16 (ἀνεῴχθησαν αὐτῷ οἱ οὐρανοί), and in John i. 32. Spiritual eyes are needful for the contemplation of spiritual transactions ; he only who possessed such, was in a condition to behold the working of the Spirit. A vague and undefined emotion, awakened by the mighty working of the

any power, until Elias shall come and anoint him and make him known to all. (See note on Matth. xvii. 10, ff.) At the close of Christ's ministry (see note on John xii. 28), a similar public approval of him took place by a voice from heaven ; so that the same event forms alike the commencement and the close of his public life.

* It is quite an erroneous notion, that Jesus made his public appearance in consequence of an exactly calculated and carefully formed plan. His inward life obeyed only the direction of his heavenly Father ; what he saw him do, that the Son also did. There was, indeed, at the same time, the clearest consciousness of what he did ; but all calculation and human forming of plans must be conceived as excluded, because it trenches upon Christ's direct oneness of life with God.

Spirit, may have pervaded the multitude at the sublime instant, when the glory of heaven descended to earth ; but the transaction itself was not seen by them. (Compare the analogous case in the conversion of the Apostle Paul, Acts ix. 7.) If we thus transfer the occurrence to the domain of the Spirit, we need not have recourse either to the historical interpretation (which speaks of Jewish notions of a brazen vault of heaven, and birds accidentally directing their flight to the place of baptism), or to its mythical explanation. The Spirit—the invisible cause of all that is visible—contains in himself the ground of all things ; the revelation and bestowment of himself is a quality of his nature. The opening of heaven—the region of the Spirit—is, consequently, nothing but the revealing of the world of spirits to the spirit. Every revelation is a rending of the heavens—a descent of the Spirit. (Isa. lxiv. 1 ; Ezek. i. 1 ;) Acts vii. 55.) Far as we ought to be from viewing the opening of the heavens materially, we should be just as far from considering it imaginary ; it is a real operation of the Spirit for the spirit. For the Saviour, this opening of heaven was an abiding one ; the flow of his inner life towards the eternal home of the Spirit, and the stream thence down to him, never again ceased. Gradually during their intercourse with our Lord, the disciples had their spiritual eye opened to this relation, as they saw continually heaven open, and the angels of God ascending and descending upon the Son of Man. (John i. 52.) The descent of the Spirit is therefore nothing but his bestowment, which is his very nature. As love, God descends, in his Spirit, into the hearts of his people. So also the sound of the voice is a necessary operation of the Spirit. The Spirit—the author of language—speaks for the spirit ; his operation is nothing but *word*. *What* he speaks the spirit understands immediately ; not by the intervention of the physical ear, but by the spiritual ear—that is by spiritual susceptibility of spiritual operations.*

With regard to the comparison of the Holy Ghost to a *dove*, the word ὡσεί, *as if, as,* used by all the four Evangelists, shews that it was meant to be regarded only *as a comparison*. The reality of the appearance is, indeed, expressly signified (σωματικῷ εἴδει, Luke iii. 22); but, as a real spiritual phenomenon, it was not visible to physical eyes, and, consequently, the impression could only be described by a comparison with visible things. According to the symbolism of the Bible, certain mental characters appear expressed

---

* It is not intended by these remarks to assert, that, in the whole transaction there was not also something visible and audible to all. The Gospel according to the Hebrews (see the author's History of the Gospels, p. 81) mentioned an additional circumstance—viz., the visible appearance of fire at the baptism. As all revelations of the divine take place with light and splendour, the idea is not incorrect; only, it is viewed materially. Just so with the voice (see John xii. 29), there may have been something audible to *all.*

in several animals, as in the lion, the lamb, the eagle, and the ox. In this system of natural hieroglyphics, the dove denotes purity and simplicity, and hence the spirit of purity may be most fittingly compared with the dove.* The coming of the Spirit like a dove denotes, consequently, that the fulness of the spirit of purity was imparted to Jesus, whereby he became the purifier of mankind. He was therefore sealed, so to speak, as the Son of God ; on which account the declaration of the voice from heaven is, *This is my beloved Son,* etc. That the term Son of God refers here to the divine eternal nature of the Son, is shewn by John i. 34. In the baptism of the Spirit, the Saviour himself was consciously perfected in that nature, and manifested first of all to John. ('Αγαπητός = יָחִיד. Εὐδοκεῖν ἔν τινι = בְּ רָצָה. Nothing but his own image is well-pleasing to God, and, consequently, only those who are in Christ, Ephes. i. 6.) There are two other points in the account of the baptism mentioned exclusively by the Evangelist John (i. 32.) First, the words ; πνεῦμα ἔμεινε ἐπ' αὐτόν—i. e., ἦλθεν ἐπ' αὐτὸν καὶ ἔμεινε, *the Spirit remained upon him*—i. e., *came upon him and remained.* In these words the Evangelist notices, in the Saviour's case, what he usually insists upon as the peculiar aspect of the Spirit's operations under the New Testament. While in the Old Testament mode of his operation he reveals himself at particular moments, he appears in the New, as permanently and uniformly efficient. In the life of Jesus we find this uniformity of divine consciousness perfectly exhibited ; while, in the developments of life in Old Testament saints, there was an alternation of elevated, and, as it were, *spiritless* seasons. Secondly, the words : οὐκ ᾔδειν αὐτόν, *I knew him not* (John i. 33), are remarkable. They appear at variance, partly, with the passage Matth. iii. 14, which supposes an acquaintance between Jesus and John ; and, partly, with their family relations, it being scarcely possible, while the mothers were so intimate, that the sons should be unknown to each other. But ᾔδειν, *knew,* evidently does not stand opposed to the supposition that John knew Jesus *externally,* and cherished anticipations of his exalted destination. But to gain divine *indubitable* certainty, that it was in the person of Jesus that the hopes of mankind were to be fulfilled, required express confirmations, such as to transcend all subjective impressions, and the deceptions to which they are liable. Such a miraculous sign was appointed him in the outpouring of the Spirit, and this sign he had at the baptism. (John i. 33.)†

---

* The comparison of the Spirit with the dove is found in the Samaritan and Rabbinical writers also. In the tract *Chagigah,* it is said on Gen. i. 2; "Spiritus Dei ferebatur super aqua, ut columba," *The Spirit of God hovered over the water, like a dove.* The Christian sects probably derived the comparison from the New Testament.

† As John grew up in the wilderness, and Jesus in Galilee, they may not have been *personally* acquainted. A sign had been promised to John by which he should recognize

Luke (iii. 23) connects with his account of the baptism, the genealogy, in which, agreeably to the popular notion (ὢν ὡς ἐνομίζετο), he commences with Joseph, Mary's husband. With this transition, Luke connects the important observation, that Jesus was thirty years old at the beginning of his ministry. 'Ωσεί, *about,* being added, seems indeed to make the date uncertain ; but as the age of the Levites' entrance on office was fixed by Numb. iv. 3, 47, at thirty years, and as the Saviour invariably adhered to the existing ordinances of the Old Testament, we may conclude with probability that the Saviour was *not less* than thirty years of age. Yet there is no reason to suppose that he exceeded the fixed number ; in the Saviour's life all is disposed according to number and measure, and it is therefore best to adhere to the age assigned. The only remaining uncertainty is, whether his public appearance falls at the beginning or the end of the year. (In the construction of the sentence, supply the verb διδάσκειν with ἀρχόμενος. It is not conformable to the connexion to construe the participle with ἦν, or ὢν with ἀρχόμενος.)

§ 3. CHRIST'S TEMPTATION.

(Matth. iv. 1–11; Mark i. 11, 12; Luke iv. 1–13.)

THE Saviour's endowment with the fulness of the Spirit is most appropriately followed by his steadfastness in the contest with the evil one. It is part of the idea of the Messiah, that he is appointed to destroy the kingdom of darkness ; his whole life on earth, therefore, appears as a conflict with its prince. The Gospel-history, however, particularizes two periods in the life of Jesus, in which he opposed the full and united power of the evil one, and overcame. These periods form the commencement and the close of his public labours, and each possesses its peculiar character. In the first temptation, at the commencement of his ministry,* temptation approached the Saviour by the avenue of *desire;* in the other, at the close of his earthly labours, by that of the *fear* of suffering and death. Every temptation appears in the one or the other of these forms ; by the conquest of both alike, our Lord stands as the *ideal* of perfect righteousness—as victor in the war with sin. The narrative before us of the temptation of Jesus through the medium of

the Messiah (John i. 33.) But when Jesus came to him (Matth. iii. 14) *before the sign,* the impression of his majestic appearance, and an inward voice alike said to him, "This is he!" And then came the sign as a sealing witness from heaven.—[E.

* Even in Jewish theology the conception had been formed from the general idea of the Messiah, that he would have to be tempted by Satan just at the commencement of his office. See *Schöttgen, Jesus der wahre Messias; aus der jüdische Theologie dargestellt.* Leipzig, 1748. 8vo. S. 754, ff.

desire, makes it approach the Saviour in the three principal forms
by which the world uniformly works—viz., the lust of the eyes, the
lust of the flesh, and the pride of life. (1 John ii. 16.) This narrative, consequently, exhibits the comprehensiveness and sufficiency of
his victory over sin, and thus forms a suitable introduction to the
description of the labours of the Saviour, who was in all points
tempted like as we are, yet without sin. (Heb. iv. 15.) The same
temptations of pleasure, which on this occasion met Jesus concentrated, and were in this form repelled by him, followed him individually through his whole earthly ministry, assuming various forms
at various times. In like manner, temptations on the side of pain
presented themselves to the Saviour through his whole earthly life,
till, at its close, they assailed him in their full concentration.

Our conception of the evangelical narrative of the temptation of
Christ is necessarily qualified by our views regarding the doctrine
of the devil, and of bad angels in general. Reserving fuller explanations on this point for the note on Matth. viii. 28, we simply remark,
that only the most arbitrary exegesis can deny the existence of evil
spirits. Even the Old Testament teaches, though for wise reasons
obscurely, that man did not produce evil from himself, but was exposed to its influence by the seductions of a wicked power, a doctrine essential to the very idea of redemption, which supposes a
bondage under a foreign force. (See Gen. iii. 1 ; Lev. xv. 8 ; Deut.
xxxii. 17 ; Psalm cvi. 37 ; Job i. 6 ; Isa. liv. 16 ; Zech. iii. 1.) In
the New Testament, Christ confirms this doctrine, partly by universally taking it for granted, as appears times without number in
his discourses, that there is a kingdom of evil in opposition to the
kingdom of good (see Matth. xii. 26, ff.), and partly by express assertions respecting it (Matth. xiii. 39 ; John viii. 44 ; xiv. 30), which
admit no other unprejudiced exposition. The expositor, then, who
feels himself compelled to include the existence of the devil among
the doctrines taught by Christ and the apostles, will be unable to
sanction explanations of the temptation, which understand the term
διάβολος, devil, in Matthew and Luke (for which Mark has σατανᾶς)
of some kind of human enemies or tempters, as, in the idea of
Christ, the idea of his contest with evil in its centralized form is
necessarily included. The whole doctrine of the Bible concerning
Christ's relation to the kingdom of evil, even though we did not
possess the narrative of the temptation, would lead to the same idea
which is there involved. But if these explanations are inadmissible,
incomparably more so are those which regard the temptations here
recorded as arising from within the Saviour. Schleiermacher is not
wrong in saying : "If Jesus ever harboured any such thoughts (as
the tempter suggested to him), even in the most evanescent manner, he would no longer be Christ ; and this explanation appears to

me the worst neological outrage that has been committed against him." (*Versuch über den Lucas*, S. 54.) The absolute purity of Jesus admits in no way of an impure thought coming *from* himself ; as the first Adam, according to the profound narrative in Genesis, was tempted *from without*, so was the second Adam also (1 Cor. xv. 47), only with this difference, that the latter came off victorious.* *Schleiermacher's* own view, however, that the temptation is merely a parabolical narrative, which was afterwards misunderstood—which view *Ullmann* also (Studien, H. 1, S. 59, ff.) approves—is sufficiently refuted by *Usteri* (Studien 1832, H. 4). Undoubtedly we possess here a pure fact, undistorted by mythical elements (*Blätter für höhere Wahrheit*, B. v., S. 247, ff.) ; yet still even from the strictly biblical point of view it may be doubted, whether we are to conceive of an external appearance of Satan standing, as it were corporeally, before Christ. This may be denied for various reasons. In the first place, we can point to no analogous fact either in the Old Testament or the New ;† for the narrative in Gen. iii. 1, take it as we may, cannot, at least, be called an *appearance* of the devil. Nor would the fact be explained even by assuming an outward appearance of the prince of darkness ; for, assuming that Jesus was physically transported through the air, it would still be inconceivable how all the kingdoms of the world could be surveyed from a mountain.‡ Besides, the words which the tempter uttered outwardly, must be conceived to have been united with an inward influence, because, without this there would have been no temptation ; this would, therefore, be the essential point, even on the supposition of an outward appearance. It is, therefore, doubtless most fitting to lay the scene of the occurrence, as an internal one, in the sphere of the soul ; we thus obtain a true conception of it, and preserve all its essential features. The temptation consisted in this, that the *soul* of Jesus was exposed to the full influence of the kingdom of darkness. This kingdom in the person of its representative, first displayed to the Saviour its bright side, and endeavoured to seduce him from the narrow path marked out for him on earth.

* The hypothesis started by *Meyer* (in *Ullmann* and *Umbreit's Studien*, 1831, H. 2), does not differ essentially from this view. He supposes that the temptation was a *dream*, and compares with it Solomon's dream, 1 Kings iii. 5, ff. For if those seductive thoughts could have arisen in Christ's heart, though only in a dream, his purity would have been sullied. But if any one chose to refer the excitement of the thoughts in a dream to a hostile power, the opinion would not indeed be offensive; but then there appears no reason why the whole occurrence should not have taken place in a waking state, as the narrative implies.

† But there was no moment analogous to this, no man analogous to Christ. The tempter could not appear under a mask to our Lord as to Adam. (Comp. my Krit. d. Ev. Gerch. § 53.—[E.

‡ Yet, on the other hand, we can scarcely conceive of a real temptation to the Saviour to display himself by throwing himself down before a multitude that existed only in vision. So also the first temptation attaches itself to a real, physical hunger.—[E.

We meet with analogous appearances in the Old Testament as well as the New. (See Ezek. viii. 3 ; xi. 1 ; Rev. i. 10 ; xvii. 3.) And if we are disposed to connect, 2 Cor. xi. 14, " Satan is transformed into an angel of light," with the temptation, that expression by no means requires us to imagine an outward appearance : it can be understood of an inward revelation of Satan, as a good angel, the more surely to deceive.

Matth. iv. 1.—Immediately after the baptism, the Saviour left the Jordan (see Luke iv. 1), and withdrew into solitude, to prepare in quiet for his lofty calling. That a literal wilderness is here meant, is seen by Mark i. 13. Tradition refers it to Quarantaria, which lies near Jericho. (*Joseph. Antiq.*, xvi. 1. *Bell. Jud.*, iv. 82.) Inasmuch as this quiet preparation, and the temptation connected with it, was based on God's plan itself, it is said : *he was led up by the Spirit*, etc. (ἀνήχθη ὑπὸ πνεύματος εἰς τὴν ἔρημον.) That this Spirit was that good spirit who filled Jesus at the baptism, is seen from Luke iv. 1, in the words : Ἰησοῦς πνεύματος ἁγίου πλήρης κ. τ. λ. But in that case it seems inexplicable how we can speak of the Saviour who was armed with the fulness of the Spirit, as being tempted (πειρασθῆναι). (The meaning of the word is always one and the same ; it is modified only according to the object or subject of temptation. Used of the evil one, it denotes *to try*, for the purpose of destroying. In this sense it is said of God, πειράζει οὐδένα, *he tempteth no one*, James i. 13. God, on the contrary, tempts in order to purify and to perfect, Gen. xxii. 1. Used of men in reference to God, it is always the product of unbelief and presumption, since it involves the contrary of humble waiting for indications from God, Heb. iii. 9.) But we must include the possibility of a fall (like Adam's *posse non peccare*) in the very idea of a Saviour ; because, without this, no merit is conceivable.* True, this possibility must be viewed as purely objective ; since in so far as God became man in the person of Christ, so far we must ascribe to him the impossibility of sinning (*non posse peccare*). This blending of the possibility of falling with the necessity of a victory over evil, is a mystery, which is one with the idea of the God-man itself. It is only by distinguishing between ψυχή, soul, and πνεῦμα, spirit, that we can attain to a clear idea of the relation. His liability to temptation was attached to his human soul ; the necessity of a victory, to the fulness of the spirit. By the former, he is made like us, and set for a pattern ; by the latter, he is above all that is human, and assists individuals to become like himself, by the power of the same Spirit. In his last great temptation, that, viz., of his final sufferings, the

---

* The consolation, too, that is afforded to unhappy man, struggling against sin, in the fact that the Saviour himself tasted the bitterness of that struggle in all its forms (Heb. ii. 17, 18), would be destroyed, if the objective possibility of Christ's falling were denied.

Saviour himself announced his being deserted of the fulness of the
divine Spirit (Matth. xxvii. 46) ; this abandonment, in which the
humanity of the Saviour stood as it were isolated, affords a view of
the nature of his conflict at that time. In the present case nothing
is expressly said of such a desertion ; but it must be presumed, particularly as the Saviour does not at once recognize the tempter. The
outward fasting in the wilderness was an emblem, as it were, of his
inward forsaken condition ; and it is only by this assumption, that
the temptation acquires essential significancy. In full possession
of the divine Spirit, temptation is inconceivable ; it is only as divested of that fulness that the soul of Jesus could humanly fight
and struggle. According to this, the scene should be conceived in
the following form :—After the effusion of the Spirit on our Lord,
he went, under the impulse of that Spirit, into the wilderness, in
order to begin his great work in the seclusion of his inner life.
There, as in the garden of Gethsemane, and on Golgotha, the fulness of the Spirit was withdrawn from him, and he was left to the
power of darkness (Luke xxii. 53) ; pleasure, in its most seductive
forms, tempted his soul. But, in perfect innocence, the Saviour
passed through the conflict ; and, when the temptation was repelled,
the fulness of heavenly power returned to him (Matth. iv. 11). If
it were said, that John i. 32 : πνεῦμα ἔμεινεν ἐπ᾽ αὐτόν, the Spirit
abode upon him, is contradictory to this view, the same might be
said of Matth. xxvii. 46, where such a state of spiritual desertion
must certainly be supposed. By whatever method the difficulty is
solved in that case, the same must be applied here. My idea of this
obscure relation is this : In the Saviour there was an alternation of
states ; he had seasons of the richest spiritual fulness, and of desertion ; but, in the first place, these states were not so variable as they
are wont to be in sinful men ; and, next, they did not penetrate to
the inmost sanctuary of his being. His soul itself was holy and
pure ; and, from its being most intimately pervaded by the Spirit,
was so entirely a spiritual soul (ψυχὴ πνευματική), that even at the
moments of complete desertion by the overflowing fulness of the
Spirit (as we must suppose in Matth. xxvii. 46), his soul acted in the
might of the divine Spirit. This unalterable repose in the depths
of his holy soul—this perfect freedom, in the inmost seat of life,
from those agitations of disquietude, which the Redeemer bore for
our good, as he did all the other consequences of sin—are denoted
by the "abiding of the Spirit," which is contrasted with the alternating conditions of Old Testament saints, who might be immediately overpowered by sin whenever dark hours arrived.*

* There seems no difficulty in reconciling John's statement of the Spirit's remaining
upon the Saviour, with his subsequent withdrawal. His descending and remaining, i. e.,
not immediately withdrawing, is in no way inconsistent with his leaving Christ afterwards
for special reasons.—[K.

Ver. 2.—In Christ's fasting for forty days, there is evidently a parallel with the fasting of Moses (Deut. ix. 9, 18) and Elijah (1 Kings xix. 8). We are, therefore, the less justified in taking νηστεύειν, *fasting*, in a wider sense—viz., "abstaining from *ordinary* nourishment," since it is said of Moses, that he ate no bread, and drank no water, which coincides with Luke iv. 2 : "He did eat nothing." The intention of the Evangelists is to place Jesus in comparison with the great prophets of earlier days (according to Deut. xviii. 15 : "A prophet *like unto me*," says Moses, "will the Lord thy God raise up"); he could not, therefore, do any thing less than they did. The number forty was certainly a sacred number with the Jews ; but it does not follow thence that it is not to be taken exactly ; but rather that the idea entertained by the Jews of the sacredness of certain numbers has itself a deeper foundation, which, taken as a general proposition, may be thus expressed :— "According to divine arrangement, which is pure harmony, every development proceeds by definite measure and number." The forty days of the temptation forms an interesting parallel with Israel's forty years' journey through the wilderness.* All the passages quoted in the history of Christ's temptation are taken from the narrative of that journey.

Ver. 3, 4.—The point of the first temptation is justly regarded as lying in the thought of employing the higher powers bestowed upon him for satisfying his own wants. The principle here maintained, of using his miraculous powers only for the good of others, the Saviour followed out with self-denying love through his whole ministry. Jesus repulsed the powerful solicitation of sensual appetite by faith in God's power, with a reference to Deut. viii. 3, where the LXX. translate כָּל מוֹצָא פִי יְהוָה by ῥῆμα ἐκπορευόμενον διὰ στόματος Θεοῦ. In this passage the manna, viewed as an extraordinary heavenly aliment (Psalm lxxviii. 25), is contrasted with earthly means of subsistence, and just so Jesus contrasts the earthly ἄρτος, *bread*, with the heavenly. According to the connexion, therefore, other kinds of earthly food cannot be meant. The ῥῆμα Θεοῦ, *word of God*, is to be conceived of here as the effectual creative cause of *all* nourishment. As every thing was made by God's word, and by the breath of his mouth (Psalm xxxiii. 6), so that same word also preserves all things, since the preservation is but a continued creation. Jesus is stayed by faith in this power of God ; so long as the Spirit did not release him from the wilderness, he was fed by the

---

* Such parallels are acknowledged by the advocates of the mythical character of the Gospel-history, *Strauss* and *De Wette;* but in such a way, that precisely because of those parallels they deny the historical reality, both of the typical event in the Old Testament, and of the antitype in the New. But in this way they are degraded into mere puerilities. For a serious person they can have no import, unless they be founded on real transactions, by which God speaks to men in the language of fact.

hidden word of God, which strengthened soul and body, without his providing any thing for himself by the miraculous gift granted to him. (On ῥῆμα θεοῦ, see note on Matth. iii. 2.)

Ver. 5.—Luke has placed the second temptation last ; evidently with less propriety.* The first two thoughts the tempter suggests to Jesus we can, for a moment, imagine as coming from a good being ; the temptation is more hidden, and Satan, consequently, does not display himself as he is ; but in the last requirement his dark origin is openly revealed, so that it is properly followed in Matthew's account by ὕπαγε, be gone. ('Αγία πόλις = עִיר הַקֹּדֶשׁ, holy city, a designation of Jerusalem as the centre of the Old Testament theocracy. Πτερύγιον = כָּנָף, a wing of the temple, in the shape of a tower, with a flat roof. The conducting him thither took place ἐν πνεύματι, in Spirit, Rev. xvii. 3.)

Ver. 6.—The point of the second temptation lies in the thought of parading the gift of working miracles, and thus attaching to himself the unreasoning multitude ; this thought, being clothed in the words of Scripture,† is suggested to our Lord in a delusive form. In this respect Jesus acted constantly on the principle here approved—his miracles always had reference to moral and spiritual ends. The quoting of the Scripture words was intended to excite his vanity from the consciousness of his being the Son of God, through the pleasure inspired by the miraculous powers residing in him. Humble' obedience, the laying aside of one's own will, can alone secure the victory in such a case. The passage is quoted from Psalm xci. 11, according to the LXX., but in an abbreviated form. In the context, the words apply to all the pious, and represent them as under God's protection. But the pious part of mankind, conceived as a whole, has its representative in the Messiah as the second Adam ; and therefore it is quite right to refer the passage to the Messiah ; the error lies only in its application to cases of our own making. The angels appear here as "ministering spirits, sent forth to minister for them who shall be heirs of salvation." (See note on Heb. i. 14.) The entire fulness of the heavenly powers is present for those that fear God, as Paul says, "All things are yours." (1 Cor. iii. 21, 22.)

Ver. 7.—Jesus meets the tempter, who plants himself on the temple, and makes free use of the word of God, with that same Word. His language expresses (Deut. vi. 16) this thought, that the perverse application of a correct principle is a tempting of God. The words are quoted according to the LXX. ('Εκπειράζειν is used

* [See Greswell's Dissertations on the Gospels, vol. ii., p. 192, ff., second edition.]—Tr.
† Concerning the use of the words of Scripture on the part of angels, see remarks on Luke i. 17.

in Luke x. 25 ; 1 Cor. x. 9, in a bad sense only ; and not, therefore, of God's temptations.)

Ver. 8, 9.—This passage, as already observed, goes specially to prove that the temptation is to be conceived as internal. A view of all the kingdoms of the world is of course impossible from any physical elevation ; even on the hypothesis of physical changes of place, we must still have recourse to a spiritual ecstacy.* But in his holy humility and self abasement, he chose the cross instead of the crown. But that the reference is not to a dominion over the Jews merely, but to universal monarchy, is evident even from the Jewish notion of a Messiah, which maintained it to be one of his prerogatives to rule over all nations. (See *Bertholdt, Christol. jud.*, p. 188.) The idea, rightly conceived, is also perfectly correct and true. This last temptation seems to turn on the proud lust of dominion. Satan here manifests himself as the "prince of this world" (John xii. 31 ; xiv. 30 ; xvi. 11), and as desirous of making Jesus his instrument (that is, of making Christ Antichrist), since he aims to delude him by the promise of dominion over the world, and by the revelation of its glory, while at the same time he possesses the power of arraying its entire forces against Jesus, in case he resists his seductions. As payment, the tempter demands worship from him. (Προσκυνεῖν, as an outward rite, such as kneeling or prostration, is here merely a symbolical expression of the inward act, at which the temptation was aimed—*i. e.*, acquiescing in Satan's will, permitting him to rule in the soul, and submitting to become his instrument.) It was precisely this which disclosed to the Saviour the dark nature of the being that suggested to him the thoughts which he repelled ; and Jesus, therefore, bids the creature of the night depart, with the word ὕπαγε, *be gone.*—Luke's narrative contains some peculiar traits. On occasion of the view of the kingdoms of the earth from the mountain, he adds : ἐν στιγμῇ χρόνου, *in a moment of time* (= ἐν ῥιπῇ ὀφθαλμοῦ, 1 Cor. xv. 52), which is still more in favour of the interpretation of this scene as a spiritual vision [but which admits a simple explanation from the superhuman power of Satan]. Luke next adds in his account of this temptation the following words to what the devil said : "for it has been delivered to me, and to whomsoever I will I give it" (ὅτι ἐμοὶ παραδέδοται, καὶ ᾧ ἐὰν θέλω, δίδωμι αὐτήν). Παραδέδοται, *it has been delivered*, conveys a hint worthy of notice, as opposing the doctrine of an original evil principle ; the prince of this world has *received* all from God, to whom alone, as the everlasting παντοκράτωρ, *almighty*, dominion is due. The confession of having received all, forms the strangest

---

* According to our view, we avoid the question altogether whether the ὄρος ὑψηλὸν λίαν was Tabor, or some other mountain—a question we are utterly destitute of data for answering.

contrast with the demand of worship. What the tempter here says of himself, is true of the Saviour in the purest and deepest sense. (See John xvii. 22 ; Rev. xi. 15.)

Ver. 10.—In answer to this last temptation, the Saviour put forward the first commandment (Deut. vi. 13), which contains all the rest in itself. Only the One, the Eternal, the True God of heaven and of earth, ought to be the object of worship. Where the assumption of this divine prerogative shews itself, the spirit of the devil is displayed. (See 2 Thess. ii. 4.) Through this maintenance of the honour of God, not only *this* world, but the *other* also, became the possession of Jesus ; to him all power in heaven and earth was given. (Λατρεύω = עָבַד is stronger than προσκυνεῖν; the latter is used also of subordination to man, the former refers only to God.)

Ver. 11.—The temptation of Jesus stands as one of those decisive events, such as are met with in a lower degree in common life also, and which determine the character of all its subsequent manifestations. As, after Adam's first transgression, all subsequent sin was nothing but the unfolding of original sin ; so this, the Saviour's first victory, appears as the foundation of all that follow. The Saviour here appears standing between the two worlds of light and darkness. As the hostile powers fled, heavenly powers surrounded him, and joined in celebrating the victory of good.* The Tempter wished Christ to serve him, instead of which the angels minister to Jesus, and announce that he is king of the kingdom of light. The circumstance mentioned in Mark i. 13: "he was among the wild beasts" (ἦν μετὰ τῶν θηρίων), has also, as *Usteri* (*ut. sup.*) strikingly observes, a typical meaning, because it is meant to represent Jesus as the restorer of Paradise. Adam fell in Paradise, and made it a wilderness ; Jesus conquered in the wilderness and made it a paradise, where the beasts lost their wildness, and angels took up their abode. But that the Redeemer's great conflict with the kingdom of darkness was not over for ever, is expressly noticed in Luke iv. 13, in the words : ὁ διάβολος ἀπέστη ἀπ' αὐτοῦ ἄχρι καιροῦ, the devil departed from him *for a season*, which close the history of the temptation.

If, according to the view given above, the temptation of Jesus took place in the depth of his inward life without witnesses, we must regard his own account of it as the only source of information, and testimony to its reality. This, and similar events, probably formed the subject of Jesus' discourses with his disciples after the resurrection, when he spoke to them of the things pertaining to the

---

* After our Lord's second great temptation in Gethsemane, there appeared to him an angel to strengthen him, Luke xxii. 43. We may suppose something of the same sort in this case.

kingdom of God. (Acts i. 3.) To become acquainted with the nature of that kingdom, it was needful that they should behold it in its establishment, and into that the temptation afforded the deepest insight. The accurate agreement in the narratives of Matthew and Luke, though writing quite independently of each other, both as to the event itself, and its place in the Gospel-history, is an *external* testimony to the event not easily invalidated. It carries its *internal* testimony within itself, and in the close connexion in which it stands with the character and work of the Saviour.

THIRD PART.

OF CHRIST'S WORKS AND DISCOURSES.

PARTICULARLY IN GALILEE.

MATTH. iv. 12—xviii. 35; MARK i. 14—ix. 50; LUKE iv. 14—ix. 50.

---

§ 1. JESUS APPEARS AS A TEACHER.

(Matth. iv. 12–17; Mark i. 14, 15; Luke iv. 14, 15.)

Ver. 12.—Were we not accurately instructed by the accounts of the Evangelist John as to the many events which intervened between the public appearance of Jesus and the imprisonment of John (see John iii. 24), we should conclude from Matth. iv. 12, and Mark i. 14, that the incarceration followed close upon the temptation of Jesus. This fact confirms the view detailed above (Introduction, § 7), that in this part of the Gospel-history, a chronological arrangement of the individual events is impracticable, since it is evidently by accident only that a comparison of John's narrative enables us to demonstrate, that the events thus connected in the narrative are separated in point of time.* For even though Luke does not mention John in this place (see, however, Luke iii. 19, 20), yet he begins his narrative (iv. 15) with the general statement, that Jesus " taught in their synagogues, being glorified of all ;" by which this section is deprived of its chronological character. Matthew (iv. 23) applies similar general formulas, and thus likewise renounces beforehand all pretensions to an exact chronological arrangement of the several events. What portion of the accounts of the first three Evangelists can with probability be assigned to the early period of Christ's public ministry, can be determined only by the help of the Gospel of John. The references to *place* are as indefi-

---

* That this does not warrant any conclusion unfavorable to Matthew as an author, is shewn by *Sieffert, ut. sup.*, S. 72.

nite as those to time ; particularly in Matthew. At the very beginning of this section (iv. 12) this Evangelist does indeed transfer the scene to Galilee and Capernaum ; but we cannot infer thence, that Matthew knew nothing of Christ's extending his labours beyond the limits of Galilee, till his last journey to Jerusalem ; for it cannot possibly be demonstrated where the separate events recorded by Matthew took place, since paying but slight regard to time and place, he arranges all according to certain general features.* Though it is probable, therefore, that as a Galilean, he narrates especially what took place in Galilee, yet his narrative assumes so general a form (see from ix. 35 onwards ; x. 1 ; xi. 1, 2, 7 ; xii. 19 ; xv. 22), that it may refer equally well to events in Judea and in Galilee.

Ver. 13.—After intimating, in general terms, that the Saviour selected Galilee as the chief scene of his ministry, Matthew informs us that not Nazareth, the dwelling-place of his parents, but Capernaum, became the centre of his labours. (Καπερναούμ, more correctly Καφαρναούμ == בַּחֲיֹם נַפָּר, *vicus consolationis.* It lay on the lake of Gennesaret [hence called παραθαλασσία, see John vi. 17], on the border of the tribes of Zebulun and Naphtali, in the neighbourhood of Bethsaida, not far from the mouth of the river Jordan.) There is no reason assigned here for his leaving Nazareth ; but, according to Luke iv. 16–30, it was the unbelief of its inhabitants that constrained our Lord to withdraw his blessed influence from these ungrateful people. The parallels to this narrative in Luke do not occur till Matth. xiii. 54, ff. ; Mark vi. 1, ff. ; and the same cure, which Luke places immediately subsequent to the occurrence at Nazareth, Mark (i. 21) transposes quite to the commencement. Although we think it highly probable, therefore, that Luke has placed the occurrence at Nazareth in a more correct chronological order, we prefer to postpone the exposition of the passage till we come to Matth. xiii. 54, ff. For we should not think ourselves justified in departing from our plan of following Matthew in this part of the Gospel-history, unless it could be proved (as it certainly cannot) that Luke iv. 16, ff., is to be understood of a much earlier, and Matth. xiii. 54, ff., of a second, and much later, visit of Jesus to Nazareth.

Ver. 14–16.—Even the choice of these districts the Evangelist does not regard as accidental, but recognizes in it the fulfilment of a prophecy of Isaiah (viii. 22, ix. 1.) The passage quoted contains the prediction, that the light of the Messiah will be manifested with the greatest splendour in the most despised regions of Palestine. (Micah v. 2 is similar.) Moreover, Matthew gives the passage abbreviated, and specifies only the names of the tribes of

---

* For a more complete discussion on this subject, see the author's programmes on the authenticity of Matthew.

Naphtali and Zebulun, and the neighbourhood of the lake of Gennesaret, which latter region experienced most richly the blessing of our Lord's presence, and witnessed the majority of his miracles. (The expression ὁδὸς θαλάσσης, *way of the sea*, = דֶּרֶךְ הַיָּם denotes, undoubtedly, the western shore of the lake of Gennesaret, here called יָם, as πέραν τοῦ Ἰορδάνου, *beyond the Jordan*, = עֵבֶר הַיַּרְדֵּן denotes the eastern shore of the same lake. The two expressions, therefore, taken together, include all its circumjacent parts ; and, according to the Gospel-history, the Saviour visited both shores of the lake of Gennesaret.) Of the inhabitants of these northern border provinces, it might be said most emphatically, that they lived in spiritual darkness ; in part, because they were far distant from the theocratic centre—Jerusalem and the temple, in which the true knowledge of God, so far as it existed among the people, was concentred ; in part, because they had contracted much that was impure, through continual contact with their heathen neighbours. But, at the same time, these very inhabitants of Galilee, whom the rigid Jews despised as half heathen, were most fitted to receive the new doctrine of the kingdom of God ; since they were freed from their gross exclusiveness by intercourse with people of the neighbouring states, while, at the same time, their degraded condition made their need of salvation very prominent. As, therefore, the sinner (as a penitent) is nearer to the kingdom of God than the righteous (Matth. ix. 13), so our Lord manifested himself to the poor Galileans in preference to the other inhabitants of Palestine. (On the opposition of φῶς and σκότος, see further in note on John i. 3, 4. Σκιὰ θανάτου, *shadow of death*, is after the Hebrew צַלְמָוֶת, which is commonly used as synonymous with חֹשֶׁךְ, *darkness*. The LXX. derived it from צֵל and מָוֶת.)

Ver. 17.—After this notice of the locality, Matthew mentions briefly the matter of the Saviour's preaching. He confines himself to the same points which he had spoken of in John's preaching (iii. 2)—repentance, urged by the near approach of the kingdom of God. The Saviour's proclamation was at first naturally connected with that of John ; yet the remark in Mark. i. 15, is certainly not to be overlooked, that πίστις, *faith*, was connected immediately with μετάνοια,* *repentance*, and that, not merely a general faith, such as formed the

---

* *Schleiermacher* remarks beautifully in his *Festpredigten*, ii., S. 93—"When Christ commands repentance, he does it with a powerful word, to which the act is not lacking. This word, which commands repentance, and which, properly speaking, creates the new spiritual world, since every one comes into existence there through repentance alone, is iust as powerful and effectual as the commanding word, which summoned into existence the external world around us." Christ's preaching of repentance is, therefore, quite different from John's ; the former was accompanied by the Spirit, who creates it : it is itself a Gospel ; the latter, like the Old Testament in general, demands without giving. Even repentance is a gift of God.

groundwork even of the Old Testament, but a πιστεύειν ἐν τῷ εὐαγ-
γελίῳ, *believing in the Gospel*. (On πίστις, see notes on Matth. viii.
1 ; ix. 2 ; xiii. 58 ; xvii. 20.)   The εὐαγγέλιον, *good news, Gospel*, implies here the *kingdom of heaven*, as actually present and represented
in the living person of the Messiah, foretold by the prophets and so
long desired.   Jesus announced that thus all that was ever foretold
and desired was fulfilled in him, and that the new principle of life
bestowed by him demands only to be received.   The phrase : ὁ
καιρὸς πεπλήρωται, *the time is fulfilled* (Mark i. 15), evidently points
like Gal. iv. 4, to an established order of development, and internal
regularity in it.   The time of the Saviour's incarnation, as well as
his public appearance among the people, were necessary epochs fixed
by divine appointment.

§ 2. Jesus Chooses Disciples.

(Matth. i. 18–22; Mark i. 16–20.)

The calling of the brothers, Peter and Andrew, and afterwards
of James and John (of whom a fuller account will be found in note
on Matth. x. 1, ff.), is left, in this place, without either an explanation of the motives for it, or a detail of the circumstances.   John assures us (chap. i.), that these disciples became known to Christ immediately after his baptism ; and this passage refers, therefore, only to
their being received to a more intimate companionship with the
Saviour.   Matthew, whom Mark here follows, makes but a passing
allusion to the calling of the apostles, in order to pass immediately
to what was with him specially important—the discourses of Jesus.
(On ποιήσω ὑμᾶς ἁλιεῖς ἀνθρώπων, see note on Luke v. 10, where
the thought stands in a more definite connexion.—Ἀμφίβληστρον,
from ἀμφιβάλλω, does not occur elsewhere in the New Testament.
It signifies a double net of considerable size, while δίκτυον, denotes
a smaller net, used for hunting or fishing.   On θάλασσα τῆς Γαλιλαίας,
see note on Luke v. 1.)

§ 3. Christ's Sermon on the Mount.

(Matth. iv. 23—vii. 29.)

The Evangelist first sketches, in its general features, the work of
the newly appeared Saviour—the same words occur Matth. ix. 35—
in order afterwards to portray fully his character as a teacher.   He
diffused blessings on all sides, and went about to do good ; like the
sun, quietly and majestically pursuing his course.   He did not *de-*

mand like the law, but *poured blessings* on men ; he shewed by actions that the kingdom of God was come ; teaching and healing, restoring soul and body, were his great business. (Synagogues [συναγωγή = הַכְּנֶסֶת בֵּית] are not mentioned till after the captivity. See *Joseph. Antiq.* xix. 6, 3, *de Bell. Jud.* vii. 3, 3. In the time of Jesus they were spread all over Palestine, as well as among the dispersed Jews [διασπορά] ; in Jerusalem there are said to have been 480 of them. Smaller places of meeting in villages, or for smaller congregations, were called προσευχαί ; [Acts xvi. 13.] They served, like the synagogues, for the daily meetings for prayer ; doctors of the law, even if they were not strictly priests or Levites, could speak in them.—Νόσος, *disease*, and μαλακία, *infirmity*, are related as sthenic and asthenic disorders, while βάσανος denotes especially such diseases as are accompanied with excruciating pains.)

Ver. 24.—The fame of Christ's healing power (the effects of which are not particularly narrated till viii. 1*) spread through the whole land to the borders of Syria, and all the sick people came to him in crowds. (Ἀκοή = שֵׁמַע ; Luke iv. 37 has ἦχος.—Syria denotes the regions of Palestine bordering on Syria, and the border districts of Syria itself, which the Saviour touched in his journeys. Mark has in the parallel passage, i. 28 ; εἰς τὴν περίχωρον τῆς Γαλιλαίας, *into the region around Galilee.* We shall afterwards speak particularly of the different forms of disease.—On the δαιμονιζόμενοι, see note on Matth. viii. 28.—Σεληνιάζεσθαι is not found elsewhere in the New Testament, except in Matth. xvii, 15.—Συνέχειν = צוּר, *to bind, to fetter;* the disease is conceived as some power that restrains the free action of the organization.)

Ver. 25.—People from all parts of the Jewish land, stimulated by the mighty manifestations of his healing power, joined our Lord, and the longer to enjoy his society accompanied him (some distance) in his journeys.

(Δεκάπολις, Mark v. 20 ; vii. 31. In *Plin.* H. N. V. 16, *regio decapolitana,* a district of ten towns, which cannot, however, be named with certainty, on the further side of the Jordan, in the tribe of Manasseh. See note on Matth. viii. 28.)

Chap. v. ver. 1.—After this preliminary description of the cures wrought by Jesus, and the impression they made upon the people, Matthew immediately introduces his readers to the long discourse of Jesus, which, from the locality on which it was delivered, is usually called *The Sermon on the Mount.* But before we consider minutely this first larger division in the Gospel by Matthew, we shall prefix some general observations.†

* Compare also the explanations on the cures by Jesus and his Apostles in general, given in the note on Matth. viii. 1.

† This important section, the antitype of the giving of the Law on Mount Sinai, has

The SERMON ON THE MOUNT, in the form in which it is given us by Matthew, cannot possibly have formed a whole when delivered by Jesus.* For the connexion of its sentiments is such as to make it appear extremely improbable that the Saviour should, in speaking, have thus passed from one thought to another. It is only the purposes of written composition, and the special objects of the Evangelist, that could warrant such a combination. But a comparison of Luke is decisive in favour of this opinion.† We do indeed find in that Gospel (vi. 17, ff.) a discourse of Jesus, evidently very nearly related to the Sermon on the Mount in Matthew, and at the beginning and end apparently identical with it, but much shorter than that in Matthew. If it should be said, Luke gives *a selection* from the full discourse in Matthew, it is true, that in Luke there are only two verses (vi. 39, 40) which Matthew has in a different connexion (xv. 14 ; x. 24 ;) and as these are both conceived in a proverbial form, they might have been repeatedly uttered. But those parts, which Matthew only has in the Sermon on the Mount, are found in Luke mostly in an entirely different connexion, and that so definitely conceived, that we are compelled to regard them as preserved by Luke in their original connexion.‡ Add to this that Luke's Gospel exhibits an accuracy of historical combination, which is wanting in that of Matthew. If, therefore, we wish to maintain the unity of the Sermon on the Mount, we are driven to the hypothesis, that those parts of it which stand in Luke in a different and distinctly specified connexion (*e. g.*, the Lord's Prayer, Luke xi. 1, ff., compared with Matth. vi. 7, ff.), were spoken *twice*. But as this hypothesis will scarcely find supporters now, there is no alternative left but to adopt the opinion, that the unity of the Sermon on the Mount proceeds not from the Saviour himself, but from Matthew. Matthew attached parts of kindred discourses to one actually delivered by Jesus on a specific occasion. The circumstances, under which Jesus spake, are exactly detailed by Luke. According to

been frequently the subject of special treatises; particularly by *Pott* (Helmstadt, 1789;) *Rau* (Erlangen, 1805); *Grosze* (Göttingen, 1819); best of all, by *Tholuck* (Hamburg, 1833. The third edition appeared in 1845). Among the Fathers, Augustine has left a separate work on the Sermon on the Mount.

* Against this view comp. my Kritik. der Ev. Gesch. § 69.—[E.

† *Tholuck* has decided that the discourse in Matthew is the original, laying particular stress on the circumstance, that our Lord might have repeated many things twice. Granting this, however, the place of the Lord's Prayer in Matthew cannot but be pronounced less appropriate than that which it occupies in Luke. That which Tholuck (Clark's Biblical Cabinet, No. xx., p. 134) says—viz., that our Lord may have repeated the prayer to one of his disciples, according to Luke xi. 1, is possible indeed, but not probable.

‡ On the connexion of the single passages in Luke, which are parallel with passages in the Sermon on the Mount, see the Commentary on Luke, from ix. 51, onward.

Luke vi. 12, ff., Jesus had gone upon a mountain* for the purpose of prayer. On the morning after the prayer, he completed the number of the twelve disciples (see note on Matth. x. 2), and, descending to the level ground (καταβὰς ἔστη ἐπὶ τόπου πεδινοῦ, Luke vi. 17), taught the people who pressed upon him. The circumstance that Jesus, according to Luke, descended from the mountain, while, according to Matthew (v. 1), he went up to it, may be thus reconciled —either Matthew connects the previous ascent with the teaching, without mentioning the subsequent descent ; or the pressure of the people, eager to be healed, caused Jesus, after his descent, to retire up the hill, so as to be able thence to address a greater multitude. This appears to have been one of the first public and solemn discourses of Jesus addressed to vast multitudes. (Hence ἀνοίξας τὸ στόμα αὐτοῦ [ver. 2], which Tholuck correctly regards as denoting the solemn and silently expected commencement of the discourse.) As such, Matthew made use of it to attach to it all those parts of other discourses, which might serve to give a general view of the peculiarities of the Gospel, in relation to the Old Testament. Neither the oral discourse of the Saviour, nor Matthew's written one, could have been intended as an initiatory discourse *for the disciples*. Both were intended as much for the multitudes as for the disciples (Matth. v. 1 ; Luke vi. 17, 20); but it was doubtless intended to unfold to the view of all the nature of the kingdom of God. In Matthew, particularly, the discourse appears like a second giving of the law, which is distinguished from that on Sinai, because, in the first place, it teaches the most comprehensive spiritual interpretation of the commandments, and, in the second, presupposes μετάνοια, *repentance* (as an effect of the law of Moses, Rom. iii. 20), and, with the law, proclaims, at the same time, the grace which accomplishes its fulfilment. This placing of the New Testament law-giving† at the commencement of the Messiah's work, is designed for the members of the Old Testament theocracy, who, on the authority of Deuteronomy xviii. 15, ff., looked upon the Messiah as a second Moses.

In both Evangelists, Matthew as well as Luke, a connexion may

---

* On the situation of the mountain, it is impossible to come to a definite opinion. Tabor has been thought of by some, probably incorrectly. Tradition speaks of a hill near Saphet (Bethulia) under the name " Hill of the Beatitudes," as that from which our Lord pronounced this discourse.

† The assertion, that Christ was not a lawgiver, contains a truth which I by no means wish to deny by my view of the Sermon on the Mount. The specific end of the Saviour's work was not to bring any new law, but to deliver from the yoke of all law. But in so far as he taught us to view the law of the Old Testament, in its spirituality, as it had not till then been viewed, he reiterated, as it were, the law of Sinai, and perfected it. Moreover, as Son of God, the Sinaitic law is his also. Moses was but the μεσίτης, *mediator*, at its proclamation ; and it was not simply law for others, but for *himself* also. See *Schleiermacher's* beautiful explanation of this point in the *Festpredigten*, B. ii., S. 66.

be traced in the discourses. It is, indeed, more close in Luke, as he gives the discourse in an abbreviated form.* For as, in the first part, four woes exactly correspond to the four beatitudes (ver. 21–26), so again, the exhortations to pure, disinterested love (ver. 27–31) correspond to the descriptions of natural interested love, which does not suffice for the Gospel (ver. 32–34), and is followed, by way of conclusion (ver. 35–38), and with a reference to ver. 27, by the re-newed exhortation to the disciples of the New Testament to live in pure, genuine love. The whole, therefore, forms a delineation of the nature of the Gospel, in contrast with the strict law ; only, that in Matthew the contrast is drawn more sharply and at greater length. At ver. 39, Luke breaks off the discourse with the remark, that the Saviour continued his address in parables. (On παραβολή, see note on Matth. xiii. 3.) The words : *But I say unto you*, pro-bably indicate an abbreviation of the discourse, as Luke has omitted here the more pointed contrast between the Old and New Testa-ments, furnished by Matthew (v. 13–43.) The parabolical parts are also incorporated by Matthew, only in quite a different order. We may, therefore, conclude, with probability, that they formed an integral part of Christ's address. The arrangement of the parables, as given by Luke, is entirely natural. For in all of them this thought is presented to the disciples, that, so far as they desired to gain influence in the world for the new higher principles of life (before described), they must first receive it entirely into themselves and live according to it. Accordingly, they must first be cured of their spiritual blindness—have the motes removed out of their eyes —themselves bring forth good fruit, and build their house on the eternal foundation of God's word (in opposition to pharisaical human doctrine), and then they may help others. The only passage which does not seem to fit in with this course of thought, is ver. 40, on which see the remarks on Matth. x. 24. On closer consideration of the context, however, this thought also appears to be inserted in its appropriate place. The previous expression, "Can the blind lead the blind?" (ver. 39), as well as the subsequent parable of the mote (ver. 41, ff.), evidently points to the Pharisees, as exercising a de-termining influence on the Old Testament life, in the form which it had taken among the Jews at that time. For these Pharisees were occupied with the hypocritical work of seeking to produce in others what was lacking in themselves ; and against this our Lord intends to warn in his parables. The thought that "the disciple is not above his master," fits thus very properly into the train of thought :

* I cannot coincide with *Schleiermacher's* view of the discourse in Luke (Ueber die Schriften des Lucas, S. 89, ff.), who thinks unfavourably of it. The discourse is, indeed, abridged (the "woes" only appear to be explanatory additions, see note on Matth. v. 3) but still, in the main, it is accurately and connectedly epitomized.

" Break loose from all attachment to your old teacher ; the law and
Pharisees cannot guide you farther than they themselves have
reached, and the perfect scholar is only equal to the teacher ; choose
me rather as your new teacher, with decision and earnestness ;
then you will not remain blind leaders of the blind, but will walk
in the light of the living."

As in Luke, so also in the discourse, as given by Matthew, a
connexion may be traced.[*] For though we must suppose that Matthew has connected kindred thoughts uttered by the Saviour on
other occasions with those uttered at this time, yet out of them the
Spirit of God in him formed a new connected whole. In the beginning and end, Matthew's version agrees perfectly with Luke's,
which circumstance sufficiently proves their identity. Only in the
fifth chapter Matthew carries out the contrast between the Old and
New Testaments much more carefully, since he accurately expounds
the nature of both in a series of propositions. In this form the discourse appears more expressly as the giving of a new and more spiritual law ; but, at the same time, with the law grace is brought
into view, since the increased strictness of the commandments follows only in the train of blessings pronounced on the poor and the
sorrowing. Hence true repentance, which necessarily includes faith,
is presupposed, in order to receive the law of love. By means of
this, really to receive the higher principle of life into oneself, and to
preserve it, and thus properly to conceive of the relation of Gospel
and Law, is the connecting thought between the beatitudes and
our Lord's new commandments. (See Matth. v. 13-20.) Of the
new commandments, six forms are specified by way of example (ver.
22-47) ; in which, however, the spirit of the New Testament was
sufficiently unfolded, so that the general proposition in ver. 48, " Be
ye therefore perfect, even as your Father which is in heaven is perfect," might conclude this comparison. Then, in the sixth chapter,
the Evangelist, with a reference to chap. v. 20, proceeds further in
the comparison of Old and New Testament piety, viewing the
Pharisees as the representatives of the Old Testament—impure representatives indeed, but at that time exercising a potent influence
on the popular religious character. The depth and truthfulness of
spiritual life form a contrast to the external show and pretence of
pharisaic piety. The usual forms in which such piety exhibited itself—viz., alms-giving (ver. 2), praying (ver. 5), and fasting (ver. 16),
form the points in which the Saviour unfolds the contrast of the
new with the old. The giving of the Lord's Prayer forms here the
central point, since its first half sets forth the spirituality of life
which characterizes the subjects of the new dispensation, and its

* See *R. Stier*, in his "*Andeutungen*," Th. i., S. 104, f. The connexion is more minutely considered at the individual passages.

second half a state of penitence, too, as essential to the subjects of the kingdom of God, but as precisely that in which the Pharisees were deficient. The close of the chapter (ver. 19–34) is occupied with a discussion on the relation of the children of the kingdom to the necessities of their life on earth, particularly food (ver. 25) and clothing (ver. 28) ; and this concludes the contrast between the New and the Old Testaments, which prevails through the whole discourse. The Pharisees, in their eagerness to gather earthly treasure (see Luke xvi. 13, 14), served two masters (Matth. vi. 24), and thus corrupted the singleness of their spiritual eye (ver. 22, 23); instead of this, childlike faith in the fatherly love of God, and consequently an entire separation from all care for earthly things, are insisted on as the marks of the children of God ; and this places our Lord's Prayer in a more striking light, as embodying all the wishes and cares of the children of the kingdom. The thoughts, which in the seventh chapter are connected more loosely, are gathered up by the concluding exhortation, and placed in connexion with what precedes. After the contrast between the piety of the Old and New Testaments, the whole is appropriately concluded by an exhortation to the hearers, in every thing to exemplify the character of the higher life in the kingdom of God. The first condition insisted upon is to have a constant regard to our own sins, with true repentance, and a warning is given against that regard to others which diverts us from right personal endeavor (ver. 1–5) ; while still, a reckless casting of what is good before men is forbidden (ver. 6). With this negative duty, the positive one (ver. 7–14) is conjoined of serious prayer and striving, as necessary conditions of the perfecting of a life in God. A demand for a searching examination of all to whose influence they yield themselves, forms the close (ver. 15–23), while the last verses (24–27) present, in figurative language, the consequences of a faithful application of the word of God, heard by us, as well as of a careless use of such a blessing.

In the form thus given by the Evangelist to the discourse of Jesus from the Mount, it constitutes a magnificent porch by which the reader of the Gospel is conducted into the temple of Jesus' ministry. It may be said, that his whole subsequent life, all his discourses and conversations, form a commentary on the Sermon on the Mount, which contains the quintessence of all that is peculiar to the kingdom of our Lord.

Ver. 3.—Matthew opens the Sermon on the Mount with a noble summary of the characteristic features of the children of the kingdom of God, and the children of the world. True, those of the latter are not expressly mentioned, but they lie, as opposites, at the foundation of the portraiture ; the blessings pronounced on the one class stand opposed to the unuttered woes of the other. Luke, who has chosen the second person as more appropriate to a discourse than the third, makes this contrast distinctly prominent (vi. 24–26) ; but as he abridges the number of the beatitudes, it is not improbable that he has expressly enunciated this contrast only for the sake of greater plainness. The discourse would have been too long and uniform, if there were a "woe" to answer to each of Matthew's sentences. But the idea that Matthew's fuller record is an amplification of our Lord's shorter discourse, is refuted by the peculiar nature of the portions found in Matthew alone ; a supplementary amplification of the fundamental thought would have been less profound and original. Nor does Luke's abridged form omit any thing essential ; the first and last blessings he has preserved, and omitted nothing but the rich amplification. In Matthew, the arrangement of the separate sentences is such, that ver. 3 corresponds with ver. 10, where the words, "theirs is the kingdom of heaven," with which the discourse commenced, recur. Consequently, there are only seven beatitudes to be reckoned, for ver. 10–12 do not add any new thought ; they merely form the transition to what follows, since they characterize the relation which the children of God bear to the world, the description of their subjective character being completed. In all the beatitudes, the one thought is expressed, that, according to God's law of eternal recompense, he who here thirsts for divine things shall obtain full satisfaction in the kingdom of God ; but, on the contrary, he who is satisfied with the perishable, shall hereafter experience, to his sorrow, the need of that which is eternal. There is, therefore, here no contrast between virtue and vice ; even the Old Testament punishes crime ; but the sensible need of salvation is placed in contrast with the deadness of the natural man, who, without a deeper craving for eternal things, can find his rest in what is transitory. Over such a woe is pronounced, because when the perishable things in which they rest, shew their true character, disquietude will thence arise. The position which Christ thus takes up, is therefore one above the law ; this last is seen to have fulfilled its office, a sense of the need of salvation is awakened (Rom. iii. 20) —the matter is now to satisfy it. The only circumstance that occasions surprise is, that several of the points particularized by the Saviour : Blessed are the meek, the merciful, the pure, the peacemakers, appear to rise above this condition of awakened need of salvation, inasmuch as they express an inward state of moral excellence. But this feature is easily accounted for, if we remember how frequently, in the language of Christ and his apostles, the germ of the new higher life is viewed as coincident with its consummation. True poverty of spirit, as the necessary condition of every development of the higher life, includes it ; and in this very unity Christ views it here. Thus understood, the first statements of the Sermon

on the Mount contain a description of the character of God's children, which is true for all grades of development, the highest as well
as the lowest. For as in the lowest, purity of heart exists in its
germ, the highest still maintains poverty of spirit.

The first word of instruction with which the Saviour breaks silence
is, μακάριοι οἱ πτωχοί, *blessed are the poor*, with the addition of τῷ
πνεύματι, *in spirit*, which must be supplied in Luke, where it is
wanting.[*] The term πτωχός, *poor*, corresponds to the Hebrew עָנִי,
which so frequently occurs in the Psalms with a kindred meaning.
It comes near to ταπεινός = שָׁפָל, *humble* (Prov. xxix 23, שְׁפַל רוּחַ), yet
is not synonymous with it, because he who is endowed with the fulness of the Divine Spirit may be called ταπεινός, *humble* (Jesus calls
himself so, Matth. xi. 29), but not πτωχός, *poor*. The word denotes
here (as the hungering and thirsting in ver. 6) the state of felt spiritual need, the sincere repentance of the soul.—Hence also, πνεῦμα,
spirit, must, by no means, be referred to genius, mental capacity
(νοῦς) (for the intellectual, as well as the feeble, must become poor);
but to the whole higher, yet natural, vital principle in man.[†] A
sense of the insufficiency of this principle for attaining true righteousness and holiness, and a desire for a higher principle that can
lead thither—*i. e.*, the Holy Spirit, are the conditions of the kingdom's entering the heart ; it is even the presence of the kingdom
itself ; for the strict sense of the present tense should be retained
here as in ver. 10, since true "poverty" includes the kingdom of
heaven in its germ, because it is the noblest fruit of preparatory
grace in the soul. The rich (πλούσιοι,) form the contrast (Luke vi.
24), who, filled with what is present and vain, have no longing for
the world to come. ("Ye have received your consolation," Matth.
vi. 2.) Hence the kingdom is not the object of their desire, and
consequently they receive it not. But the kingdom of God is here
presented to us throughout as purely inward and spiritual ; it seeks
for nothing dazzling—nothing pleasing to the eye of man ; on the

---

[*] *Strauss* takes the beatitudes in Luke in quite a different—an Ebionitic sense—viz.,
that of outward poverty and distress. Such an idea is very foreign to the New Testament. According to its representation, external poverty, apart from internal, is of no value.
But in so far as external wealth is wont *ordinarily* to be associated with a clinging of
spirit to worldly possessions, the term πτωχοί may include a reference to the poor of this
world.

[†] Πνεῦμα is not so used elsewhere in the New Testament. The sense would rather
be this, "those who are poor in the gifts of the Holy Spirit (righteousness etc.)"—*i. e.*,
who *feel* themselves to be poor. But he who so feels himself poor, already ceases to be
poor. Better then to take τῷ πνεύματι, not as designating that *in which* one is poor, but as
dative of *relation and manner*. The πτωχοί are then the *earthly* poor in the widest sense,
those whom the world regards as unfortunate, as being destitute of money and possessions,
of houses, portion, etc. Such poor, if they are *poor in spirit, i. e.*, if with a spiritual mind
they render their poverty in the goods of this world, subservient to the pursuit of the eternal riches of heaven, are pronounced happy in the kingdom of God. A similar reversal
of the judgments of the world is discernible in all the beatitudes.—[E.

contrary, it stoops to what is despised and unworthy. With the ideas of those Jews whose senses were dazzled with brilliant pictures of the Messiah's kingdom, this commencement of his discourse presented a violeñt contrast ; but to those in whom the law had fulfilled its office, and who were broken-hearted, such language was balm. But that in rendering prominent the spiritual, we are not to deny the outward features of the new kingdom, is manifest from ver. 5.

Ver. 4.—The second beatitude merely adds a subordinate trait to the fundamental disposition just pronounced blessed. Mourning (πενθεῖν), unites with the feeling of poverty a consciousness of suffering, which is to be regarded as arising from guilt. (Luke uses κλαίειν, *to weep*, with the same reference ; only he has placed those who hunger before those who weep.) Hence " being comforted" (παρακαλεῖσθαι) here involves the idea of forgiveness, which is conceived only in its beneficent *result*, expressed in Luke by γελᾶν, *laugh*, used in a noble, sacred sense. Wherefore the Messiah, the author of consolation, is called παράκλητος = םֵחֲנַם, *comforter* (John xiv. 16).

Ver. 5, 6.—It would seem that ver. 6 must be connected immediately with ver. 3 and 4, as in Luke, because this again employs the physical longing after bodily sustenance to express spiritual appetite. (On this comparison see Psalm xlii. 1 ; Isa. lxv. 13 ; Amos viii. 11.) This thought differs from ver. 3, 4, only in the object of desire ; this latter is righteousness, no longer regarded as outward, but the inward New Testament righteousness of God (δικαιοσύνη θεοῦ, see note on Rom. iii. 21). The insertion of ver. 5 is explicable on the ground, that the desire of the children of the kingdom is described in its progress. Πρᾳότης, *meekness*, is to be viewed as the first fruit of the πενθεῖν, *mourning*. A sense of our own guilt—complete repentance—renders us gentle in judging of others. He who has actually received forgiveness carries a forgiving principle within. Thereby not only is the kingdom of God in him, but he also will be in the kingdom of God.—In this place the Future retains its full import because the κληρονομεῖν τὴν γῆν, *inherit the earth or land*, is not synonymous with : ἡ βασιλεία ἐστὶν αὐτῶν, *theirs is the kingdom*, (ver. 3, 10). The phrase corresponds to the Hebrew formula יָרַשׁ אֶרֶץ (Deut. xix. 14 ; Psalm xxv. 13 ; xxxvii. 9), and may be traced to the Old Testament view of the land of Canaan, as the earthly object of the divine promises. The possession of this land is therefore the symbol of all and every divine blessing. That possession is viewed *ideally* in Heb. iv. In this place in connexion with the kingdom of heaven, which is viewed in the poor as *spiritually* present, the phrase denotes the full realization of the kingdom of God, even in its *external*, manifestation. Thus viewed, the land of Palestine stands as a symbol of the earth in general, conceived as restored and sanctified to God. The Saviour connects participation in this *realized* kingdom of God, with meekness, because that kingdom, being a fellowship of brotherly love and union, is opposed to the disunion prevailing in the world, and in its perfected harmony only that which is akin to itself can find a place.

Ver. 7.—In the following verses the consummation of the inward life, originating from a moral craving, appears in more definite traits. First, with respect to the term ἐλεήμονες, *merciful*, it differs from πραεῖς, *meek* (ver. 5), in this, that while the latter bear their brother's *guilt* with love, the former kindly assist him in his *distress*. So far as distress and guilt are connected, the two terms are quite identical. This declaration, therefore, follows the hunger and thirst after righteousness very appropriately ; the sense of our own distresses awakens sympathy for those of others. It is, however, remarkable, that even to those who show mercy, mercy is promised as something *future* ; while it would seem, on the contrary, that the experience of the divine mercy towards ourselves would first awaken compassion. The thought is rendered clear at once, if we consider that the character of the merciful must be taken relatively. Every one in whose heart compassionate love has been kindled by the experience of mercy, still stands in need of divine forbearance, because the life of love in him is, after all, only in its infancy, and is mixed with all the imperfections of the old man.*

Ver. 8.—The two following declarations must be taken with the same restriction : for absolute inward purity would necessarily be one with the present seeing of God, which yet is here connected with purity (καθαρότης), as something still future. Καθαρὸς τῇ καρδίᾳ = בַּר לֵבָב (Psalm xxiv. 4), forms the contrast to moral filth (ῥυπαρία). (James i. 21.) Purity is not specially different from righteousness (ver. 6.) In the two expressions the same condition of the soul is viewed in different relations. But what is stated in ver. 6, as desired, is here represented as (relatively) attained ; and thus the life of the children of the kingdom is again conceived in its inward progress. Although all relative purity of heart is necessarily accompanied by an inward seeing of God, since nothing but the presence of the Divine Spirit in the heart can produce purity, yet that is not to be compared with the perfected vision of the divine glory, which is, therefore, here spoken of as future. (Seeing God, Ὀπτεσθαι Θεόν = רָאָה פְּנֵי אֱלֹהִים [Psalm xlii. 3], involves, of course, the idea of the highest blessedness ; but is, by no means, to be taken as a mere figure. The expression involves rather the capacity, though marred by sin, of the human soul really to recognise its eternal source—the highest good. This capacity presupposes close relationship to the divine, for it is only *like* that can receive its *like*. Wherever, therefore, a divine nature is born in the soul, from its craving for the divine, the

---

* See remarks on the interesting parallel passage in James ii. 13.

capacity of knowing God's eternal nature is revealed ; which knowledge, conceived as complete, is subsequent to our life on earth.*
On this point see notes on Matth. xi. 27 ; John xvii. 3.)

Ver. 9.—In the last stage of moral perfection, the idea of εἰρήνη,
peace, is put forward. It is represented as realized by the members
of the kingdom. Εἰρηνοποιός is very distinct from εἰρηνεύων. The
latter signifies one who *maintains* peace already existing ; the
former, one who *makes* it when wanting. Hence, in the εἰρηνοποιός,
peacemaker, a (relative) καθαρότης, *purity*, is presupposed, because
the element of strife, sin, must be banished from his heart, and that
of peace must be active there, if his labours are to have any effect.
That the being a child of God is viewed as connected with the peacemaker, is explained by the fact, that in the term Son of God, is implied the greatest blessing which can be promised to man. For in
the υἱός, *Son*, the idea of spiritual relationship appears ; agreeably
with which the true Son is the image of the Father. The God of
peace (2 Cor. xiii. 11) begets children of peace, whose actions are
peace. This (perfected) character of sonship to God is represented
as future, or, at most, as present in its germ. (Καλεῖσθαι = εἶναι,
with the meaning of " being essentially," see note on Luke i. 35.)
The same thought is expressed Matth. v. 45. This implies, that all
the gradations of moral perfection are to be viewed in relation to their
earthly imperfection. The state of perfection hereafter is identical
with sonship to God. Accordingly, men in their sinful nature do
not appear as children of God. They need first a higher principle of
life, that must be imparted by him who is pre-eminently the Son of
God—a principle which is received in the aspiration for the divine
(in penitent faith), and is gradually unfolded till it attains that
point.

Ver. 10.—After completing the description of the inward state
of the true children of God, our Lord passes on to portray their relation to the world of unrighteousness (ἀδικία.) In so doing, he
connects ver. 3 by repeating in this verse the words : " Theirs is the
kingdom of heaven." The righteousness is here conceived as complete in the children of the kingdom, in that they are viewed purely
in contrast with the world.

Ver. 11, 12.—These two verses are merely an expansion of the
thought in ver. 10. Under the reign of unrighteousness, righteousness must necessarily suffer. The different forms of persecution by
word and by deed are then more particularly specified.† (Ὀνειδίζειν,

* When we read in John i. 18, " No man hath seen God at any time," where the idea
is implied, " No man *can* see God—He is invisible to the creature" (1 Tim. vi. 16). This
refers to the foundation of the divine essence—the Father God can be seen only in the
Son. See the fuller discussion in note on John i. 18.

† According to John xvi. 4, the Saviour did not first speak to his disciples of the
persecutions that awaited them. It is not improbable, therefore, that the mention of

is persecution by word, διώκειν by act. Luke vi. 22 has added
ἀφορίζειν, to *separate*, to exclude from ecclesiastical and political
communion. At the head of them all is put slander [πονηρὸν ῥῆμα
εἰπεῖν ψευδόμενος], such as the charges of murder and licentious
habits brought against the first Christians. Luke has given the
thought somewhat modified : τὸ ὄνομα ὡς πονηρὸν ἐκβάλλειν = ἀφορίζειν,
only a stronger expression.) But our Lord adds, as the peculiar
feature of the persecution, which is endured because of the truth,
that it is ἕνεκεν ἐμοῦ, *for my sake*. By this weighty expression, the
doctrine of Christian patience (closely allied to self-denial, which
also is to be exercised only *for the Lord's sake*), first attains its true
significancy. (See note on Matth. x. 39.) Since Jesus is himself
the truth and the righteousness, and that, too, manifested in a living
person, pure suffering for what is good requires faith in him to be
exercised by the members of the kingdom of God. Where selfishness prevails, there cannot be such suffering as bestows happiness.
But where such suffering is incurred for the faith's sake, and is
borne in faith, it perfects the inward life, and awakens the desire for eternity. This latter point is very prominent in ver. 12,
since we are there called upon even to rejoice in opposition to sufferings. (Ἀγαλλιάω, *exult* = בּיל. It is a stronger term than χαί-
ρειν, *rejoice*. Luke vi. 23 uses σκιρτᾶν, *leap*.) This joy, with respect
to ourselves, does not exclude sorrow in reference to the persecu-
tors. In the former respect, the suffering is only a testimony to
the believer that he is God's. In the "woe" (vi. 26) Luke presents
the other aspect. The exciting of human applause presupposes a
worldly spirit. Where that is given, it is to be feared that the ap-
plauded one belongs to the community of the wicked, and of the
false teachers (ψευδοπροφῆται), just as the persecuted one is thereby
numbered with the company of persecuted prophets. (The reference to the prophets gives greater prominence to that aspect of the
discourse, which shews it to have been addressed to the actual disciples, ver. 1.) The mention of the μισθός, *reward*, ver. 12, appears
remarkable, as it seems to reconduct to a legal point of view. In
the kingdom of God, the motive for actions is not the reward in
itself. The term was, perhaps, chosen with immediate reference to
the position of the disciples, as Christ's earlier discourses do often
still bear a legal colouring ; but there is, too, a reward for pure love
—a reward which is pure in proportion as the love itself is ; for the
reward of love consists in being appreciated, and in moving in its
own atmosphere.

Ver. 13.—It has been already observed, in the general survey of
the connexion in the Sermon on the Mount, according to Matthew,

them in this place is among the parts taken from later discourses. Yet they are found
mentioned as early as Luke vi. 22.

that the giving of a new (stricter) law is connected with the beatitudes, in the course of the chapter, by the supposition of a power
of the Holy Spirit being received in true repentance, which teaches
us to observe such new commands. But the relation which the
mention of the "salt of the earth" bears to what immediately precedes, and to the whole, is obscure. The most natural connexion is
.undoubtedly the following : The idea of persecution presupposes a
power of higher life in the persecuted disciples, by which sin feels
itself aroused ; but this same power, which awakens enmity among
the opponents of what is good, is the condition under which it
works effectually in susceptible minds. It must, therefore, be preserved and cherished notwithstanding persecutions. *First of all*
Jesus calls the disciples ἅλας τῆς γῆς, *salt of the earth.* (Γῆ, *earth,* is
here = κόσμος, *world,* ver. 14, and denotes mankind generally with the
additional notion of being corruptible, and requiring to be preserved
by salt.) In the general system of natural symbols, which suggested
itself in all profound research, salt always held an important place ;
Pythagoras regarded it as the emblem of the δίκαιον, *just.* Its use
at sacrifices was also full of meaning. (Comp. Lev. ii. 13. This
subject is more fully discussed in note on Mark ix. 50.) The point
of comparison between the disciples and the salt lies in the power
possessed by the latter of preventing corruption and imparting life.*
The intimation that, without this power, the salt is wholly useless,
was to excite the disciples to a careful preservation of the sacred
power entrusted to them. (Instead of μωρανθῇ, some Codd. read
μαρανθῇ, from μαραίνεσθαι, *to waste away,* which is less preferable.
Μωρός, used of salt, correponds to בֵּשֶׁל, [Job vi. 6], *insipidus, fatuus.*†
Mark [ix. 50] uses ἄναλος, *saltless, insipid*—instead of it. Luke
[xiv. 34] reminds us of the practice of applying salt as manure
[κοπρία] ; but savourless salt is useless even for that purpose—nothing remains for it but the ἔξω βάλλειν, *the casting forth*—a figure of
the spiritual destruction of backsliders.—On the parallel passages,
Mark ix. 50 ; Luke xiv. 34, 35 ; and for what follows, Mark iv. 21 ;
Luke viii. 16, see those passages in their connexion.)

Ver. 14, 15.—The *second* comparison conveys the same general
meaning. According to it the world appears as darkness (John i. 5),
which the children of the kingdom are to illuminate. The disciples
form the rays of him who is himself the light. (John i. 4 ; Phil. ii.
15.) In what follows, the circumstance is not specified, that the
illuminating power may be lost, as was done with the salt ; there
is only the exhortation to let the light shine. But, indirectly, this

* *De Wette* compares 2 Kings ii. 20, according to which passage, Elisha heals water
with salt.
† The figure turns on the fact that salt produced by evaporation of sea-water, in hot
countries, by long exposure to air and heat, loses its chloride of magnesia, and is hence not
strong enough to preserve meat.—[E.

exhortation involves the same warning which was given above ; for to him who covers his light, it is extinguished. To give vividness to his exhortation the Saviour makes use of two more comparisons. First, that of an elevated city, which strikes the eyes of all. Thus divine things have a loftiness in themselves, and, where they reveal themselves, they are seen, unless concealed for fear of persecution. Then comes the second comparison of a λύχνος, lamp, the intention of which is to give light to those who are in the house ; this intention ought not be frustrated. (In the parallel passages the same figure is employed, only that in Luke viii. 16, instead of μόδιος, first σκεῦος, and then κλίνη, are used. But in Luke xi. 33, we have κρυπτή.)

Ver. 16.—An application of these comparisons is made ; from which it is evident, that light has reference not merely to doctrine and knowledge, but must be taken generally as the inward principle of life—as the source of good works. (These are opposed not merely to evil works, but also to dead works, such as do not grow from the life of faith.) As a mark of the genuineness of the good works, it is noticed, that they must call forth praise, not for man, but for God ; it must be visible in them, that man is only the organ for the flowing forth of divine power from him to others.

Ver. 17.—The more undeniable it must have been to every one, that in Christ appeared something entirely new ; and the more expressly our Lord himself acknowledged this, and, in the sequel, contrasts himself as a new Lawgiver with the old lawgiver—the more important was it to prevent the mistake of imagining, that the manifestation of what was new in him was detached from its historical foundation. Hence Christ here declares the intimate connexion between the Old and New Testament, in a manner which must have excluded all mistake on the point, if preconceived opinions on the subject had not been allowed to exercise an influence on the exposition. First of all, the Old Testament is described as inviolable in itself; then the New Testament is regarded as the completion of the Old ; and lastly, in this completion the law is declared to be of divine and eternal authority.

The words : μὴ νομίσητε, think not, intimate a thought very likely to arise on the part of the disciples, that by the New, the Old Testament was abrogated. The Saviour distinctly excludes such an effect from the purpose of his mission (οὐκ ἦλθον.) (Νόμος καὶ προφῆται, law and prophets, = תּוֹרָה וּנְבִיאִים, is a general denomination for the entire writings of the Old Testament, and more fully still, Luke xxiv. 44. But the writings themselves are not to be regarded in their dead external character, but in the vital principle, from which they proceed, and which discloses itself in them.) The opposition of καταλῦσαι, destroy, and πληρῶσαι, fulfil, is here of greatest importance. Used of law, καταλύω means " to do away with," "to repeal." (John x. 35.) But πληρῶσαι does not seem to be in contrast with that meaning ; κυροῦν—to establish, to confirm, should rather have been used. It is better therefore to regard the figure as taken from a building whose foundations can be loosened, but which can still be completed on them. Accordingly, the Old Testament is the foundation on which the structure of the New Testament is to be placed, in order to complete it. In this comparison the Old Testament contains the outline (μόρφωσις, Rom. ii. 20*), and the New its filling up ; the two are in organic connexion, like bud and blossom. The fulfilment is therefore to be regarded as a comprehensive one ; Christ fulfils not only the prophecies and types of the Old Testament, but the moral law also he fulfils perfectly in himself and his people.

Ver. 18.—With strong emphasis the Saviour represents the impossibility of destroying (καταλύειν) the law from its very nature. ('Αμήν = אָמֵן, verily, is always used in our Lord's words, to direct attention to a thought, and to give it emphasis.) The Old Testament, as God's word, is eternal and unchangeable (1 Peter i. 25) ; hence it stands in contrast to created things. Οὐρανὸς καὶ γῆ, heaven and earth (Gen. i. 1) are put for the universe, creation in general. While this latter vanishes altogether, the former remains, even in its apparently unessential parts. ('Ιῶτα, the smallest letter of the Hebrew alphabet. Κεραία, "apex," points, by which particular letters, e. g., ד and ר, are distinguished).† Moreover, as the first ἕως ἄν, until, fixes a limit to the universe, so the second does to the law itself. (In the phrase ἕως ἂν πάντα γένηται, scil. τὰ ἐν τῷ νόμῳ γεγραμμένα, the γίνεσθαι is = πληροῦσθαι. See Luke xxi. 32.) This thought involves no difficulty relatively to the typical character of the Old Testament. In the universality in which it is here laid down, it must, however, be applied to the law in all points. And yet it would seem that its moral features must be conceived as eternal, and, of course, can have no limit assigned to them. True ; but in the world of perfection the law will be done away, in so far as it will have become the inmost life of all beings ; there is no longer need of law, for every one himself ordains what is right. As, then, there is no law for God, so there is none for the perfected world ; for, like God, it also is law unto itself.

Ver. 19.—The following words point, perhaps, to some particular occurrences ; as some of the disciples, under a false conception of

---

* The Apostle Paul explains himself in the same way, in regard to the relation of the Old Testament to the New, as the Epistle to the Galatians, in particular shews. In Gal. ii. 18, the contrast of καταλύειν and οἰκοδομεῖν is also found. It is only in appearance that such passages as Ephes. ii. 15, contain a different view of the law.

† In like manner the Rabbins say : Si quis Daleth in Deut. vi. 4, mutaret, concuteret totum mundum. It would change אֶחָד into אַחֵר—the true God into an idol. See Wetstein on the passage.

their freedom, may have assailed the edifice of the old theocracy. The passage has, at any rate, no reference to the Jewish doctors' division of the law into great and small commandments, since such a depreciation of the moral part (as the small commandments), and over-estimation of the ceremonial part (as the great commandments), being false pharisaical doctrine, necessarily excluded from the kingdom of heaven. But the expressions : " to be least·in the kingdom of heaven," and "not to enter into the kingdom," cannot possibly be synonymous. Our Lord speaks rather in general of a state of mind, controlled mainly by Christian principle, but in which man proceeds without proper reverence for God's word, and teaches so to proceed, and does away with many apparently non-essential ordinances of the law. With a *false liberty* like this, a man may indeed be of the kingdom of God in his inmost soul, but he does not belong to it with all his powers ; and for that reason, too, he is unfit to teach. The terms μέγας, *great*, and ἐλάχιστος, *least*, denote, therefore, different grades of development in the principle of the Christian life. The Scriptures often speak of different gradations like these, especially under the names of " children," " young men," and " men." (1 John ii. 13, 14 ; 1 Peter ii. 2 ; Ephes. iv. 13 ; Col. ii. 19.) The whole passage is, therefore, a warning to the disciples not to damage the cause of the kingdom of God and their own progress in it, by premature interference.*

Ver. 20.—In what follows, Jesus contrasts with the arbitrary subversion of the Old Testament the equally arbitrary retention of it in its external form ;. this was seen in the Pharisees, and totally excluded them from the kingdom. In itself, indeed, what belongs to the Old Testament can never be *un*christian ; it is only *pre*christian, and, as type, includes what is Christian. It may, however, be represented as unchristian and antichristian, if it is retained in its germ-like form, and its free development is impeded. Such was the position of the Pharisees ; they restricted the commandments of the Old Testament to their literal meaning, without penetrating to their spiritual contents. They had, therefore, a righteousness, but it was merely outward ; they *seemed* to keep the law, but this appearance was only a means for them the more certainly to break it in its most sacred forms. And as they had, too, the law written in their hearts (Rom. ii. 15), they desecrated God's sanctuary within them,

* The Pharisaic mode of feeling (v. 20) is not *contrasted* (as Olshausen would have it) with the λύειν, *breaking* of the law ; but v. 20 rather attaches itself by the *for* (γάρ) to v. 19 as an argument. Hence the λύειν v. 19, must represent the Pharisaical mode of dealing with the law, and thus (unlike κατα λύειν, v. 17) must denote the mechanical breaking up of a law into a multitude of casuistical and merely formal precepts in opposition to its spiritual apprehension and fulfilment. This subtle casuistry is in the kingdom of God *valueless* (shall be called least, etc., v. 19), and whoever reposes in it his hope of salvation excludes himself from the kingdom of God.—[E.

and closed the kingdom of heaven against themselves by *their* right-eousness, which with them never led to poverty of spirit. How the righteousness of the subjects of the kingdom was to stand related to that of the Pharisees, forms the main thought in the grand com-parative view of Old and New Testament laws, to which the dis-course now passes ; only that Christ gives nothing new ;* he merely seizes the Old Testament in its deepest living root. The Pharisees, on the contrary, confound the form with the essence, and insist on the former instead of the latter.

Ver. 21.—First of all, the precept of the Mosaic law : οὐ φονεύσεις, *thou shalt not kill*, i. e., *murder*, is discussed. The words ἐρρέθη τοῖς ἀρχαίοις, *it was said*, etc., are evidently not meant of the contem-poraries of Moses merely, as if the meaning were, " the law was given to *those of old*."† For the same law was given to the con-temporaries of Jesus, and to all times. This interpretation would also involve the inconsistency, that Jesus set himself and his doc-trine (ἐγὼ δὲ λέγω ὑμῖν, ver. 22) in opposition to the Mosaic, which he had just (ver. 18) described as eternal, divine truth. For the same reasons, it is not admissible to supply χρόνοις with ἀρχαίοις, *in ancient times;* the Saviour is not arguing against something anti-quated, but against the active errors of the present time. The words ἐρρέθη τοῖς ἀρχαίοις, must, therefore, be explained by the con-struction of the passive with the dative. On this construction, see *Winer*, Gr. of the New Testament, p. 172 (Amer. Tr.) ; and as to the Hebrew, *Gesenius' Lehrgebäude*, p. 821—so that the meaning is, " the ancients have said." ('Αρχαῖοι = קַדְמוֹנִים or רִאשׁוֹנִים, like πρεσβύτεροι, denotes the Rabbinical and pharisaical representatives of the Old Testament theocracy.) Hence arises naturally the following con-nexion. To the external conception of the Mosaic commandments on the part of the Pharisees, our Lord opposes the inward one, and observes, that it is only this which introduces to the true, full mean-ing of the law. The whole argument against the Pharisees is, therefore, a defence of Moses, whose law assumed a *form*, indeed, corresponding to the immediate demands of the people, in their lower state of culture, but, at the same time, did not prevent, but promote the highest and purest development in spiritual life. But

---

* See 1 John ii. 7, 8, where what is *new* in the Gospel is called the *old* which was from the beginning.

† *Tholuck* has again defended this view, on the ground that in connexion with ἐρρέθη the dative must denote the person, and that ἀρχαῖοι is not elsewhere used for the authors of the pharisaical tradition. But the manner in which Tholuck endeavours to gather a reference to tradition out of ἐρρέθη and ἠκούσατε, is so harsh, that I prefer the other ex-position, according to which the dative is taken as an ablative, because it suggests much more readily a reference to tradition, which is absolutely required by the connexion. Though ἀρχαῖοι does not elsewhere occur, as used of the authors of tradition, yet it may be so applied without hesitation; and Tholuck himself acknowledges that the dative is wont to be used as an ablative with εἴρηται.

the pharisaical Rabbins checked this development, by retaining on
principle the undeveloped form. The command : οὐ φονεύσεις, *thou
shalt not murder* (Exod. xx. 13), they interpreted simply of ordinary
death by violence, and referred crimes of that sort to the inferior
courts. All shortening of a neighbour's life by vexation, or in whatever way it might take place, they set aside, as not included under
this commandment. The Mosaic command is, therefore, here connected with the doctrinal interpretation of the Pharisees. From
ver. 22, it is plain that κρίσις, *judgment*, = מִשְׁפָּט, is to be distinguished
from the sanhedrim. While this latter denotes the last court of
appeal in judicial affairs in Jerusalem itself (see observation on
Matth. xxvi. 57), κρίσις refers to the inferior courts in the provincial
towns, which were constituted in conformity with Deut. xvi. 18, and
consisted of seven persons.

Ver. 22.—In opposition to this pharisaical explanation, by which
murder was understood but of the outward act, and reckoned among
minor crimes, the Saviour unfolds the comprehensive meaning of the
commandment, "Thou shalt not kill;" which forbids not only
the outward act, but also the inward disposition of hatred,
Our Lord thus seizes the act in its spiritual origin, and attacks
sin in its source, which the Pharisees hypocritically spared. Hatred
is moral murder. (1 John iii. 15.) The Saviour evidently intends, therefore, to forbid hatred in general, and the reading, εἰκῇ
= לַשָּׁוְא, *without a cause*, should be regarded as a mere correction
(*Fritzsche* on the passage justly removes it from the text), which
arose from the idea that there may even be good reason for anger.
But this anger ought to be directed against the *sin* only, not against
our *brother;* against the person (in whom God's creature is ever to
be honoured) there is no pure anger.—The one main thought, that the
fellow-subject of the kingdom admits no hatred into his heart, is expressed in a three-fold gradation. Ὀργίζεσθαι, *to be angry*, denotes,
in general, the rising of wrath in the soul, the admission of the mur-
derous spirit into the mind. In εἰπεῖν ῥακά, *saying raca*, the inward
emotion is conceived in its external manifestation against the
brother ; but Jesus does not go beyond the mental action—the word
—purposely in order to make the contrast more striking with the
pharisaical spirit, which laid stress upon the outward act only. But
the words of the angry man may attack human dignity itself : this
latter is expressed by εἰπεῖν μωρέ. (According to Tholuck's investigations, ῥακά is to be derived from רָקַק *to be thin;* whence רִיק, רֵיקָה
was formed and used among the inhabitants of Palestine as a gentle
reproach = "stupid." Μωρός = נָבָל, is a stronger term of reproach,
involving the added idea of *abandoned, impious*.) The parallel
gradation in the punishment, κρίσις, συνέδριον, γέεννα πυρός, *judgment,
sanhedrim, gehenna*, is further remarkable. These earthly punish-

ments are not to be taken as designating *divine* punishment in its different degrees, as if Christ would oppose to the law of the letter a new law of the letter. He means only to set forth the general truth that sin in its slightest manifestation is worthy of death.* Still less does he intend to establish a *human* political law. The ὀργίζεσθαι, *being angry*, cannot in itself be *a matter on which a human tribunal would pass judgment ; for the reason, that the fact can never be proved.* (Γέεννα = הִנֹּם גֵּיא, means, primarily, the Valley of Hinnom. [2 Kings xxiii. 10.] The prophets use תֹּפֶת, *Tophet*, for it, which is from תּוּף, a *place spit upon*, Jer. vii. 31 ; xix. 6.) The place for bodily filth became the symbol of the spiritual slough, where all that is estranged from God is gathered together. On the relation of Gehenna to Hades, see note on Luke xvi. 23.

Ver. 23, 24.—From the negative view, the not admitting hatred and the spirit of murder into the soul, our Lord passes on to the positive one, and teaches that the believer should quench the flame of wrath in his brother's heart also, as becomes a peacemaker (ver. 9). In this the purity of love is manifested in its greatest splendour. This precept does not apply merely to those cases where the anger of our brother is excited by injury on our part. The expression ἔχειν τι κατά σου, *hath aught against thee*, is intentionally made general. Even when one hates without cause, we are to quench the flame in his heart—that is, not merely be placable, but also not allow our brother to hate. The thought of bringing the expression of this pure love into connexion with the act of offering sacrifice, is specially profound. In that act man approaches the eternal love to claim its compassion for himself. That is the most befitting moment for exercising it on others. But to make these words of the Saviour imply a sanction of sacrifices in the New Testament, is an error. Christ evidently speaks here merely of the existing Jewish worship, which he left unassailed. (On the supposed difference between καταλλάσσω and διαλλάσσω, see *Tholuck*.)

Ver. 25, 26.—The following verses were doubtless spoken originally in a totally different connexion, as is seen from Luke xii. 58, 59, where the question is more fully discussed. But Matthew has interwoven the thought in a peculiar manner into our Saviour's discourse. The relation of a debtor, who does well to free himself from his creditor in season, not to be cast into prison by him, is employed by the Evangelist for a further illustration of the foregoing principle. He conceives of our relation to an angry brother, whom we have

---

* That this command of our Lord's, as well as all that follow, ought not to be understood literally, is plain from the passages, Matth. xxiii. 17, 19 ; Luke xxiv. 25, in which Jesus himself calls men "fools" (μωροί), and in the last passage, even the disciples. This whole interpretation of the Old Testament necessarily requires a separating of the internal and external church ; in the latter, the words of Jesus do not apply literally, they are calculated only for the former.

injured as a relation of debt. The ἀντίδικος, *adversary*, is therefore, any one who can prefer legal claims.* Such an one the Saviour advises us to satisfy by humble, childlike submission, that the hatred may not continue, and prosecute us to our ruin. To strengthen the exhortation, ταχύ, *quickly*, is subjoined, with an admonition of the transitoriness of life (ὁδός = דֶּרֶךְ). That which is not reduced to harmony here below, continues its destructive course hereafter.— Ἴσθι εὐνοῶν, *be gentle, ready to forgive*—i. e., " offer thou the hand." The idea of the continued effect of hatred, is particularly difficult, expressed, as it is, under the figure of being accused and cast into prison. (The κριτής, *judge*, is God, and the ὑπηρέται, *officers*, his angels. But the φυλακή, *prison*, is an *image* of perdition. As the kingdom of love forms a united whole, and by its power extends beyond life ; so also the accusing principle (Rev. xii. 10) constitutes a mighty power, which demands its right, till a reconciliation has been made. He who will not forgive sin below shall receive no forgiveness. (See Matth. xviii. 34.)

Ver. 27, 28.—The command οὐ μοιχεύσεις, *thou shalt not commit adultery*, is adduced as the *second* out of the Old Testament, which Jesus teaches us to regard more profoundly than the pharisaical teachers had been accustomed to do. That which they applied merely to the external act, the Saviour extends to the spiritual act, to the desire (ἐπιθυμία), and the tolerating of it in the soul. The desire in itself is an element in the sinfulness of human nature in general. It is not to be looked upon as actual sin when resisted with sincere earnestness ; (?) but the tolerating of it, and, consequently, the entering into it inwardly with the will (precisely what βλέπειν πρὸς τὸ ἐπιθυμῆσαι, *looking in order to lust*, denotes), is the act itself, even though external circumstances, independent of the man's will, hinder its execution.

Ver. 29, 30.—With these thoughts Matthew connects words which were uttered originally on another occasion, as the context of Matth. xviii. 6, ff. ; Mark ix. 43, ff., shews ; but here also the Evangelist has, with profound truth, collected different elements into a whole.† With special propriety is the assurance that the command, " Thou shalt not commit adultery," teaches inward as well as outward purity, followed by the exhortation to preserve that purity by the utmost moral strictness, and by the greatest resoluteness in self-denial, which shuns not even the keenest pain and privation. Eyes and hand are regarded here as organs of sense, which become the inlets of temptation, and, in turn, the means by which sin displays it-

---

* On the principle " Owe no man any thing, but to love one another," each is debtor to another in love.

† Considering the sententious form of the passage, it may, however, be allowable to agree with *Tholuck* in regarding the words as original in both places.

self outwardly. To sacrifice these organs, in themselves useful and valuable, for the sake of sanctification—that is, to abstain from the use of them, or to limit it, is the immediate lesson conveyed in this thought. (For the critical minutiæ, see note on Matth. xviii. 6, ff.)

Ver. 31, 32.—As the *third* example, our Lord specifies divorce. According to Deut. xxiv. 1, it was allowable for the husband to put away his wife, but he must give her a letter of divorcement, ἀποστάσιον = ספר כריתות. (On all that respects this subject, and particularly the Rabbinical explanations of the Mosaic ordinances, see more fully in note on Matth. xix. 3, ff.) According to the express assertion of Jesus (Matth. xix. 8), this regulation was made only on account of the Jews'·hardness of heart, σχληροκαρδία. The right conception of marriage, as an indissoluble union of soul, was embraced even in the Old Testament. But the Pharisees did not regard this indulgence as such, and considered it as belonging to the essence of marriage, that a husband can dismiss his wife when he pleases, in order to marry another. To this vulgar notion the Saviour opposes the *ideal* conception of marriage, and paints the evil consequences of divorce. *First*, the divorced woman (ἀπολελυμένη), who must still be conceived as bound by the marriage-tie, is exposed to the temptation of entering on another connexion. He therefore occasions her to sin, ποιεῖ αὐτὴν μοιχᾶσθαι. *Next*, he brings another man into the danger of forming an adulterous connexion with the divorced. Nothing is said of his own sin if he marries another, because that is self-evident; and the case of infidelity is excepted, because then the divorce, as a fact, has preceded the outward separation. (See note on Matth. xix. 9.) (Παρεκτὸς λόγου πορνείας, where πορνεία denotes "adultery" as well as "fornication;" and λόγος, like דבר, denotes here αἰτία, πρᾶγμα, *cause*.) The thought is in itself so easy of comprehension, that it admits of no controversy. The Saviour evidently forbids *all* divorces except in the case of infidelity, where that is itself the separation, and regards fresh connexions, formed by the divorced, as adultery. But the question as to our Lord's intention in the *application* of this principle in his church, is more difficult. Just as in the case of oaths* (ver. 33, ff.), that intention can only be gathered from a general view of the position of the church. The external church, as a

* Consult the decision of the theological faculty at Bonn on the re-marriage of divorced parties, reprinted in the *Allgemeine Kirchenzeitung*, 1836, Nos. 148, 149, and afterwards published separately. In the main, I agree with this decision. The church of the present day, grown up with the State, and filled with unbelieving members, cannot possibly be put on a par with the apostolical church. The fathers of the church felt it necessary early to permit modifications in practice. (See history of the exposition of the passage in *Tholuck's* Commentary.) Obstinate desertion and attempts to murder, early constituted valid grounds for divorce.

visible institution, cannot possibly be regarded as the expressed *ideal* of the kingdom of God. It is rather the covering merely, in which the communion of all the faithful is enveloped, as the kernel in the shell. Hence the regulations of the external church cannot answer to the *ideal* requirements of the kingdom ; but as it occupies the Old Testament level in the majority of its members, it must conform its regulations to the Old Testament. As, then, in the Old Testament, God permitted* not only divorces, but also the re-marriage of the separated parties (see *Michaelis'* commentaries on the laws of Moses, translated by Smith, bk. ii., and Deut. xxiv. 2), so the church *may* admit modifications of our Lord's law, as expressed in this passage, for the mass of its members. Nay, it *must* do so, because the application of 'the New Testament principles to unconverted and unregenerate persons cannot but have injurious consequences. The Romish Church is, therefore, wrong in putting the words of Jesus authoritatively into practice in the visible church, which has fallen back under the dominion of the law.† Still strictness should pervade the legislation of the church, and the effort be everywhere made to elevate the members more and more to a comprehension of the New Testament spirit.‡ The case is quite different with those members of the church who also belong to the Saviour's spiritual communion ; because these latter are in a position both to recognize his requirements, and, by his power, to satisfy them. This command is in full force for them and among them, just like the command not to hate, to give to every one that asketh, etc. But since, as such, they are under the Gospel, and not under the law, there is no constraint upon them. To their Lord they stand and fall. (On the whole question, consult also the observations on Matth. xix. 3, ff., and 1 Cor. vii. 15, 16.§)

* God nowhere permitted murder in the Old Testament, nowhere allowed fornication ; but he did expressly allow divorce. Those, therefore, who insist on Christ's command being literally applied in the church, as it now exists, should ponder well what they do. The subsequent commands respecting the cloak, and the smiting on the cheek, shew plainly enough that a literal fulfilment cannot be intended in the external church. The passage Matth. xix. 9, ff., is also evidently not a precept given to be exalted to a universal external law. The Saviour there speaks for those only who are able to receive it.

† Indeed, the Romish Church even increases the severity of the command on its own authority, since it does not permit divorce *quoad vinculum* even in case of adultery.

‡ The Saviour is not here legislating. He is simply explaining that divorce for other reasons than adultery, and re-marriage in such cases, is positively sinful. Thus much, at least, follows, that the Christian Church cannot bless such a positively sinful act.—[E.

§ (The above discussion may seem strange to those who are unacquainted with the opinions and practices respecting divorce prevalent in Germany. Divorce is much more common than in England, and is granted for many other causes than that of unfaithfulness. The question has been much debated, and some of the pastors have felt strong scruples in solemnizing marriages, where one or both of the parties may be persons who have been divorced. The defence offered above is very inadequate. The distinction be-

Ver. 33–37.—*Fourth* observation—on oaths. The plain requirement of the Old Testament in Lev. xix. 12, οὐκ ἐπιορκήσεις, *thou
shalt not foreswear thyself*, was distorted by the Rabbins from a
comparison of Numb. xxx. 3 ; Deut. xxiii. 21 (where vows [ὅρκοι
= נְדָרִים] which were, for the most part, accompanied by oaths, are
the subject), so that they taught the evasion of their fulfilment
towards men through a hypocritical reference of them to God. To
this hypocritical behaviour the Saviour opposes that of the children
of God. The command of Moses, " Thou shalt not swear *falsely*,"
Jesus converts into, " Thou shalt *not* swear *at all;* because he sees
in swearing, just as in the case of divorce above, nothing but a permission rendered necessary by sin. But in order to combine the expression of this abstract principle in the kingdom of God, with a
refutation of the hypocritical Rabbinical interpretation of the
law of Moses, Jesus specifies four forms of swearing familiar
to the Jews ; and demonstrates, *first*, that all of them refer to God,
and that it is only in their being referred to him that they mean
any thing ; *next*, that they are, one and all, inadmissible in the
kingdom of · God. The subjoined clauses, " For it is God's throne,"
etc., refer to that Rabbinical interpretation, that a man need not
perform oaths that do not refer to God himself. For this reason, in
the case of each form of swearing, its reference to God is demonstrated by our Lord ; and it is implied, that it is only by virtue of
this reference that it can have any meaning. (See more fully in note
on Matth, xxiii. 16, ff.)—The conceiving of heaven and earth as
throne and footstool of God (Isa. lxvi. 1) is, of course, figurative ; but the figure is founded on the true thought, that to
the Omnipresent Being heaven and earth stand in different relations.
He who is everywhere present, is yet everywhere different. Jerusalem, as the seat of the visible theocracy, is called God's city (Psalm
xlviii. 2 ;) and an oath by the city acquires its significancy from this
peculiar relation. The reason subjoined to the oath : " by the
head,"* is obscure. That oath is similar to the Mohammedan
swearing by the beard. It is explained, however, if we take in this
case negatively, what, in the other cases, was expressed positively.

tween an external and internal church results only from laxity of discipline, conjoined
with the absorption of the church in the State, which prevails in the German Govern-
ments. The external church is, in fact, those who have the name of Christians, and
nothing more, and are not, therefore, of Christ's church, and would not be in visible
communion, if a right state of things, as to discipline, were restored. It can never be
admitted, that there is any power on earth that can assume authority to relax Christ's
plain command. In the church, his command is law, and, so far as marriage and divorce
come under secular jurisdiction, the government of a Christian country is bound to follow
the precepts of Christian morals.)—*Tr.*

* The construction of ὀμόσαι with the accusative (James v. 12), or with κατά and the
genitive (as in Heb. vi. 16), is pure Greek. In the New Testament it is generally
construed with ἐν or εἰς after the analogy of בְּ נִשְׁבַּע in Hebrew.

What impotent man cannot accomplish—make one hair white or black—*i. e.*, produce the slightest change in himself—the Almighty can accomplish. Dost thou swear, then, by thyself? thy oath can have no meaning, except as thou intendest him who wills that thou thyself shouldst exist. Hence every oath, if it is to have any meaning, refers to God, since he only, the Eternal, can give a pledge for the security of what is transitory.—But as the entire prohibition of *all* swearing is joined to this thought, it is evident that we may not draw this conclusion : " Since all objects of adjuration have a reference to God, by which they acquire their import, we are to swear *only* by God ;" but, on the contrary, " Since we are to refrain from swearing in general, and all oaths refer originally to God, the eternal and true, we are not to employ *any* oath ; the simplest statement of opinion is sufficient, any thing further has sprung from the source of evil, and become necessary only by reason of sin." The idea, that only the *abuse* of oaths is forbidden, can never be defended by a true interpretation. In the passage, James v. 12, a different view might, for a moment, commend itself, on account of the different position of the words ; but even there, on a closer examination, the connexion requires the sense of prohibiting oaths in general. This absolute prohibition of our Lord can occasion no difficulty, [if we consider that here again Christ is not giving a *formal law*, but uttering a *truth*. The Jews in taking oaths, proceeded on the assumption that there are oaths which must be kept, and others which may be violated, while declarations without this sanction, may be so with entire impunity. Our Saviour sets aside entirely this artificial distinction. An oath founded on the false conception of being essential to create an obligation to keep one's word is *sin*. *Every word* must be truth, and uttered in a conscious appeal to an omnipresent and holy God. *Every word must be an oath in the true sense*. Hence follows that before the court (Matth. xxvi. 63) and even elsewhere (Rom. i. 9 ; ix. 1 ; 2 Cor. ii. 17 ; xi. 10 ; Phil. i. 8 ; 1 Thess. ii. 5 and 10) it must be allowed to call God to witness ; provided that this be done *for the sake of others*, and not under the delusive idea that it is by our adjuration that we are obligating ourselves to speak truth.—E.]

Ver. 38–42.—The *fifth* instance comprises the nature of the law in a general maxim, and opposes the evangelical *principle* to the pharisaical conception of it. The idea of retaliation (*jus talionis*), which is the foundation of law in general, is expressed in ὀφθαλμὸν ἀντὶ ὀφθαλμοῦ scil. δώσεις κ. τ. λ., *an eye for an eye, etc.* Exod. xxi. 24. But the Pharisees made such a use of retaliation, that it could not but become a cloak for revenge and uncharitableness. Christ, on the contrary, conceives the idea of law in the spirit of the purest love, and derives thence the command of self-denial and resignation.

"Eye for eye, tooth for tooth," is an eternal law in the government of the world ; but love takes the brother's fault on itself, and, by thus becoming like him, causes him to become like it. Thus, out of the *jus talionis*, love procures redemption and *forgiveness*, which is nothing but retribution reversed, and cannot, therefore, exist without the sufferings of the Redeemer. This conquering by yielding is the essence of the Gospel ; the law is founded on the ἀντιστῆναι τῷ πονηρῷ, repelling force by force.* The manifestations of love in contrast with the rude character of retaliation, are then presented in four instances, arranged in an anti-climax. Outrage on the person is the most grievous (ῥαπίζειν is of kindred meaning with κολαφίζειν, the latter, however, denoting rather blows with the fist) ; next to this in order comes the *demanding* of property (κρίνεσθαι, *to claim before a tribunal*) ; *asking*, as the mildest form of presenting a request, forms the close. Between the two latter forms, ἀγγαρεύειν, *to constrain*, is placed, as partaking of both. (The term is of Persian origin, but was adopted into the prevalent languages of antiquity ; the Aramaic language also adopted it. See *Buxtorf. Lex. talm.* s. v. אַנְגַּרְיָא.) In Luke vi. 30, the words καὶ ἀπὸ τοῦ αἴροντος τὰ σὰ μὴ ἀπαίτει, are added—the general thought for the particular instances in Matthew. (᾿Απαιτέω = נשׁה, *to exact, to demand*.)

The preceding observations on marriage and oaths apply likewise to the carrying out of this command. The Saviour does not intend by his precept for his kingdom to invalidate the truth of the maxim, " An eye for an eye," as a legal principle ; he who holds the legal position cannot, and must not, be treated otherwise than according to the law.† But for him who is possessed by the spirit of the Gospel, without having as yet overcome the power of sin, the conduct indicated by the Saviour is suitable. Where the spirit is still uncultured and hard, there it would not be love, but unkindness, to shew unappreciated love. What, for instance, could be more unkind than a literal use of the precept, π α ν τ ὶ τῷ αἰτοῦντί σε δίδου, *give* TO EVERY MAN *that asketh of thee ?* It would be to form begging vagabonds. Hence the application and exercise of the laws of love cannot be reduced to fixed rules ; love alone teaches

---

* We cannot very well take πονηρῷ as neuter here; for it is our duty, under all circumstances, to oppose what is evil in itself. But here the evil is viewed in its effects in an individual, in whom there is, at the same time, a susceptibility for good. In reference to this mixture of good and bad, the Saviour may say, that the member of the kingdom of God does not resist the manifestations of sin, in order to accomplish for the good a perfect conquest in the heart of his brother, by the manifestation of forbearing love, which is expressed thereby.

† Thus the Saviour himself answers the rude servant who struck him on the face: If I have spoken evil, prove that it is evil; but if I have spoken right, why smitest thou me? John xviii. 23. To turn to him the other cheek would have been an infraction of love, as it would have brought the man into the temptation of increasing his sin by increased turpitude. Paul behaves similarly, Acts xxiii. 3.

us to apply them properly, and enables the scribe, instructed to the kingdom of heaven, to bring out of his treasure things *new* and *old*. For *this* order of things, before the full manifestation of the kingdom of God, the law still retains its application ; yet the Gospel has its sphere, in which it is ever gradually unfolding its nature more perfectly.

Ver. 43–45.—At last Jesus comes to what is highest and final— to *love* itself. The command, לְרֵעֲךָ וְאָהַבְתָּ, *Thou shalt love thy neighbour* (Lev. xix. 18), applied it is true, *immediately*, as the context shews, to the nation of Israel, which, to them, in their partial state of development, represented that collective humanity, to which *neighbour*, in its profoundest sense referred. But the hypocritical Pharisees drew the inference from this command, that we were at liberty to hate our enemy. ('Εχθρός, like *hostis*, primarily " one not of the same people." See the passages quoted in *Wetstein* and *Schöttgen, ad loc.*) They not only *tolerated* hatred of enemies, as something at the time not quite conquerable, but they *cherished* it as something allowable, nay, included (by implication) in the command. To this outrageous interpretation of the Old Testament, Jesus opposes his own, which unfolds the undeveloped truth from its inward nature and principle. The fulness of love, taught by Jesus, and imparted from his fulness to his people, not only extends over the narrow circle of national affinities, but makes what is opposite, as well as what is akin to it, the object of its exercise. The different manifestations of love (ἀγαπᾶν, εὐλογεῖν, καλῶς ποιεῖν, προσεύχεσθαι), form a climax, and are in contrast with the forms of hatred ; these latter, indeed, as such, cannot and ought not to be loved ; but the individuals are, in whom they are seen, since there is in them the latent germ of a nobler existence, which is to be awakened by the power of love. But the love here enjoined, is no passive love, residing merely in the domain of feeling ; for that can never be excited by the manifestations of hatred, but is influenced only by kindred qualities ; it is rather love as a *power of the will*, which is able to overcome all (opposing) feelings. For this reason, too, assimilation to God is assigned as the end of the manifestation of love to enemies. (In υἱός, *son*, the representation of the image, existing in the Father, is expressed.) As God abhors *evil*, and commands us to abhor *it* (Rom. xii. 9), but blesses the evil *man;* so does he, too, who lives in pure, divine love. The Spirit of God in him teaches him to separate the evil from the man; and while he hates the former, to love the latter. But such love man cannot obtain for himself by a determination of will or by any effort, for it is divine ; he can receive it only by spiritual communication in faith. Yet this by no means excludes the effort to exercise it before it is possessed, as it is that very effort that awakens us to the consciousness of its necessity. ('Επηρεάζειν occurs, besides in this passage, only in Luke vi. 28 ; 1 Peter iii. 16. According to *Pollux*, it is a law term, meaning " to drag before a judge with ignominy and insult ;" then, in general, " to injure," " to insult.") Luke adds another trait, *lend hoping for nothing again* (vi. 35), where, likewise, sincere, disinterested love is expressed. Luke has expanded this thought afterwards, when he comes to portray the forms in which natural love manifests itself. On the whole, with the exception of one unessential transposition, Luke has the same thoughts here, and they must, therefore, certainly be regarded as original, integral parts of the Sermon on the Mount.

Ver. 46, 47.—As a parallel to this sacred love, which includes even what is hostile in the sphere of its exercise, and which is bestowed in regeneration alone, Jesus brings forward natural love, which loves only what is akin to it, and, in that, itself essentially. (Ephes. v. 28, " He that loveth his wife, loveth himself.") Such is the prevailing power of love in the Old Testament, a few traces of love to enemies excepted (as in the case of David, 1 Sam. xxvi.) which point to a future higher grade of religious life. As such it does not stand *opposed* to the higher love of Christ, but *beneath*, as something subordinate, which has its analogy even in the animal world. The τελῶναι and ἐθνικοί, *publicans and Gentiles*, in Matthew, the ἁμαρτωλοί, *sinners* (πόρναι, Matth. xxi. 31) in Luke, are mentioned as standing emblems, with the Pharisees, of what is despised. In the publican, in particular, the prominent characteristic is being involved by the calls of his station in the lowest worldly connexions; for which reason the taxgatherers are used as a symbol of worldliness and its temptations. ('Ασπάζεσθαι is a general term for tokens of love of all kinds.)—In these verses, moreover, the idea of μισθός, *reward*, appears again. (See note on ver. 12.) Natural love is represented as being accompanied by a less reward than pure love. There is evidently a condescension here to the legal level, for it is just the nature of sincere love to seek no other reward than that which is in itself. But as, in fact, the possession of it involves all that constitutes blessedness, because God is love (1 John iv. 8), and no one can love but he in whom God dwells ; it is certainly true, also, that its reward is great. But a *distinction* between love and its reward, and of an effort to attain the former for the sake of the latter, can exist only on the level of the law ; pure love seeks itself for its own sake, for it includes in itself all that can be desired.

Ver. 48.—The last words contained in this verse are, as it were, the key-stone which completes the whole. The general result not merely of our Lord's last commands, but of all that precedes, is : Let *perfection* be your aim. ("Εσεσθε οὖν is parallel with ὅπως γένησθε above, ver. 45.) For the observance of but *one* of these commands, as here laid down by our Lord, nothing short of perfection is sufficient. It does not, therefore, alter the thought, if, instead of τέλειοι, *perfect*, as it is in Matthew, we read οἰκτίρμονες, *merciful*, as it is in Luke vi. 36. For neither pure love nor mercy can be conceived *alone* in the human soul, without the other qualities involved in perfection ; so that all must necessarily be conceived as joined with the one. But to refine upon the idea of "perfect," and to understand it of a relative perfection, is evidently forbidden by the words subjoined : ὥσπερ ὁ πατὴρ ὑμῶν, *as your father*, which, as compared with ver. 45, cannot mean any thing else than that the image of God is to be represented in men, as the sons of the highest. Accordingly, the passage is parallel with that in the Old Testament, וִהְיִיתֶם קְדֹשִׁים כִּי קָדוֹשׁ אָנִי (Lev. xi. 44), which Peter adopts ; ἅγιοι γένεσθε, ὅτι ἐγὼ ἅγιός εἰμι, *be ye holy*, etc. (1 Pet. i. 16), and is explained by it. That is, as in that passage the requirement of holiness on man's part is *founded* on the holiness of God, so here also in relation to perfection ; so that this passage may be interpreted, " Be ye perfect, *because* God is perfect." The perfection of man, as well as his holiness, is not separate from that of God, such as man might possibly attain of himself ; it is the divine perfection *itself;* God himself designs to be the perfect and holy One in man. In this way the passage must be interpreted, on the principle that every speaker is the expositor of his own words, even though we should regard the notion itself as false.

Matth. vi. 1–6.—After this prefatory comparison of the holy character of the doctrine of Jesus with the unholy teachings of the doctors of the law, the thought of v. 20 is resumed. The reality is opposed to the appearance ; the latter has what is visble and transitory for its object and proper end (ὅπως δοξασθῶσιν ὑπὸ τῶν ἀνθρώπων, *that they may have glory of men*), the former what is invisible and eternal ; God in heaven is placed in contrast with men on earth. Δικαιοσύνη* *righteousness*, conveys again, as in ver. 20, the general idea of a right relation to God, viewed in the light both of the Old and the New Testament. This contrast is viewed in reference to alms (ver. 2) and prayer (ver. 5) as the prominent manifestations of the religious life. (Σαλπίζειν, *sound a trumpet*, is not to be taken literally, but figuratively, " to do any thing with ostentation." Μισθὸν ἀπέχειν, *have a reward*, is spoken of in reference to the time of the future general reward, when only what is eternal finds its reward, because it was accomplished by the working of God's eternal Spirit.) The figure in ver. 3 cannot mean total unconsciousness, which should in no case exist, but only the absence of

---

* The reading ἐλεημοσύνη, which is supported by very many Codd., is, probably, only an explanation of δικαιοσύνη, which, in later Greek, is used for "alms," like the Hebrew צְדָקָה. Paul uses it in 2 Cor. ix. 9, for "kindness," " charitableness."

self-appropriation of the act; every good deed must be referred to its origin—to the spiritual source from which it springs; there it has even now its hidden reward, and hereafter its open one. To the outward proclamation of works of love by the Pharisees is opposed the humble ignorance of one's doings. (Ταμεῖον = הָעֲלִיָּה = ὑπερῷον, a chamber, to which they could retire for prayer, in quiet, Acts x. 9; see also Isa. xxvi. 20. The term ὑποκριτής, hypocrite, occurs frequently in the Gospels—e. g., in this chap., ver. 5, 16; vii. 5; xv. 7; xvi. 3; xxiii. 13, and frequently in Matthew; again in Luke vi. 42; xi. 44, etc. The verb ὑποκρίνεσθαι occurs only in Luke xx. 20. It is properly originally = ἀποκρίνεσθαι, to answer, then particularly, "to answer as a character in a play"—i. e., "to act on the stage." Then, in general, "to assume a form not one's own"—"to represent it." In the New Testament it is always used of religious form, with which the inward nature does not correspond.)

Ver. 7–13.—These verses bring out the last remark in a special application. In Phariseeism, not only does the character of hypocrisy manifest itself in prayer, but also the heathen notion (perpetually reproduced from the heathenism inherent in human nature), that prayer avails as *opus operatum*, and, consequently, from length and copiousness of words. From the pure idea of God, the Saviour teaches us to regard the inward disposition and the purity of thought resulting thence as that which is well-pleasing to God. Matthew also presents, as a pattern, a prayer given by Jesus, which is pervaded by simplicity, depth, and humility. Luke (xi. 1) records the circumstances which occasioned our Lord to give such an injunction. The disciples felt their spiritual poverty, and supplicated his rich grace to teach them to pray. Hence, too, it is said, "thus pray ye;" for it is a prayer calculated for the position of sinful men, not for him who knew no sin. (Βαττολογεῖν[*] is not from בָּטָא, *effutivit;* but according to *Suidas* it is derived ἀπὸ Βάττου τινὸς μακροὺς καὶ πολυστίχους ὕμνους ποιήσαντος.[†] Hence βαττολογία = πολυλογία.) *Superstition* places the reason of the hearing of prayer not in the grace of God, but in its own godless work. *Unbelief* deduces the uselessness of prayer from the omniscience of God, in whom it does not itself believe. *Faith* rests its humble prayer precisely on this holy, gracious, divine knowledge. Thus our Lord teaches us to pray in faith, *because* God knows, before the petition what we need (χρεία, need, taken both bodily and spiritually), and, consequently, can himself prompt the acceptable prayer, and fulfil it accordingly.

---

[*] See the copious discussion on this rare term, which is nowhere used but by *Simplicius* in one passage (in Epict. enchir., c. 37) in *Tholuck's* Comm. (Clark's Biblical Cab., No. xx., p. 114.)

[†] "One Battus, who composed long prolix hymns."

The words οἶδε γ ά ρ, *for he knows*, are to be taken as the reason which prevents the Christians from praying after the heathen manner. The believer does not pray for God's sake (to do him a service), but for his own sake ; that God knows, affords to him the consolation that he cannot ask wrong ; for he is concerned only for God's will, not for his own. The prayer of the believer is therefore nothing less than the divine will itself becoming manifest in humanity ; thus the Lord's Prayer is conceived. It is an expression of the highest, final, divine plans in the government of the world, both as to the whole and the individual.

With reference, first, to the state of the text of THE LORD'S PRAYER,* the doxology at the close is undoubtedly of later origin, and is added for liturgical purposes. In the *Const. Apost.*, vii. 24, it appears in the process of formation; it reads, ὅτι σου ἔστιν ἡ βασιλεία εἰς αἰῶνας. Ἀμήν.—*For thine is the kingdom for ever. Amen.* But the contents are profound and agreeable to the spirit of the prayer, and, therefore, certainly belonging to a period when pure Christian feeling prevailed in the church. It is wanting in Codd., B. D. L., and in many others, as *Griesbach's* New Testament shews. Still it is found as early as the Peshito, where, however, it may be an interpolation. So also the petitions, " Thy will be done on earth as it is in heaven ;" and, " But deliver us from evil," are wanting in the text of St. Luke. They are wanting not only in B. L., but also in the earliest fathers, as in *Origen* (de Orat., p. 226, edit. de la Rue, vol. ii.), who expressly notices the omission. But it does not follow from this that they are spurious in the prayer ; Luke rather appears to have abridged here, in the same manner as we noticed at Matth. v. 1. These petitions do not, indeed, form an essential part of the prayer, since they are included in those immediately preceding ; but for an unfolding of the meaning they are an integral part.† The question, *Whether Christ meant to lay down a stated formula in this prayer ?* may be best answered to this effect, that the Saviour certainly had in view, as his primary object, to teach the disciples to pray in spirit ; but in so far as he contemplated the arising of an outward church that should require liturgical formulas, he might intend its permanent use also ; and the church has done right to retain it. But that no value is to be ascribed to the letter, is shewn by the variation with which the Evangelists themselves record the prayer. In Rabbinical and Talmudical writings (according to *Wet-*

---

* We possess separate expositions of this prayer by *Origen, Tertullian,* and *Cyprian.*

† On the form of the Lord's prayer found in Luke, see the more copious remarks in note on Luke xi. 3, ff. On the omission of the doxology, see *Rödiger's* dissertation at the end of the synopsis, p. 231, ff. A transposition of the second and third petitions in *Tertullian* is discussed by Nitzsch, in the " Studien und Kritiken," published by *Ullmann* and *Umbreit,* 1830. H. 4, S. 846, ff. *Meyer's* " Blätter für höhere Wahrheit," Th. v., S. 10, ff., give an exposition of the prayer.

stein, Schöttgen, Lightfoot, in their notes on this passage) there are very many thoughts akin to the individual petitions. We learn thence how much of what is spiritual and true is contained in the Jewish writings ; only it is generally mixed with error by the pedantic Rabbins. But it is very perverse to infer from this relationship of the prayer to Rabbinical passages, that Jesus compiled his prayer by reflection from such elements of Jewish prayers. Whatever of noble and true was presented to him in the national culture wrought only to stimulate his inward development ; and even what he did derive thence, he reproduced with fresh life from his own creative and vitalizing power. But the exposition has not only to unfold the individual thoughts, but to regard them in their connexion. Regarded as a whole, the Lord's Prayer contains but *one* thought— the desire of the kingdom of God*—into which all the prayers of God's children (and, as such, Christ here teaches us to pray) may be resolved. This one thought, however, is conceived in two relations ; *first,* in reference to God's relation to man—thus in the first three petitions, which represent the kingdom of God as advancing to completion, and the highest purpose of God expressed as a wish ; *next,* in reference to man's relation to God—thus in the last four petitions, in which the hindrances to God's kingdom are noticed. The *first* part commences, therefore, with speaking of the riches of God :—

> THY name be hallowed ;
> THY kingdom come to us ;
> THY will be done.

The *second* part, on the other hand, speaks of the poverty of man :—

> To US give daily bread ;
> To US forgive sins ;
> Us lead not into temptation ;
> Us deliver from evil.

In the significant doxology, the certain hope is expressed of the prayer being heard—a hope founded in the nature of the unchangeable God himself, who, as the chief good, will cause the good to be realized in a manifest form (the kingdom of God.) At the same time, this prayer admits of an application to the individual (who is compelled, however, in the constantly recurring plural, to regard himself in connexion with all), as well as to collective humanity ; for this very reason, that being uttered from the inmost soul of humanity, and seizing the relation of God to the sinful race in its

---

* *Luther* is right, therefore, in saying, "the true Christian prays an *everlasting* Lord's Prayer," inasmuch as his whole desire centres in God's kingdom.

deepest root, it meets the wants of the whole and of the individual equally, provided always that he is living in faith. Every prayer directed not to transitory particulars, but to eternal things, is included in the Lord's Prayer.

In the invocation : " Our Father which art in heaven" (Πάτερ ἡμῶν ὁ ἐν τοῖς οὐρανοῖς), there is implied, *first*, an elevation above what is earthly and transitory to what is eternal and enduring ; and, *next*, the consciousness of our relationship to the eternal. The name Father presupposes the consciousness of sonship (Rom. viii. 15). This sentiment marks the prayer as belonging to the New Testament ; for though Isaiah exclaims, אָבִינוּ אַתָּה כִּי, *thou art our father* (Isa. lxiii. 16), yet that must be viewed as a momentary illumination of the higher spirit of the New Testament ; in general, the relation of servant to master (in which relationship is subordinate) prevails in the Old Testament. The *first* petition : ἁγιασθήτω τὸ ὄνομά σου, *hallowed be thy name*, is closely connected with the two following. 'Αγιάζεσθαι, used of what is unholy, means "to be made holy ;"* but, used of what is holy, it means to be recognized as such" = הִקְדִּישׁ.† The spread of the pure worship of God is, therefore, the subject of this petition. Only, as *Augustine* (de Corr. et Grat. c. 6) very truly remarks, this is not here to be understood of outward progress, but of inward ; so that the meaning is, " sanctificetur nomen tuum *in nobis*. A knowledge of what is holy (not in idea merely, but experimentally), presupposes inward holiness ; for only kindred minds know what is akin (Psalm xxxvi. 10). The meaning of ἁγιάζεσθαι, *be hallowed*, in this place, is therefore much like that of δοξάζεσθαι, *glorified*, as employed by John (John xiii. 31 ; xiv. 13 ; xv. 8, and elsewhere) in the sense of being glorified. The divine name (ὄνομα = שֵׁם) is put for the divine essence itself, inasmuch as it expresses and reveals the latter in its nature. (See the *locus classicus*, Exod. xxiii. 21). The divine must therefore, first of all, glorify itself in human nature, and by that means become known to man in its true nature ; not till then can the kingdom of God come. The *second* petition : ἐλθέτω ἡ βασιλεία σου, *thy kingdom come*, regards the divine power exerting itself *within*, which is supposed, in the first petition, as appearing *outwardly* ; [from the original source of all grace the suppliant passes over to the final consummation of the plan of salvation, comp. Rev. xxii. 20 ; in the third petition again to ‚the present] ; but, in so far as the kingdom of God appears again as displaying and devel-

---

* *Tholuck* gives it the signification, "to treat as holy," "to keep holy," which supposes, however, "a being holy," if it is to be real. It seems, therefore, more natural to understand it in this place as denoting the cause, rather than the consequence.

† That God be honoured should be the Christian's first desire. God is not for the sake of man, but is God of and for himself. The name of God, *Jehovah*, designates his self-existence. Before asking God's grace toward us, we must first of all acknowledge him as the being who owes nothing to us, and to whom we owe all—as God.—[E.

oping itself, Christ subjoins, in the *third* petition, γενηθήτω τὸ θέλημά σου κ. τ. λ., *thy will be done, etc.*, in order to express the consummation of the kingdom of God, which consists in the unlimited fulfilment of God's will ; so that the three petitions stand related to each
other as beginning, end, and middle. The words " as in heaven, so in
earth," express the *unqualified* fulfilment of the will, which now ap-
pertains to the heavenly state only, but which, in the consummation, is to extend to earthly things also.

In the *second* half of the Lord's Prayer, the subjective distance
from the kingdom of God, and the steps of approach to it, are apprehended and described with the supplementary thought, " That it
may be so, give us daily the bread of life." That ἄρτος, *bread,* does
not denote bodily food merely, is seen from the context; it stands
among purely spiritual petitions, and supposes spiritually-disposed
petitioners.* True, the suppliant should set out from his physical
existence, and ascend to what is higher ; for which reason the reference to bodily nourishment, on which the existence of the whole
man depends, should not be excluded, nay, it may even be regarded
as the immediate one ; but the spiritual food must still be looked
upon as included, since otherwise the important petition for the
Spirit of God would be entirely wanting in the prayer. (On ἄρτος,
as spiritual food to man, as a spirit, see Matth. iv. 4 ; John vi. 32,
compared with 41, 48, 50, 51.—The word ἐπιούσιος, which occurs
nowhere else, is difficult.† *Some* derive it from the particle ἐπιοῦσα,
which is used like *sequens* [Acts vii. 26 ; xvi. 11 ; xxi. 18 ; xxiii.
11], particularly in the phrase ἡμέρα ἐπιοῦσα = מָחָר, which, according to *Jerome*, was used in this passage in the *Ev. sec. Hebr.* [Comm.
in Matth. *ad loc*]. But this interpretation, which *Dr. Paulus* extends even to the future in general, is in contradiction to Matth. vi.
34, where care for the morrow is forbidden. In that case the connexion of σήμερον with ἐπιούσιος is inappropriate. *Others* more correctly derive it from οὐσία,‡ in the sense of *substantialis*—so that the
term is meant to define the bread more accurately in its nature,
nourishment for the true being of man—or what is sufficient for existence—what is enough. Thus *Tholuck.*)

In the consciousness of the dependence of spiritual and bodily
life on God and his preserving power, the consciousness of *guilt* is

---

* As heaven, where angels perfectly fulfil the will of God, stands separated from
earth, where we still dwell in a state of expectancy, we need for our earthly life, earthly,
daily bread. It is better to refrain from spiritualizing the simple sense of the prayer.—[E.

† *Origen* (de Orat., p. 94) regards it as a word coined by the Evangelist himself, without giving an etymology. The derivation from the participle is admissible after the analogy of περιούσιος ἐθελούσιος. But it may be derived from the participle of εἶναι as well
as from that of *léval.* See *Tholuck* in his comm. on the passage.

‡ The word is not ἐπούσιος but ἐπιούσιος, being derived not from the noun ἐπουσια,
but from the noun οὐσία and the prep. ἐπί.—[E.

implied, which is expressed in the *fifth* petition, and from which the desire proceeds to see all hindrances arising thence taken away by forgiving love. That the prayer is that of a believer, is evident from " as *we also* forgive ;" in which words forgiveness is again (see v. 7) made dependent on the forgiving love in the heart, which alone permits us to believe in forgiveness, without denying that this love is itself the gift of grace.* The idea of debt is taken very widely, comprehending sin in general, which, even in believers, contracts new debts, that need continual forgiveness—*i. e.*, blotting out. See the similes, v. 25, and Luke vii. 41, ff. ; and in ver. 14, immediately below. A lively perception of sin is accompanied by a sense of weakness, such as may not only disobey God's command occasionally, but even fall from it altogether. This is the view taken in the *sixth* petition. (On πειράζειν, see note on Matth. iv. 1.) The dangerous nature of temptation, from which the children of God beg to be delivered, lies in the disproportion between the power of the new life, and that of evil. The fear of God, therefore, in the believer begs for the removal of the cup.† The Saviour having been already led into one temptation at the beginning of his ministry, and having overcome it to the saving of men,‡ prays himself (for he became in all things like us, only without sin), in the second temptation, at the close of his ministry : "if it be possible, let this cup pass from me." (Matth. xxvi. 39.) In this petition, therefore, the assurance

---

* The words, " as we also forgive," must not be understood as determining the *measure* of forgiveness; for if God did not forgive men in a higher degree than they themselves shew forgiveness, no one would be forgiven. God always forgives completely and absolutely; while man oftentimes, even when honestly struggling, can forgive partially only—that is, so as that something yet remains in the mind. The words are rather to be taken as a *proof* how much God is forgiving love, since he not only forgives the believer his own sin, but also enables him to forgive others. *Being able* to forgive others, is accordingly a *token* to the believer of his being in a state of grace; and the petition may therefore be thus paraphrased: "Forgive us our sins—that is, reveal the entire fulness of thy forgiving love unto us, as thou givest us to taste it in this, that in thy power we can forgive." Moreover, we must not overlook, that forgiving *sins toward man* is alone spoken of; for we cannot and ought not to forgive *sins against God.* Thus David forgives Shimei's sin *against himself,* but on his deathbed he retains the sin *against the Lord;* and thus does the Apostle Paul also, according to 2 Tim. iv. 14–16.

† Πειρασμός, *temptation, trial,* may be (a) the trial to which God puts his people for their good (Rom. v. 3; James i. 2–4; 1 Pet. i. 6, f.), for whose removal the Christian will not pray; (b) temptations of personal lust, James i. 12; to this "lead us not into temptation," is not applicable; (c) the malicious assaults of Satan from which God preserves us if we pray to him. This is here the only appropriate meaning, and to this corresponds the following, "but deliver us," etc.—[E.

‡ See in the Epistle to the Hebrews ii. 18: "For in that he himself hath suffered *being tempted,* he is able to succour *them that are tempted.*" And again, 1 Cor. x. 13, were πειρασμὸς ἀνθρώπινος seems to be placed in contrast with another—namely, θεῖος, in which God himself, as in the cases of Abraham, Job, and other distinguished believers, and particularly in that of the Saviour, led into temptation; at such trials nature shudders. To *be* led into temptation must, however, be carefully distinguished from presumptuous, determined *entering* into it, which is one with tempting God.

is not implied, that no temptation shall happen to the believer—rather, as our Lord drank the cup, so every follower *must* drink *his* cup also. (Matth. xx. 23.)

As the two previous petitions referred to salvation in particular points, so finally, the *seventh* petition embraces salvation in its comprehensive sense.* As the whole prayer implies a community of spirit in all believers, so, at the close, good appears in contrast with evil itself; by the overcoming of which the kingdom of God attains its consummation and further temptation becomes impossible. Hence, the ἀλλά, *but*, in contrast with the previous petition. Whether we take τοῦ πονηροῦ, *of evil*, as masculine or as neuter, is indifferent, provided the neuter is regarded as including all that is wicked and evil, according to which notion it is Satan's very element. The masculine is, however, more agreeable to Bible usage. (Matth. xiii. 19, compared with ver. 38 ; Ephes. vi. 16 ; 2 Thess. iii. 3.) The petition for the consummation of the work of salvation connects itself with the beginning, since that is the kingdom of God ; and the doxology, though not uttered by our Lord, but added by the church in the Christian spirit, assures to us the fulfilment of all that has been asked by the consciousness that all is God's ; and, consequently, by means of this highest and only good, all good is as certain of triumph as the evil is of destruction. At first sight, however, it would seem that power (δύναμις) should have been mentioned *before* kingdom (βασιλεία), as being the more general idea, by the instrumentality of which that kingdom is realized. But this order was probably chosen for this reason, that it is not the divine omnipotence in an absolute sense that is meant, but its manifestation in the establishment of the kingdom of God, which the whole prayer presupposes. Hence, the doxology being, as it were, an assurance of the certain fulfilment of the prayer, declares very appropriately, first, that the kingdom is the object of *God's* desire—that is, its realization is *willed* by God ; then that his power carries it forward, and hence will assuredly bring all to a *consummation*.

Ver. 14, 15.—The subsequent thoughts are in Luke (xi. 4, ff.) more immediately connected with the prayer. Matthew expands the thought in ver. 12, respecting the exercise of forgiveness, in order to the receiving of forgiveness, with which the closing petition also stands connected, inasmuch as salvation is a comprehensive forgiveness, of which only the forgiving mind is a fit subject. (A similar thought occurs in a different connexion in Matth. xi. 25, 26.) The difficulty here is that forgiveness seems to be made dependent on the existence of love, while it is forgiveness received that first produces love ; see note on Luke vii. 47. But it is not the first

---

* *Chrysostom*, the theologians of the Reformed church, the Arminians, the Socinians, and others, recognize only six petitions, as they join the sixth and seventh.

kindling of love proceeding from forgiveness, that is meant (although the very reception of forgiveness supposes receptive love) ; but the exercise of enkindled love in particular instances. (Παράπτωμα, *trespass*, a single manifestation of the general ἁμαρτία, *sin*. It is = ἁμάρτημα, Mark iii. 28. The expression, πατὴρ οὐράνιος, like βασιλεία τῶν οὐρανῶν, is peculiar to Matthew ; see Matth. vi. 26, 32 ; xv. 13.)

Ver. 16–18.—The following verses are parallel with ver. 2 and 5 —a renewed exhortation to seek for the reality instead of the appearance. After prayer and almsgiving, *fasting* is taken up as another manifestation of the religious life. ('Αφανίζω denotes primarily "to make invisible," thence "to spoil," "to destroy," as ver. 19. Here, "to disfigure"—the Latin, *squalere*. To sorrowing negligence in externals is opposed joyful attire, denoted by anointing (ἀλείψαι), and washing (νίψαι). In that (apparently open) exhibition of the religious life, therefore, hypocrisy is manifest, which might be erroneously looked for in this (apparently not open) concealment of it ; for the essence of piety is the most inward reference of our life to God. All stealthy glances towards the external are the fruit of hypocrisy. ('Εν τῷ κρυπτῷ, *in secret*, is opposed to being open before men. It is, therefore, equivalent to the inward man, to whom God reveals himself.) This fundamental thought, that God himself must be the end of human striving, extends to the close of the chapter. It is the thread by which the different thoughts hang, which, according to Luke, stood in a different relation to Christ's discourses.

Ver. 19–21.—Earthly possessions are placed in contrast with heavenly ones in their indestructible nature, and the spirit is directed thither—to the source of all truth. (Σής, *tinea* = סָס, Isa. li. 8. Βρῶσις denotes in general the consuming process to which all earthly things are subject. The meaning "rust" does not suit ; for gold and silver do not rust.* In Mal. iii. 11, it is used also for a kind of worm.) The union of the heart with the treasure is assigned as the reason of this admonition to store up heavenly possessions. The treasure is regarded as the aim of the longing and desire which proceed from the heart. The concentrating of them on created things must produce misery, since the soul is destined for what is eternal.

Ver. 22–24.—Seeking after earthly treasure (which is so very contrary to man's inward spiritual nature) implies, therefore, inward impurity. The connexion with the preceding context is not altogether simple, though not to be mistaken. This circumstance indicates, doubtless, a different original position of the thought. (See Luke xi. 34, 35.) The relations of our spiritual life are illustrated by physical ones. It is remarkable that the eye should be called λύχνος, *lamp*. It seems to be merely the capacity of receiving

* See, however, note on James v. 3.

light. But capacity to receive light implies a partaking in the nature of light. "Were not thine eye sunny," says Göthe, with great depth and truth, "how could it ever behold the sun?" (See Psalm xxxvi. 9.) Thus the eye, with the light which flows to it, is that which itself illuminates, which makes light—a view which is optically true.* The condition of the bodily eye, however, modifies its action : ἁπλοῦς, single—πονηρός = διπλοῦς, double-sighted, as it were (ver. 24), or even totally blind, to which σκοτεινόν, dark, refers. Just in the same way the Saviour views the spirit's inward eye—the reason—the power of receiving divine things.† Its capacity for the higher light implies the nature of light in it, whence φῶς ἐν σοί = λύχνος, ver. 22. Jesus accordingly does not teach the absolute moral depravity of man.‡ That noble power destined for divine things, when drawn away to what is sensual, becomes blindness. The inward light is dissipated, and the power of sight destroyed. Spiritual darkness then is more fearful than bodily blindness. Luke, however (xi. 36), brings out the other and opposite result—that is, the entire inward illumination of our being, by which the very last traces of darkness (μὴ ἔχον τι μέρος σκοτεινόν) vanish. (On the special difficulties in the passage, see note on Luke xi. 36.) This is followed immediately by the mention of *two masters,* in which comparison the double-sightedness—glancing stealthily from God to the world—is expressed in another way. The appropriateness of the contrast lies in the completeness with which· the one excludes the other. The relation of the masters to each other does not allow of *indifference* among the servants. *Hate* (μισεῖν), therefore, stands opposed to *love* (ἀγαπᾶν), and *despise* (καταφρονεῖν), to *hold fast* (ἀντέχεσθαι.) ('Αντέχεσθαί τινος, properly " to seize any thing," " to hold it fast," = הֶחֱזִיק, thence "to pursue any thing with diligence and interest," 1 Thess. v. 14 ; Titus i. 9.) Μαμωνᾶς, or Μαμμωνᾶς, (according to Luke xvi. 9), from מָמוֹן, on the authority of *Buxtorf,* (lex. talm., p. 1217), is so used in the Targums for the Hebrew בֶּצַע, בֶּסֶף, that the term may be taken as equivalent to the Greek πλοῦτος, *wealth.* *Augustine* observes on the passage : " *Congruit et punicum nomen, nam lucrum punice Mammon dicitur.*" In opposition to

* *Philo* expresses the same thought (de vit. theor. ii. 482, edit. Mangey) when he says : ἡ θεοφιλὴς ψυχὴ ἀθάνατα ἔκγονα τίκτει, σπείραντος εἰς αὐτὴν ἀκτῖνας νοητὰς τοῦ πατρὸς, αἷς δυνήσεται θεωρεῖν τὰ σοφίας δόγματα. (See also *Gesenius* in the Lexicon, *s. v.,* צָוָה, Job xx. 9.)

† The *Reason,* provided it has been made clear and pure, can receive divine things. It has a receptive faculty; but it cannot originate any thing divine out of itself. It is carefully to be distinguished from the *understanding*—the faculty of ideas. In the New Testament the former is νοῦς, the latter φρόνησις. (See the *author's* Opuscula, p. 152, sq.) *Philo* de cond. mundi, t. i., p. 12, says : ὅπερ νοῦς ἐν ψυχῇ, τοῦτο ὀφθαλμὸς ἐν σώματι.

‡ The "absolute moral depravity of man," is a subject which our Saviour has not here under consideration. The strongest affirmers of that depravity yet admit man's possession of the natural faculties for apprehending moral truth.—[K.

God, money, when personified, appears as an idol, after the manner
of Plutus, without our being able to shew that an idol of this name
was outwardly worshipped. In the Saviour's meaning, the name
Mammon applies to the author of evil, which consists precisely in
confounding what is not divine with what is. Evil we must hate
(Rom. xii. 9) if we are to love good. The natural man, from the
fear of encountering the world, where good and evil are found mixed,
endeavours to avoid this alternative ; but Christ compels a decision
of the heart to pure love, which gives at once sincere *hatred* against
sin, never against the person of the sinner. 　　　　　　　·

Ver. 25–34.—The Saviour raises man, involved in his common
earthly wants, and wasting his poor existence in the anxious satisfying of them, from subjection to the prince of this world, who
occupies his slaves with such cares, to faith in God, which gives
birth to a holy care that dispels those grovelling vexations of our
daily life. The passage, Phil. iv. 6, is a commentary on these
words. In it the Apostle puts the command : μηδὲν μεριμνᾶτε, *be
anxious for nothing,* in contrast with the direction to ask of God
what is needful. *Prayer* is, therefore, the opposite of *anxious care,*
because in prayer man commits the care to God. The *natural* man
cares without praying. The brute, and the man who has become
as the brute, care as little as they pray.—Ver. 25. The discourse
turns on the double meaning of ψυχή = נֶפֶשׁ, which denotes, 1, *life;*
2, *soul.* Viewed in their essence, the two meanings involve each
other ; but the carnal man places the principle of life in the
flesh, and regards eating and drinking as its chief requirements.
For the believer, the life of man, as such, is in the soul, and the
soul alone is to him the principle of life (that is, the ψυχή viewed as
ψυχή πνευματική), and, consequently, he provides for it chiefly. The
words : μεριμνᾶν τῇ ψυχῇ, are not, therefore, equivalent to ἐν τῇ
ψυχῇ = καρδίᾳ ; but ψυχή is the object of care—the psychical life.—
Ver. 26. Faith in God's fatherly care for the nourishing of the
body is awakened by a view of his procedure in nature. (Πετεινὰ
τοῦ οὐρανοῦ = עוֹף הַשָּׁמַיִם. The general expression is, in Luke xii.
24, made special : κατανοήσατε τοὺς κόρακας.) Man stands connected with physical nature by his body, and may, therefore, trust
himself to fatherly love in reference to that, as unreservedly as the
birds of heaven. But since a divine principle of life reigns in his
physical being, this bears him to a higher region of life.

Ver. 27.—The helplessness of the creature in all that is external
is viewed in contrast with the fulness of the Creator's power, who
daily nourishes all beings. Man cannot make a single blade grow,
nay, he cannot make any physical change in himself. ('Ηλικία is
primarily " size of body," " stature" [Luke xix. 3], then "age" [John

ix. 21.]* To add a cubit to the stature would be something monstrous in proportion to the body, which does not exceed three cubits in height. From the connexion, something small is intended here. Better, therefore, " to add a little to the age." The care for eating and drinking—the conditions of physical life—is an agreement with this.—Ver. 28. The same applies to raiment. (Κρίνον = שׁוֹשַׁנָּה, Song of Sol. ii. 1, lily. Νήθω, neo, filum ducere.)—Ver. 29. The formations of nature exceed in beauty all the formations of art. Art, therefore, can only try to imitate nature—a powerful motive to unreserved confidence in the wondrous Framer of the universe, in whose kingdom the greatest and the least appear clothed in the most splendid dress.

Ver. 30.—If God thus cares for what is most perishable, how much more for the heirs of his eternal kingdom! (In regions where wood is scarce, as generally in the East, the use of other substances, as grass and brushwood, for burning, is the natural result of circumstances. Ὀλιγόπιστος = קְטַנֵּי אֲמָנָה, Matth. viii. 26 ; xiv. 31 ; xvi. 8.)—Ver. 32. Hence is deduced the prohibition of care for the physical necessities of life ; and that care is represented as rooted in heathenism, where, instead of the living God who knows (ver. 8), we meet with a blind fate (εἱμαρμένη) which compels man to be his own God.—In ver. 33 and 34 the noble and freely expressed thought, that the believing child of God is not careful, is qualified in order to prevent the mistaken idea that the prohibition of care is to destroy all exertion for earthly things. Ζητεῖν, seek, is contrasted with μεριμνᾶν, be anxious, so that the latter signifies anxiously caring without God,† the former striving in faith in God and with God. (Luke, however [xii. 29], uses ζητεῖν as synonymous with μεριμνᾶν,) Πρῶτον, first, gives the first rank to striving for the kingdom of God, to which the striving for earthly things is subordinate. For God's fatherly care is manifested by the believer himself ; he does not expect in a spirit of tempting God, to be supported on air. The " kingdom of God" is again to be taken in its large and indefinite sense, as comprehending what is external and internal (see note on Matth. iii. 2), as also the righteousness, which, though in itself an essential feature of the kingdom of God (Rom. xiv. 17), is yet here specially noticed, in order to indicate the nature of the kingdom of God, whether inwardly or outwardly manifested, and to guard

---

* In use the reverse: primarily time of life, age, then stature.—[K.

† Luke (xii. 29) subjoins the admonition: μὴ μετεωρίζεσθε, which word does not occur elsewhere in the New Testament. In the Old Testament it is often found, as well as μετέωρος, and the derivatives, μετεωρισμός, μετεωρότης, in the sense of being lofty, proud. (Psalm cxxxi. 1; Ezek. x. 16, 17; 2 Macc. v. 17; vii. 34.) In the sense of suspenso esse animo, " filled with hope and fear"—a sense not uncommon in profane writers—it occurs only in this passage. The βεβαιότης of πίστις stands opposed to the μετεωρισμός of μέριμνα.

against false conceptions. The term π ρ ο ς τεθήσεται, *shall be added*, points to the divine as the immediate and proper object of all man's endeavours, with which temporal blessings are associated subordinately, and *necessarily*, if the endeavour after God be pure. Hence the exhortation closes with the words with which it began : μὴ μεριμνήσητε, ver. 25. The words εἰς τὴν αὔριον, *for the morrow*, do indeed seem to limit the universality of the exhortation, and to describe the care for the present as well founded. But in the idea of care a reference to the future is always included, and the present appears as provided for, as is seen in the succeeding context ; consequently the requirement *not* to care, should be maintained to its full extent (see 1 Peter v. 7); but as was observed, without thereby excluding truly believing exertion. The words immediately following : ἡ γὰρ αὔριον μεριμνήσει τὰ ἑαυτῆς, *for the morrow will take thought*, etc., confirm this view ; for in them God is represented as he who takes thought, since time itself, to which taking thought is ascribed, must be viewed in its dependence on him, by whom every need is supplied for every circumstance. Lastly, the Saviour notices that, even apart from lading himself with care for the future, the life of the believer in the present retains its burden because of the sin of the world ; so that the *taking no thought* urged upon us, cannot be *exemption from suffering*. (Κακία is purposely used, as it expresses physical ills, but in their moral origin. Ἀρκετός occurs also Matth. x. 25 ; 1 Peter iv. 3.) As regards the critical state of the verse, the Codd. vary in the words : ἡ γὰρ αὔριον μεριμνήσει τὰ ἑαυτῆς, as some omit τὰ ἑαυτῆς ; others only τά ; while some give περὶ ἑαυτῆς or ἑαυτῇ. The *various readings* do not alter the meaning essentially ; but the usual construction of μεριμνᾶν is with the accusative ;—we might, therefore, prefer ἑαυτῆς as the less common. It is more important to notice a *punctuation* different from the ordinary one, which *Fritzsche* (comment. in Matth. p. 284), has adopted in the text : μὴ οὖν μεριμνήσητε εἰς τὴν αὔριον· ἡ γὰρ αὔριον μεριμνήσει. Τὰ ἑαυτῆς ἀρκετὸν τῇ ἡμέρᾳ ἡ κακία αὐτῆς, *Be not anxious for the morrow; for the morrow will be anxious. What belongs to itself, its own evil, suffices for the day.* Ἡ κακία αὐτῆς is then taken as in opposition with τὰ ἑαυτῆς. This punctuation seems to me worthy of regard ; only the words : ἡ γὰρ αὔριον μεριμνήσει, produce, perhaps, the impression of a defective construction ; the words subjoined give more completeness to the thought. The thought, however, is not essentially altered by this punctuation.

Ver. 1, 2.—[With decision in striving after the kingdom of God, and with strictness towards ourselves, we must combine mildness towards others. The way to righteousness consists not in discovering others' sins, but our own. He then who does this must feel constrained to ask divine assistance (ver. 7–12.). To relations of union with God corresponds provident conduct towards men (v. 12–20). That Matthew (ch. vii.) has not arbitrarily put together unconnected matter is shewn by the parallel passage of Luke vi. 37, ff.] The thought is expressed more fully in Luke vi. 37, 38 ; there is something similar in Mark iv. 24. Κρίνειν, κρίμα, *judge, judgment,* is in Matthew evidently = κατακρίνειν, κατάκριμα, *condemn, etc.,* in which sense they occur, Rom. ii. 1 ; xiv. 3, 4 ; 1 Cor. v. 12, and frequently. This is seen from the parallel word, καταδικάζειν, *condemn,* used by Luke, which defines κρίνειν, and from the contrast between ἀπολύειν and διδόναι in Luke vi. 37 ; the former of which expressions denotes " acquittal by the court" (*absolvere reum;*) the latter, the " remission of what might be legally demanded." *Judging,* therefore, so far as it is *testing, is not here forbidden ; that is always required by Scripture.* (1 Thess. v. 21.) That state of mind is forbidden in which, *forgetting his own sin,* man condemns the sins of others, thus assuming the place of a holy God, and hence also judges falsely and perversely, rejecting the sinner with the sin. The phrase : " With what measure ye mete, it shall be measured to you again," is equivalent to : " An eye for an eye," Matth. v. 38. The nature of overflowing, forgiving love, which prepares us in turn to receive forgiveness, is described by figure in Luke vi. 38.— (Μέτρον καλόν = ἱκανόν, *a just measure, not falsified;* πιέζω, *to press together;* σαλεύω, *to shake and move to and fro,* in order to force as much as possible into the measure ; ὑπερεκχύνομαι = פּ֫וּק, Joel ii. 24, the *overflowing* of the filled-up measure—all in contrast to giving without love, which is done to avoid a direct violation of the law. Κόλπος = חֵיק, *sinus,* the lap of the flowing dress for receiving any thing—a figure frequent in the Old Testament. 'Ανταποδοῦναι εἰς τὸν κόλπον, Jer. xxxii. 18 ; Psalm lxxix. 12, for " to recompense.")

Ver. 3–5.—The next verses carry out, in detail, the same thought which has just been viewed in its relation to the whole character. Uncharitableness sees the faults of others, while it overlooks its own ; pure love overlooks those of others, and watches sharply its own. The same figure is found in the tract *Baba Bathra:*—*Cum diceret quis alicui, ejice festucam ex oculo tuo, respondit ille; ejice et tu trabem ex oculo tuo.* To have a splinter in one's eye is conceivable ; to have a beam, not. But to have a beam in one's eye without observing it, is certainly an image of the wildest self-delusion.

Ver. 6.—These exhortations to gentleness are followed very appropriately by the command to beware of the other extreme—that is, an indiscriminate pouring out of holy things from want of judgment. He who forbids our judging (which decides man's *culpability*), commands us to form an opinion (which marks only the *state.*) This latter is absolutely necessary for the child of God, in order to distinguish the false from the true. (Κύνες, χοῖροι, *dogs, swine,* denote the common natural condition, which shews itself in shamelessness, carnality, and lust ; these things the Christian must know as such, and not bring what is holy into contact with them ;* for their internal condition does not admit of their receiving it, and it reacts destructively on himself. Ἅγιον, μαργαρίται, *holy, pearls,* denote the holy doctrine of the kingdom of God. [Matth. xiii. 45.] For such men the law alone is fit ; the Gospel they misunderstand to the injury of those who proclaim it to them. In dog-like natures, holy things excite rage, and swinish natures tread them without thought into the mire, which is their element.)

Ver. 7-12.—Prayer for the Holy Ghost alone leads to the attainment of such a life of love as does not condemn, and yet carefully judges. [Such prayer itself then marks the direct opposite of the dog-like dispositions which repel what is holy.] The general maxim : " Ask, and it shall be given you," repeated in different forms, is exemplified by a similitude, which reasons from the less to the greater.—Ver. 8 proves ver. 7, from the general thought : " Every one that asketh, receiveth." The demonstrative force lies in the nature of him to whom the prayer is addressed. Every prayer which is really such—that is, which flows from the inward necessity of the soul, God answers. The human relation between the father and the supplicating child forms an argument *ad hominem.* Luke (xi. 12) adds a third case : " Instead of an egg, a scorpion." Here, to the idea of what is useless is added that of something repulsive and frightful. The transition : ἢ τίς ἐστιν, gives emphasis to the opposition : " or does it ever happen otherwise?" In comparison with God, the eternal good, men, in their sinful alienation, appear as evil (πονηροί;) in the relation of parental love, kindness still manifests itself in the midst of sin, how much more in the eternal God! Luke (xi. 13) calls the gift, which includes all other gifts, expressly the πνεῦμα ἅγιον, *Holy Spirit,* who must be understood there as the creative principle of holiness in man. In this Spirit we exercise pure love.—The maxim in ver. 12 is also based on proverbs current among the Jewish people. In the Talmud : " *Quod exosum est tibi, alteri ne feceris," what is offensive to thee, do not to another,* stands as one of *Hillel's* sayings. Love for ourselves should give the rule of our self-sacrificing love for our neighbour (Matth. xix. 19); only

---

* Dogs (κύνες) denote elsewhere in the New Testament not the common state of nature, but obduracy and positive and fierce hatred of the Gospel (Phil iii. 2 ; 2 Pet. ii. 22 ; Rev. xxii. 15, comp. Ps. lxxx. 14.) In like manner swine (comp. 2 Pet. ii. 22 with Ps. lxxx. 14), is an image not of natural carnality, but of that gross and obstinate sluggishness which can make no use of what is holy but to defile it. To Mary Magdalene and a publican, the Gospel may and should be preached, but the Christian must be able to discriminate such characters from the dogs and the swine. For the latter the only feasible attempt to save is excommunication.—[E.

God is to be loved *above* ourselves. Instead of οὗτός ἐστιν ὁ νόμος, as *Griesbach* reads, *Fritzsche* would read οὕτως; but, apart from critical reasons, οὗτος should be preferred on account of the deeper thought which it expresses, that in this command of love toward our neighbour, the *essential* import of the Old Testament is included. (Mark xii. 29, ff.; Matth. xxii. 40.)

Ver. 13, 14.—From what has been said, follows naturally the difficulty of a walk in self-denying love, being represented under the figure of a narrow path, which conducts through a narrow gate into the strong citadel of eternal life. The figure is so natural, so true, that it is repeated in every earnest attempt, even in subordinate stages of religious life. *Cebetis tab.* c. 12, οὐκοῦν ὁρᾷς θύραν τινὰ μικρὰν, καὶ ὁδόν τινα πρὸ τῆς θύρας, ἥτις οὐ πολὺ ὀχλεῖται, ἀλλὰ πάνυ ὀλίγοι πορεύονται, αὕτη ἐστὶν ἡ ὁδός, ἡ ἄγουσα πρὸς τὴν ἀληθινὴν παιδείαν. (The parallel passage, Luke xiii. 24, will subsequently receive a special explanation. For ὅτι, ver. 14, we should undoubtedly read τί; it corresponds to the Hebrew מָה.)

Ver. 15–20.—Yet is the way of the pure life in God not merely narrow in itself, it is rendered still more difficult by the teachings of false prophets. Here we are required to try the spirits. The *fruits* are assigned as the test. In 1 John iv. 1, 2, pure doctrine is mentioned as the criterion. Is this meant here, too, by the term fruits? I doubt it; though Tholuck has defended that view with specious reasons. The doctrines stand first; they might well be compared to the root, but not to the fruits. The fruits are necessarily of a moral nature. It is certainly difficult to distinguish between the real fruits, and the counterfeits of hypocrisy and fanaticism; but the Saviour supposes in his people a simple sense of truth, that separates the true and the false with certainty. [Yet they include not merely the life of the *individual*, but the consequences of a *system*. A school, sect, creed, that rejects the laws of Christian morality, and defends sin on theory, or that makes its theories an idol before which the ten commandments must bow down, proves itself radically false.] The sheep's clothing is, of course, not of the actual prophetic dress (Matth. iii. 4), but denotes figuratively, the outward show, in opposition to the true nature—sayings and doings apparently full of love, which are the offspring of a selfish heart. The wolf's nature seeks its own, and soon betrays itself to the child-like sense. By the processes of the vegetable world, we are shewn how the fruit characterizes the nature of that which produces it. The figure is similar in James iii. 11. (Ἄκανθα, *thorn-bush*. *Virg. Ecl.*, iv. 29 : " *Incultisne rubens pendebit sentibus uva ?*" [Ἄκανθα, אטד, *buck-thorn*, with fruits like grapes but disagreeable. Τρίβολος, דרדר, perhaps the Opuntien cactus (Indian fig-tree), which produces fruit similar to the fig, but worthless. And

as both deceive by their fruits, so still more by their splendid blossoms, while that of the vine is unpretentious, that of the fig, hidden.]
—See Matth. xii. 33 for the same figure rather differently carried out, as also Luke vi. 45, which passage will be explained with the former. On ver. 19, 20, see note on Matth. iii. 10 ; Luke iii. 9.

Ver. 21–23.—These verses make a special application of what was observed of all false prophets generally, to those who are connected with Christ, among whom insincerity may creep in. Λέγειν is opposed to ποιεῖν, as λόγος to ἔργον, or δύναμις. (1 John iii. 18 ; Col. ii. 23 ; 1 Thess. i. 5 ; James i. 22.) To say Lord, Lord (Λέγειν κύριε, κύριε), signifies pretending to an attachment which is not felt in reality. According to ver. 22, the foundation of this devotion appears to be spiritual vanity, which was nourished by the conspicuous exhibitions of the Spirit's power, which were imparted even to a Judas, along with his confession of Jesus as the Messiah. To prophesy—to cast out devils—to do wonderful works, are the most common operations of spiritual power, which, in the time of Jesus, was so mightily exerted—their nature we shall afterwards consider more precisely in their individual manifestations.* By the words : in thy name (τῷ σῷ ὀνόματι), we must understand not merely a superstitious pronouncing of the name, as was the case with the sons of Sceva (Acts xix. 13, ff.); but a receiving of the power of the Lord—yet without true spirituality. (On ὄνομα, see note on Luke i. 49 ; and again on Matth. x. 41 ; xxviii. 19.) By the words : "in that day," the revealing of the hypocrisy, unperceived by human eyes, is postponed to the time of the general judgment, when every secret must be made manifest. (Rom. ii. 16.) Hypocrisy, therefore, appears, here, as at the same time self-deception, in consequence of which a man persuades himself that he belongs to the Lord, till the discovery of the depths of the heart brings him to feel, that what he deemed his holy actions were a great violation of God's law (ἀνομία), because his final aim in them was constantly his own, not God's glory. That we are not to conceive of any exchange of words on the day of judgment, is self-evident. The situation here so vividly portrayed is the *language of fact;* the unbeliever will stand beseeching, but will be refused. (The words: ἀποχωρεῖτε, κ. τ. λ., [*depart, etc.*], are from Psalm vi. 8.) The solution of this psychological enigma—the possibility of such self-deception, is contained in the words : I never knew you, ver. 22. Γινώσκειν, *know*, like ידע, is used in the Scriptures in a deep spiritual sense, particularly in the phrases : "God, Christ knows man, the soul." (Deut. xxxiv. 10 ; 1 Cor. viii. 3 ; xiii. 12 ; Gal. iv. 9.) Knowing God is connected with being known by God as the consequence; no one can know, without being known of, God. If we connect these expressions with

* On these gifts, see the detailed remarks on 1 Cor. xii. and xiv.

the Christian doctrine of regeneration, the rich import of this contrast is evolved. The genuine knowledge of God—not a merely *notional* knowledge, but that *essential* knowledge which is eternal life itself (John xvii. 3)—becomes possible only by a revelation of the hidden God to the soul (see note on Matth. xi. 27) ; God's thus revealing himself is a knowing of the soul (γινώσκειν τὴν ψυχήν). The figure of a bridal relation of the soul to God, which pervades the entire Scriptures, thus acquires its essential import ; the inward illumination of the soul is like a visit from the heavenly bridegroom, by whose agency, the knowledge of God results to the soul, according to the Old Testament expression : " In his light we see light," Psalm xxxvi. 9. Those who say, " Lord, Lord," are, therefore, unregenerated men, who, with a false liberty, behave themselves as children of God, without having been begotten of him. The phrase : "whence ye are" (πόθεν ἐστέ), in Luke xiii. 25, is therefore, very significant. It marks their foreign origin ; they are not from above,(ἄνωθεν, John iii. 3) ; they are σὰρξ ἐκ τῆς σαρκός, *flesh of the flesh* (John iii. 6). In Luke xiii. 25–27, the elements of this passage are found in a different connexion, in which they will be considered hereafter.

Ver. 24–27.—The *epilogue* teaches the importance of applying a discourse like this, under the figure of a man who builds on a rocky foundation, and sets forth as the rock of salvation, the Word of eternal truth which was embodied in Christ's teaching. (Deut. xxxii. 15 ; Psalm xviii. 2 ; xlii. 9 ; Isa. xvii. 10.) Here the contrast is not between the bad man and the good, but between the fool and the wise man (as in Matth. xxv. 1) ; for all that hear are supposed to be well-intentioned ; but in many, spiritual prudence for their being spiritually benefitted was wanting. The similitude of building is carried out in 1 Cor. iii. 9, ff., and there (ver. 11) Christ is called the foundation, on which the superstructure of the spiritual life must rest. In Luke vi. 48, the figure of laying a foundation is further carried out by digging deep. (Βροχή, " heavy torrent of rain," = םֶשֶׁג. In Luke, πλήμμυρα = πλημμυρίς is used, which means " the flowing tide," in contrast with ἄμπωτις or ἀνάρροια, *the ebb*. Here, where it is used in its more general sense, it denotes any overflowing, desolating flood, from streams or rain storms. [To understand the comparison, imagine the rough, steep sides of the valleys, of that Jura formation prevalent in Palestine. A house built beside a torrent, on a *rock*, is unharmed by the swollen and sweeping flood. But if resting, though placed high above the stream, on a foundation of earth, the flood gradually wears away its base, till at length the undermined and growing slide of earth reaches the house itself, and plunges it into the flood.]—Ver. 26. As a contrast to the building on the rocky foundation of the eternal Word of God, which defies all temptations and dangers, there follows the figure of a baseless building on the sand, to denote the founding of the inward life on perishable human dogmas, opinions, and fancies. This building on the sand evidently refers to a spiritual work, which has some affinity with the genuine, regenerating work of the Spirit, but is destitute of the proper character of that work. [He who has received the word of Christ into his ear only, builds *on logical sand*. He is not born again ; Christ the rock lives not in him ; and he is not on the rock. He, on the contrary, who *does* Christ's words, *i. e.*, dies to the world (Matth. v. 3-12), receives the light from above (v. 13, ff.), understands in spirit, and strives to fulfil the law of God (v. 18-48), hence lives for God alone, not for his own advantage (vi. 1, ff.), and strives after eternal life (19-34), recognizes his own sinfulness (vii. 1, ff.), prays for the Holy Spirit (7), and follows Christ in the narrow way, not the multitude, nor the false prophets, (vii. 13, 15) ; he has built his spiritual edifice on Christ the Rock, and at Christ's second coming will stand.]

Ver. 28, 29.—The Evangelist concludes the whole with a reference to v. 1. Matthew, in conclusion, notices only the impression which Christ's words made on the hearers. Ἐκπλήττεσθαι is stronger than θαυμάζειν ; it expresses being inwardly affected. To this the words ἐξουσίαν ἔχειν* point, which distinguished the discourses of Jesus from those of the Pharisees ; the latter often uttered truths, but they were destitute of spiritual power; their discourses were pictures drawn in the air, without essential power and vital energy. These were breathed forth in the words of Jesus, and by them he reached the depths of men's hearts ; wheresoever, therefore, anything in unison with the truth slumbered within, it could not fail to be awakened by such a stimulus.

§ 4. HEALING OF A LEPER.

(Matth. viii. 1-4; Mark i. 40-45; Luke v. 12-16.)

After this portraiture of Jesus as a teacher, Matthew proceeds to describe him as a *worker of miracles*, since the next two chapters contain nothing but narratives of the Saviour's wonderful works. In as far as such actions are generally viewed as manifestations of mighty power, they are called in the Scriptures, δυνάμεις, גְּבוּרוֹת, *mighty works*. Regarded in their connexion with the divine purposes in relation to individuals or the whole, they are called σημεῖα,

---

* *Having authority.* I think the specific reference here is to the tone of authority which Jesus assumed, and which marked him as a spiritual *legislator*. He spoke as *himself* the source of knowledge, and the authoritative expounder of duty. With this, of course, stood intimately connected the vital power of the truths which he uttered.—[K.

אֹתֹות, *signs.* As events exciting astonishment or terror, they are called τέρατα, θαυμάσια, Matth. xxi. 15 ; מִפְלָאוֹת, מֹפְתִים. The most appropriate name for them, when used of our Lord's miracles, is ἔργα, *works* (a word found in Matth. xi. 2, and very frequently in the Gospel of John). In that name the miraculous character is, as it were, pointed out as the natural form of the Saviour's agency, since he, as possessor of divine power, must necessarily produce supernatural phenomena by means of it. *He himself* was the wonder (τέρας), his wonderful works were but the natural acts of his being. Hence it is evident that we cannot adopt that idea of a miracle, which regards it merely negatively as a suspension of the laws of nature. Starting from the scriptural view of the abiding presence of God in the world, we cannot regard the laws of nature as mechanical arrangements, which would have to be altered by interpositions from without : they have the character of being based, as a whole, in God's nature. [Yet it should be remembered that nature *here* has been disturbed by sin, and subjected to death, and hence differs from that of the *higher* regions of creation, heaven.] All phenomena, therefore, which are not explicable from the known or unknown laws of earthly development, are not for that reason necessarily violations of law and suspensions of the laws of nature ; rather, they are themselves comprehended under a higher general law, for what is divine is truly according to law. That which is not divine, is against nature ; the real miracle is natural, but in a higher sense. True, the cause of the miracle must not be sought within the sphere of created things ; it exists rather in the immediate act of God. All God's doings are, to the creature, miracles, although, viewed in relation to the divine essence, they are purely law and order. To the believer, therefore, what is apparently natural—*e. g.,* the preservation of the world—the growth of all its products—is miraculous, because he is accustomed to refer every thing to its first cause. *No miracle is therefore performed without a real power.* As we see human beings working miracles, extensively in the New Testament, we are taught the possibility of higher powers being imparted to men, which act controllingly upon surrounding objects, whether nearer or more distant. Unless we admit the presence of such a real element of power—the Spirit in his gifts (χαρίσματα, 1 Cor. xii. 10)—there is absolutely no connecting link between the miracle and the worker of it, and it becomes mere juggling or witchcraft. We might, perhaps, regard animal magnetism as bearing a certain analogy to this higher principle of power ; but we must beware of confounding that obscure, dangerous principle of sensuous life with the pure element of light, which wrought in the holy men of Scripture narrative. This is the essence of God in them ; the former power is of the creature, and defiled by sin. But that in later times spiritual power in the leaders of the church was *not* combined with miraculous gifts, results from the progress of the race, and the absence of those necessities, which called forth extraordinary phenomena to meet the exigences of a critical period.

It is a significant fact that the Scriptures assert not merely holy, but also evil,* power to be the cause of miracles. Two series of miracles extend throughout Scripture history. As the works of the Egyptian magicians stand opposed to the miracles of Moses (Exod. vii. ff.), so in the New Testament the miracles of antichrist stand opposed to those of the Saviour. (Matth. xxiv. 24 ; 2 Thess. ii. 9 ; Rev. xiii. 15.) This distinction between the divine and the satanic miracles suggests the idea, that it cannot possibly be the end of miracles *to establish the truth of any affirmation.* In the sense of Scripture, too, this is by no means the intention of miracles. It was only the people that so viewed them, because they allowed themselves to be influenced in their judgment by the impression of power, or the excitement of the senses ; for which reason they attached themselves to false prophets as willingly, and even more so, than to the true. The Saviour, therefore, severely rebukes this eagerness for sensible miracles. (John iv. 48.) But when our Lord in other places (*e. g.*, John x. 25 ; xiv. 10, 11) calls for faith in his works, and connects them with his dignity and his holy office, this is not done in order to establish the truth of his declarations ; truth, as such, rather proclaims itself irresistibly to impressible minds by its inward nature. ("Every one that is of the truth heareth my voice," John xviii. 37.) They are intended rather to *demonstrate his character as a divine messenger,* for those in whom the impression of the truth, conveyed by the spirit and language of the Saviour had wrought its effect. The proclamation of truths may be conceived, without the person who proclaims them bearing the character of a messenger from God. In such a case, the truths may predominate greatly both in word and power over what is erroneous ; but error cannot be conceived as utterly excluded in the case of any human teacher. God, therefore, invested particular individuals as his instruments with higher powers, in order to distinguish them from humanly excellent teachers, and to accredit them before mankind as infallible instruments of the Holy Spirit—as teachers of absolute truth. Hence the gift of miracles is one of the necessary characteristics of true prophets, and serves to witness their superior character—to prove that they are to be regarded as leaders and guides of the people, and freed from *all* error. For this reason, faith—that is, susceptibility to divine operations—is supposed in the case of miracles ;

---

* In so far as evil in general is merely a product of created powers, we may say that the satanic miracles are merely apparent miracles; since miracles can be performed by God's omnipotence alone.

and it is only the truth, *combined* with the testimony from miracles, that constitutes the character of a divine messenger ; by virtue of which, things may also be established as true and certain, which cannot be known to be such by an indwelling susceptibility to truth. The reverse relation obtains with the representatives of the kingdom of darkness, whom the Scriptures call false prophets, false Christs, because, notwithstanding a total inward diversity, they have an external similarity to the true messengers of God. Though these representatives of falsehood mix up much that is true in word and deed, and would fain appear as the messengers of the kingdom of light ; yet to the sincere soul, fitted to receive the truth, the entire spirit of their doings discovers itself as unholy, and therefore all the miracles conceivable fail to induce the soul to surrender itself to them ; the very association of miraculous powers with an unholy spirit is rather a proof to such a soul of their close connexion with the kingdom of darkness. When, therefore, the Saviour condemns the thirst for miracles, he rebukes the regard to externals involved in it, which is a sign of deadness to what is spiritual, and exposes to the danger of doing homage to the operations of evil, when they are conjoined with miraculous appearances. But, on the other hand, our Lord commends the desire for miracles, as a confirmation of the inward certainty, that he, whose truth and purity of action at first touched the soul, is more than a human teacher—that he is a heavenly accredited messenger of God. Miraculous power then, and every separate manifestation of it, is in itself without meaning; all turns on its connexion with the general disposition of the person in whom it is seen. The *association* of miracles with what is holy, is the sublime testimony of God to his servants ; the *association* of miracles with what is unholy, is a warning, meant to awaken horror at the emissaries of the pit ; the knowledge of what is holy and what is unholy in itself, and in its true nature, is presupposed, in order to be capable of discriminating the nature of miracles ; and this knowledge depends on sincerity and purity of heart. The impure man persuades himself that God's true miracles might have been wrought by the evil spirit, and the false ones he regards as true ; the pure man views both in their true form, because he carries in himself the rule and criterion of truth.

If now we glance at the *history* of miracles, we do not find any miracles wrought by the agency of men *before* the time of Moses ; for God's miracles, his revelations in the Son, and in angels, and so forth, are to be carefully distinguished from those in which miraculous gifts are attached to a human being. It seems as if a ripeness of human nature were requisite, to fit it to serve as the vehicle of mighty spiritual energies. For this reason, Jesus wrought no miracles as a child ; and the apocryphal books of the New Testa-

ment betray their senseless character in this, among other things,
that they describe the child Jesus as working miracles. Again,
after the time of Moses, we notice a difference between the miracles
of the Old and New Testament. The miracles of the Old Testament bear not only a more colossal, but a more external, character.
They are more calculated to move the inferior powers of the soul,
particularly the imagination. The miracles of the New Testament
are more spiritual. They display a more definite reference to the
moral world. In particular, we find the Saviour, in his miraculous
agency, following the principles maintained in the temptation. He
never wrought miracles to amaze—never for himself. The Father
only wrought miracles in him for his disciples, either in a narrower
sphere, as at the transfiguration, or in a wider one, as at the resurrection, for the confirmation of their faith. In humble quiet, Jesus
employed the fulness of divine power and life dwelling in him, to
console the unhappy, and deliver them from the source of their sor-
rows ; in this sense also to destroy the works of the devil, and to lay
the foundations of the kindgdom of God ; since our Lord always
knew how to apply outward help as a spiritual remedy. For the
miraculous cures wrought by Jesus should be regarded as acts at
once physical and moral, in which the fulness of divine life passed
over to susceptible individuals, in order, along with the organic harmony of the vital processes, to evince the possibility of a harmonious
spiritual life. The cures effected by the Redeemer were also distinguished from those of his disciples in this, that he performed
them in his own name, by the perfection of his indwelling power.
The disciples, on the other hand, wrought them only in the name
of Jesus, by his power, as his instruments. Faith was, therefore,
to them as much the medium of appropriating miraculous powers,
as to others of being healed ; and, in this appropriation through
faith, we find them in a state of gradual progression. (Matth. x. 1,
8 ; xvii. 19, ff.) For a time the gift of miracles continued after the
removal of the apostles, till, after the complete establishment of the
church, it gradually disappeared. But, together with the Holy
Spirit, there still remained the inward miracles of regeneration,
sanctification, hearing of prayer, which are greater than the outward ones. These outward miraculous gifts will not again appear
till the last times, when the situation of the church shall render
necessary the sending of new prophets. 'The view held by the
Romish church of the necessity of an unbroken continuance of
miraculous gifts, results from a confounding of external and internal
miracles. It is only the latter of which a church cannot be conceived to be destitute ; for the God whose every act is a miracle,
dwells in it.

Matth. viii. 1.— Of the first of the cures narrated by Matthew, the chronological connexion is undetermined. (See Matth. viii. 1, 5, compared with Luke v. 11, 16, 17.) Still as, according to Luke (vii. 1), Christ heals the centurion's servant at the conclusion of the Sermon on the Mount, as Matthew likewise relates (viii. 5, ff.), the position given to this event by Matthew may be chronologically correct, and the healing of the leper may have happened immediately after the Sermon on the Mount, on the road to Capernaum. (Luke [v. 12] says, ἐν μιᾷ τῶν πόλεων.) The narrative begins with the observation, that, immediately on the Saviour's descending from the mountain, crowds gathered around him. Among them a leper approached. (Καταβαίνειν ἀπὸ τοῦ ὄρους refers to ver. 1. The construction is remarkable for the repetition of αὐτῷ—a construction which occurs in this same chapter, verses 5, 23, 28, and elsewhere in Matthew. The first αὐτῷ looks like a dative absolute with καταβάντι. From this feeling, the various reading καταβάντος αὐτοῦ may be accounted for as a correction for the less usual dative.)

Ver. 2.—The leprosy shewed itself in several forms—some more dangerous, others milder. The regulations of Moses respecting the צָרַעַת leave no doubt on that point. (Lev. xiii. ; xiv.) The persons afflicted with the dangerous leprosy (see on the subject *Winer's* " Realwörterbuch," *s. v.*) were considered unclean according to the Mosaic law, and could not be received into the congregation again till their cure was ascertained. This leper, of whom Matthew tells us, might already have heard of Christ's cures, or have seen some of them. At any rate, he displays his faith in Christ by prostrating himself, and by the express petition for healing, which he supposes Jesus able to accomplish for him also. (The word προσκυνεῖν = γουυπετῶν in Mark = πεσὼν ἐπὶ πρόσωπον in Luke, corresponds to the Hebrew הִשְׁתַּחֲוָה. It is the general form of expressing respect in the East, and has not in itself any religious reference.) But, with respect to the *nature of the faith*,[*] which we must suppose to exist in the persons cured in this as in all similar cases (see note on Matth. xiii. 58), we must first of all lay it down that πίστις, *faith*, viewed in its religious bearing, in every case retains one and the same fundamental signification. This is modified only by the different objects of faith, which again are determined by the different degrees of its development. Now we must not make the essence of faith to consist in *knowledge* either of the divine in general in the Old Testament, or of the divine in Christ in particular in the New. For such knowledge, whether confused or clear in its conception, may be united with a state of the soul, which is the opposite of believing. Faith is rather rooted in a spiritual *susceptibility* to the divine, which has its seat in the *heart*, καρδία (see Rom. x. 9, 10), while knowledge (γνῶσις) depends upon the susceptibility to the divine

* See remarks on Rom. iii. 21.

in the *understanding* (νοῦς). Faith is also capable of inward gradation, according to the degree in which the divine is revealed. Particularly in the cures, where faith is made the negative requisite,
which determines the ability to receive the Spirit's powers emanating from Christ, the faith demanded or exercised is not the holding
certain doctrinal positions, but a susceptibility, both spiritual and
bodily, to the Saviour's agency. This was, doubtless, uniformly
accompanied by the belief that Christ was the Messiah, and that,
as Messiah, he could work miracles. But we might also conceive
these ideas as existing apart from that fundamental disposition,
which we have designated as susceptibility of the heart, and of the
whole nature to the divine : and thus separated they would not
satisfy any condition of miraculous healing.* This is the view suggested by the description of all the cures wrought by Jesus. In no
case does he ask after definite doctrines as objects of faith. In no
case does he mention them as a necessary quality of faith. The
Saviour leaves the mere profession of faith to speak for its quality,
because demeanour and language at once proclaimed the general
disposition of the soul, as being either open or closed to divine influences. Hence it is evident also, that the outward bodily healing
was only a symbol of the *inward spiritual healing* which was properly intended. (See note on John vii. 23.) For those same vital
powers, which removed the bodily disorganization, exercised an influence, in conformity with their nature, on the spiritual character
of the person cured. They brought him into a real connexion with
the world of good in general, and took possession of him on the
position to which he had just attained, in order to raise him still
higher.

Ver. 3.—At the sick man's request, our Lord lays his hand upon
him, and heals him. In most cures wrought by Jesus there was a
similar immediate touching ; and there can be no hesitation in acknowledging a conducting medium of healing power (only not a
necessary one) in the putting forth of the hand, just as in blessing
with the solemn laying on of hands (ἐπίθεσις τῶν χειρῶν). The analogy
of animal magnetism suggests itself, and it is certainly not accidental ; only, as was hinted above, it must never be forgotten, that
the power of Jesus Christ was divine, and magnetism, therefore,
can be referred to, only to indicate a power presenting similar phenomena in an inferior region of existence. (Καθαρίζειν = טָהַר may
signify " to pronounce clean," inasmuch as the priest who pronounced the diseased man clean, restored him to society from which
he had been cut off. [See Lev. xiii. 13, 17, in the LXX. transla-

---

* The profound mystic *Gerhard Tersteegen* calls faith, very appropriately, " the inwardly hungering desire of the spirit, which lays hold of not only the *form*, but also the
essence of what is divine." (*Weg der Wahrheit*, S. 366.)

tion.] But that an actual and instantaneous removal of the disease is intended in this case, is evident from the words " immediately his leprosy departed from him" (εὐθέως ἀπῆλθεν ἡ λέπρα) [Mark i. 42], which are explanatory of ἐκαθαρίσθη, *was cleansed.* In Matthew, too, the connecting of ἐκαθαρίσθη with ἡ λέπρα αὐτοῦ, requires in the verb the idea of removing.)

Ver. 4.—All the narratives agree in recording, that the cure was followed by the command of our Lord to tell no one of the event. Similar prohibitions are often found in the Evangelical history. (See Matth. ix. 30 ; xii. 16 ; xvi. 20 ; xvii. 9 ; Mark iii. 12 ; v. 43 ; vii. 36 ; viii. 26, 30 ; ix. 9 ; Luke viii. 56 ; ix. 21.) The Saviour's reasons for them were of various kinds. Sometimes he, doubtless, meant, in that way, to guard against popular movements to make him the Messiah-king ; at others, to withdraw the people's attention from the transactions, and prevent their rendering him external homage ; or, as Luther observes, to give an example of humility. But he may have often forbidden the announcement for the sake of those who were cured. If these persons were in danger of distraction by outward occupation, it might be the intention of Jesus to lead them thus to try themselves, and to turn their attention within. That this was sometimes his motive, is especially probable from the circumstance that we meet with instances of an opposite character, where our Lord encourages them to declare what God had done by him. (See Mark v. 19.) This appears to have been his practice towards those persons who, naturally reserved, and lost in undue self-contemplation, needed prompting to outward activity for the prosperity of 'their inward life. The circumstance last noticed affords a glance into the profound wisdom of our Lord as a teacher, who understood how to treat every one according to his wants. In the present case, it would seem from the account in Matthew, most suitable to look for the reason of the prohibition in the person cured, since the cure was wrought in the presence of many, and yet the command to tell nothing of it was directed to the leper alone. It is true, Mark had said nothing of the multitudes ; and from *his* representation, it is more probable that the command was intended to prevent popular tumults. His account is (i. 45), that the leper, notwithstanding the prohibition, published the miracle diligently, (πολλά often used in Mark—e. g., iii. 12 ; v. 23 ; xv. 3—in the sense of " greatly," " zealously,") and that, by that means, such a commotion arose, " that Jesus could no more openly enter into the city"—viz., without giving encouragement to the carnal hopes of the Messiah among the multitude. Perhaps Mark has also subjoined the words : καὶ ἐμβριμησάμενος αὐτῷ εὐθέως ἐξέβαλεν αὐτόν, *and he straitly charged him,* etc., to make the command more stringent. ('Εμβριμάομαι has here the meaning of " to command with solemnity and emphasis," as in Matth. ix. 30. 'Εκβάλλειν = הוֹצִיא. See Matth. ix. 25.)

Not less important than this *prohibition* is the *command* to go to the priests and present the appointed offering. (See Lev. xiv. 2, ff.) This command not only displays a wise care to interfere, in no respect, with the theocratic institutions, but also a tender cautiousness not to remove the subject of the cure from his moral position, but to confirm him in a faithful discharge of his obligations. We by no means find Jesus seeking to awaken in each subject of his healing power that deeper feeling which, through regeneration, should bring him into the life characteristic of the New Testament. He often leaves them, as in the case of John the Baptist, quietly to maintain their legal position (in which they had been called to perfection), and seeks only to guide them to the true righteousness which even under the old dispensation involved repentance. All the Evangelists concur in specially subjoining the words : "for a testimony to them." They intimate that the command had reference to the priests also—that is, by pronouncing the leper clean they were to testify to the reality of the cure, and, at the same time, condemn their unbelief. (The antecedent ἱερεῖ, must be taken collectively on account of the αὐτοῖς, which follows. The word ὑποχωρέω, used in Luke v. 16, does not occur anywhere else, except in Luke ix. 10, with the meaning, *clam me subduco*.)

§ 5. HEALING OF THE SERVANT OF A CENTURION.

(Matth. viii. 5–13 ; Luke vii. 1–10.)

This narrative is one of the gems among the many little episodes, complete in themselves, with which the Evangelical history is adorned. It exhibits to us a pious heart in the most amiable childlike form, freely manifesting its life of faith without any doctrinal tinge whatsoever. The centurion, probably in the Roman garrison at Capernaum, having grown up in heathenism, was, from residing among the Jews, favourably disposed towards the religion of the Old Testament. The miracles of the patriarchal times, of which he heard, he might often have longed after, without knowing that he was to see infinitely more than these. But his humility was as profound and sincere, as his faith was deep ; he esteemed himself not worthy that the ruler over spiritual powers should enter his house. In this character he recognized Jesus ; but what precise view he entertained of him, it would be hard to determine, since it was, probably, as usually happens in childlike dispositions, undeveloped, though in the main, correct. The Saviour makes no effort to extend his views : his desire is satisfied ; his faith in the gracious manifestation of divinity which had come near him, strengthened ; and aid furnished toward perfection in his present views.— With respect to the two accounts of Matthew and Luke, the latter undoubtedly possesses the superiority in point of vividness and exactness in external circumstances. Matthew gives greater prominence to that part (ver. 11, 12) in the address of Jesus, which refers to the Jews, whom the Evangelist everywhere chiefly regards. The circumstance that Luke makes the centurion send his friends to Jesus ; while, according to Matthew, he goes himself to Jesus, cannot be regarded as a contradiction ; for the latter representation is nothing but a shorter mode of expression, since, in the words of his friends, his own faith was made evident to our Lord. The occurrence mentioned in John iv. 46–53, *Semler* and others were inclined to regard as identical with this ; but *Lücke* and *Tholuck* have convincingly proved the opposite. As the narrative of a cure, this transaction is so far remarkable, that, in this case, Christ, without personal contact, merely by the magic power of his will (if I may use the expression), exercises an active power at a distance—a fact which again has its analogies in magnetism.* On the circumstance of the centurion believing, while his servant is being healed, see note on Luke xvii. 14, ff.

Ver. 5, 6.—The locality of the occurrence is fully pointed out by both narrators. It took place as Christ was entering Capernaum. Matthew makes the centurion present the request for his sick servant in his own person. According to Luke, he presented it through the intervention of others—viz., the presidents of the synagogue, to the erection of which he had contributed. This fact shews that the Roman warrior had been subdued by the power of the truth as exhibited in the Old Testament form, and had united himself to the synagogue as one who feared God (σεβόμενος τὸν θεόν), probably only as a proselyte of the gate. As a heathen, the centurion might not dare to approach the Messiah at all, and would, therefore, seek his interposition through those representatives of the Old Covenant with whom he was intimate. (Παῖς = δοῦλος, Luke vii. 2, just as נַעַר=עֶבֶד. He was afflicted with paralysis [παραλυτικός], which is generally understood to imply a partial affection only ; but as it had brought the sick man near to death [ἤμελλε τελευτᾷν, Luke vii. 2], the term is probably used for apoplexy. The Jewish elders made use of the centurion's attachment towards the Jews as a motive to induce Christ, in whom they supposed the

* There seems not the slightest necessity for these repeated, and to us offensive allusions to magnetism in connexion with the miracles of our Lord. Assuredly, it is not strange that he who controls all agencies, and works directly and indirectly throughout nature, should have wrought with a like variety of ways, upon earth. In all cases the miracle was the immediate act of omnipotence.—[K.

power of healing to exist, to exercise it in this case. Some Codd. read παρέξη for παρέξει, which, form besides in this passage, is found also in Luke xxii. 42 ; Matth. xxvii. 4 ; John xi. 40.)

Ver. 7, 8.—After Christ had expressed his willingness, and as he was approaching the centurion's house (οὐ μακρὰν ἀπέχοντος ἀπὸ τῆς οἰκίας, Luke vii. 6), the latter according to Luke's more circumstantial account, sent some friends to meet him to prevent him from giving himself personal trouble. (Σκύλλω occurs also in Luke viii. 49 ; Mark v. 35, always with the meaning, " to trouble," "to put to inconvenience.") The idea that the personal presence of the Saviour was not necessary for the healing of his servant, which he so much desired, but that the Saviour, as the Lord of spiritual powers, could help with a word (λόγῳ), is the expression of a faith both bold and free from the dominion of sense. But in the wish that Jesus should not come under his roof, various emotions are involved. In the first place, it is certainly an expression of the deepest humility, which does not esteem itself worthy of a visit from a heavenly guest (οὐδὲ ἐμαυτὸν ἠξίωσα πρός σε ἐλθεῖν, Luke vii. 7 ; οὐκ εἰμὶ ἱκανός, compare Matth. iii. 11.) Further, this humility may have been combined with fear of the presence of what is holy, as involving danger to what is unholy. (See note on Luke v. 8.)

Ver. 9.—The reasons assigned by the centurion for thinking that the Saviour need not trouble himself personally to come to the sick man, illustrate most clearly his views of Jesus. He compared Christ's relation to the world of spirits with his own military position. He derived thence, notwithstanding his subordinate rank (εἰμὶ ὑπὸ ἐξουσίαν τασσόμενος), absolute command over his inferiors. In like manner he imagined Christ commanding in the world of spiritual powers. Whether he conceived of Christ specially as Lord of the angelic host, cannot be determined. In any case his conceptions were probably dim. Heathenish notions about sons of God (as in the case of the centurion at the cross, Matth. xxvii. 54) may have been blended in his mind with views which he had heard expressed concerning the Messiah. Notwithstanding this indefiniteness in his conceptions, he possessed in his heart a deep religious life, which excited the astonishment of the Son of God himself.

Ver. 10.—The Saviour's wondering (θαυμάζειν) at the humble faith of the centurion (see note on Matth. xv. 21, ff., respecting the Canaanitish woman) points to a peculiar relation between divine and human judgments, intimated even in the Old Testament (Gen. xxxii. 24, sq.) While what is lofty in man is abomination to the Lord, the lowly find favour before him, so that he, the lofty One, dwells in the depths with the lowly, Psalm xxxiv. 18. The Saviour here employs the manifestation by a heathen of that state of soul, which is the essential condition of God's dwelling in humanity, to arouse in his Jewish companions a sense of their proper destination. Israel was called not only from its own bosom to give birth to the Saviour, but also to preserve a perfect susceptibility to his influences ; and by means of these first to build up the kingdom of God among themselves. Jesus here censures the want of that spiritual susceptibility, and hints at the mystery of the transfer of the Gospel to the heathen, intimations of which even the Old Testament contains (Isa. xix. 21, 22 ; lvi. 6, 7 ; Psalm lxxxvii. 4, ff.), without, however, connecting the diffusion of the knowledge of the true God to the heathen with the rejection of Israel.

Ver. 11, 12.—The pious centurion appears in the sequel as the representative of those heathens in general, who, by their deep longing for what is divine, surpass the Jews, who clung with the stiffness of death to mere form. Such spiritual members of Israel (Rom. ii. 14, 15 ; xi. 17 ff.) are conceived as scattered among all people and regions, but in Christ gathered together and united in the kingdom of God. John x. 16. (East and west, ('Aνατολαί, δυσμοί), to which in the parallel passage [Luke xiii. 29] north and south (βοῤῥᾶς, νότος) are added, denote all the dimensions of the earth's extent, according to the sensible impression—implying the whole of it. See Isa. xliii. 6.) The Jews, as children of the kingdom, are contrasted with the heathen, so that the latter are viewed only in a more general relation to the divine kingdom. (In like manner, Rom. ix. 25 : καλέσω τὸν ο ὐ λ α ό ν μου, λαόν μου· καὶ τὴν οὐκ ἠγαπημένην, ἠγαπημένην, after Hos. ii. 23.) The abuse of their privileges on the part of the Jews, caused this relation to be exactly reversed. The privileges in which the Jews trusted, became the possession of the believing heathen ; the punishment they desired for the heathen fell on their own heads. These privileges are comprised in the phrase : ἀνακλίνεσθαι ἐν τῇ βασιλείᾳ, recline at table; only we are not at all warranted in regarding the expression as an empty image of happiness. Jesus was addressing Jews, who had adopted into their Messianic conceptions the idea of a social meal, as a general expression of being and living together with the risen saints of old, as the representatives of whom, " Abraham, Isaac, and Jacob" (and in Luke xiii. 28, " all the prophets"), are mentioned. See *Bertholdt, Christol. jud.*, p. 196, seq.) Passages in the Old Testament (such as Isa. xxv. 6) might have contributed to the formation of this notion. Accordingly, the readiest supposition would be to regard the expressions in this passage as accommodated to the Jewish conception of the opening of the kingdom of God with a banquet, if we could persuade ourselves to incorporate into our idea of the Saviour, such a trait as an accommodation to the popular superstition which he came to destroy.* Moreover, as this

* There seems no more difficulty in supposing our Saviour to avail himself by way of

particular feature appears elsewhere in the New Testament (see Luke xiv. 14, 15 ; Rev. xix. 9), another interpretation offers itself, less at variance with the general teachings of Scripture respecting the consummation of all things, and with our idea of the Saviour. For through the whole New Testament extends the doctrine of the restoration of our sin-defiled world—(a doctrine acknowledged in other passages, as Rom. viii. 19, ff., by many interpreters, who reject it in the present)—and stands intimately connected with the resurrection of the body, presented in 1 Cor. xv., as a real restoration, not indeed of the corruptible body of death, but of that incorruptible one, which has grown up from its elements. To this restoration of the paradisaical condition of the earth, in which the acmé of Christ's power to overcome the power of sin will be manifested, the present passage refers, so that the kingdom is here the state of righteousness, outwardly and visibly attaining to power. The commencement of that state, combined with the resurrection of the Old Testament saints, is conceived as being celebrated by the Saviour visibly presenting himself in company with his people at a new covenant-banquet. As the Saviour, when about to depart, was united with his disciples for the last time at the Lord's Supper, so in the kingdom of God he will (according to Matth. xxvi. 29) again gather them, as the great family of God, at the supper of the Lamb. (Rev. xix. 9.) Hence the Jews' fundamental idea of a feast in the kingdom of God is undoubtedly correct, and likewise expressed in Christ's words in the New Testament, only that their carnal sense had, on the one hand, given it a gross material form, and on the other, viewed it isolated and without its spiritual conditions.* An external participation in the kingdom of God, realized outwardly and visibly, necessarily presupposes its inward spiritual establishment.

Not less erroneous than this Jewish materialism is Gnostic idealism, which, in the place of a real resurrection of the body, which necessarily implies a glorified world, teaches a so-called pure life of the spirit, known, indeed, to Scripture, but only to be condemned as a worthless conception. (2 Tim. ii. 18.) The Bible teaches that the soul necessarily needs an organ ; and that, consequently, the

mere allusion, of such a popular notion in regard to the kingdom of heaven, for the purpose of teaching an important truth, than in the parable of the rich man and Lazarus, to employ prevalent conceptions respecting the localities of the invisible world. In neither case does he endorse the view, for in both it is merely incidental.—[K.

* On account of such aberrations, Chiliasm has been condemned by the Church ever since the third century. But that the fundamental ideas of that system, apart from their materialized form, have their root in the Scriptures, has been acknowledged by many expositors in recent times, though with the intention of deriving arguments against the Bible. These fundamental ideas are no other than—victory of good over evil, even in outward things, and restoration of the original harmony in the visible creation also.

state after the dissolution of this terrestrial body till the resurrection is an imperfect, intermediate ' state. With the resurrection, the kingdom commences in its complete form, and to this the passage before us points.

While, then, the heathen are represented as being received into the kingdom, the Jews appear as excluded from it. (Ἔξω points to an ἔσω, since the kingdom is conceived as a limited region of existence into which nothing extraneous can make its way. On this point, see Matth. xxv. 10. Light is viewed as the element of the kingdom, to which darkness forms the contrast. In the epithet ἐξώτερον, without, the idea of distance from the element of life and joy is expressed. (Wisdom of Solomon xvii. 21 ; xviii. 1.) The weeping and gnashing of teeth in the kingdom of darkness, is parallel with the happy enjoyment of the feast in the kingdom of God, and its expression of the most exquisite sense of pain, arising from a consciousness of having missed the end of life, is the eternal truth. Moreover, as the kingdom is here in itself not strictly identical with eternal happiness, so neither is the " weeping and gnashing of teeth" identical with eternal punishment ; but as the nearer and lesser events frequently symbolize remoter and higher ones of kindred character, so here these two contrasted states may justly be considered as pointing forward to the final judgment. We can only regard the state of suffering in Sheol (a fuller discussion of which is found in note on Luke xvi. 24), which the Scripture distinguishes from Gehenna, as the immediate reference in the "weeping and gnashing of teeth." That every possibility of return is not here to be denied to the rejected Israelites, is indicated, above all, by Rom. xi. 26, where the promise of salvation is given to all Israel.

Ver. 13.—In conclusion, both historians then relate that the Saviour, overcome by the bold faith of the warrior, immediately healed the sick man. (Ἑκατοντάρχης is another form for ἑκατόνταρχος, the one used in ver. 1. Ὑγιαίνω, Luke vii. 10, means "to be well ;" so that, according to his narrative also, the cure appears to have been wrought suddenly.)

§ 6. RAISING OF THE YOUNG MAN AT NAIN.

(Luke vii. 11–17.)

This transaction, which Luke alone mentions, is distinctly connected with the foregoing context by the words ἐν τῇ ἑξῆς, on the next day, ver. 11 ; we, therefore, proceed here with this paragraph, and the more so, because verses 16, 17, where we read of the fame of Jesus beginning to extend, assign it plainly to the earlier period.

As to the general fact of a raising from the dead, it is difficult
of apprehension, on account of the uncertainty of the fact of death,
and of its nature. For the separation of the soul from the body is
not to be viewed as absolute, even where corruption is evidently
going forward, because then the resurrection of the body (as described 1 Cor. xv.) would be impossible, and, at most, it could only
be called a new creation. But if there remains, even in death, a
bond between the higher vital principle and the elements of the
body to be raised, and if medical men confess, that, even on grounds
of ordinary experience, the determining of the actual occurrence of
death is, in the highest degree, difficult, then no other assurance
againt the supposition of a trance in this and the other cases of raising from the dead recorded in the New Testament is *possible*, than
that which is afforded by the word of Christ and the apostles.
Where death is really in appearance only, as in the case of the
daughter of Jairus (Matth. ix. 24), the mouth of truth expressly
declared it, though she was thought by all to be dead ; but, where
death is actually present, it declares the fact with equal plainness.
What the short-sighted eye of man can perceive but imperfectly,
the Lord of the world of spirits saw with indubitable certainty. The
reality of his miraculous raisings from the dead rests upon his
personal veracity. But, at the same time, the view of death just
given renders it easier to picture to ourselves the awakening.
For, as at the resurrection it will take place in all through the
Saviour's life-giving power ; so, in the individual awakenings, he
revived activity in the organ that was dead, but not destroyed ; so
that the soul ($\psi v \chi \acute{\eta}$) which had escaped might again make use of it.
Hence every raising from the dead is, so to speak, a full restoration
of the entire relation between soul and body, which had been interrupted ; while, in partial restorations, it is the removal of only the
disturbance in this or that function, with which the organism of
soul and body was affected. But the same heavenly power, which
is the life itself (John i. 4), effects the latter as well as the former.
As the source of all individualized life, it can just as well recal to
its organ that which had departed, and restore to harmony what
was disordered, as create what did not exist. On questions such as
these—where the departed soul of the person raised up dwelt in the
meantime, and whether, in the meanwhile, it had consciousness or
not—the Scriptures, for wise reasons, give no information ; and it is
sufficient for us to know, that, in this respect, as in general, the
state of the dying influences their future condition. But it is all
the more important to conceive of the raising up of the dead as not
unconnected with what is moral. The corporeal resurrection was to
be a means of spiritual vivification, not merely for the relatives and
for all who saw or heard of the event, but particularly for the person

who was himself raised up.* So extraordinary an event could not but affect his inward life decisively, and render the man so raised up a living witness to our Lord's miraculous power.†

Ver. 11, 12.—The town where Jesus restored the son to his afflicted mother, was called Nain (perhaps from נָעִים, pleasant), a small town of Galilee not far from Capernaum. (On ἱκανός and πολύς, see Matth. viii. 30, compared with Luke viii. 32.) As he approached the town gate (πύλη), the Saviour saw a dead person carried out; it was the only son of a widow. (Μονογενής, as in Luke viii. 42 ; ix. 38 ; Heb. xi. 17, in the sense of "only." But in the idea of "only," as in the Hebrew יָחִיד, there is included also that of "dear," "valued.")

Ver. 13, 14.—Sympathy for the mother (on σπλαγχνίζεσθαι, see note on Luke i. 78) is specified as that which determined Jesus to waken him who reposed in the coffin. But that does not exclude a regard for the man himself in the transaction. Man, as a conscious being, can never be merely a means, as would be the case here, if the mother's joy were the sole purpose of the raising of the young man. It is rather the immediate result of the action, noticeable by the bystanders, but the less essential one ; its concealed result was the spiritual awakening of the youth to a higher existence, by means of which even the mother's joy first became true and lasting. (By σορός is not meant a closed receptacle, but an open bier. The Hebrews called it מִטָּה, lectulus.)

Ver. 15, 16.—The Saviour raised the dead man, without contact, by his mere word (compare Elisha's raising the dead, 2 Kings iv. 34), which should be viewed as the audible expression of the invisible agency of his Spirit, by which the soul and body (ψυχή and σῶμα) were restored to their true relation in the young man. In the neighbourhood, the bodily raising produced a salutary spiritual excitement, and that, in the first instance, as was natural, under the form of fear of God (φόβος τοῦ Θεοῦ). Penetrated by the holiness of Christ's work, they rightly conclude that such holiness, united to such power, indicated a definite mission of Christ from a higher world. They view the miracle, entirely in accordance with its purpose, as an evidence of his prophetic dignity. (The expression: προφήτης μέγας, a great prophet, refers to the greatness of the mira-

---

* Strauss thinks a reference to the persons raised up improbable (B. ii. S. 147, second ed.), because it is not anywhere specially noticed. But this reference did not need to be particularly mentioned, because it was a matter of course. Jesus always wrought for the salvation of men, in every word, and in his most casual intercourse with them ; how much more, then, in an awakening from the dead !

† According to John xi. 41, 42, Lazarus was raised for the glory of God; but that does not exclude a view to his own perfecting by his death and resurrection : it includes it; for a vivification of the whole man is precisely the highest glory of God.

cle ; raising from the dead was peculiar to the chiefs of the prophetic order. On ἐπισκέπτεσθαι, see Luke i. 68.)

Ver. 17.—By individual flashes of his divine power like this,
darting hither and thither, the Saviour aroused in the whole nation
the consciousness that great things were before them. From the
ardent anticipation connected with that consciousness, there arose a
deep sense of misery and present need, and a confident courage for
the future—spiritual elements which our Saviour understood how to
guide and to employ for his holy purposes.

§ 7. HEALING OF PETER'S MOTHER-IN-LAW.

(Matth. viii. 14–17; Mark i. 29–34; Luke iv. 31–41.)

After having narrated (Luke iv. 31–37) the history of the cure
of a demoniac in the synagogue at Capernaum, which, as it contains
nothing peculiar, we passed over, referring the reader to Matth. viii.
28, ff., Luke immediately subjoins the healing of Peter's mother-inlaw with the words : ἀναστὰς ἐκ τῆς συναγωγῆς. Mark also (i. 29)
introduces this narrative with the same words, while Matthew connects it loosely with the account of the cure of the centurion's servant. It is surprising that Luke here mentions Simon Peter as a
well-known person, without having previously named him ; this fact
might be accounted for on the ground of Luke's being entitled to
suppose Peter known to Theophilus. Still it can hardly be denied,
that this circumstance also strongly favours the view, that Luke incorporated memoirs into his Gospel ; and as Peter was mentioned
in them, Luke also named him, without noticing that no allusion
had been yet made to his connexion with Jesus. Matthew and
Mark had already prefixed a short mention of Peter, Matth. iv. 18,
ff. ; Mark i. 16, ff. The fact itself contains nothing particular ; the
general observations on the cures wrought by Jesus are applicable
to this case also. (See note on Matth. viii. 1.)

Ver. 14, 15.—The mention of Peter's mother-in-law (πενθερά),
implies that that apostle was married. According to 1 Cor. ix. 5,
Peter did not forsake his wife in the exercise of his apostolical calling, but had her to accompany him in his missionary journeys. (To
attempt to explain the form of the disease from Luke's expression :
πυρετῷ μεγάλῳ συνέχεσθαι, cannot but be unsatisfactory.) In this
case, our Lord again wrought by immediate contact (ἥψατο τῆς χειρός),
and restored her so perfectly that she was at once able to employ
herself. The διακονεῖν αὐτοῖς, ministering to them, must be viewed
only as the result of the cure ; its proper intention we must in this
case also regard as a moral one.

Ver. 16.—The news of the miraculous cures wrought by Jesus, attracted multitudes to him, supplicating help. They came after sunset, because the heat of day would have been oppressive to the sick. The Saviour, surrounded by crowds of such unfortunate individuals, who were bowed down by bodily pains, presents, in the healing agency by which he relieves external necessities, an emblem of the spiritual agency which he incessantly exercises within the hearts of men by the power of his salvation. Only we must suppose, that, even in the corporeal deliverance which he granted, he would constantly lead their minds beyond the crowd of earthly wants, to the malady of the soul and its cure. On the δαιμονιζόμενοι, *demoniacs*, as well as on his forbidding the demons to speak of him (Mark i. 34 ; Luke iv. 41), see more fully in note on Matth. viii. 28, ff.

Ver. 17.—Matthew, who, as writing for Jews, takes pains to connect the phenomena in the life of Jesus with the Old Testament delineations of the Messiah, here quotes Isa. liii. 4, with the formula so familiar to him, ὅπως πληρωθῇ. (See note on Matth. i. 22.) The Evangelist, moreover, again departs from the text of the LXX., who thus translate the Hebrew text : οὗτος τὰς ἁμαρτίας ἡμῶν φέρει, καὶ περὶ ἡμῶν ὀδυνᾶται, in which form the words were altogether unsuitable for his purpose. He follows the original precisely, and translates חֳלִי by ἀσθένεια, and מַכְאוֹב by νόσος ; the verbs נָשָׂא and סָבַל, used by the prophet, Matthew renders by λαμβάνειν and βαστάζειν. This independent treatment of the quotations from the Old Testament forbids us to regard the Greek text of Matthew in the light of an ordinary translation—*i. e.*, one in which the translator does not allow himself any free action. But the bringing forward of just this passage does not seem agreeable to the purpose designed by the context, particularly as in 1 Peter ii. 24, the same passage is explained of the vicarious satisfaction of our Saviour, and the whole 53d chapter of Isaiah is a description of the Messiah as suffering for sinful mankind. But the apparent difference in the explanation of the same passage by two writers in the New Testament disappears, if we keep in view, that physical sufferings (as the acmé of which we are to regard death, see Rom. vi. 23) are only the other aspect of the consequences of sin. The Saviour, who was called to restore the original state of mankind, removed external suffering no less than internal ; and, indeed, ordinarily, the former first, because deliverance from it is wont to be a means of arousing a desire for deliverance from the miseries of the soul, and quickening the faith in the possibility of that deliverance. The referring of Christ's saving efficacy to bodily sufferings no more excludes the extending of it to spiritual sufferings, than, on the other hand, the referring of it to spiritual sufferings excludes its extension to such as are bodily. The *whole* man is the object of salvation, body as well as soul. The only point of difficulty is, that λαμβάνειν, *taking*, and βαστάζειν, *bearing*, are used of Christ's relation to the infirmities and diseases, as well as of his relation to the inward sufferings of humanity. (See John i. 29, where our Lord is called, ἀμνὸς τοῦ Θεοῦ ὁ αἴρων τὴν ἁμαρτίαν τοῦ κόσμου, *the lamb of God that taketh away, etc.*) It would seem that the exercise of healing energy was by no means any thing so difficult and productive of suffering, as that βαστάζειν, *bear*, would be an appropriate term to apply to it. Hence we are tempted to interpret λαμβάνειν, *take*, and βαστάζειν, *bear*, as simply = ἀφαιρεῖν, *take away*, which, however, is not at all in accordance with the context of the passage Isa. liii., where the Saviour appears in the character of a sufferer. This difficulty is solved, however, if we conceive the healing energy of the Saviour more in its essential character. Viewing the Saviour, as we must, as truly human, as well as truly divine, we cannot but think, that the healing energy of our Lord consisted in a pouring and breathing forth of his vital fulness —that, moreover, his whole soul entered, with heartfelt sympathy, into the necessities of the sufferers—that he really suffered with them. As, therefore, physical exertion produced physical weariness (John iv. 6), so also spiritual exertion would exhaust him spiritually. Hence we may say, that in respect to infirmities and diseases also, Jesus laboured in his soul, and bore the sin of the world.

§ 8. PETER'S DRAUGHT OF FISHES.

(Luke iv. 42–44; [Mark i. 35–39;] Luke v. 1–11.)

The idea just suggested receives confirmation from the succeeding verses in Luke and Mark. For early next morning the Saviour retired into solitude (εἰς ἔρημον τόπον) for prayer. Mark uses ἔννυχον λίαν instead of the more usual expression ἡμέρας γενομένης in Luke. Ἔννυχον, for which some Codd. read ἔννυχα, occurs only in this passage. We are frequently told that Jesus spent the night in silent prayer. (See Luke v. 16; vi. 12; ix. 28.) We must believe that this retirement for solitary prayer proceeded from a real necessity, unless our Lord is believed to have done something unmeaning, or merely apparent—which would favour Docetic notions. According to the Scriptures, Jesus was in all things (κατὰ πάντα) like men, excepting sin, that he might be merciful (ἐλεήμων, Heb. ii. 17). And it is in just this view of our Lord that rich consolation is afforded, and the possibility is provided of taking Christ for our example. Regarded in his character as man, the prayers of Jesus (which must, indeed, be conceived as uninterrupted, agreeably to his own com-

mand to us [Luke xviii. 1], but still as having their points of elevation in peculiarly consecrated moments) were, so to speak, seasons
of heavenly refreshment and strengthening from above, in order to
overcome the power of darkness that incessantly assailed him. But,
at the same time, these moments of prayer are to be viewed as seasons when the Saviour was absorbed in the contemplation of the
high purposes of the Father with him, and in the depths of divine
love, in order to consecrate himself more and more to the completion of his work.

Ver. 43.—The people, however, touched with the impression
which the demeanour of Jesus produced, hastened after him into the
wilderness ; and Peter, always the most active among the apostles,
goes to Jesus to inform him that the multitude was seeking for him.
But our Lord withdraws, with the observation, that he must extend
his ministry over the whole of Israel. The ministry of the Saviour,
according to its entire plan, was not intended to be exercised continually in the same place, but to arouse from its death slumber the
mass of the nation. Hence he never stayed long in a place, but
journeyed hither and thither. Meantime he limited his more special
oversight of souls to the narrower and wider circles of his disciples,
who so yielded themselves to his sanctifying influence, that they
forsook all—came out from their previous connexions, and followed
him. (Mark [i. 38] uses the expression ἐχόμεναι κωμοπόλεις, which
occurs only in this passage. By κωμοπόλεις, he means villages
of some size, approaching towns in extent. The participle ἐχό-
μενος is to be taken as in ἡμέρα ἐχομένη [Luke xiii. 33 ; Acts xiii.
44], in the sense of "near," "neighbouring." The words in Mark :
εἰς τοῦτο ἐξελήλυθα, for this have I come forth, which corresponds to
Luke's expression : εἰς τοῦτο ἀπέσταλμαι, for this am I sent, are also
remarkable. It is true, there is the various reading in Mark, ἐλή-
λυθα, which, as being the more common phrase [ἔρχεσθαι sc. εἰς τὸν κόσ-
μον], must be regarded as inferior in value to the less common. Ἐξέρχεσθαι, come forth, refers to the formula used by John : ἐξέρχεσθαι ἐκ
τοῦ Θεοῦ, ἐκ τοῦ πατρός, come forth from God, from the Father, with
which ἐκ τῶν οὐρανῶν would be synonymous. [See John viii. 42 ;
xiii. 3 ; xvi. 27, 28 ; xvii. 8.] In ἐξελήλυθα, have come forth, a distinct reference is implied to the original relation of the Son to the
Father ; while ἀπέσταλμαι, have been sent, refers only to the appearance of Jesus as determined by God.)

Luke v. 1.—With an indefinite transition, the narrative of
Peter's draught of fishes is appended ; for the multitude, whose inconvenient proximity is here spoken of (ἐπικεῖσθαι, to crowd, to press
upon, a sign of eagerness indeed, but still an annoyance to Jesus), is
not the same as that mentioned in ver. 42, because the clause interposed, he was preaching in the synagogues, etc. (ἦν κηρύσσων ἐν ταῖς

συναγωγαῖς τῆς Γαλιλαίας), resumes the indefinite character. It is, therefore, uncertain whether this narrative should be connected immediately with the preceding.

With respect to the narrative itself of Peter's draught of fishes, it has been already remarked, in the note on Matth iv. 18, that in the mere outline there given of the calling of Peter (on which event John alone sheds adequate light), the mention of the circumstance, that Peter was called to become a fisher of men, was introduced into the picture merely as an individual feature, without our being able to maintain that this expression of our Lord's was uttered immediately at his first meeting with Peter. Luke details here more circumstantially the occurrence, in connection with which our Lord designated Peter a fisher of men; but he takes for granted that Jesus had, on a former occasion, become acquainted with Peter, and only shews how, on this occasion, the exalted greatness of Jesus opened upon him with unsuspected splendour, and thus powerfully attached him to his person. (The Lake of Gennesaret, on the shore of which Christ here appears as teaching, derives its name from the district Γεννησάρ. Josephus says [B. J. iii. 10, 7] : Ἡ δὲ λίμνη Γεννησὰρ ἀπὸ τῆς προσεχοῦς χώρας καλεῖται. The lake is also called θάλασσα τῆς Γαλιλαίας, Matth. iv. 18. In the Old Testament it is called יָם כִּנֶּרֶת, Sea of Chinnereth, Josh. xiii. 27. The Chaldee spelling of the name has the various forms, גְּנֵסַר, גִּינְסַר, גְּנוֹסָר [See Winer's "Realwörterbuch," s. v.] The extent of the lake is given by Josephus (ut sup.) as 120 stadia in length, and 40 in breadth.

Ver. 2, 3.—The pressure of the people caused Jesus to leave the land and enter one of the boats. This was drawn up on land, as was usually the case with small vessels ; Jesus desired Peter, to whom the boat belonged, to push it off from the land into deep water (ἀπὸ τῆς γῆς ἐπαναγαγεῖν), and then taught from the ship, unmolested by the crowding of the multitude. This setting of the boat afloat is to be distinguished from the bringing it out into the midst of the sea (ἐπαναγαγεῖν εἰς τὸ βάθος = altum., ver. 4), which was done for the purpose of fishing.

Ver. 4, 5.—After his discourse was finished, and the people, consequently, dismissed, our Lord orders Peter to cast out the net for a draught. (Χαλάζω, properly " to slacken," " let go"—e. g., a bow, then " to sink," " let down.") Peter, disheartened by a whole night's unsuccessful toil—a circumstance which shews, that at that time the Apostles still pursued their business, at times at least—complies, more out of deference to the dignity of Jesus, than from faith in a successful result. (Luke alone uses Ἐπιστάτης, Master. See viii. 24, 45 ; ix. 33, 49 ; xvii. 13. He calls Jesus by that name instead of the Hebrew " Rabbi," which he could not assume, as being known to his Greek readers. But he uses διδάσκαλος, *teacher*, for it also—*e. g.*, vii. 40.)

Ver. 6, 7.—Peter complies with the Saviour's desire, and they enclose a multitude of fishes in their net, so that it broke, and their companions were obliged to bring the other boat along-side, in order to take in the abundance bestowed. (Bυθίζεσθαι occurs only in this passage with the signification of "sinking deeper," "sinking." The word is used figuratively in 1 Tim. vi. 9.)

According to the conception of the historian, the abundant produce of this draught, which forms a contrast with the unsuccessful fishing through the night, when Peter toiled alone, are to be viewed as the *result* of Christ's presence, and the *effect* of his power. Christ is, therefore, here set forth as the Sovereign of nature, who, by the secret magic of his will, had power to direct even what is unconscious, according to his purposes ; just as the same power of the unsearchable God, who governs the universe, year by year conducts the fish of the sea and the birds of the air in their migrations by invisible clues. Phenomena, analogous to the great miracles of nature, appear clustered around our Lord, as around their centre ; he rules as a visible, personally present God, in the wide realm of existence ; by invisible, mysterious ties, all is connected with the word of his mouth—the expression of his holy will. And what are apparently unconscious movements and impulses of nature, appear, when controlled by his will, directed to the highest moral ends.

Ver. 8, 9.—The sense of a special divine agency, which proclaimed itself to them as emanating from Jesus, overwhelmed them all with astonishment (θάμβος) and fear ; but in the excitable Peter, expressed itself at once in act and word. His sinfulness appeared to him in such glaring contrast to the heavenly power displayed before him in the Saviour, that he fell down, partly adoring and partly praying : Depart from me (ἔξελθε ἀπ᾽ ἐμοῦ). In all this is evidently involved the idea that what is divine, and what is not so, are incompatible with each other. He who beholds God must die (Judges vi. 23 ; xiii. 22 ; Dan. x. 17)—an idea which is perfectly true of the revelation of the divine character in the law—on whose level Peter still stood—made in the thunders of Sinai, Exod. xix. 12. But in God's gracious revelation in the Saviour, his nearness to sinful man is not only endurable, but even animating and refreshing ; since, not on a sudden, but gradually, it makes old things pass away, and creates things that are new. For this reason also our Lord quiets his anxiety, and calls upon him to be a fellow-worker for the kingdom which he had come to establish.

Ver. 10.—The words "henceforth thou shalt catch men" (ἀπὸ τοῦ νῦν ἔσῃ ζωγρῶν ἀνθρώπους), express the main point in the whole transaction, to which not only the draught of fishes, but also the strengthening of the Apostles in the faith, were subordinate. We observe here, for the first time, a characteristic of Christ's actions, which we shall have frequent occasion to notice in future. The Saviour *teaches by actions*—he speaks by deeds to those around ; penetrating with deep spiritual glance into the essence of things, he is enabled to deal with the formations of nature in such a manner as to use them as a rich system of symbols or hieroglyphics.* Something analogous may be observed even in the conduct of noble and exalted personages on earth. The ideas which inspire them are shadowed forth in their doings ; and under their influence the most insignificant relations become ennobled. A system of symbolical actions of this kind is expressly seen in the ministry of the ancient prophets. (See Jerem. xiii. 1, ff. ; Ezek. xii. 1, ff. ; xxiv. 1, ff.) Of all the actions of Jesus, none presents this characteristic so undeniably as the cursing of the fig-tree (Matth. xxi. 18, ff.), which without such a theory, involves inexplicable difficulties. The advantages of a language of fact like this, are self-evident ; where fancy and feeling predominate, as is always the case wherever the mind has not risen above that state which is marked by the absence of reflection, a lively, concrete fact always produces infinitely more effect than an abstract argument. In reference to the question as to the import of this transaction, we are met by the circumstance, that an occurrence similar to this, which introduces the more immediate connexion of Peter with the Saviour, concludes it also. (John xxi.) A symbolical intimation of the subsequent spiritual ministry of Peter, who is regarded as the representative of the apostolical body, meets us at the beginning and the close of Peter's connexion with his Lord on earth. In the expression : Thou shalt catch men (ἔσῃ ζωγρῶν ἀνθρώπους)—instead of which we find in Matth. iv. 19, and Mark i. 17, I will make you fishers of men (ποιήσω ὑμᾶς ἁλιεῖς ἀνθρώπων)— that they have to gain over others to themselves, is not the only point of comparison with the spiritual work of the Apostles ; other and more minute relations evidently present themselves. In the first place the idea of catching includes the relation of the con-

---

* Augustine observes appropriately on this point: *Interrogemus ipsa miracula, quid nobis loquantur de Christo; habent enim, si intelligantur, linguam suam. Nam quia ipse Christus verbum est, etiam factum verbi verbum nobis est*—i. e., " Let us ask the miracles for their testimony concerning Christ; for they have, when understood, a language of their own. For because Christ himself is the Word, also the deed of the Word is a word to us." (Tract xxiv. in Joann. Opp., vol. iii., p. 349, edit. Bened.) With these words a beautiful passage from *Hamann's* works (pt. i., p. 50) may be compared, who, instructed by that Spirit, who always teaches the same truth in all places and at all times, writes quite independently of that Father, as follows :—" Every Bible narrative bears the image of man—a body, which is ashes and worthless—that is the outward letter; but besides that a soul—the breath of God, the life and the light, which shines in the dark, and cannot be comprehended by the darkness."

scious agent to an unconscious subject, and the latter's being overcome by the former. This is precisely the relation that subsisted
between the Apostles—as the representatives of the βασιλεία, kingdom—and the world. While the former represent the higher principle of life, those who are in the world are in a state of ignorance
as to the nature of the higher life. Next, the figure of catching
fish refers to the transference of the convert from the old element
of life, to the pure, holy element of the Gospel, on which import of
the figure the hymn, ascribed to Clement of Alexandria, dwells in
the following strain :—

Σῶτερ Ἰησοῦ	Saviour Jesus !
Ἀλιεῦ μερόπων	Fisher of men,
Τῶν σωζομένων	Even the saved !
Πελάγους κακίας	From the ocean of sin
Ἰχθῦς ἁγνοὺς	Enticing the holy fish,
Κύματος ἐχθροῦ	From the hostile wave
Γλυκερῇ ζωῇ δελεάζων	By thy sweet life.

Allusions to this transition from the old element of life into the
new one of Christianity, are often found in the early ages of Christianity in the use of the name Ἰχθὺς, fishes, of Christians. (See
Suiceri thes. eccl., s. v., ἁλιεύς.) Even in the Old Testament there
exist the elements of this comparison. See Jerem. xvi. 16, where
the first hemistich runs thus in the LXX. : Ἰδοὺ, ἐγὼ ἀποστέλλω
τοὺς ἁ λ ι ε ῖ ς τοὺς πολλοὺς, λέγει κύριος, καὶ ἁλιεύσουσιν αὐτούς. Parallel with this the second hemistich has—Ἀποστέλλω τοὺς πολλοὺς
θ η ρ ε υ τ ὰ ς καὶ θηρεύσουσιν αὐτούς.

Ver. 11.—This miraculous event drew the bond between the disciples and the Saviour more closely ; they left their worldly employment, and, following Christ, espoused that spiritual calling
which he pointed out to them in its analogy with their former external one. The leaving and following (ἀφιέναι and ἀκολουθεῖν) are
not, however, to be viewed as an outward act merely, but pre-
eminently as an inward transaction, of which the external was but
a visible expression. The power of the higher life in Christ which
seized them, liberated them spiritually from earthly fetters, and
joined them to their Lord by invisible bonds. Externally they did,
even at a later period, return to their craft. (See note on John
xxi. 3, ff.)

§ 9. JESUS STILLS THE SEA.

(Matth. viii. 18–27 ; Mark iv. 35–41 ; Luke viii. 22–25.)

Matthew apparently connects the following event with the healing of Peter's mother-in-law yet really with a situation (viii. 18) which cannot have immediately succeeded that event. Mark connects it directly with the parables of the sower, lamp, and corn-field ; in Luke it is, attached to the preceding context merely by the loose expression, ἐν μιᾷ τῶν ἡμερῶν, *on one of the days.* The first verses of this section in Matthew (viii. 19–22) are, moreover, parallel with a passage in Luke (ix. 57, ff.), separated from the first passage (viii. 22, ff.) by a wide interval. Further, the words Matth. viii. 19–22, are rather an introduction, than an integral part of the narrative. Luke introduces them at a later period (ix. 57, ff.) in a more precise connexion, and in a more complete form. For the in-terpretation of them we refer, therefore, to that passage. Matthew seems to have inserted them here in the section which treats of the miracles of Jesus, to bring out the contrast with the all-command-ing will of Jesus ; and to make apparent, that the greatness of the requirement to follow him who had not where to lay his head, is, on the other hand, modified by the fact that he governs the elements. With respect to the fact itself, it exhibits Christ as the Lord of nature in a new aspect, and as calming and pacifying its throes and convulsions. Sin, which, in its fearful effects, disturbed even the physical portion of existence, is thus represented as overcome by the Prince of Peace in the most various forms of its manifestation. (Isa. ix. 6.) In so far as what is external is always a mirror of what is internal, this, and similar events in the evangelical history, express the analogous power of the Saviour over the agitations of the in-ward life. (See note on Matth. xiv. 21, 22.) The Saviour in a ship, accompanied by his disciples, tossed on the waves of the sea, is a natural antitype to the ark containing the representatives of the in-cipient human race, and a prefiguration of the church in its relation to the sea of evil (πέλαγος κακίας) in the world.

Ver. 23, 24.—Our Lord, intending to pass over to the eastern shore of the lake (ver. 18), entered the ship, and fell asleep. Mark, with his usual care, finishes the picture more minutely. On the one hand he observes, that in company with that one ship other smaller ones crossed (iv. 36), and on the other, he describes precisely the Saviour's position. (He was lying in the hinder part of the vessel [πρύμνα, Acts xxvii. 29, 41], resting his head. Προσκεφάλαιον is probably a support to lean against ; in other cases, generally a "pillow.") While Jesus slept, a sudden hurricane arose. (Instead

of λαῖλαψ, which Mark and Luke use, Matthew has σεισμός, which
denotes properly "earthquakes," then "violent agitations" in general.* The LXX. use it for רַעַשׁ).

Ver. 25, 26.—Though of *little* faith, because they feared being
swallowed up together with the sleeping Saviour (on ὀλιγόπιστος, see
note on Matth. vi. 30), yet the disciples are *believing*, since they ask
deliverance from the Lord ; and the Saviour, not putting their
faith to shame, produced a perfect calm. (Γαλήνη = שְׁתִיקָה, Psalm
cvii. 29, in Symmachus.) It is remarkable, that Jesus' word appears not merely as checking the lawless course of the elements, and
reducing the scattered powers to oneness and harmony, but that,
according to Mark, he quiets the waves of the sea by a direct address
to it : σιώπα, πεφίμωσο. There is undoubtedly more implied in this
than a mere oratorical personification. It indicates a view of nature,
as of something living, which is affected by divine, as well as by
hostile, influences. Our Lord, by viewing the commotions of nature
as the echo of the general interruption of harmony, refers them to
their original source. (On ἐπιτιμᾶν, expressing a command of divine
power, see note on Matth. viii. 29.—Φιμόω, *to close the mouth*, 1 Tim.
v. 18 ; φιμοῦσθαι, *to be dumb, silent*, κοπάζω = ἡσυχάζω, used of the
wind, Matth. xiv. 32 ; Mark vi. 51.)

Ver. 27.—The more colossal and externally striking the effects
of the Saviour's power are, the more they impress the natural man.
In themselves the hidden spiritual effects are infinitely mightier and
more exalted ; they strike at the root of sin, while the former touch
only its remote and secondary effects.

§ 10. Cure of the Gadarene Demoniac.

(Matth. viii. 28–34; Mark v. 1–20; Luke viii. 26–39.)

We avail ourselves of this most important and difficult of the
miraculous cures—the first, according to Matthew's arrangement,
among the narratives of the treatment of what are called δαιμονιζόμενοι, *demoniacs*—to develop in a connected way, agreeably to the intimations contained in the Scriptures, the view which we entertain
on the condition of such persons, and on the several phenomena
which the Scriptures mention in connexion with them. The entire
Scriptures are undeniably pervaded by the idea,† that what is holy

* Properly, *shaking, violent agitation*, then specially, *earthquake*.—[K.

† The vigorous opposition offered to the doctrine of the existence of the devil and bad
angels, may, in part, arise from pure motives—viz., the desire to prevent the great abuses
which have been made of the doctrine; but, in part, are prompted by those of a totally
different kind—viz., a laxity of morals, and an unwillingness to acknowledge to themselves,
in all its deformity, the nature of that evil which men detect plainly enough in them-

and what is unholy in mankind, has not its root in themselves, but in a higher region of existence, whence arise those influences of good and evil, which may be receeived or rejected on the part of men, according to the position and the faithfulness of the individual. With a comprehensive glance, the doctrine of Scripture conceives the good as well as the evil in the universe as a connected whole—only with this difference, that the good, being the divine itself, always appears likewise as the *absolute;* the unholy, on the contrary, is indeed represented as a real interruption of harmony, but still only as something dependent on the will of the creature. The Scriptures know of no second principle, and the church has invariably condemned the doctrine of Manicheism as incompatible with the idea of God. By removing the source of evil out of human nature, *redemption* is recognized as possible. For it is only the germ of good in man, viewed in its state of bondage under a hostile power, that can be

selves. They ought to separate the abuses from the thing itself, and then it would be seen how, in this information respecting the relations of the world of spirits also, the Scriptures are perfectly adapted to the wants of men. Many a soul despairs in the conflict with evil thoughts, or yields itself up to them, which might be well able to overcome them, were it taught to distinguish itself from the Evil One, and to ascribe the fiery darts by which it is assailed, to the wicked being who directs them against it. (Ephes. v. 16.) If we carefully banish the devil and his angels, we retain a world full of devilish men, and for ourselves a heart full of devilish thoughts, as Göthe appositely remarks: "They got rid of the wicked *one*, but the wicked *ones* remain;" for evil itself, with its frightful manifestations, cannot possibly be removed; it stands engraved in history with indelible lines. Hence the doctrine, that the source of evil is in a higher region of life, is a blessing to mankind; it contains the key to the doctrine of redemption. On this account also, it is so deeply based in the teaching of Scripture, that it will never be possible to overthrow it in the church, except, indeed, the church should ever so far forget itself as to admit accommodation to evident errors into the idea of its Saviour, which would be equivalent to self-destruction. But, as truth in general will remain unconquered, so will also the truth respecting evil, which consists precisely in our knowing *that* it exists, and *how* it exists. For it is the real victory of evil not to be known. But with regard to the *use* to be made of the doctrine, great care is certainly commendable in this respect, as all deeply impressive ideas, like edge tools, must be applied prudently. The use made of the doctrine in Scripture supplies most excellent hints on this subject. *First*, we find that, in the earlier periods of the Old Testament, the doctrine appears only in obscure intimations; it is not till the times of the captivity, when the worship of the true God was firmly established among the people, that the germs were further unfolded. In this fact, we have a plain hint not to propound the doctrine either before children, or before minds so immature that they may be regarded as childish; before such, it is better, after the example of the Old Testament, to refer the manifestations of evil to the permission of God, without entering more minutely on the subject. The Saviour *teaches* concerning the devil only in the presence of his disciples. *Next*, the doctrine of the kingdom of darkness and its agency ought never to be brought forward in any other way than in connexion with the doctrine of redemption. The consciousness of grace which overcomes all, is the surest means to prevent all misconception of the doctrine. *Lastly*, the doctrine, in general, is not so much included among the subjects of the formal κήρυγμα τῆς ἀληθείας, just as it does not appear so in the New Testament, and in the Confessions of Faith; it is more particularly important in the private cure of souls. In the manifold enigmas of self-examination, we shall find that this doctrine has not only a deep psychological root, but that a beneficial effect may be expected from its being wisely employed.

redeemed ; but the hostile power, as well as man himself, if he has consciously resigned himself to it altogether, and is, therefore, absorbed in it, is not an object of redeeming power. The kingdom of evil, then, regarded in its individuality, and conceived as the opposite (though only relatively) of the kingdom of good, is called in the Scriptures, the devil and his angels (διάβολος καὶ ἄγγελοι αὐτοῦ) (Matth. xxv. 41 ; Rev. xii. 9) ; also, the kingdom of Satan (βασιλεία τοῦ σατανᾶ) (Matth. xii. 26.) The terms, devil (διάβολος) and Satan (σατανᾶς) (= שָׂטָן = κατήγωρ τῶν ἀδελφῶν, accuser of the brethren, Rev. xii. 10), are used only in the singular for the central power of evil, who is conceived as carrying in himself potentially the power of his kingdom. In one passage (Matth. xii. 26), it is true, Satan seems to be used as equivalent to δαιμόνιον ; but even there, it is only in appearance. The subordinate spirits, corresponding to the angels of God, are called δαιμόνια, demons, less frequently, δαίμονες, (Matth. viii. 31 ; Mark v. 12 ; Luke viii. 29) ; frequently unclean spirits (πνεύματα ἀκάθαρτα) ; and (in Ephes. vi. 12), πνευματικὰ τῆς πονηρίας, spiritual (essences of) wickedness. The signification of the word δαίμων = δαήμων, is, among ancient writers, more comprehensive ; it denotes "one who is well informed, knows ;"* and because knowledge manifests itself as the essence of the spirit, it denotes spiritual existences in general. (The character of the knowledge is more accurately specified by adjuncts, as ἀγαθοδαίμων, κακοδαίμων). In the same way as good is viewed in its different modifications in the angels of light, evil is individualized in the angels of darkness in its modifications. (On the classes among the demons, see note on Ephes. vi. 12.) The germs of this mode of viewing the subject are found in the very earliest writings of the Old Testament, and we may imagine a development of these germs in the popular mind by continued enlightenment through the spirit of truth, without calling to our aid the foreign influence, which some have thought to have been exercised over the Jews during the Babylonish captivity.†

* More probably from δαίω, divide, allot.—[K.

† This view, which has become so current, is involved in considerable historical difficulties. For since those regions, to which Nebuchadnezzar removed the Jews, were under the dominion of the Chaldeans, by whose popular worship such an effect cannot be supposed to have been wrought upon the Jews, since they had no doctrine of evil spirits (Münter's conjecture in his " Religion der Babylonier," S. 87, ff., that there was some instruction on the subject of demons in the Chaldean esoteric doctrines, is mere hypothesis) ; the question arises—Whether the system of the Zendavesta, to the influence of which it is ascribed that the Jews became acquainted with the doctrine of demons during the captivity, ever was prevalent in the Chaldee kingdom? There were Magi in Babylon, it is true, even before the capture of that city by Cyrus (see Bertholdt's third Excursus to his commentary on Daniel) ; but whether these Magi were worshippers of Ormuzd, and acquainted with Ahriman, is very doubtful, because (see Gesenius' second appendix to his commentary on Isaiah) none of the Chaldee names of gods have the least similarity to the Persian. But if the religion of the Zendavesta had been esoteric only in the Chaldee em-

But then if we start from the magnificent conception of the unity of the kingdom of darkness, the question occurs—What peculiar form of the influence of the powers of darkness do the Scriptures denote by the name δαιμονιζόμενοι, *demoniacs?* For although they likewise connect moral evil in mankind with the influence of the devil (*e. g.*, John says of Judas Iscariot : Satan entered into him, chap. xiii. 27), yet the representatives of evil among mankind (false prophets and antichrists) are never called demoniacs. In the case of the latter, on the contrary, we always perceive appearances of sickness, generally convulsions of an epileptic nature, and a derangement or loss of personal consciousness. But still this state of sickness does not appear as the characteristic of demoniacs ; for it is evident that the same maladies may, in one case be of demoniacal origin, in another, not ; for instance one who is dumb in consequence of organic defect, perhaps an injury to the tongue, would never be called a demoniac, though we read in Luke xi. 14 of a demoniac who was dumb. Many demoniacs shew themselves to be maniacs (*e. g.*, the Gadarene, whose history we are discussing) ; but it does not, therefore, follow that every madman, even such as were disordered by organic injuries of the brain, was considered by the Jews a demoniac.[*] All the descriptions of demoniacs indicate a strange *mixture* of psychical and physical phenomena. In the *first* place, the condition of the demoniacs appears always to suppose a certain degree of moral delinquency ; yet so, that their sin manifests itself, not so much as wickedness, properly speaking, as predominant sensuality (probably lasciviousness in particular), which was indulged in opposition to their better self. Thus in such

pire, then, again, it is not easily conceivable how the poor Jewish exiles should have become acquainted with it, and that so far as to have received thence new doctrines into the circle of their ideas. The whole subject needs, as before observed, a more thorough historical investigation. [The Bible doctrine of fallen angels is the reverse of the dualistic doctrine of the Zendavesta.] But *that* idea is not less to be rejected, that the belief of the existence of evil spirits is a notion belonging to the infancy of mankind. The history of the development of demonology in the Scriptures, as well as the nature of the case, proves the contrary. The purer, the deeper, and the truer the conception of the divine, as the good, the more thoroughly does man know evil in its nature, and comprehend it in its development. The Scriptures represent the false prophets and false Christs as its most perfect forms, and place them at the end of the world's course. The fact that our most modern systematic theology, even since its restoration after its self-destruction, has been still so little able to adopt the doctrine of the kingdom of darkness (as is seen in *Schleiermacher's System*, for instance), proves, that the Christian consciousness has not allowed itself to be thoroughly penetrated with the light of Christian principle.

[*] *Josephus* (*Ant.* vii. 6, 3) pronounces the demons to be the souls of wicked men, and, on the same supposition, *Justin Martyr* explains the nature of the demoniacs. (Apol. I. c. 16, p. 14, edit. *Braun.*) This view must, however, be regarded merely as the private opinion of a few, and is not to be taken as the prevailing popular sentiment. *Josephus* (*Ant.* viii. 2, 3) narrates the cure of a demoniac. *Philostratus* (iv. 20, 25) records of Appollonius Tyaneus also that he exorcised evil spirits. Compare *Baur's* "Leben des Appollonius," S. 144.

persons, the noble, deep-seated germ of life might be preserved, and out of it the desire for deliverance might be developed, if the consciousness of the frightful condition of knowing themselves to be bound under the power of sin was awakened within them. *Next*, there appears, as a characteristic of demoniacs, a weakening of the bodily organization, particularly the nervous system, occasioned by the sin in which they indulged ; and from the very intimate connexion of the nervous life with all mental activity, the enfeebling of the former must very easily produce derangement in the whole internal life. This derangement appears the more striking in such unfortunate beings, the more excitable their conscience seems to have been ; testifying to them that their misery was the result of their own fault, without their being in a condition, by their own power, to extricate themselves from the fetters of sin and the kingdom of darkness, to the influence of which they had resigned themselves. On the other hand, one who, in his inmost soul, had resigned himself to sin, yet rather intellectual than sensual, might be a πονηρός, *wicked*, but not a δαιμονιζόμενος, *demoniac*. For in such persons there is still a certain unity of nature, which may in the end become despair (as in the case of Judas), but not madness, which presupposes a violent inward conflict between the better self and the power of darkness, by which it feels itself enthralled. It coincides with our view, *first*, that in all the descriptions of demoniacs we find mention made of physical sufferings. Convulsions, epilepsy, raving, and lunacy (according to Matth. xvii, 14, ff.), are particularly noticed—the kind of maladies which agree well with our hypothesis. The agreement appears to be less, where demoniacs are called dumb or deaf ; but even such forms of physical suffering may be easily brought to harmonize with our general view, if only, as just observed, we do not conceive of organic destruction of hearing and speech in the case of demoniacal deafness and dumbness, but rather nervous paralysis, ascribed by the troubled conscience of the sufferers to the influence of the kingdom of darkness, which they were conscious they had permitted to enter their souls. Hence the common opinion, which pronounces the demoniacs to be sick people, is partially true ; but only partially, as it confines itself to the outward effects, while the representation of Scripture regards the phenomena in their moral origin [as the influence of fallen angels on the nervous system.] *Next*, it is equally in accordance with our view, that a desire for deliverance, a hope of being cured, is expressed by all the demoniacs. And though this longing is, as it were, but a *spark* of hope and faith, which yet glows within ; still even this implies a susceptibility to the powers of the higher life which the Saviour presented to them. Accordingly, the demoniacs do not appear by any means as the most wicked, but only as very miserable men. The decidedly wicked man, who has admitted the hostile influence, undisturbed and unopposed, into the inmost recesses of his heart, cannot be healed. Faith—susceptibility to a higher principle of life—is wanting in the most secret depths of the soul. In the demoniacs, the contest against evil presents apparently a more hideous form ; but that there still remains a contest against it, speaks for the existence of a germ of noble life ; so that in the case even of the demoniacs, *faith* is the necessary condition of their being healed. But *again*, our view is in accordance with the circumstance, that, in the descriptions of the demoniacs, we often find a subjection of the nervous system, and with this, of the voluntary bodily functions, especially language, to the will of the demons. They speak their character, or rather the demon speaks through them, but always so that there reappears at moments the consciousness of their individuality. This state is quite parallel with the trance (ἔκστασις), or being in the spirit (ἐν πνεύματι εἶναι), and speaking with tongues (γλώσσαις λαλεῖν) ; that is, the effect produced in these latter states by the holy element of the spirit (πνεῦμα), or light (φῶς)—see 1 Cor. xiv., where the suppression of the consciousness (νοῦς) by the overpowering holy force manifestly appears—is, in the former case, produced by the unholy element of darkness (σκότος). We are not, therefore, by any means, to conceive of the state of the demoniac, as if two or more persons were contained in the individual ; but the suffering person appears with his own human consciousness suppressed, and a controlling foreign influence on his nervous life ; but as there are alternating seasons in which the hostile power is ascendant, and in which it retreats, so, after a paroxysm, the human self again shews itself in lucid intervals, with a full sense of the wretchedness of such a bondage. And, *lastly*, we discover also in the demoniacs an enhanced faculty of foreseeing, a kind of somnambulic *clairvoyance*, by which, in particular, they recognize the important relation sustained by the Saviour to the entire realm of spirits. This very circumstance agrees perfectly with the hypothesis, that nervous affections form the basis of such states, so far as they are corporeal ; and how easily unnaturally increased nervous action is united with the gift of clairvoyance, is sufficiently familiar from the history of animal magnetism. It is thus that the contradictory language of the demoniacs is to be explained ; at one time they manifest a deep insight into the truth ; at another, rude popular notions are mixed up in their words, so that the whole of their conversation has the fearfully vivid character of the erring and confused talk of madmen, who not unfrequently give utterance to striking thoughts, but so connect them with other elements, that the splendour of the thought is only a more melancholy testimony to the greatness of the derangement in the seat of life whence it issued.

On these grounds, we have still to explain why demoniacs are no longer to be found.* First, it is certainly undeniable, that the spirit of the Gospel has had a beneficial influence on mankind even in this respect, and that thus various manifestations of evil (particularly in its rude forms) have been mitigated. It is a mistake when some have gone so far as to maintain, on the authority of 1 John iii. 8, that the devil has no more opportunity to exert his influence in the church of Christ (least of all can the passage referred to supply any proof of that opinion). It might be allowed of the *ideal,* invisible church—as the community of believers ; but the external church evidently forms a mixed communion, in which the power of Christ's redeeming work is, indeed, in a state of advancing development, but has not yet, by any means, sanctified the whole ; for which reason, the influences emanating from the kingdom of darkness must not be conceived as destroyed, but only as modified. *Next,* the fact in question may be accounted for from this, that the knowledge of evil spirits and of their influence is not now so prevalent. In many maniacs or epileptic persons there may be a state very similar to that of the demoniacs, (?), only the sufferer himself (as medical men commonly do) looks upon his state in a different light.† But it is evident that the circumstance of the unhappy being's knowing or not knowing of his state, is something purely accidental. In this is but reflected the character of the time, just as

---

* I assume here, according to the prevalent opinion, that such is the fact, and that no demoniacs are now to be met with. But it must not be forgotten, that eminent medical men are of a different opinion—*e. g, Esquirol* in Paris (compare the " Magazin für ausländische Heilkunde, von Gerson und Julius." Sept. 1828, S. 317). *Kerner's* views on the subject are well known. The missionary *Rhenius* gives an account of a remarkable demoniac in the East Indies, in the year 1817. (In *Meyer's* " Blätter für höhere Wahrheit," B. 7, S. 199, ff.) Were the apostles to visit our madhouses, it is questionable how they would designate many of the sufferers in them.

† On the same grounds it is accounted for, that there is no mention made of demoniacs in the Old Testament. The doctrine of demoniacs and their influence had but little currency among the people before the captivity; even if therefore, the kingdom of darkness did produce similar manifestations (as at the present day), yet they were not *recognized* as such. After the captivity, forms quite analogous to those of the New Testament may have existed ; but the prophetic writings of that period contain little historical matter, and hence it is easily explained how we meet with no references to the subject in them. At the time when the Apocryphal books were written, spiritual life in general was at a low ebb among the Israelitish people; and for that very reason the opposing principles were but little developed. For that *such frequent* manifestations of the hideous power of darkness appear in the New Testament side by side with the nobler manifestations of the divine, is, doubtless, to be accounted for from the excited character of the whole period, which caused all the opposing principles to come out more distinctly. But with respect to the cause of the Evangelist *John's* silence about demoniacs, that cause is to be sought only in his relation to the synoptic Evangelists ; the latter had narrated a sufficient number of the cures of demoniacs; and for that reason John (to whom, in general, the actions of Jesus serve only as points of connexion for the discourses to be communicated) passed them over in silence. At least the view which John entertained of the devil (according to viii. 44 ; xiii. 27) was not, in any respect, different.

the name is which the madman applies to his demon. At most, therefore, we can only say, that the cases have become much more rare, and this shews how the restorative power of the Saviour will, at some future period, harmonize all discords in the life of man, both of his body and of his soul. [It seems, however, more probable that that fearful letting loose of demoniacal agency ran parallel with the special revelation of Deity in the incarnation, and that therefore they were *only then* permitted by heaven.]

If, after these remarks, we turn to the history of the *Gadarene demoniac* before us,˙ which has, moreover, special difficulties, we have to observe, in general, that Matthew speaks of *two* sufferers, while the other two Evangelists know of only *one*. A similar case of the number being doubled occurs in Matth. xx. 30, where he speaks of two blind men, though Mark (x. 46) and Luke (xviii. 35) make mention of one only. This difference belongs to the class discussed in the Introduction (§ 8), which we must take to be such as they manifestly are—as discrepancies—without seeking for explanations ; as, for instance, that one carried on the conversation, and is, therefore, alone mentioned, and so forth. In this case it is extremely improbable that there should have been two persons afflicted in this manner. Probably Matthew has combined this occurrence with a kindred one, which might happen all the more easily, as he uniformly presents the frame-work of his narrative only in general outline. *Further*, there is an uncertainty about the spelling of the name of the place, after which the demoniac, of whom our narrative speaks, was called. In all the three Gospels there are the various readings, Γεργεσηνῶν, Γαδαρηνῶν, Γερασηνῶν; from which we may conclude, that they did not originally agree in the reading. The difference of the reading arose from the effort to establish uniformity. It must indeed be allowed, that the possibility of such a variation in the name of the place results from the character of the locality itself. In Decapolis (see note on Matth. iv. 25), where according to Mark v. 20, the occurrence took place, lay the well-known town of Gadara, the capital of Perea, sixty stadia distant from Tiberias, and renowned for its warm baths. Farther to the north lay Gerasa, a place on the eastern boundary of Perea ; at some distance from the sea indeed, but yet so that the territory of the town extended down to it ; and hence the "countries" (χῶραι) of the two towns might easily be confounded. (On the two places, see *Winer's* " Reallexicon," s. v.) *Origen* (Opp. vol. iv., p. 140) does indeed report, that in his day the precipice was shewn down which the swine were said to have cast themselves, and calls the neighbouring town Gergesa.* But the entire account speaks

* *Origen* speaks of the reading Γερασηνῶν as the common one in the Codd. of his day. He says, that the reading Γαδαρηνῶν is found in only a few copies, and decides in

only of a tradition, and, hence the existence of a town of that name
is rendered doubtful, since there are no other reliable traces of its
existence at the time of Jesus. (On the ancient Gergesa, see Deut.
vii. 1 ; Joshua xxiv. 11 ; *Joseph.* Ant. I. 6, 2.) In the text of
Mark and Luke, the reading Γαδαρηνῶν is undoubtedly the correct
one. In Matthew, on the other hand, that reading is certainly only
taken from the other two Evangelists. But whether Γεργεσηνῶν or
Γερασηνῶν is preferable in Matthew, it would be difficult to decide.
In the edition of *Griesbach-Schulz*, the former reading is adopted
on the authority of the Codd. ; but yet it may be questionable,
whether this reading was not introduced into the Codd. simply on
the authority of *Origen*, and whether the original reading in Matthew was not Γερασηνῶν. *Fritzsche* is also against Γεργεσηνῶν, but
decides in favour of Γαδαρηνῶν, in which case the original reading
must have been the same in all the three Gospels, which from the
many variations in the name, is improbable.

Ver. 28.—The description of the demoniac, in the present narrative, shews him clearly to be a maniac. The madness seized the
unhappy man convulsively at separate moments ; then, after such
paroxysms, a period of quiet supervened. Mark depicts the poor
man's state most vividly in his description (v. 3–5.) He shewed
tremendous muscular power, as is usual in cases of mania. In order
to restrain him they had chained him (πέδη = περισκελίς, *fetter for
the foot*, is a species of the general term ἅλυσις, *chain*); but he
broke the bonds, and would not even endure clothes on his body.
The hostile power, to which he had allowed an entrance into his
soul, drove him to solitary places, where he lived in the tombs, and
his appearance terrified the passers-by. We are to imagine the
μνήματα, *tombs*, to have been at a distance from the town, as well as
hewn in the rocks ; for which reason Mark (v. 5) connects ἐν τοῖς
μνήμασι καὶ ἐν τοῖς ὄρεσιν, *in the tombs and the mountains*. But, from
time to time, his better nature awoke within, and gave vent to itself in a doleful cry of anguish, and in self-inflicted torments, to
which the consciousness of guilt drove him (κράζων καὶ κατακόπτων
ἑαυτὸν λίθοις, Mark v. 5.) The narratives of Mark and Luke only,
furnish a vivid picture of Jesus' meeting with this unhappy man,
and the way in which the Saviour dealt with him. Matthew (ver.
29) begins at once with the exclamation : τί ἡμῖν καὶ σοί, *What hast
thou to do with us ?* which renders the picture of the action obscure.
According to Mark and Luke, there was first a salutary emotion
which at the sight of the Prince of Peace came over the poor man,
who had felt within himself the fierce raging of the powers of evil.

favour of Γεργεσηνῶν, on the ground of the traditional report. The passage about Gergesa is as follows :—Γέργεσα ἀφ' ἧς οἱ Γεργεσηνοί, πόλις ἀρχαία, περὶ τὴν νῦν καλουμένην
Τιβεριάδος λίμνην, ἀφ' οὗ δείκνυται τοὺς χοίρους ὑπὸ τῶν δαιμόνων καταβεβλῆσθαι.

He hastened up to Jesus, and fell at his feet—evidencing, in this act of homage, the obscure confession, that he expected help from him. We should, indeed, utterly disarrange the connexion if we were to take the words "crying with a loud voice" (κράξας μεγάλη φωνῇ), which Mark and Luke connect with the προσεκύνησε, *worshipped*, as contemporaneous with it. Then the worshipping could only be an action proceeding from the dominion of demoniacal power, and the object of the humble petition could not have been to be healed, but μή με βασανίσῃς,* *do not torment me.* But it is evident, that in that case the demoniac would not have hastened to meet Jesus; but would have fled from him. And, moreover, this view does not accord with Mark v. 8: ἔλεγε γάρ κ. τ. λ. (Luke viii. 29 has παρήγγειλε γάρ κ. τ. λ.) The γάρ is evidently intended to mark the reason of the exclamation : τί ἐμοὶ καὶ σοί; and the aorist is, therefore, to be construed as a pluperfect. See *Winer's* Grammar, § 41, 5.

Ver. 29.—The whole then is conceivable in the following form : With a presentiment of help, the unhappy man, when he came within view of the Saviour, hastened towards him, and fell at his feet ; Jesus commanded the unclean spirit to depart from him, and in an instant his condition was reversed. A violent paroxysm seized him, and, under its influence, he spake, with a suppression of the human consciousness, in the character of the demoniacal power, and cried, " What have I to do with thee ?" (τί ἐμοὶ καὶ σοί), although he had just before sought the Lord with purely human feelings. (The common term for the command to the demons to come out, is ἐπιτιμᾶν = גָּעַר, in which the idea of severe reproof is implied.) This change in the temper of the demoniac in connexion with the fact, that his healing was not contemporaneous with the command of Jesus to the spirit, is a very important circumstance for the comprehension of this narrative, and of the state of the demoniacs in general. According to our general view detailed above, it is most simple to conceive of the matter thus. By the contraction of deep guilt, and long continuance in the practice of sin, the situation of this pitiable being had, probably, become so dangerous, that a violent penetration of the holy power of Jesus into him might, indeed, have availed to repulse the power of darkness, but would, perhaps, have destroyed the bodily organization of the demoniac. Even Christ's first effort, expressed in the words, Come out of the man (ἔξελθε ἐκ τοῦ ἀνθρώπου), was followed by a violent paroxysm (although we must conceive of the Saviour's power as purposely moderated), and, under its influence, the unhappy man spoke in the character of the dominant power of darkness, his consciousness being

---

* Similar expressions from demoniacs occur also in the exorcising of a devil by *Apollonius* of *Tyana* ; but *Philostratus* probably had reference in them to the narratives of the New Testament. See *Baur ut sup.* S. 145.

absorbed in it. To bring him out, again, from this state, and recover him to a consciousness of himself, Jesus, diverting him from
the inventions of his fancy, inquired his name, which must necessarily bring him to reflection on himself. In the words of the
demoniac, τί ἡμῖν (ἐμοί) καὶ σοί, *What have we (or I) to do with
thee?* (corresponds to מַה־לִּי וָלָךְ, Joshua xxii. 24 ; 2 Sam. xvi. 10),
which are here intended to denote the consciousness of complete
distinction of nature, as well as in the invocation " Son of God,"
we have a plain instance of the gift of *clairvoyance* common with
persons of this kind. For although the name is not here used with
any definite doctrinal idea, yet it denotes a holy character, in whom
the better self, in its enlightened seasons, surmised a helper, but in
whom the hostile power, when it gained the predominance, saw the
judge. Just because of this character of the confession, the Saviour
often *forbids* it—e. g., Mark i. 34 ; Luke iv. 41, οὐκ ἔφιε λαλεῖν τὰ
δαιμόνια, ὅτι ᾔδεισαν αὐτόν. (See also Acts xvi. 17.) Believing confidence alone, and not knowledge associated with terror, makes the
confession of his name desirable. That it was not forbidden in this
case, was on account of the state of the unhappy man, who had to
be treated with great care. According to two of the Evangelists, this
confession was immediately followed by the petition, " do not torment
me." If we were to regard the man as the subject speaking, fear of
suffering, which he imagines coming upon him from Jesus, would not
agree with his previous approach to our Lord ; from which it must
be supposed that he expected good from him. But if we suppose
that it is the demon speaking through the man, the singular does not
agree with the subsequent statement, that many evil spirits have
possession of him. But that the latter view is the more correct, is
shewn by πρὸ καιροῦ, *before the time*, Matth. viii. 29. For this suggests the idea, that a period of the victory of light is at hand, in
which all the powers belonging to the kingdom of darkness shall be
consigned to the abyss (ἄβυσσος.) (See note on Luke x. 18.) But
this idea, correct in itself, bears, in its connexion, as uttered by the
demoniac, the character of insanity. First, confounding himself
with the hostile power that ruled in him, he utters in *behalf* of it a
prayer which stands in contradiction with the inmost longing of his
real self ; then again, in the conversation carried on, for the most
part, in the character of the powers of evil, there is blended much
derived from the habits of the sufferer as a man, particularly the
phrase, " I adjure thee by God" (ὁρκίζω σε τὸν Θεόν) (Mark v. 7),
which, of course, suits only his character as a man. But this very
confusion in the talk of the demoniac evinces the truth of the narrative ; just as evil is in itself contradictory, so the discourse of the
unfortunate subject of evil likewise appears self-contradictory.

As was hinted above, the Saviour would not dispel the power of

darkness suddenly, because the conflict of warring powers in his de-
pressed organism, instead of healing, would have annihilated him :
hence he wisely prepares the way for a complete cure. After the
first paroxysm, therefore, Jesus asks, as was observed (according to
Mark v. 9 ; Luke viii. 30), in order to recover him to a consciousness
of his individuality, Τί σοι ὄνομα ? *What is thy name ?* But the in-
sane man, persisting in his confusion of himself with the power
which ruled over him, cries out, Legion (Λεγεών) ; and the Evangelists add, that this name was suggested by the impression, that more
than one evil power was exerting its influence over him. In this
trait, error and truth are combined with fearful vividness, just as
they were interwoven in the unhappy man's mind. The impression
was true, that not merely one part of his being was given over to the
influence of the demoniacal world, but that his *whole inner man* was
laid open to them (see Mark xvi. 9, where it is said of Mary Magdalene, that she had seven devils—i. e., was become the possession of the
kingdom of sin in all the departments of her being). But this correct
idea the sufferer expresses in the form of calling himself Legion ;
Mark (v. 9) adds, " for we are many"—very expressively choosing the
first person. This name was evidently derived from the immediate
experience of his senses. The view—which he might at some time
have had the opportunity of taking of a compact Roman legion—
that terrible instrument of the Roman dominion over the world, at
the sight of which the Jew especially trembled—gives him the idea,
that a compact host of Satanic powers was come down upon him.
In his present state of mental aberration, he confounds himself
with this host, conceives of it as a unity divided into many, and gives
himself the name Legion.* The utterance of this name is then
followed (Mark v. 10 ; Luke viii. 31) by the repeated (see Matth.
viii. 29) petition, in which the afflicted man again speaks in the
character of the power that controlled him, not to deprive the devils
of their power, and send them to the abyss (ἄβυσσος). (This term
is used also in Rom. x. 7, and frequently in the Apocalypse, ix. 1,
2, 11 ; xi. 7 ; xvii. 8 ; xx. 1, 3. It is used like Tartarus (τάρταρος)
[2 Peter ii. 4], and Gehenna (γέεννα), and corresponds to the Hebrew תהום, which, by the by, is not used in the Old Testament for
the dwelling-place of evil spirits. In the Old Testament שׁאוֹל comprehends, in its more general signification, what we find distinguished
in the New. The ᾅδης or the φυλακή of the New Testament, as the
assembling place of the dead, must be conceived as strictly separate

---

* A similar instance of diversity regarded as a divided unity, may be found in the
Rabbinical language, in which לְגִיוֹן denotes "the commander of a legion." (See *Buxtorf, Lex. Talmud*, p. 1123.) We might imagine that the poor man had an indistinct idea
of being possessed by an archfiend (ἄρχων τῶν δαιμόνων), so that *potentia*, the power also
of the angels subject to him, was exercised upon him.

from the ἄβυσσος. See note on Luke xvi. 28.) But again, popular notions are mingled in this petition, as the additional clause in Mark ἔξω τῆς χώρας, *out of the region,* shews. These words are, doubtless, connected with the popular Jewish opinion, that certain spheres of operation were assigned to the bad angels, as well as to the good. The demon desires not to be removed out of his. If a removal out of one region into another was regarded as impossible, their being driven out of the region assigned would be precisely equivalent to their being sent down into the abyss.

Ver. 30–32.—Thus far the evangelical narrative gives a most vivid picture of this occurrence, which, up to this point, appears closely allied to all other narratives of this sort. But now a circumstance is subjoined, which is the more difficult, because the New Testament supplies nothing analogous to it ; and for that reason it is a tempting subject for the mythical interpretation.* But it must be confessed, that, independently of the general reasons against that interpretation, it is opposed, in this case, by the exact accordance of all the three narratives, which is rarely found in mythical subjects. It is recorded that a great herd of swine (Mark v. 13, states the number as 2000) presented itself to the view of the demoniac,† who, speaking in the character of the hostile power, begged that the demons might be allowed to enter the animals. Jesus permits it, the demons enter the swine, and they precipitate themselves from the cliff (κρημνός) into the lake. The fact of the devils' passing into brute creatures, is here quite as difficult as the subsequent circumstances.‡ For although an influence of what is spiritual over what is physical, both on the part of righteousness and of sin, is recognized throughout the Scriptures (see Gen. iii. 17, ff. compared with Rom. viii. 18, ff.), yet the entering into the swine is for this reason specially difficult, that it corresponds with the entering into man, in a way which too much identifies the animal with the human elements. [Yet we have seen that the influence of the demons is

* As in the New Testament the swine of the Gadarenes, so in the Old, Balaam's ass (Numb. xxii. 28, ff.) forms an offence and a stumbling-block. In both events spiritual effects are seen in connexion with the brute creation.

† The Evangelists seem not to agree exactly here, since Matthew says, the herd was at a distance from them ; but the other two, that they were there. The idea of at a distance must be taken relatively ; the herd was on the *same* plain, which extended down to the lake (ἐκεῖ), but at a considerable distance (μακράν) from the scene of the dialogue.

‡ Dr. Strauss here, as everywhere, settles the matter at once, and cries Myths, nothing but myths! He smiles when he sees any one taking pains to solve the difficulties which the case presents. And yet this great master of negation, in his review of *Kerner's* work on similar phenomena of the present day, is compelled to acknowledge that he is unable to devise any solution of them at all plausible. What presumption to deny that similar phenomena may have existed in the apostolic times, which his wisdom may not be able to understand! for he has no other reason whatever for his assertion, that these narratives of the New Testament are myths, than their extraordinary character. (See " Jahrbücher für wissenschaftliche Kritik." 1836, Dec. S. 111, ff.)

on the nervous, *i. e.*, the animal system. That the nervous life of brutes is as excitable as that of men, none will question.] Besides, it seems unaccountable why the Saviour should yield to a passing whim of the sufferer, as one might be inclined to regard his request, to which the Evangelists ascribe such real consequences ; first, the entering into the animals, then, their destruction. To suppose this destruction occasioned by a violent assault of the unhappy man, is as contradictory to the narrative, as to view it as *accidentally* coinciding with his prayer. But if we assume that, in the view of the narrators, the destruction of the animals was occasioned by the spirits, we do not see what reason can be conceived why the demons should have entered the swine in order themselves immediately to destroy these subjects of their power. [They did not enter the swine with *the design* of destroying, but of vexing them. But the shock on the nervous system of the animals was too violent to be resisted. They became frantic and furious, and plunged into the sea. Somewhat otherwise Olshausen.] ·On this obscure passage I beg leave only to offer a few hints and conjectures, which may lead to farther inquiry. The expression, εἰσέρχεσθαι εἰς τοὺς χοίρους, must, in any case, be regarded as implying an *influence* on the animals ; but this must have been immediately intended for their destruction, and that on account of their *possessors*. On the part of evil, the intention of their destruction might then have been to limit the Saviour's power in its beneficent influence, as the effect of it actually was (Matth. viii. 34) to prepossess the minds of the people against our Lord. On the part of Christ, the permission might have been intended, in respect to the sufferer, to lighten, by yielding to him, his subsequent paroxysm and render possible his cure ; in respect to the owners of the animals, to *prove* them by this worldly loss, and lead them to a decision for or against God and his cause ; or, if we suppose that the animals belonged to Jews (which would not be impossible, since Jews and heathen were often mingled in the border provinces), it must have been a warning visitation, because a culpable love of gain led them to keep animals, which by the law were unclean. This interpretation, at least, keeps in view the *moral* aspect of the transaction, and thus sets aside the question how Christ could be so unjust as to destroy 2000 swine : a question exactly parallel with the inquiry how God can be so unjust as to allow in any case the existence of a murrain. The simple answer to the question is, that where cattle die, men are to be quickened, in order to learn that there is a God, and that all that he does is right.

Ver. 33, 34.—Matthew follows up the account of the destruction of the herd with that of the flight of the herdsmen, and the crowds of inhabitants coming out of the city. Of the state of the patient he gives no further account. But Mark and Luke describe him most vividly in his totally altered condition after his complete recovery, which was doubtless preceded by another violent paroxysm. He sat quietly and clothed at the feet of Jesus, an object of surprise and admiration to the inhabitants. They acknowledged, that nothing but supernatural holy power could have accomplished the cure of one so shattered. Matthew, in common with the other two Evangelists, records, that the inhabitants besought Jesus to leave that region.* This might have been an expression of the fear of God (as in Luke v. 8) ; but as the Saviour immediately leaves them, anxiety lest they should suffer further loss of property from the Deliverer of souls, may have mingled in this request—a meanness of disposition which must have taken from our Lord all hope of sowing with profit the seed of eternal life in a soil so overgrown with thorns and thistles. Mark (v. 18–20), and Luke (viii. 38, 39), give some particulars of the man's future course, which are unnoticed by Matthew. He desired to accompany the Saviour ; but the latter discouraged him, and sent him back to his friends, *charging* him to tell what God had done for him. The reason of this charge (see note on Matth. viii. 4) must be sought in the *man himself* who was healed. The deeper the malady had been rooted in him, the more advantageous it would be for him to take an active part in the duties of life, since being much occupied with himself might have drawn him back to his old sins. Moreover, such employments would form a salutary check on his undue partiality for solitude, which was, in all probability, closely connected with the vices that had laid the foundation of such a surrender to the evil powers. And, lastly, the telling of his being healed by the Messiah of Nazareth, naturally confirmed his faith in his deliverer.

§ 11. CURE OF A PARALYTIC.

(Matth. ix. 1–8; Mark v. 21; ii. 1–12; Luke v. 17–26.)

Matthew proceeds in his delineation of Jesus as a worker of miracles, without reflections and eulogies, merely by the simple narration of mighty acts that fill the soul with holy astonishment. His call by our Lord (ver. 9, ff.) does, indeed, seem interposed as something foreign to the subject ; but it is manifestly narrated not on its own account, but for the sake of what stands connected with it (ver. 11–13). The Evangelist means to exhibit the contradiction which existed between the judgment of the Pharisees, uttered at the feast in Matthew's house, and that of the people, as to the person

---

* The phrase ἐξέρχεσθαι εἰς συνάντησίν τινι, is not found anywhere else in the New Testament, except in Matth. viii. 34. In the Old Testament the LXX. use it several times—e. g., Gen. xiv. 17 ; Deut. i. 44.

of Christ, and, at the same time, to shew how our Lord fulfilled his high calling in such miraculous cures. It must be confessed, that the verses 14–17 have a less direct reference to the context of the ninth chapter. They seem to have been occasioned by the previous narrative of the feast, and to serve merely to complete the narrative of a day so important to Matthew.

If, too, we compare the *place* of the first event of this chapter in Matthew, with that which it occupies in Mark and Luke, we again meet with a remarkable variation. According to Matth. ix. 1 2, the cure of the paralytic is in immediate connexion with the account of the demoniac, as having taken place directly after arriving at the other side of the lake. Mark and Luke, on the other hand, assign this event to an earlier period. The former connects it with the history of the cure of the leper (Mark i. 40, ff.) Luke does, indeed, likewise connect it with this event (ver. 17); but with the loose expression : ἐγένετο ἐν μιᾷ τῶν ἡμερῶν, *it came to pass on one of the days.* The account of his call, and the circumstances connected with it, which, in Matthew, follow the cure of the paralytic, are, indeed, placed in the same sequence in Mark and Luke; but the narrative of the woman with the issue of blood, which comes next in Matthew (ix. 18, ff.), is recorded by Mark (v. 22, ff.), and Luke (viii. 41, ff.), much later. The difficulties arising hence in a chronological arrangement of the several sections of the Gospels appear to us insuperable.

Matth. ix. 1.—Mark does indeed also mention the circumstance, that Jesus returned to the west coast of the lake after the cure of the demoniac ; but his narrative becomes indefinite in the words : " And he was by the sea-side," and he then introduces the narrative of Jairus' daughter with the phrase : " And lo." Matthew makes him go immediately to Capernaum (ἰδία πόλις), which Mark (ii. 1) also mentions as the place where the paralytic was. Mark and Luke carefully describe the scene in the house where Jesus was. People filled the porch of the house (τὰ πρὸς τὴν θύραν scil. μέρη = vestibulum), so that the entrance was closed up. Among those present, Luke enumerates learned Jews (νομοδιδάσκαλοι, *teachers of the law* = γραμματεῖς, *scribes*, םיִרְפֹס), some of whom were even from Judea and Jerusalem ; but that they were come to Capernaum purposely on account of Jesus, is a gratuitous conjecture. Our Lord is represented as being employed partly in teaching (ἐλάλει αὐτοῖς τὸν λόγον scil. περὶ τῆς βασιλείας, Mark ii. 2), and partly in healing.

The words in Luke v. 17 (δύναμις κυρίου ἦν εἰς τὸ ἰᾶσθαι αὐτούς), lit. *there was the power of the Lord to heal them*, are very obscure. There is no previous substantive to which the word αὐτούς, *them*, refers ; we might take it as an indication that Luke, in the narrative of the event, had incorporated a document with his gospel, without taking care to alter what in it had reference to some antecedent. But the words δύναμις κυρίου ἦν, *there was the power of the Lord,* are still more difficult. To refer κύριος, *Lord,* to God, so that we should have to supply, "with Jesus" (μετὰ 'Ιησοῦ), in the sense of the power of God being with him, so that he *could* heal, makes too harsh an ellipsis. But as referred to Christ, the thought can be no other than this, that the power of healing that dwelt in him *manifested itself;* so that ἦν *was,* would have to be interpreted with a pregnant meaning, perhaps with ἐργαζομένη, *working,* supplied.

Ver. 2.—On this occasion, among other sick people, they brought a paralytic (see note on Matth. viii. 6) to Christ, who could not, however, as he was laid upon a bed, be brought to him in the usual way, because of the crowd. Mark and Luke relate in detail the manner in which those who carried the sick man made their way to Jesus. The whole description can be understood only from the oriental construction of houses, in consequence of which the flat roof might be reached either by a ladder from the outside, or from a neighbouring house. Still the breaking up of the top-floor, which was generally laid with tiles (διὰ τῶν κεράμων, in Luke), appears somewhat strange ; but perhaps the description is to be understood of their somewhat enlarging the entrance into the house from above. ('Αποστεγάζω, *unroofing,* Mark ii. 4, is a strong term to express the undertaking of the people, so strong in faith. Χαλάω == χαλάζω, used by Mark, is several times found in Luke also, v. 4, 5 ; Acts ix. 25 ; xxvii. 17. Κράββατος == *grabatus,* corresponds to κλινίδιον in Luke.) In this proceeding, though extraordinary, and in some measure even annoying, the compassionate Saviour saw only the faith of the parties concerned. (The faith of the sick man is viewed as one with that of the friends who assisted him ; he doubtless encourged them, and imparted to them his own lively emotions.) In this case, again (see note on Matth. viii. 1), definite doctrinal ideas do not form the substance of this faith, which consists rather in the inward need of help, that feels itself powerfully attracted to that quarter whence it expects help. That this sense of need was, in some of the cases of cures only external, is seen from the narratives such as that in Luke xvii. 12, ff., of the ten lepers. Usually, however, the *external* need was associated with the *internal,* and, in every instance, the latter was *intended* to be aroused by the former ; and where that did not happen, reproof was administered. The words immediately addressed to the sick man by our Lord : *Thy sins are forgiven thee,* shew that in this case there was no want of inward susceptibility. Perhaps this address was occasioned by penitential expressions on the part of the paralytic, which the words (in Matthew) θάρσει τέκνον, *son, be of good cheer,* might suggest. His peculiar sin might have brought on the illness under which he was suffering, and thus have excited a sense of his sinfulness. But even if that was not the case, still Christ might have felt himself called to pass at once from the outward phenomenon to its moral source, in order to prepare for the inward cure by the outward one. The connexion of sin and disease, or suffering of any kind, is a necessary one. The Jews, like the unspiritual man in general (see John ix. 2, 34), erred only in this, that, from a case of affliction, they felt themselves warranted to criminate the patient *personally*, which necessarily gave rise to false and unrighteous judgments. The just conclusion is to regard the suffering of the individual as proof of the guilt of the whole race, and consequently of himself; that produces humility and meekness. (See note on Luke xiii. 4.) But in whatever light we view the condition of the sufferer, Jesus announces to him the forgiveness of sins. This is to be viewed as the root of the new life that was to be awakened in the soul of the penitent, which, however, could only gradually (as we see in the case of the apostles) transform the whole inner man; so that ἀφέωνται (the Doric form) is to be taken not as a wish, but as creative and effective : " Thy sins are forgiven ; I forgive them thee even now." But in those words, the Saviour had regard not only to the good of the sufferer, but also to the spiritual awakening of the people, and even of the Pharisees, as the sequel of the conversation shews.

Ver. 3.—The Pharisees had a correct insight into the nature of forgiveness of sins ; they recognized in it a prerogative of God ;—that is, so far as it is intended to be not merely a kind wish or an empty declaration, but a *living effect*, it presupposes a knowledge of the secrets of the heart, and a divine power of life, which is capable of overcoming the sinful power, and of translating into the element of the spirit. Hence, so far as the church forgives sins (John xx. 23), God is in it, and the persons who pronounce the forgiveness are only the organs of the forgiving power of God. But as Jesus here forgives sin, not in the name of another, but in his own, and in full inward power, their accusation would have been true, if, as they imagined, Jesus were a mere man. They regarded the forgiveness of sins as a sacred act of God, which no one could perform without robbing God of his honour ; and in that they were perfectly right. (The profound sense which the Scriptures attach to βλασφημέω, βλασφημία, is unknown to the profane writers of antiquity; it there denotes primarily only " to speak injuriously of any one," then " to utter something of evil omen," the opposite of εὐφημεῖν. It is monotheism only that leads to the notion of blasphemy [corresponding to the phrase יְהֹוָה שֵׁם נָקַב in the Old Testament], which denotes not only cursing and blaspheming God, but also, in particular, the assumption of the honour of the Creator on the part of the creature, John x. 33.) But as the Redeemer is the only-begotten Son of the Father, he exercised even this prerogative ; and blessed was the man who believed in him, for he experienced the saving power of the Lord in his heart. But we must allow, that thoughts like those of the Pharisees might have occurred to a mind, not indeed decidedly irreligious, but more prone to speculation ; for faith in the revelation of God in Christ is something very great. Such genuine doubt, or, rather, such an uncertainty, would have exhibited itself very differently from what it did in the Pharisees ; in them the Saviour sharply reproves such thoughts, as sinful. The reason was probably the following :—The conspicuous majesty of Jesus, which was reflected purely in childlike minds, reached their hearts also ; but they opposed themselves to these sacred impressions, from the feeling that, if they gave entrance to them, they must renounce altogether their principles and their practices. Standing thus in inward opposition to God, they were glad to make use of circumstances, which might be perplexing even to sincere minds, as a welcome means of enabling them to justify their conduct in their own eyes. (Εἰπεῖν ἐν ἑαυτῷ, ἐν καρδίᾳ = בְּלִבּוֹ יֹאמַר. Luke uses διαλογίζεσθαι, by which the activity of the λόγος = νοῦς is expressed. But the διαλογισμοί, according to the invariable use in Scripture, are referred to the καρδία, לֵב. See note on Luke ii. 35.)

Ver. 4, 5.—Jesus, penetrating their thoughts (Mark ii. 8 rightly assigns the spirit as the principle of knowledge in him), reproves their sin, but does not deal with them as incorrigible persons. Knowing the impurity of their hearts, and the difficulty of believing, our Lord endeavours, by an external fact, to aid in overcoming these difficulties. Accordingly, the miracle (see note on Matth. viii. 1) appears here in its proper intention of deepening the impression on the heart, presupposed by it, in order to bring to the conviction that the worker of miracles does not teach *what is true* in his own name, but the *truth* by commission from above. ('Ενθυμεῖσθαι, Matth. i. 20 ; Acts x. 19, and ἐνθυμήσεις, Matth. xii. 25 ; Heb. iv. 12, are nearly related to διαλογίζεσθαι and διαλογισμός, like θυμός to καρδία. But the former terms have generally a bad meaning associated with them. We might denominate θυμός the disturbed καρδία, and the ἐνθυμήσεις the impure actions thence proceeding. The question of our Lord, τί ἐστιν εὐκοπώτερον, *which is easier ?* is accommodated to the external mode of conception, which the miracle was intended to assist. According to it, what is external is called greater, more difficult, than what is internal—that is, the forgiveness of sins ; the spiritual eye, indeed, takes the opposite view of them.)

Ver. 6, 7.—As Son of Man, Jesus expressly claims the authority to forgive sins, which involves the declaration of his higher nature. In the expression : Son of man on earth, there is the implied contrast with God in heaven ; so that the Messiah appears as the representative of God upon earth. The idea of the Jews, that the forgiveness of sins would be among the prerogatives of the Messiah (*Schöttgen*, "Jesus der wahre Messias," Leipzig, 1744, S. 307. *Bertholdt Christol. Jud.*, p. 159, seqq.), evidently expressed the recognition of his higher nature ; hence Jesus desires to rouse to a conviction of the true nature of the Son of Man. (*Fritzsche* removes the difficulties in the construction of the clause, τότε λέγει τῷ παραλυτικῷ [Matth. ix. 6], by the ingenious conjecture τόδε ; but, as the Codd. exhibit no various reading, he has properly refrained from introducing it into the text. According to the common reading, we must take the words as parenthetical, and interposed by the Evangelist.)

Ver. 8.—The narrative is silent as to the effect of the miracle on the Pharisees, because there was nothing pleasing to report ; but it is observed of the simple people who were open to divine influence, that they proclaimed God's praise with wonder, entirely in accordance with the Saviour's intention, blessing the author of all good for the revelation of his glory in him. (See Matth. v. 16.) The concluding clause in Matthew, τὸν δόντα ἐξουσίαν τοιαύτην τοῖς ἀνθρώποις, *who gave such authority to men*, is not to be interpreted as if (ἐξουσία being taken as the cause for the effect) it was in praise of the blessings flowing from God to men through Jesus ; ἄνθρωποι, *men* = γένος τῶν ἀνθρώπων, *human race*, rather includes Jesus himself, in whose gift of miracles the divine power was so gloriously manifested. Without being able to define doctrinally the view held by the multitude regarding the person of Jesus, we may say, that this thought has its full eternal truth. For, as certainly as the Word of the Father was revealed in the person of our Lord, so certainly was Jesus also truly man ; and what of divine fulness was manifested in him had been imparted to the human race in general in *his* humanity. (Instead of θαυμάζειν, *wonder*, used in Matthew, Mark has ἐξίστασθαι, *amazed*, and Luke ἔκστασις ἔλαβεν ἅπαντας, *amazement seized them all*. The latter expression is the stronger ; it denotes being in transports. [See Mark v. 42 ; Acts iii. 10.] In other places this expression has a qualified signification [see note on Acts x. 10], and is used, like *being in the Spirit* (ἐν πνεύματι εἶναι), of a state of prophetic rapture. In Luke v. 26, παράδοξα = θαυμαστά, corresponds to the Hebrew נִפְלָאֹת].

§ 12. THE CALLING OF MATTHEW. OF FASTING.

(Matth. ix. 9–17; Mark ii. 13–22; Luke v. 27–39.)

It is but incidentally that Matthew touches upon his call to the apostleship, and without making himself personally prominent.[*] Sacred as was to him the moment which called him into immediate proximity to the Redeemer, his spiritual eye remained, nevertheless, exclusively fixed upon the sublime object which he wished to represent to his readers. He alludes to his call, only for the sake of the events connected with it. Both Mark and Luke give to him, who was called on this occasion, the name of *Levi;* but the similarity of the narrative and the identity of the discourses connected with it, compel us to regard the names, though different, as denoting one and the same individual. All attempts to represent them as denoting different persons, have proved futile.[†]

Ver. 9.—Ματθαῖος. = מַתְיָה, Θεόδωρος. The τελώνιον = בֵּית הַמֶּכֶס, which, according to *Buxtorf* (Lex. Talmud. p. 1065), properly signifies "an exchange." The call ἀκολούθει μοι, like the δεῦτε ὀπίσω μου (iv. 19, comp. with ver. 22), implies, not only the outward attendance to which the Lord here invites him, but also the internal spiritual following, which is its proper ground. A previous acquaintance with Matthew must be supposed, for otherwise the Redeemer could not have invited him to leave his official position ; and without doubt, Matthew had already taken the necessary steps to relieve himself from his office. (?)

Ver. 10.—Matthew joyfully received into his house the Saviour who had called him to a nobler office ; he prepared for him a δοχὴ μεγάλη, *great feast*, = מִשְׁתֶּה, Gen. xxvi. 30. This word is also met with in Luke xiv. 13. (Concerning τελώνης and ἁμαρτωλός compare the remarks on Matth. v. 46.) The Evangelist contrasts our Saviour, choosing a publican for an apostle, with the Pharisees who would not even permit any intercourse with those unfortunate beings, who were devoted to the world, but whose hearts, notwith-

---

[*] This keeping of their own persons in the background, on the part of the Evangelists, is a peculiar feature of the Gospels; the Evangelists thereby show themselves to be pure historians, altogether absorbed by the sublimity of their subject. Against the authenticity of Matthew, as little can be inferred from the circumstance of his not making himself known, as against that of John, for the same reason. The position of this event appears, no doubt, to be unchronological; but, in the first place, Matthew does not pretend to any chronological order; and, in the second place, the present call of Matthew presupposes an earlier invitation on the part of Christ.

[†] Mark (ii. 14) calls Levi τὸν τοῦ Ἀλφαίου. This Alpheus is, at all events, a different person from the father of James (Matth. x. 3); for the existence of any relationship between James and Matthew, cannot be rendered probable by any circumstance whatever.

standing, were often filled with the noblest longings. Yet do these Pharisees not appear as wicked and malicious ; but rather as incapable, from their narrow view, of comprehending the freeness of Christ's love. Our Lord, therefore, opens to them an insight into a purer life than any which they conceived.

Ver. 12, 13.—Jesus describes, in few words, his holy office as the Physician of mankind. The man exposed to contagion may do well in shunning the diseased person ; but the physician hastens to him to relieve his suffering. Jesus represents himself as ἰατρός, *i. e.*, physician of the soul according to Exod. xv. 26, where Jehovah himself says to wretched Israel : כִּי אֲנִי יְהֹוָה רֹפְאֶךָ. In the parallel passage in which Jesus speaks of his vocation (ἔρχεσθαι, *come*, = to the more usual ἔρχεσθαι εἰς τὸν κόσμον, *come into the world*, signifies the appearing on earth of one belonging to a higher order of things), δίκαιοι, *righteous*, stands, as explanatory of ἰσχυροί, *whole, sound*, as ἁμαρτωλοί, *sinners*, of κακῶς ἔχοντες, *afflicted, sick*. Without denying the universal sinfulness of mankind, we yet see that the sacred writers frequently draw a line of distinction between men. (Comp. the remarks on Luke xv. 7.) Sin, as it were, concentrates itself in some individuals. But these are often the very persons on whom the Redeemer, in his grace, first has compassion. The righteous (those who are according to the law less culpable) then frequently act the part of the jealous brother on the calling home of the prodigal son. (Comp. the remarks on Luke xv.) Calling (καλεῖν) expresses the act of the Redeemer in reference to the sinners (ἁμαρτωλοί) ; it signifies the gracious call of our Lord to his feast of joy. (Comp. on this word and its relation to ἐκλέγειν, *select*, the remarks on Matth. xxii. 14.) Luke adds εἰς μετάνοιαν, *to repentance*, which, in Matthew and Mark, is an interpolation ; the repentance (comp. the remarks on Matth. iii. 2) being viewed as the first step towards the kingdom of God. Matthew, moreover, adds to this idea a reference to Hos. vi. 6. (The word πορεύεσθαι, *go*, is redundant, according to the analogy of הָלַךְ). In the words of the Old Testament seer, the dazzling brightness of the rising sun already clearly shines forth ; the life manifested in self-denying love appears as outshining all sacrifices חֶסֶד חָפַצְתִּי וְלֹא זֶבַח, *I will have mercy, etc.* Hence, in these words the sacrifices do not appear to be abrogated, but on the contrary, consummated, in the true sacrifice, of which all the others are but types. The word חֶסֶד = ἔλεος, signifies love, as it manifests itself to the unhappy, and hence is not a matter of personal enjoyment, but of self-sacrifice. Such an explanation of the holy Scriptures to the scribes was to them a powerful exhortation to repentance.

Ver. 14.—Afterwards, the same Pharisees (according to Luke), or some disciples of John who were present (according to Matthew), or both together (as Mark, reconciling the difference, says), bring forward another peculiarity of the disciples of Jesus, viz., their abstinence from fasting and stated prayer (Luke v. 33)—on which things even the Baptist, in conformity with his Old Testament tendencies, laid great stress.

Ver. 15.—The Redeemer, as one who always penetrated to the depths of the spirit, immediately goes to the root of these outward peculiarities, and then sets before them the essential difference between the Old and New Testament dispensations. In the first place, says Jesus, the peculiar nature of the kingdom of heaven lies not in such external matters ; in his church, life would hereafter exhibit itself in another way, more analogous to the New Testament. He therefore compares himself to a bridegroom, and his disciples to the friends of the bridegroom (comp. the remarks on John iii. 29), and deduces from this comparison, what is necessary for his purpose. As marriage is the season for the most heartfelt joy, so also the Lord's appearance in the world ; streams of light and life filled the heart ; eating and drinking, and full enjoyment, appear as the outward manifestation of inward joy. Sorrow, indicated by fasting, could take place only at the death of the bridegroom ; but then, indeed, so much the more bitter and acute. The striking points in the comparison are, *first*, that the disciples are designated υἱοὶ τοῦ νυμφῶνος, *children of the bridechamber*, (= παρανύμφιοι, *i. e.*, companions of the bridegroom to the bridalchamber ; νυμφών =חֻפָּה), since they, together with all believers, are the bride herself. (Comp. Eph. v. 23.) There is, however, another admissible view of the disciples, viz., as the first rays which the rising Sun of the spiritual world sent forth among mankind ; they introduced, as it were, the heavenly bridegroom to his earthly bride. *Secondly*, it is not quite clear how the words ὅταν ἀπαρθῇ, *when he shall be taken away*, are to be connected with the expression νηστεύσουσιν, *they shall fast*, by which they are followed. If we regard it as signifying the death of the Redeemer on the cross, the meaning would appear to be, that the church would fast during the whole time of his absence, until his coming again to glory. But this idea seems unsuitable, for the reason that the resurrection of the Redeemer immediately dispelled the sorrow for his death ;—and yet the Saviour could certainly not have intended to say that his disciples would fast only on the one day during which he remained in the grave. We must therefore look for a more spiritual meaning, which removes the difficulties, and apprehends the permanent application of our Lord's language. For his words are spirit and life (John vi. 63), and, as such, they must have a spiritual significancy applicable to the church at all times. What Christ here says, holds of his disciples in every age ; sometimes they rejoice, sometimes they fast. It is evident that the question is not so much respecting the bodily presence of our Redeemer (ἐπιδημία αἰσθητή), which, for Judas certainly, was not a time of nuptial joy, as his eternal spiritual presence in the soul (ἐπιδημία νοητή). But this presence of our Redeemer is more glorious and efficacious after the resurrection than before. Referring the words of Jesus to this, we obtain the profound idea, that even in believers there are internal vicissitudes—vicissitudes of light and darkness (James i. 17), inasmuch as, at one time, there prevails a nuptial joy, and, at another, grief for the departed bridegroom ; and that, accordingly, their outward life also assumes a different character. Yet the joyous disposition is conceived as predominating under the New Testament ; the graver and sterner under the Old.

Ver. 16, 17.—Since, however, there was something in the remarks of the Pharisees and the disciples of John (ver 14) which challenged a reply, the Lord finally declares, by means of two similes (Luke v. 36, uses, on this occasion, the expression παραβολή, which is here applicable only in its wider sense ; comp. on this the remarks on Matt. xiii.), that the two dispensations do not admit of being confounded. The new spirit requires a new form ; and even though, in the New Testament life, we meet with forms allied to those of the old dispensation, they still differ from the phenomena of a life purely under the law. Both similes certainly express the same idea, but are conceived from different points of view ; and the difference in the points of view explains the difference in the similes themselves.*

In the former, that which is new is considered as merely incidental, remedying the deficiencies of the old—for in this light the Gospel must have appeared to the Pharisees from their own limited point of view. In the latter simile, on the contrary, that which is new appears as essential, while that which is old is regarded as merely formal—such, in truth, was the real relation of the two. By the

---

* *Neander*, in his Kl. Gelegenheitsschr. S. 144, so explains these similes as not to refer them to the relation between the Old and New Testament, but to the disciples of John, who appear as the interrogators; so that Christ explained to them the cause of their astonishment at the difference between their own way of living and that of Christ's disciples. It arose, he says, from this, that the disciples of John were still moving in the sphere of obsolete Judaism, and hence could not comprehend the spirit of his new doctrine. For this reason, it would be of no use to invite them to adopt the new manner of life of his own disciples. The old garment of the old nature cannot well be mended with a single patch of new cloth ; wherever regeneration has not taken place, a reform in detail will not be durable. Although this view contains much that is commendable, yet I prefer that explanation which preserves the contrast between the Old and New Testament ; the whole connexion imperatively demands this. The difference between the similes is sufficiently explained by the remark on the different points of view from which they are taken, and which will also aid in the solution of other difficulties in the parables of the evangelical history. (Comp. the remarks on Luke xviii. 1, seq.)

combination of the two similes, our merciful Lord, graciously condescending to human weakness, satisfied the wants of all. The
Pharisees themselves could not but perceive that they were unable
to screen the imperfections of their dispensation (*i. e.*, of the Old
Testament) by the superinduction of the evangelical element ;
that could as little have a beneficial effect, as an unmoistened
piece of new cloth, if put on an old cloak. ('Επίβλημα is found
only in this passage ; according to Suidas, it is τὸ τῷ πρωτέρῳ
ἐπιβαλλόμενον. The patch of cloth being viewed as filling up a rent,
is called πλήρωμα, 'Ράκος, from ῥήσσω, signifies a " piece torn off"—
a rag, or patch ; ἄγναφος, " not fulled or dressed.") Luke v. 36,
views the simile in a different light. He conceives a piece torn off
from a new garment, and applied to the mending of an old one.
This produces a double disadvantage. For, in the first place, damage is done to the new garment, and in the second, the new piece
does not agree with the old garment. This mode of viewing the
simile is evidently founded on the attempt to render these two
similes more homogeneous ; for, according to the view of Luke, the
New Testament, as the new cloak, would be contrasted with the Old
Testament ; but for this very reason the representation of Matthew
and Mark is to be preferred ; the account of Luke appears to be
somewhat modified. (The reading ἀπὸ ἱματίου καινοῦ σχίσας in the
text of Luke is no doubt genuine ; it was perhaps omitted only in
order to assimilate the narrative of Luke to the description given
by the other two Evangelists.) In the second simile, the relation subsisting between substance and form, as viewed from the
New Testament standing-point, is brought prominently forward ;
by its innate creative power, the substance must produce a form
analogous to its own character ; wherever human self-will should
attempt to shut up the spirit into the old form, the immediate
result will be the breaking of the form, while, at the same time,
the substance also will not be able to manifest itself in a regular
way ; its innate power will indeed shew itself, but only in irregular
phenomena, which are by no means advantageous to the whole.
The simile is as simple and intelligible as it is wonderfully profound,
and fraught with a beautiful meaning. Especially the comparison of
the principle of evangelical life with the most spiritual production of
nature suggests many ideas. (The ἀσκοί, *utres*, according to eastern
custom, skins smeared with pitch on the inside, were used for the preservation of wines ; this kind of vessel was very convenient for
transportation on asses and camels.) Luke adds (v. 39) another
very characteristic feature which relates to the Pharisees. The
gracious Saviour himself finds an apology for hearts long habituated
to the old, and sees nothing unreasonable in their stepping slowly
and reluctantly out of the sphere of their old religous customs, and

venturing into a new and heaving element of life. The Old, although in itself more rigid (as is the Old Testament compared with the New), becomes more pleasant through the influence of habit ; the New, the wine yet fermenting and foaming, we at first (εὐθέως) do not relish. Yet, this very expression gently invites us to enter into the new spiritual life which the Redeemer brought to mankind.

§ 13. HEALING OF THE WOMAN WITH THE ISSUE OF BLOOD. RAISING FROM DEATH THE DAUGHTER OF JAIRUS.

(Matt. ix. 18–26 ; Mark v. 22–43 ; Luke viii. 40–55.)

After recording these conversations at the feast given in his own house, Matthew proceeds to set forth Jesus as a worker of miracles. *Storr* (Evang. Gesch. des Joh. S. 303) is no doubt right in saying that Matthew has here (up to v. 35) brought together what occurred in his own house, and before his own eyes. With regard to the chronology, therefore, we must here unhesitatingly follow Matthew, inasmuch as the other two Evangelists, pass immediately, by indefinite formulas, from the above comparisons to other events. (Comp. Mark ii. 23 ; Luke ii. 1.) It must indeed appear strange that Matthew should describe, in a manner so little graphic, the very events which occurred immediately after his calling, and in his own immediate presence ; while both Mark and Luke present them in a form so striking and picturesque. True, the features which they add to the narrative are, as usual, to some extent, unessential ; for instance, the name of the ruler, the age of the damsel, the circumstance of the woman suffering from the issue of blood having sought aid from physicians. But there are other traits more essential to the narrative, as, for instance, the sending of messengers to inform Jairus of the death of his child, and the notice that Jesus perceived that virtue had gone out of him. We can, therefore, even here, not mistake the fact that Matthew writes without precision, and apparently not as an eye-witness ; the question only is, whether this fact entitles us to infer that Matthew is not the author of the gospel. All that can with safety be drawn from this circumstance, is a want of clearness and liveliness in his narrative, and a limited power of conceiving external circumstances. But all this may very well consort with the character of an apostle, for whom not genius, but spirituality of mind is requisite. Matthew, moreover, did not lay himself out specially to notice extraneous circumstances, as did Mark. Finally in both the narratives contained in this section, our Redeemer again appears as a messenger from heaven, such as mankind, in their most secret longings, sigh for as their *ideal*. With the holiest, purest purposes of love, he combines a fulness of divine energy which, in a life-giving stream is poured out over the moral wastes through which he passes. Raised above all miseries and necessities, he does not withdraw from them, but, on the contrary, he lovingly descends into the depths of wretchedness, swallows up for ever death and sin, and wipes away the tears from the faces of the poor. (Isaiah xxv. 8.) Such a Saviour the Prophets had prayed for with ardent desire, and, with confident hope, had promised at the command of the Spirit;—and in the New Testament we see him rule thus, God and man at the same time—incomparable, and attracting to himself, with a magic power, all hearts susceptible of noble impressions. He is truly the Saviour of his body—the church ! (Eph. v. 23.)

Matthew, ix. 18, brings what follows into direct connexion with what precedes by the words ταῦτα αὐτοῦ λαλοῦντος αὐτοῖς, *while he was speaking to them these things*. (Ἄρχων is here = ἄρχων τῆς συναγωγῆς [Luke viii. 41], or ἀρχισυνάγωγος [Mark v. 22], *i. e.*, the ruler of the synagogue who presided over the meetings, ראשׁ הַכְּנֶסֶת.—Instead of εἰσελθών, no doubt εἰς ἐλθών must be read, as Matthew frequently uses εἰς for τίς [viii. 19 ; xvi. 14 ; xviii. 28 ; xix. 16], according to the analogy of the Hebrew term אֶחָד and the Aram. term חַד.—The name Ἰάειρος is = יָאִיר, Numb. xxxii. 41 ; Deut. iii. 14.) According to Matthew, Jairus, at the outset, declares the damsel already dead ; while according to Luke and Mark, this announcement is made by messengers at a later period. But, precisely because Matthew wished to omit this circumstance, he was obliged at once to bring forward the event as completed ; the child was dying when her father hastened to Jesus to seek for aid. Others think that experiments were still being made for the purpose of reviving her ; in which case, the message of the servants would refer to the futility of these attempts. Luke viii. 42, observes incidentally, that the child was twelve years of age, and the only daughter of the ruler. (Μονογενής is to be understood as in Luke vii. 12.)

Ver. 19.—The disciples went with our Lord, who obeyed the call of the agonized father, and both Mark and Luke depict the scene, by stating that a crowd of people followed and thronged Jesus (Mark v. 24, συνέθλιβον ; Luke viii. 42, συνέπνιγον.) Rudeness, curiosity, and kind-heartedness, were mixed together in the motley crowd ; Jesus bore with them all.

Ver. 20.—There now pressed forward a woman diseased with an issue of blood ; she had suffered for twelve years, had employed physicians and human aid, but all in vain ; her disease had even rendered her poor. (The term δαπανάω of Mark is = προσαναλίσκω of Luke, and signifies " to expend," with the accessory notion of

" spending in vain." Βίος [Luke viii. 43] = *opes, facultates, means of living*, as in Luke xv. 12, 30 ; xxi. 4.) She appears as one utterly destitute of comfort, and of hope from human aid, in her extreme distress. The faith of the woman was great, but yet she imagined that, at all events, she required an actual touch in order to be healed ; she came behind Jesus that she might touch the hem of his garment. Unlike that centurion so strong in the faith (Matt. viii. 8), she did not know that the power of Jesus was efficacious even afar of. False modesty also may, perhaps, have prevented the sufferer from disclosing herself to Jesus ; she hoped to obtain aid though she were only to touch his garment. She evidently entertained the idea of a sacred atmosphere encircling the heavenly visitant, into which she must strive to enter. The garment she considered to be the conductor of the power. (Comp. Matt. xiv. 36.) It is not likely that the notions of the woman were free from a materialistic view of the miraculous power of Jesus ; but, happily, she was to be cured, not by the imaginations of her head, but by the faith of her heart ; and this was ardent, and well pleasing to the Lord. (Κράσπεδον = ציצת, Numb. xv. 38 ; Deut. xxii. 12.) (Comp. the remarks on Matt. xxiii. 5.) Mark and Luke alone describe explicitly the effect of this believing touch, and that which was consequent upon it. Mark v. 29, makes use of the significant expression ἐξηράνθη ἡ πηγὴ τοῦ αἵματος, *the fountain of blood was dried up*, to signify a radical cure of the deep-rooted disease ; and adds, ἔγνω τῷ σώματι, *she perceived in her body*, to shew that she experienced a peculiar bodily sensation which gave her the conviction that the malady was removed. (Μάστιξ sc. τοῦ Θεοῦ ; comp. 2 Maccab. ix. 11. Every disease is, rightly understood, the consequence of sin, and hence, also, a punishment of God, which is intended to lead to a knowledge of sin. Comp. the commentary on Matt. ix. 2.) But with this, both the Evangelists connect an account of the conduct of Jesus towards the healed woman, which is altogether peculiar. Mark v. 30, observes that Jesus had perceived that virtue had gone out of him ; Luke viii. 46, adds an explanation that Jesus himself uttered the words, ἔγνων δύναμιν ἐξελθοῦσαν ἀπ' ἐμοῦ. The disciples, in their want of spiritual discernment, imagined that the question of Jesus was occasioned by the pressure of the people, and wondered at the conduct of Christ, but he looked around him with a searching eye (περιεβλέπετο, Mark v. 32), and the woman, feeling that she was discovered, approached and confessed, δι' ἣν αἰτίαν ἥψατο αὐτοῦ, *for what cause*, ect, and did so before all the people, as Luke ver. 47, very significantly adds. What strikes us in this description is, that Jesus makes use of the expression δύναμις ἐξελθοῦσα ἀπ' ἐμοῦ, *power going from*, etc. From this, the notion imperceptibly begins to arise, that the power has wrought by a process involuntary on the part of Christ—a supposition unsuited to the transaction. The words in themselves, however, evidently do not imply that the virtue emanated from Christ involuntarily ; but we can have as little hesitation in admitting that virtue really proceeded from Christ, as in admitting the doctrine of the church, that the Spirit proceedeth from the Father and the Son, and is poured out into the hearts of believers. The fulness of spiritual life which our Redeemer had in himself, manifested itself, as it is the nature of the Spirit to do, in its creative and curative character ; and that is expressed in the words δύναμις ἐξέρχεται, *power goeth forth*, as the radiance of fire beams forth light and warmth.*

On the other hand, this significant mode of expression contrasts strikingly with that empty view, according to which Jesus is said to have cured and operated without the pouring forth of virtue. But the view that the efficacious working of Christ took place, in this case, involuntarily, seems to be favoured by the question, " Who has touched me ?" when connected with the passage, " I felt that power went out of me." If Christ, indeed, did not know *that*, and *whom* he was curing, the whole transaction appears magical and unworthy of the Lord. Each of his cures must be considered as an action of which he was conscious, and which stood in close connexion with the person to be healed, and with his moral condition. And this feature will become apparent even in the case before us, if we look to the following considerations :—Her moral cure was the very circumstance which induced our Lord to draw her from her concealment into the light, for he had recognized her timid faith, and did not wish that she should be put to shame. Without addressing her, he compels her to come forward spontaneously, and to overcome the false modesty which had prevented her from coming freely and openly before our Lord, and laying her necessitous case before him. Though even her secret approach to the Lord for the purpose of touching his garment, undoubtedly exhibits faith, yet her mode of procedure was not altogether pure and single-minded ; fear of man, and false timidity, were at the foundation of it, and had, as yet, to be overcome. Now, it would have been too hard to have required her, before her cure, to speak openly in the presence of the people. Our gracious Lord, therefore, softened the difficulty by making this demand subsequent to the cure, and this helped her along the narrow way. But from the act itself he could not altogether free her, as it was subservient to her spiritual birth, and to the new life. We thus gain the true moral standing-point,

---

* Hence it is that passages like Matt. xiv. 36 ; Mark iii. 10, vi. 56 ; Luke vi. 19, in which we are told that many people supplicated Jesus to be permitted to touch his garment, and that they were healed, offer no peculiar difficulties, because the cures plainly appear to be actions of his will.

and perceive in Christ every thing well considered and ordered for man's temporal and eternal welfare, according to the measure of his infinite love. Only one question more may be asked, viz., whether it was not substantially an untruth to ask, " Who is it that touched me ?" if he knew that it was she. But if we consider that Christ only wished to bring her to a confession, and that any dissembling of his knowledge of her is utterly out of the question, we can no more find in this a stumbling-block, than in the case of a father who should put to the entire number of his children the question—Who has done this ? well knowing the guilty one, yet desirous of obtaining the free confession of his guilt.*

Ver. 22.—After this victory of the woman over her old nature, it was now time to comfort her, and to foster the faith which had at first manifested itself but timidly. In the process of healing, the the *power* of Christ appears as the efficient cause, and the *faith* of the woman as the essential condition ; both combined to complete the work. Our Lord gave her peace not in words only, but in its substantial spiritual effects.

Mark and Luke continue to report what turn the events took whilst Jesus was going to the house of Jairus. There came messengers (ἀπὸ τοῦ ἀρχισυναγώγου sc. δοῦλοι) announcing the death of the child (compare the remarks above on Matth. ix. 18), and requesting that Jesus might not be farther troubled. The Redeemer comforts the trembling father, wavering in his faith, and arrives at length at the house. Both the narrators here mention, by way of anticipation, that Christ took in with him only certain persons. Matthew, with greater care, mentions it once more in its proper place, in the 40th verse.

Ver. 23.—According to the custom of the Jews, who rapidly hastened on their funerals, Jesus already found funeral music (αὐληταί), and howling (Mark has ἀλαλάζειν), and wailing (κόπτεσθαι, *pectus plangere* = *lugere*) people before the house. The Redeemer interrupted their noise with the words, οὐκ ἀπέθανε τὸ κοράσιον, *the maiden is not dead*, without giving heed to their mocking. This declaration of Christ is so simple and plain, that no one ought ever to have tampered with it.†

* According to *Euseb.* H. E. viii. 18, there was set up in Cæsarea Paneas, cast in bronze, the statue of Christ, with the woman suffering from the issue of blood, in the act of touching his garment. We have no reason to doubt the veracity of this narrative, inasmuch as the fact is, in itself, anything but improbable.

† Christ will not have the *raising of the dead*, as such, to be openly and immediately known, and thus his reputation with the unconverted multitude increased. (Comp. Mark v. 23 ; Luke viii. 56): hence he speaks to the mass of mourning women and musicians the enigmatical words, "the child sleepeth, she is not dead." The less discerning among the crowd would misunderstand his language, and suppose that he had performed not a resurrection from the dead, but a miraculous cure: yet was the child so manifestly dead

The miracles of our Lord need no adjuncts from human hands ; the very absence of ostentation adds to their grandeur. The addition, "but sleepeth," does not permit us to understand the first expression, as if it meant " she is not dead, because I have the intention of raising her, or, inasmuch as what I intend to do must be regarded as already accomplished." The contrast, " she is not dead, but sleepeth," which all the three Evangelists repeat *verbatim*, admits of no prevarication. We have here, consequently, *no raising from the dead in the true sense of the words*. It is likely that the child was in a deep trance ;[*] but viewed even in this light, the act performed by our Lord is not less significant. He presents himself, in such a plain declaration, in the purest moral grandeur. The real moment of death, which man can never ascertain, is perfectly known to Jesus ; and of this he declares that it has not yet arrived ; but the very circumstance that he knew this—that he knew it before he came—that he knew how to fix the time and circumstances—all these constitute the miraculous part of this act. What was unknown to all of them (Luke viii. 53 has the words εἰδότες ὅτι ἀπέθανεν, *knowing that she was dead*, because they had tried every means to restore her) he knew, without having even seen the child ; and he openly declared what he knew, and produced thereby life and faith. His miracle was not diminished, by this open declaration, in the eyes of those present, but was, on the contrary, rendered great and glorious. (Mark v. 42 ; Luke xiii. 56.) Having here again in view the moral impression, Jesus collected from among the rude mass (who are as prone to mockery as to stupid amazement) a small number of susceptible souls ; to them he permitted the undisturbed enjoyment of beholding the returning life of the damsel, in all its manifestations, in order that thereby they might be excited to solemn and sacred thankfulness to God. This impression, however, our

that they laughed Jesus to scorn, and it was at most not until *after* they saw the child living and healed that they could become doubtful whether the death had been a real or only apparent one. The enlightened must have recognized in the words of Jesus the meaning that *for him and his power* death was but a sleep, and that for these mourning women there is at hand no dead body to be the object of their wailings, but a sleeping child, that is on the point of being awakened.—[E. That Ebrard is right as to the *fact* I cannot doubt. His correctness in assigning the *cause* of the Saviour's language, is more questionable. It seems clear that the Evangelists intend to describe a raising from the dead; and the words of the Saviour, *interpreted according to his ordinary modes of speech*, interpose no difficulty to this view. Strictly speaking, she was *dead*, but viewed with reference to the *result* she was only asleep. There was one present to whom her death was the same as the state of sleep, and this is expressed in the Saviour's sharp and terse manner by the language, "She is not dead, but sleepeth."—[K.

* Physicians distinguish *syncope* from *asphyxia ;* by the latter they understand the suspension of all the vital functions; and it is this which must here be supposed. The history of Eutychus (Acts xx. 7, seq.) is quite similar to this. Of the youth mentioned Paul says, ἡ ψυχὴ αὐτοῦ ἐν αὐτῷ ἐστιν, which words explain the expressions ἐπέστρεψε τὸ πνεῦμα in our narrative (Luke viii. 55.)

Lord commanded them to conceal in the depths of their souls, lest, by their busy talkativeness, they should immediately destroy again the slight spark of life which was but just enkindled. (Mark v. 43 ; Luke viii. 56. Comp. also the remarks on Matth. viii. 4.) Mark with still greater care, reports what happened in presence of the parents, and of Peter, John, and James. (Concerning the presence, on many occasions, of these three apostles only, compare the remarks on Matth. x. 2.) Jesus seized the hand of the damsel and called, טְלִיתָא קוּמִי. (The substantive is the Syriac form of טָלֶה, which properly signifies " lamb," but is frequently used of children also.) It may be best to consider here the call of Christ, his life-giving word, as the means of resuscitation. Not the slightest mention is made of the application of any other means, and there is no reason for supposing that such were used, though it is not absolutely impossible that such should have been employed, inasmuch as Jesus, upon other occasions, makes use of such means. (Comp. the remarks on Mark vii. 23.) But just because everything is recorded in a plain and straight-forward manner, and in its proper place, it is as natural to suppose that, where no such thing is spoken of, it did not take place. Christ and the apostles, who were free from all charlatanry, represent the most wonderful occurrences in the plainest and simplest manner ; and as our Lord, after having fed thousands with a few loaves, yet, in strict accordance with human nature, gives orders to gather carefully the fragments that remained ; so also he, who himself is the life, and who hereafter shall awaken all the dead by his voice (John v. 25), orders that the little child, whom he had awakened from her trance, and whom he declares not to have been dead, should be supplied with food. (Mark v. 43 ; Luke viii. 55.) He thus permits everything to go on in a natural and simple way, and manifests thereby a truth of the inner life which forms, in a peculiar manner, the true foil to his great actions.

§ 14. HEALING OF TWO BLIND MEN AND OF A DUMB MAN.

(Matth. ix. 27–34.)

Matthew alone relates that, during the time which Jesus spent in his house, he healed therein two blind men, and a dumb man. The words, αὐτῶν δὲ ἐξερχομένων ἰδού κ. τ. λ., *and as they came out, etc.* (ver. 32), connect immediately the healing of the dumb man with that of the blind men. The similar narrative in Matthew, xi. 22, seq., must therefore be regarded as a different event. The accusation of the Pharisees, ἐν τῷ ἄρχοντι τῶν δαιμονίων ἐκβάλλει τὰ δαιμόνια, *he casteth out devils by the prince, etc.*, will, when that passage is under consideration, be subjected to more special inquiry.

As the narratives of the two cures here effected offer no difficulty which are not solved by the remarks previously made, one circumstance only need be mentioned, viz., that the κωφὸς δαιμονιζόμενος, *dumb demonaic*, verse 32, must be distinguished from a dumb man suffering from organic imperfection. The former is dumb through demoniacal influence. This, no doubt, must have assumed the form of a kind of mania, which must not, however, be viewed as imaginary, but as the consequence of the agency of hostile powers. Their being overcome by the light-giving power of the Redeemer, restores in the sufferer the right psychical and physical relations. This scriptural mode of viewing things, which ascribes real effects to real causes, and which, specially, never admits psychical phenomena without spiritual or demoniacal influence, appears equally simple and profound.

§ 15. THE SENDING FORTH OF THE APOSTLES.

(Matth. ix. 35; x. 42; Mark vi. 7–11; Luke ix. 1–5.)

After having represented Jesus in chapters viii., ix. as a worker of miracles, Matthew gives, in chap. x. a series of our Lord's discourses, put together in the same manner as in the Sermon on the Mount. He opens it by a transition, expressed in general terms, such as we have already met with in Matthew iv. 23, et seq. He remarks that Jesus went about teaching and healing. We find in this passage no limitation to Galilee. The words of Matthew are, on the contrary, so general, that it is clear that he did not at all intend to fix the localities. But then the Evangelist sets forth how the immediate perception of the condition of the people, which our Redeemer obtained in his wanderings, excited in him the most heartfelt compassion for the miserable situation of the people of God; and it was this which formed the motive for his sending forth of the disciples. (Concerning σπλαγχνίζεσθαι, compare the remarks on Luke i. 78. Its real and primary meaning is maternal compassion for the helpless child. Instead of the more common word ἐκλελυμένοι —ἐκλύεσθαι, used of the failing and exhaustion of all strength, Gal. vi. 9, Heb. xii. 3, the less frequently used expression ἐσκυλμένοι should, no doubt, be received in the text, as is done by *Griesbach:* "Worn out by the cares of life, and scattered [ἐρριμμένοι] by wolves like sheep without a shepherd." Concerning this figure, compare the remarks on John x. 3, et seq.) The general idea connected with this, ὁ μὲν θερισμὸς πολύς κ. τ. λ., *the harvest indeed*, etc., stands in Luke, x. 2, in a more close and definite connexion, as spoken on the occasion of the sending forth of the seventy disciples; for which

reason we refer to our remarks on that passage. Matthew introduces it here, only because it indicates the prevailing disposition of
the Saviour's soul ; from this proceeded the sending forth of the
twelve apostles, which stands in immediate connexion with it.
The thought indicates the character of the time and of the
people ; their preparation for the reception of the divine doctrines ;·
and their need of such teachers, as could effectually supply their
true wants.

The body of the twelve apostles is here evidently assumed as
already existing ; of its formation the Evangelist reports as little as
of the calling of the individuals singly, if we except the fragmentary
notices in chap. iv. 18, et seq. Mark and Luke appear here likewise more exact in their statements. They connect with the list of
the apostles, the remark that Christ had expressly chosen and installed them as a body. (Mark iii. 14, καὶ ἐποίησε δώδεκα, ἵνα ὦσι μετ᾽
αὐτοῦ. Luke (vi. 13) is yet more definite, προσεφώνησε τοὺς μαθητὰς
αὐτοῦ, καὶ ἐκλεξάμενος ἀπ᾽ αὐτῶν δώδεκα, οὓς καὶ ἀποστόλους* ὠνόμασε).
Luke gives prominence only to the significancy of their *installation*.
He remarks, chap. vi. 12, "he went forth into the mountain to pray,
and spent the night in prayer to God" [ἐξῆλθεν (ὁ Ἰησοῦς) εἰς τὸ ὄρος
προσεύξασθαι, καὶ ἦν διανυκτερεύων ἐν τῇ προσευχῇ τοῦ Θεοῦ]. It would
appear then that our Redeemer prepared himself by a night spent
in prayer, and in the morning installed the twelve apostles. If we
consider that, in the election of this body of men, in whose hearts
the first germs of truth were to be deposited, everything depended
upon a right selection of persons, we shall estimate the importance
of the moment. It was a moment in which the foundation-stone
of the church was laid. The twelve apostles, as the representatives
of spiritual Israel,† were to form among themselves a complete
unity ; it was therefore necessary that in their fundamental dispositions they should mutually supplement each other, and carry within
themselves the germ of all the various tendencies which on a larger
scale afterwards manifested themselves in the church. It is only
as a discerner of hearts (John ii. 25) that the Lord was enabled to
establish such a band of closely united spirits, who were to stand as
the representatives of the whole spiritual creation which was to be
called into existence. In himself, everything was united in a holy
unity ; but, as the ray divides itself into its colours, so that one
light which beamed forth from Christ fell, in variously modified

---

* The term ἀπόστολος appears here as a real official title of the twelve. (Concerning the relation of this term to similar expressions, compare the comment. on 1 Cor.
xii. 28.)

† This is figuratively represented in Rev. xxi. 14. The twelve apostles, as distinct
from Paul, seem likewise to have had a special reference to Israel after the flesh. (Compare the remarks on Matth. x. 5, 6, and the Introduction to the Epistles of Paul.)

splendour, upon the hearts of his twelve apostles. Thus alone was it possible, that, through this medium, not only a few men, but all, according to their wants and dispositions, might be equally satisfied by the Gospel. A striking feature in this election of the twelve is, that Judas Iscariot,* the betrayer of the Lord, was admitted into this narrow circle. But faith perceives even in this a wonderful, gracious dispensation of our Lord. Evil is everywhere entwined and mixed up with the good, that it may be overcome by the redeeming power of Christ. As in paradise there was a serpent, and in the ark a Ham was saved, so must there be a Judas among the twelve, if their circle was truly to represent Israel. Not that he was predestinated to evil—Scripture knows no *reprobatio impiorum* (compare Rom. ix.)—but in order to give him occasion for overcoming, by the help of the Lord, the evil which was in him. True, the unhappy man, as he did not avail himself of the opportunity, was to become the instrument of our Lord's betrayal ; *but it was by no means his destiny.* The God of mercy ordains everywhere, in the present order of things, the intermixture of good and evil, that the latter may be overcome by the former ; or, if it *will* not be overcome, to consummate the good by collision with the evil. For although Judas brings our Lord to the cross, yet by this very act he aids in procuring an everlasting redemption.

Of the first sending forth of the twelve apostles, which happened under the eye of the Lord himself, both Mark (vi. 7–11) and Luke (ix. 1–6) give an account, but without communicating so detailed instructions as does Matthew in chap. x.† In this discourse (chap. x.) Matthew evidently unites various elements. Luke narrates in chap. x. the sending forth of the seventy disciples, on which subject Matthew is silent, and communicates, on this occasion, a discourse of Jesus addressed to them. This discourse, and chap. xi. of Luke, wherein Christ gives special admonitions to his disciples, contain many elements of the instructions to the apostles, communicated by Matthew in chap. x. True, there is nothing in Matthew unsuitable to the occasion ; so that, in this respect, we might unhesitatingly assume that Jesus had thus spoken ; yet it is not probable, since in Luke the same passages stand in more appropriate connexion, while in Matthew, the connexion of the separate thoughts is often but loose. The simplest supposition is that Matthew intended to put together, in this chapter, the principles which Jesus impressed

---

* For further remarks on Judas Iscariot compare the comment. on Matth. xxvi. 24, and John xiii. 27.

† The hypothesis raised by *Dr. Paulus* (in his Commentary, vol. ii., p. 34), that Luke and Mark are narrating a subsequent mission of the twelve apostles, has originated only from the attempt to bring the separate evangelical narratives into a close connexion in point of time ; but it is altogether void of internal probability.

upon his apostles, at different times, concerning their relation to the world. This becomes the more probable, because many expressions occurring in the instruction (com. specially the remarks on Matth. x. 23) went beyond the knowledge which the apostles had at the time when they were sent forth. The special reference of the instruction to the impending mission of the twelve has assumed, in the hands of the Evangelist, a general character ; so that in this discourse of Jesus to his disciples, we have received instructions for them and for their whole apostolic work, nay, for all the missionaries of all times. How far this may have been the intention of Matthew, I leave undecided ;* but the Spirit, who spoke through him, has given that rich fulness to his representation.

Ver. 1.—Jesus on sending out the twelve apostles by two and two (Mark vi. 7), for their mutual assistance, gives to them, in the first place, a seal of their official authority, viz., the power of healing (ἐξουσία). It is obvious that the communication of such power of healing could only be by a communication of the power of the Spirit. Hence we find in this passage the first trace of a communication of the Spirit of Jesus to his disciples, which is increased in John xx. 22, and consummated on the day of Pentecost. From this also comes the relation in which the miraculous cures of the apostles stood to their other ministrations. The outward work of healing was the most subordinate and the first ; their purely spiritual labours in preaching the word they could begin only after the Pentecost. So also the Saviour began by healing the body ; but afterward, he exercised his redeeming power by healing the soul also. It is therefore no great loss which the church sustained, if, at a subsequent period, the gift of healing departed from her ; the higher gift, the word by which souls are redeemed, remained. A remarkable instance of such communication of the Spirit to others is found in Numb. xi. 17, et seq., where it is related how Moses laid upon the seventy elders of Israel the Spirit which rested upon himself. This is by no means a view of the Spirit bordering on materialism, but is, on the contrary, a representation of him in his essential nature. As God is love, and, as being love, it is his nature to communicate himself ; so it is also the nature of the Spirit, as a divine substance, to communicate himself unceasingly, creating life, and, as a stream, strengthening and refreshing the heart. A Spirit who would or could not communicate himself would be no spirit, or not a divine spirit. Now Christ, as the image of the invisible Father, continually pours out a fulness of living Spirit, but communicates to every one according to his wants and suscepti-

---

* Compare on this point my "Festprogramm über die Aechtheit. des Mat.," Abth. ii, S. 17.

bilities. As Jesus had purposely not chosen any noble or learned disciples, but those who were poor and despised in the eyes of the world (1 Cor. i. 27), they needed all the more a divine power to guide them in the discharge of their functions. This power, however, was to act, pure and undisturbed, through them, as pure organs ; and the less their minds had been formed by human influences, the more they were fitted to become such instruments of the Spirit.

Ver. 2.—Here follows the list of the apostles, which, for the convenience of the reader, we present, together with the other lists of the same (as given in Mark iii. 13, et seq.; Luke vi. 12, et seq.; and Acts i. et seq.), in the form of a comparative table :—

MATTHEW.	MARK.	LUKE.	ACTS OF THE APOSTLES.

1. First Class.

MATTHEW.	MARK.	LUKE.	ACTS OF THE APOSTLES.
1 Σίμων.	1 Πέτρος.	1 Σίμων.	1 Πέτρος.
2 ’Ανδρέας.	2 ’Ιάκωβος.	2 ’Ανδρέας.	2 ’Ιάκωβος.
3 ’Ιάκωβος.	3 ’Ιωάννης.	3 ’Ιάκωβος.	3 ’Ιωάννης.
4 ’Ιωάννης.	4 ’Ανδρέας.	4 ’Ιωάννης.	4 ’Ανδρέας.

2. Second Class.

MATTHEW.	MARK.	LUKE.	ACTS OF THE APOSTLES.
5 Φίλιππος	5 Φίλιππος.	5 Φίλιππος.	5 Φίλιππος.
6 Βαρθολομαῖος.	6 Βαρθολομαῖος.	6 Βαρθολομαῖος.	6 Θωμᾶς.
7 Θωμᾶς.	7 Ματθαῖος.	7 Ματθαῖος.	7 Βαρθολομαῖος.
8 Ματθαῖος.	8 Θωμᾶς.	8 Θωμᾶς.	8 Ματθαῖος.

3. Third Class.

MATTHEW.	MARK.	LUKE.	ACTS OF THE APOSTLES.
9 ’Ιάκωβος ’Αλφ.	9 ’Ιάκωβος ’Αλφ.	9 ’Ιάκωβος ’Αλφ.	9 ’Ιάκωβος ’Αλφ.
10 Λεββαῖος. Θαδδαῖος.	10 Θαδδαῖος.	10 Σίμων ὁ Ζηλ.	10 Σίμων ὁ Ζηλ.
11 Σίμων ὁ Καν.	11 Σίμων ὁ Καν.	11 ’Ιούδας ’Ιάκ.	11 ’Ιούδας ’Ιάκ.
12 ’Ιούδας ’Ισκ.	12 ’Ιούδας ’Ισκ.	12 ’Ιούδας ’Ισκ.	

The arrangement observed in these four lists, according to three classes, is so similar, that it cannot be supposed to have had an accidental origin ;* and yet they so differ from each other, that we are prevented from referring them to one written source. Hence it is most natural to suppose that each Evangelist arranged them according to their importance, as acknowledged by the universal consent of the church. Those who were less known and influential had the last place assigned to them ; those who were best known had the first. Slight modifications, of course took place in this ar-

---

* All agree as to the place of Peter, Philp, James the son of Alphæus, and Judas Iscariot; but they differ as regards the places of those between the above named. Yet the classes themselves remain unchanged.

rangement—for instance, Matthew and Luke place together the
apostles who were brothers, in consequence of which Andrew stands
before James and John ; on the other hand, in Mark, and in the
Acts of the Apostles, the three principal apostles are placed foremost, Peter being at the head. Among those who were nearly equal
in importance, as Philip, Bartholomew, Thomas, and Matthew—
arbitrary transpositions take place. But the notion, that some of
the apostles were of greater importance than others, is irresistibly
forced upon us by the evangelical history—Peter, James, and John,
especially, appear pre-eminent among the twelve. On several important occasions, Jesus took these alone into his intimate companionship. (Besides Mark v. 37, Luke viii. 51, comp. also Matth. xvii. 1
[Mark ix. 2 ; Luke ix. 28]; Matth. xxvi. 37 [Mark xiv. 33], and
John xxi. 19, 20, where Peter and John only were taken.) The
disciples thus surrounded the Lord in gradually expanding circles.
Nearest to him stood the three, then followed the other nine, then
the seventy, and last of all the multitude of his other disciples.
Yet, undeniable as was the difference among the disciples of Christ,
this does not imply any special secret doctrine for those who stood
nearer to him. The mystery of Christ, the highest and simplest
truth, was to be preached from the house-tops. Some, however,
apprehended this mystery itself far more profoundly than the others,
and were hence better fitted to move in immediate proximity to
the Lord. As regards the apostles individually, Peter is put at the
head by all the Evangelists ; Matthew calls him *first*, which certainly is not accidental. (For particulars, comp. the remarks on
Matth. xvi. 18.) Concerning the *cognomen* Πέτρος, *Peter*, comp.
the remarks on John i. 42.—Andrew stands much in the back-
ground throughout the gospel history. (Ἀνδρέας = אַנְדְּרְיָה, which
may be derived from נֵר.) James the son of Zebedee, appears only
in connexion with the two coryphæi of the apostles, viz. John
and Peter.* According to Acts xii. 2, he died early the death of a
martyr. (Concerning Philip, comp. the remarks on John i. 45 ; he
also was from Bethsaida. Bartholomew (בַּר תָּלְמַי = son of Ptolemy)
seems according to John i. 46, to be identical with Nathaniel of
Cana. (John xxi. 2.) The evangelical history is silent regarding the
latter ; Philip is introduced speaking, in John xiv. 9.—Thomas,
Θωμᾶς, תְּאם, Δίδυμος. Comp. concerning him, the remarks on John
xx. 24.—Matthew, Ματθαῖος, with the addition ὁ τελώνης, *the publican;* this addition points to Matthew, the author of the gospel, inasmuch as it is wanting in all other lists of the apostles, and an
addition of this kind is made to no other name.† It was only the

---

* On the cognomen Βοανεργές, given to John and James (Mark iii. 17), comp. the
remarks on Luke ix. 54.

† *De Wette* (in his comment. on this passage) calls this remark unimportant; but is

author himself who could, with propriety, have added it; in his mouth it was a recollection of the undeserved mercy which had been bestowed upon him. Concerning the various persons called James, compare the remarks on Matthew xiii. 55, and the introduction to the Epistle of James. Simon, with the cognomen the Canaanite (ὁ Κανανίτης), is described in a manner not to be mistaken, by the explanatory cognomen ὁ ζηλωτής, *the zealot*, which Luke gives him in his Gospel, as well as in the Acts of the Apostles. (Κανανίτης, from קנא, to be jealous.) He had, no doubt, belonged to the sect of the Jewish zealots, of whom mention is made by *Josephus* (B. J. iv. 3, 9.) His demagogical zeal, hitherto directed only to outward things, was subsequently directed towards the attainment of spiritual freedom. Greater difficulties present themselves respecting the person of Lebbeus, whom Mark calls Thaddeus. In the first place, the reading of the text of Matthew, is doubtful. The addition ὁ ἐπικληθείς, *surnamed*, is omitted in many codices. Nor does it appear to me, indeed, to belong to Matthew, who in no other passage makes use of this phrase in connexion with a name. It is probable that it may have crept into the text from some gloss; inasmuch as, on the margin, the very probable supposition was expressed, that the Thaddeus of Mark was identical with the Lebbeus of Matthew. *Mill* supposed that this addition had a reference to the name of Matthew. He regarded the Lebbeus = Levi, and hence supposed that some one had made this addition in order to direct attention to the circumstance, that Matthew is called Levi by both Mark and Luke. The identity of the names cannot however be proved. Λεββαῖος, is probably derived from לב, *heart*, so that it signifies *cordatus*. Thaddeus (Θαδδαῖος), is perhaps synonymous with Theudas (Θευδᾶς) (see *Buxtorf*, Lex. Talm. p. 2565; s. v. תד *mamma* = to the Hebrew שד). Both the names are wanting in Luke (in the Gospel as well as in the Acts of the Apostles); instead of them he has Ἰούδας Ἰακώβου, *Judas (son) of James*, who is not mentioned by either Matthew or Mark. That there was a Judas (not Iscariot) among the twelve apostles, clearly appears from John xiv. 22; and it may be that he is the same person as this Lebbeus or Thaddeus. The ancient church at a very early period, adopted this view. (*Hieron.* ad. h. l. calls him triple-named, τριώνυμος.) The view adopted by modern commentators, that we ought to supply after Ἰακώβου, *of James*, not as commonly υἱός, *son*, but ἀδελφός, *brother*, is altogether without foundation. This Judas

any other apostle designated after this worldly calling? Is Peter designated the fisherman, or anything of that kind? Moreover, the expression "publican" has, in a secondary sense, an opprobrious signification, as appears from the phrase "publicans and sinners." Such a cognomen only Matthew himself could assume. Least of all would some later author of the gospel have chosen it, as it would have been the interest of such an one to extol Matthew.

would then appear to have been the author of the Epistle of Jude, which forms part of the canon of the New Testament, and a brother of James, the son of Alpheus, and of Simon Zelotes ; and all these, the ἀδελφοὶ τοῦ Κυρίου ;—a view which we shall endeavour to refute when we come to treat of Matthew xiii. 55 ; John vii. 5, and in the introductions to the Epistles of James and Jude. There exists no reason whatsoever for departing from the common mode of supply- ing the ellipsis ; and, for this reason, we must consider this Judas, with the cognomen Lebbeus, or Thaddeus, to be a different person from Judas, the brother of our Lord. The passage ·of John vii. 5, must here serve as a clue to lead us to the truth ; for, according to this passage, the brethren of Jesus did not believe in him, and could, therefore, by no means, have been in the number of the twelve apostles. Finally, Judas Iscariot, 'Ιούδας 'Ισκαριώτης = אִישׁ קְרִיּוֹת, a man of Karioth. (Josh. xv. 25.)* This explanation is given also in several MSS. on John vi. 71 ; xii. 4, in the words ἀπὸ Καριώτου. Other derivations, as, for instance, from שֶׁקֶר, falsehood, lie, are ob- viously intended to convey an allusion to his treacherous deed ; but in this very circumstance, the pure character of our gospels is mani- fested, that as they abstain from every kind of laudatory expression concerning Christ and his acts and discourses, so, in like manner, they avoid all reproachful allusion to Judas. The only remark which they make, as historians, when referring to the name of Judas, is ὁ παραδοὺς αὐτόν, who delivered him up. With this single exception, they allow the stupendous facts in the history of Jesus to speak for themselves ; and the simple, truthful descriptions make light and shade appear in the most striking contrast. And thus, viewing everything in its purely objective light, they despise all paltry, per- sonal censure.

Ver. 5.—To this company of the twelve apostles, Jesus, accord- ing to Matthew, now directs his discourse. It may appear strange that it should proceed on the principles of Jewish exclusiveness, in- asmuch as the apostles are prohibited from going to the Samaritans and Gentiles. Luke, x. 1 has not this limitation in the discourse of Jesus to the Seventy ; but these Seventy appear as the represen- tatives of the whole Gentile world, and Luke alone gives an account of them, as he wrote for Gentiles. Jesus, however, never comes for- ward as a destroyer of the exclusive privileges of the Jewish people, which had been vouchsafed to them by God himself (compare the remarks on Matth. xxi. 33) ; on the contrary, he acknowledges them (Matth. xv. 24), and confines his own ministry, on the whole, to

---

* De Wette, agreeing with Lightfoot, has again declared in favour of the derivation of this appellative from the word אסקורטיא, "a leather apron," or אסכרא, "strangling." The parallel passages in John, however, seem to be altogether opposed to this deriva- tion ; the assertion that קְרִיּוֹת אִישׁ or קְרִיּוֹתָי could not have been added as a sur- name to the proper name, is altogether destitute of proof.

Palestine. He, indeed, hints at a time at which this exclusiveness will be done away (John x. 16) ; but he ministers, in the meantime, among Gentiles and Samaritans only occasionally, whensoever their faith constrained him to do so. (Compare Matth. xv. 21, seq., and John iv.) We cannot suppose that in this Christ was accommodating himself merely to the weakness of the disciples ; but rather to the demands of the times, and the immediate destination of the twelve. The Gospel was first to be offered to Israel as *a nation*. Had they received it, the prophecy of Micah (iv. 1, ff.) would have been immediately fulfilled. They rejected it, and it was only at a subsequent period that Paul received the express command to labour for the Gentile world (Acts ix. 15) ; and when the Redeemer departed from the earth, he extended the sphere of action of the twelve also to all nations (Matth. xxviii. 19). But it was necessary, first of all, to prepare, in the nation of Israel, a hearth to receive the sacred fire, and to keep its heat in a state of concentration. It was only after the Church had thus been safely established in the midst of the people of God, and after the unbelief of the mass had been fully manifested, that the stream of life was poured out over the wide Gentile world.

Ver. 6.—Πρόβατα ἀπολωλότα are here used in the sense of *sheep who have gone astray, and have been separated from their shepherd* (compare the remarks on Luke xv. 4) ; with evident reference to Jeremiah l. 6 צֹאן אֹבְדוֹת הָיָה עַמִּי.

Ver. 7.—The main burden of their preaching is to be, that the kingdom of heaven is at hand (compare the remarks on Matth. iii. 2 ; iv. 17); but in the form used by John the Baptist. (See Mark vi. 12, they preached that men should repent.) The direction given to the disciples, and their special object, were at this, their first mission, altogether different from what they were after the outpouring of the Holy Spirit. The apostles themselves, as yet, occupied Old Testament ground, and, like the Baptist, preached repentance, and baptized with water (John iv. 2) ; subsequently, after the soil had been prepared by the previous preaching of repentance, they proclaimed the remission of sins.

Ver. 8.—With this is connected the promise of miraculous healing, as the first outward manifestation of the coming redemption. (Compare the remarks on Matth. xi. 5.) The exhortation " freely give" was the natural result of circumstances. The disciples might easily have been induced to receive presents, and have thus been imperceptibly led to regard not the faith, but the wealth of the sick, thus inflicting injury on their own souls. They had claims only for the necessaries of life. (Very considerable critical authorities omit the clause "raise the dead" (νεκροὺς ἐγείρετε) ; others place it after λεπροὺς καθαρίζετε, *cleanse the lepers*, and this shows it to be not very unlikely a marginal gloss. *Mill* and *J. D. Michaelis* therefore consider it a subsequent addition. We might indeed suppose it added to honour the apostles. But as no instance of such a miracle is recorded, this very fact perhaps accounts better for the omission of the clause. But it does not follow that because no such example is given, no such case actually occurred.)

Ver. 9, 10.—This endowment with spiritual riches, our Lord follows up with the exhortation to go forth in the external garb of poverty. But the remark that they need no outward preparation for their journey, is, in reality, only another view of their riches. By going forth without human resources, they lived upon the rich treasure of their heavenly Father. The correct exposition of our passage is best obtained from a comparison with Luke xxii. 35–37. In that passage, Jesus, a short time before his sufferings, reminds the apostles of that rich and glorious time when he could send them forth with no earthly equipment, and remarks that the times were now different (as these were the days in which the bridegroom would be taken from them)—that now every one must prepare himself as well as he could, and to the utmost of his power. The leading thought, therefore, is this ; we live at a time of rich blessings (it is the hour in which the light is in the ascendant, contrasted with Luke ii. 53, " This is the hour and power of darkness ;" concerning which passage, comp. the Commentary), when no human preparation is required—"love will guide you, love will provide you !" The details given must not be too much pressed, but must be taken in all the freedom in which the apostles themselves received them. Mark, vi. 8, permits them to take a staff ; but the two other Evangelists forbid even that ;* Matthew forbids also even the sandals ; Mark permits them. It is a mere trifling with words to insist here on a difference between ὑποδήματα, *shoes,* and σανδάλια, *sandals.* The words, " The labourer is worthy of his meat" (Matth. x. 10), afford the true point of view. The Redeemer, who had himself no place where to lay his head, puts his disciples likewise on a footing of pure faith ; as the labourers of God,† they had to expect from him what was necessary for their bodily wants ; for the exercise and proof of their faith they went forth without any such careful preparations as the man destitute of faith makes, and must make. Some of the disciples might even have had some money with them ; but in this they would not have acted in opposition to the command of Jesus,

* *Gratz,* in his commentary on Matthew, vol. i., p. 519, is of opinion that Jesus only forbade them to take with them a supply, but not that he prohibited the taking of the staff which was in their hands, or the shoes which were on their feet. Very strange, certainly! for who ever carries with him a supply of sticks on a journey!

† The expression ἐργάτης, *labour,* is a figurative one, according to which mankind are compared to a vineyard or arable field, in which spiritual labour is to be performed (Concerning this, comp. the remarks on Matth. xiii. 1, seq.)

unless they had taken it *from unbelief*. The command must thus be viewed spiritually—in its relation to the disposition of mind and to faith ; and, in this respect, it has its eternal truth, applicable to all labourers in the kingdom of God, at all times and in all places. Yet this word of the Lord must never be viewed without its necessary complement from Luke xxii. 35, seq.

Ver. 11.—There now follow more special precepts with regard to their spiritual ministry. The words ἐξετάσατε τίς ἄξιος, *inquire who is worthy*, must not be referred to virtuous and noble dispositions, but to the poor (Matth. v. 3), the longing, the needy in spirit (Matth. ix. 12); to these alone could the proclamation of a Redeemer be an εὐαγγέλιον, *good news*. [The work of evangelization is never to be prosecuted at random. It should seek first those who are in some degree ripe for it, and spread from them as a centre.] In the same town they were not to change their residence. He exhorts them to strive after peace and quietness, in the bustle of their travelling. (In Luke x. 7, the same idea is expressed, with an additional remark ; concerning which, see the comment. on that passage.)

Ver. 12—The apostles, as the recipients of the spiritual powers which our Redeemer possessed without measure (John iii. 34), and had communicated to them according to their capacities for receiving them, are enjoined to communicate their gifts. As the sun sheds abroad his rays upon the good and the evil, so they also shall bless the house into which they enter ; their blessing when given to the impure, will *return* to them. This mode of expression flows from a partially material conception of spiritual influence ; like the light, it pours itself forth, and returns again to its source ;* blessing and intercession are, according to this view, an exhalation and inhalation of the Spirit. These, indeed, are figurative expressions, but they embody a substantial and profound meaning. Led by the Spirit, the apostles enter into a house and say, Peace be to this house (εἰρήνη τῷ οἴκῳ τούτῳ) (Luke x. 5), not as a mere empty phrase, like the כֶּם לָכֶם שָׁלוֹם of the Jews, but as the most genuine expression of their character and office. The blessing remains where it finds a welcome place (ἄξιος, *worthy*, is again to be understood, in the evangelical sense, of all those who are in want of, and long for salvation and mercy) ; where it finds no welcome, it returns to those who pronounced it, as to its living source. Hence the Spirit appears as that which is life itself, having its fountains from which it emanates and into which it returns, if it does not find a place wherein to settle, in order to create a new fountain. (John iv. 14 ; vii. 38.)

---

* This mode of viewing is rendered specially prominent, in the representation of χάρις and πνεῦμα, as given by John. Comp. the remarks on John vii. 38, 39.

Ver. 14.—Wherever the feeling of need, and the longing for that which is divine are wanting, thence the messenger of Christ departs ; he comes only to bring to the sick the message of healing. The shaking off the dust (ἐκτινάσσειν κονιορτόν), is a symbolical representation of total and utter separation and renunciation. (Acts xiii. 51 ; xviii. 6.) To express an 'idea by means of action is very common in the Old as well as in the New Testament, and indeed throughout the whole of the East; this mode of speech is more impressive for sensual man than mere words. (Comp. the remarks on Matth. xxvii. 24.)

Ver. 15.—Sodom and Gomorrha are held forth as the symbols of God's justice punishing alienation from himself. The greatness of the guilt is proportioned to the clearness and purity in which the heavenly element has presented itself to him who hardens himself against its impressions. He who turns away the messengers of Christ, shews himself more hardened than the old sinners of Sodom, because they represent that which is divine, more purely than did Lot and his pious contemporaries. (Concerning the whole idea here hinted at, comp. the more extended remarks on Matth. xi. 22, 24.)

Ver. 16.—From this exhibition of the lighter side of the apostles' ministry, the Saviour turns to its darker side, viz., their relation to the enemies of his kingdom. As the wolf is the symbol of cunning malice, so is the sheep of simple purity ; it stands defenceless against the wild power which knows no restraint. This is a very significant picture of the position of every follower of the Lamb (Rev. xiv. 4), among the perverse race of the children of this world. Continuing the use of significant animal symbolisms, the Lord exhorts to prudence—a virtue specially difficult for the believer to attain ; he fears the character of the old serpent, and prefers to *suffer* rather than to *deceive*. In the περιστερά, *dove*, the symbol of the Holy Ghost (Matth. iii. 16), purity of soul is expressed ; (ἀκέραιος == unmixed, pure, without guile) ; in the ὄφις, *serpent*, (Gen. iii. 1), cunning and prudence. (Φρόνιμος, Φρόνησις, derived from φρένες, signifies, in biblical anthropology, understanding, and power of reasoning, which is shewn in adapting itself to circumstances.) (Comp. the remarks on Luke i. 17.) It is difficult to combine this wisdom of the serpent with the guilelessness of the dove ; but the very command of Jesus testifies that it is not impossible. Yet, in the course of Christian development, let prudence suffer rather than simplicity, if their union is as yet unattained.

Ver. 17, 18.—Their impending suffering for the testimony of Jesus, is now more definitely brought before them. The Lord intimates that their life, which as yet moved in a narrow sphere, would be brought out into the publicity of the great world, and that earthly tribulations of all kinds await the preacher of heavenly peace. (Comp. the remarks on Matth. xxiv. 9.) The συνέδρια, *councils*, are the courts of justice in the provincial towns. (Comp. the remarks on Matth. v. 21. In like manner, it is used in Mark xv. 9.) The discourse ascends from the minor to the major. The ἡγεμόνες, *governors* (comp. the remarks on Matth. xxvii. 1), are the Roman pro-consuls ; the βασιλεῖς, *kings*, are the tetrarchs (Acts xii. 1 ; xxvi. 1.) Concerning the words, εἰς μαρτύριον, comp. the remarks on Matth. viii. 4. In the sufferings which the children of God have to experience from the world for the name of Jesus, their true character—that of suffering and self-sacrificing love—will make itself manifest.

Ver. 19,ˣ20.—As a consolation in the prospect of such sufferings, our Lord promises them special help from above. The disciples, inexperienced and unskilled in speaking, are directed to the spirit of all wisdom. The words, μὴ μεριμνήσητε, πῶς ἢ τί λαλήσητε, *take no thought how or what ye shall speak*, exclude all human calculation, and refer the disciples to a higher principle, to the Spirit from above. The idea that it is a gift of God to know how to speak a word in season, is expressed in Isaiah l. 4. (Comp. the remarks on Luke xxi. 15.) This does not, of course, exclude the use of the natural powers—these are rather to be sanctified by this Spirit. The word μεριμνᾶν, *take thought*, must therefore refer to the anxious collecting of one's own strength, as is done by the unbelieving natural man, who is ignorant of any higher source of life and power. Such a reliance on a higher power, however, would be *fanaticism*, if, first, the conditions of help from above, viz., repentance and true faith, were wanting, and if, secondly, impurity should design to apply it to wicked purposes. To confirm them in the conviction of such help from above, Jesus adds : For it is not ye that speak, etc. Individual characters thus disappear altogether in the great struggle between light and darkness ; God's cause is at stake, and that is pleaded by his Spirit in those instruments which he consecrates to himself. By views like these, the individual gains an invincible power, inasmuch as he is taken from his isolation, and recognizes himself as the member of a great invincible community. The *Spirit of the father* (πνεῦμα πατρός) is contrasted immediately with the spirit of the disciples themselves ; the heavenly principle appears, therefore, as already operating in them, although it had not yet displayed itself in its full power. (Comp. the remarks on John vii. 39.)

Ver. 21.—Hitherto the discourse has contained nothing inapplicable to existing circumstances ; but the following verses seem to have another reference, viz., to such circumstances as are described in chap. xxiv. They point to a sphere of action of a wider extent than that which would present itself to the disciples in this, their first mission. Our Redeemer would no doubt speak to them of persecutions, even unto death,* only in the last days of his earthly ministry. (Comp. the remarks on Matth. xxiv. 10, 12.) The relations of the disciples, however, were analogous in the various periods of their ministry ; and, in so far, these verses also have here their full application. The Gospel is now represented as overruling the natural relations of earthly life. The element of new life, which it has brought into the world, is arrested in its course by no barriers of relationship or family ties ; every where it appropriates to itself susceptible minds. But, precisely for this reason does it also call forth opposition in minds that do not lay themselves open to its influence, and the Gospel of peace brings the sword into the bosom of families ; for, being the Word of God, it divides asunder the joints and marrow (Heb. iv. 12.) The history of the spreading of Christianity proves the literal truth of these prophetic words of our Redeemer. (Comp. the *Acta Martyrii perpetuæ et Felicitatis*, printed in *my Monum. Hist. Eccles.* vol. i., p. 96, seq.) But as phenomena of that kind could not have happened at the time when the Redeemer spoke those remarkable words, they bear a prophetic character.

Ver. 22.—The hatred of all men, actuated by purely worldly principles, is specially directed against the name of Jesus. Natural virtue the world may find to be amiable, for the world perceives it to be a product of its own life ; but it hates what is specifically Christian, for it feels that therein is its death (James iv. 4.) The reference to the impending persecutions required some hint concerning the earnestness and endurance necessary for the struggle. Salvation is connected with endurance. The words εἰς τέλος, *to the end*, admit, primarily, a reference only to individuals, not to the tribulation of the entire body ; for death brings to every individual believer, the end of trouble, and the beginning of everlasting safety. Yet the passage reads (and ver. 23 confirms the impression that the sense of these words extends farther) as part of some prophetic discourse concerning the second coming. That the mention of this second coming, seems unsuited to the occasion of the first mission of the disciples, will presently be more fully developed.

Ver. 23.—In view of the impending persecutions, Jesus once more recommends prudence ; he advises them to avoid them as much as possible, that they may not receive injury in their souls by wilfully entering into danger, or continuing in it. The church has ever acted according to this precept ; it was only *Montanistic rigour* that would prohibit a fleeing from persecution. (The passage κᾂν

---

* Decisive, in this respect, is the passage John xvi. 4, the exposition of which may be compared.

ἐκ ταύτης κ. τ. λ. is, no doubt, genuine ; its omission in some MSS. originated, most probably, from the similarity in the terminations of the clauses, *homoioteleuton*.) In the closing words, the reference to the second coming of Christ, and to the end (which was already perceptible in ver. 22) clearly appears. The Son of Man is to come again before the disciples who were sent forth should have wandered through all the cities of Israel (τελεῖν sc. ὁδόν). Here a difficulty arises, inasmuch as it seems not to have been the purpose of this mission that the apostles should travel through the whole country ; but that it took place, in a great measure, for the training of the disciples themselves. From the feeling, therefore, that the connexion demanded a reference to something about to happen immediately, the explanation originated ; "You will not need to hasten through all the towns of Judea, in the persecution which you are to meet with ; I will be with you again ere that." But yet to this sense of the words, although grammatically admissible, does not suit, in the first place, the earnest ἀμήν, *verily;* and, secondly, Jesus does not come to them, but they come back to Jesus (Luke ix. 10); and finally, the phrase, "the Son of Man cometh" (ἔρχεται ὁ υἱὸς τοῦ ἀνθρώπου), has a definite doctrinal signification—it always refers to the second coming (παρουσία). But of this (viz., the παρουσία) Jesus cannot, according to the whole context, have well spoken. Nor is any thing gained by referring the coming of our Lord to the resurrection, or to the pouring out of the Spirit, or even to the destruction of Jerusalem ; for all these events were too remote from the disciples during the first period of their living with Christ. It is a matter of course that the *return* should be dependent upon the *departure* from them ; but of the latter the Redeemer had not yet spoken. It was only at a subsequent period, viz., shortly before, and at his transfiguration, that he gave to his disciples an insight into these two events (Matth. xii. 40 ; xvi. 21, 27 ; xvii. 1, seq. ; Luke ix. 22, 31) ; it was only on this solemn occasion that, by means of heavenly messengers, the Lord himself, in his human consciousness, was made acquainted with the divine counsel, in its whole extent, concerning the redemption of mankind through his sufferings. Thus these words which make mention of the second coming of Christ involve, by way of anticipation, a wider range of vision. They blend with the earlier, the subsequent mission of the disciples, and thus form a system of *general* instruction for the disciples in preaching the Gospel. It is true that this liberty which the Evangelists, especially Matthew, allow themselves (as appears on a close examination) in the treatment of our Lord's discourses is, after all, somewhat remarkable. (Concerning this, compare § 8 of the Introduction. But that which would have destroyed the character of the Gospel, if it had been done by an uncongenial spirit, tends

only to add to its splendour, if done by the kindred divine Spirit.
The various sentiments of Christ resemble pearls and jewels which
the Evangelists freely use, in order to produce the most varied and
beautiful works.* (Compare on this passage the comment. on
Matth. xxiv. 1.)

Ver. 24.—Jesus continues to intimate to the disciples their future destinies, by comparing them with himself. The passage is
given in a different connexion by Luke (vi. 40), and with the addition κατηρτισμένος δὲ πᾶς ἔστι ὡς ὁ διδάσκαλος, but in which the word
κατηρτισμένος must be understood as signifying, *perfectly educated,*
accomplished; so that the meaning of the words would be, " the
accomplished disciple resembles his master in all things." (Compare remarks on these words in the comment. on Matth. v. 1, with
reference to the connexion of the discourse in Luke [chap. vi. 20,
seq.]) The thought is rendered difficult by the reflection which
forces itself upon the reader, that many disciples surpass their
teachers.† An appeal to the proverbial mode of speech, contained in
these words, is evidently of no avail, for another proverb says,
" Many disciples are superior to their teachers" (πολλοὶ μαθηταὶ
κρείσσονες διδασκάλων.) The first requisite of a good proverb (and
certainly the Lord can have employed none but *good* ones) is, that
it be the expression of truth. This difficulty, however, is removed,
if we consider that the disciple who surpasses his master, ceases, at
that very moment, to be his disciple in the true sense of the word;
as a disciple, he can go no farther than his master ; hence, if he goes
farther than the master, he must have had some other master, and
if he has no human one, the Spirit must have been his teacher,
who has brought out that which was dormant in him. These words,
viewed thus, have their *relative* truth everywhere : but, in an *absolute* sense, they beautifully express the relation of the disciples to
Christ. He, the image of the Father, could not be surpassed,
either by his disciples or by any other ; he is Lord and teacher, in
the absolute sense, and compared to him, no one ever gets beyond
the sphere of dependence and instruction. In this relation, then, it
is likewise absolutely true, that whatever happened to the master,
must also happen to the disciple.

Ver. 25.—As the height of the hostile disposition, it is stated
that the world will call diabolical, that which is in its purest mani-

---

* Why might not Jesus himself, in prophetic anticipation, have here foretold to the
disciples once for all, the collective result of their entire future, and now but commencing
ministry : to wit, that they must *flee* from city to city, but that he would come in judgment on Israel, in the destruction of Jerusalem, before they should have completed in
their flight the entire circuit ?—[E.

† There seems no necessity of finding a difficulty here. The words convey the general and unquestionable truth, that the disciple naturally takes the impress of his master.—[K.

festation, *divine;* and this, at the same time, implies the contrast, that the world regards the diabolical element as the divine, and thus seeks to effect a total confusion of the elements of good and evil. If such be the case with the sun, what must happen to his rays ; if the master be treated thus, what must be done to his servants, in whom the glory of the Lord is only reflected ? (Οἰκιακός, comp. ver. 36, *domesticus,* with reference to the οἰκοδεσπότης.) The passage refers us back to Matthew ix. 34, ἐν τῷ ἄρχοντι τῶν δαιμονίων ἐκβάλλει τὰ δαιμόνια, by the *prince of the devils, etc.* (Comp. xii. 24.) This expression is not different from ἐπικαλεῖν Βεελζεβούλ, *calling on Beelzebub,* for, in order to be able to cast out devils *through* him, he must be in the individual that casts them out. As regards the name, Βεελζεβούβ is = זְבוּב בַּעַל. He was a god of the Ekronites, so called because the power was ascribed to him of removing troublesome flies, as Jupiter also had the cognomen ἀπόμυιος, μυίαγρος. In the New Testament, however, the reading Βεελζεβούλ, *Beelzeboul,* is to be preferred, inasmuch as the Jews, out of derision, changed the name of the idol into a form suggestive of contempt. For, this form of the name (derived from בַּעַל and בֶּאֱל) signifies the lord of mire. (Comp. *Lightfoot* on Matth. xii. 24.) The interpretation of this name, as given by Dr. Paulus, is very ingenious. According to him, the form must be resolved into the words בַּעַל זְבוּל, lord of the dwelling, viz., of the subterraneous one ; to this would very well answer the οἰκοδεσπότης, *householder,* of Christ. But that the prince of darkness is named after a national deity, arises from the circumstance that, according to the constant view of Scripture (comp. the remarks on 1 Cor. viii. 5), heathenish life, devoted to idolatry, appears as the element of darkness.

Ver. 26, 27.—Christ keeps the minds of the disciples in a state betwixt fear and implicit faith ; by the former, he urges them to earnestness, by the latter, he preserves them from despondency. It appears very striking, that their confidence is based upon the certainty of a future disclosure of all that is concealed. This is the fundamental idea of all the four clauses of these two verses. True, the unveiling of what is hidden, can never, in itself, be the foundation of faith ; if the mystery were something evil, it would rather give rise to fear. But, for the bosom which conceals within it that which is holy, but as yet unintelligible to those around, no certainty can be more consoling than that of its coming manifestation, for with this comes also the triumph of the good. Ver. 20 contains the explanation of the preceding verse ; the two clauses contained in each, must be viewed in conformity with the law of *parallelismus membrorum.* The words ἐν τῇ σκοτίᾳ, *in darkness,* are opposed to κεκαλυμμένον, *covered,* and signify the unintentional darkness which rests on anything ; in this case, for instance, on Galilee, a country hitherto unknown, but out of which, nevertheless, a new life arose. The " hearing in the ear" (εἰς τὸ οὖς ἀκούειν), on the contrary, corresponds with " that which is hid" (τὸ κρυπτόν), and denotes here the intentional concealment of that which is hereafter to be communicated, as in the case before us, the opening of the mysteries of the kingdom of God within the narrow circle of the apostles. The future free proclamation of the divine counsel in all its relations, and the disclosure of all the mysteries in the church by the Spirit, are hinted at in these words. The church knows of no mysteries to be kept back. (In the phrase κηρύσσειν ἐπὶ τῶν δωμάτων, *proclaim on the house-tops*, the form of the ancient houses and roofs must be borne in mind.)

Ver. 28.—The general exhortation " fear not then" (verse 26) is, in the 28th verse, brought into connexion with the true object of fear, whilst its false objects are excluded. With reference to verse 21, Jesus remarks, that the enemies of *physical* life should not be objects of fear to a child of God, inasmuch as their power cannot reach his *true* life. The words " cannot kill the soul" (μὴ δύνασθαι τὴν ψυχὴν ἀποκτεῖναι), contain an allusion to their purely external power, which is not able to penetrate into the domain of spiritual life, in which the faithful move. This power, however, is ascribed to some other agent, and of him the Lord *commands* them to be afraid. The following reasons, *apparently*, compel us to understand thereby the prince of darkness : 1st, If those words were to be referred to God, the expression *fear* (φοβεῖσθαι), must be understood in two different senses, in the same verse,* the first time, in the sense of *be afraid* (*metuere*), the second time, in the sense of *reverence* (*revereri*); 2d, Verses 29 and 30 would scarcely agree with it, inasmuch as God is represented in them, as a protector in danger and distress ; and on this, verse 31 founds the exhortation " fear not therefore" (μὴ οὖν φοβηθῆτε), which would then form a contradiction to the " fear" (φοβηθῆτε) found here, and so emphatically repeated in Luke xii. 5 ; 3d, It appears unsuitable to say of God, that he destroys souls, inasmuch as it is he who saves them. But still it would be a *decisive* argument against this view, that, in Scripture, the devil *never* appears as he who condemns to hell ; his whole activity depends upon the permissive will of God. (James iv. 12.) Moreover, as verse 33 clearly indicates the possibility of apostacy and denial, the passage is best understood of a powerful *exhortation* given by the Redeemer to the disciples to earnestness, and diligence in preserving and making sure their calling. True,

---

* No stress is to be laid on the change in φοβεῖσθαι τινά and ἀπό τινός; the former combination also may also signify *metuere ;* but, in the sense of *revereri*, it certainly is not found in connection with ἀπό. In the usage of profane writers " to be afraid of," " to reverence," is expressed by φοβεῖσθαι πρός τι.

in this case, we cannot avoid changing the meaning of "fear" (φοβεῖσθαι); such cases, however, are not unfrequent. And the "fear not therefore" of ver. 31, refers under this interpretation to the assumed fidelity of the disciples. (Concerning γέεννα, comp. the remarks on Matt. v. 22.)

Ver. 29, 30.—As an antidote to fear, Jesus refers the apostles to the almighty aid of God, for whose kingdom they were contending. How should he, who feeds the sparrows and numbers the hairs of the head, not guard the lives of his faithful servants ? Στρουθίον, sparrow, is here, as frequently in the LXX. = צפור. An ἀσσάριον, was the tenth part of a δραχμή.)

Ver. 31.—The consolatory power of this doctrine is founded in the special providence of God. Everywhere, as in nature, it combines the greatest and the least into one harmonious whole. Thousands are fed, and the crumbs are collected ; our Redeemer rises from his grave, and the linen is carefully folded together.

Ver. 32, 33.—The whole assumes more and more a general character: the discourse gradually extends to the whole collective body of the disciples of Jesus, in their conflict with the world. Christ also appears here as he whose recognition has a decisive influence on man's everlasting weal or woe ; whose testimony is accepted before God and his angels. The believer's confession before men (as the enemies of that which is good) is contrasted with Christ's confession before the heavenly host. Whosoever takes upon him the ignominy of appearing as a true worshipper of Christ will be received as such when Christ reveals himself in his glory. But this declaration is immediately followed by its contrast (verse 33) ; as the latter fills with fear, so the former allures. The whole declaration has, of course, a reference to believers only, who have recognised the Lord in his true character, and who now either venture to confess their faith, or conceal it through fear ; the latter course must extinguish the light of faith which was kindled in them, and exclude from the kingdom of God.

Ver. 34.—As the fear of strife and persecution might easily deter from an open confession, our Lord distinctly points out that the Gospel, from its very nature, must occasion strife. Not as though strife itself were the object of the Gospel (its object is peace, the end of strife), but strife is the necessary consequence of Christ's coming into the world, or into a heart. Just because in Christ there appears absolute holiness, whilst the world comprises in itself good and evil mixed together, therefore the spirit of Christ (μάχαιρα, sword, Ephes. vi. 17), cuts off the evil (διαμερισμός, separation, Luke xii. 51), and along with it him who clings to it.

Vers. 35, 36.—Jesus sets forth the results of this separating power of the Gospel, in the same manner as in verses 21, 22. The sword of the Spirit severs the most intimate connexions based upon human relationships, and earthly love ; destroys them if they attempt to hold fast the unholy element ; and ennobles them if free scope is everywhere given to the Holy Spirit. That which our Lord here points out as his requisition upon believers, viz., to be separated from all earthly ties, even the most intimate, for the sake of union with himself, was already declared by Moses of the Levites : " Who said unto his father and to his mother, I have not seen him ; neither did he acknowledge his brethren, nor know his own children : for they have observed thy word, and kept thy covenant. They shall teach Jacob thy judgments, and Israel thy law." (Deut. xxxiii. 9, 10. Comp. Gen. xii. 1.)

Ver. 37.—The love of Christ must be stronger than either the love of father or of mother [and must prove itself the stronger in all cases where they come into *conflict, i. e.*, where parents appeal to filial duty to enforce their command of disobedience to Christ]. (Compare the remarks on Luke xiv. 26, where the still stronger expression occurs : μισεῖν πατέρα κ. τ. λ.) Very significant is the clause, " is not worthy of me," for Christ himself is the aim and object of believers; they long for himself as he is in the power of his resurrection and in his sufferings. (Compare the remarks on Philip. iii. 10.) This effect of the Gospel—its claiming the whole man— makes the world rage with fury ; for this reason it makes to itself another Christ, who allows good and evil to dwell peaceably and quietly together. But if Christ had not been the Truth and Life itself (John xiv. 6), it would have been a violation of the most sacred duties to demand that, for his sake, the dearest ties of relationship should be disregarded. It is only God whom we must obey rather than father and mother ; and Christ, only because we behold in him the Father (John xiv. 9). And therefore, by assigning to him a rank above all that is most dear and sacred, no duty is violated ; on the contrary, every duty is purified and ennobled. The command, " Honour thy father and thy mother," is thus not abrogated, but fulfilled (Matth. v. 17), inasmuch as man recognises himself in Christ Jesus as a child of the Father, of whom the whole family in heaven and earth is named (Ephes. iii. 15).

Ver. 38.—With this demand of a separation from all earthly ties which faith in the Redeemer, if it be a living one, at all times presupposes, is connected the intimation of a course of life full of sufferings, the end of which is death. How deeply must our Lord have been conscious of the glory and blessedness to be given by him, if he did not hesitate to draw such a picture of the life of his followers ! The words, σταυρὸν λαμβάνειν, *take his cross*, spoken before the crucifixion of our Lord, must be explained from the general custom of malefactors being themselves obliged to carry their cross to the place of execution. In the mouth of Jesus, they assume a prophetic character, as they were spoken previous to his sufferings. *Fritzsche* (on this passage) distinguishes between λαμβάνειν and αἴρειν τὸν σταυρόν, and refers the latter expression to the *spontaneous* taking up of the cross. The ἀκολουθεῖν ὀπίσω, *following after*, refers evidently to the subsequent *bearing* of the cross, with the death of the cross, as its final consummation. The life of the followers of Christ upon earth, is necessarily toilsome, inasmuch as they live continually in the midst of dangers, and sacrifice their own will to the will of God ; and, hence, it resembles a continual dying on the cross. Although, according to the context, that which has been here said has a primary reference to a life in the first ages of Christianity—a life exposed to *bodily* dangers and persecutions, yet it retains its truth for all time in reference to the inward struggles of the believer ; and hence this same figurative mode of expression is used throughout Scripture. (Gal. ii. 20, v. 24 ; Romans vi. 6.)

Ver. 39.—From this one aspect of the Christian's sufferings, viz., persecution and perils of death, the eye is directed to a view still more general ; the death of the old life is the condition of the birth of the new life. That " the losing one's life" (ψυχὴν ἀπολέσαι) can mean not merely the loss of bodily life for the sake of Jesus, is evident, partly from the fact that some of the apostles did not die by persecution, while yet their blameless continuance in life cannot be set down to their disadvantage ; and partly because we may conceive even of death by persecutions which, originating (as not unfrequently happened) in vanity or fanaticism, did not correspond to the present requirements. The losing one's life therefore can be understood only in a spiritual sense, and it is only by such a death that the bodily death is sanctified. In the expression ψυχή, the signification *soul* and *life* are again blended together. (Compare the remarks on Matth. vi. 25). In this passage, then, a *twofold* soul is spoken of, of which one is lost, if the other be preserved. If we translate ψυχή by *life*, it implies a twofold existence, a higher and a lower, between which man has the choice. (The same thought is expressed in the same words in Matth. xvi. 24, 25, and in John xii. 25. Instead of *find* (εὑρίσκειν), John, however, has *love* (φιλεῖν), which is more intelligible ; *find* (εὑρισκεῖν), here signifies *to gain, to attain to*).* The passage will become most distinct by being paraphrased thus : ὁ εὑρὼν τὴν (σαρκικὴν) ψυχὴν, ἀπολέσει αὐτὴν (sc. πνευματικήν): καὶ ὁ ἀπολέσας τὴν ψυχὴν (σαρκικὴν), εὑρήσει αὐτὴν (πνευματικήν)—he that findeth his (fleshly) life shall lose it (*i. e.*, his spiritual life) : and he that loseth his (fleshly) life, shall find it (*i. e.*, his spiritual life). That which constitutes true personal identity (the *ego*) remains the same, but, in the exercise of true self-denial, it becomes dead to sin ; the

* Compare Hebrews x. 39, where the words are : περιποίησις ψυχῆς

unbelieving man, on the contrary, remains in his natural state of being, and the germ of the higher life can never attain to dominion in him. The expression here made use of by our Redeemer is most simply explained by supposing that the soul of man is conceived as standing between two powers, the influence of which he may receive within himself, and by means of which he may be transformed into their nature. Now, as man by nature is more especially exposed to the one (the evil power), the work of renovation implies the renunciation of the old sinful life which has become part of the man, and, instead of it, the entrance into the new life of light. This transition is a death ; but, out of this death a new and higher life springs up. The addition of ἕνεκεν ἐμοῦ, *for my sake*, is of importance, inasmuch as it opposes itself to all self-devised means of sanctification and perfecting of spiritual life. A crucifying of the flesh, and self-denial undertaken *for one's own sake*, for one's own perfecting, are an abomination in the sight of our Lord, since they are always in such a case, the proofs of secret presumption and pride.* On the contrary, they must be done from love to Jesus, from a principle of

* The religions of Asia, especially Buddhism, prominently point out and enjoin the duty of self-denial; but as it is practiced out of Jesus, and without the perfect *ideal* of holiness in man, it leads to the most eccentric and foolish exhibitions. The addition, therefore, of ἕνεκεν ἐμοῦ is of the highest importance to the precept of self-denial, and furnishes, at the same time, a remarkable proof of the divine dignity of Jesus; for it would have been the highest presumption on his part to require, that all things should be counted but loss for his sake, unless he had been higher than all created beings. In the work of *J. J. Schmidt* (Ueber die ältere religiöse, politische und literarische Bildungsgeschichte der Völker Mittelasiens. Petersburg, 1824), several characteristic features of such false self-denial are communicated. "Shaggiamuni (the Buddha of the Mongol tribes), when in the form of a king's son, once met on his walk a tigress with her young, nearly dead of hunger. Penetrated with compassion, and there being nothing at hand to refresh and revive her, he withdrew himself, under some pretext, from his retinue, went up to the tigress, and laid himself down before her, that he might be torn in pieces by her. But, perceiving that she was too much exhausted to be able to injure him, he first made incisions in his skin, and allowed her to lick up the blood which flowed from the wounds, whereby she was so much strengthened, that she was able to devour him altogether." What a caricature, compared with the sight presented by the life of a true follower of Christ, walking in true, genuine, Christian self-denial! The duty was conceived of in a far more worthy manner, by the nobler Mahommedan mystics, especially by *Dshelaleddin Rumi*, who thus beautifully expresses the necessity of the death of the old man, in order that the new man may be brought to life:

> Death ends indeed the cares of life,
> Yet, shudders life when death comes near;
> And such the fond heart's death-like strife
> When first the loved one does appear.
> For, where true love is wakened, dies
> The tyrant *self*, that despot dark.
> Rejoice then, that in death he lies,	,
> And breathe morn's free air, with the lark.

But certainly it must be admitted, that, between the conception of the duty, and the realization of it in the life, there is a wide difference.

obedience to him, and by the working of his Spirit ; it is then only that they bring forth beautiful fruits, and produce that "holiness, without which no man shall see the Lord." (Heb. xii. 14.) The medium between indolence on the one hand, and self-righteous activity on the other, is difficult of discovery ; but the author of the faith must here also be himself the finisher of it. (Heb. xii. 2.)

Ver. 40.—As a consolation under the difficulties which our Lord has set before his disciples, there follows, in conclusion, a rich thought, pointing out how infinitely dear to the Lord of the universe are the combatants for truth.* As Christ is the representative of the Father, so he considers his disciples as his own representatives ; whosoever, therefore, receives the disciples, receives the Lord of the universe himself. (Mark ix. 37.) The following verses, however, shew that δέχεσθαι, receive, must be taken emphatically thus : " whosoever receives you, fully conscious of what you are, and for the sake of this your spiritual character, receives God," and hence derives all the blessing from it, which is conferred, according to the history of the Patriarchs, by a visit from the Lord. There is implied, therefore, in the receiving (δέχεσθαι), not an outward receiving merely (hospitio excipere), but, more especially, the opening of the heart and of the whole inner life, so that a man may be able to receive the disciples of the Lord, although he should not have where to lay his head.

Ver. 41, 42.—But in order to place in its true light the greatness of the glory of true believers, and to pourtray the blessedness of those who receive them, the Redeemer closes with a remarkable parallel. His disciples, the representatives of the principles of the new Christian life, are compared by him to the Old Testament saints, prophets, and righteous men (προφήταις καὶ δικαίοις), and he thus infers, that as much as the former stood higher than the latter, by so much higher and more glorious would be their reward. As regards, in the first place, the gradation, the name μικροί, little ones, here given to believers, is remarkable. We might here refer to the Rabbinical usus loquendi, according to which, קטן, small, forms the contrast to רב, great, the latter signifying teacher, master; the former, disciple, servant. But this does not meet the case ; the expression seems intended to indicate a peculiarity of the disciples of Jesus. (Comp. Matth. xviii. 6.) According to the context, it would seem to point out, first, the needy condition of the disciples, who, like helpless children, seem to be given over as a prey to misery in this world, but are sustained by the help of the Father from above.

* The reverse side of this picture is pointed out by Luke x. 16, in the words ὁ ἐμὲ ἀθετῶν κ. τ. λ. Allusions to this thought are also met with in the Rabbinical writings; e. g., si quis recipit viros doctos, idem est ac si reciperet Schechinam, i. e., manifestationem summi numinis. Comp. Schöttgen on this passage.

Next, it has reference to the child-like, innocent, and, specially, the humble feeling of the regenerate, who, although exalted and glorious, are yet conscious of their glory without any feeling of presumption. (The passage in chap. xvii. 6, explains this more fully.) This humbleness (μικρότης) of the disciples, is contrasted with the Old Testament piety, which, although inferior, yet bears a somewhat more pretentious character; its two principal forms are pointed out, viz., προφητεία, *prophecy*, and δικαιοσύνη, *righteousness*. In the former, is specially displayed the fulness of illumination by the Spirit of God, which however, as in the case of Jonah, might well be combined with meagre personal attainments; in the latter, preciseness in obeying the law. (Comp. the remarks on Luke i. 6.) Righteousness appears here as the higher gradation of religious life under the Old Testament, inasmuch as it presupposed a higher degree of personal attainment than prophecy. But, above these two, stands the New Testament life, in which an inward regeneration is manifested in the outward life. These three gradations of character, *prophet* (προφήτης), *righteous man* (δίκαιος), and *little one* (μικρός), are brought into connexion with those who receive them, and to every one is promised the μισθός, *pay*, *reward*, of him whom he receives. (On the signification of μισθός, comp. the remarks on Matth. v. 12.) The term is, in a legal point of view, wholly appropriate; but in the evangelical point of view, only in so far as love, which appears in it as the active principle, carries its reward in itself. But as a condition of the reward, it is farther added in what manner the reception is to take place—εἰς ὄνομα προφήτου, δικαίου, μαθητοῦ, *in the name, etc.* This εἰς ὄνομα, *in the name*, contains the key to the whole rather obscure passage; it is identical with the Hebrew בְּשֵׁם (it is not necessary to suppose an exchange of the prepositions εἰς and ἐν), so that the name signifies the character and true nature of the person to be received. Hence the passage is full of rich meaning. It points out the moral principle, that every action must be measured by the disposition from which it proceeds, and that the disposition is the result of the whole inward state of man. Hence, it is not the *isolated act* of receiving, which is considered as the ground of the reward, but the *disposition of soul* from which the act proceeds; and the reception itself, turns not more on the person received, than on the clearness with which his true character is apprehended. Hence the sense of these remarkable words is this: whoever receives an Old Testament prophet, for the sake of his spiritual character, and is endowed with the ability of receiving him, and recognising him as such, will be rewarded according to his Old Testament position; the same takes place with regard to the righteous; but he who receives a disciple of Jesus, *i. e.*, a child of God, and a citizen of the heavenly kingdom, and refreshes him by the merest trifle (a weaker counterpart of δέχεσθαι)—who is thus able to recognise in him, under his insignificant outward appearance, the effulgence of that which is divine—who is able to love it and to do good to it, in its representatives, he thereby shews that he has dispositions in harmony with this New Testament dispensation, and hence will also receive the reward which, under it, is certain. But this reward is an eternal one (οὐ μὴ ἀπολέσῃ τὸν μισθὸν αὐτοῦ); and in this it is implied, that the Old Testament awards to its saints promises of a more earthly character. The thought is highly spiritual; and hence has been so frequently misunderstood by interpreters. For it evidently involves also the thought, that while he who occupies a lower position, can never be received in a higher character, because the higher life is wanting in him; yet the higher may be received in a lower character. The disciple of Jesus has already passed through the law. Many a benevolent, pious Jew, might therefore receive the apostles as prophets or righteous men, because, from his point of view, he could not apprehend them more profoundly. But he who, in the messengers of Christ, was able to recognise their new and nobler character, and from love to this, received them, he received from them the full, rich blessing of the new birth; while those, also, who occupied the lower ground, if turning toward them with a heart of love, would receive an appropriate reward. Hence the little ones appear here as bestowing blessings in every direction; indeed "as dying, but yet living; as poor, and yet making many rich; as having nothing, and yet possessing all things." (2 Cor. vi. 9, 10.)

§ 16. JOHN THE BAPTIST SENDS HIS DISCIPLES TO JESUS. DISCOURSES OF JESUS ON THE OCCASION OF THIS MISSION.

(Matth. xi. 1–30; Luke vii. 18–35; x. 13–15, 21, 22.)

Ver. 1.—Matthew closes the preceding discourse with the words: διατάσσων τοῖς δώδεκα μαθηταῖς, instructing his twelve disciples, and thereby clearly indicates the wish that the preceding discourse should be understood as designed for the disciples who were sent forth. Of the journey itself, however, he says nothing. Luke ix. 10, on the contrary, mentions the return in the same way as in chap. x. 17, he mentions the return of the seventy. With an indefinite καὶ ἐγένετο, and it came to pass, Matthew proceeds to another subject, viz., the report of the question put by John the Baptist through his disciples. The same report is connected, in Luke vii. 18, with the history of the raising of the widow of Nain's son, but likewise very loosely, by the general formula: And they reported to

John, etc. (καὶ ἀπήγγειλαν Ἰωάννῃ κ. τ. λ). But we are struck by the exceedingly exact agreement of the Evangelists in this section, not only in single expressions (as ver. 23), but also in the Old Testament quotation from Malachi iii. 1 (Matth. xi. 10). The LXX. give an exact translation of the Hebrew text ; but both the Evangelists differ alike from both.* We have here again, in Matthew, a discourse composed of various elements, whilst Luke gives in another more definite connexion, that which is here brought together. From the narrative of the mission of the two disciples of John, Matthew only takes occasion to report the discourses of Jesus which describe the different positions of the people, with respect to him. Jesus was as little understood by the proud, as was John the Baptist. The humble recognised the divine element under even the most varied forms, because indeed, it was only this of which they were in search. With this, chap. xii. connects itself very suitably.

Ver. 2.—From the mission of the disciples of John, we are led to make some inquiries regarding the spiritual condition of the Baptist. He appears here in prison (at Machaerus according to *Josephus, Arch.* xviii. 5); it is only in a subsequent chapter (xiv. 3 seq.) that Matthew, by way of supplementing, gives the necessary information about his imprisonment. The Baptist hears in his prison of the works of Jesus, and is therefore induced to send to him two disciples, with the question : Art thou he that cometh, or do we look for another ? (σὺ εἶ ὁ ἐρχόμενος, ἢ ἕτερον προσδοκῶμεν); (The expression ὁ ἐρχόμενος, *he that cometh*, has a fixed doctrinal signification, viz., the Messiah, perhaps from the passage in Psalm cxviii. 26, בָּרוּךְ הַבָּא בְּשֵׁם יְהֹוָה,† *blessed is he that cometh*, etc. In Heb. x. 37, Christ, with reference even to his second coming (παρουσία) is called ὁ ἐρχόμενος, i. e., he at whose future coming all prophecy will be fulfilled.) The question of the Baptist seems, then, to indicate an uncertainty as to whether or not Jesus was the longed-for Saviour ; and such a question must certainly appear very strange from the mouth of the Baptist, after the strong declarations of his faith, and after the disclosures made to him concerning his relation to Jesus. (Compare Matth. iii. and specially John i. 23.) Hence many have been disposed to consider this question as intended to strengthen the faith of his disciples who were beginning to faint; others, as containing a call upon Jesus to hasten the carrying out of his plans. The former opinion has absolutely no weight ; for the disciples of the Baptist would have been completely satisfied by the decided

* On this point compare Matth. iii. 3 ; Mark i. 1.

† *Hengstenberg* (Christology, vol. iii., p. 292, et seq.) derives, on very plausible grounds, the expression from Malachi iii. 1 ; but it is very probable that several passages of the Old Testament concur in giving it this fixed doctrinal signification.

declarations of their master (John i. 29), as we see in the case of the apostles. The second opinion is not without truth. John might, in fact, regard Jesus as proceeding too cautiously, inasmuch as he did not understand his secret working upon the souls of men. But it is difficult to conceive that John, if his own faith remained unshaken, should have merely wished to urge our Lord to a different mode of procedure ; the very form of the question obliges us to refer it rather to the state of mind of the interrogator himself. For, if we look at the passage before us with unprejudiced eye, it appears more natural to seek for the ground of the question in the mind of John himself. Our inward experience can alone teach us to understand such events. In the life of every believer, there occur moments of temptation, in which even the firmest conviction may be shaken : nothing is more simple than to imagine such a time of darkness and abandonment by the Spirit, in the life even of John.* We are too much accustomed to think of the character of Scripture saints only under a certain form, and as liable to no change ; but (excepting the Lord himself, whose character was peculiar, and must be regarded *per se*), it is evident that internal changes of light and darkness must be supposed in all individuals, even when such are not reported ; inasmuch as, by this very struggle, the life of the saint is perfected. Hence, wherever communications simple and clear are brought before us as the one in question concerning John, there is no reason whatever for doubting. In his gloomy prison at Machaerus, the man of God was no doubt sur-

* That after the events recorded, Matth. iii. 16, and John i. 33, John the Baptist could have come to any real doubt of the Messiahship of Jesus, is scarcely conceivable, and seems to be denied by the Saviour, Matth. xi. 7. He did not doubt his Messiahship, nor was he impatient that Jesus did not by miracle deliver him from prison : but the Saviour's free, unlegal, New Testament mode of working, he could not comprehend. In his opinion Jesus should have carried out the outward separation of the people, commenced in his own ministry, instead of casting the pearls of his miracles and teachings before the undiscriminating mass. This misapprehension he embodies in the question, " Art thou really he ? From thy mode of working one would hardly believe it !" To this corresponds the reply of our Lord (v. 4), and to this the language in which Jesus (v. 7, 8) defends John against the suspicion that like a shaken reed he now doubted what he had once testified, or like a weakling had become impatient of his imprisonment. To this finally answers the declaration (v. 10, ff.), that the greatest under the Old dispensation failed to apprehend the spirit of the New, in which all legal outward forms are broken up by the violence with which the kingdom of heaven is seized upon.—(E.) The correct view seems to me fully given neither by Olshausen or Ebrard. That the question is not one of simple inquiry for information is clear. That John was in a measure stumbled at the proceeding of our Lord, whose Messiahship he did not question, seems equally clear. But that John was stumbled rather at our Saviour's slowness in assuming to himself that temporal dominion which doubtless formed a part of his view of the function of the Messiah, than at his free, *unlegal* procedure, seems to me almost certain. The miracles to which the Saviour points in self-vindication, contrast most naturally with false conceptions of outward greatness and glory, which John may have entertained. The following discourse adapts itself equally well to this view.—[K.

prised by a dark hour, in which he was struck by the quiet unob-
trusive ministry of Christ, and began to doubt the experience of
which he had heretofore been the subject. This is clearly implied
in the words of Jesus : *Blessed is he whosoever, etc.* (μακάριός ἐστιν
ὃς ἐὰν μὴ σκανδαλισθῇ ἐν ἐμοί) (ver. 6), which contain, at once, censure and comfort. For, indeed, it would have been a sad thing for
the poor prisoner if he had not stood firm in the hour of temptation, if he really had been offended; but now he was only tempted
to be so—and blessed is the man that endureth temptation (James
i. 12). But as, without a struggle, there is no victory for sinful
man, so the Baptist also could not be spared such a struggle. The
very circumstance, however, of his having sent to Jesus himself for
enquiry, shews that he endured the temptation and conquered.
That he asked him in this manner proves that he was tempted ;
but that, in his temptation, he asked no one else, but applied to the
Saviour himself, proves his faith ; and so much the more, as the
free life of the Redeemer, so different from his own, must have appeared rather strange to the austere preacher of repentance. (Compare the remarks on Matth. xi. 19.) The question of John is nothing else than the prayer, "Lord, I believe, help thou mine unbelief ;"
and this prayer is answered by our gracious Lord. Whosoever asks
God whether he be God ; whosoever asks the Saviour whether he
be the Saviour, is in the right way to overcome every temptation—
it is only thus that he can attain certainty. Hence it is, that the
words of Jesus concerning John (ver. 7, seq.) form no contradiction
to the supposition that he sent the messengers in an hour of severe
temptation. He even thereby proved that he was not a reed shaken
by every wind, but that he stood firm and unshaken amid all storms.
But when there is no storm, how can firmness be proved ? It was
then, during the time of his shining, and when the fulness of the
Spirit dwelt on him, that God made use of the Baptist for *his own*
great purposes among mankind ; but in the time of his poverty and
abandonment, God perfected him within himself.

Ver. 4, 5.—With reference to prophetic passages, such as Isaiah
xxxv. 5, 6 ; lx. 1, Jesus answers the question by pointing to his
deeds ; the messengers find the Redeemer in the midst of his messianic labours ; all that they can report is that he is redeeming.
They saw his outward agency ; the spiritual significancy of those
outward miracles his discourse unveiled to them. The bodily healing but prefigured the healing of the soul. (Concerning πτωχός,
comp. Matth. v. 13.) Εὐαγγελίζεσθαι, has here the signification of
"hearing the gospel," "receiving the glad tidings." The passage,
Isaiah lxi. 1, which is here referred to, forbids the interpretation,
"the poor preach the gospel." Indeed, a glorious mode of proceeding ! alone fitted to convince of his messianic dignity. Not a word

of John individually—only the μακάριός ἐστιν, *blessed is he,* reaches him for consolation and warning. But if it be asked, why the Lord did not speak more fully, we answer that such struggles must be fought only in the inner man ; the question was to the Lord a sign of the approaching victory. He left him, therefore, entirely to himself, without further interference with him. (Concerning σκανδαλίζεσθαι, comp. the remarks on Matth. xviii. 8.)

Ver. 7.—But before the people, who might easily have misunderstood such a question, Jesus expressed himself more fully, and depicted to them the noble image of the stern warrior, that, on the one hand, they might know what they might expect from him, and, on the other hand, might also recognise what he could not give to them. Some of the disciples of John, who were present, may have given immediate occasion to these remarks. Of himself, he maintains a calm and dignified silence ; upon all he impresses the words : Blessed is he whosoever shall not be offended in me. The manner in which our Lord, from the 7th to the 9th verse speaks to those surrounding him concerning John, is somewhat obscure. It is difficult to apprehend in their right relation his various reproving questions. The reed shaken by the wind (κάλαμος ὑπὸ ἀνέμου σαλευόμενος), may be figuratively understood of a lightminded man (as in Ephes. iv. 14 ; Heb. xiii. 9); or, without any figure, of the reed which grew on the banks of the river Jordan, and with which the wind sported. In the latter case, the sense would be the following : " You must certainly have had some object in view, in hastening to the wilderness : it can certainly not have been to get a view of some empty, every-day object, as, a shaking reed, or soft garments." The third question must then indeed denote the proper object ; they wished to see a prophet, and *that* John the Baptist certainly was. Yet the thought in this shape would be rather meagre—it would have been better, in that case, to put only the single question, " You wished to see a prophet, did you not ? well then, you have seen him, and the greatest one too ; only obey him !" But, if we turn to the other mode of interpretation, we here too meet with difficulties. The thought, "have you gone out to see a light-minded or luxurious man ?" is too harsh, for who goes to the wilderness for such a purpose ? Or who could imagine John to be such an one ? But, if it be said that the unsuitable question was only intended to shew that they certainly thought no such thing, the question again is, For what purpose are these things brought forward ? The passage continues dark, until verse 16, seq. are compared. That passage shews that Jesus, in his questions, has only in view the character of the mutitude, and portrays *their own* contradictions. *They* evidently went in crowds to the wilderness *to see* a prophet (as if there were any thing in a prophet to be *seen*, while they did not desire to *hear* him); they might well have known how a true prophet would manifest himself to them, and yet when they perceived his moral earnestness, they did not like him ; their impure hearts had longed for a prophet after their own taste. Our Saviour, who searches the hearts of men with eyes of fire, lays open to them this their inconsistency, in hastening out to the prophet, and then desiring that he might not be what he is, and might be something which he cannot be, viz., *such an one as themselves.* They themselves are the reed shaken by the wind, as is fully demonstrated in verses 16, 17. " You imagined that you would find a pseudo-prophet, one who would yield to all the caprices of sin, and one altogether like yourselves ? You imagined that you would find a sensual teacher, flattering your sensuality ? you imagined that you would behold a prophet, just as your fancies had depicted him to you, mighty, glorious, but sparing sin ? Indeed you have obtained one, but one who is another Elijah." Then follows, first, a farther delineation of the Baptist, and of the character of his ministry, with which is connected a parallel between Jesus and the Baptist—with the remark, that the same character of the multitude that did not like John, had taken offence at him, although his mode of life was altogether different from that of the Baptist; and they had been offended at him for this sole reason, that they could never, in any form of the divine, whatever it might be, find the likeness of their sinful selves ; and that it was only themselves they were everywhere seeking. The haughty judges of the children of light, who dislike in them now this, and now that, must, therefore, before all things, come down to humility ; the babes (νήπιοι, ver. 25) who possess it, for this reason also, apprehend the divine element in its most varied forms of manifestation, because they never anywhere care about the form, but always and everywhere about the *substance.*

Ver. 9.—The description of John the Baptist begins with the words " Yea, and more than a prophet" (ναὶ καὶ περισσότερον προφήτου). That the Baptist was more than a prophet (*i. e.*, that in the clearness of his view, he had attained to a point beyond that of the prophets), is inferred from Malachi iii. 1, in which a messenger is described as preparing the way for the Messiah. (Concerning this, comp. the remarks on Matth. iii. 3.) By means of this office, the Baptist received a peculiar position, inasmuch as he occupied the intermediate space between the Old and New Testament ; yet in the general direction of his life he still belonged to the Old Testament, and only formed the link by which the two spheres of religious life are connected. (Comp. what has been remarked on Matth. iii. 21.)

Ver. 11.—But the Redeemer proceeds yet farther in his exaltation of the Baptist ; as he had placed him above all the prophets, so he

places him now above all the γεννητοὶ γυναικῶν, *born of women.*
The words ἐγείρεσθαι ἐν = בְּ הָקִים, have the signification "to be
raised up," "to be called forth" for a particular purpose, from a
great multitude ; so that we may supply ὑπὸ τοῦ Θεοῦ, *of God* (John
vii. 52).—Γεννητὸς γυναικός, *born of women* = אִשָּׁה יְלוּד, Job xiv. 1 ;
xv. 14. (Γεννήματα γυναικῶν signifies man in general, but with the
accessory idea of frailty or impurity.) The expression, therefore,
has its contrast in the phrase γεννητὸς ἐκ τοῦ Θεοῦ, *born of God;* thus
were the first man and Christ, and thus are believers, who are begotten of the Spirit, through Him. (John i. 13.) To this contrast
the closing words of the verse refer, in which the least in the kingdom of heaven is placed above John. (Concerning the expression
μικρότερος ἐν τῇ β., *least,* etc., compare what has been remarked on
Matth. v. 19, where the μέγας and ἐλάχιστος ἐν τῇ β. are contrasted
with each other.) Even in the lowest degree of the Christian life,
which has been brought to mankind by Christ Jesus, man stands
higher than John.* Concerning this remarkable thought, it must,
in the first place, be well observed, that the being greater (μείζων
εἶναι), ascribed here by the Redeemer to those living in the kingdom
of God, must be understood in a Christian sense, so that even the
greatest is, at the same time, the humblest, divested of all selfishness and sin, entirely in the sense of Matth. xx. 25, 26. Those in
the kingdom of God, occupy in so far, therefore, a higher ground, as
the possibility of attaining this position, of being divested of self,
lies within their reach. This is therefore the general character of
all the members of the kingdom of God ; and the difference between
them consists only, partly in the degree in which they have received
into all the faculties and powers of their nature the principle of
higher life, freeing from all sin, and hence also from pride ; partly
also, in the more or less copious endowment with those powers
which determine the varied spheres of activity in individuals.
Again, it is self-evident that the being in the kingdom of God cannot here refer to every one who is a member of the visible church of
Christ ; inasmuch as there are many bad fishes in the large net of
the kingdom of God. (Matth. xiii. 47 seq.) The expression is
rather limited here by the preceding γεννητοὶ γυναικῶν, *born of
women;* whence we must infer, that the kingdom of heaven contains only the born of God. The kingdom of heaven is here, then,
the kingdom of God in the *ideal* conception. This community, with
all its members, our Redeemer, in verse 11, places above that community to which John, with the Old Testament prophets, belonged.

---

* The comparative μικρότερος needs not to be taken as the superlative. Compare
Winer's Gr. S. 221. The reference of the expression to Jesus himself: " I, the lesser one,
am greater in the kingdom of heaven than he," is evidently quite inadmissible. It would
have been mock-humility, if Jesus had called himself less than John.

The whole passage, therefore, is applicable to those only who are truly regenerated. To many members of the visible church, not even a position equal to that of the representatives of the Old Testament can be granted. But a considerable difficulty still adheres to this passage, inasmuch as the question here arises, as to whether no regeneration took place at all under the Old Testament. To answer this question, we must distinguish between regeneration in a narrower, and a wider sense. In the narrower sense, the expression signifies the communication of a higher life [of Christ's glorified humanity], which can be effected only through the operation of the Holy Spirit, whose outpouring on mankind depended upon the glorification of Christ. (John vii. 39.) In this more confined sense then, the regeneration of the Old Testament saints is out of the question. Abraham, Isaac, and Jacob, as well as all the Old Testament saints, beheld the Redeemer only as Him who was to come, without having experienced the real effects of his power. (Heb. xi. 13 ; 1 Pet. i. 10–40.) They were, therefore, in the *Sheol*, and attained to the resurrection only through Christ. (Comp. the remarks on Matth. xxvii. 52, 53.) In the wider sense, however, every important and eventful change in the inner man may be called regeneration,* and such a one was no doubt experienced by Abraham and Jacob, on account of which, and especially on account of the new name given to them, they may be justly regarded as types of the new birth. The sense of the words "There hath not risen among them that are born of women a greater than John the Baptist," may, accordingly, be still more exactly determined. It is not likely that Jesus intended to subordinate Abraham and Jacob to the Baptist ; these stand not only as the ancestors, according to the flesh, of the people of God, but specially also as the fathers of all the faithful, in a far brighter splendour. [Yet in their relations to the salvation of the New Testament, they surely stood below the Baptist.] For, among individuals under the Old Testament dispensation, various degrees of attainment, and various positions may be distinguished as clearly as among the members of the New Testament church. A distinction between prophets and righteous men has been already made above. (Matth. x. 41.) Here we might to a certain degree, find a third class alluded to, viz., the regenerate of the Old Testament. The Baptist would in that case, be repre-

---

* Better, conversion (E). As human nature is substantially the same in all ages, there can be, it would seem, no *radical* difference in the process by which men in different ages are brought into a state of reconciliation with God. There must always have been a virtual new birth by the influence of the Holy Spirit. Under the old dispensation his workings were comparatively limited and secret ; under the new he was poured out in such abundant measure as to characterize it as the special economy of the Spirit. There must have been a time when the Old Testament saints felt the first impulse of love to God, and that must have been a season of internal regeneration.—[K.

sented only as a righteous man, in the noblest legal sense,* as a
true representative of the law, but from whom was concealed the
higher life of the Spirit, such as was experienced by Abraham and
Israel, who appear far more as the representatives of the higher order
of the evangelical life which was hereafter to be revealed, than of
the legal state.

Ver. 12.—From the personal delineation of the Baptist, our
Redeemer proceeds to describe the peculiar character of the time ;
and this leads him to the objurgatory discourse in verse 16. "As
the man is great whom God has raised as the precursor of the kingdom of the Messiah, so the time also in which he works, is rich
in blessings : the more culpable, therefore, are they who do not avail
themselves of it." The days of John, must be understood of the
time of his publicly appearing to preach repentance (the *terminus
a quo*); in the words ἕως ἄρτι, *until now*, the *terminus ad quem* is
only in so far intimated as that the favourable time still lasted,
which must, however, be by no means considered as now brought to
a close. The conception of a season favourable to the growth of all
that is good, is expressed in a peculiar manner, by the words : The
kingdom of heaven suffereth violence (ἡ βασιλεία τῶν οὐρανῶν βιάζεται). In Luke xvi. 16, a similar expression is found : The kingdom
of God is preached, and every man presseth into it (ἡ βασιλεία τοῦ
Θεοῦ εὐαγγελίζεται καὶ πᾶς εἰς αὐτὴν βιάζεται). With this thought corresponds entirely what follows in our passage, καὶ βιασταὶ ἁρπάζουσιν
αὐτήν, *and the violent seize upon it*. No doubt the words of this
verse must be understood as presenting one aspect of the phenomena of which the Lord speaks. In that time of powerful excitement, there was manifested among mankind generally, but es-
specially among the Jews, a fervent longing, a desire after a change
of condition, which broke forth the more violently the longer it was
repressed. In so far as this longing was, in its ultimate principle,
really pure, so far the kingdom of God might be regarded as its object ; but, in so far as it contained a depraved element and was
blended with much that was erroneous, it is called βιάζεσθαι, *suffering violence*, and a ἁρπάζειν, *seizing*, is ascribed to it. For although
these terms are meant, in the first place, to express only the greatness of the zeal and earnestness for that which is divine, which acted so powerfully at the time of our Lord, yet it is impossible not to

---

* *Hengstenberg*, in his Christology, vol. iii., p. 472, has misunderstood this my view,
as though I denied repentance and faith to the Baptist; I only meant to say, that he does not
pre-eminently represent faith; Paul could therefore not have used the Baptist as the representative of the life of faith, as he did Abraham in Rom. iv. We cannot conceive of any
righteous person of the Old Testament as being destitute of faith, according to Heb. xi.,
only, that Old Testament faith did not, like that of the New Testament, imply the possession of divine things, but only the *hope*, as it is clearly expressed in the passages quoted.
(Heb. xi. 13; 1 Pet. i. 10, seq.)

see, in the choice of the words, a gentle censure upon its mode of manifestation. Had the Redeemer been disposed to bring forward the other view of the same phenomenon, he might have said : "Heaven is, as it were, now opened ; streams of the Spirit are poured out over mankind with life-giving energy." But it was better adapted to his purpose to set forth the activity of men. With this Luke vii. 29, 30, connects itself very naturally ; as, in this passage, the ardent desire of the poor after truth is contrasted with the haughty contempt of it on the part of the Pharisees. (Δικαιόω forms a contrast with ἀθετέω—the former signifying " to regard as just," " to approve," in which signification it is found, immediately afterwards, in Matth. xi. 19 [see farther remarks in comment. on Rom. iii. 21], the latter signifying " to despise.")

Ver. 13.—The peculiar condition of the spiritual world, prevailing at that time, is still more distinctly brought out, according to Matthew, by the declaration of Jesus, that the law and the prophets prophesied only until John ; that with him then, the great turning point of the old and new worlds had come. The thought appears in a different connexion in Luke xvi. 16 ; but, in Matthew, it is so intimately connected with the whole, that we are disposed to consider it as having been spoken on this occasion. For, if the whole Old Testament dispensation closed with John, it was natural that, with his appearance, a powerful spiritual movement should pervade humanity, which, like the travail of a parturient woman, should precede the birth of a higher order of things. But in the expressions in this verse, we are, in the first place, struck by the connexion of νόμος, law, with the prophets ; so that it also appears as prophesying. The νόμος = תּוֹרָה, law, signifies here the element from which the prophets, as its representatives, proceeded, and it is the nature and power of the law to prophesy of Christ. By awakening the consciousness of sin, it calls forth also the longing for the Redeemer, without entirely satisfying it. Next we inquire how the word προεφήτευσαν, prophesied, is to be explained. It might be understood : " the prophetic agency continues until John—himself included." But, in the first place, John himself was not properly a prophet in the Old Testament sense ; he only bore witness of him who was now present, and invited to repentance ; in the second place, moreover, prophesy continued even after John (Acts xi. 28). It is, therefore, better to understand it of the prophecies themselves, and its meaning to be : " with John the prophecies are fulfilled ; they do not extend beyond him." But this thought seems without foundation ; inasmuch as so many prophetic oracles reach down to the establishment of the kingdom of God on earth, in the remotest future. Yet the words which follow in verse 14, compel us to decide in favour of this view ; in them John is represented as

Elijah, and this points to the end of all prophecy. (Mal. iv. 5.) Hence, it is probable, that we must add this passage to the many other passages in which both according to the words of Christ, and those of the apostles, every thing appears consummated at their time. The explanation of these striking declarations lies simply in this, that up to the time of John the Baptist the time of *prophesying* continued, and with Christ commenced that of *fulfilment*.

Ver. 14.—As if for addition and confirmation, Christ subjoins, moreover, that this John was also the promised Elijah. As regards, in the first place, the notion of the appearance of Elijah, to which the words ὁ μέλλων ἔρχεσθαι, *that was to come,* refer, it rests on Mal. iv. 5: הִנֵּה אָנֹכִי שֹׁלֵחַ לָכֶם אֵת אֵלִיָּה הַנָּבִיא, *Behold I send Elijah,* etc. The LXX. have very correctly referred these words to the Tishbite ; and so likewise has Sirach xlviii. 10 ; according to grammatical rules the word הַנָּבִיא requires a reference to a definite historical person. It might be made a question whether the reference to this definite person could not be explained figuratively by the ἐν πνεύματι καὶ δυνάμει 'Ηλίου, *in the spirit and power of Elijah,* as in Luke i. 17. This would even appear more probable,[*] if the New Testament itself did not furnish more exact information concerning it. According to Matth. xvii. 3, Moses and Elijah appeared as heavenly messengers to the Redeemer in his transfiguration ; whereby the figurative explanation of that promise is rendered improbable. Striking, however, is the declaration in the passage before us, that John is Elijah ; whereas he himself declares he is not. (John i. 21.) But even if the words " if ye will receive it" did not indicate it, yet the whole connexion of this passage with the other passages which treat of Elijah, clearly shows that the Redeemer called him so *only in a certain sense,* viz., because he wrought in the spirit and power of Elijah, as Scripture says. (Luke i. 17.) Elijah the zealous preacher of repentance, is, as it were, the type of John. The question, however, is, whether we are to believe that that Old Testament prophecy has been entirely fulfilled in the appearance of John or of Elijah himself, at the time of Christ's transfiguration. We feel inclined to doubt this, when we read that the prophet Malachi (iv. 5), adds that Elijah will be sent, לִפְנֵי בּוֹא יוֹם יְהוָֹה הַגָּדוֹל וְהַנּוֹרָא, *before that great and terrible day, etc.*[†] It seems, therefore, not an

---

[*] Yet this view is surely the correct one. The prophecy (Mal. iv. 5) that Elijah should prepare the way for the Angel of the Covenant, Christ, cannot be fulfilled in the appearance of Moses and Elijah at the transfiguration, but in John the Baptist, as is said Luke i. 17 ; John i. 21. John only denies that he was the *risen* Elijah, the same person as the Old Testament prophet. That he is the second Elijah prophesied Mal. iii. he does not deny.—[E.

[†] The day of the Lord, according to the Old Testament prophets, begins with Christ's incarnation.—Rev. ii. 6, Moses and Elijah are employed as sensible images of the Law and the Gospel.—[E. The account of the day of the Lord in Malachi has its best commen-

improbable supposition, that this prophecy, although fulfilled in a certain sense, must be regarded as yet not wholly fulfilled. (Comp. remarks on Rev. xi. 6.) As it is the nature of Old Testament prophecy that its subject may appear in a previous manifestation, without its import being thereby fully exhausted, so also here. The time of Christ was by no means the prophesied great day of the Lord ; but, that whole time which reached to the destruction of Jerusalem had a certain resemblance to the last days ; and so it had also an element (John the Baptist) which prefigured the future appearance of Elijah. It is likely that, from such a train of ideas, the indefinite " if ye will receive it" arose.

Ver. 15.—To direct attention to those appearances in the present time, Christ adds the solemn, earnest words : He that hath ears to hear, let him hear (ὁ ἔχων ὦτα ἀκούειν, ἀκουέτω) (ἀκούειν = שָׁמַע, intelligere; hence ὦτα = אָזְנַיִם, of the faculty of the understanding.*) According to the intention of Christ, his discourse must have contained something not less worthy of investigation than requiring it, and by this, the admonition was called forth. From the remarks already made, it will appear that the words have not yet lost their profound meaning.

Ver. 16, 17.—That which was alluded to in ver. 7, is now in figurative language more fully set forth. Our Redeemer reproves his fickle contemporaries by comparing them to capricious children whom it is impossible to please in any way, and who understand neither mildness nor severity. (Concerning γενεά = דּוֹר, those living together at one period, comp. remarks on Matth. xxiv. 34. The text of Matthew has been altered here in various ways ; instead of ἀγοραῖς—ἀγορᾷ has been adopted ; instead of ἑταίροις—ἑτέροις, in place of which Luke has ἀλλήλοις. The usual reading, however, deserves the preference, both from internal and external reasons.) The piping, mourning (αὐλέω, θρηνέω), refer to children's plays, both amusing and grave. But the whole figure would be misunderstood, if the speaking children were made to represent Jesus and John, who again are the representatives of mildness and severity ; whilst the other children spoken to represented the capricious multitude. On the contrary, both classes of children—those who speak as well as those who are addressed—are to be viewed as the representatives of the capricious contemporaries of Jesus, so that the sense is this : " The generation resembles a host of ill-humoured

tary in John's description of Christ, Matth. iii. The reference obviously is to the searching, descriminating, spiritual character of the new kingdom. There is then no difficulty in making the "great and terrible day of the Lord" identical with the Saviour's appearing to set up his new kingdom. John the Baptist is clearly the promised Elijah.—[K.

* Similar formulas are used by Jewish teachers, e. g., in the Zohar: qui audit audiat, qui intelligit intelligat. Besides, in the Gospels, the formula, ὁ ἔχων ὦτα κ. τ. λ. is found very frequently in Revelations; but it is altogether wanting in the Gospel of John.

children, whom it is impossible to please in any way; one part desires this, and the other that, so that they cannot agree upon any desirable or useful occupation.*

Ver. 18, 19.—This figurative discourse is immediately followed by the literal declaration; John was too severe for them, and Jesus too mild. (Concerning the phrase δαιμόνιον ἔχει, comp. the rem. on Matth. xii. 24.) The difference between the Old and New dispensations appears here in a striking manner, in the description, though frequently misunderstood, of their respective representatives. In John, we see the strict observer of the law, who exhibits in his demeanour an austere and rigid morality, and abstains from all contact with the sinner; in our Redeemer, on the other hand, we see the impossibility of sinning, joined with compassionate love, which urges him not to withdraw even from the most wretched, since their impurity cannot tarnish his heavenly purity, whilst his divine light is able to illuminate their darkness. John is a noble human phenomenon, a flower of earth; Jesus appears as a heavenly form, the offspring of a higher world. Blessed at that time, and blessed now are those who are not offended at him, but receive him as he is! The words, " and wisdom is justified of her children" (Luke adds all), form the close of this thought. These, like so many other words of the Lord, resemble many-sided polished jewels, which send forth their splendour in more than one direction; a peculiarity found in many pregnant maxims, even of human sages. Considered by themselves, they possess a manifold significancy; but in the connexion of discourse, one meaning, of course, becomes prominent. The expression, "children of wisdom," evidently points to a contrast with what precedes, where the children of folly are described from the folly of their judgments. (The καί must therefore be taken = ἥ in an adversative sense, and δικαιοῦσθαι as above in Luke vii. 29, in the sense, "to declare just," hence "to acknowledge as such," "to praise," "to laud.") The thought would then be : "wisdom (which is found fault with by foolish men) is justified, and defended, and represented as wisdom by her children, viz., by their treatment of her requisitions." With this agrees Matth. xi. 25, seq. in which the νήπιοι, babes, are described as the truly wise. (Neither the aorist, nor the signification of the δικαιοῦσθαι, favours the translation, " wisdom is blamed by her children.") But this thought acquires a pe-

---

* The sentiment, I think, stated in more precise language is: This generation is like those children sitting in the market place to whom their fellows call, saying, We have piped, etc. The simple point of the comparison is that, as these children would neither join their fellows in strains of merriment or grief, so the men of this generation find fault equally with the austerity of John, and the more genial character of the Saviour. Olshausen's explanation does not, I think, make allowance for the want of strict *exactness* in the Saviour's mode of expression. He says, "it is like children sitting and calling," etc., when the precise *meaning* is, " it resembles what occurs when children sit," etc.—[K.

culiar charm, when we consider that Scripture does not speak of
wisdom in the abstract, but as a~heavenly person, yea, that Jesus
calls himself *the Wisdom*. (See note on Luke xi. 49, compared
with Matth. xxii. 34 ; John i. 1, and Sirach xxiv. 4, seq.) In this
case, then, the Redeemer here appears as speaking with reference to
his divine nature, and the aorist ἐδικαιώθη, *was justified*, acquires a
peculiar significancy. The same phenomenon which he reproves in
the present, viz., that foolish men take offence at the ways of wisdom, has repeated itself at all times ; but at all times the children
of wisdom have justified their mother, and will do so even now.
The Redeemer appears here, therefore, as the bestower of all spiritual blessing from the beginning of time, as the generator, from the
beginning of the world, of all the earthly representatives of wisdom
whom he now, closing the series of manifestations, represents personally, in all her fulness and glory. (We must reject all expositions
of the passage which exclude the contrast with that which precedes ; as, for instance, that according to which λέγουσι, *they say*, is
to be supplied after καί, *and;* so that even the clause ἐδικαιώθη, κ. τ.
λ. is put into the mouth of the censorious Jews, according to whom
the τέκνα σοφίας would be merely *supposed* children of wisdom.)

Ver. 20.—The reproving discourse which follows, is found, in its
original connexion, on the occasion of the sending forth of the
seventy, in Luke x. 13, seq. ; but Matthew has, very properly, introduced it in this part of his narrative. The whole discourse of
the Redeemer was a censure upon his contemporaries ; but, in the
following words, the reproof is uttered, in its utmost severity, against
those who had most clearly seen his glory. The whole passage
again represents the same principle, but only from a different point
of view, which we dwelt upon in Matth. x. 41. As a reward is not
regulated by the deed itself, but by the disposition from which it
springs, and the consciousness by which it is accompanied ; so
punishment also will not be determined by the outward aspect of
the deed, but by the inward disposition of which it is the evidence,
and by the consciousness which it presupposes. The guilt of Tyre,
Sidon, and Sodom, is in this passage represented as less ; *first*, because their inhabitants occupied a less advanced position than did
the Jews at the time of Christ ; and *secondly*, because that which
was divine appeared to them in a far less glorious form. At the
time of Christ, however, the feeling of need was active, and was met
in his person by the purest manifestation of divinity, condescending, moreover, to human weakness, by external acts of the most
striking character. But, nevertheless, men hardened themselves
against these powerful impressions of the Spirit, and did not repent ;
this, therefore, enhanced their guilt exceedingly. By the greater
guilt of the latter, however, the guilt of the former is, in no way,

diminished ; it remains what it is, though spoken of relatively as compared with the more fully developed manifestations of sin.

Ver. 21.—Chorazin (Χοραζίν), a small place in Galilee, on the shores of the lake of Gennesaret, near Capernaum, is mentioned only here. Some expositors write, without any reason, χώρα Ζίν. It is evident that towns are here spoken of (ver. 20). In the same quarter was situated the better known town Βηθσαϊδά (derived from בַּיִת and צַיְדָה, i. e., fisher's town). The two together appear as the representatives of that highly favoured region, where the footsteps of the Lord were seen so long, and his hand dispensed so many blessings. Tyre and Sidon, on the contrary, are mentioned as the wealthy and voluptuous representatives of gross sensual enjoyment, which, as such, had been frequently denounced by the prophets of the Old Testament. (Is. xxiii.) Repenting in sackcloth and ashes, is the well-known Old Testament description of an earnest disposition to repentance, which manifests itself in corresponding outward acts. (1 Kings xxi. 27 ; 2 Kings vi. 30 ; Jonah iii. 6, 8.)

Ver. 22.—The term ἡμέρα κρίσεως, day of judgment, is used, in its most general sense, to denote the period which will at length come, when good and evil which, in the present course of the world, are mixed together, shall be separated. (Comp. further remarks on Matth. xxiv.) Ἄνεκτος or ἀνεκτός, from ἀνέχω, " tolerable," " endurable." (See the same thought, Matth. x. 15.) The comparative, as well as the whole context, points to different degrees of punishment for the wicked ; some are, as it were, in mitissima damnatione as Augustine says. This idea of degrees of punishment seems to imply, that it may be even remitted ; and this must be unhesitatingly conceded of the lesser forms of sin. (See more particularly at Matth. xii. 32.)

Ver. 23.—The same thing applies, in a higher degree, to Capernaum. (See note on Matth. iv. 13.) This insignificant Galilean country-town had become the fixed residence of the Messiah, and had thereby gained a higher importance. The choice of the town for his abode, on the part of the Redeemer, is evidently not accidental, but intimately connected with the reputation and susceptibility of its inhabitants. Here the nucleus of the kingdom of God might, and should have been formed. Instead of that, however, only a few joined themselves with entire devotedness to the Lord ; the others, destitute of faith, persevered in their unholy walk. The more dazzling, therefore, the light was to which they opposed themselves, the longer it shone upon their dark hearts, the heavier was their punishment. This is described in ἕως ᾅδου καταβιβασθῇ, thou shalt be brought down to hell, in uttering which, our Redeemer probably had before his mind Old Testament passages, such as Ezek. xxxi. 10 ; Is. xiv. 15, lvii. 9. Καταβιβάζεσθαι occurs nowhere else in the New

Testament ; it is the reverse of ὑψωθῆναι, hence *dejici*, "to be brought down." Οὐρανός, *heaven*, is contrasted with ᾅδης* or ᾅδου οἶκος, δῶμα = בֵּית. Such expressions, taken from the Greek mythology (as 2 Pet. ii. 4, alludes even to τάρταρος), the language of Scripture admits without hesitation, if they were prevalent in the mouths of the people, and had a true foundation. The true and simple fundamental idea of heaven and hades, is this ; that evil and good, which, even on earth, though outwardly blended, are separated in their nature and essence, are to have an ultimate and complete separation. In so far then as the day of judgment (κρίσεως, *separation*) reduces to its ultimate principle that which appears here mixed together, the being cast down into hades signifies the return of individual evil to its element.† At the great separation, which is impending over the universe, every individual life will be attracted and governed by the power of that element to which it granted admission into itself. He who admitted the Spirit and light of Christ, will be drawn by him into his kingdom of light ; he who allowed the spirit of darkness to rule in his heart, will become a prey to the power of darkness ; each according to the degree of his guilt, which only God can determine (see note on Matth. vii. 1), since it is dependent upon the degree of the impression which the light made upon man, and against which he hardened himself. Strange that some expositors should have explained this passage of external prosperity. "Thou art a very wealthy and prosperous town, but thou shalt greatly decline." Whatever man cherishes in his heart, he reproduces even in the word of God ; he makes a god for himself, and makes his Redeemer speak as suits him best, and as he would have spoken. (Comp. 2 Pet. ii. 20.) The more guilty Capernaum is then contrasted with Sodom, with the remark : it would have remained until this day. These words, unless they are empty words, are remarkable, as showing that our Redeemer ascribes, even to that which is past, no absolute necessity. He evidently acknowledges, even here, the freedom of self-determination, and the possibility of things having been otherwise, if men had been obedient to God, This, in a moral aspect, so important a view of history, as being wholly based upon the free actions of individuals, lies at the foundation of the whole Scripture doctrine.

Ver. 25.—That the following words were not spoken in immediate connexion with the preceding, Matthew himself indicates by the words : ἐν ἐκείνῳ τῷ καιρῷ, *at that season*. This formula of transition seems to place an interval between that which precedes

---

* Concerning ᾅδης, compare the remarks on Luke xvi. 28.

† "Being exalted to heaven" and "brought down to hades," seem to be strong figurative expressions, denoting on the one hand high spiritual privilege, on the other, corresponding degradation and ruin, of course, with a spiritual reference.—[K.

and that which follows. Luke x. 21, seq. gives a definite and ap- / propriate connexion of the words. We have, therefore, reason to suppose that Matthew again followed his practice of bringing into a new connexion the elements of our Lord's discourses, as it was not at all his object to exhibit the life and acts of Jesus chronologically, but only under their more general points of view. The same Spirit, who had spoken through our Lord, guided the disciple also in the arrangement. This may again be seen in the position of the following verses ; they form a very appropriate contrast with the preceding objurgatory discourse against the unbelieving ; they are the commentary on the words in ver. 19, Wisdom is justified of her children. The entire passage (ver. 25–30), moreover, is remarkable for its majestic course of thought. It is conceived in the spirit of John. We see hence, that it is the same Jesus who speaks in Matthew and John ; his discourses are received by different individuals; and each reproduces him in the aspects under which, with his peculiar mental traits, he had been enabled to apprehend him. Ver. 25, 30, now open to us an insight into the innermost recesses of our Redeemer's heart—a heart burning with love to his brethren. Conscious of his divine majesty and glory, he humbly condescends to the lowly, and seeks to comfort the forsaken. The real substance of Christianity, the condescension of the Divine to the weak and poor, is here celebrated in inspired language. Compared with this, all human greatness, wisdom, and glory, sink into the dust. (Matthew begins : Jesus answered and said (ἀποκριθεὶς εἶπεν ὁ Ἰησοῦς), ἀποκρίνεσθαι, answering, being used according to the analogy of the Hebrew עָנָה. [Comp. note on Luke i. 60.] Luke x. 21, on the other hand, points out the rejoicing and exulting of the Lord's spirit, in the words " exulted in spirit" (ἠγαλλιάσατο τῷ πνεύματι). Here τῇ ψυχῇ, in soul, could not have been appropriately used, as it would have pointed rather to the human nature of the Redeemer, as in Matth. xxvi. 38. The joy here spoken of is purely objective, in which the world of spirits shares, and which is exhibited in its perfection, in the inner life of the Lord). Christ commences with the praise of God, for his sovereign providence. (Ἐξομολογεῖσθαι = הוֹדָה seq. Dativ. " to praise," " to laud," Rom. xiv. 11, and frequently in the LXX.) According to the well-known Old Testament designation, Lord of heaven and earth, God is represented as the Lord of the universe, in evidently intended contrast with the νήπιοι, babes = μικροί (Matth. x. 42), πτωχοὶ τῷ πνεύματι. For the idea of the babe implies not only that which is undeveloped, but also that which is inexperienced and helpless ; as it stands here in contrast with σοφοί, wise, and συνετοί, prudent. The former of these two expressions refers rather to that which is divine, the latter to that which is earthly ; the σοφία is the result of the νοῦς (reason), the σύνεσις, of φρένες (understanding).*   Hence it cannot be said precisely, that the wise and prudent possessed a *false* wisdom and prudence; they had in their knowledge much that was true, and were, in this respect, more advanced than the disciples of the Lord. But their wisdom and prudence was, at the best, *earthly*, marred, therefore, by many defects, and unable to penetrate the depths of that which is divine. Christ, on the contrary, brought a *heavenly* wisdom ; and the first condition for the reception of it was poverty, the being emptied of man's wisdom. For this reason, human wisdom became in itself an obstacle to the reception of the pure light which beamed down from the opened heavens, whilst the simplest and lowliest men—such as were conscious of their poverty and blindness in things divine and human, but burned with a long- ing after truth—received it more readily and deeply. (Comp. 1 Cor. i. 19.) It is this wonderful dispensation—that the Lord of heaven and earth espoused the poorest and the most wretched—which our Saviour here celebrates with exultation. The term ταῦτα, *these things*, comprehends, therefore, all which was peculiar in the life of Christ, and which has been conferred upon mankind through his ministry. The men who could comprehend it, received it by a revelation (ἀποκάλυψις). Human wisdom is a fruit of intellectual activity and spontaneity ; the heavenly wisdom, on the contrary, is an effect of a divine influence on man's receptive faculties, and is the root of the life of faith. But, whilst faith belongs altogether to the heart, wisdom, in its heavenly form, is a blossom of the in- tellect (νοῦς). With the revelation, however, is contrasted a con- cealing (ἀπόκρυψις), an expression which might be considered as favouring the doctrine of absolute predestination. (Comp. Matth. xiii. 13, 14.) There is, however, nothing which prevents us from understanding ἀποκρύπτειν, *concealing*, in this passage as meaning merely " not to reveal ;" so that the sense would be, " they are left to their earthly wisdom." We here, therefore, pass over the refer- ence to predestination, which will hereafter frequently occupy our attention.

Ver. 26.—Once more our Redeemer breathes forth his feelings of thankfulness to the Father ; ναί sc. ἐξομολογοῦμαί σοι. (Concerning εὐδοκία = רָצוֹן, see note on Luke ii. 14.) Inasmuch as the divine will is the pure manifestation of the divine nature, since God can never will any thing but what he is, this implies the idea, that even this gracious endowing of the poor, and of babes, with true heavenly wisdom, is an effect of the pure self-denying love of God, manifest- ing itself in the communication of his own nature. The *love* of God, the absolute reverse of envy, induces him to descend into souls and into precisely those of the poor and needy. Without being en-

---

* Comp. the Author's *Opusc. Theol.* (Berol. 1833), p. 159.

lightened from above, man does not know nor understand this wonderful love of God, since he loves only splendour and fulness—not poverty ; but Jesus is himself the clearest proof and manifestation of it ; in him dwelt the fulness of the Godhead in the bosom of humanity ; and yet this divine manifestation was most unpretending and humble. From the Father, the Lord of heaven and of earth, our Lord passes to himself, the visible representation of this pure love of God, and describes himself as working, just in the same manner which he celebrated in the Father ; he invites all the needy, all the wretched, to enjoy the fulness of God which is in him.

Ver. 27.—The transition from the Father to the Son may be explained by the following thought : "The organ through which the Father reveals himself, as the eternal mercy, is the Son himself." First, the Redeemer proceeds from the thought of his divine power, in the words : " All things are delivered unto me by my Father" (πάντα μοι παρεδόθη ὑπὸ τοῦ πατρός). The πάντα, all things, refers back to the κύριος οὐρανοῦ καὶ γῆς, Lord of heaven and earth, in ver. 25, so that the passage forms a parallel to the words of the Lord : ἐδόθη μοι πᾶσα ἐξουσία ἐν οὐρανῷ καὶ ἐπὶ γῆς, all power is given, etc. (Matth. xxviii. 18), in which Christ, the Son of God, is represented as the ruler of the world, to whom the same honour and worship are due as to the Father, and in whom alone the Father reveals himself to mankind. (John xiv. 9.) But as the kingdom belongs originally to the Father, it is only given (παρεδόθη) to the Son, in so far as he is at the same time Man; for which reason, at the end of the kingdom of God, the Son gives it back into the hands of the Father. (1 Cor. xv. 28.) Starting from this fundamental relation, our Redeemer then points out the special relation of his people to the Father, in reference to their knowing him (ἐπίγνωσις), and thence deduces the doctrine, that all that true revelation to the babes, comes only through him; that therefore all knowledge gained without him and out of him, is merely human knowledge, and, therefore, unsatisfactory. In the first place, then, the Lord represents the mutual relation between Father and Son, by saying : οὐδεὶς ἐπιγινώσκει τὸν υἱὸν εἰ μὴ ὁ πατήρ, οὐδὲ τὸν πατέρα τις ἐπιγινώσκει εἰ μὴ ὁ υἱός, no one knoweth the Son except the Father, etc. It is remarkable, that the Fathers often invert this passage in their quotations. (Comp. on this subject my Gesch. der Evang. S. 292, f.) Irenæus even says in a passage (Adv. Hær. iv. 14), that the heretics had intentionally made this inversion, according to which they read first: οὐδεὶς ἐπιγινώσκει τὸν πατέρα εἰ μὴ ὁ υἱός, no one knoweth the Father except the Son; but that is very improbable, because Irenæus himself frequently inverts the two members of the verse. Now the reading itself is not contested by the MSS; the question then only is, why the position of the members should be just as it is. The knowing of the Son is no doubt here placed first, because it forms the principal subject; Jesus wishes to impress upon his followers that no man can come to the true knowledge of God, except through the Son, for " no man can come to the Father except by me." (John xiv. 6.) If Jesus had wished to represent it absolutely, "no man knoweth the Father except the Son" would very likely have been placed first. It is precisely in the contrast of the two members, that the peculiar mutual relation, existing between the Father and the Son, is indicated, according to the words, Thou Father, art in me, and I in thee.* The Father beholds himself in the Son, as his image, the effulgence of his glory (εἰκών, ἀπαύγασμα τῆς δόξης, Heb. i. 3); the Son finds himself again in the Father, so that the Son is the self-manifestation (*Selbstobjectivirung*) of the Father, which, as a divine and hence everlasting act, has begotten the Son as an everlasting Being. (On the relation between the Father and the Son, see more fully on John i. 1.) This mutual act of recognising and being recognised, between the Father and the Son, is communicated to mankind by the Son as the *Word*, as the manifestation of the Father, who is concealed within himself. (Comp. remarks on 1 Cor. xiii. 12 ; Gal. iv. 9.) This revelation, it is true, depends on the will of the Son (ᾧ ἐὰν βούληται), which, however, must not be conceived of as an *arbitrary* one, but as guided by compassionate love and wisdom. If any oné should here object, that if the Son communicates to any the knowledge of God, as indeed he has communicated it from everlasting to certain individuals, it is then no longer the Son *alone* who knows the Father, but these also along with the Son ; we would answer that in the individual knowing God, it is Christ himself, by his Spirit, who knows the Father (Gal. ii. 20); if, therefore, the whole church hereafter shall know the Father by the Spirit of Christ, yet it is still only the Son who in this infinite number of individuals, recognises the Father, inasmuch as they are all one in Christ. (Gal. iii. 28 ; 1 Cor. xii. 12.) Hence it is clear, that the ἐπιγινώσκειν, *knowing*, is no mere intellectual knowledge of divine things (precisely the nature of human wisdom, whose knowledge of God has no power of creating divine life), but the life of God in man, and of man in God, which, it is true, is not *without* knowledge, but unites in one knowledge and the essential substance. The knowing of God is, therefore, based upon divine love, upon God communicating his nature to the beings whom he has created. " It is only light that beholds light; only that which is divine recognises divinity."

Ver. 28.—The following verses, which we find only in Matthew, and which seem here in their appropriate place, are a commentary

---

* Concerning the recognition of the Father through the Son, and of the Son through the Father, compare the pregnant texts, John x. 14 ; 1 John ii. 13, 14.

on the words in ver. 5 : *the poor have the Gospel, etc.*. He to whom
all things are delivered by the Father, calls to himself the heavy
laden—not the rich, the great and the glorious—that is to say, he
gives himself to them. The two terms, κοπιῶντες καὶ πεφορτισμένοι, *labouring and heavy-laden*, denote the same condition (that
of being under sin and its consequences) ; the former pointing out
its active, the latter its passive feature. The sense of suffering beneath the yoke of sin, originates in man only from divine influence ;
the ungodly man feels at his ease under it. So far as the divine
principle in men strives after deliverance from sin, they are called
κοπιῶντες *labouring* ; so far as they feel its pressure, and their inability to free themselves from it, they are called πεφορτισμένοι, *heavy-
laden*. The removal of this whole condition is promised by the Redeemer in the rest (ἀνάπαυσις). Faith in him brings back the lost
harmony in the inner and outer life, and with it, rest to the soul.
(Comp. Jer. vi. 16. The idea of rest corresponds with John's ζωὴν
ἔχειν καὶ περισσόν, *having life and that abundantly*. [John x. 10.]
As soon as the magnet of life has found its pole of attraction, peace
and rest follow. The *rest* (ἀνάπαυσις), in its higher degree, and un-
changing state, is *peace*, εἰρήνη.)

Ver. 29, 30.—But as the holy principle in man is encumbered
with the heavy burden of sin within and around him, the claims of
the divine life appear at first burdensome and oppressive. The
discord in man is not immediately removed after his entering into
the element of the good. For this reason, the Redeemer speaks
also of a yoke and a burden (ζυγός and φορτίον), which he himself
imposes. But it appears easy and light when compared with the
burden of sin. For, from the latter, man's nobler nature suffers directly, it causes the deepest oppression of the soul ; and this feature
characterized the oppressive yoke of the Pharisaical ordinances, inasmuch as they were born of sin, and checked in its development
the divine life. (Comp. remarks on Matth. xxiii. 4.) The burden
of Christ, on the contrary, is only felt by man so far as he is still encumbered with sin ; his nobler nature feels Christ's Spirit and life
to be a homogeneous element ; and thus the believer can exult and
sing praises inwardly, although, outwardly, he be perishing daily.
(2 Cor. iv. 16.) This struggle with sin, the believer must *enter
upon*, according to the command of Christ, (ἄρατε, *take*, signifies the
positive activity in entering upon the struggle—comp. remarks on
Matth. x. 38), and *learn* of Christ. In a manner not to be mistaken, then, Jesus here represents himself as King and Prophet,
who imposes the yoke of his rule, and offers his doctrine for acceptance ; but his is a mild rule and teaching, when compared with the
service of sin, and all which has originated from it (for instance the
Pharisaical observances) ; and it is this mildness which the Re-

deemer urges as a motive for taking his yoke. Besides this train
of thought, there seems to be another in this passage. The expression *my yoke*, may not only be explained : "the yoke which I, as
ruler, impose upon others," but it may also be understood : "the
yoke which I myself bear ;" so that it is equivalent to the cross of
Christ. Viewed in this light, the words *for I am meek*, etc., also
acquire a new signification. From the meekness of Jesus in carrying his cross or yoke, his disciples should learn the same disposition
of mind ; for thereby every burden becomes easy, and every suffering is overcome. If any one walks under the burden of sin, as a
common burden ; if he bears all the sufferings of time as the consequences of the universal guilt of mankind, then it may be said he
walks in self-denying love, takes upon him the yoke (does not merely allow it to be imposed upon him), and thereby finds rest for
his soul ; for disquietude originates in self-will, which refuses to
bear a due share of the burden of sin. According to this train of
thought, our Redeemer regards himself also as a bearer of the cross
and yoke, as in all things he was made like unto men, his brethren ;
only, that he did not bear the burden on his own account, but on
ours. It is only to this mode of interpretation, that the expression
"lowly in heart" (ταπεινὸς τῇ καρδίᾳ) is suitable. A ruler may, with
reference to his subjects, be said to be πρᾷος, *meek*, but not ταπεινός,
lowly. As little, therefore, as God is ever said to be lowly, just so
little is the Redeemer in his divine nature ; ταπεινοφροσύνη, *lowliness*,
is the character only of the creature ; and Christ calls himself lowly,
only in so far as he is man, and all human, as well as divine attributes, appertain to him. Holy Scripture expresses the act of the
incarnation of the Son of God by κενόω, and the humiliation of the
Son of God as man by ταπεινόω. (Comp. remarks on Philip. ii. 6-
8). This shews, that in this passage the Redeemer did not intend
to speak of himself only as the Son of God, but pointed also to his
human nature (and the divine and human nature must be considered to be united in his holy person—a union miraculous, and to us
inconceivable); he to whom all things were delivered by the Father
himself, bears the yoke with us, and hence puts his hand along with
us to the heavy burdens of life ; and, though the only Lord, he is,
at the same time, a servant. (Comp. Matth. xxiii. 4-11.) He not
only gives commands, but enables us also to obey them, inasmuch as
he, by the power of the Spirit, causes that they do not appear heavy.
(1 John v. 3.) The expression τῇ καρδίᾳ, *in heart*, describes the humility of the Redeemer, as in entire accordance with his holy will,
and originating in the very depth of his heart ; hence humility appears in him as the cheerful result of free choice. There is, then,
certainly a difference between *lowly in heart* and *lowly in spirit*
(ταπεινὸς τῷ πνεύματι) = רוּחַ שְׁפַל, Prov. xxix. 23. (Comp. Ps. xxxiii.

18 [LXX.] with πτωχὸς τῷ πνεύματι, Matth. v. 3.) The latter expression denotes an attribute of sinful man, and marks what is laudable only in so far as the knowledge of poverty and wretchedness is a condition of all help from above ; but in this sense the expression cannot be applied to Christ. He was lowly in heart but elevated and rich in spirit, inasmuch as the bent of his will, and the disposition of his heart, are not towards what is high, but towards what is lowly. *His* humility is therefore compassion ; but the use of ταπεινοφροσύνη, used alike of the perfectly holy *One*, and of sinful man, is peculiar to the language of Scripture. Even in the Old Testament, the LXX. use it for expressions, such as אֶבְיוֹן, עָנִי, דַּל, corresponding with the terms πτωχός and ταπεινός of the New Testament. Among the ancient profane writers, the term is very rarely (for instance by Plutarch) used in a noble sense. The peculiar use of the *word* is connected with a peculiar *idea* which belongs to revealed religion. Whilst we everywhere meet, in the natural man, with a striving after that which is *high*, which originates in a dim consciousness of his *deep* fall, Scripture teaches, more darkly in the Old Testament, more distinctly in the New, that the safest way to salvation, and to the highest exaltation, is to humble ourselves to the lowest poverty. It is only in the lowest depths of repentance, and of bitter self-knowledge—producing a compassionate love to all our fellow-men—that the soul can receive the powers of divine life, and rise again to the highest exaltation. In the life of our Redeemer who, from love, became like unto sinful man, this way, which alone leads to peace, is exemplified.

§ 17. The Disciples Pluck Ears of Corn.

(Matth. xii. 1–8; Mark ii. 23–28; Luke vi. 1–5.)

In the subsequent twelfth chapter of Matthew, the Evangelist reports several events (among others, a cure in ver. 9, seq.), which, however, pervaded by a common bond, likewise show the design of Matthew to arrange the life of Jesus according to certain general classes of subjects. It is the rising hostility of the Pharisees to Jesus, by which all the single events in this section are connected, and on account of which the various occurrences seem to be reported. It is probable, from the more minute account of John, that the hostility of the Pharisees to Jesus assumed a decided form, only after he had come to Jerusalem for the celebration of the feast. (John v. 1, seq.) As, however, Matthew pays no attention either to time or place—restricting his communications neither to Galilee

nor to any other locality*—as he narrates without mentioning
places, and aims only to exhibit to his Jewish readers the life
of Jesus in its various aspects, we must here also give up any
exact arrangement of the single occurrences, and this the rather,
because inferences respecting it, drawn from the internal character
of the narratives, cannot but be arbitrary. (Comp. *Dr. Paulus'*
Commentary, Th. ii. Anf.) An impartial comparison of the other
two Evangelists, leads to the same result. For, although Mark
connects the narrative of the cure of the withered hand, immediately
with the plucking of the ears of corn, yet he differs, in chap. iii.
7–19, so very much from Matthew, and brings forward in these
verses circumstances so entirely different, that we gain nothing for
a chronological arrangement by his coming back (iii. 20) to events
which Matthew also reports in this chapter. Luke differs from
Matthew still more strikingly ; inasmuch as, in the passage parallel
to Matth. xii. 22, seq., he enters upon the record of the last journey
of Jesus to the feast (Luke xi. 14, seq.), and then returns, at the
end of the chapter, to viii. 19, seq.

The first narrative then—that of the plucking of the ears of
corn by the disciples—is introduced by Matthew, with the very indefinite expression : " at that time" (ἐν ἐκείνῳ τῷ καιρῷ)—a formula
admitting of wider and narrower limits, and corresponding to the
general phrase : " and it came to pass," of Mark. But Luke here
uses a peculiar expression : ἐν σαββάτῳ δευτεροπρώτῳ. From this
formula, we might be able, perhaps, to infer something decisive in
favour of a chronological arrangement, if its signification were not so
completely indeterminate. The word seems to have been formed
by Luke himself, and is not met with either in the Biblical writings,
or any where else. According to the common opinion, which was
first advanced by *Scaliger*, the expression : δευτερόπρωτον σάββατον
is meant to designate the first Sabbath after the second day of the
Passover ; so that it might be resolved into : σάββατον πρῶτον ἀπὸ
δευτέρας ἀπὸ τοῦ πάσχα. For, according to the Mosaic institution
(Levit. xxiii. 11–25), the first ears of corn were offered to the Lord
on the second day of the Passover (הַשַּׁבָּת מִמָּחֳרַת) ; and from this day,
seven Sabbaths were counted to the day of Pentecost. The Sabbath following this second day of the Passover, is thought to be designated by δευτερόπρωτον. The plucking of the ripening ears by
the disciples agrees very well with this supposition ; yet, it must
be considered that the harvest was protracted until the day of Pentecost, which indeed was the real Feast of Harvest ; the disciples
might, therefore, have walked through the fields at a later period

---

* The opinion frequently expressed by modern critics, that Matthew intended to give
only reports of Christ's sojourn in Galilee, has been refuted in the Author's " Programme
über die Aechtheit des Matthæus."

also. Furthermore, Jesus must have left Jerusalem very soon, if he walked through the fields of Galilee on the first Sabbath after the feast, which, as it is well known, was celebrated during seven days. Finally—the explanation itself is indeed ingenious, and possibly correct, but proofs of it are wanting. We may well imagine, that every first Sabbath of two closely following each other, and, as it were, belonging to one another, was thus named ; and such a case frequently occurred. For, in the three great festivals, the first and the last of the seven days were celebrated, and these might very easily be followed or preceded by a Sabbath, so that these two days of rest followed each other. The same was the case with the Pentecost and new moons. The first of these two days of rest was then called δευτερόπρωτον. In favour of this explanation, although it likewise cannot be proven, would be the omission of the article, which points in a manner not to be mistaken to several σάββατα δευτερόπρωτα. (The Hebrew נָבָה or שַׁבָּתוֹן is translated by the LXX. sometimes σάββατον, sometimes σάββατα, and both the forms occur in the New Testament likewise.) [It is best to assume a weekly Sabbath, falling between the two festal Sabbaths of a festal week. Comp. my Krit. d. ev. Gesch. § 79.]

Ver. 2.—The plucking of ears of corn, in so far as it was done for appeasing hunger, was permitted by the law (Deut. xxiii. 25) ; it was only forbidden to use the reaping-hook. But the Pharisaic *Micrology*, which had perverted the simple Mosaic commandment of external rest into a grievous institution, added the plucking of ears of corn on the Sabbath-day to the forbidden labours. They divided all business into thirty-nine main classes (called fathers), many of which, moreover, had subdivisions (called daughters).

Ver. 3, 4.—Jesus, therefore, endeavours to raise them from their limited standing-point to a spirit of greater freedom, and this, in such a manner that, from the law itself, he points out to them its free application ; whence he would derive the result, that the law, with its arrangements, must be understood and treated spiritually. The first example adduced is that of David. The well-known narrative of this occurrence, which took place when David fled before Saul, is found in 1 Sam. xxi. 1, seq. The loaves of shew-bread (ἄρτοι προθέσεως = פָּנִים לֶחֶם), were placed on small tables in the sanctuary of the tabernacle. (Exod. xxxv. 13, xxxix. 36.) The addition made by Mark ii. 26, ἐπὶ 'Αβιάθαρ, *under Abiathar*, presents some difficulties. For, according to the narrative in the Old Testament, it was not Abiathar, but his father Abimelech, who was at that time high-priest ; and the expression ἐπί, cannot be otherwise understood than *at the time* when he was in office. (Compare Luke iii. 2, iv. 27 ; Acts xi. 28.) *Beza* considered this passage an interpolation ; but there is no ground for this opinion. The MSS. with a very few exceptions, favour the reading. It is most simple and natural to say : the Evangelist has confounded father and son, which might easily happen, as Abiathar was the better known of the two. If any one will not admit this (to which I, however, can see as little objection as to the adoption of various readings), we might suppose that the father likewise bore the name of Abiathar, although no proof for this can be given. [Jesus does not, in this example, teach that *one may break a commandment*. He reasons from the less to the greater. "David broke even an express ceremonial law ; my disciples have not even done that (as the Pentateuch nowhere forbad plucking ears on the Sabbath). If now David—in the *spiritual* perception that the object of this shew-bread ordinance was sensibly to set forth good works, not to leave God's anointed one to a death by starvation—overstept the letter of the ordinance, how much more may my disciples appease their hunger in a way which no law forbids !" Thus his answer does not raise the inquiry whether the fourth commandment is binding, but *how* it is to be fulfilled, whether in Pharisaic *literalness*—which regards plucking the corn as a violation of the Sabbath, but not hostility and falsehood toward Jesus !—or in its spirit.]

Ver. 5.—Matthew and Mark, taken together, give us the discourse of Jesus complete. Matthew first adduces another example from the Old Testament, from which it may be seen that the law concerning the rest of the Sabbath must be understood spiritually. (Compare John v. 17, where Jesus, from the unceasing creative activity of God, vindicates an unlimited activity for himself also.) According to Numb. xxviii. 9, certain sacrifices had to be offered up by the priests in the temple on the Sabbath ; this duty presupposed work of various kinds, and yet the priests were without guilt in it. [From this Jesus draws the simple conclusion that in the fourth commandment, not *action* absolutely is forbidden, but action in our own and worldly concerns. Activity in the work of God is both allowed and commanded.] The clause : σάββατον βεβηλοῦν = חִלֵּל שַׁבָּת (Ez. xx. 16), is therefore to be understood in this way : "they would (according to your false notions), desecrate the Sabbath." Evidently the words : ἐν τῷ ἱερῷ, *in the temple,* are here intended to form a contrast with βεβηλοῦσι, *profane,* "they desecrate it in that place where, on account of its holiness, it should be least expected."

Ver. 6.—From the temple, Jesus passes over to the then existing circumstances. Of the two readings, μείζων and μεῖζον, the latter, as being more difficult, is no doubt to be preferred. It is supported, moreover, by very important authorities among the MSS. The μείζων could only form a contrast with νόμος, *i. e.,* the author of the law—Moses—whilst the neuter draws a parallel between the relations of the priests to the temple in general, and the relation be-

tween the disciples and Christ. The sense then is : " We have here
to do with a much greater matter than the temple service ; if even
in the latter, the letter of the law could be understood and treated
with spiritual freedom, how much more here." True, these relations derived their superiority solely from his personal importance,
and hence even the reading μείζων gives no bad sense. In verse 8,
the same thought is expressed with greater precision.

Ver. 7.—This whole reasoning from the Old Testament, must
already have convinced the Pharisees how little they had understood
the sense of the sacred Book. According to Matthew, our Redeemer still continues to bring this more definitely before them. They
had wished to censure the disciples as transgressors of the law, and
in this very censure they had transgressed it themselves. Their
leaning towards externals had prevented them from entering into
the spirit of the Old Testament writings, and so they had not understood the meaning of the profound words of Hosea vi. 6 : ἔλεον
θέλω καὶ οὐ θυσίαν, *I desire mercy and not sacrifice.* (Comp. note
on Matth. ix. 13.) In these words even prophecy pointed forward
to the spiritual elevation to which mankind were to be raised by the
Gospel ; in which, it is not the external deed, but the internal disposition, and especially that of self-denying merciful love, which is
truly well-pleasing in the sight of God. This compassionate love
was wanting in the censure of the Pharisees. They had no concern
for the real improvement of the disciples, no pure zeal for the cause
of God. They rather sought from envy and inward malice to
fasten blame on the disciples, and under show of zeal for the Lord
in reality persecuted the Lord himself in his disciples. They condemned the guiltless (κατεδίκασαν τοὺς ἀναιτίους) ; for the disciples
had not plucked the ears of corn for mere pastime, but from hunger
(ver. 1) ; they had abandoned their own possessions, and were
famishing amidst their toils for the kingdom of God. Hence, they
were in a position similar to that of David, the servant of God, who,
in the service of the Lord, hungered likewise with his followers ;
and to that of the priests who were obliged to work in the temple
on the Sabbath, and who thus, from the Pharisaical point of view,
seemed to break the law of the Lord.

Ver. 8.—The conclusion of our Lord's discourse points back to
his own exalted rank, and hence to that of his disciples. · In Mark
ii. 27, it is preceded by a rich idea : " the Sabbath was made for man,
not man for the Sabbath." Inasmuch as " Sabbath" stands here *per
synecdoche* for the law with all its ordinances, the Pharisaic *casuistical* view of the Old Testament is, in these words, contrasted
with the Christian, free, and spiritual view of it. According to the
former, the commands themselves, and the external legal observance of them, are the *end* to which man is only subservient. In

such a view of it, the law is a grievous burden. According to the Christian view, however, man, and his training for heaven, are the *end;* whilst the commands and the external observance of them, are only means for this end. From this point of view, the law appears, in its true import, as a gift of love from our paternal God, who trains man by means of external ordinances, only until he becomes able to receive the inward law in his heart. (Jerem. xxxi. 33.) It is impossible that, in the concluding thought, which is common to all the three Evangelists: The Son of Man is Lord of the Sabbath (κύριος τοῦ σαββάτου ὁ υἱὸς τοῦ ἀνθρώπου), the term, *Son of Man,* should be parallel to *man,* in Mark ii. 27; for although sinful man does not exist on account of the law, but, on the contrary the law exists on account of man, yet it would be altogether unsuitable to say, that man is *the lord* of the law, or of any one of the legal institutions. *He* only could say so of himself, who was the ideal of man. *Son of Man,* must then be here understood as the contrast of *man,* and hence the Messianic dignity of the Redeemer is declared in this expression. Being the Lord of heaven (1 Cor. xv. 47), although walking here on earth in the humble form of a man, the Messiah is raised above every legal institution, inasmuch as his will is the law itself; yet, he nowhere appears as abrogating any law, but as fulfiling it in a spiritual sense. (Matth. v. 17.) Thus our Redeemer fulfils the Old Testament law of the Sabbath also, by recommending internal repose of the soul, and rest in God. [The sense is not: " I am Lord of the Sabbath *law,* and hence may break it ;" but, " I am Lord of the *Sabbath;* the Lord whose work must be done on the Sabbath. What therefore my disciples do on the Sabbath in *my* service (as they then in his companionship and service appeased their hunger), this is not breaking, but sanctifying the Sabbath. I am the Lord of the Sabbath, hence it is for me to determine what is hallowing the Sabbath." Here, again, the question is not of the validity of the fourth commandment, but of the true, spiritual mode of fulfilling it.— Christ is the Lord of the Sabbath as he is the Lord of life, and as such has interpreted the command, Thou shalt not kill, while yet he has himself so perfectly fulfilled it, that, far from killing others, he submitted to death like a lamb, and prayed for his murderers. It no more follows from his being the Lord of the Sabbath, that he *dispenses* with the fourth commandment, than from his being Lord of life that he dispenses with the sixth. He teaches us only to fulfil it *in its spirit,* as he has done, not by literal inactivity, but by rest from secular labour, and by spiritual and heavenly employment.]

§ 18. JESUS CURES A WITHERED HAND.

(Matth. xii. 9–21; Mark iii. 1–6; Luke vi. 6–12.)

Ver. 9.—The same subject is still farther developed on another occasion, when Jesus healed a sick man. He avails himself of this event, to open the eyes of the Pharisees to a more spiritual discernment of the Old Testament ; for, notwithstanding their repugnance to him, our Redeemer did not yet give them up. It is impossible not to observe how vague are the formulas of transition used by Matthew. The words : μεταβὰς ἐκεῖθεν, departing thence, would lead us to connect this event with that immediately preceding ; but from Luke vi. 6, we see that at least eight days intervened, and that the occurrence now to be narrated happened on another Sabbath. The words, "he came into their synagogue," prove as clearly that he paid no attention at all to the localities ; for nothing had been previously mentioned to shew who are meant by the their (αὐτῶν.) (The χεὶρ ξηρά, withered hand = ἐξηραμμένη by Mark, as the expression so naturally derived from the appearance indicates, is a hand lamed by paralysis, and deprived of vital power ; a mere luxation is here out of the question.) *

Ver. 10.—According to Matthew, the Pharisees endeavoured to entrap Jesus by an insidious question ; Luke and Mark allude, in general, to their malicious intentions, but do not introduce them as speaking. (The word παρατηρέω is often used by Luke in the signification, insidiose observare [Luke xiv. 1; xx. 20.] In Gal. iv. 10 it has another cognate signification, superstitiose observare. The notion of anxious observation is common to both.) Christ, however, perceived their intention, not merely from the question (for that might have originated from a well-meaning disposition also), but by his power of discerning hearts, which was very different from mere reflective conjectures concerning their intention (Comp. remarks on John ii. 25.—Concerning the διαλογισμοί [Luke vi. 8], comp. note on Luke ii. 35; Matth. ix. 4).—Mark and Luke, again, detail the outward circumstances of this event far more graphically than Matthew. They describe how Jesus ordered the sick man to come forward, so that he might be seen by all ; and how he then, by directing their looks to the sufferer, endeavoured to rouse the consciences of those men who were dead in a fancied observance of the

---

* In the apocryphal additions to the genuine Gospel of Matthew, as Jerome found them in the Gospel of the Nazarenes, this sick man was declared to have been a cœmentarius. Jerome (Comm. in Matth. p. 47) writes that he said: "Cæmentarius eram, manibus victum quæritans; precor te, Jesu, ut mihi restituas sanitatem, ne turpiter mendicem cibos." (Comp. my Gesch. der Evang., p. 78.

law. The question, however, which Jesus puts to the assembled Pharisees (Mark iii. 4; Luke vi. 9) is singular in its character. For the question at issue seemed to be not about doing good or evil, but about *doing* or *not doing*. But it is from this contrast, so apt to mislead them, that our Saviour wished to free them, and to point out to them that the *not doing* might often be a sin. Now, however, it was clear that man should not sin on the Sabbath, any more than on another day ; and hence (so Christ argued) it might, under peculiar circumstances, not only be permitted, but even be a duty, to work on the Sabbath day. [Here also the only question is of the *mode* of observance, not of the sanctity, of the Sabbath. Rescuing, ransoming, saving, *belongs* to the Sabbath. Doing evil and indulging in malice, as the Pharisees did, is desecrating the Sabbath.]

Ver. 11.—Matthew goes on to narrate how the Redeemer appealed to the consciences of all those who were present—asking, whether, they would not, on the Sabbath, draw out a sheep, from a well into which it had happened to fall. Jesus draws an inference *a minori ad majus:* how much more is the faithful Shepherd of souls bound to save on the Sabbath day a little sheep of his flock which had fallen into the pit of perdition ! This indeed is a veritable Sabbath-work, a true service of God ! (The same thought, in a somewhat different connection, is found in Luke xiv. 5. For βόθυνος, *pit*, Luke has φρέαρ, *well* = באר.) The Pharisees held their peace (Mark iii. 4), and hence confessed themselves overcome by the truth of the discourse (Luke xiv. 5). This susceptibility, coupled with so much hardness, awakened anger in the heart of the Redeemer : περιβλεψάμενος αὐτοὺς μ ε τ’ ὀ ρ γ ῆ ς σ υ λ λ υ π ο ύ μ ε ν ο ς ἐπὶ τῇ πωρώσει τῆς καρδίας αὐτῶν (Mark iii. 5). A sorrowful, sympathizing anger is not at all a contradiction. It is only in sinful man that boiling rage stifles the more gentle feelings of sorrow and sympathizing grief. In our Redeemer, as in the heart of God, the glow of anger is identical with love ; whilst he hates sin, he has mercy upon the sinner. (The substantive πώρωσις is, besides in this passage, found only in Rom. xi. 25; Eph. iv. 18. The verb, on the other hand, occurs frequently. It is derived from πῶρος, *callus*, and signifies " obduracy," " insensibility," especially to moral impressions.)

Ver. 13.—After this address, which so deeply struck their hearts, our Redeemer cures the sick man. ('Αποκαθίστημι of bodily healing = שוב Exod. iv. 7 ; in like manner Matth. viii. 25. It signifies, primarily, *in integrum restituere*, to restore to the former, original condition. Thus often in a spiritual sense. Compare note on Matth. xvii. 11.)

Ver. 14.—The disclosure of sin either awakens repentance, or, if man is insensible to it, anger;· so also with the Pharisees. The host of priests, attacked in their most secret sin, joined for the defence of their kingdom. There was no longer the opposition of individuals, but of a powerful body, whose enmity was called forth by the light which emanated from Christ. According to Mark iii. 6, the crafty priests immediately attempted to form a coalition with the secular powers; " They took counsel with the Herodians (μετὰ τῶν 'Ηρωδιανῶν συμβούλιον ἐποίουν). These Herodians were courtiers and adherents of Herod Antipas, the ruler of Galilee (Matth. xxii. 16 ; Mark xii. 13), whom the Pharisees undertook to gain over to their interests, because they could effect nothing without the secular power.* Their wicked intentions became evident even at that time ; they hardened their hearts against the beneficent influences of the Holy Spirit ; ἐπλήσθησαν ἀνοίας, they were filled with folly, as Luke vi. 11 very significantly expresses it, for every departure from God is folly.

Ver. 15.—But as the hour had not yet come, in which the Lord was to be delivered into the hands of his enemies (Matth. xxvi. 45), he left them and withdrew into retirement. The narrative of Matth. xii. 15, 16, finishes with the same kind of general formula, as we have already frequently met with (iv. 23, seq.; ix. 35, seq.). According to the parallel passage (Mark iii. 7, seq.), Jesus went to the Lake of Gennesaret, and, among the multitudes who sought him there, there were not only persons from Idumea, Tyre and Sidon, but also from Judea and Jerusalem—(Comp. iii. 22, where γραμματεῖς ἀπὸ 'Ιεροσολύμων καταβάντες are expressly mentioned); which clearly proves that Jesus had already exercised his ministry in Judea and Jerusalem. It is probable that many events narrated by Matthew and Mark happened in, or around Jerusalem ; only, the Evangelists omit any mention of the locality ; no intimation is to be found that, before his last journey to the feast, Jesus limited the sphere of his ministry to Galilee. According to the farther account of Mark (iii. 19), the throng of people was so great, that they became troublesome to our Lord (θλίβειν), and he was obliged to enter into a vessel in order that thence he might be able to teach them. (In the phrase : ἵνα πλοιάριον προσκαρτερῇ αὐτῷ, the expression προσκαρτερεῖν is used in the sense of præsto esse, " to be at one's disposal.") Here also Jesus endeavoured earnestly and impressively to inculcate (ἐπετίμα), that his abode and dignity should not be made known, (ἵνα μὴ φανερὸν αὐτὸν ποιήσωσι, Mark iii. 12 ; Matth. xii. 16.) According to the context, this command of Jesus chiefly implies that he wished every political movement in his favour to be avoided on the part of those Jews who were filled with false notions concerning the Messiah, that he might thus take from his adversaries every

* The uncritical *Epiphanius* describes the Herodians as a religious sect. (Epiph. Hær. Ossen. p. 44.)

even apparent occasion of accusing him. (Compare, concerning this, the remarks on Matth. viii. 4.)

Ver. 17—Matthew avails himself of this quiet retirement of Jesus, which contrasted so strikingly with the tumultuous enter-prises of the false Christs of a later period, to 'quote a remarkable passage of the Old Testament (Isaiah xlii. 1–4) in which this cha-racter of the Messiah is pointed out. The Messiah is there described as possessing the same gentleness and meekness as he had displayed in his discourse, Matth. xi. 28–30. (On the ὅπως πληρωθῇ, comp. remarks on Matth. i. 22.)

Ver. 18.—This quotation of the Old Testament is also treated in a peculiar way. Matthew follows neither the LXX., nor the Hebrew text *verbatim;* on the contrary, he makes use of the text for his purpose in a free translation. The LXX. have, in the first place, added to the translation their own exposition ; they add to Isaiah xlii. 1: Ἰακὼβ ὁ παῖς μου, Ἰσραὴλ ὁ ἐκλεκτός μου. The reference of this passage to Israel, *i. e.*, to the whole body of the truly faith-ful among the people, is, indeed, not incorrect : but Matthew could not make use of it for his purpose (at least, not without an explan-ation); hence he adheres to the words of the original text בְּחִירִי, עַבְדִּי which presented a more natural reference to Jesus, and translates by ἰδοῦ the הֵן omitted by the LXX. But, with full warrant, the Evangelist refers these words to Jesus, inasmuch as our Redeemer was not only a member of the collective body of the true worship-pers of God in Israel, but their representative ; and many expressions, especially ver. 4 (לְתוֹרָתוֹ אִיִּים יְחֵלוּ), shew that the prophet had such an one in his view. The word ἡρέτισα (Heb. אֶתְמָךְ, LXX, προσεδέξατο) from αἱρετίζω, which is found only in this passage, differs from the signification of the word in the original text ; yet the word תָּמַךְ " to seize," " to lay hold on," = αἱρέω, might perhaps be taken in that sense. The word יוֹצִיא the LXX render better by ἐξοίσει, than Mat-thew by ἀπαγγελεῖ. Perhaps Matthew chose the expression on ac-count of the subsequent prophetical discourses of Christ concerning the judgment.

Ver. 19.—The words of this and of the following verses, extol the gentle character of this beloved Son of God. Matthew has trans-posed the first two expressions, the words, of the Hebrew text being לֹא יִצְעַק וְלֹא יִשָּׂא, he *shall not cry,* nor *strive* (the LXX have ἀνήσει instead of ἐρίσει.) In the subsequent clause בַּחוּץ (LXX, ἔξω) is rendered freely, ἐν ταῖς πλατείαις, and has no doubt a reference to the ἀναχωρεῖν (εἰς τὴν ἔρημον) in ver. 15.

Ver. 20.—As ver. 19 described the quiet, noiseless ministry of Christ (for all the noise and tumult connected with his ministry proceeded not from Jesus, but from the people ; our Lord always endeavoured to quell the tumult), which the carnally-minded Jews

had not at all expected of the Messiah, inasmuch, as, in their vain
mind, they imagined that he would appear in noisy splendour, and
tumultuous glory; so this verse expresses his condescending affabil-
ity, ministering to the necessities of the suffering and feeble. The
expressions, κάλαμος συντετριμμένος, a *crushed reed*, and λίνος τυφό-
μενος, *smoking flax*, are natural figures of the broken, perishing life;
it is represented as the business of the Messiah again to strengthen
and excite it. The last words from Isaiah xlii. 3 : לֶאֱמֶת יוֹצִיא מִשְׁפָּט,
he shall bring forth judgment unto truth, which the LXX. renders
εἰς ἀλήθειαν ἐξοίσει κρίσιν, Matthew has rendered with a deviation :
ἕως ἂν ἐκβάλῃ τὴν κρίσιν εἰς νῖκος, which latter expression would
rather suggest לָנֶצַח. (Comp. 2 Sam. ii. 26.) We may suppose that
the Evangelist had another reading before him, or, that the words
εἰς νῖκος are explanatory of εἰς ἀλήθειαν; for the carrying out of the
κρίσις to the ἀλήθεια is indeed the victory.*

Ver. 21.—Matthew has omitted the first words of Isaiah xlii. 4,
thinking them less adapted to his purpose ; but he quotes the concluding words לְתוֹרָתוֹ אִיִּים יְיַחֵלוּ, the isles shall wait for his law,
which he renders : τῷ ὀνόματι ἔθνη ἐλπιοῦσι, in his name shall the
nations trust; and this agrees verbatim with the LXX. We cannot but notice here the exact agreement with the LXX, in opposition to the Hebrew text, when looking at the former deviation ; and
this can hardly be otherwise explained than by a different reading.
For the very word לְתוֹרָתוֹ must have appeared to Matthew very suitable for his purpose. As regards the Messianic explanation of this
whole passage, it has lately been defended by *Umbreit*, in his beautiful treatise on the servant of God (*Heidelberger Studien und
Kritiken*, B. I. H. 2.) This intelligent expositor has very correctly
understood the idea of the suffering and victorious innocence, and
of the moral power of the servant of God, who is no other than the
Lord and King Jehovah; only he appears to overlook the identity
of the servant of God in the various passages. The difficulty of
referring the various, and apparently contradictory, attributes to
one individual, disappears when we suppose the idea of a multiplicity being represented by a unity. The various expositions of
this difficult passage concerning the servant of God (from Isaiah
xl. to lxvi.) according to which, either the whole nation of the pious
or the prophets in the nation, are thereby understood, are not in
strict contradiction to the Bible or Messianic exposition, inasmuch
as all this is implied in the idea of the Messiah. The Messiah represents the *ideal* of the true Israel, whilst the pious and the prophets represent it as it actually existed.

* Others, as for example *Gesenius* (on this passage), translate אֱמֶת by " *mildness*,"
a signification justly not admitted by *Umbreit*, in the treatise which will be presently
quoted.

§ 19. OF THE CALUMNIES OF THE PHARISEES. JESUS' SEVERE
REBUKES OF THEM.

(Matth. xii. 22–45; Mark iii. 20–30; Luke xi. 14–26, 29–32.)

To suppose a more intimate connexion of the narrative which
follows, with what precedes, is in Matthew, out of the question, inasmuch, as, after the general formulas in ver. 15, 16, the narrative
is taken up by a simple τότε, *then*. In Luke xi. 14, seq., we find
ourselves transported into a perfectly strange region ; and Mark iii.
20 again leads us back to the sending forth of the twelve Apostles,
where the report of their return is followed by an indefinite : καὶ
συνέρχεται πάλιν ὄχλος, *and a multitude again come together*. The
addition, however, in ver. 22, "the scribes that had come down
from Jerusalem," renders it probable, that a feast in Jerusalem has
preceded. But, on the one hand, it is uncertain which of the feasts
is to be understood ; and, on the other, we might suppose the journey of the scribes not at all connected with a feast ; a supposition
admissible, only, if these doctors were Galileans. But since this is
not mentioned, we may conceive that they were emissaries sent out
by the chief men of Jerusalem, and these might arrive at any time
in Galilee. At all events, it will not do to attempt to determine
what has been left undetermined. In Mark iii. 21, another remarkable circumstance is added, which will presently occupy our attention (at Matth. xii. 46); but then he immediately states the
impudent charge of the Pharisees against the Lord, without referring
to the cause which called it forth. Matthew thus represents the
opposition of the Pharisees in its gradual growth, until it reaches
its climax, in accusing Christ of a connexion with the kingdom of
the evil one, and of madness.

Ver. 22.—According to Matthew, the cure of a demoniac, who
was at the same time dumb and blind, was the occasion of the impudent accusations of the Pharisees. (Luke xi. 14 points out his
dumbness only, without however denying that he was blind also.)
The sick man must have suffered from the extraordinary form of
disease, as it is only thus that the remarkable astonishment of the
multitude, and the inferences which they draw from the cure, can
be accounted for. (Matth. xii. 23 uses the phrase : ἐξίσταντο πάντες
οἱ ὄχλοι. The verb as well as the noun ἔκστασις are, in the New
Testament, frequently used to express violent terror or astonishment ; [Mark ii. 12, v. 42; Luke v. 26 ; Acts iii. 10.] Concerning
υἱὸς τοῦ Δαβίδ, compare remarks on Luke i. 35.) It is clear, however, that the sick person is called demoniac, not because he was

dumb or blind, or, as in the present case, both at the same time, but because these affections in him were accompanied by other physical and psychical phenomena which pointed to spiritual influences. (Compare the remarks on Matth. vii. 9, 27, seq.)

Ver. 24. The more striking was the deed of Christ, and the more the wonder and sympathy of the simple multitude were excited by the cure of a most unfortunate being who seemed to be cut off from all living intercourse—the more fearful was the wrath of the priestly company, who doubtless perceived that the ministry of Jesus would annihilate their dominion. They breathed blasphemy into the hearts of the simple-minded, by insinuating that the powerful effects which were moving them, were the work not of the Holy One, but of the unholy one. As mighty effects infer mighty causes, they accused him of a union with Beelzebub. (Compare the remarks on Mark x. 25.) The accusation formerly made (δαιμόνιον ἔχει, Matth. xi. 18) was less severe. It is true the phrase δαιμόνιον ἔχει, he hath a devil, is by no means = μαίνεσθαι, being mad, as John x. 20 clearly shews, where both the phrases are connected by means of καί, and hence cannot be identical unless we suppose the writer to have made use of a gross tautology. The madness indeed, may be conceived of as the consequence of the demoniacal possession, and being, as such, if not necessarily, at least commonly connected with the δαιμόνιον ἔχειν, it might be supplied even here. But, in itself, δαιμόνιον ἔχειν, signifies only " to be ruled over, to be guided by an evil spirit" = ἔχεσθαι ὑπὸ δαιμονίου. The difference therefore betwixt this expression and that used in xii. 24, consists in this, that here a direct influence of the ἄρχων τῶν δαιμονίων, the prince of the devils, is asserted, while, in the other passage, merely that of an evil being in general ; and farther, that the performance of miracles by means of the power of darkness, presupposes a peculiar wickedness of disposition ; whereas in the having a devil, there is assumed rather an unconscious state of dependence upon the evil one.

Ver. 25, 26.—Jesus knew their hearts (see Luke vi. 8), and the evil thoughts that were in them. (Concerning διαλογισμοί, διανόημα, ἐνθυμήσεις, comp. remarks on Luke ii. 35 ; Matth. ix. 4.) He first endeavoured to instruct them by means of arguments, and a representation of the circumstances. (According to Mark iii. 23, ἐν παραβολαῖς, on which comp. Matth. xiii. 3. The parabolical character of the discourse is particularly obvious in Mark iii. 27.) This endeavour of the merciful Redeemer who knew what was in their hearts, is consolatory. We infer from it, that he perceived in their hearts the germs of something better, to the quickening of which he might direct his instructions. Had these unfortunate men, who called light darkness, and converted that which was holy into an unholy thing, not been blinded by passion, they would then have committed the sin against the Holy Ghost (Matth. xii. 32), and thus have been deprived of all hope of forgiveness. But it is inconceivable that our Saviour should have addressed to those who could not be redeemed, words having a tendency to deliver them from their error ! For Jesus endeavours, first, to lay open before them the contradictory character of their charge. He compares a kingdom, a town, a family, in short any united community, with the kingdom of Satan, and argues thus : As nothing of this kind can maintain its existence without a certain order and union of the members, so neither can the kingdom of darkness. (Μερίζεσθαι, διαμερίζεσθαι, denote " to be in a state of internal division, mutual strife ;" they are the reverse of ἐνοῦσθαι. In like manner ἐρημοῦσθαι, οὐχ ἵστασθαι denote " to be cut off from existence and subsistence" = τέλος ἔχειν, Mark iii. 26.) The whole argumentation, however, seems somewhat obscure. We might in fact regard it as the very essence of the kingdom of darkness, that peace and unity are wanting, and that strife rules in their stead. How then can an inference *against* strife be drawn from the nature of the kingdom of darkness ? We might answer to this remark of Christ against the charge of his opponents : "this very circumstance, that evil is in strife with itself, proves that it cannot have a lasting existence." But the difficulty will be removed, if we consider that the Lord does not say : " No kingdom, town, or family in which there is strife (namely, among the members who constitute the community), can stand ;" for in that case we should be obliged to say that there is no kingdom, town, or family at all, for there is none in which there is not some strife. He, on the contrary, only very wisely expresses himself thus : No kingdom, nor any similar united community, can stand, if, as such, it be divided against itself. If, then, strife be not silenced in a kingdom, so far as it stands in opposition to another kingdom, it must be regarded as dissolved: but if, *in this opposition*, it keep together as a living unity, then the internal divisions among its individual members do not make its existence impossible. Jesus thus does not deny that there are divisions in the kingdom of darkness, for that is rather its nature ; but this he maintains, that it forms a united community in opposition to the kingdom of God. It is for this reason also that it is said: "if Satan cast out Satan." This passage therefore cannot be made use of to prove that σατανᾶς stands for evil angels in general. (Compare above the remarks on Matth. viii. 28.) On the contrary, it signifies, as the article shews, the prince of the devils. This ruler, being the representative of the whole, cannot be *against himself*, otherwise he could not (and with him his kingdom, which is himself) maintain such an opposition to that which is good. Moreover, that here " a kingdom of the evil spirits is assumed, cannot possibly be doubted when viewed exegetically," even according to the opinion of *Dr. Paulus* (Com. Th. ii. S. 89). Hence it will be necessary to have recourse to artificial means, to remove this troublesome doctrine from Holy Scripture.

Ver. 27, 28.—After having thus proved the absurdity of the supposition, that Beelzebub would attack his own kingdom, Jesus passes to another óbjection. Jews also cast out demons (οἱ υἱοὶ ὑμῶν* —the Pharisees and Scribes are considered as fathers in the faith, and hence, as fathers of the faithful Jews), by whom (ἐν τίνι) do they cast them out? This question is based on the principle : no effect without a cause ; now, as the Pharisees acknowledged the cures of Jewish exorcists, they were obliged to assign a cause for them. They could not assume an evil power, partly from what has been previously said, and partly because the general popular notions would not have admitted of it ; hence there remained no alternative, but to assume a *good* power. From these slight demonstrations of a good power appearing seldom, and isolated, the Lord reasons to the host of cures of otherwise incurable diseases, which he had effected, and hence concludes that the kingdom of God is at hand. The kingdom of God must here be taken generally as that order of things, in which divine influences are triumphant in the present economy of the world. This then was very properly connected with the appearance of the Messiah, and in so far the expression signifies the Messianic times. (Instead of ἐν πνεύματι, Luke xi. 20 has ἐν δακτύλῳ Θεοῦ, according to the analogy of the Hebrew אֶצְבַּע [comp. Exod. viii. 19 : הִיא אֱלֹהִים אֶצְבַּע.] It is = יָד, χείρ, *hand*, a figurative expression for power, with the accessory idea of a manifestation of divine power, more secret and difficult to be perceived.) There is no doubt that the Jewish notions of evil spirits, and of their casting out, were mixed up with much superstition. *Josephus* (Bell. Jud. vii. 6, 3) relates, that there grew a root in the neighbourhood of Machaerus, by means of which evil spirits were cast out, whom he considers as the spirits of wicked men (πονηρῶν ἀνθρώπων πνεύματα). The same writer relates in his Antiq. viii. 21, 5, an instance of exorcising by means of such roots, with the aid of Solomonic formulas of incantation. In like manner, an evil spirit is cast out by means of the liver of a fish in Tob. viii. 2. But such an admixture of superstition does not prove there is at the bottom of the thing itself no truth to which the false notions were attached. We may well imagine, that many Jewish exorcists, by faith in the help from above, performed acts which had some resemblance to the cures effected by Jesus (Acts xix. 14) ; only, that they must be regarded as feebler and isolated effects of spiritual power.

Ver. 29.—How thoroughly Jesus comprehends the struggle be-

---

* *Chrysostom* understands by this expression, the apostles; no doubt he thought that he could not ascribe to the Jews the gift of casting out demons.

tween good and evil, is shewn by the third parable* in which he
infers, from the nature of the contrast, that such phenomena as
were seen in his ministry, could be explained only as the result of
an absolute preponderance of power. The kingdom of darkness, as
a united community, is here contrasted with the kingdom of light;
both the kingdoms being viewed in their personal representatives.
But though the contrast is viewed as a *real* one, yet it by no means
appears as an *absolute* one, inasmuch as in the good there is always
the power of conquering. Luke carries out the figure more carefully. The evil one is represented as an armed man protecting his
castle ; (αὐλή stands here for palace, as in Matth. xxvi. 3, a large
building surrounded with courts or porches.) A mightier only
can conquer him, deprive him of his armour (πανοπλία), and divide
the spoil. (Σκῦλα, Matthew and Mark have σκεύη = כֵּלִים, which
frequently signifies " armour," in which sense it may form a parallel
with the πανοπλία. As the contrast to σκῦλα, which are distinguished from the armour, it might be taken in the sense of furni-
ture, possessions in general.)

Ver. 30.—After these discourses of Jesus addressed to the understanding, his language assumes another character—that of *sternness*. To the Pharisees and Scribes—who, as representatives of the
theocracy, ought to have been *for* the Redeemer and his cause, if
they had truly acted up to their calling, he represents, that, in their
position, mere *indecision for* him, was *decision against* him. (The
two parallel members contain the same thought. The contrast
of συνάγειν, *collect*, and σκορπίζειν, *scatter*, is, perhaps, borrowed
from the figure of collecting treasures of any kind.) With all the
sternness expressed in this discourse, the thought still breathes
gentleness ; our Redeemer does not regard them as absolute enemies, but still views them as undecided friends ; distinctly pointing out, however, at the same time, that indecision was their ruin.
Should it be said that this language may perhaps refer to other
Pharisees who had not uttered that bold accusation, we answer,
that there is no indication of it in the discourse, and that Christ's
former mode of addressing his calumniators, allows also in the present case the more lenient interpretation. But this proverbial saying forms an apparent contradiction to the similar one : He that is
not against you, is for you (Luke ix. 50 ; Mark ix. 40.) This declaration, however, refers to persons not definitely called to labour
for the kingdom of God, in whom, therefore, the absence of decision
against the truth may be as certainly considered a favourable sign
of their good disposition, as the indecision of the Pharisees was to

---

* The parable is based upon the passage Is. xlix. 24, 25, where the גִּבּוֹר corresponds
to the ἰσχυρός. The description of Luke agrees entirely with the prophetic discourse according to the version of the LXX.

him a sign of their evil disposition. It is here quite out of the question to refer this proverbial saying to the kindgdom of darkness, in which case the μετ' ἐμοῦ and κατ' ἐμοῦ (*with me* and *against me*), could be applied only to the subject suggested by the context, while the first person would be used only proverbially, so that this sense would arise: "the common remark, he who is not with me, etc., may with full truth be applied to the devil."

Ver. 31, 32.—With this idea is then connected a description of the fearful guilt into which all plunge themselves who were against Jesus (κατ' ἐμοῦ). But to place this guilt in its true light, our Lord compares it with other very culpable actions—especially with blasphemies. This difficult passage requires a careful consideration on account of its doctrinal importance.*

In the first place, as regards the various expressions used by the Evangelists, there is, in Luke xii. 10, a similar thought, but more briefly expressed. It stands there in quite a different connexion. A comparison of it with others, contributes nothing to our understanding of the passage. Mark has the words in the same connexion as Matthew, but more briefly, and with less peculiarity. It is in Matthew alone that the thought appears fully brought out ; and he proves again here that he can make up, by care in communicating the discourses, for his want of vividness in narrative. If, then, we follow Matthew, the substance of the thought is, that all sins may be forgiven with the exception of one, which Matthew calls: "speaking a word against the Holy Ghost, blasphemy of the Spirit" (εἰπεῖν λόγον κατὰ τοῦ πνεύματος ἁγίου, βλασφημία τοῦ πνεύματος). Mark, on the contrary, calls it, βλαφημεῖν εἰς τὸ πνεῦμα τὸ ἅγιον. In order to illustrate the idea, it is, moreover, added, that even βλασφημίαι (according to Mark), and speaking against the Son of man (εἰπεῖν λόγον κατὰ τοῦ υἱοῦ τοῦ ἀνθρώπου, according to Matthew), will be forgiven —but not the sin against the Holy Ghost. It cannot, therefore, be said that ver. 31 and 32 express the same truth ; for although ver. 31 contains the preliminary remark, that the sin against the Holy Ghost cannot be forgiven, yet ver. 32 points out the new and important thought, that even the sin against the Son may be forgiven, but that the sin against the Holy Ghost can not. The expressive remark, moreover, is added : οὔτε ἐν τούτῳ τῷ αἰῶνι, οὔτε ἐν τῷ μέλλοντι, *neither in this world, nor in that to come.* This simple thought, however, it is very difficult to explain ; partly, because it stands quite isolated, inasmuch as no other passage of the New Testament speaks *expressly* of this sin ; partly, because it is in it-

---

* On the sin against the Holy Ghost, compare the instructive treatises by *Grashoff* (Stud. 1833, H. 4), *Gurlitt* (Stud. 1834, H. 3), *Tholuck* (Stud. 1836, H. 2.) Yet, from the fear of too great digression, I have been only very *rarely* able to take notice of the points therein suggested.

self dark, and stands in connexion with other difficult doctrines, *e. g.*, with the doctrine concerning the Holy Ghost. Nor can difficulties such as these be removed by means of grammatical and philological enquiries ; each one solves them in accordance with his own fundamental views. The right explanation of such a passage necessarily involves sympathy with the Spirit of Christ ; without this it will be inevitably misunderstood. After a comparison of Heb. vi. 4, seq. ; x. 26, seq.; 1 John v. 16, we must, *in the first place*, discard all such views as would limit the sin against the Holy Ghost by such relations of place and time, as to render it impossible to be either previously or subsequently committed.* *In the second place*, we must discard such explanations as weaken the moral import of the words, by affixing to the words, "that the sin against the Holy Ghost cannot be forgiven" (notwithstanding the addition, "neither in this world nor in that which is to come") the meaning : that it can be forgiven *with greater difficulty* than other sins. *Finally*, the *Christian* expositor must likewise discard every explanation of this remarkable passage which understands, by the sin against the Holy Ghost, an act detached from the whole moral condition of the individual sinning ; it must always be considered as the fruit of a previous sinful course of life. As the first two modes of exposition destroy the profound meaning of the word of God, and connect the most important moral relations with special localities on the one hand, and indefinite language on the other ; so the latter view evidently leads into errors which perplex the conscience, inasmuch as some unfortunate man, in an unguarded moment of his life, may easily be plunged into a sin which somewhere, and at some time, has been explained as meaning the sin against the Holy Ghost. As regards, now, the biblical exposition itself, the passages already quoted (Heb. vi. 4, seq. x. 26 ; 1 John v. 16) lead us to think of a fearful progress in sin, in which man is as little inclined to believe, as in that advance in moral goodness, which is taught in, the doctrine of Christian sanctification ($\delta\iota\kappa\alpha\iota o\sigma\acute{v}\nu\eta$ $\tau o\tilde{v}$ $\Theta\epsilon o\tilde{v}$). For although the phrase : blaspheme against the Holy Ghost ($\beta\lambda\alpha\sigma\phi\eta\mu\epsilon\tilde{\iota}\nu$ $\epsilon\iota\varsigma$ $\tau\grave{o}$ $\pi\nu\epsilon\tilde{v}\mu\alpha$ $\tau\grave{o}$ $\acute{\alpha}\gamma\iota o\nu$) is wanting in those passages, and in fact the matter at issue is different, the question being *there* of the loss of spiritual life already received, *here* of the refusal to receive it ;† yet the compari-

---

* Who does not here recall to mind the strange definition which *Reinhard* gives of the sin against the Holy Ghost, in his *Dogmatik*, S. 321: Delictum quorundam Judæorum (!) qui summa pertinacia ducti, miracula Jesu, quorum evidentiam negare non poterant, a diabolo proficisci criminabantur. " *The crime of certain Jews, who, in their perverseness, charged that the miracles of Jesus, which they could not deny, proceeded from the devil.*" This exposition is so much the more unsuitable, as the gospel history does not at all tell that the Pharisees who used this language (Matth. xii. 24) *had committed* the sin against the Holy Ghost; it appeared only possible that they might commit it; and it is against this that Jesus warns them.

† *Lücke* remarks on 1 John v. 16 (S. 233) that the sin against the Holy Ghost is a

son of such parallel passages is by no means *unimportant*, inasmuch as we recognize from them the severe import of the *shall not be forgiven*. As a parallel in another point of view, we have the remarkable passage in Matth. x. 41, 42 ; for as in that passage, already explained, a progress in good was taught with its accompanying reward, so here is a parallel progress in evil, with its accompanying ruin. The several steps, however, are here not so clearly defined as in Matth. x. 41, 42; but it is evident from a closer examination that here, three degrees of sin are to be distinguished, as there, three degrees of righteousness. It is generally acknowledged that the blasphemy of the Spirit or the speaking against the Holy Ghost, is the lowest stage ; but in what the speaking against the Son of Man is distinguished from it, is doubtful. Some understand the Son of Man = man, as in Mark iii. 28, " all sins shall be forgiven to the sons of men." (Υἱοὶ τῶν ἀνθρώπων in this case = אָדָם בְּנֵי.) But this view is inadmissible, for this simple reason, that the singular " the Son of Man" (ὁ υἱὸς τοῦ ἀνθρώπου) with the article, is never used as a general designation of man ; it is, on the contrary, the name of the Messiah, and stands parallel with the πνεῦμα ἅγιον, *the Holy Spirit.* The sin against the Son of Man is pointed out by the formula, καὶ ὃς ἂν (ἐάν is a less authorized reading) εἴπῃ λόγον, as a distinct and peculiar crime. After it had been remarked in the second clause of ver. 31, that the blasphemy of the Spirit (βλασφημία τοῦ πνεύματος) will not be forgiven, the sin against the Son of Man is further specially mentioned, with the remark, that even *it* may be forgiven.—The *third* class of sins is more obscurely indicated, inasmuch·as the *Father* is not expressly mentioned along with the Spirit and the Son ; but the reference to the Father is necessarily implied in the words, All manner of sin and blasphemy shall be forgiven to men. (Matth. ver. 31. Comp. also Mark iii. 28.) For every sin, but especially every blasphemy, has, at bottom, a reference to God.*
Blasphemy cannot by any means be uttered against an angel or a

---

species of the sin unto death (ἁμαρτία πρὸς θάνατον), spoken of by John in the passage referred to. I am disposed rather to place them in an inverted relation; for we might also say the sin which John describes is a sin against the Holy Ghost. The difference between the two expressions seems to consist only in this, that the name, *sin against the Holy Ghost*, points to the object to which the sin refers, whilst the name, *sin unto death*, places in the foreground the consequence of the sin to the individual who commits it. (Compare *Lehnerdt's* Treatise on 1 John v. 16. Königsberg, 1832.)

* It is only apparently that this is contradicted by some passages, in which, as in Acts vi. 11, βλάσφημα ῥήματα λαλεῖν is applied to men; for in that passage Moses is viewed as a divine ambassador. It is therefore the will of God that is blasphemed in his person ; for which reason the words, εἰς Μωϋσῆν καὶ τὸν Θεόν are added as an explanation. In Rom. xiv. 16, τὸ ἀγαθόν stands for that which is divine, as 2 Pet. ii. 2, ὁδὸς τῆς ἀληθείας for the ordinance of God. Of course what applies to Moses applies to the apostles also. (Compare Rom. iii. 8; 1 Cor. iv. 13; x. 30). This with reference to the remarks of *Grashoff*, loc. cit. S. 955, seq.

man. There appear, then, three gradations in sinfulness. *First*, sins against God the Father; *then*, against the Son; and *finally*, against the Holy Ghost. For the two first degrees there is a *possibility* of forgiveness (on the supposition of repentance and faith); it is only for the last that it is excluded. This gradation is the safest guide for a correct explanation of the passage. As we already remarked, when commenting on Matth. x. 41, 42, the value of a deed must be determined both according to the object to which it refers (so that, in a political point of view, it is not a matter of indifference whether I confer a benefit on a king or on a peasant, nor, in a spiritual point of view, whether I confer it on a prophet or on a righteous man), and to the degree of moral development of the person who performs it. Precisely so with the growth of sin. The internal condition of the agent, and the relation of the act to the object, determine the degree of guilt. The Redeemer was dealing here with persons who recognise their occupation with divine things as their calling, and who had attained a certain grade of spiritual culture ; the higher this was conceived to be, the more perilous was their position, if notwithstanding, they gave themselves to sin. A child is incapable of committing blasphemy, because it has no knowledge of God ; and even though it should repeat blasphemous words, it would utter only *words*, because its inward sense cannot comprehend their meaning. But the Pharisees, who knew of God, but hardened themselves against his exhortations, required the warning, that man can become so completely callous to divine impressions, that reconciliation is no longer possible. Such a word, uttered in the power of love, might yet rouse their hearts from their carnal security, in which they were staggering along on the brink of the abyss. But the Saviour of the world wishes to deprive no one of the comfort of forgiveness ; he proclaims it to all sin and blasphemy, on the supposition, of course, of true repentance and genuine faith. The sins (ἁμαρτίαι), as distinguished from blasphemies (βλασφημίαι), are sins committed against man or any other creature; while blasphemies are sins against the Divine Being himself. To commit the latter, presupposes a knowledge of God, and a depravity prevailing over the light of this knowledge.* Such an internal state is represented as yet affording hope of redemption ; the superior power of grace may yet stir up the hidden susceptibility of good. But if the higher revelations of the Divine in Christ Jesus be perseveringly rejected ; if, while heightened religious culture opens the mind to spiritual influences, there be, from impurity of life, a shutting of the heart against the light, pardon and redemption become

---

* Of so-called cursing or swearing, and thoughtless abuse of the name of God, we cannot here think; inasmuch as it is done thoughtlessly, the sin consists mainly in the very thoughtlessness which can effect such guilt.

impossible, inasmuch as the susceptibility to holy impulses becomes utterly extinct. Thus the successive stages of sin appear dependent on the degree of religious culture, and the deeper knowledge of things thereby rendered possible. He who has only a general knowledge of God, can sin only against God the Father. He who is more advanced, and able to recognise the Son of Man, is in a position also to reject the deeper and more spiritual revelations of Divinity manifested in him; but he who has experienced in his heart the workings of the Holy Ghost, may be guilty of sin and blasphemy against the Holy Ghost.* Hence a high degree of the knowledge of God is not a guarantee against sin; on the contrary, the greatest sin presupposes the greatest knowledge;† it is only purity, sincerity, and humility of heart which, in every degree of development, afford such security. But inasmuch as this very disposition was wanting in the Pharisees, they were *on the way* toward the commission of the sin against the Holy Ghost.

Without entering, at present, into a minute discussion of the doctrine of the Trinity, let us simply conceive of Father, Son and Spirit, as gradations in the revelation of the Divine Being. The knowledge of God as the Father has reference to the power and wisdom; that of the Son, to the love and mercy; that of the Spirit, to the holiness and perfection of the one Divine Being. He who according to his progress in spiritual knowledge is able to recognise the holiness and perfection of the Divinity (and that not merely in imagination, but in reality), and who, nevertheless, shuts his heart to their influences, nay, calls even holiness unholiness —proves that his inward eye is darkness. Accordingly, the speaking against the Son of Man must not be understood merely of speaking against the Messiah's unpretending humanity;‡ it must be distinctly pointed out, that he who so sinned, felt the impression of the divinity which shone forth in Christ, and yet allowed no room for

---

* The resisting the Holy Spirit (Acts vii. 51), the grieving of the same (Eph. iv. 30), even the embittering and provoking of the Holy Spirit (Isa. lxiii. 10), are still to be carefully distinguished from the blasphemy against the Holy Ghost which is really the unpardonable sin against the Holy Ghost. GRASHOFF (loc. cit. S. 947) considers the blasphemy against the Holy Ghost as a *species* of the *genus* Sin against the Holy Ghost— a view, however, which does not seem to be countenanced by our text.

† The Reformed theologians taught *rightly* that the sin against the Holy Ghost is committed by unregenerate persons, and consists in fact in the rejection of converting grace, but denied *incorrectly* that along with this there is with the regenerate the sin of apostacy (Heb. vi.) The Lutherans maintained *rightly* the possibility of apostacy, but *incorrectly* confounded this with the sin against the Holy Ghost.—[E.

‡ This view would be, on the whole, similar to the one referred to above, according to which ὁ υἱὸς τοῦ ἀνθρώπου is = ἄνθρωπος. For whosoever *really* saw in Christ only what is human, because he possessed no deeper susceptibility for the Divine, sinned no more in cursing Christ than he would by doing so to any other man. It is the inward intention, of which, it is true, God alone is the judge, by which the deed must be measured.

this impression. He who opposes himself to the melting power of such a revelation, sins heinously; yet by perfect holiness, and its fear-inspiring impression, the hardening produced thereby may yet be overcome; but where this also is rejected, there is spiritual death. We wholly lose the point of view necessary to a right understanding of the passage, in understanding the Holy Spirit ($\pi\nu\epsilon\tilde{\upsilon}\mu\alpha$ $\H{\alpha}\gamma\iota o\nu$) only of the general power of God manifested in miracles.* It is inconceivable how, in the non-recognition of *such* a power, creating merely an impression of might, an unpardonable sin should be committed; and the more, as evil miracles also have been performed by satanic agency, and these so deceptive, that they would have deceived, were it possible, even the elect (Matth. xxiv. 24). Nay, it is here that forgiveness seems to find its appropriate sphere. The $\pi\nu\epsilon\tilde{\upsilon}\mu\alpha$ $\H{\alpha}\gamma\iota o\nu$ in our passage is the highest revelation of God, as the absolutely Holy and Perfect One. In so far, then, as in the person of Jesus, the Godhead dwelt, and Father, Son, and Spirit are inseparably united, the depravity of men, might, according to their degree of culture, in sinning against him, sin against Father, Son, and Spirit, according as they perseveringly resisted the effect of divine power, love, and holiness which proceed from him. On the other hand, purity of heart, coupled with an equal advance in knowledge, might, through him, receive Father, Son, and Spirit. But where the mind was wholly blind to that higher revelation of the Divine in humanity, which appeared in Christ Jesus, there could one still believe that he saw in Jesus a prophet or a righteous man of the former dispensation, and receive from him the blessing which was adapted to his grade of culture. Thus our Redeemer became all things to all men; to the pure in heart, a dispenser of blessings for every grade of their development; to the impure a reproving Judge, first, to lead them to repentance; and then to judgment, when their obduracy had closed the way to repentance (Luke ii. 34). It is manifest, then, that the sin against the Holy Ghost can be also committed now; for since the Divinity in Christ manifests itself continually in the church, sin, in individual men, even where there is the highest degree of knowledge, may oppose itself to his beneficent influence. Otherwise either the period to which the possible commission of this sin was confined, seems left in obscurity, or our Lord deals with it with an extraordinary severity. But if, as frequently happens with persons who are touched by the power of grace, earnest repentance is accompanied with the idea that they may have committed the sin againt the Holy Ghost, and be thereby excluded from forgiveness—a thought which on sensitive spirits may

† $\Pi\nu\epsilon\tilde{\upsilon}\mu\alpha$ $\H{\alpha}\gamma\iota o\nu$ has always a reference to what is moral. The notion of mere power occupies a subordinate place in it. But $\pi\nu\epsilon\tilde{\upsilon}\mu\alpha$ by itself signifies, for instance in Matth. xii. 28, power only with reference to its higher origin.

work most perniciously, and at least exclude them for a time from the consolations of the word of grace—he who is entrusted with the care of souls, or is called on for advice, may with full confidence, invite all such to cry in faith for mercy. For whoever vexes himself with the thought that he may have committed the sin against the Holy Ghost, proves, by his very grief and self-accusation, that he has not committed it ; he who has really committed it will defend himself against all reproach. Nay, even though sin should have developed itself in any soul in a very alarming form, so that, as in the case of Judas Iscariot, the grief of repentance should threaten to degenerate into despair, even in such a case, the exhortation to believe in pardoning love is still admissible, inasmuch as the sin against the Holy Ghost is unpardonable, not because God is unwilling to forgive, but because man has become unable to believe that God can forgive. If, then, the proclamation of grace takes hold of the heart, it is actually proved that the sin against the Holy Ghost has not been committed.

The passage under consideration is, in dogmatic theology, also referred to as a leading proof-text for the doctrine of the eternity of punishment. All other passages which treat of an αἰώνιος κρίσις, *eternal condemnation*, are less definite than this, in which ἐν τῷ αἰῶνι μέλλοντι, *in the future world*, is expressly added. It is true that the term αἰών, αἰώνιος, *age*, *eternal* (in the phrases : εἰς τὸν αἰῶνα, αἰώνιος κρίσις in Mark), as also the phrase : αἰὼν οὗτος and μέλλων (in Matthew) have a vague sense, capable of various interpretations. The Bible knows no metaphysical expressions, and hence, has not one for eternity in the sense of *timelessness* (*Zeitlosigkeit*), absence of time. All the biblical expressions for this idea denote long periods connected with one another. The phrase : εἰς τὸν αἰῶνα, *for ever*, is quite parallel with the other phrases : εἰς τοὺς αἰῶνας, εἰς τοὺς αἰῶνας τῶν αἰώνων (Gal. i. 5), which denote the *æternitas a parte post* or the *future*, conceived as an indefinitely extended period ; but the phrase : ἀπ᾽ αἰῶνος, *from everlasting*, is = ἀπὸ τῶν αἰώνων, πρὸ τῶν αἰώνων, by which the *æternitas a parte ante*, or the *past*, is conceived as an indefinitely extended period. Αἰών is therefore like עֹלָם = αἰῶνες, עֹלָמִים, as is proved by the formula συντέλεια τοῦ αἰῶνος, which is identical with συντέλεια τῶν αἰώνων. Comp. 1 Cor. x. 11, the expression : τὰ τέλη τῶν αἰώνων.) But as the same expressions are applied to the eternity of God, as well as to a long enduring period, according to the conception of the creature ; as the terms : κρίσις, κόλασις αἰώνιος, *eternal punishment*, κρίμα, πῦρ αἰώνιον, *eternal fire*, form the contrast to ζωὴ αἰώνιος, *eternal life* ; no objections can be raised against the eternity of punishment from philological grounds. But the feeling against the doctrine of the eternity of the punishment of the wicked, which shews itself among the de-

fenders of a restoration of all things (ἀποκατάστασις τῶν πάντων)—and
they have been found at all times, and are, at the present time,
more than at any former period, though it may often have its foundation in a vitiated moral state, yet has no doubt a deep root in noble
minds—is the expression of a heartfelt desire for a perfect harmony in the creation. But, viewing it from a merely exegetical
point of view, we must confess that no passage of the New Testament affords a clear and positive testimony for the fulfilment of this
longing. The scriptural terms used to denote the resolving of the
discord arising from sin into a harmony—ἄφεσις, καταλλαγή, ἀπολύ-
τρωσις, remission, reconciliation, ransom—all denote a being fettered
by the evil ; hence a mixture of good and evil is found in human
nature after the fall. Hence, the terms above mentioned can, according to the doctrine of Scripture, never be applied to the spirits
of the kingdom of darkness, nor to men who, by persevering and
continued resistance to the drawings of grace, have become
the subjects of that kingdom. Should it be urged that evil, as
a thing created and temporary, must share also the general destiny of what is temporary, viz., cessation and annihilation, and that
the ages (αἰῶνες) of the course of this world, though they may bring
lasting punishment to the wicked, must yet at last themselves come
to an end ; there is indeed a text of Scripture pointing to this passing away of time itself with all temporary phenomena, into the
abyss of eternity when time shall be no longer, viz., the mysterious
words in 1 Cor. xv. 28 (on which compare the commentary). But
the mysterious character of the passage itself, along with the circumstance that no mention is made in it of evil and its dissolution,
authorises scarcely more than conjectural inferences regarding the
eternity of punishment ; the words of our Redeemer, in Matth. xii.
32, remain as an awful testimony to the fearful character of sin, and
its consequences.* But along with this they are also a consolation,
in that even they promise the possibility of forgiveness of sins committed against the Father and Son, hence of sins of a very heinous
character. For the addition : οὔτε ἐν τῷ μέλλοντι αἰῶνι, *nor in the
world to come*, is certainly not overstrained, if we infer that all other
sins can be forgiven in the world to come, always supposing, of
course, as has been already remarked, repentance and faith. (Comp.

---

* If we were to interpret our passage from 1 Cor. xv. 28, in such a manner as to
make it affirm that the sin against the Holy Ghost will be forgiven, neither in this αἰών,
nor in the αἰών to come, but that after that αἰών, age or *world*, forgiveness might be obtained, this would evidently contradict the meaning of the writer. For in Matth. xii. 32,
the "shall not be forgiven" is, in a decided manner, contrasted with the "shall be forgiven:" the addition, οὐκ ἐν τούτῳ τῷ αἰῶνι, οὔτε ἐν τῷ μέλλοντι, *not in this world, nor in
that to come*, is only employed completely to exhaust the *not;* hence to strengthen, not to
weaken it. Matthew by no means imagines that, subsequently to the αἰὼν μέλλων, there
is still to come another period of the world's existence; it is, on the contrary, completed
in the αἰὼν οὗτος and μέλλων.

rem. on 1 Peter iii. 18, seq.)   This is also indicated by such passages
as Matth. v. 26, compared with xviii. 34, for the being cast into prison
till one shall have paid the uttermost farthing, is evidently very different from κρίσις αἰώνιος, *eternal punishment*. (Comp. the remarks on
Matth. xviii. 34 ; Luke xvi. 19, seq.) But that the doctrine of the forgiveness of some sins in the αἰὼν μέλλων, *world to come*, is not in contradiction with the doctrine of the judgment, is shewn by the following exposition of the relation of αἰὼν οὗτος to the αἰὼν μέλλων. For
the former expression, the New Testament uses also ὁ νῦν αἰών (Tit.
ii. 12 ; 2 Tim. iv. 10), καιρὸς οὗτος (Mark x. 30), αἰὼν τοῦ κόσμου τούτου (Ephes. ii. 2), αἰὼν ἐνεστὼς πονηρός (Gal. i. 4). Instead of αἰὼν
μέλλων we find also the expressions : αἰὼν ὁ ἐρχόμενος (Mark x. 30),
αἰὼν ἐκεῖνος (Luke xx. 35), αἰῶνες ἐπερχόμενοι (Ephes. ii. 7). The
phrase : κόσμος μέλλων does not occur. The old controversy about
the relation of the Rabbinical terms עוֹלָם הַזֶּה and הַבָּא, which was
carried on with so much vehemence between *Witsius* and *Rhenferd*
(comp. *Koppe's* Exc. i. on the Epistle to the Ephesians), as to
whether the Messianic period or eternity is to be understood by
αἰὼν μέλλων, is somewhat barren, and does not touch the substance
of the contrast ; the αἰὼν μέλλων, *coming age*, comprehends indeed
both (just as the βασιλεία τοῦ Θεοῦ, comp. remarks on Matth iii. 2),
the phrase, however, having a preponderating reference now to the
one, now to the other relation. In general, the αἰὼν μέλλων forms
the contrast to the whole temporary order of things, the peculiarity
of which is, that in it good and evil are mixed together. In so far
it stands intermediate between the kingdom of light and that of
darkness, and forms the contrast to the kingdom of heaven. For,
although the good has assuredly its root in the temporary order of
things, yet the evil apparently prevails, on which account, Gal. i. 4,
the present age or world (αἰὼν ἐνεστώς) is even termed πονηρός, *evil*,
βασιλεία τοῦ ἄρχοντος τοῦ σκότους, *the kingdom of the prince of darkness*. With this temporary order of things is contrasted the future one, which terminates the blending of good and evil, and establishes in its purity the dominion of the former. The term : αἰὼν
μέλλων, with its synonyms, is therefore related to the βασιλεία τοῦ
Θεοῦ ; it only views the same phenomenon from a different point,
and is somewhat differently *used*. It is not applied to *individuals*,
as is the βασιλεία τοῦ Θεοῦ (comp. remarks on Matth. iii. 2) ; it is
nowhere said : the αἰὼν μέλλων exists for some one, or in some one.
It has reference always to the collective body of the church, or of
mankind. But, on the other hand, the *usus loquendi* is in so far
the same, that the expression αἰὼν μέλλων, as well as the kingdom of God is used in a twofold sense as to its manifestation ; sometimes it appears as having already come and taken effect ; at others,
as still future. Instances in which the αἰὼν μέλλων appears as al-

ready existing, are 1 Cor. x. 11 ; Heb. vi. 5, ix. 26, in which the συντέλεια τῶν αἰώνων (= τέλη τῶν αἰώνων) as the transition from the αἰὼν οὗτος to the μέλλων, is conceived as being present. This must be accounted for in the same manner as in the βασιλεία τοῦ Θεοῦ, regarding which, the same *usus loquendi* prevails. As, with the person of Christ, and the foundation of the church, the kingdom of God was present in its germ, so in this slumbered the world to come as now present ; just as, according to John, eternal life exists for the believer, not only as future, but as already present to him. (Compare the remarks on 1 John iii, 14.) Generally, however, the αἰὼν μέλλων is viewed as being yet future, and, accordingly, its appearance takes place with the συντέλεια τοῦ αἰῶνος (τούτου), when the Divine will be manifested as the ruling and conquering power, and sin, as cast out. This period the apostles conceived of as very near at hand, and, moreover, they did not distinguish in their conception its separate and individual features—especially not the first and the second resurrection—any more than those of the kingdom of God (βασιλεία τοῦ Θεοῦ.) The analogy of the Old Testament prophets, who, in their prophecies concerning the advent of the Messiah, were not accustomed to distinguish between his twofold coming, may explain this phenomenon. (Comp. further at Matth. xxiv. 1.) If then, in our passage, a remission is thought possible in the world to come, that signification of the term predominates, which excludes eternity, and the preceding general judgment. The αἰὼν μέλλων is here viewed as the world to come, which, at some future period, shall reveal itself in the victory of good here on earth, and sinners in the Sheol are assumed as belonging thereto. The preaching of the Gospel to the unbelieving contemporaries of Noah (1 Pet. iii. 18), involves such a forgiveness in the αἰὼν μέλλων, for all who are disposed to believe in it.

Ver. 33.—That which follows seems to countenance the opinion that the Pharisees to whom Christ was speaking, had, by their very speech (ver. 24), committed the sin against the Holy Ghost. The words in Mark iii. 30 : " because they said, he hath an unclean spirit," seem likewise to favour this view ; since, by these words, the discourse on the sin against the Holy Ghost is connected with the preceding blasphemous speech of the Pharisees. But, as already stated, the preceding discourses of Jesus (ver. 25, seq.), especially when compared with 1 Cor. ii. 8 ; Acts xiii. 27, 28 ; Luke xxiii. 34, render this, in my opinion, very improbable. For, even admitting, as we may well do, that the ἄρχοντες, *rulers*, mentioned there, are different from those spoken of in our passage, yet, as they even crucified the Lord of glory, they can surely have been hardly less guilty than those who denied the divinity of his miracles. It is, however, mentioned that they crucified him from ignorance (ἄγνοια), and how much soever their ignorance may have been the consequence of their sin and guilt, yet the sin against the Holy Ghost can be committed only where there is knowledge and consciousness, since it must be conceived of as the highest development of sinfulness. The words in Mark iii. 30, retain indeed their full import, if the discourse on the sin against the Holy Ghost be referred to the probable final issue of the sin of those Pharisees. For if any man, who has attained to that degree of knowledge which the Pharisees, as the heads and teachers of the people, possessed, could say of the miracles of the Son of God, who displayed before them all his glory, that they were wrought by the evil spirit—that man is certainly on the direct way to the sin against the Holy Ghost, although he may not yet have made sufficient progress to be able to commit the sin itself.

Ver. 34, 35.—Our Saviour contrasts good and evil with each other, as they are contrasted in the phenomena of nature :—the good tree bringeth forth good fruit ; the corrupt tree evil fruit. (Comp. remarks on Matth. vii. 18, seq. The ποιεῖν [ver. 33] in a sense analogous to the Latin *facere, ponere,* " to set," or " plant a tree," etc.) Comp. here the kindred passage, Luke vi. 43–45. For there, precisely as here, Luke compares the inward productive power of man (ϑησαυρός, ver. 45) with the creative power of the tree, and adds : that as the fruit of a tree indicates its character, and we may infer from the one the nature of the other, so with man ; wherever the root of the spiritual life is poisoned, there evil deeds will spring forth. (Luke adds, very suitably, in ver. 45, ϑησαυρὸς τῆς καρδίας, *treasure of the heart ;* the heart (καρδία) is here again conceived as the centre of the soul (ψυχή)—hence, of all personal life and self-determination.) It is clear then, that from the general principle, the tree is known by its fruit, our Lord infers that the Pharisees are evil, and hence unable in this their condition, to do any thing which is good. He calls them : γεννήματα ἐχιδνῶν, *race of vipers* (see comment. on Matth. iii. 7), and pointed from the wicked speech which they uttered, to the inward source from which it flowed. (All external things are expressions of the internal :—στόμα, *mouth,* the counterpart of καρδία, *heart:*—abundance (περίσσευμα) = treasure (ϑησαυρός), the fulness of the inner life which, even in the feeblest, manifests itself in some form of outward action). The whole passage, however, apart from its connexion with what precedes, has no inconsiderable difficulties. For the comparison seems to place moral existence on a par with physical, and to establish among men, a *necessary* diversity of character, necessitating a corresponding diversity of outward conduct. As then the Pharisees are here called evil, it would seem that the sin against the Holy Ghost was to be ascribed to them as a necessary consequence of the wickedness of their hearts—a view which would overthrow our previously expressed opinion. This doctrine, however, that there exists a *necessary* difference betwixt the good and the evil, would be in immediate opposition to the whole teaching of the Bible. As we can conceive of none among our fallen race who, from his good treasure produces by inward necessity only what is good, so also of none who, in like manner, produces only what is evil. In all fallen men, good and evil appear mixed together. The true solution of the difficulty is doubtless this : The point of comparison is not *the natural necessity* of the result, but the mutual correspondence of the *nature* and the *fruit*. Man cannot act in contradiction to the inward elements of his being. If these are worldly, all his acts are worldly ; if these are transformed by a heavenly birth, his acts are pure and virtuous. The viperous race which, as such, *cannot* do any thing which is good (πῶς δύνασθε in ver. 34 must be understood in its proper sense of an ethico-physical inability for that which is good) may, by grace, cease to be what they are, and may by repentance and faith, change their nature. Thus even the Baptist preached (Matth. iii. 7, 8) ; " generation of vipers, who hath warned you to flee from the wrath to come ?"—*i. e.*, while maintaining your present character—for the old man must die—" bring forth, therefore, fruits," etc. And thus also does Christ preach here. And just because he preaches repentance to the viperous race, they cannot as yet have committed the sin against the Holy Ghost, since, in that case, to proclaim repentance to them would have been mockery. The corrupt tree, then, which in its natural state bears bitter fruit, must be ennobled by a noble graft ; and so must the natural man be renewed by regeneration, into the image of him whose heart overflows with grace and salvation.

Ver. 36, 37.—The efforts of our Redeemer to rescue the Pharisees who were plunging into the abyss of sin, are plainly pointed out in the subsequent verses, in which he places before their eyes the significance of sin in its spiritual aspect. Recognising only the *deed* as real guilt, they may have considered their sin as a very trifling one, inasmuch as they had only *spoken*. Jesus now leads to a higher and more spiritual view, which makes the spirit and intention, though disclosed only in *words*, the object of divine judgment. The idle word, ῥῆμα ἀργόν (it must be taken as Nomin. absol.), is purposely chosen in contradistinction to the wicked word (ῥῆμα πονηρόν) which they had spoken ; ἀργόν = ἀεργόν, ἄχρηστον denotes a slighter culpability,[*] and hence gives emphasis to the thought. The " rendering an account" (λόγον ἀποδιδόναι) indicates immediately, only that, in the eye of God, even the most secret emotions of

---

[*] *Chrysostom* has already remarked this. He understands by ῥῆμα ἀργόν not only wicked, but also useless words, τὸ μάταιον, τὸ γέλωτα κινοῦν ἄτακτον.

evil find their punishment. And the deeper the significance of speech, the more culpable its abuse ; nay, in speech, as the expression of the soul, is man's entire character revealed. With *words* are contrasted *deeds*. The latter appear to sensuous man of greater importance because they are more obvious to sense. But every deed is, at bottom, only an embodied word, and every word may give birth to a deed. In this spiritual character the word is here considered by the Redeemer, and is, therefore, made the object of judgment. As man speaks, so he is ; as he is, so he is judged. The λόγοι are thus not merely external, but more especially internal words, the movements of the internal and moral life. He, therefore, who hypocritically speaks good words shall also be judged according to his words, because they are hypocritical. (Δικαιοῦσθαι is the reverse of κατιδικάζεσθαι, hence *pro justo declarari*, but with the supposition of being just and righteous [see remarks on Rom. iii. 21]. The words ἐκ τῶν λόγων indicate the influence of the λόγοι on the κρίσις).

Ver. 38.—In Matthew, this section is immediately followed by a rebuke addressed to certain Pharisees who wished to see a sign. Luke reports the elements of this discourse in a different order indeed, but with a literal agreement. The connexion in Matthew is simple and plain ; so that the position of the words here is unobjectionable ; yet as Luke's whole account bears stronger marks of originality, we shall here also give him the preference. But whether the " certain ones" who ask the sign in this place, be or be not identical with the Pharisees who, ver. 24, spoke the blasphemous words (concerning whom Luke, xi. 15, likewise said, τινὲς ἐξ αὐτῶν), is of little importance to the exposition. The expressions employed by our Lord to repel them (ver. 39), shew that they occupied the same moral position as the others. Yet, by Luke xi. 16, where their request of a sign appears to be anticipated, the supposition is rendered very probable, that one party expressed themselves in this way in order to put Christ to the test, and the others, in another (Luke xi. 16, ἕτεροι δὲ πειράζοντες σημεῖον παρ᾽ αὐτοῦ ἐζήτουν ἐξ οὐρανοῦ). The sign appears at the same time more distinctly defined as one from heaven.

A σημεῖον, sign (אות) ; is a miracle, not in itself, but in its relation to something else, in so far as it proves, signifies, indicates something ; as in the case before us, the Messiahship of Jesus. (Comp. Comment. on Matth. iv. 12.) Apart from every thing miraculous— as a mere testimony for the disposition of the heart (as *Dr. Paulus* would have us to understand it), the word is never used in the New Testament. The σημεῖα ἐξ οὐρανοῦ, *signs from heaven*, (or ἀπὸ τοῦ οὐρανοῦ according to Mark viii. 11, or even ἐν τῷ οὐρανῷ, Rev. xii. 1) are contrasted with the σημεῖα ἐπὶ τῆς γῆς, *signs on the earth*, and seem to carnal man to be required of the Messiah, since they imply greater power.

Ver. 39.—Jesus dismissed them and their demand with a rebuke. (Γενεά = דּוֹר means primarily " age," " period of life ;"* then, those living together at the same period. [Comp. remarks on Matth. xxiv. 34.] In the same connexion as in this place, the word μοιχαλίς, *adulterous*, is found also in Matth. xvi. 4—a passage parallel to the present both as to its fact and expression. The expression must be explained by the uniform Old Testament mode of speaking, which conceives all that is unbelieving and unholy as born of unholy love, and therefore presupposes a separation of the soul from the Lord. The spiritual turning away of the soul from the Creator to the creature, according to a profound conception of the soul's relation to God (to which we shall frequently refer hereafter)† is represented as adultery. Compare *Gesenius'* Hebrew Lexicon, s. v. זָנָה, זְנוּנִים, זְנוּת.) The dismissal of these sign-seekers evidently militates in no degree against the value which we elsewhere (John v. 20, x. 25) see Jesus putting upon his miracles. For, as his miracles had always a moral aim, they suppose a susceptibility of mind for that which is holy. Where this was wanting, they had so little effect, that even the most stupendous miracles could be ascribed to an unholy power (ver. 24). It thus appears, as the curse of sin, that divinity, in its exalted and blissful manifestations, withdraws from it. To the evil generation belongs only the invisible sign of the prophet Jonas.

Ver. 40.—To what extent our Redeemer intends to give to the Pharisees the sign of the prophet Jonas, is indicated by the Evangelist himself in the words : ὥσπερ γάρ κ. τ. λ. There can be no doubt that there is more than one point of similarity in the parallel between the resurrection of Jesus and the fate of Jonas, which is here brought forward. In the first place, both had reference to the persons themselves (on account of which Luke, xi. 30, employs the words : ἐγένετο Ἰωνᾶς σημεῖον, Jonas himself was the sign) ; secondly, both the deliverance of Jonas out of the fish, and the resurrection of Jesus were unseen signs, given only to the faith (of the adversaries) ; thirdly, the ἐν τῇ κοιλίᾳ κήτους, *in the belly of the fish*, forms a parallel with ἐν τῇ καρδίᾳ τῆς γῆς, *in the heart of the earth*, as a contrast to the demanded sign from heaven. The main point of resemblance, however, which forms the connecting link between the two is this, that as the preservation of Jonas was not seen by the Ninevites, so also the greatest miracle which takes place on the person of the Son of Man was to remain invisible to the Pharisees ; the mystery of the Lord's glory is concealed from the vulgar eyes of the

---

* Rather, primarily *birth*, than *descent, generation, race*.—[K.

† Comparisons with John viii. 41 are here quite inadmissible; μοιχαλίς does not signify "begotten in adultery" (*spurius*), but practising adultery.

adulterous generation. The recently attempted explanation of this passage which understands the sign of Jonas to be his preaching to the Ninevites (making v. 40 a misconception by Matthew of the words of Jesus), springs from an utter mistaking of the entire connection, and sufficiently refutes itself. The Saviour's reference to the history of Jonas contains finally a hint important to the biblical interpreter for the explanation of that portion of the Old Testament : but with this we are not at present concerned. Jesus elsewhere (Matth. xvi. 1, ff.) makes use of what occurred to Jonas, to compare with it his resurrection. The three days and three nights must be explained according to the Hebrew mode of speaking ; a νυχθή- μερον = בֹים does not require that just three times twenty-four hours should have elapsed. The Redeemer rested in the grave on three days, and thereby fulfilled the prediction. The accuracy of Scripture never degenerates into minute and anxious precision. Like nature, it combines regularity with freedom ; and hence it affords scope to liberty, and states and fulfils all prophecies in such a manner that they may either be believed, or contradicted. The Holy Scriptures would altogether miss their aim if, by mathematical precision and strictness, they should *compel* belief. The parallel between ἐν τῇ κοιλίᾳ τοῦ κήτους, *in the belly of the whale, sea-monster,* and ἐν τῇ καρδίᾳ τῆς γῆς, *in the heart of the earth,* must not be overlooked. The former words are a quotation from the LXX., which translates גְּדוֹל דָּג, Jon. ii. 1, by κῆτος. The καρδία = לֵב, signifies the interior in general. The term seems unsuitable for expressing repose in the grave ; nor is the parallel very appropriate. Might not these words have a further reference to the condition of the soul of Jesus after death ? (Compare Comment. on 1 Pet. iii. 19 ; Ephes. iv. 8.) The words convey but intimations, and when spoken, may not have been understood either by the Pharisees or by the disciples—as was the case with so many other declarations, the full meaning of which was opened to them only at a subsequent period. Moreover, the Lord had not as yet distincly spoken of his death. The whole, therefore, remained, as was proper, in enigmatical obscurity ; it was for the present, as it were a hieroglyph, the deciphering of which was reserved for the future. One might say that in such passages the Redeemer prophesies of and for himself; for, although doubtless the whole great course of his work was laid open before his soul when he began it by being baptized in the Jordan ; it is yet not improbable, that its great individual incidents—especially his death and all the details connected with it—were but gradually brought with greater distinctness before his human consciousness. The history of the transfiguration (Matth. xvii. 1, seq.) seems to countenance this view. (Compare, for fuller remarks, the Commentary.)

Ver. 41, 42.—The mention of the history of Jonas leads the Lord to yet another point that makes manifest the debasement of the men of his time. Although no visible sign had been vouchsafed to the Ninevites, they yet believed when Jonas preached and called them to repentance : and the Queen of the South hastened uninvited to Solomon, that she might learn wisdom from him. But the Pharisees would not even accept what was offered to them. . In these comparisons, the reproof was so much the more severe, as, in both cases they were Gentiles—above whom the Jews were so fond of exalting themselves—who gave those proofs of faith ; just as in the similar comparison in xi. 20, seq. The judgment and resurrection are here again mentioned as the period of final, unerring decision, when every thing will be manifested in its innermost nature. (Νινευῖται = ἄνδρες Νινευί = נִינְוֵה אַנְשֵׁי נִינְוֵה, according to a well-known Hebraism ; Josh. viii. 20 ; x. 6. The βασίλισσα νότου is the מַלְכַּת שְׁבָא, 1 Kings x. 1. The νότος, *south*, points in an indefinite manner to the south, to *Arabia Felix*. The πέρατα τῆς γῆς, *extremities of the earth* = הָאָרֶץ אַפְסֵי is a well-known phrase in the Old Testament, taken from the popular view of the world.) The less was the splendour by which the Ninevites and the Arabian queen were overcome, the more culpable must appear the conflict with holiness in its perfect ideal. (Πλεῖον Ἰωνᾶ, Σολομῶνος ὧδε, comp. Matth. xii. 8.)

Ver. 43.—Luke—who, throughout the whole of his eleventh chapter, has arranged in a peculiar manner the various elements, as we shall afterwards see, and who in ver. 27 and 28 inserts a separate little narrative—brings the following words (Matth. xii. 43–45) into immediate connexion with the demoniac and his cure, from which, in Matthew also (xii. 22, seq.), every thing sprang. These words may indeed have had their place after the history of the cure ; but Matthew has arranged them, according to his custom, in an independent, and by no means unskilful manner. He connects them, after the closing words of ver. 45, " so shall it be also with this wicked generation," with the main part of the conversation regarding the wicked and adulterous generation (ver. 39). It might indeed appear strange how such language could be applied to the Pharisees, who, after all, must be understood as referred to in the γενεὰ μοιχαλίς, ver. 39. As no demon had been expelled from them, we cannot see how he could return into them. Nay, as there was neither spiritual desire nor faith in their hearts, we can as little see how the casting out of a demon could be spoken of, even although we were to understand this return as something to be expected in the future. It is only from a misunderstanding of the passage that unbelief itself could be regarded as the demon to be cast out. But as the Pharisees, as *pars pro toto*, may, with full propriety, be regarded as representing the whole people who had imbibed their spirit, so might the Jewish people of that time, viewed as a greater individuality, be regarded along with the Jewish people of former times as a person in different stages of development. That among the people there were always some, such as the apostles and other noble-minded individuals, who did not share in the general corruption, forms no argument against such a view; for all these did not, as such, properly belong to the people; they rather stood above them. The Babylonish captivity appears in the history of the Jewish nation as a period of purification, as a true casting out of the demon of idolatry amidst fearful paroxysms. After their return, the Jews appear in greater purity than they ever did before. But instead of idolatry the more dangerous Pharisaism returned; and this was, after all, the same spirit of idolatry in different forms. It was in the fetters of this spirit that our Redeemer found the nation, which would not now suffer itself to be emancipated, so that it resembled a demoniac who had sunk back into his old disorder. A profound and significant application of the comparison! It is only the future tense in ver. 45: οὕτως ἔσται ἐν τῇ γενεᾷ ταύτῃ, thus shall it be, etc., which may appear inconsistent with the view which we have stated, inasmuch as, according to it, every thing appears as past. But the "shall be" can evidently refer only to what immediately precedes it: "the last state worse than the first;" and indeed the evil consequences of the relapse of the Jewish people manifested themselves very strikingly only after they lost their independence. To refer the οὕτως ἔσται, "so it shall be," to the whole parable, so that the casting out of the demon and his return with seven others were still in the future, would make the whole passage unintelligible; for, neither among the Pharisees alone, nor in the whole nation, do there appear any events which might be viewed in this light.

In the words of ver. 43, 44, we have parabolically represented a national Jewish idea, indeed we may say a conception of universal humanity. Evil, viewed as discord, as desert, reappears in the physical world, as it were, an echo and a copy of evil in the spiritual. The deserts of earth are witnesses of the sin of mankind—a visble proof of the disappearance of Paradise. As then kindred object appear to man as in close connexion, deserts are considered as habitations of evil spirits; so that what was made desolate by sin became also the local abode of evil. (Isaiah xiii. 21; xxxiv. 14; Rev. xviii. 2; Tob. viii. 3; Baruch iv. 35.) Of this simple idea, which has its foundation in the depths of human nature, our Redeemer here avails himself, that he may draw a graphic picture of evil. The whole description bears a parabolic impress; and hence the several features should not be over-strained. Still they rest not upon an empty accommodation to a national and baseless superstition, but upon the simple truth, that in the great creation all the parts form a whole, and the spiritual world is reflected in the physical. Hence, over-come by the power of God, the evil spirit appears in the represen-tation of Jesus, escaping to the desert (τόπος ἄνυδρος = ἔρημος, i. e. מִדְבָּר, צִיָּה אֶרֶץ, Isaiah xxxv. 1 ; Joel ii. 20) seeking rest (on ἀνάπαυσις, see remarks on Matth. xi. 29), the loss of which is a characteristic of evil. But change of place cannot give rest to a spirit—it finds its rest only in God, its primeval source. It is therefore represented as returning to the soul which had become the abode of evil.

Ver. 44.—Carrying out the figure of the dwelling, Jesus de-scribes the guilt of a man freed for a time from the power of the evil one. The term σχολάζων, vacant, unoccupied, points out the guilt incurred by negligence and sloth—the cause of a relapse into sin ; the terms σεσαρωμένον, swept (from σαρόω, "to sweep," Luke xv. 8), and κεκοσμημένον, garnished, denote only the alluring and charming character of the abode which a purified soul offers. Here also the figure is based upon the notion that sin, as moral defilement, has its analogy in the visible world ; he who is unclean is allured by what is clean and pure, which, however, is defiled by contact with him. All these are figures ; but how deep is the truth which lies in them ! The soul appears here as the bride wooed by heaven and hell. She may receive the former or the latter; but the spirit whom she receives transforms her into his own nature, and makes her his bodily.

Ver. 45.—Just as good is making perpetual inward progress—as it is impossible to conceive of its being stationary—so evil always grows and matures. The wicked man raised to the sphere of the good, but sinking back, must fall the more deeply the higher he had risen (John v. 14). There are gradations also among the bad (πνεύματα πονηρότερα, compare remarks on Ephes. vi. 12). The discourse closes, at length, with the general idea, that every relapse is more danger-ous than the disease itself. This was likewise evident in Israel. At the time of the Babylonish captivity, the chastening rod of the Lord still produced its effect ; but when the Creator came unto his own (John i. 12), his own had become estranged from him, and re-ceived him not. (Τὰ πρῶτα is, as it were, the original, simple state of suffering : τὰ ἔσχατα, the state of relapse.)

§ 20. THE ARRIVAL OF THE MOTHER AND BROTHERS OF JESUS.

(Matth. xii. 46–50; Mark iii. 31–35; Luke viii. 19–21.)

The importance of Mark for the right understanding of many sections of the Gospel history, through the addition of minor traits, becomes here very palpable. The accounts of Matthew and Luke leave it obscure why Jesus did not even admit his mother and his brethren to his presence. The declaration also that his disciples are his true relatives would be somewhat startling, if Mark did not come to our aid.* At the beginning of the section previously explained (Mark iii. 20, 21), he relates that Jesus had gone into a house with his disciples, and that this house was surrounded by crowds of people, so that while engaged in spiritual labour, they could not find time even to appease their hunger (ὥστε μὴ δύνασθαι αὐτοὺς μήτε ἄρτον φαγεῖν). Here his relatives (οἱ παρ' αὐτοῦ) came to lay hold of him (κρατῆσαι, "to seize" "to arrest"), in order to bring him to a place of safety ; for they said that he was beside himself (ἐξέστη). (Concerning ἐξίστημι compare remarks on Matth. xii. 23 ; here it is = insanity (μαίνεσθαι), the consequence of the demonical possession of which he was accused by the Pharisees ; by the hostile power, man seems to be driven out of himself, and of his self-possession). This remark explains the whole scene. The wicked Pharisees had brought their blasphemous assertion even to the relatives of Jesus, who had been induced thereby to make an attempt to bring him back from his, in their view, destructive course. Without this hint we should have been obliged to content ourselves with Luke's statement in ver. 19, "they were not able to come at him on account of the crowd," by which, however, the whole occurrence would have remained enveloped in considerable obscurity. We can easily conceive from John vii. 5, how the unbelieving brethren might be carried away by such a rumour ; but it is not so easy to understand how even his mother could give credit to it ; we should suppose her faith to have been immovable. But, in the first place, it may, from the account of the Evangelists, be supposed that Mary in nowise shared the opinion of his brethren, but merely accompanied them on their journey, in order, perhaps, to mitigate their perverted zeal. No decisive argument can be advanced against such a supposition. But, on the other hand, it is by no means improbable that Mary experienced moments of weakness, when her faith was fainting and struggling. The long series of years which had elapsed

* Against this identification of the event narrated (Mark iii. 31, ff.), with that in Matth. xii. and Luke v., compare my Kritik. der Evang. Gesch., 2 Ed., § 63 and 70. Matthew attaches the incident of Mark iii. 20-21, closely and definitely to his selection of the disciples (the discourse on the Mount). On the evening of this day it occurred, while Jesus was still in a journey. How could then his mother and brethren in Nazareth learn that he was thronged by the people, and unable to eat ? How resolve at once to traverse Galilee in search of him ? How find him ? And granting they had found him, how could this be expressed by "came out to lay hold of him," since assuredly the "coming out" makes a manifest contrast to the "house," Matth. iii. 20, and must signify a coming out of the house in front of which Jesus was teaching, not a setting forth from Nazareth. But entirely decisive against the identification is the fact that Mark himself afterwards, v. 32, relates the visit of his mother and brethren as a separate event. Had it been his mother and brethren who, v. 21, had already sought to take him, how could he be informed afterwards for the first time that they wished to see him ?—[E.

since the great events which she had experienced, the form which
her son's ministry assumed—a form so entirely different from any
which she may have imagined—may have been a severe trial for her,
and, like John the Baptist, she may have doubted (Matth. xi. 2,
seq.) She had certainly not given up her faith, but it is possible
that, according to the prophecy given to her (Luke ii. 35), it was
just now severely assailed, and the anxious mother came rather to
obtain consolation from her son and Lord, than really to *take him
home*, and yet, influenced by the tormenting rumour, asking at the
same time, Art thou he who is to come ?   It is traits like these
that instil so much life into the evangelical history.   It is wholly erroneous, as already remarked, (Matth. xi. 1), to conceive of all the
heroes of the Gospel-history as unwavering characters.   The stupendous events in the life of Jesus must, doubtless, have been connected
with great fluctuations in all those who surrounded him, and these
form integral features of the rich picture which cannot be effaced.
It is not to the prejudice of the holy character of the Scripture personages, that they manifest such inward fluctuation.   No saint has
ever become so without heavy struggles, in which the billows may
often have passed over his head.   Through these the Son of God
himself led the way for his people.

Ver. 46.—While Christ was yet talking to the people, his mother
and brethren (concerning them compare Matth. xiii. 55) arrived.
They stood ἔξω (see Mark iii. 34) outside the house, and sent in
messengers.

Ver. 47, 48.—On receiving information thereof, Christ refused
to see them.. This, it is true, is not stated in express words ; but
the form of the language : " but he answered and said," compels us
to this view.   He neither *went out*, nor did he allow them to *come
in;* on the contrary, he continued his discourse.   It is probable, indeed, that he may have seen them *after* the close of it, but not *before* it.   The whole answer would otherwise lose its point.

Ver. 49, 50.—Mark adds here the graphic : περιβλεψάμενος κύκλῳ,
looking round about, as he called the whole company of his disciples,
" my mother, my brethren" (ἡ μήτηρ μου καὶ οἱ ἀδελφοί μου).   But
ver. 50, extends the expression from those present to a wider
circle, inasmuch as the doing of the will of God (according to
Luke : λόγον τοῦ Θεοῦ ἀκούειν καὶ ποιεῖν) is laid down as the test of
spiritual relationship.   The terms mother and brethren, suggested
by the circumstances, here therefore include the general idea of relationship ; this is conceived by Jesus in its most abstract form, as a
moral and spiritual union in that loftier whole, embraced in the
kingdom of God.   The striking point in this representation is, that
our Redeemer seems entirely to rank himself as a member of this
great community—nay, even as a subordinate member, since he

speaks of his mother. True, we might here appeal to the current maxim, that, in expressions of this kind, the words must not be overstrained. But, on the other hand, we might also say, that this view expresses the lowliness of the Son of Man, who said : they are my mother and my brethren, where he might have said : they are my children. But even this would not fully exhaust the thought ; and it would appear as though the words: "behold my mother" were used by the Lord to indicate a' peculiar view of the church, according to which the same community of the faithful who, when considered separately, are his brethren, may, when viewed as a unity, be called his mother, inasmuch as, in the church, divinity continually assumes the form of humanity, and Christ is perpetually born anew in her. [Doubtless the sense of the whole is simply this, they are my kindred, nearer to me than any earthly relatives.]

§ 21. A WOMAN ANOINTS JESUS.

(Luke vii. 36—viii. 3.)

Matthew, in this instance, connects the following 13th chapter with the preceding (in harmony also with Mark iv. 1), by a chronological statement, so definite that we must consider them as belonging to each other. Hence, this is the most appropriate place for introducing a narrative which is found in Luke alone ; and brought by the Evangelist into the closest connexion with the account of the parable of the sower. True, we cannot even in this case, think of asserting a strict order ; for, while in Matth. xiii. 1 we find : ἐν ἐκείνῃ ἡμέρα, on that day, so that the parable must have been spoken on the same day with the events of the preceding chapter, we read in Luke, after the narrative of the anointing : ἐν τῷ καθεξῆς (sc. χρόνῳ) ἐγένετο, by which formula all that follows is, at all events, transferred to a later day. This section ought then to have been placed before Matth. xii., provided that all in this and chap. xiii. took place on one and the same day. But as Matthew's dates leave it altogether uncertain where the day begins ; and Luke says nothing on the time of the anointing, it was impossible to fix the exact time with any greater certainty. For this reason, we are led by its agreement with what follows to insert it here.

With regard to the occurrence itself, the first question which presents itself is—In what relationship does it stand to a similar event narrated in Matth. xxvi. 6–13 ? (Compare also Mark xiv. 3, seq. ; John xii. 1, seq.) *Schleiermacher* (in his *Versuch über den Lucas*, S. 110, ff.) has lately, in an acute and ingenious manner, objected to the diversity of the occurrences, which was, for a long time, unquestioned. He declares them to be identical, and thinks that the account, as given by Luke, had been misunderstood by the reporter from whom Luke received it, and noted down by him in its present form. At first sight there appears much to favour this view. It appears strange to assume two narratives in which a woman anointed Jesus at a feast given in the house of a certain Simon. It appears strange that a woman of bad reputation, but otherwise unknown to the master of the house, should have obtruded herself on such an occasion. But assuredly it is still more extraordinary, that the occurrence should be the same, and that in Luke we have only a distorted representation of it.* For, in the first place, it is to be sure easily explained how Mary could so freely, in the company, express her devotion to Jesus, as, according to the accounts of Matthew, Mark, and John, the feast was given by a family on friendly terms with Lazarus ; and Simon the leper, whom Matthew and Mark mention as the host, must be considered as a relative or intimate friend of this very family. But for this very reason, it is altogether inexplicable how this same friendly host should have expressed himself in a way which was, even in the remotest degree, liable to be so misunderstood, as Luke's narrative would in that case make it. It is improbable that he should have uttered any suspicion whatever against the Saviour ; and still more improbable that he should have uttered an insinuation of that kind against the sister of Lazarus. Even supposing that it was not his intention to denote, by the term *sinner* (ἁμαρτωλός), a sinful woman in the ordinary sense, and that this severe view of the word arose from the misconception of the reporter whom Luke followed ; yet it is clear that something which *could* be thus misunderstood, must have been said by Simon the leper. For such a supposition, however, there is, according to the accounts of Matthew, Mark, and John, not the slightest occasion ; nay, everything is against it. The expression of the woman's love seems to have been singularly touching ; Judas merely blamed the waste of the precious ointment. Supposing the circumstances to have been such as those so minutely described by the three Evangelists, any occasion for all the speeches which, in Luke, are connected with it, is absolutely inconceivable ; on the contrary, everything testifies against the assumption that any such speeches were uttered by the Lord in the midst of his favourites of Bethany. Hence, assuming the identity of this transaction with the anointing by Mary, the sister of Lazarus, at Bethany, Luke has not only misunderstood, but *totally distorted* it ; the occurrence has become specifically different. But this is partly incompatible with the

---

* I attach no weight to the circumstance that, according to Luke vii. 37, the event happened in a *town*, whereas Bethany was a κώμη (John xi. 1); the two appellations may not have been so strictly distinguished.

authority of the biblical writings, and partly also with the position of John, who was no doubt acquainted with Luke's Gospel also, as *Schleiermacher* himself supposes. This scholar even claims to find traces—although he has not mentioned them—of the fact that John knew both the accounts. These traces I have not been able to discover ; but so much appears to me certain, that if a narrative so completely distorted could have crept into Luke's Gospel, John would not have omitted to notice it as such. If, then, the identity of the events involves difficulties so substantial, it will be more natural to maintain their diversity. For, although it may be strange that a similar occurrence happened twice in the house of a certain Simon, yet it is by no means impossible or contradictory ; especially as the name Simon was one of so very common occurrence among the Jews. And whatever seems offensive in the circumstance of a woman intruding herself at a feast, is partly mitigated by eastern usages, partly perhaps in the case of this woman, by special relations, altogether unknown to us. Were it, *e. g.*, a woman from the Saviour's more immediate circle, her approach to him is easily explained. Nor, *finally*, can any argument for the identity of the occurrence be founded on Luke's omission of the anointing at Bethany, as similar omissions occur in all the Gospels, in John, *e. g.*, of the institution of the supper. In the opinion of many ancient interpreters, this woman, who, according to Luke, anointed Jesus, was Mary Magdalene ; but the opinion is wholly without proof. Nay, as she is immediately (in viii. 2) named without reference to the event here narrated, it seems improbable that it was she, unless we assume that Luke purposely omitted to mention her name, and the words, ἀφ' ἧς δαιμόνια ἑπτὰ ἐξεληλύθει, *from whom seven devils had gone out*, are meant as an indication of her guilt. As there is thus an entire want of any definite account, we leave the person undetermined.

Ver. 36.—It is possible that this Pharisee himself had been healed by Jesus, and that, not feeling any true gratitude, he thought that he might acquit himself of his obligation by an invitation. (See remarks on ver. 47.)

Ver. 37.—The city (πόλις) is here commonly understood to be Nain, from the preceding account (vii. 11) of his raising the widow's son from the dead at Nain ; but the formulas of transition in ver. 17, 18, 20, 36, are by far too general to establish this supposition. The woman is called ἀμαρτωλός, *i. e.*, guilty of sexual offences (John viii. 7, 11). Ἀλάβαστρον stands for σκεῦος ἐξ ἀλαβάστρου.

Ver. 38.—The scene must be conceived of in accordance with ancient customs : the banqueters lay stretched out (*accumbere*, ἀνακλίνεσθαι), their feet being bare or covered only with sandals. The fervour of grateful love manifested itself in her affectionate approach ;

but her feelings of shame and contrition allowed her to approach only the *feet* of the Redeemer. The case was different with Mary the sister of Lazarus; her love was not less ardent, but there was less of the sense of shame; she annointed the *head* of the Lord. (Comp. remarks on Matth. xxvi. 7; Mark xiv. 3. Both here narrate probably with greater accuracy than John xii. 3.)

Ver. 39.—The heartless Pharisee, incapable of being moved by such an exhibition of love,* takes occasion to make his reflections on the character of Jesus. It is inconceivable that this should have happened at the feast in Bethany; for such a person there was no room there. (Εἰπεῖν ἐν ἑαυτῷ = אָמַר בְּלִבּוֹ.) As regards earthly purity, there is some truth in the thought that the pure is contaminated by a touch of the impure (see remarks on Matth. xi. 19); but the overwhelming power of Jesus, undreamed of by the Pharisee, renders it in his case utterly untrue.

Ver. 40, 41.—The Pharisee who was not so wicked as he was coarse-minded, is instructed by the merciful Friend of Sinners, by means of a narrative, in which he represents both the relation of the woman, and that of the Pharisee himself, to God. (Χρεωφειλέτης = ὀφειλέτης, found elsewhere only Luke xvi. 5.—Δανειστής = נֹשֶׁה, fenerator, 2 Kings iv. 1. In the New Testament found only here.)

Ver. 42, 43.—The comparison between the *more* and the *less* of love, necessarily leads to a parallel between the Pharisee and the woman; and hence the supposition is very probable, that the Pharisee too was indebted to Jesus for some previous kindness. [?]

Ver. 44-46.—The conduct of the Pharisee is contrasted with the fervent love of the woman, who did more than was demanded either by custom or by the circumstances. The water for the feet (Gen.·

* I cannot refrain from quoting here the words of a noble man who reproves, with reference to the anointing of Jesus, the uncharitable criticising, by a cold and dead generation, of the ardour of his own love for the Saviour, and of its manifestation. The excellent *von Roth*, has published the following words of *Hamann*, in the preface to his edition of *Hamann's* works (S. ix. of vol. 1): " Jerusalem—it is the city of a great king! To this king whose name, like his glory, is great and unknown, flowed forth the little river of my authorship, despised like the waters of Siloah that go softly (Is. viii. 6). Critical severity persecuted the dry stalk, as well as the flying leaf of my muse; because the dry stalk whistled and played with the little children, who sit in the market-place, and because the flying leaf was tossed about being giddy with the *ideal* of a king, who could say of himself with the greatest meekness and humility: " One greater than Solomon is here." As a devoted lover wearies the ready echo with the name of his beloved mistress, and does not spare any young tree of the garden or forest with engraving the initials and characters of her beloved name: thus was the remembrance of the fairest among the children of men (Ps. xlv. 3), even in the midst of the king's enemies, like unto a Magdalene—ointment poured out, and flowing down like the precious ointment upon the head of Aaron, which ran down upon his beard—flowing down to the skirts of his garments. The house of Simon the leper was filled with the odour of the gospel-anointing; but some merciful! (or rather merciless) brethren and critics, were angry with what they called the ordure, and their nostrils were filled with the odour of death only." Precious and profound words! and full of hints for those who can see and hear.

xviii. 4 ; Judg. xix, 21), the kiss (Gen. xxxiii. 4 ; Exod. xviii. 7), and the offering of ointment, have reference to well known Jewish, or rather universal Eastern, custom. The distinguished Pharisee had omitted the offer of such courtesies, because, very likely, he considered the invitation itself a sufficient honour. Jesus reproves this coldness towards his benefactor—a coldness coupled, at the same time, with such self-conceited exaltation above the woman.

Ver. 47.—The contrast before referred to appears here anew. Although the words : ᾧ δὲ ὀλίγον ἀφίεται, *he to whom little is forgiven*, state the thought only generally, yet they may very appropriately include the σοὶ ὀλίγον ἀφίεται, *to thee is but little forgiven*, which was not uttered solely from polite considerateness. The first member of this verse presents some difficulty ; for, according to it, love does not appear as the *consequence* (as in the second member of the verse—quite in accordance with the parable), but as the *cause* of forgiveness. The ὅτι, *because*, as well as the Aorist ἠγάπησε, *loved*, represent love as that which precedes, and is the ground of, forgiveness. It has indeed been asserted (comp. *Schleusner's Lex.* ii. 325), that ὅτι stands for the Hebrew מִי, דְּבַר עַל, יַעַן in the sense of διό, *wherefore* ; but neither the passages in the Old Testament referred to (Ps. xvii. 6 ; cxvi. 10 ; Deut. xxii. 24, and others) are to be thus understood, nor is the word ever found, with this signification, in the New Testament. (Passages such as John viii. 44 ; 1 John iii. 14, are erroneously referred to.) *Further.*—To escape the difficulty offered by the Aorist, ἀγαπᾶν is taken with the signification : " to give a proof of love," so that the sense of the verse would be : " thou mayest, therefore, infer that many sins are forgiven to her, for she has given me [in consequence thereof] a great proof of her love." But such a view is opposed by the signification of ἀγαπᾶν, as it immediately appears in the second member of the verse, for it signifies a *state*, and not a mere *action*. The sense evidently is, not that she *has* loved, and that her love is now past, but that she is constantly living in love. It is thrown back into the past, merely in order to connect it with the forgiveness ; we must, therefore, rather attempt to overcome the difficulty involved in the thought. The Roman Catholic Church has so far misinterpreted[*] it, as to infer from it the dependence of forgiveness upon merit ; for she understands *love* (ἀγαπῆσαι) of *active* benevolence, the fruit of our natural powers, and essential to forgiveness. According to the parable, however, this cannot be the sense. But the ability to receive forgiveness presupposes

---

[*] *De Wette*, in commenting on this passage, makes the remark: " We are now beyond any polemical opposition to the Roman Catholic doctrine of justification by works." I very much doubt this. The natural resort of an unrepenting heart is the effort to gain salvation through works; and this manifests itself even within the evangelical church, in forms not exactly Roman Catholic.

love existing in the heart as a *receptive* power, which must be the more intense, the greater the guilt to be forgiven appears to man. If this receptive love (which is identical with penitential faith), really receives within itself the grace of forgiveness, it then unfolds and manifests itself actively, as in the case of this woman towards Jesus. In this love, she, as it were, makes the power which enkindled life in her, the *receptive pole* of her activity, so that in these words of our Lord, love is represented in its wondrous forms of manifestation, by virtue of which it appears sometimes as active, sometimes as passive, but always the same. The sense of the words, therefore, may be thus exhibited : he who is to believe in forgivenes must carry within himself an analogous fund of (receptive) love, which, as soon as the pardoning power of love, as it were the *positive pole*, approaches it, manifests itself in the same ratio as the guilt, which is taken away, increases. At the same time, there is implied in this, an allusion to the peculiar arrangement of the Lord, that where sin abounds, grace does much more abound (Rom. v. 20) ; not that sin can produce any thing which is good, but only because the compassion of the Lord reveals itself in the brightest manner towards those who are most miserable. The Pharisee was not without love ; he loved a *little*, thinking that he had received *little ;* but the woman who had received *every thing*, loved ardently, with all the energy of her life.*

Ver. 49, 50.—With this is connected a solemn repetition of the forgiving words : ἀφέωνταί σου αἱ ἁμαρτίαι, *thy sins are forgiven thee*, to the amazement of those present. Compare concerning this the remarks on Matth. ix. iii. where faith and its relation to forgiveness are treated of.

A transition, describing in general terms the ministry of Jesus (Luke viii. 1–3), introduces us to the parables. Our Redeemer went about through cities and villages preaching the kingdom of God, and was accompanied by living witnesses of his redeeming power. The persons specially named are, 1. Mary of Magdala. (Compare remarks on Matth. xv. 39.) Her condition previous to her restoration is described as having been peculiarly distressing (on ἑπτὰ δαιμόνια, compare Matth. xii. 45); all her faculties and powers seem to have been a prey to the workings of darkness.† 2. Joanna the

---

* Compare what has been said in Matth. xiii. 58, on the relation of receptive love to faith. The important passage Hos. ii. 19, 20, ought also to be compared, as, in the words of the prophet, faith and love penetrate each other.

† The same is remarked of Mary, in Mark xvi. 9, in a connexion altogether different. It therefore appears that her deliverance from demoniacal influences was considered as something altogether peculiar. Her former condition was pre-eminently distressing, but so much the more gloriously was the power of the Lord manifested in her, and so much the more evident was her love to the Lord. Everywhere (compare the history of the Resurrection) she is named first among the women.

wife of Chuza. ('Eπίτροπος = οἰκονόμος, *steward*.) 3. Susanna,
שׁוֹשַׁנָּה, *lily*. The two latter are only mentioned here ; but Mary
Magdalene is known from the history of the Passion. (Matth.
xxvii. 55.) According to that passage, however, others also, and
probably those mentioned here, adhered stedfastly to the Lord,
even to the cross   These women afforded him support from their
private property (ὑπάρχοντα, *opes, facultates*), and ministered unto
him. The rarer the glimpses furnished in the Gospel history of the
external circumstances of the Redeemer's companions, the more
attractive are they to the reader ; they throw a peculiar light upon
his whole conduct while on earth. His indwelling divinity clothes
itself in a genuine human garb : his glory is strictly internal, and
displays itself in outward brightness only to bless others. He who
supported the spiritual life of his people, did not disdain to be supported by them bodily. He was not ashamed to descend to so deep
a poverty that he lived on the charities of love. It was only others
whom he fed miraculously ; for himself, he lived upon the love of
his people.* He thus loved, and allowed himself to be loved, in
perfect, pure love. He gave everything to men, his brethren, and
he received everything from them, and enjoyed in this the pure happiness of love, which is perfect only when it is at the same time
giving and receiving. What a trait in the character of the Messiah ! Who could have invented it ! He who feeds thousands by
a word, lived himself on the bread of the poor. Such a life must
have been led, to be so recorded.

§ 22. THE COLLECTION OF PARABLES.

(Matth. xiii. 1–53 ; Mark iv. 1–20, 30–34 ; Luke viii. 4–15 ; xiii. 18–21.)

The progress of Matthew's history, brings us to a collection of
parables. There is something extraordinary in this collection, inasmuch as it seems not to be in accordance with this mode of teaching, to accumulate parables. For as they are intended to present
truth under a veil, and to stimulate to meditation and inquiry, their
significance would be weakened by bringing many together in an
oral discourse. In consequence of the varied relations contained in
the parables, the mind would rather feel distracted and bewildered
than stimulated ; and hence their aim would be missed. But the

---

* It is remarkable that it is only women of whom it is said αἵτινες διηκόνουν αὐτῷ
ἀπὸ τῶν ὑπαρχόντων αὐταῖς, *who ministered to him with their substance*, and who, with a
touching attachment, were devoted to the Lord, as is shewn by the history of the Resurrection. The weaker half of the human race were the first to arrive at the knowledge of the strength which they possessed in Christ.

case is different in a written discourse. The reader can reflect at
leisure on the individual parable, compare one with the others, and
thereby obtain a clearer insight into the peculiarities of each. To
the purposes of writing, therefore, a collection of parables is admi-
rably adapted. But although according to what has been stated, an
accumulation of recorded parables, is at once appropriate in itself, and
specially adapted to Matthew's mode of collective representation,
we may still ask whether it were not better to assume here not so
much a collection of parables spoken at different times, as a strictly
exact exhibition of the Saviour's mode of communicating them
in succession. To support such an opinion, we might refer to several passages in Luke—especiaily to xiv. 28 ; xvi. 31, where Jesus
utters a series of parables, while yet everything proves that they are
uttered in their original connexion. To this we must add the common reference of all the parables here collected to the kingdom of
God, so that there was no risk of the hearers being distracted, inasmuch as one parable explained the other—add also Matthew's mode
of delineating the scene (v. 1, seq.), in that Jesus teaches sitting on
the sea-shore, and surrounded by a crowd of people, and finally
brings, xiii. 53, his instructions to a close. But to this view we must
object (?) that Luke, in that case, must have transposed some of the
parables, inasmuch as he narrates what is contained in Matth. xiii.
18–21, in quite a different, although a very appropriate, connexion.*
Moreover, we saw already, in the Sermon on the Mount, in what an
indefinite sense Matthew uses such opening and closing formlas. (?)
As he evinces no local or chronological interest, we cannot lay much
stress upon them. It cannot well be reconciled with the scene as
described in Matth. xiii. 1, seq. that, according to ver. 10, the disciples came to him, and asked him concerning the meaning of
the parable which he had spoken. That evidently could not have
been done in presence of the assembled multitude, but belonged
solely to the private circle of the disciples. Mark iv. 10, confirms
this supposition ; for he adds that this question was addressed by
the disciples to the Lord, when he was *alone.* Here, thus we perceive, [only] that the writer has anticipated the interpretation of
the first parable, since it could have taken place only after Jesus
had withdrawn from the crowd, and was alone with his disciples, just
as is stated in ver. 36, on the occasion of the second interpretation.
According to ver. 36, it appears doubtful whether the Lord spoke
the last three parables to the people, or to the disciples only. Mark
and Luke quite agree with Matthew in the order of the first parable, but the subsequent ones are differently arranged. We can
finally by no means deny an intimate connexion of the parables
related in Matthew xiii.; on the contrary, it distinctly comes out in

---

* When carefully examined, Luke gives absolutely no connexion.—[E.

the communication of them. The seven parables which Matthew communicates in this chapter are intended to characterise the various relations of the kingdom of God. The *first* parable considers the relation of various classes of men to the divine word ; the *second* considers their relation to the kingdom of the wicked one ; the *third* and *fourth* depict the greatness of the kingdom of God, in contrast with its insignificant beginnings ; the *fifth* and *sixth* point out the value of the kingdom of heaven ; and, finally, the *last* pourtrays the mixed condition of the church on earth until the day of judgment.

With regard to the parable itself, and its use in the New Testament, the Greek terms παραβολή, παροιμία, completely correspond with the Hebrew בְּשָׁל. Both words are used with a certain indefiniteness. Just as בָּשָׁל frequently signifies a proverbial saying (*Gnome*) a normal precept, so also does παραβολή when the proverb involves a comparison. (Luke iv. 23 ; Matth. xv. 15.) Common similes also, even without being proverbial or normal, occur under the same designation. (Mark iii. 23 ; Luke v. 36 ; vi. 39.) Most commonly, however, the name is used in the first three Gospels (for neither the term nor the thing itself is found in John's Gospel, or in any of the other writings of the New Testament) of a peculiar mode of teaching, of which there are some analogous examples in the Old Testament (Is. v. 1 [which *Mashal* is used by Jesus himself. Comp. Mark xii.], Ezek. xvii. 1, seq. ; Judg. ix. 7, seq. ; 2 Kings xiv. 9 ; 2 Sam. xii. 1), and which is most nearly related to the fable (λόγος, ἀπόλογος, αἶνος). The *parable* differs from the *comparison* chiefly in this :—that in the latter the subject is not individualized, and conceived as a fact. True, it is often rather indicated, than fully developed, as, *e. g.*, in Matth. xiii. 44, 45—the parables of the hidden treasure, and the merchantman. But, even in this unfinished form, it differs from the mere simile or allegory, inasmuch as the basis of the definite supposed fact may still be recognised in it. But it is more difficult to point out the difference between the *parable* and the *fable*. The ancients, especially *Aristotle* (Rhet. ii. 20), whom *Cicero* (de Invent. i. 30) and *Quinctilian* (Inst. v. 11) follow, place the difference only in the more or less ample treatment, inasmuch as to them the fable appears as the more finished production —the parable as the less finished. But among recent writers, *Lessing* makes this difference, that the fable represents the single fact as *real*, the parable, only as *possible*. According to *Herder*, it consists in this, that the fable avails itself of irrational nature, the parable, of the rational one. None of these opinions is free from difficulties. To judge from the biblical parable, it also represents the occurrence as a real one, and not merely as possible, as, *e. g.*, the very first parable of the sower. (Matth. xiii. 4.) This makes against the view taken by *Lessing*. Against that of *Herder* are the Old Testament parables above referred to, especially Ezek. xvii. 1, seq., in which the inanimate creation is the subject of the action, and yet none could style it a fable. And on the other hand, in the fables of Æsop, men are frequently made the vehicle of instruction. The difference is, without doubt, altogether internal. The ground occupied by the writer of fables is lower, and hence his aim also is subordinate. The fable restricts itself to earthly virtues, or commendable qualities. Now, as earthly virtues—prudence, cunning, laboriousness, and the like—have their representatives in certain classes of animals, the irrational animal-world may be most advantageously used for this form of instruction. If men are introduced in a fable, they always appear in a character allied to the animal-world. But the parable introduces us into a higher—a purely moral domain. It seeks to exhibit heavenward tendencies of life, or divinely instituted relations. Hence, its element is pre-eminently in the world of men. Where the parable touches upon the irrational element, it conceives it as subject to a higher and divine control. Humanity, where it enters the realm of fable, appears in its subordinate features ; irrational nature displays in the parable its diviner element. The whole spirit and aim of Scripture are adverse to the admission of the fable ;* for its constant endeavour is to reach and elevate the divine principle in man ; the parable is its true element. One might almost style the whole Old Testament history a continuous parable, conveying divine instruction. In the New Testament, the Son of God concealed the truth revealed in him under parabolic veils, in order thus to afford instruction for all degrees of development and knowledge at the same time, and to cause alike that one class should be initiated into the profoundest mysteries of the kingdom, and another be left in darkness regarding its nature.†

Ver. 1, 2.—Our Redeemer went from his dwelling-place (probably in Capernaum) to the sea (the Lake of Gennesareth), and, in order to withdraw himself from the crowd, he entered into a ship which happened to be there. The people were standing on the land (ἐπὶ τῆς γῆς) by the sea (πρὸς τὴν θάλασσαν, Mark iv. 1).

Ver. 4-9.—The parable of the sower is one of the few of which we possess an authoritative explanation by the Lord :—and this is

---

* At the most, Judg. ix. 7. seq. might be regarded as a fable, but, owing to the circumstances connected with this passage, it is on purpose that no higher point of view is brought out in it.

† Modern literature has been enriched with some very instructive works on the parables. *Rettberg* and *Schultze* are the authors of prize essays on this subject for the Göttingen University (both published in Göttingen, 1828). A more ample treatise, *De Parabolarum Jesu natura interpretatione*, etc., was written by *Ungen* (Lipsiæ, 1828). The most recent, and the fullest exposition is by *Lisco*. It is translated into English, by Fairbairn (Clark's Bib. Cab., vol. xxix).

of the greatest importance, not only for the understanding of the
single narrative, but also for the deduction of principles bearing
upon the exposition of all the parables. We may, especially, gather
from it what is usually most difficult in the exposition of parables :
namely, *how far the single features of the parabolical discourse have,
or have not any significance.* In the same manner as skepticism
may do away all that is profound in the word of God, by saying,
that this or that is mere ornament, so may superstition make a
mountain out of every mole-hill. (Ver. 4, to τὰ πετεινά Luke adds :
τοῦ οὐρανοῦ, analogous to the Hebrew הַשָּׁמַיִם עוֹף. Βάθος τῆς γῆς =
βαθεῖα γῆ.—Καυματίζεσθαι signifies "to be burnt up, scorched by the
sun ;" ξηραίνεσθαι "to wither," "to dry up altogether." Ver. 7,
ἀναβαίνειν = עָלָה, צָמַח, "to grow up," "to spring up." Mark iv. 8,
has the same numbers as Matthew—only inverted—which shews
that no stress is to be laid on their position. The well-known formula of emphasis : ὁ ἔχων ὦτα κ. τ. λ. calls to examination.)

Ver. 18–23.—We immediately subjoin to the parable the explanation by the Lord, which the disciples asked from him when
they were alone (καταμόνας, Mark iv. 10). The intervening important discourses we shall afterwards consider. The words : ἀκού-
σατε τὴν παραβολήν, must not be translated, hear the *exposition* of
the parable ; (*Schleusner* has even a special number, s. v. παραβολή,
in which he assigns to it the signification of : "explanation of a
parable") ; on the contrary, it is only by comprehending it that a
history becomes a parable. Our Lord draws a parallel between the
four kinds of fields, and the four kinds of disposition of heart in those
who receive the word of God, scattered abroad (Luke viii. 11). The
parable here passes at once to direct discourse ; for, whereas in the
parable the seed is mentioned which developes differently, according to the nature of the soil into which it falls, here the individuals
are introduced in whom this development takes place. The direct
discourse is, in a peculiar manner, mixed up with the parabolical
language, as in Matthew, in the phrases : ὁ παρὰ τὴν ὁδόν, ἐπὶ τὰ
πετρώδη, εἰς τὰς ἀκάνθας σπαρείς, *that sown by the way-side, on the rocks,
among the thorns.* In Luke only (viii. 14, 15) the neuter several
times occurs. As regards the description of the first disposition of
heart, it is not represented *per se*, but only in its consequences, which,
however, admit of an inference as to the disposition itself. A hearing (ἀκούειν) of the word is supposed, but not an understanding
(συνιέναι) ; on the contrary a losing of it. Although a positive
cause, lying external to the individual described, is assigned for this
losing ; namely, the prince of darkness who is anxious to prevent
the gaining of souls (ἵνα μὴ πιστεύσαντες σωθῶσιν, Luke viii. 12), yet,
it is quite evident that the possibility of such an agency of the
prince of this world has its reason in the disposition of the mind.

The figure (the ὁδός, *way, road,*) indicates a hardness which arose from, and was brought about by, external causes. There is in them a want of susceptibility, an inability to believe, which prevents them from receiving the word. Even though in such persons, that which is divine should find a certain entrance into the heart (ἐν τῇ καρδίᾳ * Matth. xiii. 19), yet it is not received in its nature and essence (μὴ συνιέντος); it does not sink deep enough to be secured against the attacks of the hostile principle ; but into the γῇ καλή, *good ground* (ver. 23), the evil power does not enter, and hence ,the divine element may there freely display itself. It is remarkable, that in this first part of the parable, the birds (πετεινά) (ver. 4) are explained by the evil one, πονηρός, (according to Mark, σατανᾶς, according to Luke, διάβολος †)—an explanation which, if it had not been given by the Lord himself would scarcely have been received. The figure (τὰ πετεινά) would have been resolved into the general notion of injurious influences. But here we have evidently a passage in which, as in v. 39, our Redeemer speaks of the devil in a *didactic manner,* and that too, unsolicited, and in the most intimate circle of his disciples. The second state of mind described, is a kindred one, although differing widely, in its outward manifestation. In the heart there is the same want of susceptibility to divine influences (τὰ πετρώδη); its higher and nobler impulses are all on the surface.‡ The beginning of life raises fair expectations (μετὰ χαρᾶς λαμβάνει λόγον θεοῦ), but the plant cannot take deep root (ἰκμάς [Luke viii. 6] = ὑγρότης); the nourishing moisture is wanting ; such an one therefore is *for a season* (πρόσκαιρος, explained by Luke by πρὸς καιρὸν πιστεύει,) the contrast to αἰώνιος, *permanent* (2 Cor. iv. 8). In the hour of temptation (ἐν καιρῷ πειρασμοῦ), which Matthew and Mark by the terms θλίψις, *affliction,* and διωγμός, *persecution,* characterise more specially as coming from without, they fall away (Luke, ἀφίστανται ; Matthew and Mark, σκανδαλίζονται: compare concerning σκάνδαλον, the remarks on Matth. xviii. 8). The use of ἥλιος, *sun* (Matth. xiii. 6) in parabolical language, in the signification of " scorching heat," is

* In the phrase ἐσπαρμένον ἐν τῇ καρδίᾳ, it is not necessary to interchange εἰς with ἐν ; it means: the seed which was scattered abroad, and is now in the heart.

† It is to me incomprehensible how *Schleiermacher* (*Glaubenslehre,* B. 1, S. 213) can say that " the terms here are of doubtful interpretation, and that the enmity of men to the divine word is as obvious as the reference to the devil." The terms: ὁ σατανᾶς, ὁ διάβολος (with the article, and without any thing preceding to which they might possibly be referred) cannot by any means be explained as referring to man.

‡ The figure is drawn from fields common in the Jura formation. The dry, parched limestone is covered with a thin soil. Amidst the coolness of spring the seed germinates, but the growing warmth of the sun heats the rock and dries up the seed; an image of the religion of *feeling* which admits the animating and comforting influences of the Gospel, but falls away when it seeks to make *a new man* (as the stony heart remains) ; of the religion of *fashion,* which also receives Christianity until conflict arises.—[E.

found in the Old Testament also (Ps. cxxi. 6 ; Isaiah xlix. 10, comp. with Rev. vii. 16). In the third state of heart, it is not insensibility which prevents the development of the divine word. Thorns choke the germ: foreign elements are blended in the mind with the principle of divine life. [The image is clear : the heart does not remain essentially stony : a real conversion has taken place, but wicked desires are not thoroughly eradicated. Their evil seed lurks in the heart, and springing up with the good seed chokes it.] As that which prevents the growth of the heavenly germ, two forms are pointed out, in which sin manifests itself in the present course of the world (αἰὼν οὗτος). First, the μέριμνα, care, the oppressive, burdensome part of this earthly life, whereby men are drawn away from God ; and, secondly, the ἀπάτη τοῦ πλούτου, deceitfulness of riches, the alluring part of it, which, in a delusive manner, seems to appease the cravings of the soul. This second form of the pernicious influences of the worldly principle is more fully described by Luke viii. 14, in the additional clause : ἡδοναὶ τοῦ βίου, pleasures of life. (Βίος signifies here, like seculum, man's temporal existence as it appears blended with sin [comp. 2 Tim. ii. 4]. From this the Church Fathers derived : βιωτικόν, βιωτικά = secularia, " what belongs to," "what concerns this world." Comp. Suiceri Thes. s. h. v. and Luke xxi. 34 ; 1 Cor. v. 3, 4.) Mark uses instead of ἡδοναί, pleasures, the expression αἱ περὶ τὰ λοιπὰ ἐπιθυμίαι, lusts of other things, so that other allurements of the world of sense are conjoined with wealth, as exercising equal influence. These heterogeneous things withdraw from the divine the undivided attention which it requires, and hence it cannot unfold itself in its power. (Συμπνίγουσι τὸν λόγον, ἄκαρπος γίνεται, οὐ τελεσφοροῦσι, according to Luke. The word τελεσφορέω is found only in Luke viii. 14 ; it signifies "to bring to the end," " to finish.") But the fruit of the Spirit is the end of the inner spiritual life, which the word of God, sown into the heart, is to attain (Gal. v. 22), inasmuch as this supposes that it has exercised its full influence upon the whole inner man. That this spiritual fruit grows up from the divine word sown in the heart, is precisely the characteristic feature in the fourth and last disposition of heart which the Redeemer calls figuratively good ground, a spiritual soil, with full receptivity, in which the progress of development is interrupted by none of the above-mentioned obstacles. The various expressions of the Evangelists render most perceptible the influence of the heavenly doctrine upon such hearts. According to Matthew, with hearing is connected a συνιέναι, an understanding, a grasping of divine truth in its peculiar nature, as contrasted with that in ver. 19. According to Mark, it is a παραδέχεσθαι, a receiving into the depth of life, opposed to the losing in ver. 15. According to Luke, it is a κατέχειν, retaining, which points out the activity of the will in preserving the acquired principle of divine life, and in repelling all heterogeneous influences, opposed to ver. 14; Luke has, moreover, the significant expression: ἐν ὑπομονῇ, *enduringly*, in order to represent the bringing forth of fruit, as the result of the gradual penetration of the inner life by divine influence, and by no means depending on the mere instantaneous determination of the will. Matthew and Mark farther point out, in figurative language, the various degrees of fruitfulness. Without overstraining the meaning of " an hundred, sixty, thirty," we may yet assert that the numbers not only indicate different degrees of natural endowment, on which depends the abundance of fruit (comp. Matth. xxv. 14, seq.), or the degrees of carefulness expended on its growth ; but also, that even in this part of the great kingdom of God, everything is distributed according to *order* and *rule;* that thus the powers and susceptibilities implanted in various individuals are not lavished indiscriminately, but bestowed according to law and order.

In the accounts of Luke viii. 16-18, and Mark iv. 21-25, there follow immediately upon the explanation of the parable thus given by the Lord, certain words which are wanting in Matthew, but which are not without importance for the deeper understanding of it. The connexion of these verses with the foregoing parable is obvious, if we bear in mind that the Saviour, in passing on to another comparison, shows how the apostles were the good ground, and therefore called to bring forth seed and fruit, which in turn were to be still further fruitful. The light which has been kindled, and which is intended to diffuse its radiance, is thus equivalent to the seed scattered abroad and designed to grow up,* and the general idea which follows, " for there is nothing hidden," etc., contains merely the affirmation that everything wrapped up in the divine word shall gradually unfold and disclose itself. To this is subjoined the admonition, βλέπετε οὖν πῶς ἀκούετε· ὃς γὰρ ἂν ἔχῃ δοθήσεται αὐτῷ, καὶ ὃς ἂν μὴ ἔχῃ καὶ ὃ δοκεῖ ἔχειν, ἀρθήσεται ἀπ' αὐτοῦ, *beware then how ye hear, for whosoever hath, etc.* The same words stand at Matth. xiii. 12, but are somewhat differently introduced. The original connexion may probably have been preserved by Luke and Mark. For according to them, the words evidently aim to guard against a possible misunderstanding of the parable, to wit, that the states of mind, described as existing in different men, and the consequent variety of effects wrought in them by the word of God, originate in any inherent *necessity*. The admonition βλέπετε κ. τ. λ., and especially the remark ὃς γὰρ ἂν ἔχῃ κ. τ. λ. takes for granted the freedom of choice

---

* The same intermingling of the two comparisons of seed and light is found also in Philo; ἀθάνατα ἔκγονα μόνη τίκτειν ἀφ' ἑαυτῆς οἷα τε ἐστιν ἡ θεοφιλὴς ψυχὴ σπείραντος εἰς αὐτὴν ἀκτῖνας νοητὰς τοῦ πατρὸς, αἷς δυνήσεται θεωρεῖν τὰ σοφίας δόγματα. *De vita theoret.* Opp. v. ii., p. 482. Mangey.

and the influence of self-determination, amidst all differences of internal organization. For, according to the connexion, the having and not having (as conjoined with the "seeming to have") refer to the fruit really or only apparently produced. The having (ἔχειν) admits also of being referred to the good ground, to which the fruit stands related, as cause to effect ; but the former view is to be preferred. Thus understood, the entire sentiment (*Gnome*) is, that the divine principle, where it has once manifested itself in fruit-producing power, developes itself with ever increasing purity and excellence ; but where it fails to be efficacious, the man not only sinks back to his former state, but still lower, and loses even that which he vainly imagined himself to possess. This idea plainly leads to the further conclusion that the states of mind depicted in the parable are not to be conceived of as definitely restricted to certain classes of characters, but as possible to be realized in the same person *successively* in different periods and situations of life, so that equally, on the one hand, may the hard stony heart, by a faithful use of grace, be ennobled into a good and fruitful soil for the divine word, and the good ground, on the other, by faithlessness, be desolated and destroyed. [Most certainly the four varieties of soul represent not four classes of natural endowments, but four modes of relation to the Gospel, e. g., the rocky soil marks the man who is never spiritually converted ; the thorny soil, him who is indeed converted, but by unfaithfulness in pursuing sanctification, falls from his state of grace, etc.*] Mark makes an addition (Mark iv. 26–29), which presents the comparison of the seed sown in the field with a modification not found in the other evangelists. It stands in immediate connexion with the preceding idea, that wherever the divine principle takes root in a soul, it manifests itself in ever increasing blessing according to the power which dwells in it, and which is ever tending to outward manifestation. The comparison therefore sets forth this indwelling energy (and in this respect it is allied to the parable of the leaven), quite as strongly as it does the inability of him who soweth the seed of the divine word to effect its growth, that growth proceeding wholly from itself as the general law of all development implies. (Mark iv. 26, 27, contains a representation of the gradual growth of the seed without the co-operation of the sower; Καθεύδειν, ἐγείρεσθαι, *sleeping* and *waking*, is merely a description of what happens in ordinary life, which excludes any further attention to the seed that has been sown. Independently of the efforts of man the earth itself [αὐτομάτη] brings forth fruit. What properly belongs to the seed is here attributed to the earth, as determining its

* The first variety marks a heart uninfluenced by divine truth; the second, a superficial, not a real conversion; so the third, if the unfruitfulness is to be taken as absolute.—[K.

growth ; otherwise, it is of no importance to the understanding of the similitude. The expression αὐτόματος, *self-moved, spontaneous,* does not occur elsewhere, except at Acts xii. 10. The growth by progressive stages, is described by the words χόρτος [the first springing of the corn which is grass-like], στάχυς [the sprouting of the ears], σῖτος [the ripened grain]. In verse 29th, παραδῷ, scil. ἑαυτόν, *produces itself,* is used after the analogy of the Latin *se dare, tradere,* as *Virgil,* Georg. i. 287, *multa adeo gelida melius se nocte dederunt.* Compare also the Hebrew םלֵשׁ, the Chaldee, םלֵשׁ, Ezra vii. 19 [see *Buxt.* Lex. Talm. p. 2422]. Δρέπανον sickle, stands for the labourers bearing the sickle ; the θερισταί, see Matth. xiii. 39.) There is only one difficulty in this parabolical discourse, as given by Mark, the circumstance namely, that the sower, who after scattering the seed goes away, is none other than the Son of man, as our Lord's explanations afterwards shew (Matth. xiii. 37), and as is indeed indicated by the very fact, that the Lord, when the harvest is come, sends the reapers into the field, an act which, according to Matth. xiii. 39, must be referred to the time of the judgment (κρίσις). But in what sense it can be said of the Lord that he lets the field grow without caring for its advancement, one does not well see, inasmuch as grace is required equally at the commencement and throughout the course of the divine life. Every thing would appear to harmonize better if we could understand by the man who sows, any and every teacher who may be labouring in the Lord's vineyard, and who certainly after implanting the word in the heart, must leave it to its own further development. Perhaps, however, such difficulties shew that the similitudes ought not to be pushed thus far. The very nature of a similitude implies that on some point or other, the thing compared must differ from that to which it is likened, else the two would be identical. But in this case we are precluded from this recourse, by observing that this abandonment of care for the seed sown is the specific point of the comparison. Unless, therefore, the whole is to have the appearance of inanity, meaning and force must be given to this point. Perhaps then, according to Matth. ix. 15, the meaning of the entire parabolical discourse may be taken in this way : although spiritual life in its development in man, is never absolutely without the grace and presence of the Lord, yet may it be said that there are two special periods when that grace is pre-eminently active. The first is the commencement of the life (the sowing), the second is the ripening of the fruit (the harvest). Between these points lies a period, during which it may be said, that comparatively the soul is without the Lord, the divine life implanted in man developing itself according to its own inherent power, and to this season perhaps, a season of internal struggle and conflict, the Lord here refers. Thus understood, the comparison gains for itself, at least, a specific meaning, and its connexion is made clear with what had gone before. Nor does this explanation exclude a reference to individual human teachers, only this does not appear as the thing primarily intended.

It is in another sense, however, that the words : ὃς γὰρ ἂν ἔχῃ κ. τ. λ., *for whoever hath, etc.*, are interwoven into the discourse by Matth. in the verses of which we are now to give the explanation. According to ver. 10, seq. the disciples came to Jesus and asked him generally what was his purpose in thus speaking in parables (διατί ἐν παραβολαῖς λαλεῖς αὐτοῖς;). The Lord replies, that he employed them on account of the differences in the character of his hearers, some of whom he wished to understand him, others not. In speaking by parables, this twofold object would be gained, for everything that it was needful for him to state would thus be declared, but in a form so veiled that only those understood it who were designed to understand it. Among these the disciples are mentioned first of all, and in this connexion is it said " for whosoever hath," etc., (ver. 12.) The idea thus appears under a different form from that in which we find it in Luke and Mark. The apostles are represented as they who *have*, on whom, for this reason, there flows in the abundance (περίσσευμα), but the rest as they who have not, who lose for this reason what they already have, to whom the appearance of the light itself tends to bring destruction. Before considering, however, this idea, which is further developed in the following verses, we must attend to the expression : μυστήρια τῆς βασιλείας τῶν οὐρανῶν (τοῦ Θεοῦ), *mysteries of the kingdom of heaven (of God).* It marks the general object of the parables, and in those very parables which follow throughout this chapter, reference to it is express and constant. The word μυστήριον then, from μυέω to *initiate*, is in the New Testament used to denote the divine counsels, decrees, doctrines, which, as such, could never have become known to men as such, to men if left to themselves. (So the Heb. רָז in the Old Testament.) Nowhere, however, are these decrees, etc., represented as absolutely and eternally hid, and incapable of being known ; but God, who at the prompting of his own love reveals himself and all that is in him, is constantly (by his ἀποκάλυψις) revealing his mysteries ; yet not in such a way that they cease to be mysteries (μυστήρια) ; they retain for ever their divine character, which exalted them above all the powers of discovery belonging to man himself; instead of hidden, they have become unveiled μυστήρια. (1 Cor. ii. 7 ; Rom. xvi. 25.) According to this view, the mysteries of the kingdom of heaven denote the whole system of divine counsels, ordinances, and doctrines, which have been revealed through Christ, and through the new economy which he founded. They stand in contrast, as it were, with the mysteries of the law (μυστήρια τοῦ νόμου), which, after the fulfilment of the Old Testament economy, had to make way for a new system of mysteries. This whole collection of mysteries, however, was made known only to some (ὑμῖν δέδοται γνῶναι), from others it was hid (according to Mark τοῖς ἔξω, to those *without*, as opposed to the apostles τοῖς ἔσω, those *within*. Compare Paul's mode of expression on this subject at 1 Cor. v. 12, 13 ; Col. iv. 5 ; 1 Thess. iv. 12.) In the δέδοται, *it is given*, there is an unmistakeable reference to the decree of God. It implies first, the positive exercise of divine grace, in communicating the blessing, and, negatively, the inability of man's will to attain of itself the thing bestowed. He uses the expression in the same sense as at Matthew xix. 11 ; xx. 23, and especially at John iii. 27 ; vi. 65 ; xix. 11, with the addition of ἄνωθεν, ἐκ τοῦ οὐρανοῦ. But this idea, that the passage asserts the giving and the withholding a knowledge of the secrets of the divine kingdom, forms precisely the great difficulty that meets us in this and the following verses (ver. 13-15), where at greater length it is explained, and founded on Old Testament prophecy.

According to the narrative of Matthew xiii. 13, the idea certainly seems put in such a form as to intimate that Christ's speaking in parables was simply a *consequence* resulting from the blindness and insensibility of a portion of his hearers. For the expression employed is, I speak in parables *because* seeing, etc. (ἐν παραβολαῖς λαλῶ ὅτι βλέποντες οὐ βλέπουσι κ. τ. λ.), while Mark and Luke in the corresponding passage give, *in order that* seeing they may not see (ἵνα βλέποντες μὴ βλέπωσι), words which obviously mean that their failing to understand him was the *object designed* by our Lord in using the language of the parables. But that in Matthew's account of our Lord's discourse he meant to convey no meaning different from that of the other evangelists, is shewn first by the quotation from the Old Testament, which of itself expresses as strongly the same idea, and in the next place, if we take the ὅτι in ver. 13, to denote the *cause* which led to his speaking in parables, it implies something self-contradictory. " For this reason do I speak to them in parables, *because* they do not understand," is a mode of thought which admits of no justification.* For if they wholly failed to comprehend him, we do not see why the Lord did not speak at once in simple unfigurative terms, in which there would, at least, have been a better chance of his being understood than in speaking before men of dull apprehension in language obscure and veiled. And according to this view, the possibility of his being understood

---

* The words could only be so interpreted if the parables were to be considered as means for *facilitating* the understanding of the subject referred to. But against this view the passage ἐκείνοις δὲ οὐ δέδοται (v. 11), is so decisive that the point admits of no further discussion.

must, to a certain extent, be assumed, as otherwise it would have been more to the purpose for him to have refrained from speaking altogether. On the other hand, the idea is a very simple one:—"I speak in parables *in order that* they may not understand," and this view has been attempted to be got rid of simply on account of the dogmatic difficulties it involves—difficulties which do not concern the interpreter of Scripture. According to the connexion, therefore, the words in Matth. xiii. 13 should be translated only in this way, " I speak to them in parables, *for* seeing, they see not," so that the result is represented as an effect contemplated and designed. This is plainly shewn also immediately afterwards at ver. 15, by the expression μήποτε ἴδωσι, *lest perchance they may see*, in the prophecy of Isaiah (comp. Mark iv. 12.) Attempts have been made, it is true, to put such a meaning on the μήποτε here, and the ἴνα in Luke and Mark, as to take away from both particles the idea of *design*. And it is not to be denied that μήποτε (as was already remarked in regard to ἴνα on Matth. i. 22), sometimes, in the New Testament, wants the sense of intention, or design. Especially convincing in support of this view of μήποτε, is the passage 2 Tim. ii. 25, μήποτε δῷ αὐτοῖς ὁ θεὸς μετάνοιαν, which it is utterly impossible to translate, "*in order that* God may not grant them repentance," but rather " whether God (εἰ ποτε) will not bestow on them repentance." According to this the passage before us (ver. 15) might be rendered—whether they might not see, whether they might not hear. The reference however to the prophecy (Isa. vi. 9, 10), which is also introduced in the same sense at John xii. 39, seq.; Acts xxviii. 26, seq., admits no interpretation of the passage except the teleological. Matthew and also Luke in the Acts of the Apostles, follow with unimportant variations the reading of the LXX. while John, on the contrary, has given a translation of his own which expresses however the idea with the utmost distinctness. He writes οὐκ ἠδύναντο πιστεύειν, *they could not believe*, and ἴνα μὴ ἴδωσι, *that they may not see*, so that only the utmost violence of interpretation will allow the passage any other sense than this, that the design was they should not understand. The connexion of the words also in the Old Testament clearly shews the same meaning. (Compare Gesenius in his Commentary on the passage Isa. vi. 9, 10.) It is represented as the penalty, as the curse of sin, that it prevents man's understanding the revelation of divine truth. (The βλέπειν and ἀκούειν, *seeing* and *hearing*, as contrasted with the οὐ συνιέναι, οὐκ ἰδεῖν, *not understanding*, *not seeing*, denote the opportunity given of understanding the divine will as being unfolded in their immediate presence, while they did not possess the susceptibility necessary for embracing it. This want of susceptibility—the inability to believe—is denoted by ἐπαχύνθη = הַשְׁמֵן, " *to become fat*," in the sense of "*to become unfeeling or insensible.*" It stands as parallel to the הַכְבֵּד and הָשַׁע which in the Greek are rendered βαρέως ἀκούειν, καμμύειν. Καμμύειν is a barbarous form for καταμύειν = κλείειν τοὺς ὀφθαλμούς. The verb ἐπιστρέφειν = שׁוּב, *to abandon a path which had been already entered on,* denotes here, as frequently elsewhere the turning of the soul from darkness to light. In the last clause, καὶ ἰάσωμαι αὐτούς, a various reading, ἰάσομαι, is found, which certainly has been transferred from the LXX. in order to soften the passage by giving to the words the sense of "but I will heal them." This interpretation however does not agree with the connexion of the Hebrew, in which וְרָפָא בֹּ וְשָׁב, holds a position entirely parallel. In Mark accordingly, the whole force of the idea is preserved, though the figure of "healing" (ἰάσομαι), is explained by the words "that their sins may not be forgiven them," a rendering transferred also to the Chaldee version.) In its original connexion, the passage Isa. vi. 9, 10, refers primarily to the contemporaries of Isaiah. Matthew sees in it a reference to the contemporaries of Jesus, not judging capriciously, but taking a profound view of its real import. For the phenomena of the prophetic times did not differ from those of the age of our Saviour ; regarded in their essential relations, they were identical. Divine truth, as disclosed in the discourse of Isaiah, was met by the insensibility of the people whom he summoned to spiritual effort, and the curse of their sin was that they did not even recognise the evidences of divinity. In the time of Jesus the same nation went through the same experience, with only this difference, that in Jesus there was exhibited to the people the purest manifestation of Divinity, of which Isaiah presented but a faint reflection. Inasmuch then, as even this splendour of divine light was unrecognised by them, the curse of sin was exhibited in all its magnitude, and the prophet's words met here their entire fulfilment. [The great body of the people were carnally-minded. Hence Jesus was *compelled* to select his disciples, and hence also to reveal truth in the enigmatical form of parables, intelligible to the spiritually-minded disciples, but destined to remain inexplicable to the carnal populace—to all, in fact, who are carnally-minded.]

Ver. 16, 17.—In contrast with the curse, which strikes these hardened hearts, follows the blessing which is imparted to the believing and receptive spirits of the disciples. The ὀφθαλμοί, ὦτα, *eyes, ears,* are mentioned as the organs of reception in general, which have their analogies in the inner man. At Luke x. 23, these words occur in an entirely different connexion, to which we shall attend hereafter. He adds, that Jesus addressed these words to the disciples when by themselves (κατ' ἰδίαν = καταμόνας, Mark iv. 10, 34), a fact which might have been inferred even from their contents.

The comparison of his disciples to the προφῆται, *prophets*, and the δίκαιοι, *righteous men*, of the Old Testament (Luke, instead of the δίκαιοι, has the word βασιλεῖς, *kings*, an expression, however, which must in this case be held as applying to *righteous* kings), would have been unintelligible to the multitude. Finally the idea expressed in ver. 17, is simply an exposition of the frequently occurring πλεῖον 'Ιωνᾶ, πλεῖον Σολομῶνος ὧδε, *a greater than Jonah, than Solomon is here* (Matth. xii. 41, 42). All the longing desires of the pious throughout the Old Testament centred in the Messiah. To behold him was the loftiest object of Old Testament hope. This blessing was granted to the disciples, and all their happiness, all their glory, consisted in this, that they were illumined by the radiance of the Sun of righteousness. The special grace thus vouchsafed is brought to their remembrance by Christ, not to exalt them above the Old Testament saints, but to lay them low before the Lord.

Ver. 24–30.—From this same figure of seed-sowing, arises a second similitude, which however contemplates a different aspect of the kingdom of God. Of this parabolic statement also, an authentic explanation is given by the Lord, ver. 36–41, which again we shall take up immediately. (The ὡμοιώθη ἡ βασιλεία τῶν οὐρανῶν ἀνθρώπῳ, *the kingdom of heaven is likened to a man*, is an abbreviated form of expression—one point of the similitude is brought prominently forward, and on it the comparison is concentrated. Here it is the man who scatters the seed, and so at ver. 33, it is, the ζύμη, *leaven*, at ver. 44, the θησαυρός, *treasure*, at ver. 47, the σαγήνη, *net*, at ver. 45, the ἄνθρωπος ἔμπορος, *merchant*. The word παρατιθέναι = םוֹשׂ, is here selected with reference to the enigmatical character of parabolical language—he laid the parable before them, for solution. In the σπείρειν ἐν τῷ ἀγρῷ, we must beware of supposing that there is any confounding of εἰς and ἐν, he sowed *upon* his field as the place of his labour. The night-time is described (ἐν τῷ καθεύδειν τοὺς ἀνθρώπους), as at Job xxxiii. 15. Ver. 25.—ζιζάνια, in the Talmud זוּנין. Comp. *Buxtorf. Lex. Talm.* fol. 680, Suid. ἡ ἐν τῷ σίτῳ αἷρα, i. e., lolium [*Virg.* Ecl. v. 37, *infelix lolium*] *cockle, darnel*. The weed shewed itself first at the springing time [βλαστάνειν], and latterly when the fruit was forming [καρπὸν ποιεῖν], and it could not therefore be then stifled by the grain. Ver. 28.—'Απελθόντες συλλέξωμεν, *go and gather up*, represented as spoken, after the analogy of the Hebrew, הָלַךְ, in the house of the οἰκοδεσπότης, but neither here nor in any other passage where הָלַךְ is used are we to regard it as an empty pleonasm. Ver. 30.—Θεριστής = ὁ θερίζων, occurs only here : δέσμη is also an ἅπαξ λεγόμενον = אֲגֻדָּה. Exodus xii. 22. An Old Testament comparison lies at the foundation of this whole parable of the burning up of the tares. Comp. 2 Sam. xxiii. 7, where the same reference had already been made to the final judgment. The ἀποθήκη corresponds to the Hebrew, אָסָם, "*granary, store-house.*"

Ver. 36–43.—The explanation of the parable was in this instance also communicated to the disciples when alone, after the people had been dismissed (ver. 36). In brief clauses our Lord expounds the several portions of the comparison, the last point, however, the final separation of the good from the bad, on which the whole turns, being given with more minuteness. But for this express exposition by Christ another interpretation would unquestionably at first sight have suggested itself. Jesus explains the field as being the *world* (κόσμος), the good seed as the children of the kingdom (υἱοὶ τῆς βασιλείας), the tares (ζιζάνια) as the children of the wicked one (υἱοὶ τοῦ πονηροῦ), and consequently the whole human race, good and bad together, are viewed as the corn that is growing up in the world, a word which here seems like *orbis terrarum,* to denote the universal earth. The generality of this reference does not appear at first sight to agree with the connexion, since the subject of discourse is not the whole world (ver. 24), but the kingdom of heaven. That in the world at large evil intermingles itself with good, is obvious at a glance, but it is strange that in the kingdom of God itself, even to its close, the same intermixture should be seen, for the express design of that kingdom is to represent the good. Beyond all doubt, then, this similitude must be understood of the kingdom of God, which, however, is here in so far termed the world, as viewed ideally, it is destined to pervade the whole world, or conversely, the world is ideally represented as destined of God to become his kingdom.* The derangement of this original purpose by the influence of the kingdom of darkness, the Saviour here explains, and defines the relative connexion of good and evil in the church of God on earth, as well under the Old as the New Testament, down to the final judgment. The Son of man, consequently appears here again, in his ideal dignity (comp. Dan. vii. 13), as the adversary of the devil, as from the beginning onward he has been working out the victory of good among the human race. This, moreover, is another of the passages in which Christ refers in his teaching literally and directly to the devil. The disciples had requested an authoritative exposition of a similitude that was dark to them. In no point of view was there an occasion for concession to popular prejudice (even if the idea of such accommodation were not essentially inconsistent

---

* The (as yet vacant) soil on which the seed is sown is the *world.* The *field,* which consists of tares and grain in inseparable mixture, is the *church.* The kingdom of God exists not in visible separation from the world, but as mingled with the world—as a *church.* Hence again the church is not identical with the kingdom of God, but a blending of the kingdom of God and the world.—[E.

with the holy character of Jesus), and still less for recourse to proverbs or any thing else of the kind. While, however, the parable as a whole is clear, yet on particular points we are met by important difficulties. Thus the contrast of the child of the kingdom (υἱὸς τῆς βασιλείας), and of the wicked one (τοῦ πονηροῦ), seems to point to an absolute severance of individuals, which might again seem to favour the doctrine of predestination. But the prohibition forbidding the rooting out of evil (ver. 28) at once sufficiently shews that neither the children of the kingdom are conceived of as entirely dissevered from evil, nor the children of the wicked one as wholly dissociated from good. The one class appear only as in a certain respect the concentration of good (not however that any irresistible grace preserves them from falling back), the other as the concentration of evil (not however that any decree of reprobation forces them into wickedness, and holds them back from the possibility of repentance), drawn by birth, circumstances, education, now more towards the one element, now more towards the other. For though all men are involved in sin, yet are they not all in an equal degree under its power; sincerity, uprightness, and susceptibility for everything good, being beyond all mistake manifest in some, while others display malice, obstinacy, hardness of heart. It is strange however, that this prohibition to separate these elements before their becoming ripe should be the thing *omitted* in the Lord's explanation, whether it be that Matthew has abridged his exposition, or whether it be that the Saviour wished merely to set prominently forth the great final separation, thus sufficiently indicating that until that separation take effect, no arbitrary, and therefore merely pernicious attempt to dissever them ought to be made.* It is indeed self-evident that this does not prohibit the severance of sinful from virtuous elements ; it means only that no *person* should be shut out from intercourse with the good *as incorrigible*, [nor should the church attempt judicially to burn and destroy the supposed children of evil. What is forbidden to the angels will hardly be successfully accomplished by men]: there is always the possibility that the beneficent influence of good may awaken in him the slumbering elements of improvement. At the same time, however, it admits of no doubt, that according to the meaning of this parable, all *violent* interference with the course or life led by the sinful members of the church (not merely death, but also final excommunication), as well

* The view of this parable recently put forth by Steiger (Ev. K. Z. Feb. 1833, p. 113, seq.) to the effect that it is simply prophetico-historical, *i. e.*, that it contains no admonitions intended to guide the conduct of believers, but merely instructs us in the truth that the church shall never on earth be pure, is obviously untenable, for in that case the account of the servant's zeal in wishing to root out the weeds, and the Lord's prohibition, would be mere decorations incidentally introduced to adorn the similitude—a supposition which clearly is most arbitrary, and destructive to the character of the parable.

as every arbitrary effort to realize absolute purity of communion on earth (Donatism), is forbidden, because the former leads to harshness and injustice, the latter inevitably to pride and blindness. For as *within* man, even the best, there exists a mixture similar to that which prevails *without* him, the effect can only be most pernicious, if, overlooking the sin that is in his soul, he holds himself forth to others as a *pure* member. The view here inculcated leads simply to humility, mildness, and yet to constant watchfulness, for the improvement of one's self and others. For no admonition, or appropriate church discipline or other methods of dealing with the lives of sin ful members of the church, *not forcible* in their nature are excluded. What man however is unable to separate, that the all-knowing God dissevers finally in the συντέλεια τοῦ αἰῶνος τούτου, *end of this world*. The meaning of this expression cannot here be very accurately determined ; generally and comprehensively it denotes simply the conclusion of the course of this world's affairs, as the period in which good and evil are blended. That this severance is advancing of itself step by step, that it has been going on throughout the course of the world's history, that it was decisively manifested in the founding of a visible kingdom of God, and will be finally consummated in the universal judgment—are truths not touched on in the passage here before us. There is merely presented to us the great principle of divine judgment as unfolded in the Bible, that one day the holy and the unholy shall be mutually and wholly separated, but up to that period they shall remain ripening together, each according to its own nature. (Comp. in regard to συντέλεια τ. α. what is said at Matth. xii. 31 ; and xxiv. 1). On account of the judgment as here given, the kingdom of God is contemplated as the only true and proper existence, from which it is merely required that foreign admixtures be expelled, in order to manifest its real nature (The sending of the ἄγγελοι, and the entire imagery under which the punishment is set forth, will be explained more fully at Matth. xxiv. 31; xxv. 30, 31. The σκάνδαλα, *stumbling-blocks, causes of stumbling,* be it also observed, and the ποιοῦντες τὴν ἀνομίαν, *they who practice iniquity,* are not to be taken as synonymous—the former is the more forcible expression. Κάμινος πυρός = πῦρ αἰώνιον. As to κλαυθμὸς καὶ βρυγμὸς ὀδόντων, see on Matth. viii. 12.) After the expulsion of evil as the element of darkness, good reveals itself in its pure nature as light. (Τότε οἱ δίκαιοι ἐκλάμψουσι, as children of light—children of God the πατὴρ τῶν φώτων [James i. 17]. The words are chosen with reference to Dan. xii. 3. Comp. Wisdom iii. 7, 4 ; Ezra vii. 55.)

The *third* parable, of the mustard seed, is at once seen to be far less fully carried out than the two which precede it. It approaches the character of a mere comparison, for it is simply the nature of the mustard seed itself, and of the plant growing out of it, which is employed to illustrate the kingdom of God. In Luke this parable, and the following one of the leaven, also occur, but in another connexion, which we shall afterwards consider more at length. (In the parable the μικρότερον, and the μεῖζον, with the genitive following them, have certainly the force of the superlative, only too much stress in this respect must not be laid on them. Λάχανον, = יָרָק, vegetables, cabbage-like plants generally. The πετεινὰ τοῦ οὐρανοῦ, birds of heaven, appear here in a connexion wholly different from that at Matth. xiii. 4, as representing all those who seek protection and refuge in the kingdom of God, according to Ezek. xvii. 23, which passage seems to lie at the foundation of this whole comparison. As in various classes of objects various characteristics are expressed, so in the parabolic language of Scripture, they may express a variety of conceptions.) The idea set forth in this parable is obviously this—that in the unfolding of the kingdom of God, its commencement and consummation stand in reversed relation to each other. Starting from invisible beginnings, it spreads itself abroad over an all-embracing sphere of action. But as the kingdom of God itself may be conceived now in its aggregate character, now in special relations to single nations, or individuals, so also with the parables which set forth and illustrate its separate features. The rich thoughts deposited in them possess the same truth for the whole body, as for the private members, because truth is universally alike and consistent with itself.

Ver. 33.—The *fourth* parable of the leaven is closely allied to the foregoing, illustrating like it the all-pervading power of the heavenly element, and the efficiency of which does not depend on the extent of the mass on which it may have to act. The two parables differ simply in this, that, in the former, that of the mustard seed, the divine kingdom is exhibited as manifesting its powers *outwardly;* in that of the leaven as unseen, as working *in secret.* The leaven shows it at the same time acting on another element which it strives to draw, and transmute into its own nature, while the mustard seed illustrates the single point of its growth. (Ζύμη, *leaven,* is used, Matth. xvi. 6; 1 Cor. v. 7; Gal. v. 9, in a bad sense, with reference to the passover feast, Ex. xiii. 3. Its pervasive, seasoning power, forms here the single point of comparison with that divine element which wisdom, the heavenly mother, deposited in humanity, to leaven and hallow it. The word ἐγκρύπτειν, *hide,* indicates its secret invisibly-acting influence. Ἄλευρον, stands for the substance of the φύραμα, the meal, of which the dough was to be formed. The measure σάτον, according to Josephus [Antiq. ix. 2], contains μόδιον καὶ ἥμισυ Ἰταλικόν.* The mention of the particular measure indivi-

* Nearly 1½ peck English—[K.

dualizes the comparison as the nature of a parable requires. It were wrong expressly to apply the particular number to spiritual subjects, yet are we not perhaps altogether to deny some reference here to spirit, soul, and body, as the three powers of human nature to be sanctified by divine influence).

Ver. 44–50.—The last three parables, which however are given more as hints than in full detail, exhibit the kingdom of God in a way peculiar to themselves. They bring out the relation which men sustain to it, while the preceding ones had considered partly its nature in itself, and partly its relation to men. This peculiarity makes it not improbable that, as indicated in ver. 36, these latter parables were spoken confidentially to his immediate disciples, with whose relations to the kingdom of God, they singularly harmonize, as indeed with those of all who are connected with it like them as preachers of the Gospel. The first two parables respecting the *treasure* in the fields, and the *pearls*, stand related to each other in the same way as those of the leaven and the mustard seed. They represent the absolute value of divine things as compared with the relative value of every prized earthly treasure, and enjoin the sacrifice of the latter for the sake of the former. The abandonment, for the sake of heavenly treasure, of a man's whole possessions, whether external (property, goods, possessions), or internal (opinions, usages, general aims of life), the apostles had begun to put in practice, and the Saviour here intimates, that step by step they would be required to carry it out. But the two parables, though thus allied, have their points of difference. In both the precious object (the ϑησαυρός, or the μαργαρίτης), appears, it is true, as concealed, but they represent human effort in reference to the concealed treasure under different aspects. In that of the *pearls* a noble *active* nature is exhibited, which, under the pressure of inward impulse, seeks after (ζητεῖ), truth, and strives with lofty aim ; till at last in divine objects as revealed in Christ their centre, it discerns the substance of all that is desirable, and by complete self-renunciation secures its possession. The similitude of the treasure in the field, on the other hand, delineates a more *receptive* turn of mind in reference to spiritual things. They come unsought, unlooked for, yet has the soul the will and the power, at any price, to acquire possession of them ; active exertion (the ζητεῖν) is wanting. The history of a Peter and a Nathanael exemplify these different forms of development in human life (comp. John i.) In the parable of the treasure hid in the field, not only is bold, joyful, self-sacrificing zeal (ἀπὸ τῆς χαρᾶς αὐτοῦ ὑπάγει), commended, but praise seems also given to prudential management in divine things, inasmuch as the man who finds the treasure hides it again, and then buys the field from the owner without saying any thing of the treasure contained in it. Whatever might surprise us in this will be considered and explained when we come to the more difficult passage, Luke xvi., respecting the unjust steward. Another thing peculiar to the parable of the pearls is the contrast between unity and plurality. It expresses in a peculiar way the absolute importance of the one thing, and the merely relative value of everything else. Naturally this one thing can be no mere doctrine, no dogma, but something essential; it must be the divine itself in humanity, as exhibited in the person of Christ. That man should in his own experience find God in himself, and himself in God—this is the one pearl for whose acquisition he must, in a peculiar sense, be willing to part with all things that he may win all things. The oneness of the pearl, however, does not contradict the idea that there are a multitude who seek it, for precisely because it is in itself divine, therefore may each man seek and find it. It exists everywhere, inasmuch as the divine germ lies slumbering in all hearts, and requires only to be awakened by quickening, and life from on high.

The last similitude, of the *fishing-net*, is again closely allied to the second, of the tares in the field. Both represent the intermingling of good and bad in the kingdom of God, which are to be separated only at the end of the day. For, what in the parable of the tares is denoted by the harvest, is here shadowed forth by the completing of the draught of fishes. In verses 49, 50, the parabolic discourse is so explained as to correspond, word for word, with verses 41, 42, and our observations on the former passage therefore apply equally to this. The difference between the two similitudes might perhaps be most properly stated thus. In that of the tares, the kingdom of God is conceived in its ideal character, as identical with the whole world, while in this of the fishing-net, on the other hand, it is taken according to its actual appearance, as a smaller whole defined and marked off within the world, but including within itself the tendency to universal diffusion. This is indicated by the circumstance, that it is from the *sea*, which here conveys the idea of universality, that fishes are taken into the net of God's kingdom. Thus explained, the passage is another evidence that the Saviour himself did not in his visible church on earth acknowledge an absolutely pure communion. It belongs to the wondrous economy of God's grace, that in the whole course of man's temporal affairs, evil obtrudes itself by the side of good. As in the ark a Ham appears along with Shem and Japhet—as in the company of the twelve, a Judas—so has the spiritual Israel, the spiritual Jerusalem, a Babel in its bosom. By this arrangement the opportunity of repentance is extended to the wicked, and the child of light perfected in his conflict with the enemy. Not till the κρίσις ἐσχάτη, *last judgment*, will an entirely pure fellowship of saints be exhibited. The para-

ble gives us further an important hint as to the ἄγγελοι, to whom
the work of making a separation is entrusted. For they are obviously the same persons who first cast out the net, then draw it to
shore, and afterwards separate the fishes. If we compare then
Matth. iv. 19, where the Lord promises to the apostles that he will
make them fishers of men, it appears that by the ἄγγελοι, we
are to understand no spiritual beings from the heavenly world, but
men whom God has furnished as his messengers and servants, by
infusing into them heavenly powers for trying and proving the spirits of others. Thus had the כֹּהֵן, *priest*, already been styled at Mal.
ii. 7, מַלְאַךְ יְהוָֹה צְבָאֹות, *messenger of the Lord of hosts*. Although
therefore the apostles in one sense are themselves fishes (ἰχθῦς)
caught in the net of God's kingdom, yet are they in their renewal
and regeneration transformed into partners in the spiritual work of
him who first took them by the might of his love, an intimation
which is not without importance for the understanding of other
passages, such as Matth. xxiv. 31 ; xxv. 31, compared with Jude
ver. 14 ; 1 Cor. vi. 2, 3 ; xi. 31.

Ver. 51, 52.—Matthew concludes this collection of parables
with the question of Jesus to the disciples, συνήκατε ταῦτα πάντα,
have ye understood all these things ? If we compare Mark iv. 13,
we find a word of reproach uttered by Jesus against the little power
of understanding possessed by the disciples, and this question may
therefore be translated—have ye now then at last comprehended all
this ? Not that they should have gained an understanding of it
without explanation, but along with and by means of it. For Mark
observes, iv. 34, κατ᾽ ἰδίαν τοῖς μαθηταῖς αὐτοῦ ἐπέλυε πάντα, *he pri-
vately explained*, etc. (The verb ἐπιλύειν, points plainly to what
was enigmatical [חִידֹות] in the parabolic discourses of Christ). On
receiving the affirmative reply of the disciples, the Saviour gives
under another similitude a view of the peculiar nature and ministry
of a γραμματεύς, *scribe*, in that more exalted sense in which the character ought to belong to the apostles. The διὰ τοῦτο, *on this account*, refers back to the preceding ναὶ κύριε, *yea, Lord*, of the
apostles, the force of it being—" on this account can ye now fulfil
your calling for," etc., etc. Obviously, however, the reading τῇ
βασιλείᾳ must here be preferred to the other ἐν βασιλείᾳ or εἰς βασιλείαν, which can have arisen only from a misunderstanding of the
passage. For it is not simply the members of God's kingdom who
are here spoken of, but those who act as *teachers* in behalf of the
members. The expression γραμματεὺς τῇ βασιλείᾳ μαθητευθείς is therefore to be explained as meaning a scribe who has been instructed,
and who, by means of instruction, has become capable of labouring
for the kingdom of God ; who therefore himself, in the first instance,
belongs to it, and has then penetrated into its deep things that he

may be able to lead others the further. Obviously our Lord intends to contrast his apostles with the Jewish סוֹפְרִים, the γραμματεῖς τῇ βασιλείᾳ τῆς γῆς μαθητευθέντες, *scribes instructed for the kingdom of earth*. These latter learn earthly wisdom after a human method for earthly ends ; the apostles, and by consequence, all who resemble them, draw instruction from the eternal Word (John i. 1), the fountain of all wisdom and truth, for heavenly objects. The relation in which these spiritual scribes stand to the church is compared by the Lord to the relation in which the father of a family stands to the members of the household. He has wisely provided his stores, and out of them divides to every individual according to his wants. (The θησαυρός is here equivalent to the ταμεῖον, in which the new and old supplies lie treasured up. The ἐκβάλλειν is equivalent to הוֹצִיא, promere). Probably something more definite than mere diversity is denoted by the καινὰ καὶ παλαιά, *new things and old*. It is most naturally referred to the great distinction between the law and gospel, in the due apportioning of which lies fundamentally the whole employment of one instructed for the kingdom of heaven, since our spiritual life is ever oscillating betwixt these opposite points, as will be further explained on Rom. vii.

Ver. 34, 35.—In conclusion, let us consider the words with which Matthew indeed closes these parables that were uttered in the hearing of the people—but which have a general application to the ` parabolic mode of speaking. Matthew, with whom Mark (iv. 34), agrees, observes that in general Jesus never spoke, χωρὶς παραβολῆς, *without a parable*—that is, never to the multitudes, for to his disciples he even expounded them. In considering this idea, we must in the first place understand the παραβολή in the general sense of comparison, *similitudo;* though we scarcely see, even when it is thus explained, how the position can entirely be made good, that Jesus never spake without comparisons. The shortest mode of explanation is to view the negation as merely a relative one, or if this seems inadmissible, it may then be said that the καθὼς ἠδύναντο ἀκούειν, *as they were able to hear*, of Mark iv. 33, supplies us with a solution, inasmuch as though the Saviour did not always speak literally in similitudes, yet was he never understood *aright* by that multitude, so little fitted for the reception of spiritual truths. With this, the quotation that follows well agrees, which marks distinctly the mysterious character that pervades the whole ministry of the Messiah. (In regard to the formula ὅπως πληρωθῇ, see on Matth. i. 22. The passage quoted is found at Ps. lxxviii. 2, in a poem by Asaph. According to the account of *Jerome* [in his commentary on the passage], the name of Isaiah stood in the passage of Matth. as given in the old MSS., but without doubt it was interpolated, because the writer of the Psalms did not seem to the transcriber to be a

prophet—a name which it was usual to restrict to the persons primarily so called.)   The first half of the verse agrees with the Hebrew
and the LXX., the second, however, varies from both.   The words
אַבִּיעָה חִידוֹת מִנִּי־קֶדֶם are translated by the LXX., φθέγξομαι προβλή-
ματα ἀπ' ἀρχῆς.   The words as given by Matthew are so peculiar that
they furnish another argument for the independence of the Greek
text.   The phrase ἀπὸ καταβολῆς κόσμου, in the sense of ἀπ' ἀρχῆς,
does not once occur in the Old Testament ; in the New Testament,
on the contrary, it is very common, Matth. xxv. 34 ; Luke xi. 50 ;
John xvii. 24, and often besides.   At the foundation of it lies that
figure which compares the world to a building whose erection commences with the foundation (καταβολή).   Only in this passage, however, do we find the verb ἐρεύγω, which the LXX. also employ at Ps.
xviii. 2, in translating הִבִּיעַ, and which is very commonly used by the
Gnostics to express their emanation-doctrine of the streaming forth
of being.   The expressions מָשָׁל, parable, and חִידוֹת, dark sayings,
imply the idea of dark, enigmatical discourse, veiling profound and
mysterious thoughts.   The חִידוֹת מִנִּי־קֶדֶם, dark sayings from of old, are
the eternal mysteries of the world and of human history which Christ
unfolds for those who comprehend his discourse, but which remain
hid from the multitude.   The poet utters the words of the quotation
in connexion with the rest of the psalm, and מָשָׁל, parable, and,
חִידוֹת, dark sayings, refer primarily to the leadings of God's ancient
people.   This then is another passage which seems to countenance
the idea that the phrase ἵνα πληρωθῇ does not imply the fulfilment
of a prophecy.   But that Matthew saw in it such a fulfilment—
(even though erroneously), is clearly shewn from his translating
מִנִּי־קֶדֶם, from of old, by ἀπὸ καταβολῆς τοῦ κόσμου, from the foundation of the world, while from the connexion of the psalm it refers
primarily to the times of Moses.   The expositor therefore ought not
in this case to reject the most obvious meaning of the formula—a
meaning which the writer himself plainly intended to give it.   If we
ask, however, how it is conceivable that the Evangelist can see in
these words the fulfilment of a prophecy, the explanation may be
given in the following way.   What the prophets utter as men inspired by the Spirit of God and through his power, is really spoken
by the Logos, the Son, who in all inspired Scripture reveals himself
through them.   In thus far then it is Christ's part alone to say,
I will open my mouth in parables, for without his power it is impossible for any to find out or reveal divine secrets, and what the poet
of the psalm says respecting wisdom and revelation, he utters only
through him.

§ 23. JESUS IN NAZARETH.

(Matth. xiii. 53–58 ; Mark vi. 1–6 ; Luke iv. 14–30.)

The older expositors (Storr also, and Dr. Paulus at the present day), assume that these narratives refer to separate visits paid by Christ to Nazareth. According to this view, Matthew records a later visit of the Saviour to teach in his native town, Luke an earlier. As to this, the only question is, how to connect Christ's presence at Nazareth on the first occasion with the imprisonment of John (for according to the parallel passages [Mark i. 14 ; Matth. iv. 12], the two events seem to stand in connexion), and next, how to find for the second visit a proper place in the history, inasmuch as Mark puts it in a different connexion from Matthew. Schleiermacher, however, has conclusively proved (on the writings of Luke, p. 63), that the narratives refer to the same occurrence. [? ?] For if the narrative of Matthew were transferred to the later years of Christ's life, it is not easy to suppose that the inhabitants of Nazareth could ask "whence hath this man his wisdom ?"* and still less can it be thought that the events recorded by Luke are posterior to those related by Matthew. In internal character the two narratives are entirely alike, and the single argument for their diversity is the chronology. This very fact, however, is another proof that there is, especially in Matthew and Mark, absolutely no prevailing reference to the succession of time. Matthew, at the commencement and conclusion of his narrative, uses general formulæ, xiii. 53, μετῆρεν ἐκεῖθεν καὶ ἐλθών κ. τ. λ., *he departed thence and came*, xiv. 1, ἐν ἐκείνῳ τῷ καιρῷ, *at that time*. Mark vi. 6, breaks off so indefinitely that even if he had in general followed the thread of chronology, he here obviously let it fall from his hand with the words, " and he went about the villages teaching." The words of transition— μετῆρεν ἐκεῖθεν, ἐν ἐκείνῳ τῷ καιρῷ are obviously so vague that they do not even amount to anything so definite as *afterwards* or *at the same time*, even in the wider sense of these expressions—they are rather, looking to the general aim of the Evangelist, to be understood as meaning generally, " Jesus came once upon a time to his native city." In its connexion in which it stands in Matthew, the whole narrative is introduced, not for its own sake—it serves simply to complete and crown the collection of parables. The whole emphasis lies on the words πόθεν τούτῳ ἡ σοφία αὕτη καὶ αἱ δυνάμεις ; *whence hath this man this wisdom and these miracles ?* This wis-

* They hesitated not to ascribe wisdom to Jesus, but the more they acknowledged and admired it, the more they wondered how the well-known *carpenter's* son had *attained* to it. How widely this narrow-minded sentiment of wonder differs from the *rage* inspired by his language of rebuke, Luke iv. 14, ff., is obvious.—[E.

dom of Jesus was unfolded in the parable here recorded, and the relation in which those around him stood to it, is shewn in the following narrative. They knew it well, but took offence at his immediate earthly connexions, and despised on this account the blessing which Jesus had come to bring to them. Luke, on the other hand, relates the occurrence for its own sake, and is doubtless more accurate in the chronology, although the vagueness of the formulæ (Luke iv. 14, 15), does not admit an exact determination of the time ; it is more than probable, however, that the occurrence belongs to the commencement of our Lord's ministry. Him, therefore, we shall follow mainly in our exposition, adding at the end the particulars given by Matthew and Mark.

Luke iv. 16, 17, represents most graphically Christ's entry into the synagogue at Nazareth. According to the usage of the ancient synagogue, men who were deemed trustworthy, even though not rabbis, might deliver there doctrinal addresses. They usually stood up while reading God's Word (ἀνέστη ἀναγνῶναι, ver. 16*), the servant of the synagogue (ὑπηρέτης, ver. 20) handed the roll, and the teacher, after reading the section, sitting down delivered his discourse (ver. 20). After a section from the books of Moses, there followed a passage from the prophets. The account given in this narrative corresponds closely to the usual practice, the only doubtful point being whether the Redeemer read the passage from the prophets set down for that Sabbath or not. To me the latter view seems probable. Otherwise we must assume that first an extract from the law, and next this passage from Isaiah, was read, but in this way the deep impression of these prophetic words must have been greatly weakened. Besides, the very language ἀναπτύξας τὸ βιβλίον εὗρε κ. τ. λ., unfolding the book he found, etc., points to a selection—not indeed consciously designed, but under the guidance of the Spirit—of the precise passage which predicted the appearance of the Messiah.

Ver. 17.—The βιβλίον is to be conceived of as a roll, so that ἀναπτύσσω retains its literal sense of unfolding or unrolling. The person who presented it was undoubtedly the חַזָּן, the ὑπηρέτης, ver. 20 (comp. Buxt. lex., p. 730).

Ver. 18, 19.—The passage Isaiah lxi. 1, is quoted by Luke freely, and therefore with some variations, from the LXX. Many changes, however, have been adopted from the translation into our text, as

---

* In reference to this custom quotations are given by Lightfoot on the passage. In the first it is said—Non legunt in lege nisi stantes. Imo non licet legenti, alicui rei inniti. Unde autem tenetur legens stare? Quia Scriptura dicit: tu autem mecum sta. The reader in the prophets was called מַפְטִיר, i. e., according to Buxt. Lex. Talm. p. 1719, dimittens, he who read last and dismissed the people. According to this, one may suppose that the reading of the passage from the law was already completed, and that Jesus, as maphtir, now concluded the service of God.

for instance the additional clause, ἰάσασθαι τοὺς συντετριμμένους τὴν καρδίαν after the ἀπέσταλκέ με. The clause ἀποστεῖλαι τεθραυσμένους ἐν ἀφέσει, on the other hand, is found neither in the Hebrew text nor LXX. translation of the passage, and consequently must have been inserted by the Evangelist quoting from memory. The passage, finally, in its prophetic connexion, belongs to that majestic prediction respecting the עֶבֶד יְהֹוָה, servant of Jehovah, which fills the second half of Isaiah. It contains [the prediction of that future servant of God who will execute alike for Israel and the heathen, what Israel could not accomplish for the heathen, nor the prophet for Israel. Comp. Is. xliv. 1 and 21 with xlviii. 1–8, then, xlix. 5 with v. 6.] In this light does the Redeemer now make himself known while explaining the words of the ancient seer as fulfilled in himself.

The expression πνεῦμα ἐπ᾽ ἐμέ = רוּחַ עָלַי, Spirit upon me, occurs also in the same form at Isaiah xlii. 1, lix. 21. It denotes the exalted character of him who was sent from God, and furnished with power from on high. The words ἔχρισέ με, anointed me, refer more definitely to his being furnished with spiritual power for the royal and priestly offices of the Messiah, whose various forms of manifestation are subsequently specified. Οὖ εἵνεκεν = יַעַן is nothing more than the simple ὅτι, and assigns the ground of the spiritual anointing, "for he anointed me to preach good tidings to the poor." The εὐαγγελίσασθαι πτωχοῖς, bring glad-tidings to the poor (לְבַשֵּׂר עֲנָוִים), points out that which was the primary work of the Messiah. The πτωχοί, like the πτωχοὶ πνεύματι of Matth. v. 3, are those who have been awakened from natural death to anxiety, who have been awakened to the need of an atonement. The good news is brought to these men through the very appearance of the Messiah, through faith in him and through his help against sin with all its inward and outward consequences. The ἄφεσις, deliverance, and the ἀνάβλεψις, recovering of sight, are specially brought forward as the real results effected by the Spirit-anointed Redeemer. The same saving power of the Messiah is represented now as breaking the bonds of sin, then as removing the insensibility of the spiritual eye; so that it is merely two aspects of the same thing which are brought forward, and these under physical analogies. The expression κηρύξαι, proclaim, (לִקְרֹא) however, does not imply that the deliverance and recovery of sight were merely distant and future, but close at hand, so that the annunciation and the thing announced go together. The beautiful idea of the clause ἰάσασθαι τοὺς συντετριμμένους τὴν καρδίαν, heal the crushed in heart, which expresses the gentle ministry of the Saviour in restoring all that is prostrated and crushed, is omitted by the Evangelist, that by an apparent pleonasm he may repeat the idea of the deliverance. But the τεθραυσμένοι puts us at once in mind of the συντετριμμένοι (θραύω, to break up, to crush in pieces. Θραύεσθαι, to be in a state of brokenness, equivalent to the Hebrew רָצוּץ, Is. lviii. 6). And the ἀποστεῖλαι ἐν ἀφέσει, is in the same passage parallel to the שַׁלַּח חָפְשִׁים. The ideas of healing, deliverance, restoration to our original state, are here intermingled. There is, moreover, something remarkable in the relation between the words τυφλοῖς ἀνάβλεψιν, ἀποστεῖλαι τεθραυσμένους ἐν ἀφέσει, and the Hebrew text of the passage, Isa. lxi. 1. Both there and in the LXX. the last words are wholly wanting; the first do not accurately correspond to the Hebrew text. The words of the latter run לַאֲסוּרִים פְּקַח־קוֹחַ, the opening of the prison, etc., and they are rendered τυφλοῖς ἀνάβλεψιν. The expression פְּקַח־קוֹחַ had been read as one word, in the sense of the opening of closed eyes ; אֲסוּרִים, captives, was seemingly taken to mean, men with eyes bound up; but this does not agree with the connexion of the passage in the prophet, which admits no other rendering than "release to those that are bound." The words ἀποστεῖλαι τεθραυσμένους ἐν ἀφέσει, which are entirely awanting in Is. lxi. 1, have undoubtedly been taken by Luke from the parallel passage, Isa. lviii. 6, and interwoven here with the former. In this expression he again follows the LXX. It thus appears that the writers of the New Testament deal very freely by those of the Old. With memories uncertain and wavering like those of other men, interchanging passages, confounding words, the Spirit of truth, who inspired and led them, yet so manages all, that nothing untrue, nothing that may mislead, has resulted, but that truth itself is rather presented in a new aspect, and its real nature the more completely revealed.[*] Finally, the concluding words, κηρύξαι ἐνιαυτὸν κυρίου δεκτόν, to proclaim the acceptable year of the Lord, are again taken from Is. lxi. 1. The LXX. have simply rendered קְרָא by καλέσαι. The שְׁנַת־רָצוֹן, acceptable year, like the יוֹם which follows it, denotes the whole period of New Testament life, during which they who receive into their souls the mind of Christ the beloved (the accepted one), appear as themselves also through him well-pleasing to God.[†] Ephes. i. 6.

Ver. 20.—It is doubtful whether the Saviour read merely these words, or also the following verses. To me the former supposition seems the more probable. He wished simply to proclaim a joyful message, and invite the inhabitants of Nazareth to embrace it—the immediately succeeding verses, however, contain a threaten-

[*] In regard to the quotations from the Old Testament in the New, compare the striking treatise by Tholuck, in the supplement to his Commentary on the Epistle to the Hebrews. Hamburg, 1836.

[†] It is strange that several of the fathers understood this passage to mean that Christ preached only one year (and some months). (Comp. Clem. Alex. Strom. 1, p. 407. Orig. de princ. vol. i., p. 160). As to the erroneous nature of this view, see more at length in the Comm. on John ii. 13, v. i. vi. 4.

ing of the day of wrath. (Πτύσσω is found only in this passage, *to lay together, to roll up*. ᾽Ατενίζω, *to look sharply, steadily*, a favourite word with Luke.)

Ver. 21, 22.—The expression ἤρξατο λέγειν, *he began to say*, is by no means redundant ; it indicates the solemn and weighty manner in which he entered on his discourse. In the clause ἡ γραφὴ πεπλήρωται, *the Scripture is fulfilled,* Luke gives shortly the contents of Christ's address. That this passage particularly must be understood as an authentic exposition of the Old Testament prophecy, can admit of no doubt. · (On πληρωθῆναι, see at Matth. i. 22). To suppose here any concession to popular interpretations, would be to strike at the very foundation of the Gospel. The preaching of Jesus in Nazareth was a preaching of grace ; the unbelievers themselves admitted this, but they took offence at his earthly connexions, and lost by neglect the acceptable year of the Lord. The expression, λόγοι τῆς χάριτος, *words of grace*, refers primarily to the outward charms of the Saviour's speech, but these must be considered simply as the visible result of the grace which revealed itself in him. He manifested before his hearers the fulness of his grace and truth. (John i. 14).

That it was the well-known family connexions of Jesus at which the inhabitants of Nazareth took offence, is shewn both by Matthew and Mark. They recount the names of all his family, and wish, as it were, to mislead themselves into the conviction that he is merely one of them. Like all sensual men, strangers to the spiritualities of the unseen world, they look on all that is divine, for the perception of which they want the spiritual sense, as something absolutely unattainable, and they hold themselves far off from it, should it seek to penetrate, with its transforming power, their own sphere of life. This is especially true when its influences are brought to bear through those whom they see moving in earthly relations analogous to their own. In the phrase " the carpenter's son," the prevalent popular idea was embodied, and that impression was wisely permitted, because the idea of the heavenly origin of Jesus could be of use only to believers. Mark, however, in the parallel passage, terms Jesus himself " the carpenter," inasmuch as the Saviour, in his earthly relations, and before his public appearance as the Messiah, undoubtedly followed the calling of Joseph,* a circumstance which formed part of his humiliation. Christian antiquity saw, in the facts thus recorded, nothing offensive, for the life of Jesus was in all its relations unostentatious and obscure. Adopting apocryphal additions, *Justin* tells us ταῦτα γὰρ τὰ τεκτονικὰ ἔργα εἰργάζετο ἐν ἀνθρώποις ὤν, ἄροτρα καὶ ζυγά, διὰ τούτων καὶ τὰ τῆς δικαιο-

---

* Mark does not name Joseph, he only says of Jesus that he was υἱὸς Μαρίας, which probably indicates that Joseph was already dead.

σύνης σύμβολα διδάσκων καὶ ἐνεργῆ βίον, *for he laboured while among men, in the mechanical employment, making ploughs and yokes, in these, both exhibiting the symbols of righteousness, and inculcating an active life.* (Dial. c. Tryph. Jud., p. 316. Paris, 1636). As respects the ἀδελφαί, *sisters,* here named, and the ἀδελφοί, *brothers,* who are left nameless, a question may arise as to whether they were full brothers, or step-brothers, or cousins. The second opinion, that they were step-brothers, is the least supported by proof, having nothing to rest on but the tradition that Joseph, at a former period of life, had been married to a woman named Salome. It may, therefore, be at once set aside. Between the two others, it is hardly possible, owing to the defect of proof, to decide with historic certainty. At first sight, however, everything seems to conspire in favour of the opinion that the brethren and sisters of Jesus were really *Mary's own* children, and great pains have recently been taken to establish this view.[*] 1. Their names are given in immediate connexion with that of the mother. 2. We have no ground for supposing that Joseph's marriage with Mary was a marriage only in appearance, and Matth. i. 25, rather seems to be a positive testimony on the other side. (Compare, however, the Comm. on the passage). Yet a careful examination tends rather to discountenance this, and support the latter opinion, that the so-called brethren of the Lord were cousins to Jesus. For first of all, the point is established, that none of these four brethren of Jesus can have belonged to the number of the twelve apostles, although among them there were two who bore the similar names of James and Judas. For, according to John vii. 5, they did not believe in Jesus. And at Acts i. 14, they are still markedly separated from the apostles, although they appear here as believers.[†] It is expressly stated, however, respecting Mary, the wife of Cleophas, and sister to the

---

[*] Compare Stier's Andeut. Part i. 404, sq., and Clemen in Winer's Zeitschrift für wiss. Th. Part iii.. p. 329, sq. Also Schneckenburger's Beitr. p. 214, sq., annot. in Iac. epist. p. 141. Tübing, Zeitschr. 1829, p. 47, sq., 1830, p. 2, ff. If, however, Joseph had been the father of the persons who are termed Christ's brethren, and if Mary, the mother of Jesus, had been their mother, some of them would surely, for once at least, have been styled "the son of Joseph," since it was common for the Jews to use the name of the father in denominating each other. In our opinion, the "brethren of Christ" mean at least sometimes "sons of Cleophas."

[†] Those who maintain the identity of the apostles, James and Judas, with the ἀδελφοὶ τοῦ κυρίου of the same name, appeal especially to the fact that Alpheus, who is mentioned as the father of James (Matth. x. 3), is the same person with Clopas or Cleophas, the husband of Mary, who was sister to the mother of Jesus (John xix. 25). According to the mode in which Greek names are formed from the Hebrew, it was possible that חלפי may have been changed into Ἀλφαῖος, by leaving out the aspirate, while by laying stress upon it, the name would be formed into Κλωπᾶς. It is inconceivable, however, that the same writer would have constructed the name in both these Greek forms, as we find them in Luke, who now writes Κλεόπας (xxiv. 18, and now Ἀλφαῖος (vi. 15), [but not to designate one and the same person].

mother of Jesus (John xix. 25), that she had sons, two of whom, James and Joses, are named to us by Matthew (xxvii. 56). According to this, then, the two mothers who were of the same name themselves, must have had sons whose names were also alike. This certainly is possible, yet the number of persons in the New Testament bearing similar names must in that case be immoderately increased. But how John xix. 26, can accord with the opinion that Mary had sons of her own, it is impossible to see. Beyond all doubt she would have been taken charge of by them, and not entrusted to John, who stood without the circle of the family connexion. When we consider that according to Hebrew usage אָח is the common term for cousin ; and that two of the so-called brethren are demonstrably the Lord's cousins ; the preponderance of proof unquestionably inclines to the conclusion that Jesus had no brethren of his own after the flesh.* If Joseph died young, we may suppose that Jesus and Mary dwelt in the house of her sister, and that Jesus grew up along with her sons ; this circumstance would explain very simply how it happens that Mary, the mother of Jesus, should sometimes be named along with the son of her sister.

Luke iv. 23.—Jesus looked at once through the hearts of the men of Nazareth, and saw that they could not through the veil which his lowly circumstances threw around his spiritual glory, penetrate into his essential nature. He held up, therefore, before them, as in a glass, the likeness of themselves, giving them thus to see that they were incapable of knowing him. He cites to them from the Old Testament examples to shew that even in the times of their fathers, the heavenly message found no acceptance among the immediate companions of the prophets, and that, unable to unfold its power in them, it had taken refuge among the heathen. The Saviour's first words, however, intimate clearly that the inhabitants of Nazareth had desired to see his miracles, and had remarked that he might perform a miracle on himself, changing himself from a poor man into a rich—from a lowly man into a mighty. This carnal appetite for the marvellous, the Saviour here, as elsewhere, repels. (Compare on Matth. xii. 38, 39, xvi. 1, seq.) He performs no miracle to dazzle by its splendour, but to heal, and to strengthen the poor, the week, the needy. (Πάντως ἐρεῖτε, ye will assuredly say to me. The word πάντως often occurs in Luke [Acts xviii. 21 ; xxi. 22 ; xxviii. 4]. Respecting παραβολή, see on Matth.

* The opinion that Joseph and Mary had children born to them, I am further led to reject, on the ground that, according to the Old Testament predictions, it is difficult to conceive of any continuation of the family of David in the line from which the Messiah was to come forth. We conceive of it as a fitting thing that in Jesus, springing as the everlasting Ruler from the house of David, the line itself should close. What we read of David's descendants at a future period (compare Euseb., H. E., iii. 20) refers beyond doubt to the children of some collateral line.

xiii. 1. Here it denotes like בְּשָׁל a proverb.) The meaning of Ιατρέ, θεράπευσον σεαυτόν, *Physician, heal thyself*, is simply this— Shew your skill on yourself; are you great—do you allege that as a Saviour you can give deliverance ? then deliver yourself from poverty. Thus did the blinded people mock his love when on the cross (Matth. xxvii. 42), and thus does selfishness ever manifest itself in the heart that is alienated from God. Pure unselfish love, however, gives rather than takes (Acts xx. 35), becomes poor in order to make others rich (2 Cor. viii. 9). Wetstein on the passage, cites, moreover, from the Rabbins proverbs of the same import; for example, from Tanchuma on Genes. p. 61, medice, sana claudicationem tuam. In the things of this world, the idea is in some respects true, in the kingdom of grace it is false. The concluding words of the verse shew further with what latitude the general formula of transition, at Luke iv. 14, must be taken. Jesus had, after his temptation, been to Capernaum, and there performed miracles (εἰς is the correct reading, and means *in behalf of, for the benefit of* Capernaum), the report of which had reached Nazareth. This proves that even in Luke the chronology is hard to trace, and that we cannot even in his case conclude from the immediate collocation of events, that they followed each other directly in point of time. In the words ποίησον καὶ ὧδε, *do also here*, the pride and arrogance of the natural man are most plainly explained. They demand miracles, as though they had, from being his countrymen, a special right to them. Yet do they mock him who claims to be more than they, disparaging themselves in their self-contradictory pride. Meanwhile they cannot subdue the impression which his divine presence had made on them, for they are astonished. (V. 22.)

Ver. 24.—This verse forms, in the account of Luke, the climax of the narrative. With Matthew and Mark it attaches itself incidentally to the narrative, which is regarded under an entirely different aspect. Most appropriately does Luke introduce this occurrence at the outset of Christ's ministry, and narrate it with such care, for the reception he met with when commencing his official labours in his native town, mirrored forth the peculiar experience of his whole subsequent career. Matthew and Mark further add : the prophet is of no esteem "in his own house, and among his own kindred." By these words the picture is compressed within narrower limits, but its leading outlines remain the same. As Christ's brethren believed not (John vii. 5), so neither did the inhabitants of Nazareth believe, and like the latter, so the whole nation disbelieved ; " he came unto his own, and his own received him not." (John i. 11.) The kingdom of God passed over to the heathen, and to them even Luke himself went as a preacher. As, however, after the resurrection, the brethren of Christ were among the believers (Acts i. 14), so also shall Israel turn to the Lord, at the time of the great resurrection (Rom. xi. 25.) That which happened, however, to Christ personally, he applies to *all* prophets, οὐδεὶς προφήτης δεκτός ἐστιν ἐν τῇ πατρίδι αὑτοῦ, *no prophet is accepted, etc.* For in the case of every prophet, the divine element in him comes into conflict with sin in his contemporaries, and the closer their relation in the flesh, the more incomprehensible to the worldly man is their wide separation in the spirit. The spectacle of the prophet entangled in the same irritating cares of daily life that are common to all his fellows, rendered it more difficult under this lowly guise, to recognise his heavenly character.

Ver. 25–27.—The examples by which the Lord illustrates the working of this divine power, passing by those who are near and acting on those at a distance, are taken from 1 Kings xviii. 1, seq., xvii. 12, seq. The three years and six months are also given at James v. 17, but, according to 1 Kings xviii. 1, the time seems merely to have extended over the second, and into the third year. If, however, we compute it, not from the coming of the rain, but from the flight of Elijah, 1 Kings xvii. 9, as *Benson* has proposed, the difficulty disappears. Σάρεπτα = צָרְפַת a small town betwixt Tyre and Sidon. The whole stress is to be laid on the fact, that heathens instead of Israelites saw the miracles of the prophet.

Ver. 28, 29.—These parallel cases from among the heathen, wounded the vanity of the Nazarenes; they drove out their prophet, and so made the words of Jesus true. Nay, they even intended to take his life, as they wished to cast him down from the hill on which their town was built. (Compare on Matth. ii. 23.) (Ὀφρύς, *eye-brow, steep precipice.* Hesych. τὰ ὑψηλὰ καὶ ὑπερκείμενα χωρία.)

Ver. 30.—The unbelieving, miracle-seeking Nazarenes, met, in his escape, with a proof of his wonder-working power, of which, however, they took no heed.—Διελθὼν διὰ μέσου αὐτῶν ἐπορεύετο, *passing through their midst, he went away,* relates the Evangelist. These words in themselves certainly do not indicate anything miraculous ; some fortunate accident might have made it possible for an individual to escape from the excited population of a whole city. But he who acknowledges no mere accident, and least of all in the history of the Son of God ; he who enquires exegetically into the view of the writer, must be forced to confess the idea here expressed to be this : Jesus departed through the midst of them without restraint or hindrance, because he was JESUS; his divine power held their limbs and senses bound. No one could take from him his life, unless when he freely gave it. (John x. 18.) In the same way also is the narrative at John viii. 59 to be understood.

Matth. (xiii. 58) and Mark (vi. 5) remark in conclusion, that Jesus performed few miracles in Nazareth. According to the more minute account of Mark, he healed a few sick persons by laying his hands on them. Probably this was *before* his address in the synagogue, for *after* it the scene of uproar immediately broke forth. We need not suppose that this contradicts Luke iv. 23, if we assume that these cures had taken place in quiet family circles, for surely the good seed was not wholly wanting even in unbelieving Nazareth. The expression, however, employed by Mark, is remarkable, ἐθαύμαζε διὰ τὴν ἀπιστίαν αὐτῶν, *he marvelled at their unbelief* (a painful contrast with Matthew viii. 10, where Jesus wonders at faith), and οὐκ ἠδύνατο ἐκεῖ οὐδεμίαν δύναμιν ποιῆσαι, *he was not able to do there any mighty work.* These words strikingly explain the relation of faith to the miraculous power of Christ. Faith appears here once more (compare on Matthew viii. 1), as a condition indispensable to the manifestation of that miraculous power, which, as the positive pole requires the negative, demanded susceptibility of mind before it could impart its gifts. The οὐκ ἠδύνατο, *he could not,* is therefore to be taken quite literally, as denoting an internal impossibility—obviously not a physical, but a divine, a *moral* impossibility. As God *can* save no impenitent sinner, none, who refuses humbly to mourn over his guilt, so Jesus *cannot* heal where faith is wanting. Hence it appears that the object of the miracles is not to produce faith : they *presuppose* faith as existing, but where it already is they can purify and confirm it, and at the same time awaken the mind to correct knowledge. For, clearness of understanding is not necessarily united with depth and liveliness of faith. It is not likely that the views of that heroine of faith, the Canaanitish woman (Matthew xv. 22), were very clear, but her heart burned with love, and her whole soul was susceptible to heavenly influences. Hence she was enabled to compel (if I may so speak), the reluctant Saviour to perform a miracle. (Compare on Matthew xv. 28.) Faith, therefore, in all stages of its development, proceeds from the heart ; its resting-place is in the immediate sphere of the inner life ; it is *receptive* love, as grace is *communicative* love. But the divine principle (grace), which unites itself to faith, is to pervade the powers of knowledge and understanding, nay, indeed the whole man, in all his faculties. By knowledge, however, no man attains to faith, nor shall any be saved by mere intelligence ; but a believing heart may well secure salvation, even amidst great obscurity in our perceptions of truth. (Compare Proverbs iv. 23.)

§ 24. THE BAPTIST'S DEATH.

(Matth. xiv. 1–12; Mark vi. 14–29. Luke iii. 19, 20; ix. 7–9.)

The immediately following chapters in Matthew (xiv.—xvii.) do not share the character of the preceding ; no thread can be traced guiding the arrangement of their several portions. Not till the 17th chapter, does the distinctive peculiarity of Matthew, that, namely, of combining fragments of various discourses, again appear. The chapters which here immediately follow, I am inclined to regard as supplements of a historic kind to the preceding sections (*Rubriken*). Although the unchronological character of Matthew still remains, yet in the frequent mention made of Christ's death we observe a gradual drawing near to the later period. The first incident in chapter xiv., the account of the Baptist's death, is obviously of a supplementary character—the fact of his execution is supposed to be long past. Luke (iii. 19, 20) had anticipated it. The mention of the views current regarding Christ, points, however, to a period when the reports respecting him had already obtained wide circulation, and the acquaintance of the disciples with their nature is easily explained, if we consider that their mission must have brought them into contact with persons of various kinds. From this point down to the end of this section, the relation of Mark to Matthew is peculiar. He follows him closely and throughout, only in two cases (vii. 32–37 ; viii. 22–26), inserting short narratives of cures which Matthew does not give. The account Matthew xvii. 24–27, of the coin in the mouth of the fish, he omits. Mark's peculiar style of narrative remains unchanged in these portions ; he presents far more graphically than Matthew the details of his narratives, but dwells exclusively on their outward features.

Ver. 1.—The expression ἐν ἐκείνῳ τῷ καιρῷ, *at that time*, is here used in all its vagueness, inasmuch as the preceding occurrence happened at the commencement of the Lord's ministry, while the account of Herod which follows belongs to a later period. (Concerning Herod [Antipas] and τετράρχης, compare on Matthew ii. 22 ; Luke iii. 1.) The frivolous worldling seems at first to have given himself little trouble about Jesus : he never heard of him till his fame had been widely spread.

Ver. 2.—Matthew merely records the impression which the information about Christ made on the tetrarch ; Mark and Luke state, in addition, the various rumours respecting him which were in circulation among the people. Subsequently they both repeat them on an occasion when Matthew also gives them (xvi. 14), and we defer therefore the fuller consideration of them to Matthew xvi. 14. As to Herod, Mark, agreeing with Matthew, relates that he believed Jesus to have been John raised from the dead. He expresses this opinion directly to those about him. · (Παῖς = δοῦλος, עֶבֶד). According to Luke, it was the mere *report* of this which disturbed him (διηπόρει, Luke ix. 7), yet his wish to see Jesus (Luke ix. 9), would rather lead us to the opposite conclusion, namely, that he himself disbelieved the report of John's resurrection. (Compare Luke xxiii. 8.) This seeming contradiction disappears, however, when we consider how completely this worldly man must have been involved in darkness. At the first hearing of the report his heart would be shaken with fear, for conscience would testify that from a desire to please others and against his better knowledge (see Mark vi. 26), he had caused the Baptist to be murdered. A mind so superficial, however, would soon pacify itself and become convinced of the improbability of the whole matter. His Sadduceeism would come to his aid (see on Mark viii. 15, compared with Matthew xvi. 6), and put to flight every idea of a probable existence beyond the grave. Consistency in the views of such sensualists is not to be looked for ; they deny the reality of divine things, yet amidst their very denial their heart quakes with the secret belief of them. With metempsychosis we have here nothing to do, for it is clear they did not believe that John's soul had passed into another body, but that he was himself personally risen from the dead. Not even at John ix. 3, are we to look for traces of a belief in metempsychosis, or the pre-existence of souls, during the times of the apostles. (Compare the Comment. on that passage.)

Ver. 3, 4.—The aorists are, in the connexion, clearly to be understood as equivalent to the pluperfect tense. (Compare *Winer's* Gram., p. 251.) The place of John's imprisonment was, according to *Josephus* (Antiq. xviii. 5, 2), the fortress of Machaerus. The notorious Herodias, with whom Antipas lived in incestuous connexion, was the daughter of Aristobulus, a son of Herod the Great. The latter married her to his son Philip (who is not to be confounded with Philip the Tetrarch, see on Matthew ii. 22), who was disinherited by his father, and lived subsequently merely as a private individual. For this reason, his wife, Herodias, preferred the connexion with the tetrarch, Antipas, that she might become a reigning princess. Antipas discarded in her favour, his former wife, the daughter of Aretas, the Arabian prince. (Compare *Josephus*, Antiq. xviii. 5, 1.) John, the stern preacher of repentance, had dared to rebuke this scandalous union, and drawn upon himself the unmitigated hatred of Herodias. In Antipas himself, it would appear, there often arose feelings of a better nature. (Mark vi. 20.)

Ver. 5.—Mark paints (ver. 20) Herod in more favourable colours, so that it is Herodias who appears as the special enemy of John. ('Ενέχω, v. 19, *to be angry, in anger to lay snares for;* Luke xi. 53.) Matthew, however, ascribes to Herod the intention of putting John to death, only, he remarks, that he feared the people. Mark's language, "knowing him to be a righteous and holy man," seems to indicate that his conscience had been roused, and this is confirmed by what follows. The eager hearing of John refers not to the time of his imprisonment, during which any interview between the prince and the Baptist is hardly conceivable, but to an earlier period, before his incarceration. At such a conference John might well have called his attention to the unlawfulness of his union with Herodias, as well as to other criminal acts. (Compare Luke iii. 19; 'Ηρώδης —ἐλεγχόμενος ὑπ' 'Ιωάννου περὶ 'Ηρωδιάδος—καὶ περὶ πάντων ὧν ἐποίησε πονηρῶν.)

Ver. 6.—Γενέσια may be understood of his *birth-day*, or of the commencement of his reign. Even so early as Joseph's time, the Pharaohs kept the ἡμέρα γενέσεως. (Genesis xl. 20.) Mark employs the general expression ἡμέρα εὔκαιρος = בוט םוי *festive day*, and describes the guests at the feast. The expression μεγιστᾶνες, "*lords*," seems of Persian origin. *Josephus* (Antiq., ix. 3, 2) ranges them along with the satraps. The LXX. use the word among others for רַבְרְבָן Daniel v. 1. In the New Testament it occurs again only at Rev. vi. 15; xviii. 23. Here it seems to denote the highest civil officers at the court, as χιλιάρχοι does the highest military officers. The πρῶτοι τῆς Γαλιλαίας, *first men of Galilee*, would, in that case, mean the wealthiest men of the province. We are doubtless to understand the dancing of the daughter of Herodias to have been the mimic dance, but not necessarily unchaste. On the part of his step-daughter (Salome was her name) this is hardly conceivable.

Ver. 7.—The verb προβιβάζειν occurs at Acts xix. 33, in its most immediate sense of *to draw forth, to lead out;* figuratively, it means to *instruct* any one, to *train* for some purpose. At Exodus xxxv. 34, it stands for הֹרָה. The wicked mother directed the maiden to John the Baptist, and she asked for his head. The weak Antipas granted it, though with a reluctant mind. ('Εξ αὐτῆς sc. ὥρας, Mark vi. 25.)

Ver. 9, 10.—The weak fear of man extracted from the tetrarch the order for the beheading; he was ashamed before the assembly to recal his too hasty promise. The state of Pilate's mind was similar when the demand was made that he should suffer Jesus to be led forth to death—only he was overcome by fear, Antipas by shame. Mark vi. 27 uses the Latin name σπεκουλάτωρ, by which the executioner was commonly designated. The mode of writing the word varies between spiculator (from spiculum, a spear with which they were armed), and speculator—the former seems preferable.

Ver. 11, 12.—As the execution seems to have been so soon carried into effect, the feast must have been held in the castle of Machaerus itself, or in the neighbourhood. The faithful disciples buried the body (Mark vi. 29, has πτῶμα) of their master as their last token of respect.

§ 25. FEEDING OF THE FIVE THOUSAND.

(Matth. xiv. 13–21; Mark vi. 30–44; Luke ix. 10–17; John vi. 1–15.)

The date of the feeding of the five thousand is fixed with certainty by John vi. 4 (see on the explanation of ἦν δὲ ἐγγὺς τὸ πάσχα the Comment. on the passage). The connecting of Christ's retirement into the desert, with his receiving the news of John's death, is extremely simple and probable. As his hour was not yet come, he went into retirement, partly that he might avoid all hostile machinations, partly that he might in prayer to God and converse with his disciples, meditate on, and make known those mighty events in the kingdom of God which were gradually approaching. (Compare on Mark i. 35.) As the people crowd thither after him, the scene of the subsequent feeding of the multitude is ushered in.

Ver. 13.—Matthew states in general Ἰησοῦς ἀνεχώρησεν ἐκεῖθεν εἰς ἔρημον, Jesus retired thence into a desert, leaving undetermined what the thence refers to, for his last account of Jesus (Matth. xiii. 53–58) mentions no locality. But the expression "in a ship" points to his passing over to the opposite side of the sea of Gennesareth, an inference which John vi. 1, and Luke ix. 10, confirm.[*] The latter mentions Bethsaida. This town, however, must not be confounded with the city of the apostles (John i. 44), which lay on the western shore of the sea. This second Bethsaida was situated on the eastern bank, near where the Jordan flows into the lake. At first it was a village, but Philip the tetrarch raised it to the rank of a city, and named it Julias. (Josephus, Antiq., xviii. 3; Wars of the Jews, ii. 13; compare Von Raumer's Palest., p. 100). According to Mark (ver. 31), this retirement was intended also for the disciples, that they might rest from the labours (ἀναπαύεσθε ὀλίγον) occasioned by the pressure of the people. They had even been prevented from taking their necessary food. Eager, however, for help (though only outward help, immediately), the people hastened after them into the uncultivated region whither our Lord had withdrawn, and

---

[*] De Wette (on Luke ix. 10) thinks that Luke places this feeding in a different locality from Matthew and Mark; that he knows nothing of a passage across the sea, and refers to the Bethsaida on the western shore. But this is sufficiently disproved by the single circumstance that there was no desert near the western Bethsaida: it was surrounded by the most fruitful land.

he had compassion on them. (See respecting σπλαγχνίζεσθαι on Luke i. 78.) He taught, therefore (Luke and Mark), and afterwards performed cures (Matthew). On the words (especially as given by Mark), compare the passage Matth. ix. 36. They contain allusions to Old Testament passages, such as Numbers xxvii. 17 ; Isaiah liii. 6. Luke (ix. 11) mentions as the subject of his teaching, the Βασιλεία τοῦ Θεοῦ, *kingdom of God,* under which expression is here comprehended, in an indeterminate and general way, that more exalted heavenly life which Christ was come to render the dominant principle on earth. (Compare on Matth. iii. 2.)

Ver. 15, 16.—In narrating the course of the miracle, John deviates from the synoptical Gospels. He states that the Saviour put to Philip the question, how shall we buy bread for so many ; while the synoptical writers tell us that the apostles had applied to Jesus to dismiss the people, that they might disperse themselves and find provisions in the villages that lay immediately around. It is easy, however, to reconcile both accounts. As the day was now far gone (Mark vi. 35, ὥρα πολλή, like the expression ἡμέρα πολλή, in the LXX. at Genesis xxix. 7), some of the disciples' enquired of Jesus as to the time when the people would be dismissed. John mentions another circumstance occurring, either before or after the inquiry of the disciples, the question, namely, put by Jesus to Philip. Even though, as Bengel supposes, the charge of providing food had been entrusted to him, the special object in putting the question was certainly a moral one. Philip must have his mind awakened (John vi. 6, ἔλεγεν ὁ Ἰησοῦς πειράζων αὐτόν, *Jesus spoke proving him*), that he might be able to apprehend aright the approaching miracle. Philip, however, appears here as at John xiv. 8, unable to free himself from his earthly modes of conception ; he refers to the sum of money that would be required for feeding them. (200 denarii = 40 rix dollars. This sum is given also by Mark vi. 37.)

Ver. 17.—Another equally immaterial difference in the narrative, is John's expressly naming Andrew (vi. 8) as the person who mentioned the boy with the five loaves and the two fishes (ὀψάριον properly means merely *by-meat,*[*] any thing eaten with bread ; the other Evangelists define it by ἰχθύες, *fishes*), while Matthew, Mark, and Luke make the apostles say that there was no food whatever at hand. These last Evangelists have looked on Andrew as speaking for all the apostles, and expressing their mind. The expression παιδάριον ἕν, *one little boy* (the ἕν is not to be taken as having the force of the indefinite article, but as distinctly intimating that none else besides this boy had brought food with them), forbids our supposing that the five loaves and two fishes were merely the disciples'

---

[*] According to lexicographers, however, ὀψάριον was, at a later period, used as precisely equivalent to ἰχθύδιον.

own supply of food. John immediately places, in direct contrast, the whole number present (ταῦτα τί ἐστιν εἰς τοσούτους), with the whole supply of provisions. (The assigning of the number at 5000 is alike in all the narratives, only Matthew and Mark do not mention it till the conclusion. Matthew remarks, enhancing it still more, besides women and children. The mode of arranging them at the meal greatly facilitated the reckoning. The agreement in the numbers, as well of those who were fed, as of the provisions set before them, is not to be overlooked. It is a strong testimony to the truth of the narrative ; later tradition would have corrupted the numbers.)

Ver. 18, 19.—The Saviour causes the crowd to be ranged in regular order, and proceeds to divide the small supply of food. (The ἔρημος, where the Saviour was at this time, was grassy pasture ground, without towns or villages. In the same way מִדְבָּר is used to denote pasturage. We are not therefore to conceive of any thing like sandy wastes, but rather of steppes. Συμπόσιον denotes here the persons who partake of a meal together, like our German word Gesellschaft, a company. Luke uses instead, the term κλισίαι, the reclining or sitting together at food, table-parties; each company of fifty is conceived as forming a party by itself. The repetition of the word denotes, according to Hebrew usage, the separate distribution, instead of the Greek ἀνά. In graphic language, from a vivid conception of the scene, Mark styles the separate companies πρασιαί, defined and separate spaces, e. g., garden-beds, as in Homer. He adds, that some of these parties consisted of 100, others of 50, nay, he does not forget to notice the freshness of the grass. (ἐπὶ χλωρῷ χόρτῳ—χλωρός = יָרֵק in the LXX.) These traits originate wholly in his peculiar mode of representation which deals with events chiefly in their external features. In detailing the division itself, Mark (41) adds expressly, καὶ τοὺς δύο ἰχθύας ἐμέρισε πᾶσι, and he divided the two fishes among them all. These words clearly intimate the view of the narrator, that the two fishes were the object subdivided among all ; Jesus had only this small supply for satisfying the multitude. The words of John, ὅσον ἤθελον, as much as they would (vi. 11), exclude all idea of a merely seeming satisfaction of their wants ; every one partook as much as he desired; that was the standard which, on this occasion, regulated the supply.

Ver. 20, 21.—The command to gather up the fragments admitted of being carried into execution, for our Lord was standing in one fixed place when he broke the bread and the fishes (fragments of which latter, the minute and accurate Mark informs us were also collected), at which point they would naturally collect themselves, and means might also be taken beforehand for keeping them clean. The twelve baskets (in which all the four Evangelists are agreed), shew that the fragments that remained over were of greater amount than the original loaves. Probably each apostle took a basket to complete the gathering of the fragments; hence the twelve. This union of careful savingness with creative power is a feature so peculiar, that it impresses, beyond all mistake, a heavenly character on the narrative. Such things are not invented! Nature, that mirror of divine perfections, places before our eyes the same combination of boundless munificence, and of truest frugality in imparting her benefits.

The Evangelists close their narratives with nothing certainly like exclamations or expressions of surprise—John only remarking what an impression the incident had made on the people. They concluded from it that Jesus was the promised prophet, and wished to make him by force the sovereign of their worldly kingdom. Whether such an ebullition is conceivable, if the multitude (a caravan returning from a festival, as is conjectured) had satisfied themselves with the provision which themselves had made for the journey, and in the most courteous way, left untouched the small supply of food placed before them by the apostles, we leave intelligent and believing readers to infer for themselves.

The fact itself thus recorded obviously belongs to that class of Christ's miracles which stand related to *nature*. In the other, and first class of miracles, there is, for the Christian mind, this facility towards the understanding of them, that we have, in the faith of the individual who (for example in the case of a cure) is the object of the miracle, a channel for the communication of the wondrous power and its effectual operation. But in cases where physical nature is seen as a simply passive object, the miracle easily assumes the appearance of being *magical*. The best way of escaping from this false impression is, never to view those miracles which refer to the natural world dissociated from the moral world, but as living in union with it. The mere increase of food is not the point on which stress is here to be laid, but its increase for persons who were in a certain state of mind. It is when such miracles are thus conjoined with the wants of human nature, as these were manifested in the individuals actually present, that they appear in their true character. As the Lord, in general, performed no cure save where he found faith, so he generally bestowed no food save where he found spiritual hunger.* As regards the fact itself, we pay no attention to those representations, which, in contradiction to the true exegesis, explain away all that is miraculous;† but just as little ought we to tolerate

---

* It is repugnant to common sense when, in reply to this, Strauss asks (vol. ii., p. 206), what was done then with unbelievers? The supposition is, that where Christ performed a miracle *all* were believers.

† Pfenninger says of it: "What usually takes place in three-quarters of a year be-

any views of it which are anti-natural. This, however, must be done, if we suppose the material to have been increased without a real interposition of Divine power. Rather let us believe that the same power which flowed forth from Jesus to heal the sick, here produced, in obedience to his will, another physical effect. There it appears rather as setting in order, as restorative—here rather as creative.* The correct view of the matter then is undoubtedly this, that under the hands of the Saviour, and by his Divine power, an increase of the means of food took place. As by the touch of his hand, he healed and blessed, so by this he *created*. With this, however, we are still to regard these phenomena as greatly accelerated natural processes [?]; for real formations can be produced only by a series of real developments. Yet these developments are capable of being accelerated and that to an extent which it is impossible for us to limit. But the right conception of a miracle, which discerns in it a higher principle of causality, compels us to such suppositions. No phenomenon is conceivable except in connexion with adequate powers of causation. But in the person of Jesus all the higher powers which control the processes of nature penetrated directly and profoundly to the very heart of natural life, while with sovereign and creative, because Divine energy, he pervaded all elementary formations, arranging and guiding them to more exalted ends. As to the increase of the means of food, similar things were seen formerly, under the Old Testament. Elijah, with twenty loaves (2 Kings iv. 42, seq.), fed one hundred men. Oil and meal increased to the widow at Sarepta. (2 Kings iv. 1, seq., comp. also 1 Kings xvii. 1, seq.) Manna and quails nourished

tween seed time and harvest, is said here to have been done within a few minutes, while the food was being divided. Thus the narrative will have us believe in an increase wondrously hastened forward, *and I could more easily discredit the fact were I the most believing of men, or I could credit it were I the most unbelieving, sooner than really and truly believe that the narrative does not intend to make us believe it.*" The pitiful remark of Strauss, in reply to this profound view of Pfenninger, that for the production of bread, besides the natural process of growing, there is required also the artificial work of grinding and baking, originates assuredly in something worse than mere intellectual incapacity, namely, in his entire disbelief in a living God. But for this, he would not have had such difficulty in supposing that the Divine agency had replaced the work of man.

     * Yet in no gospel narrative is a *pure* exercise of creative power ascribed to the Saviour. As nature, out of the seed corn, evolves a new creation, so Christ turns water into wine and increases the already existing bread, but without a substratum to begin with, he makes neither wine nor bread. I observe that in these remarks I refer only to the recorded facts; how far it is conceivable that Christ's miraculous powers might have been put forth in a different form, is another question. According to gospel history, the Saviour constantly appears as the *restorer* of creation. He creates no new men, but he transforms the old; he makes no new bodily members formerly wanting, but he restores the old that were useless. The same thing applies to the miracles of the Old Testament; for even in the case of the manna, the supernatural increase of a natural production may be supposed, and not the creation of matter absolutely new.

the Israelites in the desert. (As to the typical meaning of this, see on John vi.) What was there done by God in heaven and from afar, is here effected by God visible and near at hand. (Ps. cxlv. 15, 16.)

§ 26. JESUS WALKS ON THE SEA.

(Matt. xiv. 22–36; Mark vi. 45–56; John vi. 16–21.)

The following narrative of our Lord's walking on the sea is in so far akin to the preceding, as it also manifests Christ's dominion over the natural world ; yet exhibited in an entirely different relation. For we meet here not so much an influence brought to bear on nature, as a personal withdrawal from the control of earthly natural laws here, *viz.*, that of gravity. The difficulty which is commonly found in this occurrence, disappears, or at least is considerably diminished, if, along with that close affinity which connected the body of Christ with those of other men, we recognise definitely its distinctive peculiarities. It is common to conceive of the glorifying of our Lord's body, as effected either at the resurrection or ascension, and as the work of a moment. But if we suppose the Spirit's work, in glorifying and perfecting Christ's body, to have been spread over the Saviour's whole life (certain periods being still distinguished as seasons of special efficiency), much that is obscure will be made clear. A body absolutely earthly, chained down by unseen bands to earthly matter, cannot shake itself free from its origin, but that a higher bodily nature, teeming with the powers of a loftier world, should rise above the earthly level, is less surprising.* This transaction, then, of Christ's walking on the sea, is not to be viewed as a work wrought *upon* him and effected by magic, as though some external power had laid hold on him and borne him up, but as the result effected by his own will, the forthputting of an energy inherent in himself. If this power was seldom used, it was because the Saviour never did wonders for the sake of doing them, but to serve some useful end. Thus in the present instance, the manifestation of his hidden glory was designed to build up his disciples in the faith. They saw more and more with whom they had to do, and perceived that he was the revelation of the invisible Father (Matth. xvi. 16) ; their Jewish prepossessions, as to the Messiah, were more and more cleared up in his light.

---

* The absurd questions which Strauss (vol. ii., p. 182, second edition) gets up in reply to this explanation, he might have spared himself, had he been willing to reflect that the freeing of Christ's body from its bondage to the earth, is not inconsistent with its being entirely at the disposal of his own free will.

The Old Testament representations of Jehovah's glory were in living reality set before their eyes in the life of Jesus. He alone spreadeth out the heavens *and walketh on the waves of the sea*. (Job ix. 8.) We will not disturb those heavenly images of a Divine government among men, by reviewing the attempts that have been made in defiance of just exegesis, to reduce their weighty significancy to the level of every-day generalities. Such pictures, taken from the Lord's life, set before us in miniature his whole mighty work and influence on the inner world of the human spirit; they are full of exhaustless meaning.—As respects the form of the narrative, the superiority in vivid and graphic description belongs to Matthew. The incident which befel Peter, who wished to come to Jesus over the water, is, for example, recorded by Matthew alone. John's account is short, and like most narratives of events contributed by that Evangelist, is given chiefly for the sake of the discourses which are connected with it. The motive which led to the breaking up of the assembly, and the removal of the disciples, is, however, distinctly assigned by John, who thus confirms the accuracy of the connexion between this and the preceding occurrences as stated by the three other Evangelists. The miraculous supply of food excited in these worldly men a desire to make Jesus the Messianic king. From their importunities he withdrew by retiring to the solitude of a mountain for prayer (Matth. xiv. 23), but he caused his disciples to go before him by ship to the other side of the sea. Mark vi. 45 specifies Bethsaida, John vi. 17, Capernaum, as the point to which their course was directed. As the two places, however, were close to each other, the disciples may have intended first to put in at the one point, and then sail on to the other. (The expression ἀναγκάζειν, *constrain*, in Matthew and Mark, ver. 22 and 45, means merely earnest impressive exhortation, and this was needed apparently because the disciples were unwilling to separate from their Lord.)

Ver. 24, 25.—John (vi. 16) mentions the evening as the time of their setting sail. From his supplemental remark "and Jesus had not come to them," it would appear that they had continued to look for Jesus rejoining them, and it was probably their thus waiting for him which delayed so long the period of their setting sail. As the darkness of night now came on, and a storm arose, the scene assumed that terrific character which is in harmony with the entire narrative. Through gloom and tempest came the Lord, walking over the raging waves, to the help of his disciples in their tossing boat. Matthew and Mark observe that the wind, besides being fierce, was contrary to them (ἐναντίος), so that the force of the waves struck the boat more violently (βασανίζεσθαι). According to John, they had already rowed a distance of 25–30 stadia (ἐλαύνειν), and consequently more than half-way across (the sea was 40 stadia broad, about one Ger-

man mile,* *Joseph.* Bell. Jud., i. 3, 35), when they saw Jesus walking on the sea. According to Matthew and Mark, it was now
towards the morning, about the fourth watch. (Φυλακή = אַשְׁמֻרָה.)
Before the Exile the Jews had divided the night into three parts ;
afterwards they adopted the four Roman divisions of three hours
each. In the expression ἀπῆλθε πρὸς αὐτούς, *he went away to them,*
the idea of his leaving the place where he was formerly staying, is
concisely conjoined with that of his going to meet the disciples.

Ver. 26, 27.—The disciples seeing Jesus walking on the sea took
fright ; they believed they saw a φάντασμα. Πνεῦμα, *spirit,* stands in
a similar connexion at Luke xxiv. 37. The term is to be understood
in all its latitude like our word *apparition,* (*gespenst*), which according to popular notions, means any sort of incorporeal appearance,
without very accurately defining the idea of it. That anything of a
bodily nature could walk on the sea, was inconceivable to the disciples, and there came upon them, therefore, the terror which usually
accompanies unwonted spiritual phenomena. The word uttered
by Jesus ἐγώ εἰμι, *it is I,* reassures the disciples. In him they had
already recognised unwonted and extraordinary characteristics ;
they saw in him the ruler of the invisible world ; through him they had
been brought into friendship with that world ; and they knew that
he ever came to their aid in moments of danger. The expression
ἐπὶ τῆς θαλάσσης or ἐπὶ τὴν θάλασσαν (in Matthew), and afterwards at
Matth. xiv. 28, 29, ἐπὶ τὰ ὕδατα, certainly *may* mean *beside* the sea,
inasmuch as the bank of the sea or river is conceived of as elevated above the level of the water. (2 Kings ii. 7 ; Dan. viii. 2 ;
according to the LXX.) Of itself, however, ἐπί never means *ad
juxta* (compare *Fritzsche* Comm. in Matth., p. 503), but *to* or *towards*
anything, *versus.* (Acts xvii. 14.) The parallel passage, John xxi.
1, is very accurately explained by Fritzsche, ἐφανέρωσεν ἑαυτὸν ὁ
Ἰησοῦς τοῖς μαθηταῖς ἐπὶ τῆς θαλάσσης (οὖσίν), *Jesus shewed himself to the
disciples (when they were) on the sea,* in such a way that the formula
bears its usual meaning. But that in the passage before us there
is no evading the obvious import of the words that Christ walked
over the waves of the sea, appears plainly from the narrative taken
as a whole. If differently understood, it becomes either trivial or
deceptive. The opinion which would hold it a myth is sufficiently
refuted by the calm tone of the narrators. Least of all can Matthew's account of Peter's walking on the sea be reconciled to it.
This stands forth as a naked fact.

Ver. 28-31.—The peculiar conduct of Peter, the account of which
is here contributed by Matthew, is entirely in keeping with that disciple's character. Hence also a similar incident is told of him after
the resurrection of Jesus (John xxi. 7, seq). Fiery and ardent, full

* One German is equal to about 4⅔ English miles.

of burning love for the Lord, he cannot wait patiently the moment
of his near approach, but hastens to meet him with most daring
courage. As John is called the disciple whom the Lord loved, ὃν
ἠγάπα ὁ Ἰησοῦς (John xxi. 7), so might it be said of Peter that he
loved the Lord. In other words, as the nature of John was pre-eminently receptive and profound, Peter was distinguished for activity
and force. As however this power of love wherewith he embraced
the Saviour was not yet freed from selfishness, it betrayed him into
mistakes of the most various kinds. In the present case also, his
impetuous haste brings about a fall. The whole of this little history
is a rich picture of our interior life—a commentary on the words of
the prophet, the heart of a man is a froward and timorous thing (Jer.
xvii. 9). Without the command (not a mere permission) of the Lord,
Peter will not venture from the ship. Trusting to the ἐλθέ, come,
he walks forth, but at sight of the hurricane, he sinks. (Καταπον-
τίζεσθαι occurs again at Matth. xviii. 6, in the sense of sinking, or being
sunk into the πόντος.) Yet his faith remains so far firm that he
only seeks aid from Jesus. (Here he already calls him κύριε, Lord,
with reference to his higher nature, the knowledge of which had
previously been revealed to Peter [see on Matth. xvi. 16]. So also,
on seeing this dominion exercised by Jesus over the powers of nature,
the other disciples take occasion to make the confession at ver. 33,
ἀληθῶς Θεοῦ υἱὸς εἶ, truly thou art the Son of God. Comp. on Matth.
xvi. 16.) Christ gave him help along with a word of rebuke, ὀλιγό-
πιστε, of little faith, which, however, is a different thing from ἄπιστε,
faithless. The point of reproof was merely that the faith which
existed in him was not beyond being shaken. (Διστάζω occurs again
at Matth. xxviii. 17. Literally it means to turn in two different
directions, hesitating and undetermined which to follow. Whence
it denotes in general to be in doubt, and is equivalent to ἀμφισβη-
τέω.) Here again, as in all the miracles of Christ, faith is shewn to
be the medium through which they are wrought on men. So long
as the soul of Peter was purely and simply turned towards the Lord,
he was capable of receiving within himself the fullness of Christ's
life and Spirit, so that Christ's power became his power; but when,
by giving scope and weight to an alien power, he became less susceptible to spiritual influence, that power entered his heart, repressed
the influence of Christ, and the sea-walker sunk back into the
earthly element. Analogous to this is the way in which faith in the
Lord's strengthening and upholding power conducts us securely over
the agitated sea of our sinful life, while, alas! it but too often happens that the failure sinks us down into the waters. That the gospel
narratives admit such spiritual applications, is no accidental feature,
nor is the application itself to be viewed as arbitrary and capricious.
Much rather does it spring from the weight and significance of the

Saviour's character, as the centre of all spiritual life, that every thing in him and with him rises into a higher significancy. Ver 32, 33.—According to Matthew and Mark, the disciples, in the strongest terms, express their astonishment (Mark v. 51, λίαν— ἐκ περισσοῦ—ἐξίστασθαι) and adoration. (The meaning of προσ- κυνεῖν, worship, which had otherwise been vague, is at Matth. xiv. 33, accurately defined by the confession which follows that he was the Son of God. See as to this more at length on Matth. xvi. 16). Christ, along with Peter, stepped on board the ship, the wind calmed down (ἄνεμος ἐκόπασε, see above, Mark iv. 39, = γαλήνη ἐγέ- νετο), and they gained the further shore. The account given at John v. 21, ἤθελον λαβεῖν αὐτόν, they would take him, seems to differ from the others, as though the disciples had intended taking him on board when they suddenly found themselves already at the land. Read by itself the statement of John would leave the impression that the εὐθέως τὸ πλοῖον ἐγένετο ἐπὶ τῆς γῆς, the ship became straight- way at the land, also seemed to him something miraculous. But as the disciples had in the first instance sailed half the distance before they saw Jesus, as they had the wind against them, and as during the scene between Christ and Peter, they assuredly forgot their oars, they cannot well have very speedily reached the shore. The meaning of εὐθέως, straightway, however, is vague, and none of the narrators give marks to fix the time ; we can therefore conceive of a rapid rowing forward of the ship through the calm, and an immediate landing thereafter. The only difficulty that remains is the ἤθελον λαβεῖν, wished to take, in so far as it is usually held to imply the non-fulfilment of the purposed intention, in which case there would result an open contradiction to the two other narrators. We might certainly at once, in this as in other cases, admit a contradic- tion, inasmuch as the Gospel history makes no claim to exemption from trifling and unimportant irregularities. At all events, we would rather do so than either hold ἐθέλω to be here redundant, or that it means to do a thing eagerly and joyfully (so that the sense should be—they took him eagerly and joyfully on board), a con- struction for which there is no support in the usage of the New Testament.* The following, however, appears to me a simple way of solving the difficulty. The disciples were afraid that they saw a spirit, which naturally they wished as far as possible from their ship. Jesus, however, explained to them that it was he. To this it is simply added that on receiving this explanation they strove to take him in, with the natural ellipsis, and they took him in accord- ingly—after which they directly gained the land. (The verb θέλειν then retains in this case its literal meaning of active volition, see

* In profane writers, especially in Xenophon (Cyrop., I. 1, 3, 1, 5, 19. Anab., II. 6, 6, and 11), this use of ἐθέλω frequently occurs.

Passow in Lex sub voce. For, in order to take in Christ while the ship was on her course, certain preparations were needful, such as the taking down of the sail, etc. The whole of these operations are denoted by the ἤθελον λαβεῖν, and the expression consequently implies the effectual carrying out of these preparations. The clause, therefore, if completed, would run thus : ἤθελον οὖν λαβεῖν αὐτὸν εἰς τὸ πλοῖον καὶ ἔλαβον, *they wished to take, etc., and took*).

Ver. 34–36.—Both Evangelists conclude this narrative with the general remark that immediately after the return of Jesus many sick persons applied for his help, and strove simply to touch the hem of his garment. (Compare what is said on Luke viii. 44.) Mark is more copious in his language, but without adding any new ideas, only that when he passes on to relate their arrival at the opposite shore, immediately after stating the astonishment of the disciples at Christ's walking on the sea, he adds : οὐ συνῆκαν ἐπὶ τοῖς ἄρτοις, *they had not understood in relation to [the miracle of] the loaves* (elliptically for ἐπὶ τῷ θαύματι τῷ ἐν τοῖς ἄρτοις γενομένῳ). Mark means to say that they might have been able from that miracle of feeding the multitude to recognise sufficiently his Divine nature, if their capacity for receiving the truth had not been so weak. (Respecting πωροῦσθαι [callo obduci, then *to become hardened, insensible*], see Mark viii. 17 ; Rom. xi. 7. It is parallel to παχύνεσθαι, Matth. xiii. 15. Προσορμίζεσθαι, *anchor*, Mark vi. 53, from ὅρμος, occurs only here.)

§ 27. OF WASHING THE HANDS.

(Matth. xv. 1–20 ; Mark vii. 1–23.)

On the chronological relation of this event to the preceding, little can be said, owing to the vagueness of the connecting formula. It would be rash to draw any inference from the presence of the Pharisees and Scribes who came down from Jerusalem. For the fact that they came from Jerusalem does not prove that they *belonged to* Jerusalem, and just as little that they were sent for the purpose of watching him. We can only infer from the form of Christ's discourse against the Pharisees, that the occurrence belongs to the latter period of his ministry, for during his earlier labours he did not usually express himself so strongly against them.

Ver. 1, 2.—It was so completely in keeping with the spirit of Phariseeism to rebuke every deviation from their sacred external ritual that the question of these Pharisees may be accounted for without supposing that they were designedly lying in wait for Christ. Such scruples arose from the peculiar character of their minds.

The παράδοσις τῶν πρεσβυτέρων, *tradition of the elders*, consists of those δόγματα ἄγραφα, *unwritten decisions*, which gradually among the learned men of the Jews had formed around the Mosaic law a new and holy circle of commands. Mark feels himself called on, for the sake of his non-Jewish readers, to explain more particularly the practice of eating with the hands washed. (Κοινός = אמצ Acts x. 14, conjoined with ἀκάθαρτον, here it is equivalent to ἄνιπτος.) He observes that among the Pharisaic Jews it was the general custom (πάντες οἱ Ἰουδαῖοι is to be taken in connexion with κρατοῦντες τὴν παράδοσιν, for the Sadducees did not observe such ordinances). The meaning of πυγμῇ νίψονται τὰς χεῖρας is uncertain. Undoubtedly, however, πυγμή is to be taken in the usual sense of *hand*, *fist*, so that the method in which the Jews washed before eating is here pointed out. The hands seem to have been used alternately, the one in washing the other. The Syriac translators have rendered it *frequently*, *generally*, as though they had read it πυκνῇ. Either the translator heard the word wrong, or he did not know how to interpret πυγμῇ. Mark, after explaining the practice of washing the hands, next proceeds to other usages of the same kind; for ablutions of all sorts (among the rest those applicable to the priests, Exod. xxix. 4; xxx. 18, seq., compared with Heb. ix. 10), were common among the Jews. He confines himself, however, to those washings which accompanied meals. The term βαπτίζεσθαι is different from νίπτεσθαι; the former is the dipping and rinsing, or cleansing, of food that has been purchased, to free it from impurities of any kind; νίπτεσθαι includes also the act of rubbing off. In precisely the same way do the Rabbins distinguish between נְטִילַה and נְטִילַּת יָדַיִם. (Compare *Lightfoot* on the passage. Βαπτισμός is here, as at Heb. ix. 10, *ablution*, *washing* generally.) The words ποτήριον, ξέστης, χαλκίον, are different names for vessels. Ποτήριον denotes a drinking vessel; ξέστης, corrupted from the Latin *sextarius*, a vessel for holding or measuring fluids; χαλκίον a vessel of brass, the nature of which we cannot more accurately determine. The κλίναι, *couches*, must, in this connexion, be referred to the couches on which the ancients were wont to recline at meals. (Compare Mark iv. 21).

Ver. 3, 4.—In the following discourse, addressed by Jesus to the Pharisees (down to ver. 11), Mark varies from Matthew, inasmuch as he makes the Saviour begin with the quotation from Isaiah, while in Matthew it forms the conclusion. The latter is unquestionably the more natural position. Appropriately the description of the Pharisees stands first, and then follows the passage from the prophet, as in confirmation of what had been said. The leading idea of the whole passage, however, is neither more nor less than the opposition of human institutions to the divine command. The real test of a spurious faith is the substituting of the former of these for the latter, or the placing it above the latter. In this way the spirit is withdrawn from the service of God: it becomes a mere human service. This perversion of the Divine ordinances by human, the Saviour explains by an example, shewing how Pharisaic hypocrisy subverted a holy precept of God by an ordinance calculated to promote their own earthly interests. Jesus quotes Exod. xx. 12; xxi. 17, in order to shew what, according to the Divine ordinance, is the true relation in which children stand to their parents. The Mosaic regulation, the Lord (Mark vii. 10) here acknowledges as one which proceeded directly from God, because God spake through Moses, and his ordinances possessed Divine authority. Κακολογεῖν, *curse* (= βλασφημεῖν), stands in antithesis to τιμᾶν, *honour*, in the same way that μακροχρόνιος γίνεσθαι, *be long lived*, in the first (not fully quoted) passage, does to the verb ἀποθνήσκειν, *die*. The highest curse and the highest blessing were thus, under the theocratic dispensation, conceived under sensible forms.

Ver. 5, 6.—This holy commandment the Pharisees taught men to evade by the ordinance—" Temple offerings take precedence of all gifts in behalf of parents." As to the construction, we observe, *first*, that the clause δῶρον (sc. ἔστω), ὃ ἐὰν ἐξ ἐμοῦ ὠφεληθῇς, is obscure. The parents are conceived as making a request, and the children as refusing it, with the explanation that what might have been due to them (ἐάν stands for ἄν, compare *Winer*, p. 285) they had already decided to give to the temple. (Δῶρον = קָרְבָּן, applies as well to bloody as to unbloody offerings.) On this they found the inference that it is not incumbent to give them anything. Probably it is to be presumed either that the priests took a small portion of the gift instead of the whole, or that they were able to instil it into the children that they would acquire special merit by those temple-offerings. It is not conceivable otherwise that any child could have been induced to act thus towards his parents. The *second* difficulty lies in the expression καὶ οὐ μὴ τιμήσῃ. Mark guides us here to the right meaning. In the first place, the future τιμήσει is a false reading; it does not agree with εἴπῃ. In the next place, the καὶ οὐ corresponds to וְלֹא, and introduces the answering clause (the apodosis of the proposition) :—" if any one says, what would have been yours is consecrated to the temple, he need not (οὐ μή, he shall not) honour father and mother." The verb τιμᾶν (in the sense of giving bodily support), is thus chosen simply to bring out more markedly the contradiction to the Divine commandment. It is needless to suppose that anything is to be supplied, e. g., ἀναίτιός ἐστι. Hence our Lord deduces the inference that by their human institutions they subvert the Divine (ἀκυρόω is used especially in regard to laws. Gal. iii. 17).

Ver. 7-9.—After this Jesus applies the prophetic words of Isaiah xxix. 13, to the piety of the Pharisees. The two evangelists agree word for word (only instead of ὁ λαὸς οὗτος, Mark has οὗτος ὁ λαός) in the quotation. The LXX. deviates from the original much in its expressions, although the idea is the same. This agreement of Matthew and Mark in a passage containing a deviation, and which is quoted from memory, would lead to the inference that the one had used the other's gospel, or that they had drawn from some common source [possibly from a Chaldee Targum]. (The text of Matthew in this quotation is in several MSS. corrected after the LXX. Mark being less read and less expounded, is free from such interpolations.) The simple idea then expressed by the prophet is this—the outward service of God, unless the whole inner man take part in it with the living energy of mind and will (both being comprehended in the καρδία = לֵב) is in the highest degree offensive to God. Isaiah spake these words to the Jews of his day, as the connexion of the passage shews, yet both evangelists remark that Christ observed καλῶς προεφήτευσε περὶ ὑμῶν, *well did he prophesy concerning you*, an expression which may serve as a commentary to the words ὅπως πληρωθῇ, *that it may be fulfilled*. An explicit reference in these words to the contemporaries of Jesus, the Saviour, and also the evangelists, must have discovered in this passage, in thus far, that as Christ was the central point of all life and being under the theocracy, every mental tendency and aim, even though partially embodied in earlier representatives, yet gathered around *him* in the full development and display of their inherent qualities. The whole Old Testament history was prophetic of Christ and of those around him in this respect, that everywhere, in the continually recurring contest between light and darkness, between truth and error, there were displayed the types of that which in its highest energy developed itself in and around Christ. (As to ὑποκριτής, see on Matth. vi. 2).

Ver. 10, 11.—The general idea which from this conversation pressed itself on the Saviour's mind, namely, that purity is to be sought for within the soul and not in externals, he puts forward before the great mass of the people, as the germ of many other fruitful thoughts (ὄχλος in contrast to the μαθηταί), for the benefit of all those who were able to penetrate its meaning and properly to apply it. As the idea, however, was expressed figuratively (in reference to the words ἐν παραβολῇ, see on Matth. xiii. 3), Jesus, at a later period, after he had dismissed the people (Mark vii. 17) prompted by a request from the disciples, whose organ (according to Matthew) Peter once more was, gives an exposition of it. (Matth. xv. 17-19.)

Ver. 12-14.—Matthew adds, however, a parenthetical explana-

tion regarding the Pharisees and their relation to the kingdom of
God—an explanation called forth by the anxiety of the disciples
lest the Pharisees should have taken offence at his discourse, and
lest this should lead to fatal results. (As to σκανδαλίζεσθαι, see on
Matth. xviii. 6.) The words of Christ in which he allays their
anxiety on this point, refer also to the parable of the field and the
different kinds of seed, to the end of the bad seed and of the plants
which spring from it. (Matth. xiii. 24, seq., especially ver. 30,
συλλέξατε τὰ ζιζάνια κ. τ. λ.) The term ἐκριζωθήσεται, shall be rooted
up, therefore expresses the idea of the final judgment, and the
Saviour chose for the statement of this idea a figurative form of
expression already familiar to the disciples. It is a false interpretation, however, to refer the φυτεία, plant, to the doctrine of the
Pharisees, and not to themselves personally. (Literally the φυτεία
is the act of planting itself, then, the thing planted = φύτευμα.)
That were a false attempt to weaken the idea of the κατάκρισις, condemnation, (the total cutting off from the communion of the good),
which is openly announced here as formerly at chap. xiii. 30. Undoubtedly the Pharisees are God's creatures as well as other men, but
in as far as their false systems, in their moral estrangement from
God, had become blended with the very essence of their being, and
in fact could exist only there, in so far do they belong not to God
but to the devil. The expression, which my heavenly Father hath
not planted (ἣν οὐκ ἐφύτευσεν ὁ πατήρ μου ὁ οὐράνιος), must therefore
be completed by supplying, as the Evangelist intended, but the devil,
who according to Matth. xiii. 25, 38, casts in the bad seed. (The τέκνα
διαβόλου mean the same thing, see on John viii. 44.) An absolute
predestination or material difference (in the Manichean sense) between the good and the evil is not to be understood here ; no one is
by birth a child of the devil, he becomes such only by his corrupt
will and continued striving against grace. But what applies to the
leader, Jesus attributes also to the followers (see on Matth. xxiii.
15). The perverted suffer along with the perverter, obviously
according to the principle laid down at Luke xii. 47, 48. The
figurative form of the expression of the thought is finally intelligible in itself. Luke vi. 39, inserts it amidst the contents of the sermon on the mount. (As to βόθυνος, see Matth. xii. 11.)

Ver. 15, 16.—Hereupon follows the request of the apostles
(Peter being their representative), that he would explain the figurative discourse (παραβολή, see on Matth. xiii. 3). Jesus rebukes their
defective powers of comprehension (σύνεσις understanding, νοῦς,
reason; comp. on Luke ii. 47), and then explains to them the similitude. (The expression ἀκμήν literally means on the moment in the
Greek profane writers, and hence becomes synonymous with ἔτι,
still.) The explanation itself, however, is still very difficult.

Ver. 17.—In the sentiment formerly stated (ver. 11), it must have appeared at the very outset a difficulty to the disciples that Christ's explanation, "not that which entereth into the mouth defileth" (τὸ εἰσερχόμενον εἰς τὸ στόμα οὐ κοινοῖ), seemed to contradict the Old Testament, which taught the distinction between clean and unclean meats. As Christ acknowledges the divinity of the Old Testament (Matth. v. 17), he must see an importance even in its laws respecting food. That, therefore, these were wholly void of meaning, the Saviour in explaining the words, does by no means say. He only gives prominence to the contrast between what is external and internal, and calls attention to the circumstance, that food, as something external (ἔξωθεν εἰσπορευόμενον εἰς τὸν ἄνθρωπον), could never reach or pollute the *soul*. He does not however say, that what is *outward* may not cause *outward* pollution, or that it is thus of no consequence what a man may eat. This was hint enough to the disciples that our Lord left to the Jewish laws all their significancy as to externals (and as types of what was spiritual), and only intended to rebuke the Pharisaic substitutions of the outward for the internal.* Mark, who here formally paraphrases the words of Matthew, leads to a right apprehension of the first half of the thought. The food taken into the outward organ for its reception,(the mouth),enters not into the inner man (καρδία = לֵב), but goes into the κοιλία, *belly*, to nourish the bodily organism. The additional clause καὶ εἰς ἀφεδρῶνα ἐκβάλλεται, *and is thrown out*, etc., is partly intended as the climax of those explanations, which shew how thoroughly external the process of taking food is, and partly designed to intimate that nature herself has assigned the means of separating the nourishing element in food from that which is impure. Mark, in his explanatory way, expresses this in the words καθαρίζον πάντα τὰ βρώματα, *cleansing all our food*. The neuter gender (the readings καθαρίζων, καθαρίζει, are the corrections of transcribers to diminish difficulty) refers to the whole of what precedes, in such a way that τοῦτό ἐστι καθαρίζον must be supplied.

Ver. 18, 19.—The internal however is here set in contrast with that which is outward, and to this is referred the defilement of the real (the spiritual) man. To this defiling of the soul the Pharisees gave no heed while carefully avoiding that which was external. In this second idea, however, there are internal difficulties. For, *first*, it would seem that it is not the mere *issuing forth* (the manifesta-

* It is unquestionably wrong to look on this as containing an abrogation of the Old Testament laws respecting food, such as we afterwards find at Acts x. 10. The Old Testament, as typical and external in its ordinances (σκιὰ τῶν μελλόντων, Heb. x. 1), could effect only outward purification (Heb. ix. 23, τὴν τῆς σαρκὸς καθαρότητα), but this the Pharisees, according to their usual mistake of the outward for the inward, confounded with spiritual purity, and to point out this error is the object of Jesus.

tion of feeling by word or deed), but the presence of corrupt feeling which pollutes, and this idea assuredly (as Matth. v. 28 shews) the Saviour was far from wishing to exclude. *Again*, if the heart appears as the source of evil actions (ver. 19, ἐκ τῆς καρδίας ἐξέρχονται διαλογισμοὶ πονηροί), we do not then see how man can *be made* unclean ; in his inmost soul he is unclean already. It is the pure only, not the impure, that admits of being defiled. This leads us to determine with more exactness the meaning of ἐκπορεύεσθαι ἐκ τοῦ στόματος, *come forth out of the mouth* (the opposite of the foregoing εἰσπορεύεσθαι), an expression which seems intended to mark the relation of the will to evil thoughts. The general fact that evil thoughts enter into the mind of man, is a consequence of the universal sinfulness of the race, but that any particular evil thoughts gain power over him sufficient to manifest themselves in outward act, is the result of the will, and its voluntary choice. By *actual sin*, however, the *habit of sinning* is strengthened, and thus also the nobler germ of human nature is defiled. The heart, here, therefore, is not the *source* of evil thoughts, but the canal, as it were, through which they flow, and through which in like manner the Spirit of grace pours good thoughts into man.* In no respect is man the absolutely free and independent *creator* of his own thoughts and inclinations (which Pelagianism would make him), but he possesses the power equally of rejecting what is bad and admitting what is good into his soul, or the reverse. It is very obvious, therefore, what value is to be put upon the opinion of those who infer from these words that the heart produces at will evil thoughts (or good), and that these do not originate in the kingdom of darkness. " Doth a fountain send forth from the same opening sweet water and bitter ?"† James iii. 11. (Comp. as to καρδία and διαλογισμός at Luke i. 51 ; ii. 35 ; Matth. ix. 4.) In the enumeration of the several forms of evil propensities which is also given by Mark more at length, ἀσέλγεια is not to be referred to sexual impurity, as elsewhere at Rom. xiii. 13 ; 2 Cor. xii. 21 ; Gal. v. 19, al. freq., for it stands quite apart from πορνεῖαι and μοιχεῖαι. It is best understood as denoting an evil disposed wilfulness and its results. The

* *Krabbe* (on Sin and Death, Hamburg, 1836, p. 131, note) thinks that "καρδία is the innermost will in so far as it, acting unconditionally, co-operates for the production of actual sin." But that is what I doubt—whether the human will can act unconditionally and independently of everything beyond itself. A good action has for its condition the influence of God, an evil action that of the kingdom of darkness and its prince. How this does not subvert the true freedom of the will, is shewn in our remarks on Rom. ix. 1.

† Does the passage mean any more than that true purity depends not on external rites, but on the state of the heart? Moral defilement consists in evil thoughts. In the first place, they *mark* a polluted character, and secondly tend to *aggravate* its pollution.—[K.

expression ὀφθαλμὸς πονηρός, however, corresponds to the Hebrew רַע עַיִן, Prov. xxiii. 6 ; xxviii. 22 ; which denotes an envious, malicious glance. It is connected with the idea that such a look is capable of inflicting injury. (Comp. Matth. xx. 15.) The last expression ἀφροσύνη == ἄνοια, refers to forms of sin and wickedness in which stupidity is prominently exhibited—"senseless wicked acts."

§ 28. THE HEALING OF THE CANAANITISH WOMAN'S DAUGHTER.

* (Matth. xv. 21–31; Mark vii. 24–31, [32–37; viii. 22–26.])

Without marking accurately either time or place, Matthew (and Mark also, who follows him), proceeds to the narrative of a cure, in which, however, our interest is awakened, not so much by the act of healing itself, as by the antecedent circumstances. Mark once more distinguishes himself by giving minute traits which illustrate the outward action, but he leaves out also essential features, for example the statement at Matth. xv. 24, as to the relation of the heathen to the people of Israel, which casts so much light on the whole transaction.

Ver. 21.—The μέρη Τύρου, *district of Tyre*, Mark describes more definitely by μεθόρια, *borders*. The Lord *approached* these boundaries, but that he really passed over them, is rendered improbable by the idea stated at ver. 24.* The woman, however, came to meet him. (Ver. 22, ἀπὸ τῶν ὁρίων ἐκείνων ἐξελθοῦσα.)

Ver. 22.—The woman is called by Matthew (in the true phraseology of Palestine), χαναναία, *Canaanitess*, but by Mark ἑλληνίς συροφοινίκισσα, Syrophenician Greek ; (the better manuscripts have this form instead of συροφοίνισσα, which certainly is a more correct Greek form of the word, but on this very account is less deserving of being admitted into our text.) The addition of τῷ γένει, *by race*, obviously marks her descent from the inhabitants of that region ; ἑλληνίς refers to her language and education, which, as was usual in those countries about the time of Christ, were Grecian.

Ver. 23, 24.—She prays in behalf of her demoniac daughter, but the Lord refuses her as a heathen with the words οὐκ ἀπεστάλην κ. τ. λ. (comp. on Matth. x. 5, 6). Intentionally and wisely did the Saviour confine his ministry to the people of Israel. Only on certain heroes of the faith from amidst the heathen world did Jesus

---

* De Wette asserts (on this passage) "it is not said here that Jesus entered on foreign ground with a view to exercise his ministry." But after commencing his official career, he continually exercised it, and he did so specially in the present case. It is thus, to say the least of it, not probable that he crossed the boundary.

bestow grace as the representatives of nations who as yet were far from the covenants of promise.

Ver. 25, 26.—To the woman who still impressively repeated her request, Jesus again addressed the same reply, but in a sharper form. Representing himself as the steward of the mysteries of God and dispenser of all the heavenly powers of life, he compares the Israelites to the children of the family, and the heathen to the dogs. (Κύνες is used contemptuously as at Philip. iii. 2. Neither the Old Testament nor the New recognises the noble nature of this animal. Comp. on Luke xvi. 21. The diminutive certainly has a milder sense. Still the thought remains very sharp and bitter, and *he designs it to be so.*) [The woman must, above all, recognise the divinely granted prerogative of Israel.]

Ver. 27.—The woman's faith, however, humbly receives the reply in all its bitterness, and child-like she takes the position assigned her, claiming no place within the temple ; she is content to remain standing as a door-keeper in the outer court, and pleads simply for that grace which was fitting for the occupant of such a station. (Adopting the figure she entreats a gift of the ψιχία, *crumbs.* The expression occurs again only at Luke xvi. 21, in regard to Lazarus the sick man, and in a similar connexion. It is from ψίω, to *rub down, to crush in pieces.*)

Ver. 28.—Overcome as it were by the humble faith of the heathen woman, the Saviour himself confesses *great is thy faith,* and straightway faith received what it asked. This little narrative lays open the magic that lies in a humbly-believing heart more directly and deeply than all explanations or descriptions could do. Faith and humility are so intimately at one, that neither can exist without the other ; both act as with magic power on the unseen and spiritual world ; they draw the heavenly essence itself down into the sphere of earth. In this cure faith is again obviously seen not as knowledge, not as the upholding of certain doctrines for true, but as a state of the mind—the tenderest susceptibility for what is heavenly—the perfect womanhood of the soul. When *yearning* faith, by coming in contact with the object it longs for, becomes *seeing* faith, out of such a mental state there certainly spring beliefs and doctrines of all kinds, which, as being the product of this inward and immediate operation, may themselves be termed faith. Usually, however, the Christian finds more difficulty in understanding the conduct of Christ than in the depth of this heathen woman's faith. It would seem as if he who knew what was in man (John ii. 25) must have been constrained at once to help *this* woman, as her faith could not have been concealed from him ; and even although for wise reasons he was led to confine his ministry to the Jews, yet as in other instances he made exceptions (comp. on Matth. viii. 10), so might he have done in her case *at once* without laying on her the burden of his severity. Nay, the severity seems so very severe, that it were difficult to find a place for such a trait in the beauteous portraiture of the mild Son of man. It is Christian experience alone which opens our way to the right understanding of this. As God himself is compared by our Lord to an unjust judge who often turns away the well-grounded supplication (Luke xviii. 3, seq.), as the Lord wrestles with Jacob at Jacob's ford, and thus exalts him to be Israel (Gen. xxxii. 24, seq.), as he seeks to kill Moses who was destined to deliver his people (Exod. iv. 24), so faith often in its experience finds that the heaven is of brass and seems to despise its prayers. A similar mode of dealing is here exhibited by the Saviour. The restraining of his grace, the manifestation of a treatment wholly different from what the woman may at first have expected, acted as a check usually does on power when it really exists ; the whole inherent energy of her living faith broke forth, and the Saviour suffered himself to be overcome by her as he had when wrestling with Jacob. In this mode then of Christ's giving an answer to prayer we are to trace only another form of his love. Where faith is weak, he anticipates and comes to meet it ; where faith is strong, he holds himself aloof that it may in itself be carried to perfection.*

Ver. 29–31.—According to both Evangelists, Jesus after this left the western boundary of Palestine, and turned back to the sea of Genesareth. (As to Δεκάπολις, see on Matth iv. 25.) Without marking more closely the connexion, local or chronological, the narrative ends in one of those general concluding formulæ, which plainly shew that the author never intended to produce a history marked by chronological arrangement. To me it seems not unlikely, from the frequency with which such forms of conclusion occur in Matthew (comp. iv. 23–25 ; ix. 8, 26, 31, 35, 36 ; xiv. 34–36), and their uniformity, that he interwove into his work minor treatises which had perhaps at an earlier period been written down by himself.[?] There is a peculiarity in the use of κυλλός which occurs in this passage in the enumeration of the sufferers who assembled around Jesus. The same word is found at Matth. xviii. 8, conjoined as in this case with χωλός, and there it obviously means *one maimed*. But never in any other case is it recorded as an express fact that Christ really restored bodily members which had been cut off, and a cure of this kind would ill accord with his usual mode of healing. It is better therefore to take κυλλός here in the sense usually assigned it by profane writers, viz. : *bent, crooked, bowed down*. As the denial of Christ's higher, heavenly, miraculous power is an error, so it contradicts the gospel narrative

---

* As to the faith of the woman, in behalf of her daughter, see on Matth. xvii. 14, seq.

to hold that this miraculous power put forth its energy without internal law or order, to guide its manifestations. Never does the Lord create members to replace those which had been cut off, but he heals those which had been injured : never does he create bread absolutely from nothing (without a previous substratum), but he increases that which previously existed. The question, then, whether he was not able to have done such things, must be cast aside, as entirely impertinent ; it is enough for us that he did them not. Still the principle stands fast which is implied in the very idea of Christ's Divine nature, that boundless as was his power, it was yet perfectly regulated by laws, inasmuch as the Spirit himself is law, and all spiritual phenomena are embraced within a cycle of higher and heavenly laws, whose revolution constitutes the system of nature. This is confirmed by the short narrative of the heal- ing of the man who was deaf and dumb (κωφὸς μογιλάλος, i. e., hard of hearing, and for this reason as not hearing his own voice, speaking unintelligibly ; according to ver. 35, therefore, he at once spoke on his hearing being restored), which Mark here inserts (vii. 32–37), and which he alone records. Minute and circumstan- tial in his narrative, he recounts here, as in the similar account of healing the blind man (viii. 22–26), many particulars as to the ex- ternal mode of Christ's cures which bring them vividly before the mind's eye. With these notices may be compared the account of the disciples performing cures with oil (which Mark vi. 13 alone gives), and the narrative in John ix. 6, of Christ's applying spittle in the same way when healing one born blind. The oil is to be regarded as merely an ordinary outward means of cure (Luke x. 34), which the disciples, distrusting, as it were, the full effi- cacy of their miraculous powers (Matth. xvii. 20), applied at the same time. It is a wholly unscriptural view that Christ, along with their heavenly miraculous power, had enjoined his disciples to employ the expedients of domestic medicine : he rather permitted them the use of the oil in accommodation to their weakness. Leav- ing this out of view, there remain in these narratives the following peculiarities. (1.) It is a new thing that Jesus should take those who are about to be healed apart by themselves (Mark vii. 33, ἀπολαβόμενος αὐτὸν ἀπὸ τοῦ ὄχλου κατ' ἰδίαν ; viii. 23, ἐξήγαγεν αὐτὸν ἔξω τῆς κώμης). We are not to suppose that this was done from anxiety lest the people on seeing his treatment of the sick should be led into various superstitions. This would have applied equally to the sick themselves who belonged to the people, and shared their views. A single word, moreover, would have provided against such superstition. It is better to seek the ground of it in the personal interests of the sick. As their moral healing was the ultimate end of their physical cure, the Saviour ordered everything external so as to contribute to that object. Amidst the din of popular tumult beneficial impressions could with far more difficulty be made on them. And with this also agrees the command given to both, that they should preserve silence as to their cure. (Comp. vii. 36 ; viii. 26. See what is said on this at Matth. viii. 4.) (2.) Another peculiarity is the gradually advancing process of cure in the case of the blind man. According to Mark viii. 24, after the first touch of Jesus he saw darkly and obscurely. "I see men as trees (the power of measuring extension by the eye was probably as yet wanting) walking." After the second touch he was wholly restored. Obviously, therefore, the cures performed by Christ were no magical transactions, but real processes. In the case of the blind man the course of the cure may have been retarded for this reason, that his disease was deeply seated, and a too rapid process of recovery might have been injurious. We remarked something of the same kind in dealing with the history of the Gergesene (Matth. viii. 28), from whom the demon did not depart till the command of Jesus had been twice given. (3.) The application of *spittle* is peculiar to these narratives, which is also mentioned again at John ix. 6. In regard to this, we must at once reject, as unworthy of the dignity of Christ, the opinion which holds that he was himself misled by the popular notion that attributed to the spittle healing virtues, and which, further, infers from this that the thing here recorded must be understood even in cases where it is not mentioned, and so would transform Christ into an ordinary physician, acquainted with the use of certain remedies. We are equally to reject the other opinion that Christ employed this means in order to aid the weak faith of those who were to be healed.* For on the one hand the Saviour does not employ means to remedy weakness of faith, and on the other, it is incongruous to endeavour by means so purely external to reach a spiritual want. We must therefore have looked on the employment of the spittle as exercising real influence, even though we had been unable to trace in it any link of connexion. But as we already observed that the laying on of Christ's hands (so here the holding of his finger to eye and ear) must, as it were, be considered as the medium of conveyance for spiritual power (it is only in particular cases that this power imparts itself from a distance, and without visible means of communication ; see on Matth. viii. 10), so it is in a way analogous to this that we are to look on the use of *his own* spittle. (Mark vii. 34, gives in Aramaic the exclamation of Christ, ἐφφαθά—διανοίχθητι, *be opened*. It is the authoritative summons of

* In the case of the deaf and dumb, however, it is not to be overlooked that the actions of Christ (the touching of his ears and tongue, the looking up to heaven), were obviously calculated to make him aware of what was about to be done with him in order to rouse his faith, which could not be done in his case by words.

Christ adapted to the present case ; it is the expression of his Divine
will, of whose fulfilment that Son who had called on the Father
[εἰς τὸν οὐρανὸν ἀναβλέψας ἐστέναξε, ver. 34], was fully assured. The
form of the word is the imperative of the Aramaic conjugation
Ethpael, ἐφφαθά = ἐθφαθά [in Syriac חֲתַפְתָּא from the root חתף].—Ver.
37. The exclamation καλῶς πάντα πεποίηκε, *he hath done all things
well*, almost reminds us of the history of creation, where it is said
πάντα, ὅσα ἐποίησε, καλὰ λίαν, *all that he had made was very good*,
Gen. i. 31. The ministry of the Messiah seems to be viewed as a
καινὴ κτίσις = חֲדָשָׁה חֲרִיאָה בְּרִיאָה, *new creation*. According to Mark viii.
22, the healing of the blind man took place at Bethsaida [see as to
it on Matth. xi. 21], by which we are here probably to understand
the place of that name on the eastern shore of the sea of Genesareth.
Yet is the description of the locality even in Mark indefinite, so that
we cannot with certainty decide where the cure took place.—Ver.
25. The expression ἐποίησεν αὐτὸν ἀναβλέψαι, is not to be referred to
the restoration of the sight, that is afterwards expressed by ἀποκαθίσ-
τασθαι, in integrum restitui. Rather is the ποιεῖν ἀναβλέψαι equivalent to the Hebrew Hiphil, " he caused him, after laying his hands
on him the second time, to look up," and then he saw τηλαυγῶς.
That word, which is found only here, literally means " *shining afar,
radiant*," from τῆλε, *in the distance*. Here, as shown by the connexion, it means " *plainly, distinctly*.")

§ 29. Feeding of the Four Thousand.

(Matth. xv. 32–39 ; Mark viii. 1–10.)

The account which follows of feeding the four thousand is
attached by Matthew to the preceding context without any mark to
determine the time when it happened, and by Mark with the
indefinite words ἐν ἐκείναις ταῖς ἡμέραις, *in those days*. The latter
gives us once more separate minute traits, which make the narrative more graphic, as for example, ver. 3, " some of them have
come from afar," and in ver. 1 the amplification of Matthew's brief
expressions. The latter alone informs us that the number of four
thousand is reckoned apart from the women and children (ver. 38).
The narrative itself certainly contains no new points when compared
with the first account of feeding the five thousand, Matth. xiv. 13,
seq. The single circumstance to be inquired into, therefore, is
whether we are to regard the entire occurrence as distinct from the
other,. or whether, by a mistake of Matthew (and after him of
Mark), the same instance of feeding has been twice recorded. This
latter view has been put forward by Schleiermacher (on Luke, p.

137), and Schultz (on the Lord's Supper, p. 311). De Wette also and others see in this second account a repetition of the first fact drawn from tradition. The chief ground for this supposition would seem to lie in the circumstance that we cannot conceive how the disciples, if they had once had experience of such a miracle, could ever in similar circumstances have asked unbelievingly πόθεν ἡμῖν ἐν ἐρημίᾳ ἄρτοι τοσοῦτοι ὥστε χορτάσαι ὄχλον τοσοῦτον, *whence have we in the desert so many loaves?* etc., (ver. 33.) But less weight is to be attached to this remark when we find that on various occasions the disciples forget things which it should have been impossible for them to forget. For example, the plainest declarations as to Christ's sufferings and death they seem never to have heard when the event really took place. Assuming then that some considerable time elapsed between these two miraculous entertainments ; that meanwhile they had frequently met with cases in which themselves and those around them had suffered momentary want (take, *e. g.,* the plucking of the ears of corn), but in which the Lord did not choose thus to interpose his aid, we may perhaps conceive that in the moment of feeling want, it did not occur to the disciples that the Saviour would be pleased a second time thus to manifest his power. We are the more disposed to this explanation, as there is otherwise not the slightest improbability of the repetition under analogous circumstances, of the same fact, any more than that healing processes were similarly repeated. To admit, on the other hand, that the narrative in this case is not authentic, is to open the way for consequences affecting the authority of the Gospel which a Christian mind could never admit, unless they rested on such sure historical proofs, as are here utterly wanting. A new and fully detailed history of events which absolutely did not take place could be given neither by an apostle of the Lord, nor by an assistant whose gospel rested on apostolic authority. Still less could both narrators subsequently (Matth. xvi. 9, 10 ; Mark viii. 19, 20), put into the mouth of our Lord himself an allusion to an event which had never happened.* If the narrative forced us to such assumptions as this, the authority of both gospels would be overthrown. The supposition that a fully detailed narrative of fact is a pure in-

* The passage here quoted is also of importance for our object in this respect, that the remark of the disciples, ὅτι ἄρτους οὐκ ἐλάβομεν (Matth. xvi. 7), shews that even *after* the second miraculous feeding the disciples could not imagine that their being in the company of the Son of man made it needless for them to take provisions for the body. Jesus finds it necessary to rebuke them for this unbelief, and reminds them of *both* miraculous entertainments. One can hardly conceive a stronger proof that the second feeding is authentic. Meanwhile superficial modern criticism knows how to set it quite easily aside by the cheap assertion that it was only after the formation of the two fabulous reports as to the feeding, that this whole conversation was—invented. At this rate any fact one chooses may be struck out of the narrative.

vention is quite another thing from the admission of some trifling
historical oversight—for example, whether there were one or two
blind men. Add to this, that on closer examination the invention of the fact by tradition is wholly improbable. For in the first
place, if this second narrative of feeding the .people had owed
its origin to tradition, much would have been added to it by
way of embellishment. The unadorned style in which the second
event is told, precisely as was the former even in the separate words,
vouches for its apostolic origin. Nay, this narrative, so far from any
effort to display the fact in brighter colours, sets it forth as of less
importance. In the former case there were 5000, here only 4000,
and yet there are here seven loaves while formerly there were only
five, although the less the number of loaves the more marvellous
must the miracle appear. It is precisely in these little circumstances that the handiwork of tradition would most easily be
detected. What could any one gain by inventing the account of
Christ's having fed 4000 men, when in fact he had already fed
5000 ? Not thus are framed the fictions of tradition. If we
had read here of Christ having fed 10,000 men with one loaf, the
probability of forgery had been greater.* Is any one ready to say
that this second fact may be the real one while the former is the
fictitious, in which the number of the fed is increased and of the
loaves diminished? This however is the most improbable of all
views of it—that any one should place last the real fact as being
the less important and put first the false. Obviously an unconscien-
tious narrator will overdo the truth itself, and for this reason he
places last the invented fact as being the most striking. We can
discover then only proofs for the authenticity of this second feeding
as narrated, none whatever to shew that it is spurious ; for, in
regard to the disciples, we can easily admit that previously to their
being furnished with power from on high their memory was often
weak ; indeed they themselves state quite plainly that it was so
with them. They walked in a new world full of spiritual and
bodily wonders, amidst which they could not find themselves at
home until the Spirit came upon them, and brought to their minds
all things that the Lord had said to them and done. (John xiv.
26.) (As to Magdala [Matth. xv. 39], and Dalmanutha [Mark viii.
10], see on Matth. xvi. 5.)

* With great *naïveté* Strauss (vol ii., p. 203) describes these as " eager remarks into
which one had better not enter." By all means, for this wanton critic had nothing to
allege against them, except that the first feeding also was a myth, *i. e.*, a lie. Thus,
with this man, one lie is built upon another. One who honestly calls things by their
right names, which certainly makes a fatal impression, does not, Strauss thinks, know how
to penetrate the depths of the mythic view.

§ 30. WARNING AGAINST THE LEAVEN OF THE PHARISEES.

(Matth. xvi. 1–12 ; Mark viii. 11–21.)

Along with his narrative of the second miraculous feeding, the Evangelist conjoins the account of an incident which shews the weakness of the disciples. When Christ used the words προσέχετε ἀπὸ τῆς ζύμης τῶν Φαρισαίων, *beware of the leaven of the Pharisees,* they thought they were reproved on account of having forgotten to take bread, while the Saviour was thinking only of the spiritual influence put forth by the Pharisees. Everything in this section is connected with Christ's words of rebuke and warning against the Pharisees ; but since neither in the preceding nor following context are they further spoken of, it is rendered probable that the evangelist merely points out the occasion when those words, so intimately connected with the account of the feeding, and on which he laid such peculiar stress, were spoken. It can moreover excite no surprise that the Pharisees, when they demand of Jesus a sign (and a sign from heaven too, Luke xi. 16), should have been rebuked in terms similar to those of Matth. xii. 38, seq., by a reference to the sign of Jonas. There is nothing to justify the assumption (which Schulz defends loco citat.) that Jesus spoke the words only once, but that the narrator, drawing from impure tradition, has twice recorded them. It is possible that Matthew here incorporates portions of discourses originally uttered in another connexion (for example, verses 2, 3, which are given by Matthew alone, but which yet appear to me to be quite as appropriately placed here as at Luke xii. 55, 56, where see the exposition of the words), but the whole is to be viewed as a new occurrence. For if the Pharisees more than once eagerly desired a sign from heaven—which from their devotedness to externals, may easily be supposed—it is equally conceivable, that the Saviour more than once addressed them as a γενεὰ πονηρὰ καὶ μοιχαλίς, *evil and adulterous generation,* and alluded to the great Jonah-sign. (For the exposition of Matth. xvi. 1–4, see on Matth. xii. 38, seq.)

The peculiar essence of the narrative Mark, as is clear, has rightly seized. He brings forward with great care, as the essential point, all that relates to the conversation of Jesus with the disciples (viii. 13, seq). They pass together across the sea to the further shore. This points us back to Matth. xv. 39 ; Mark viii. 10, where Magdala and Dalmanutha are mentioned as the places to which Christ betook himself. The latter of these places is mentioned only here, but it lay probably in the neighbourhood of Magdala, which is named by Matthew. Μαγδαλά (from בְּגַדֹל a *tower,* for which reason it is not to be written μαγαδάν or μαγεδάν), lay on the eastern shore of the sea, in the district of the Gadarenes. One of the Marys (with the surname *of Magdala*) was undoubtedly a native of this town. On their voyage across, the conversation here recorded took place, and to their accounts of it both Evangelists prefix the remark that the disciples had forgotten to take bread. (The careful Mark even adds that they had *only one loaf,* εἰ μὴ ἕνα ἄρτον οὐκ εἶχον μεθ' ἑαυτῶν. Such traits indicate the extreme accuracy of the sources of information employed by Mark ; it is not thus that myths are formed. It would ill accord also with the idea that the second narrative of feeding the multitude is fictitious.) The remark of Jesus, ὁρᾶτε καὶ προσέχετε ἀπὸ τῆς ζύμης τῶν Φαρισαίων, *take heed and beware of the leaven,* etc., must be accounted for, and for this reason did the narrators prefix the request for a miracle which shortly before the Pharisees had addressed to Jesus.

An apparent contradiction seems to arise between Matth. xvi. 6 and Mark viii. 15, inasmuch as the former conjoins the Sadducees, the latter Herod, with the Pharisees. Herod, however, stands merely for his party (Matth. xxii. 16 ; Mark iii. 6), in which the laxity of the Sadducees in moral and religious opinion, was mixed up with political objects. (Comp. on Matth. xiv. 2, which passage does not contradict this view.) If, therefore, the Sadducees and Herodians are not identical, yet are they nearly akin—doctrine holding the more prominent place with the former, politics with the latter. Against their entire scope and influence the Saviour directs his warning. For although ζύμη, *leaven,* is immediately explained at Matth. xvi. 12, as διδαχή, *doctrine,* yet this is not to be regarded separately from their entire moral condition ; for, outwardly considered, there was much truth in the doctrine of the Pharisees (Matth. xxiii. 3). Their *doctrine, teaching,* was merely that which came forth from them, and consequently it was that which, as it were, infected others and spread the plague of these men. At Luke xii. 1, therefore, it is said most correctly " the leaven of the Pharisees is hypocrisy" (ἡ ζύμη τῶν Φαρισαίων ἐστὶν ὑπόκρισις), for with them the danger lay in their hypocrisy, with the Sadducees in the Epicurean pursuit of enjoyment—with both in their alienation from God, and mental idolatry. The term *leaven* belongs to those figurative expressions in Scripture which may be applied in either of two opposite ways. (See on Matth. xiii. 33.) The application of it to the corrupting (fermentation-causing) element of evil, is the original one. It rests even on Old Testament usage, the purification of the house from leaven, for the paschal feast is the symbol of inward purification and sanctification (1 Cor. v. 7).

Ver. 7.—The disciples who lived as yet rather in the world of sense than of spirit, mistook the connexion of Christ's remark with his former conversation with the Pharisees. They did seek for some connexion, but permitted themselves at once to make a transition from the leaven to the bread. They attributed to Jesus, doubtless, their Jewish prepossessions as to food (that Jews ought not to eat with heathen), and looking to the hostile relation in which he stood to the Pharisees, they deemed that he meant to prohibit their receiving food from them. This took place internally ($\delta\iota\epsilon\lambda o\gamma\iota\zeta o\nu\tau o$ $\dot{\epsilon}\nu$ $\dot{\epsilon}a\upsilon\tau o\tilde{\iota}\varsigma$), and found utterance in the words, " It is because we took no bread" ($\tau a\tilde{\upsilon}\tau\acute{a}$ $\dot{\epsilon}\sigma\tau\iota\nu$ $\ddot{a}$ $\lambda\acute{\epsilon}\gamma\epsilon\iota$) $\ddot{o}\tau\iota$ $\ddot{a}\rho\tau o\upsilon\varsigma$ $o\dot{\upsilon}\kappa$ $\dot{\epsilon}\lambda\acute{a}\beta o\mu\epsilon\nu$. The whole is so drawn from life, that fiction derived from later tradition is utterly out of the question. This occurrence also supports most decisively the second account of feeding the multitude.

The Saviour rebukes their weak faith, and reminds them of the two visible proofs of help received from him in time of need. Outward bread, the Saviour means to say, would not fail them, only let them not slight the enjoyment of the true and pure bread of life— *that* would be the surest preservative against hankering after the leaven of the Pharisees. (Mark expands the discourse further ; Matthew gives shortly and concisely its essence. We might say that Mark rather rewrote and expanded than epitomised Matthew.)

§ 31. CONFESSION OF THE DISCIPLES. PROPHECY OF JESUS RE-
SPECTING HIS OWN DEATH.

(Matth. xvi. 13–28; Mark viii. 27—ix. 1; Luke ix. 18–27.)

Matthew and Mark transfer the scene of the following narrative into the region of Cæsarea Philippi. (The town is not to be con-founded with Cæsarea Stratonis, which lay on the sea. [Acts xxiii. 23, seq.] Cæsarea, called Philippi from the tetrarch of that name who enlarged the city, lay on the north-east side of Palestine [*Joseph.* Antiq. xviii. 2, 1]. It was not far from Magdala and Gerasa. Originally the town was called Paneas. Philip, in honour of the emperor, named it $K\alpha\iota\sigma\acute{a}\rho\epsilon\iota a$, as Bethsaida was, in honour of the emperor's sister, called 'Io$\upsilon\lambda\acute{\iota}a\varsigma$. [*Joseph.* ibid.]) Luke gives no note to mark the time, but subjoins this incident immediately to his account of the first feeding of the multitude. Schleiermacher (loco citat. p. 138) draws from this an inference unfavourable to the genuineness of the narrative of the second feeding as given by Matthew and Mark. Could we cut out it and all connected with it, he remarks, Matthew and Luke would appear to harmonize in respect to the chorography. The supposition that the second feed-ing must be transferred to the western side of the sea (while the

first took place on the eastern shore), certainly appears according to
Von Raumer's remark (Palestine, p. 101), to be untenable. Meanwhile what has been already advanced should be sufficient to shew
the impossibility of identifying the two, and thus no weight is to be
laid further on the circumstance to which Schleiermacher has drawn
attention. In the important narrative which follows, Matthew appears as the leading historian. He subjoins (xvi. 17–19), to the confession of the disciples, through Peter as their organ, a remarkable
declaration by the Lord, as to which the two others are silent.*
Mark, it is true, once more subjoins in his account several minute
and peculiar traits (for instance ver. 27, that the conversation was
carried on even during the journey), but into the essential meaning
of the remarkable transaction he gives no deeper insight.

Ver. 13, 14.—The conversation on the road to Cæsarea (ἐν τῇ
ὁδῷ Mark viii. 27), begins with the question of Jesus, τίνα με λέγου-
σιν οἱ ἄνθρωποι, *who do men say that I am?* (some manuscripts have
falsely left out με, it was omitted simply because of the following expression, τὸν υἱὸν τοῦ ἀνθρώπου, which contains more closely the definition of με. The whole clause is to be taken thus, ἐμὲ τὸν υἱὸν τοῦ
ἀνθρώπου [ὡς οἴδατε] ὄντα. Then would the disciples be led forward
from the idea of the υἱὸς τοῦ ἀνθρώπου, to that of the υἱὸς τοῦ Θεοῦ.
[V. 16.]) The question itself undoubtedly had its immediate ground
in the special circumstances of the time. Its object, however, was to
awaken the disciples to profounder views of the dignity of Christ.
According to the disciples, then, some merely saw in Jesus, John
the Baptist (risen from the dead), others Elias. (Compare on
Matth. xiv. 2, and the parallel passages, Mark vi. 15, Luke ix. 8.)
These men therefore did not see in Jesus the Messiah himself, but
certainly they saw a person who stood in close connexion with his
(speedily to be expected) advent. (According to Malachi iv. 5, the
appearance of Elias was expected before the Messiah. See more
particularly as to this, on Matth. xvii. 10, seq., and Luke i. 17.)
There were, however, still others who held Jesus to be Jeremiah, or
some one of the old prophets (προφήτης τις τῶν ἀρχαίων, Luke ix. 8–
19). All viewed him thus as a remarkable phenomenon, and placed
him at least in close connexion, according to their several prevalent
ideas, with the coming Messiah. They did not declare their belief
in him as the Messiah himself, doubtless for this reason, that the
whole ministry of Christ appeared to them to stand in contradiction

---

* It is remarkable that Mark, whose Gospel, according to the tradition of the ancient
church, rested on the authority of Peter (comp. Introd., § 5), should be the writer who
omits to notice the important place which Peter held. One might have attributed this to
modest reserve, were it not that in the passage parallel to Matth. xiv. 29–31, Mark has
also passed over in silence a special communication respecting Peter, which, however, is
not to his praise. The supposition that Mark in writing his Gospel, used that of Matthew,
can in truth with great difficulty be reconciled with these facts.

to their Messianic expectations. The supposed reappearance in Christ of one of the ancient prophets is doubtless to be understood of a belief on the part of the Jews in their actual resurrection, not of the reappearance of their souls in his person (according to the doctrine of μετεμψύχωσις or μετενσωμάτωσις). For since, according to Jewish opinion, the *first* resurrection (see on Luke xiv. 14, compared with Rev. xx. 5) was connected with the appearance of the Messiah (his first appearance in humiliation not being dissevered from his second in glory, but associated with it as the prophets do), and the setting up of his kingdom, so the idea very readily suggested itself that forerunners of the resurrection would precede that mighty period. From no express statements of the Old Testament, except in the case of Elias, did the opinion derive any support, for unless violence were done to it, the reference to the passage, Isaiah lii. 6, seq., is inapplicable. In the New Testament also there is nothing to favour it (see however, on Moses and Elias at Matth. xvii. 4), and we can attribute it therefore only to Rabbinical legends. Around the person of Jeremiah especially there had gathered a circle of traditions (comp. 2 Maccab. ii. 7, 8 ; xv. 14) ; they termed him, by way of eminence, προφήτης τοῦ Θεοῦ, *prophet of God.* Isaiah was also named among the forerunners of the Messiah, 4 Esra ii. 18. (Comp. on all connected with this, Berthold Christ. Jud. § 15, p. 58, seq.)

Ver. 15, 16.—Alongside of these opinions of the people respecting Jesus, is presented that of the disciples. They declare him to be the Χριστός = מָשִׁיחַ, *Messiah,* himself, and thus dissever themselves from the popular views, which held him to be a forerunner of the Messiah. How far, however, it was this confession of Jesus as the Messiah which gave occasion to the following words of Christ, μακάριος εἶ κ. τ. λ., *blessed art thou,* etc., is not very obvious, for they were already spoken respecting the disciples when they first attached themselves to Jesus. (John i. 41, 42.) The whole relation of the Saviour to his disciples, which must be viewed as implying an ever advancing development, requires that in this case, their confession should have been fuller and more complete than before. For the understanding then of this remarkable passage, Matthew is specially important, who, though deficient in graphic portraiture, yet, with all his simplicity and plainness, shews frequently great profoundness of conception. Thus, after Χριστός, *Christ,* he adds, by way of explanation, ὁ υἱὸς τοῦ Θεοῦ τοῦ ζῶντος, *the Son of the living God.* This remark is most important in tracing the meaning of the expression *the Son of God.* For obviously, the expression cannot be precisely identical with Χριστός, since in that case there would arise a tautology. Its aim must rather be to determine with more exactness the import of Χριστός. The natural explanation, therefore, is this—at first the disciples, in acknowledging Christ

as the Messiah, had merely, according to their Jewish prepossessions, seen in him a distinguished man raised up and endowed
by God for special purposes.* Their closer intercourse with the
Saviour opened to them, through the working of the Spirit, a
view into his higher nature ; they recognised in him a revelation of
God, and without thinking of any theory as to the generation
of the Son, they termed this revelation, in that personal manifestation in which it stood visibly before them, *the Son of God.*
(Comp. on Luke i. 35.) The article points to the definite, Divine,
central manifestation which they perceived in Jesus, having been
by the prophecies of the Old Testament instructed as to its real
nature. We must conceive of the disciples as living in this, and
step by step advancing in their knowledge of it. When Matthew
expressly adds " Son of the *living* God," this epithet (חַי אֱלֹהִים)
obviously has reference not to idols, there being no reason for here
contrasting the true God with them, but to the reality of the Divine
manifestation in Christ. The image of Divinity, as reflected in him,
was so strong and powerful, that through it the Father, as his
original, was for the first time properly revealed in his wondrous
essence. All former life-revelations of the Living one were dead,
when compared with the living fulness which flows forth in all the
varied exhibitions of the Saviour. (John i. 4.)

Ver. 17.—According to this view, the import of the blessing
pronounced by the Saviour on hearing this confession becomes
obvious. For, if this confession of Jesus as the Son of God is
genuine, it necessarily involves a revelation of Divinity in the soul
itself, since no man knoweth the Son but the Father, and he to
whom the Father reveals him. (Compare on Matth. xi. 27 ; 1 Cor.
xii. 3.) But the revelation of the Divine within the soul as that
which gives life and being from on high, of itself imparts blessed
ness. (The μακάριος εἶ, *blessed art thou,* is as at Matth. v. 4, not a
mere expression of praise, but an express assurance of that eternal
and blessed existence which the preceding confession implies.) The
confession leads our Lord to infer an antecedent revelation (ἀποκάλυψις) ; for the Divine glory of Christ was concealed under an outwardly mean appearance, and could therefore become known only
through an inward manifestation. This revelation he expressly

---

* The common opinion among the Jews as to the Messiah, is exhibited by Justin
Martyr (Dial. c. Tr. J. p. 266, 267), when he lets him be called ἄνθρωπον ἐξ ἀνθρώπων and
be chosen of God to the Messiahship κατ᾽ ἐκλογήν, because of his virtues. Probably the
disciples, during the first period of their intercourse with the Saviour, saw in him only
the son of Joseph, until it gradually became clear to their minds that the Redeemer of the
human race must of necessity come forth in a strength mightier than theirs whom he was
to redeem, and the direct accounts of Mary, who, not without a reason, was detained till all
Christ's work was finished on earth, must then have converted their presentiment into a
certainty, by the report of the historical events.

denies to flesh and blood, but traces to the Father. (The addition ὁ ἐν τοῖς οὐρανοῖς = ἐπουράνιος, stands in contrast to the ἐπίγειος, which is implied in σὰρξ καὶ αἷμα.) This formula (flesh and blood) denotes what is human abstractly considered, which, as such, is transitory and vain. The phrase corresponds to the Hebrew בָּשָׂר וָדָם which is very common among the Rabbis [comp. Lightfoot on the passage], and had previously occurred also in the Apocrypha [Sir. xiv. 18], and in the New Testament, Gal. i. 16 ; Heb. ii. 14 ; 1 Cor. xv. 50 ; Ephes. vi. 12.) The reference here therefore is to other men as well as to the natural human powers of Peter himself, so that the sense here is " nothing human, no power or faculty of man, has been able to impart to you this knowledge, only the Divine can teach us to know the Divine." This declaration was made by the Saviour to Peter, along with the address Βὰρ Ἰωνᾶ, son of Jonah. It is exceedingly probable that this is intended to form a contrast to the foregoing Ἰησοῦς υἱὸς Θεοῦ, Jesus, Son of God. Simon stands here like Jesus, as a personal designation ; son of Jonas is probably used here in a figurative sense. Primarily indeed it is a genealogical designation (see on John i. 43 ; xxi. 16, 17),* but as Hebrew names generally are descriptive, Christ here looks to the import of the name. Perhaps he referred it to יוֹנָה, a dove, and in that case this meaning would arise, " Thou Simon art a child of the Spirit (alluding to the Holy Ghost under the symbol of a dove), God the Father of spirits, Heb. xii. 9, hath revealed himself to thee." Where God reveals himself there is formed a spiritual man.

Ver. 18, 19.—Here follows a new installation of the apostles. After they had in a true sense acknowledged Christ, the Lord could disclose to them also the real import of their own office. Let us first examine the meaning of the words, that we may then determine more nearly their reference to Peter. The symbolic name which the Saviour gave to Peter immediately after his first reception as his disciple (comp. on John i. 43), he here renews with a definite explanation of its meaning. Peter is to be the rock of the edifice of the church. (The church is represented as a ναός, temple, a common figure, compare 1 Cor. iii. 9 ; 2 Cor. vi. 16 ; 1 Peter ii. 5. The Old Testament temple is viewed as the type of the church, as σκηνή, tabernacle, is regarded in the epistle to the Hebrews, chap. viii.) The church, as a spiritual structure,† must rest naturally on a spirit-

---

* Βάρ Dan. vi. 1, vii. 13, = Heb. בֵּן. It may be presumed that Jesus in this conversation with his disciples spoke Aramaic. Ἰωνᾶ, contracted from Ἰωαννᾶ (comp. John i. 43.) = יָרֳחָן according to the LXX. at 1 Chron. iii. 24, Ἰωανάν.

† In the gospels this is the only passage where the ἐκκλησία stands as = βασ. τ. Θ. In another sense the expression occurs at Matth. xviii. 17. In the writings of Paul, on the other hand, ἐκκλησία is the usual expression for the visible communion of Christians. Βασ. τ. Θ. is used by him rather for the ideal, heavenly fellowship. In the Hebrew קָהָל corresponds to ἐκκλησία

ual foundation ; Peter, therefore, in his new spiritual character, appears as the supporter of Christ's great work among mankind, [and this evidently as destined, Acts ii., to lay the foundations of the first Christian church]. Jesus himself is the creator of the whole—Peter, the first stone of the building. (Compare 1 Pet. ii. 5.) The firmness of the building shews itself in sustaining the onsets of assailing powers. (Matth. vii. 24, seq.) These are here termed πύλαι ᾅδου, *gates of hell*, *or hades*.* Hades (שְׁאוֹל) the abode of dark destructive powers, is often represented as a palace, strongly fastened, thus marking its security and its formidable power. (Job xxxviii. 17 ; Ps. ix. 14 ; Isaiah xxxviii. 10.) This war-palace stands opposed to the holy temple of God (comp. on Luke xi. 21, 22), and appears with all its powers as assailing it, but not overcoming it, for against ᾅδης, *hades*, is arrayed οὐρανός, *heaven*, in the fulness of its power.† Still retaining the same figure, then, the Lord of this temple names Peter as its guardian ; he receives the key of it with full authority to use it,‡ and consequently to grant admission or to shut out. (Isaiah xxii. 22 ; Rev. iii. 7, explain this symbolic expression.—That the same Peter is first termed the πέτρα, *rock*, then the מְפַתֵּחַ, *opener* [see Isaiah xxii. 22], of the building is to be explained from that free treatment of figurative expression which, with all their accuracy, prevails in the discourses of our Lord. The terms δέειν and λύειν, for *shutting* and *opening*, are to be explained from the simple custom of antiquity of fastening doors by tying. John, in the really parallel passage, xx. 23, resolves the figure by the terms ἀφιέναι, *remit*, and κρατεῖν, *control*, *retain*.) This representation exhibits an earthly and heavenly character and functions as united in the church. Controlled by heavenly powers, the acts of its earthly agents bear not merely human impress and authority, but have their sanction in heaven. Obviously it is only the ideal church which is here spoken of with its ideal representatives.§ In so far as

---

* Compare Euripides Hecuba v. 1, where it is said of the lower world, σκότου πύλαι ἵνα Ἀΐδης ᾤκισται.

† I doubt much the correctness of this interpretation. The citations prove no such *war castle*. I regard *Hades* as put for the abode of death, and the gates (as the entrance), by metonymy, for Hades itself. Thus the sense is: "Death shall not prevail against it: it is indestructible.—[K.

‡ Jeremiah i. 10, forms a striking parallel to the prerogative of forgiving or retaining sins here imparted to the disciples. For the Lord there says to the prophet, "I put my words in thy mouth, see I set thee this very day over nations and kingdoms that thou shouldest root out, break in pieces, throw down and destroy, and build and plant." What in the Old Testament is given in an outward, is in the New Testament given in an inward form.

§ To the apostles was granted the power, absolute and unconditioned, of binding and loosing (so that he who was shut out from the church was excluded at the same time from heaven), just as to them was given the power of publishing truth, unmixed with error. For *both* they possessed miraculous spiritual endowments (Gal. i. 8, 9 ; 1 Cor. v. 1–5, and xvi. 22). To the ordinary ministers of the church, who possess not this extraor-

a sinful element exists in the external church (Matth. xiii. 47), the words admit of no application to it. Of the real everlasting church, however, they are forever true. Further, the power which here is merely *promised*, is, at a later period (John xx. 23), actually imparted. It remains for us to speak of Peter's relation to the other disciples. That which at ver. 19 is spoken to Peter, is at Matth. xviii. 18, John xx. 23, addressed to all the apostles. The contents of ver. 18 are again found at Rev. xxi. 14, and Gal. ii. 9, applied to all the apostles. We find therefore nothing in these words *peculiar* to Peter ; he merely answers as the organ of the college of apostles, and Christ acknowledging him as such, replies to him and speaks through him to them *all*. This, however, should not be overlooked, that Peter is and was intended to be really the active representative of the company of apostles (as John may be termed their *passive* representative, comp. on John xxi. 21). For it is impossible to conceive that the same thing which the Lord here addresses to Peter could have been spoken to Bartholomew or Philip ; no one save Peter could have been called the representative of the apostles. The personal difference between the apostles individually and the pre-eminence of Peter, has been denied merely on polemic grounds in opposition to the Catholic Church, which certainly deduced inferences from it for which there was not in Scripture the slightest ground (comp. on Matth. x. 2, and John xxi. 15). But that which is through Peter bestowed on the apostles, was again through the apostles conferred on the whole church, as is obvious from its essential nature in accordance with which the existing representatives of the church (*i. e.*, the really regenerate), exercise the spiritual powers granted to it by the Lord ; not, however, at their own pleasure, but according to the intimations of that Spirit whom to know and to obey is implied in the very character of the believer. That the apostles, then, and their genuine spiritual successors, bore the word of truth in one direction and not in another, that they followed up their labours on one man and not on another, in this consisted the binding and the loosing. The whole new spiritual community which the Saviour came to found took its rise from the apostles and their labours. No one became a Christian save *through them*, and thus the church through all time is built up in living union with its origin. Christianity is no bare summary of truths and reflections to which a man even in a state of isolation might attain ; it is a life-stream which flows through humanity, and its waves must reach every separate individual who is to be drawn within this circle of life. The Gospel is identified with, and grown into union with, the persons. That which lies enfolded in Christ Jesus as in the central principle of the new life, diffuses itself immedi-

dinary gift, this power of the keys (discipline), as well as the gift of teaching, has passed over in but a *limited* form.—[E.]

ately over the circle of the twelve, and thence over those wider circles of spiritual life which were gradually formed in the church. Already, however, have we referred to the fact, that the Lord's words to Peter were spoken to him as a new man, and are true only when viewed with reference to this new nature. That the old man Peter was incapable of labouring for the kingdom God—to say nothing of its being a rock—is shewn by the following context, v. 22, seq. The usual explanation, therefore, of the passage which the Protestant Church* is wont to oppose to the view of the Catholics, according to which the *faith of Peter and the confession of that faith*, is the rock, is entirely the correct one—only the faith itself and his confession of it must not be regarded as apart from Peter himself personally. It is identified with him—not with the old Simon but with the new Peter. (Peter, as the new name, being understood as denoting the new man. Rev. ii. 17.) Hence the power of binding and loosing can be affirmed only of the Divine nature in Peter (and the other disciples), for God alone (in so far as he works through one man or in the whole church) can forgive sin (see on Matth. ix. 4, 5). Although, therefore, the forgiving of sins is a prerogative of the church in all ages, yet since the Holy Ghost has ceased to display in the church his concentrated and miraculous agency it is imparted only conditionally, *on the supposition, namely, of true repentance and living faith*, whose existence the clergy cannot discern, since the gift of trying the spirits has ceased (1 Cor. xii. 10), but the Lord alone.

Ver. 20, 21.—On this advance in knowledge the Saviour immediately founds their introduction to a closer acquaintance with his work as the Redeemer ; he openly declares to them that he, the Messiah, the Son of the living God, must suffer, but that in suffering he should be perfected. He wished by degrees to accustom them to bear this thought. The former prohibition to speak of his dignity (see on Matth. viii. 4), has in its renewal here, reference undoubtedly to the people who were accustomed to associate with the term " Messiah" a series of superficial ideas which could only have been obstructions in Christ's way. (For further details as to ἀρχιερεῖς, γραμματεῖς, and πρεσβύτεροι, see on Matth. xxvi. 57; John xviii. 12.) Respecting the prophecy which he here utters in regard to himself, we remark, that to understand it figuratively in the sense, " I shall be apparently overcome, but soon and gloriously shall my cause assert itself," is too shallow to claim our approval. Christ speaks too often, and in circumstances the most varied, of his death and his fate generally (see on John ii. 19 ; Matth. xxvii. 63, according

---

* This explanation some of the fathers of the church had already given. Gratz, following Du Pin (de antiqua ecclesiæ disciplina), has brought together the passages in his work on Matth., part ii., p. 110, seq.

to which last passage, the Pharisees place a watch at his grave for
the reason that he had spoken of his resurrection), to permit our
referring his language to anything but literal death. In the δεῖ
παθεῖν, *must suffer*, however, his death is viewed as a necessary one.
At the parallel passages, Matth. xx. 18; Mark x. 33, there stands
the simple future παραδοθήσεται κ. τ. λ. What this δεῖ, *must*, was
intended to mean is shewn plainly by Luke xviii. 31 (parallel to the
last quoted passages), where it is said τελεσθήσεται πάντα τὰ γεγραμμένα διὰ τῶν προφητῶν τῷ υἱῷ τοῦ ἀνθρώπου, *all things written by the
prophets, etc.* (Comp. Luke xxiv. 26, 27, 44, 46. In the last passage it is said, οὕτω γέγραπται καὶ οὕτως ἔδει παθεῖν τὸν Χριστόν.) The
prediction of the Messiah's sufferings in the prophets was not, however, arbitrary, but stood in necessary connexion with the Divine
counsels. Only for the sake of the disciples does the Lord go back
to Scripture, explaining it to them authoritatively, and comforting
them by the fact that even the Old Testament recognises a suffering
Messiah. It might, however, be conjectured that the disciples had
after the event, put all these statements in more specific detail into
the mouth of Jesus, for example, the chronological reference in the
case of the resurrection. So also of Matth. xx. 18, 19, and the
parallel passages in Mark and Luke, in which all the particulars of
Christ's sufferings are fore-mentioned, that he should be reviled,
spit upon, scourged. The character of the Gospel history would
not indeed be *essentially* altered, even should we assume that the
Evangelists after the event filled up with more minuteness our
Lord's briefer declaration. But bearing in mind that even in the
Old Testament, especially at Ps. xxii. 17, 19 ; Is. l. 6 ; liii. 4, seq.,
the Messiah's sufferings had been stated in detail, we cannot take
offence at the speciality of these predictions. But to raise a doubt
of the Saviour's general foreknowledge of his own death, is absolutely
inadmissible. Nor can we draw from the deep sadness of the disciples at his death, any inference against a previous mention of
the resurrection, for the reason that the doctrine of a suffering
Messiah had almost wholly ceased to be recognised among the Jews.
(See on John xii. 34. Comp. *Hengstenberg's* Christology, p. 252,
seq.) When Christ therefore died, the disciples, who were still
influenced by popular opinion, thought not of his resurrection, since
they were staggered in regard to *everything*. The contrasts which
the life of Christ presented before their eyes, were so overwhelm-
ingly great that they were stunned and confounded. [Their partial
theoretical belief was lost in the awful fact.]

Ver. 22, 23.—But if we find in the disciples an incapacity to
penetrate in thought the mysterious contrasts presented by the life
of Christ even at his crucifixion, previous to which they had experienced so much, how much more at the period here referred to.

They could not endure that the Son of God should be a sufferer. The manner in which our Lord, however, repels the words of Peter, who again speaks as the representative of all the apostles, points to something more than the mere failure to apprehend a difficult idea. Peter wholly misunderstood his relation to the Lord ; he came forward to admonish and correct him, and that which Christ had represented as necessary (for his work) he seeks to put far from him. (The ἵλεώς σοι, scil. εἴη Θεός = לְךָ חָלִילָה 1 Chron. xi. 19.) But even this does not exhaust his meaning. The expression σκάνδαλόν μου εἶ, *thou art a snare to me*, which follows, shews that Peter's remark was not merely a sin in him, but a temptation to the Lord. Peter, we find here, perhaps from vanity at the praise just uttered, sunk back to the level of the natural man—and along with him the other disciples whom Jesus here rebukes through Peter, just as, at ver. 18, 19, he had conjoined them with him in praise. (Mark viii. 33, indicates this by his expression ἰδὼν τοὺς μαθητὰς αὐτοῦ.) It is the part of the natural man, however, τὰ τῶν ἀνθρώπων φρονεῖν, *to savor the things of men*, and of the new man τὰ τοῦ Θεοῦ φρονεῖν, *to savor the things of God*. It is not the wicked man (ἄνθρωπος πονηρός), who is here spoken of, but only the natural man (ψυχικός, 1 Cor. ii. 14), who, incapable of rising to the apprehension of the Divine, draws it down to his own human level. Where we thus recognise as intelligible the co-existence of the old and the new man (in those who are regenerate but not yet perfected), and the alternate predominance now of the one and now of the other, we also understand how Jesus can rebuke that same Peter whom he had just praised. This diversity of language is dependent on the varied prevalence of the new or the old man in the same individual. It still remains for us to say something more particularly of the ὕπαγε ὀπίσω μου, σατανᾶ, *get behind me, Satan*. These words are to be explained by the following σκάνδαλόν μου εἶ, *thou art a snare to me*, by the addition of which, Matthew greatly facilitates our understanding the whole of this remarkable scene, and again furnishes proof how exact he is in the substance, while neglecting the outward features of his narrative. Unquestionably the Saviour must be conceived as having maintained one *continuous* conflict with temptation. Its great capital periods, at the commencement and close of his ministry, exhibit merely in a concentrated●form, what ran through his whole life. Here, then, for the first time, it assumes the form of suggesting the possibility of escaping suffering and death. It was all the more concealed and dangerous that it came to him through the lips of a dear disciple, who had just solemnly acknowledged his Divine dignity. What we remarked in the case of the history of the temptation (see on Matth. iv. 1, seq.) must in this instance also be faithfully kept in view. From the clear and pure fountain of

Christ's life no unholy thought could flow ; but precisely because he was to be a conqueror of sin, it had to draw near, that in every form he might overthrow it ; and in his human nature, which only by degrees received within itself the whole fulness of the Divine life, sin, when it drew near, made upon him an impression. Such a sacred moment have we here. With the glance of his soul, the Saviour at once penetrated the source whence sprang this *far be it from thee*, and killed the springing evil in its very root. This explains at once the import of the σατανᾶ, which was addressed to Peter (στραφεὶς εἶπε τῷ Πέτρῳ). The opinion that Peter is here termed a wicked counsellor, or even an adversary* (from שָׂטַן), stands completely self-refuted ; the rock of the church cannot possibly be at the same time an adversary, and assuredly Peter did not, by having spoken these words, cease to be the rock of the church. The σατανᾶς, *Satan,* is none other than the ἄρχων τοῦ κόσμου τούτου, *ruler of this world*, who has his work in the children of unbelief (Ephes. ii. 2), and also in the children of faith, in so far as the Spirit of Christ has as yet not sanctified them, *i. e.*, in so far as the old man, still exposed to sinful influences, yet lives in them. This influence had Peter (as the organ of the others, who are to be conceived of as under the same guilt) admitted into his heart without knowing what he did. Our Lord, however, brings him to the consciousness of what he was doing, by naming the element from which sprang the thought that he had been weak enough to utter. Thus, as in the foregoing confession (ver. 16), the Divine element was seen predominant in Peter, so evil now asserts its power over him ; and here, therefore, we have in his case an exhibition of that ebbing and flowing of spiritual life, which every one experiences who has felt in his heart the redeeming power of Christ. Where sin is powerful, there does grace excel in power (Rom. v. 20) ; conversely, however, where grace is mighty, there sin also puts itself mightily forth.

Ver. 24–26.—Immediately after these words, Jesus, transferring his discourse from the immediate circle of his disciples to a more extensive audience (according to Mark and Luke), subjoins an admonition upon self-denial. The thoughts themselves we have already unfolded at Matth. x. 37, seq. ; the only inquiry here is, what association of ideas connects these verses with the foregoing. The fact that Christ must die, does not seem to imply as a necessary consequence, the death of his disciples, for indeed Christ died expressly that we might live. Of *bodily* death this is undoubtedly true, but the life and death of Jesus is a pattern for his church (1

---

* As regards the mere usage of the words, this explanation may be justified by referring to such passages as 1 Kings xi. 14 ; 2 Sam. xix. 22. In the New Testament, however, σατανᾶς never occurs in the sense of *adversary*.

554 MATTHEW XVI. 24–28.

Peter ii. 21). What the Saviour experienced, all his redeemed ones must experience *spiritually;* they taste the power of his resurrection, but previously also that of his sufferings (Phil. iii. 10). To be made alive in the new man (in the ψυχῇ πνευματικῇ), necessarily implies the dying of the old. (Compare the remarks on Matth. x. 37, seq.) The expression of Peter (ver. 22) had flowed from the natural dread of conflict, sufferings, and death, and hence our Lord exhorts all that would follow him to undertake these willingly, and for the sake of heavenly things to sacrifice all the earthly. The gain of the world with its sensuous enjoyments (ver. 26) could never satisfy man's immortal part. Is the world then, the object of his efforts? He loses, in that case, his real happiness. The sacrifice of heavenly treasure alone brings real pain, that of our earthly, pure joy. The latter may be compensated, the former never.* In the words τί δώσει ἄνθρωπος ἀντάλλαγμα, *what will a man give, etc.*, there is an implied declaration that only God could find an ἀντάλλαγμα for the souls of men. (Comp. on Matth. xx. 28.) 'Αντάλλαγμα, *exchange,* is nearly allied to λύτρον, *ransom,* although not entirely synonymous. It denotes the *purchase-money,* the object for which a man exchanges any thing, as Sir. vi. 15, φίλου πιστοῦ οὐκ ἔστι ἀντάλλαγμα. Thus, while the ἀντάλλαγμα proceeds on the idea of *possession,* λύτρον refers to a state of *slavery,* out of which the λύτρον gives deliverance. In this respect, the expression ἀπάλλαγμα, would correspond to λύτρον, but it does not occur in the New Testament. The verb ἀπαλλάσσειν, however, in the sense of *to set free,* occurs at Heb. ii. 15. To this admonition to self-denial Mark and Luke subjoin the corresponding threatening. (As to the contents of the verse, compare the parallel passage Matth. x. 32, 33.) The shunning to enter into conflict and suffering, is in fact to be ashamed of the Lord, and to sacrifice the eternal to the temporal. And this will, at the day of judgment, display its fatal results. (As to the formula ἔρχεσθαι ἐν δόξῃ μετὰ τῶν ἀγγέλων τῶν ἁγίων, see on Matth. xxiv.)

Ver. 27.—From what has gone before, it is plain, that the formula ἀποδώσει ἑκάστῳ κατὰ τὴν πρᾶξιν αὐτοῦ, *he will render to each man according to his conduct,* must be understood in such a way, that the πρᾶξις denotes not individual ἔργα, *acts,* of this or of that kind, but the whole inward course of life (the τὸν κόσμον or ψυχὴν κερδαίνειν), which flows from faith or from unbelief, and shews itself in the fruits of the one or of the other.

Ver. 28—To render his mention of the ἡμέρα κρίσεως, *day of judgment,* more impressive, the Saviour sets forth its threatening nearness. As at Matth. x. 23, I here refer once more to the leading passage Matth. xxiv., inasmuch as this same idea, that the day of

* The same thought was expressed formerly at Ps. xlix. 7–9.

the Lord's second coming was near, must be understood in the same
way throughout the New Testament. Here, the death ˙(θάνατον
γεύσασθαι = מָיֵּת בּיעַמ), of some who were present—as the longest
livers, is assigned as the period of the Parousia.* (The words ὧδε
ἑστῶτες, *those standing here*, are to be understood of the whole multitude who surrounded him, the apostles as well as the others.)   One
involuntarily calls to mind here the enigmatical words at John xxi.
22, on which compare the commentary.   The parallel passages in
Mark and Luke refer not so much to the coming of Christ, as to
the coming of his kindom (Mark adds ἐν δυνάμει), and these expressions may be understood as describing the powerful manifestations
of living Christian principle, without reference to the personal return
of Jesus.   But the immediate connexion of these words with the
foregoing context, in which the ἔρχεσθαι ἐν τῇ δόξῃ, *coming in his
glory*, refers so unmistakeably to the Parousia, does not admit of
this explanation.   The coming of the kingdom coincides with his
coming personally.

§ 32. THE TRANSFIGURATION OF JESUS.

(Matth. xvii. 1–13 ; Mark ix. 2–13 ; Luke ix. 28–36.)

The following important occurrence demands some preliminary
remarks, that we may contemplate it from the right point of view,
and all the more as it has been subject to the utmost diversity
of opinions.   At the outset, we summarily reject those views which
reduce the fact itself to a dream or an optical delusion ; views in
which thunder, lightning, and passing mists, take the place of the
voice of God, and the cloud of light.   Other explanations, however,
which find here either a myth, or a vision without any outwardly
visible fact, must be more closely examined.   *Primarily*, then, as respects the mythical hypothesis, it has historical analogy to support
it.   But he who is unable to place the Judæo-biblical history on a
level with the course of historical development among other nations,
must be precluded, as was formerly observed, by this general character of the Bible narrative, from admitting in any case the slightest
mythic element.   In it, we have a history of God amidst the human
race, in which everything appears actually realized, which springing
from the real longings of the soul, human fancy has invested, in the

* I think it can scarcely be doubted that " the coming of the Son of Man in his kingdom" refers here to the following scene of the transfiguration. The words, " shall not see
death until they see the Son of Man," refers not to *length* of life, but to *privilege:* some
shall have the privilege of beholding him in his glory even *before they die.* So some ancient commentators. The transfiguration is thus regarded as a type of the Saviour's
future glory in his kingdom.—[K.

histories of other nations, with the attractive garb of fable. Besides, in this narrative of the transfiguration, particulars are given which directly contradict every mythical conception. The mythic style of narrative, is, in its very nature, obscure and indefinite, but here, as everywhere, the evangelists maintain their historic sobriety. Contrary to their usual practice, they relate unanimously that the transfiguration took place six days after the events previously recorded. If we consider that they wrote thirty years at least after the event, it is obvious how deeply the solemn occurrence must have imprinted itself on their memories, from their retaining the date with such exactness. According to Luke ix. 37, the healing of the sick boy, which all the evangelists agree in placing directly after the transfiguration, took place on the following day.* A thing of this kind ill agrees with the mythical forms of composition. The history obviously reads like the simplest narrative of a fact. As to the view, however, that we have here the record of a vision, the occurrence is certainly styled an ὅραμα, thing seen, vision (=חָזוֹן, מַרְאָה), at Matth. xvii. 9; this term, however, is by no means restricted to an object of internal contemplation; it is often used in cases of objects outwardly and visibly present. It merely denotes, in general, objects which become known to us by the sense of sight, in contradistinction to those made known to us verbally (comp. Acts xii. 9). And further, the explanation of the occurrence before us as a vision is untenable, from the fact that we have no example of a mere vision occurring at once, and in the same way to several persons, and these so widely diverse in character and relation, as were Christ and the three disciples. We take our stand, then, on the simple literal sense of the narrative, which in the first place is assuredly that intended by the narrators; and in the next place, vindicates itself perfectly to every Christian intelligence. For if we assume the reality of the resurrection of the body, and its glorification, truths which assuredly belong to the system of Christian doctrine, the whole occurrence presents no essential difficulties. The appearance of Moses and Elias, which is usually held to be the most unintelligible point in it, is easily conceived of as possible, if we admit their bodily glorification. In support of this idea, however, Scripture itself gives sufficient intimations (Deut. xxxiv. 6 compared with Jude 9; 2 Kings ii. 11, compared with Sir. xlviii. 9, 13), which men have accustomed themselves to set down as belonging to biblical mythology—but how justly is another question.

Taken then as literally true, the incident has a twofold significance. *First*, it is a kind of solemn installation of Jesus into his

---

* Gratz (Part ii., p. 166) appeals also to 2 Pet. i. 17. As however the genuineness of the epistle cannot be certainly established we must not bring forward this interesting passage *in the character of a proof.* Yet ought it assuredly to be read.

holy office before the three disciples, chosen to be present at it. It was intended that they should be confirmed in the truth of the foregoing confession (Matth. xvi. 16), and more fully enlightened as to the dignity of Jesus. In this point of view, the Old Testament furnishes, in the history of Moses, a parallel to the transfiguration. Along with Aaron, Nadab, and Abihu, he ascended Mount Sinai, received there the law, and shone to such a degree that he had to cover his countenance. (Compare Exodus xxiv. with xxxiv. 30, seq.; 2 Cor. iii. 7, seq.) So also Christ is here installed as the spiritual lawgiver, inasmuch as the voice said αὐτοῦ ἀκούετε, hear him, (Matth. xvii. 5.) His word is law to his people. But secondly, the fact has reference to Jesus himself. For, the transfiguration takes its place along with the baptism, the temptation, and other occurrences in which Jesus is himself the object, and his spiritual life exhibited in its course of development. Throughout his earthly ministry the Saviour appears in a twofold point of view ; on the one hand as already and actively redeeming ; on the other as inherently advancing his own perfection. (Heb. ii. 10, ἔπρεπε τῷ Θεῷ τὸν ἀρχηγὸν τῆς σωτηρίας διὰ παθημάτων τελειῶσαι, it became God to perfect, etc.) Only by degrees, did the humanity of Jesus receive into itself the fulness of the Godhead. The transfiguration formed a stage in this process of development. It represented in figure the kingdom of God (in that the risen saints shall dwell around Jesus), and the heavenly messengers opened to him more fully and deeply the counsel of God in the work of redemption (Luke ix. 31). If we regard the glorification of the body as not effected instantaneously, but as gradually prepared for, the transfiguration will in this respect also have had an important significancy. (Compare the Commentary, Part II.) [Luke ix. 31, is of importance for the understanding of this event. Jesus had a few days before announced his death, and vanquished the temptation to escape from it suggested by the language of Peter. Now also Moses and Elias speak of his coming decease at Jerusalem. Law and promise demanded his death, and the Saviour is ready. Upon this the voice of the Father is again heard pronouncing him the genuine Saviour, the obedient Son, and expressing God's approval of his acts, and this alike before the lawgiver and the chief of the prophets, as before " the two witnesses of Christ," as they are called, Rev. xi. 3.]

Ver. 1.—With perfect unanimity, which runs with trifling exceptions through the whole narrative, the evangelists relate that the transfiguration took place after six days, reckoning from the occurrence which precedes it. (The eight days in Luke indicate merely another way of enumerating the days.) The mountain they describe in the most general terms (ὄρος ὑψηλόν), and we are left to conjecture in determining where the event occurred.* The preceding incident took place at Cæsarea Philippi (Mark viii. 27), and there has therefore been a disposition to seek the mountain on the eastern side of the sea of Gennesareth. But it is impossible to shew that, during the six intervening days, Christ had not changed his locality. The early fathers of the church conceived it to have been Mount Tabor (Hos. v. 1, in the LXX. Ἰταβύριον), doubtless only because it is the highest mountain in Galilee. It seems strange, that in this case Jesus takes only three disciples with him, for it would appear that the same confirmation of their faith was equally necessary for the others. We have already remarked, however, at Matth. x. 1, that the disciples stood in various relations to the Saviour. The three here named appear in the Gospel narrative as his most immediate and confidential companions. As they here beheld him glorified, so at a later period (Matth. xxvi. 27), they witnessed his deepest sufferings. The ground of this distinction which the Saviour made among the twelve, was obviously not caprice, but a difference in their dispositions and vocations. This made necessary a different training. An esoteric, secret course of instruction communicated by the Lord to these three is not to be thought of. Everywhere, stress is laid by Christ, not on the imparting of a doctrinal system, but on the renewal of the whole man.

Ver. 2, 3.—While Jesus then, was engaged in prayer (Luke ix. 29), there took place a change in his person—his face and his dress shone brightly. It is not said by the narrators, whether this glory was internal or came from without. But as Moses and Elias are mentioned in immediate connexion with it, and as they also shone (according to Luke ix. 31), it is probably the design of the narrators to represent the whole scene as illumined by a bright light (δόξα, כָּבוֹד), for it is ever in this form that the supernatural presents itself to men. We may therefore conceive of the two things as united in the person of Jesus ; he was irradiated by light shed on him from without, and he himself shone from within. Mark paints, after his manner, the outward brightness of the clothing (ix 3); the indefinite term, however, μεταμορφοῦσθαι, transfigured, employed by Matthew, is paraphrased by Luke with the words τὸ εἶδος τοῦ προσώπου αὐτοῦ

* It is remarkable that the most important incidents in the life of our Lord, (the transfiguration, sufferings, death, ascension), took place on *mountains*, as also that it was his custom to ascend mountains for prayer. In the same way, in the Old Testament, sacrifices were offered on mountains, and the temple also was built on a mountain. This is connected with the Scriptural system of symbols, according to which mountains were compared to the vault of heaven. Hence so often in the Old Testament does the expression occur "mountains of ascent, everlasting hills" (Gen. xlix. 26 ; Deut. xxxiii. 15 ; Ps. xi. 1 ; lxxii. 3 ; cxxi. 1 ; Hab. iii. 20 ; Rev. xiv. 1). It is interesting to observe the parallelism of this with the idol-mountains of the ancient natural religions (compare Baur's Theology, Part I., p. 169). The learned man we have named compares even the German name Himmel (*heaven*), with the Indian Himalayas, the primeval idol mountains of the Hindoos.

ἕτερον ἐγένετο. The narrator may by these words merely mean to say that his countenance wore an unwonted, an elevated expression. The characteristic shining or radiance Matthew brings forward with special prominence (comp. Dan. xii. 3 ; Rev. x. 1). It is a natural symbol, to conceive of Divine and heavenly objects as luminous ; in no nation or individual are they presented under the emblem of darkness. The fulness of the radiance betokens very naturally the degree of purity in the revelation from on high. In these figurative forms of speech does universal humanity express itself ; for they correspond to those essential traits which reveal themselves to every mind. (Paul uses the word μεταμορφοῦσθαι in describing the internal processes of regeneration, Rom. xii. 2; 2 Cor. iii. 18.) It is strange that any question should be raised as to how the disciples could have known Moses and Elias, partly because of the obvious answer, that in the conversations as to the occurrence, which immediately follow, Jesus may have informed them, and partly because to any one imbued with the Spirit of Scripture, such characters as Moses and Elias must be conceived as bearing an impress that could not be mistaken.

Luke ix. 31, 32, gives some additional particulars, which are of the highest importance for our understanding the whole occurrence. He remarks, first, that Moses and Elias had spoken of the decease of Jesus (ἔξοδος in the sense of *the end of life, death*, as at Wisdom vii. 6 ; 2 Peter i. 15), which awaited him in Jerusalem. We have here a peculiar feature, beyond the conception of a myth, setting in immediate contrast with this state of glorification, the deepest humiliation. It would seem, however, as if the Saviour's glory was exhibited to him in its reality, in order to strengthen him for victory. Yet even after this, his soul faltered, although he here tasted the glory! (The expression ἔλεγον ἔξοδον, *spake of his decease*, it may be added, is unquestionably to be understood as referring not so much to the fact of the death itself, as to its more immediate circumstances and relations. Moses and Elias appear merely as ἄγγελοι, as messengers from the higher world.) Luke however relates further, that Peter and his two companions were heavy with sleep, and, upon rousing themselves (διαγρηγορήσαντες), beheld the glory of Jesus and of the two men. Even in the same way did sleep overcome these three disciples amidst the sufferings of Jesus at Gethsemane (Matth. xxvi. 40), where Luke relates (xxii. 45), that they slept from grief (ἀπὸ τῆς λύπης). Great mental agitations, whether of joy or sorrow, are fatiguing. Their solemn situation amidst the loneliness of night upon a mountain—with the Saviour apart—all this must have taken hold of their souls, and produced physical exhaustion. Nothing however can be more incorrect, contradicting both history and Scripture, than to conclude that owing to this drowsiness they were unable correctly to observe what passed. The accuracy of their narrative rests obviously not so much on their own observations as on their subsequent conversation with Jesus. Had the disciples fallen into any mistake, the truthfulness of Jesus would at once have undeceived them. Far rather does the simple narrative of the circumstances as they happened, even of such as seemed unfavourable to themselves, vouch for their honesty and straight-forwardness.

Ver. 4.—Peter, the speaker, breaks silence (ἀποκρίνεσθαι = עָנָה, see on Luke i. 60), and expresses his astonishment at this spectacle. Elsewhere, fear is the feeling awakened by the phenomena of the spiritual world (see on Luke i. 12, as also at ver. 6), as is immediately shewn in the disciples, when they heard the voice. To account then for so remarkable a declaration of Peter, Mark and Luke immediately subjoin the words μὴ εἰδὼς ὃ λέγει, *not knowing what he saith*. These words refer not by any means to the drowsiness of the disciples, but to their state of ecstasy. The elevation of the scene hurried them away ; they were lifted, as it were, above themselves. (The expression κύριε in the address is explained more clearly by the parallel terms ῥαββί* and ἐπιστάτα in Mark and Luke. It has not here as yet the pregnant meaning which it has acquired in the writings of Paul, who uses κύριος, *Lord*, = יְהוָֹה, *Jehovah*.) Among the Evangelists, Luke already here and there (xi. 39 ; xii. 42 ; xiii. 15), makes this use of ὁ κύριος in contradistinction to κύριος. (Compare however on Matth. xxi. 3.) The meaning of the expression σκηνὰς ποιήσωμεν, *let us make tabernacles*, obviously is merely this—would that for a lengthened period we might remain in this place and in this company ! (Compare the remarks on ver. 10.) The words express the longing of his soul after the kingdom of God, in which the saints and those who are raised from the dead shall be for ever around the Lord. Inasmuch as Peter speaks of three tents, he places himself and his two companions humbly in the background as the servants of the three. The whole form of the address however shews that Peter acknowledged Jesus as the primary figure in the picture ; the representatives of the old covenant appear to him as merely subordinate, as messengers from the heavenly Father to the Son.

Ver. 5.—Suddenly however the scene changes ; even the three disciples who were admitted to see Jesus in his glory, were shut out by a bright cloud from the company of the other three. Most graphically is the scene presented to us by Luke. The two messengers, Moses and Elias, made a movement to one side, went apart (Luke ix. 33, ἐν τῷ διαχωρίζεσθαι αὐτοὺς ἀπ' αὐτοῦ) : while Peter was yet speaking the bright cloud came, and Jesus with the two entered

---

* As to the name ῥαββί compare on Matth. xxiii. 7.

into it. All the three were thus enclosed as in a sanctuary; the disciples stood without. On this, they became greatly afraid, partly because they felt themselves alone, dissevered from their Lord, and partly because the new phenomenon of the luminous cloud over-whelmed them with terror. (I prefer with Griesbach the reading νεφέλη φωτός, although the most numerous and best MSS. have φωτεινή. For, φωτός was probably changed into φωτεινή because of the apparent contradiction with ἐπεσκίασεν. It seemed impossible that a cloud of light could darken or overshadow, while it was easy to conceive of a bright cloud casting a shadow. The reading φωτεινή consequently better admits of the usual sense of νεφέλη being retained. According to the view of the author, how-ever, the words ἐπεσκίασεν αὐτούς, overshadowed them, are used in regard to the light-cloud, only in so far as it prevented the disciples from seeing. The most intense light is = σκότος, darkness. Hence, in the language of Scripture the expressions are used synonymously, God dwelleth in φῶς ἀπρόσιτον, light unapproachable, and in dark-ness, 1 Tim. vi. 16 ; Exod. xx. 21. The voice then, which spake from the midst of the cloud, leaves us in no doubt what we are to think of it. It is the voice of the Father who instals the Son (Ps. ii. 7, בְּנִי אָתָּה) as the governor of his kingdom, and commands that he be obeyed. (Compare as to αἰτοῦ ἀκούετε, the passage Deut. xviii. 18, in which the first Lawgiver promises a second and more exalted). The cloud was the Schechinah (compare Buxt. Lex. Talm. s. h. v. Bertholt. Christ. jud., p. 111), the symbol of the Divine presence, into which Moses entered on Mount Sinai (Exod. xx. 21), and which descended upon the Tabernacle and in the Temple (Exod. xi. 34 ; 1 Kings viii. 10). As regards the voice and the words uttered, all that is necessary will be found in our remarks on Matth. iii. 17. We must not however overlook here the additional clause αὐτοῦ ἀκούετε, hear him, which is wanting on the occasion of the baptism. (It is taken from Deut. xviii. 15, אֵלָיו תִּשְׁמָעוּן.) These words deter-mine the peculiar character of the scene. The Messianic Son of God, who has already laboured and taught under the Divine com-mission, is now formally appointed the Lord and Ruler of the earth, in presence of the representatives of the heavenly and earthly world. What the tempter had set before the Lord (Matth. iv. 8, πάσας τὰς βασιλείας τοῦ κόσμου, all the kingdoms of the world), is here conferred on him by the Creator of all things, and indeed not merely the dominion of earth but also that of heaven. To this solemn trans-action does the Saviour look back, when he says ἐδόθη μοι πᾶσα ἐξουσία ἐν οὐρανῷ καὶ ἐπὶ γῆς, all power was given* to me in heaven and on earth (Matth. xxviii. 18). The gospel history thus enables

---

* The Aor. ἐδόθη, was given, seems to point to a special occasion of the bestowment of the power, and may confirm the author's view.—[K.

us to follow plainly the separate periods in the perfecting (τελείωσις) of the Son of God. Here, at his appointment to his everlasting kingdom, it is at the same time shewn to him how he must by his own blood purchase his church.

Ver. 6-8.—Now the disciples lost all consciousness, they sank on their faces, and saw Jesus alone. (Compare as to the sinking down of the disciples, Dan. x. 8, 9 ; Rev. i. 17. In both cases the touch of the hand acts restoratively, it infuses power into men disabled by the sight of the Divine Majesty.)

Ver. 9.—In a historical point of view this verse is specially remarkable, from the fact that it forms the immediate basis on which rests the credibility of the occurrence which precedes it. The conversation respecting it with the Saviour precludes the suspicion of any misunderstanding which he deemed it necessary to remove.* Further, the prohibition to mention the event indicates that Jesus did not impart the same information equally to all the disciples, but that he had even in the circle of his disciples, a still more select and favoured company. It would certainly be a mistake, to infer from such an indication that there was any system of doctrines which Jesus communicated to some and withheld from others. This is the error of the Alexandrine fathers and Gnostics. But not less were it an error, to deny any distinction in the communications made by Jesus to his different disciples. It is difficult however to assign here the ground of the prohibition (compare on Matth. viii. 4). Any abuse or misunderstanding of such a fact, of which there was obviously a risk only in the case of the general multitude, might, so far as the disciples were concerned, have easily been guarded against, by correct information. To me it seems probable that this prohibition rested on no other ground than the exclusion of the *other* disciples from being present at the occurrence—they could not as yet bear everything. (At John xvi. 12, the same thing is, in regard to other events, applied to all the apostles.) According to Luke ix. 36, the disciples obeyed. Matthew himself therefore received his information of the event only after the resurrection. We must obviously conceive of the disciples as engaged at that time in the liveliest interchange of all their experiences. Mark remarks (ix. 10), that this word sank deeply into the hearts of the disciples (κρατεῖν = פְּזֵר, to seize on, to hold fast, as something important. Compare at Luke ii. 51, the verb διατηρεῖν), and occasioned also separate conversations among them. It was the ἀνάστασις, resurrection, at which they stumbled. The idea they were accustomed to form of it they could not reconcile with the character of the Messiah whom they had just seen in heavenly glory, for it presupposed his death.

* The idea, that the prohibition was given merely to prevent these disseminating their misapprehension, stands self-refuted.

This little trait singularly confirms the truthfulness of the narrative.

Ver. 10–13.—Luke here closes the narrative, but Matthew and Mark give a selection from a most important conversation which arose in consequence of the occurrence just recorded. It referred to Elias, whom the learned among the Jews usually associated with the appearance of the Messiah. There is an obscurity however in the introduction to the discourse, which commenced, according to Matthew, with the question of the disciples, τί οὖν οἱ γραμματεῖς κ. τ. λ.; *why then say the scribes ?* etc. The οὖν, *then*, points back to something that had gone before, and the whole inquiry leaves the impression that the disciples believed the opinion of the learned Jews to have been incorrect, for which reason Christ confirms it as right. It is most natural certainly to view the reference as pointing back to ver. 4, where Peter hoped that Elias would now remain with them, and enter on his labours. Instead of that, he at once disappeared, and for this reason he asks what they were to make of the above opinion.* Jesus declares it, according to Mal. iv. 5, to be wholly correct, and defines the kind of labours in which he was to engage by the words ἀποκαταστήσει πάντα, *he shall restore all things* (= בישׁיה, in the passage referred to). For as the Tishbite once laboured of old as an *emendator sacrorum*, so shall he also come forth at his second appearance. He is no creator of a new order of things in the spiritual life, but (by legal strictness and severity) he stems the course of sinful confusion, and re-introduces a state of order. Into this scene the Messiah steps forth as a Creator. Christ however intimates that one had already exercised for him this office, but the scribes had put him to death. The disciples (according to earlier intimations, see on Matth. xi. 14) understood him to mean the Baptist. What is expressed however so decidedly here, that Elias is already come, must be modified according to the statement of Matth. xi. 14. (Compare the remarks on the passage referred to.) For, the appearance of Elias at the transfiguration as little exhausted the prediction of the prophet (Mal. iv. 5), as did the sending forth of the Baptist.[?] Each was merely a prefiguration, adapted to Christ's first appearance in his humiliation (which the Old Testament never clearly distinguishes from his second coming in glory), but the prophecy itself remains awaiting its fulfilment at Christ's future appearance (compare on Rev. xi. 3, seq.)† While

* Peter appears merely to wish to know this, whether *this* appearance of Elias is the one referred to in prophecy. Jesus corrects him. "Elias certainly cometh (= it is predicted that he shall come), but I tell you that he is come already (the prophecy is already fulfilled in John the Baptist"), comp. Luke i. 17.—That the real Elias is to appear before Christ's second coming, is not intimated in the passage.—[E.

† As to the history of the interpretations which have been given of the passage in Malachi, compare Hengstenberg's Christology, vol. iii., p. 444, seq.

Jesus, at Matth. xvii. 12, draws a parallel between the fortunes of
John and his own coming fate, Mark reads the prophecies of the
Old Testament as predicting the sufferings of John. Καθὼς γέγραπται ἐπ' αὐτόν, as it is written of him, he writes at ix. 13. Now nothing of the kind is expressly predicted of John, nor does the history
of Elias admit of being typically referred to him, for Elias did not
die in the persecution.* It is probable therefore that the evangelist
brings together here (as at Matth. ii. 23), in one collective quotation,
all the passages of Scripture in which the persecution of prophets
and pious men is spoken of. Besides, the answer of Christ in
Mark, acquires, through the peculiar collocation of the thoughts, a
character quite different from that which it bears in Matthew. It
has been conjectured that the text is corrupt, but without any
ground. Obviously, according to Mark, the Saviour sets over against
the inquiry of the disciples another question, in order to rouse them
to reflection. The sense is then as follows, " The Scribes say Elias
must first come ;" Jesus replied, " Elias certainly cometh first
(πρῶτος = πρότερος), and setteth all in order ; but how in that case
can it stand recorded of the Son of man that he must suffer much
and be rejected ?" By the question thus retorted, Jesus wishes to
rouse his disciples to the conviction, that the prediction respecting
the preparatory ministry of Elias is not to be understood absolutely.
He certainly setteth all in order, but the sins of men prevent his
efforts taking effect. And in conclusion, the assurance is subjoined,
that Elias is already come in the Baptist (i. e., in John working
in the spirit and power of Elias. See on Luke i. 17.)

§ 33. HEALING OF THE LUNATIC.

(Matth. xvii. 14–23 ; Mark ix. 14–32 ; Luke ix. 37–45.)

The three evangelists are still parallel in this narrative, and the
indication of the time given by Luke, ἐν τῇ ἑξῆς ἡμέρᾳ, again conjoins the narrative so introduced in the closest way with what had
gone before. Mark exhibits himself once more in this history in
his well-known character. The epileptic boy he paints with a
master-hand, and the whole scene amidst which the cure was
wrought. We see the ever swelling current of people as they
pressed to the spot, and the paroxysms amidst which the beneficent
power of Jesus overmasters the destructive power which controlled

---

* Hengstenberg (Christol., vol. iii., p. 478) is of opinion, indeed, that Jezebel had intended to kill Elias, and that although her purpose did not, like that of Herodias, take
effect, yet no weight is to be laid on this difference. But in this opinion I cannot share.
A type demands in every case facts, not mere intentions.

the child. The narrative of this cure demands in itself only some brief remarks, for previous analogous passages make it sufficiently intelligible. Some things, however, peculiar to this cure, will require extended explanations.

Ver. 14, 15.—Matthew calls the sick boy (he was his father's only child, Luke ix. 38) a *lunatic* (σεληνιαζόμενος). According to ver. 18, however, he, like Luke and Mark, viewed the disease as brought by an evil spirit (πνεῦμα). Now the representations of Mark and Luke agree perfectly with epilepsy,* which, as is well known, being founded on a morbid excitement of the nerves in the lower part of the body, is connected with the changes of the moon. It is not unlikely that the secret sins of the boy (comp. on ver. 21) had destroyed his health. [?] Mark and Luke plainly intimate that the disease was not continuous, but that the child fell into paroxysms. (Mark ix. 18, ὅπου ἂν αὐτὸν καταλάβῃ. Luke ix. 39, μόγις ἀποχωρεῖ ἀπ' αὐτοῦ, i. e., the paroxysms endure unusually long.) The gnashing and foaming (τρίζειν καὶ ἀφρίζειν), and the dying, wasting away of the invalid (ξηραίνεσθαι), most graphically represent his condition. (The ἄλαλον, *speechless*, of Mark refers only to articulate speech, which in such moments would be suspended; it does not therefore stand in contradiction to κράζειν [to utter inarticulate tones] as employed by Luke.)

Ver. 16, 17.—The disciples had not been able to heal the sick child. It is a wholly groundless conjecture that not all the disciples, but only certain of their number (and those the weakest in faith), are here alluded to. The words of reproof are general—so general indeed that they may not only have included all the disciples, but the people at the same time, and especially the father of the sick boy. The apostles appear here merely as the representatives of the whole, but on them the rebuke certainly falls most heavily. Jesus, however, did not stand there for the sake of the apostles alone, nor with them alone had he to deal; the burden of all rested on him. (The verb ἀνέχεσθαι = סָבַל to bear the load of sin. The expression γενεὰ διεστραμμένη agrees with Deut. xxxii. 5, where the LXX. give it as the rendering of פְּתַלְתֹּל דּוֹר)

Mark ix. 20–27, alone paints with exact and lively portraiture the process of the cure. As the boy drew near to Christ, a paroxysm seized him. Jesus upon this began a conversation as in the case of the Gergesene (compare Mark v. 9, seq.), but here only with the father, owing to the unconsciousness of the son. The object of this conversation was, by means of the peace and security which it

* I agree substantially with the view given of this narrative in the very successful exposition of Dr. Paulus (Comment. Part II., p. 571, seq.), with only this difference, that he has missed here, as elsewhere, the fact that the evangelists mean to refer the origin of the disease ultimately to the spiritual world.

breathed, to still the raging element and inspire confidence. The father now obtained an opportunity of recounting the sufferings of his miserable child ; the convulsions, he states, often threatened in a moment to destroy even his life, by casting him into fire or water which might be near. The hostile influence awakened within him an impulse to self-destruction. Jesus thereupon commends to him the all-prevailing power of faith (see as to this subject on Matth. xvii. 20), and calls upon him to believe. The unfortunate man exclaims (almost with spasmodic impulse), πιστεύω, βοήθει μου τῇ ἀπιστίᾳ, I believe; help my unbelief. Thus the Saviour first shews himself here in the father as a producer of faith (μαιευτὴς πίστεως) before he heals the son. In the struggles of earnest desire, the power of faith is by the help of Christ produced in the unbelieving soul, and then the deliverance is vouchsafed. This passage is one of the most important to our understanding the nature of faith, as laid down in the Gospels. It is not the acknowledgment of certain doctrinal truths that is here spoken of (that is merely a consequence resulting from it); Jesus here imparts no instruction ; and the disciples also, supposing they had healed the sick child, would assuredly not have prefaced the cure by a discourse on the Messiahship of Jesus. Faith is rather an internal moral state—we have called it a receptive faculty (comp. on Matth. viii. 10), into which Divine influences find ready admission. Here, however, we see that this state of soul is not to be looked on as altogether independent of man's own efforts. Earnest striving and prayer are fitted to call it forth. Both these imply, it is true, that the germ of faith already exists (there must always be an ὑπόστασις ἐλπιζομένων, substance of things hoped for, in the soul, if man is to be able to pray), but no one is to be regarded as by nature wholly destitute of the germ of faith. By a continued course of sin, however, it can be destroyed, and so a man be brought to the πιστεύειν τῶν δαιμόνων, faith of devils (James ii. 19), which, properly speaking, is no faith. (Compare Neander's small Gelegenheitschr. p. 31, seq.) There is yet, however, a difficulty here in the circumstance, that the faith of the father seems to benefit the son. (In the same way, at Matth. viii. 5, seq., where the officer believes and the servant is healed, and at Matth. xv. 22, seq., where the mother's faith stands in a similar relation to the cure of the daughter.) As unbelief is the ground of a refusal to heal (compare on Matth. xiii. 58), it may naturally be presumed that the persons cured also exercised faith. We might hence assume in these cases two entirely distinct processes : First, the healing of the sick person, whose faith Jesus perceived, though it did not then express itself ; next, the awakening in the parents or masters, of a faith which still was not connected with the cure. Yet a connexion precisely of this kind seems to be here asserted.

At Mark ix. 23, the cure of the child is expressly conjoined with the faith of the father. There seems then in these cases a special bond of union. If then we put the inquiry, whether the child not grown up could be conceived of as exercising faith on behalf of his parents, as well as the parents on behalf of the child, none perhaps would answer in the affirmative, and hence it seems not improbable that the child is regarded as essentially dependent on the parents. It is here very natural to suppose such an union of posterity to their parents as is expressed in Heb. vii. 5, and which also lies at the foundation of the whole account of the relation in which Adam and Chrst stand to the human race. (Comp. on Rom. v. 13, seq.) Something analogous also seems, according to Matth. viii. 5, seq., to be pointed out in the relation between the master and his servant; it is, however, self-evident that in this union the relation is merely to be viewed as accidental, for it may be conceived of as reversed. Upon this conversation with the father follows the cure itself, which, as in the case of the Gergesene, again produces a violent paroxysm, ending in the entire prostration of all his powers. (Comp. Mark v. 15.) The boy was so exhausted by the violence of the reaction, that they thought him dead (Mark ix. 26), but the touch of Jesus renewed the powers of life.

Ver. 19, 20.—After the cure the disciples came to Jesus, and within their narrower circle ($\kappa a \tau$' $l\delta i a \nu$, Matth. xvii. 19), inquired why *they* could not heal the sick child. Luke wholly omits this important conversation. Mark so curtails it that its essential meaning cannot be perceived, and it seems to bear on its surface a somewhat different sense; and here again his graphic power shews itself rather in outward portaiture. Matthew, on the contrary, goes into the *essence* of things, especially in regard to the discourses of Jesus, and we willingly excuse therefore his want of exactness in outward details. Such points speak decisively enough for the apostolic origin of his Gospel. On the part of the apostles, also, Jesus now reproves the $\dot{a}\pi\iota\sigma\tau i a$, *unbelief*, and plainly charges their want of faith with guilt. They, too, might have cried out " help our unbelief." The position of the apostles (as of men in general), relatively to that which is Divine, thus appears here as not essentially different from that of those who were to be healed. Does man wish to receive heavenly powers? he must stand waiting and expectant. Still the faith of the apostles was an active principle, compared with the purely receptive faith of the subjects of the healing power. Thus we plainly see here *different gradations of faith.* (Compare what is said more in detail on Rom. iii. 21.) With the reception of the principle of life, there comes an increase in the soul's susceptibility of it, and thus faith goes on to perfection in itself. The apostles had already for a long time been in communion

with Jesus, and never had been without faith in him, yet Christ
marks here within them the want of the germ of real faith (κόκκος
σινάπεως), or as one might call it, of *creative* faith, for in this character it ought to shew itself *in them*. Faith is thus a living internal state, inherently developing itself, since the Divine principle
becomes gradually predominant and effectual within the soul ; but
in all stages of its development, the fundamental condition of the
heart (in which faith dwells [Rom. x. 9], and not in the understanding), continues one and the same. (Compare on Matth. xxi. 21)—
Jesus now holds up to their view the portraiture of perfect faith,
whose effect it is that to men *nothing shall be impossible*. (Compare Mark ix. 23, πάντα δυνατὰ τῷ πιστεύοντι.) Nothing can be a
greater mistake than to divest these words of their profound import
by explaining them as hyperbolical. We read at Matth. xix. 26,
respecting God, " With God all things are possible" (compare the
parallel passages Mark x. 27 ; Luke xviii. 27). These words guide
us to an understanding of the true meaning of this eulogium on
faith. Just because faith is a susceptibility to Divine influence, it
imparts to him in whom it is developed, the very nature of divinity;
and under the guidance of the Divine power which animates the
believer, he is brought, according to the degree of development imparted to him, into those circumstances in which he must through
faith come off victorious. The *all things*, therefore, is to be taken
in its widest sense, only not to be referred to the various caprices
which might spring from mere unbelieving curiosity, but to the
real wants of the believer. Such a case of need the disciples had
encountered, but they had neglected earnestly to supplicate the
requisite power from on high. The mode, finally, of portraying the
omnipotent power of faith is figurative. It is conceived first in its
minimum state, then in its maximum of power. (See as to the κόκκος
σινάπεως on Matth. xiii. 31. The overturning of mountains is an
expression selected unquestionably in allusion to passages of the
Old Testament. Compare Job ix. 5; Zech. iv. 7. In the New
Testament, Paul repeats the statement at 1 Cor. xiii. 2. Another
similar figure to denote what is impossible for man, but possible for God in believers, is seen at Luke xvii. 6. In Matth.
xxi. 21 [Mark xi. 23], the figure of the overturn of mountains is
repeated.)

Ver. 21.—The connexion of the following verse with the preceding context is obscure. " This kind (scil. τῶν δαιμόνων,* according
to what goes before) goeth not out but by prayer and fasting."

---

* *Sieffert* (ut supra, p. 100) wishes to refer τοῦτο τὸ γένος to the unbelief of the
apostles themselves. But I know of no instance in which unbelief, which was something
negative, could be compared with demons who must be driven out. This view of the
passage seems to me inadmissible.

(The fasting being viewed as a means of cure accompanying prayer.) The close connexion of the words with the reproof administered to the apostles for their unbelief, leads obviously to this meaning— "this obstinate enemy was not to be overcome in the same way as many others. It was needful for you, with prayer and fasting, earnestly to strive after more of the power of faith, and then might you have been victorious." The prayer and fasting relate thus to the disciples themselves. And yet both may be referred also to the person cured ; ye ought to have enjoined on him similar duties, and then ye would have been enabled effectually to heal him. The reference in this view to Luke ix. 42, "he restored him to his father," is certainly most correct ; it is not unlikely that the Saviour had exhorted the father to a wise treatment of his son. According to the connexion of ideas in Mark, the reference of prayer and fasting is mainly to the cured boy, who probably had by sins of impurity plunged himself into this nervous disorder.* In Matthew it is perhaps best to combine both references.

Ver. 22, 23.—In the concluding verses the evangelists are entirely agreed in introducing a new mention of the Saviour's sufferings (compare on Matth. xvi. 21). The words stand without any visible connexion with what precedes. It is, however, not improbable that from time to time the thought of his approaching sufferings struck Jesus, and then as is here presented in the narrative, he suddenly expressed what he felt to his disciples, especially when he withdrew from his larger sphere of labour into solitude and the circle of his confidential friends. (This is indicated at Mark ix. 30, by the words οὐκ ἤθελεν ἵνα τὶς γνῷ [sc. αὐτόν].) This declaration, however, must only have been at the time of a fragmentary nature, for the disciples could not reconcile themselves to the idea of their Messiah's sufferings—that Messiah from whom they expected the end of all suffering (Mark ix. 32 ; Luke ix. 45, ἠγνόουν τὸ ῥῆμα τοῦτο). Meanwhile the utterance of that deep and anguished feeling carried them away involuntarily (Matth. xvii. 23, ἐλυπήθησαν σφόδρα), but the majestic gravity which marked his entire character and bearing, deterred them from asking further as to the transaction he had alluded to (ἐφοβοῦντο ἐρωτῆσαι in Mark and Luke); there thus remained for them only the obscure impression of some mighty and fearful event awaiting them.

* See on the contrary παιδιόθεν, *from a child,* Mark ix. 21.—[E.

§ 34. The Coin (Stater) in the Fish's Mouth.

(Matth. xvii. 24–27.)

Before proceeding to the occurrence itself which is here recorded, we must cast a glance at the connexion. Mark ix. 33, as
also Matthew, makes the Lord come to Capernaum, but connects
immediately with his arrival the narrative of the conversation as to
who should be the greatest in the kingdom of God. He relates
most minutely that this conversation took place in the house, and
was introduced by a question put by Jesus, as to what they had
talked of by the way. Now, according to the view of Dr. Paulus
(Comment. Part ii., p. 621) Peter was not present at the commencement of this conversation, but came in subsequently while it was
going on (Matth. xviii. 21), and it is simply to account for his absence that this narrative of Peter's taking the fish is inserted by
Matthew. But, for this conjecture the whole account gives not the
slightest occasion ; nay, Mark ix. 35 rather mentions the twelve as all
present at the commencement of the conversation. The expression
προσελθὼν αὐτῷ, *coming to him*, at Matth. xviii. 21, merely means
that Peter came close to him when addressing Jesus. If the evangelist had distinctly intended to represent Peter as absent, he would
have stated so in plainer terms. It is far more natural to suppose
that Matthew added in conclusion this little narrative of Peter's
taking the fish, because it happened just at the time, and in order
that he might introduce once more in chap. xviii. a more lengthened collection of various fragments of discourse which he did not
wish to interrupt. Moreover, Christ's conversation with Peter as to
the tribute, might have been considered of importance in respect to
the discourse which follows, as will be afterwards shewn. The
character of the discourses given in Matth. xviii., by no means
demands, as will afterwards be shewn, the absence of Peter, even if
they were spoken successively in the same order in which we read
them in Matthew. Peter's taking the fish was undoubtedly (in
their proximity to the sea) the work of a few moments, and we may
therefore justly suppose him present at what follows.

As regards the incident itself, however, recorded in Matth. xvii.
24–27, it is not to be denied that the natural explanation which
Dr. Paulus (*ut supra*) has given of it, brings forward points that deserve consideration. The narrative, as ordinarily understood, contains much that might surprise us. It is strange, in the first place,
that the coin should have been in the *mouth* of the fish. It seems
more to the purpose to conceive of it as in the belly, especially as
the fish was caught by an ἄγκιστρον (*hamus, fishing-hook*), the use

of which presupposes the opening of the mouth. In the next place, the object aimed at seems to stand in no fitting relation to the miracle. The miracles of Jesus have always a definite reference to the well-being of man, or they are designed to authenticate his Messiahship, and prepare the way for faith in it. We trace here no connexion with either of these objects, for the occurrence referred to Peter alone, who was already convinced of the Messiahship of Jesus ; the address of Jesus (ver. 25) presupposes faith as already existing in him. Besides, as Jesus was in Capernaum, even if his bag was empty (John xii. 6 ; xiii. 29), he might in this place have obtained the small sum in a more simple way. Thus the proposal to explain the expression εὑρήσεις στατῆρα, *thou shalt find a stater* (ver. 27), as meaning " thou shalt obtain the coin (stater) for the fish" (by selling it), will appear as not so entirely inadmissible. [?] For, even with this explanation, the transaction, taken symbolically bears a beautiful meaning, as shewing how Christ, as the Lord of nature, draws what he needs from the great treasure-house of the Father. We are at first the more tempted to accede to this view, from the remarkable fact that at the close of the history the usual conclusion of miraculous narratives is wanting—namely, that Peter, at the command of Jesus both did and experienced what had been said to him. But looking without prejudice at the narrative, we cannot conceal the difficulties presented by this explanation of Dr. Paulus. Taking the words at ver. 27 as we find them "and on opening its mouth thou wilt find a stater" (καὶ ἀνοίξας τὸ στόμα αὐτοῦ εὑρήσεις στατῆρα), it must be confessed that the narrator means to say that the stater (coin) would be found in the mouth. Granting indeed that εὑρίσκειν *may* mean *to acquire, to obtain* (without defining the way in which a thing is obtained), still the fact that the acquisition of the piece of money is so immediately connected with* the *opening* of the *mouth*, unquestionably is in contradiction to the opinion that the money was to be raised from *the sale* of the fish. The remark of Paulus on this point, that the opening of the mouth refers merely to his taking the fish off the hook, and that this was needful because it would otherwise have died more speedily, and so would have been of less value, is obviously too far-fetched. It is clear that this mode of explaining away what is supernatural is suggested not by the text itself, but by reflection. In the next place, it is not to be overlooked, that plainly only *one* fish was intended to be caught. Paulus will have it that ἰχθύς, *fish*, is to be taken collectively, but the addition of πρῶτος, *first*, altogether forbids this. (Compare *Fritzsche* on the passage.) But in poor Capernaum, where fish were common, the sum of money here named could not possibly have been obtained for a single fish. As then it is the interpreter's first duty to render faithfully the text of his author, we must maintain, that Matthew means to relate that Jesus commanded Peter to take a fish, and foresaw that it would bear a stater in its mouth. The result, however, thus yielded by our interpretation, we cannot leave standing in opposition to the character of Christ ; and it becomes a question, whether, notwithstanding the above objections, this miracle can be made to harmonize with his general procedure. The main question to be settled is this, whether the form of miraculous action here exhibited was in opposition to the fundamental laws which controlled the Saviour's action : the other objections will then disappear of their own accord, or will lose their weight. It must be maintained as a leading principle, that every miraculous act of Christ had an object connected with his whole Messianic work. What can have been the object of the present miracle ?

Peter's answer to the collectors, that the Lord would pay the contribution, implied a failure to recognise his peculiar position ; and although Jesus might appeal to his Divine Sonship, which, at a former period, Peter had already confessed, yet the Saviour seems to have wished still more deeply to impress on his mind a view of his exalted dignity. [Peter had, rashly and unauthorized, conceded that Jesus was bound to pay the tax, comp. ver. 25. This the Saviour teaches him ; this too he intends to teach the receivers of the tribute, and that by actual proof. He shows them that he is Lord not only of the temple, but of the whole world, and that his submission to the tribute was purely voluntary, not in the sligtest degree obligatory.]

Ver. 24.—As respects the relative value of the money which this narrative refers to, the στατήρ is = 4 drachmas or Roman denarii. These formed a Jewish shekel. The δίδραχμον is therefore = half a shekel, i. e., to about 10 good groschen. The stater thus amounted to 20 good groschen.[*] This sum of itself,[†] and still more the conversation which follows, shews that it is not a civil tax but a temple tax that is here spoken of. According to Exodus xxx. 13, seq., every Israelite was required to pay such a contribution ; and in the time of Josephus (Antiq., xviii., 9, 1), even the foreign Jews paid it. The question put by the collectors of this assessment, whether Jesus would pay it, doubtless arose from their believing that, as a theocratic teacher, he would regard himself as free from such an impost. But Peter, to whom the question was addressed in the absence of Jesus, believed, that with his strictness in religious observance, he would make it a point to pay the sacred tax, and answered affirmatively.

* The good groschen is equal to rather more than 3 cents. The Marien-groschen is of less value.—[T.

† The double article also οἱ τὰ δίδραχμα λαμβάνοντες, indicates a reference to certain appointed persons entrusted with the collection of the temple offerings.

Ver. 25, 26.—Jesus perceived at once that on the part of Peter this arose from defective views. In his answer he had contemplated Jesus rather under the aspect of his legal piety than of his ideal dignity, and Jesus therefore anticipated his remark (προέφθασεν αὐτόν) by the question "What thinkest thou, Simon?" he awakens by this inquiry the perception of his elevation, as well as that of Peter himself, above the temple-service of the old dispensation. Jesus here runs a parallel between earthly kings and earthly tribute (τέλη, *custom-duties on goods*, κῆνσος, *head-money on persons*), and the heavenly King, and spiritual contributions ; as with the kings their own are free from taxes, so also in the things of heaven. For, what God's children possess belongs to God—they have no property exclusively their own—they contribute out of and into their own purse—they are therefore free. Jesus places himself here on a level with Peter, but it is obvious that from this figurative mode of speaking nothing can be inferred respecting the import of " *Son of God.*" The meaning is simply this—we belong to a higher order of things than that to which the commandment in question (Exod. xxx. 13) applies ; not for us did God give it, we pay to the temple not a poor tax, but we ourselves belong to it wholly, with all that we are and have. Jesus thus elevates Peter to his own spiritual level—a position for which he certainly was not yet fully trained, but to which, as a renewed man, he already belonged. The Lord's words at the same time clearly prove that he in general acknowledged and honoured the Old Testament economy as of Divine institution ; unless this be assumed, the words had no meaning. But he contemplated the whole temple service in its preparatory character, and led on the disciples so to view it.

Ver. 27.—While thus conscious that he stood above the Old Testament economy (comp. xii. 8), the Saviour yet subjected himself to it ; as, in general, up to the completion of his work on earth, he in no respect assailed or withdrew from the the existing order of the Divine service. Only with Christ's atoning death was the law completed and finished, and a new form of religious life arose in the church, in which the commands of the Old Testament acquired their true spiritual meaning. Here, in this subordination to the law, does Jesus make obvious the weakness of those around him (see as to σκανδαλίζεσθαι on Matth. xviii. 6); he wished neither to give them offence nor lead them to believe that he did not reverence the law of the Old Testament. It is certain, also, that at the basis of this lies the general principle " it is becoming us to fulfil all righteousness" (ποέπον ἐστὶ πληρῶσαι πᾶσαν δικαιοσύνην. Comp. on Matth. iii. 15.)

§ 35. On the Character of the Children of the Kingdom.

(Matth. xviii. 1–35; Mark ix. 33–50; Luke ix. 46–56.)

The words ἀναστρεφομένων αὐτῶν ἐν τῇ Γαλιλαίᾳ (Matth. xvii. 22), again seem to unsettle the whole chronological connexion by their vagueness; nor do the parallel passages in Mark and Luke give any more certain data. The contents, however, of the succeeding context, make it probable that no great interval in this instance elapsed between what had preceded and what now follows. The conversation as to pre-eminence in the kingdom of God in which the disciples were engaged on the way to Capernaum (Mark ix. 33), may have been occasioned by the transfiguration, and the preference there shewn for certain of their number, and as all the three narrators give exactly the same connexion of events, the possibility becomes a probability. It is true, however, that the Evangelists record the event each with details of his own. Luke is the shortest; he has merely the admonition to humility. Mark gives also the warning against offences greatly expanded, as is his manner. Matthew adds still further particulars. It is not impossible so to conceive of the antecedent circumstances, that all these different points may on this occasion have been made by Christ the subjects of conversation, simply on account of what had fallen out among the apostles. The evangelists themselves give details from which we may infer the following to have been the course of events. The disciples not merely conversed as to their pre-eminence in the kingdom of God, but fell into a sharp contest on the point. (Hence the admonition at Mark ix. 50, εἰρηνεύετε ἐν ἀλλήλοις.) In the altercation, they not merely boasted the one over the other, but by hard words wounded each other's feelings; nay, the disciples by this gave such offence to each other, or to any individual who might be present, that their faith might have been shaken alike in the reality of any higher life as existing among the Saviour's companions, and in his own exalted character and destination. This would explain how Christ should successively have discoursed of humility, of offences, of grace towards sinners, of reconciliation. This view, however, rests simply on conjecture as to the contents of that conversation between the disciples. It is also possible that Matthew, according to his custom, has again united together portions of kindred discourses.* The tie which in this chapter connects the various elements, is the endeavour to depict in the Saviour's words the true

* Compare here the remarks on Matth. xiv. 1, and the introductory observations to chap. xix. 1.

character of the children of God. Much had occurred which might be viewed as attributing to the disciples something of outward importance ; especially might Christ's very address to Peter as to the temple-taxes (Matth. xvii. 25), be so misunderstood.* To this error Matthew now opposes the spiritual nature of discipleship as standing in direct contradiction to an earthly domination. Yet the Saviour does not deny a difference of position to be occupied in the future kingdom of God ; he merely sets forth that frame of mind by which all abuse of this truth is obviated.

Ver. 1.—Most graphically does Mark ix. 33, seq., again depict the scene. The conversation as to who should be the greatest had taken place by the way. In the house our Lord questions the disciples on it, and they, conscious of guilt, are silent, whereupon, by a symbolic act, he sets clearly before their view the nature of God's kingdom. First, however, it is to be carefully marked here, that the Saviour by no means denies that the apostles possess special dignity in the kingdom of God ; which indeed he could not do, for it is promised them by himself (comp. on Matth. xix. 28). Further, he does not deny that there is a distinction between his different disciples, for this he himself in like manner confirmed (see on Matth. xvii. 1). Thus the error of the disciples did not consist in assuming a distinction among the members of the kingdom, or in cherishing the conviction of their own exalted calling. It lay rather in their forming low and earthly conceptions of that calling, in confounding supremacy in the kingdom of God with dominion in the kingdoms of earth. True, the very idea of a kingdom, presupposes government and subordination ; but in the kingdom of God the government is specifically different from earthly rule. This distinction the Saviour here developes, inasmuch as, according to Mark ix. 35, he represents the *first* in the kingdom of God as the *last*, the *lord* as the *servant of all*. (Comp. on Matth. xx. 28.) Thus in the Divine kingdom the power of self-sacrificing, devoted, self-abasing love (which, in the Saviour himself, is seen in its glorious perfection), is the one turning-point on which all pre-eminence depends ; while conversely, in the world, he who rules is wont to make use of the governed simply for himself, his own benefit, his reputation and glory. The fleshly minds of the disciples therefore, mistaking the idea of God's kingdom, had induced them in the future manifestation of Christ's glory to look for the gratification of selfish hopes. These the Lord overthrows by intimating that only he who has divested himself of all self-seeking, and who lives in pure love and lowly self-renunciation, shall there reign, or exert commanding influence. (The τίς μείζων ἐστίν, *who is the greater*, clearly indicates that all the disciples were united in the belief that

---

* So we find it in Clemens Alex. quis dives salvetur, chap. 21.

they, as standing in immediate connexion with the Lord, were called
alike to exercise the most important influence in the kingdom of
God :—their only point of dispute was who among themselves should
be the greater, the more influential. The occurrence related at
Matth. xvii. 1, might easily occasion such reflections.)

Ver. 2–4.—Very naturally, according to the account of Matthew,
is there subjoined here the symbolic act of Jesus in placing a child
(παιδίον is not =עֶבֶד, a slave or servant, but with reference to regeneration a child, one who is new-born) in the midst of them, and in
him setting forth the character of those who should have influence
in the kingdom of God. That it is not the character of this individual child that he here speaks of (according to the legend, it was
the martyr Ignatius), is shewn at once by the immediately following
words, become as children. Jesus merely brings forward in this
individual child the general character of children, as a model for
the members of the kingdom of God. For, although the general
sinfulness of human nature certainly shews itself at once in children,
yet does humility and an unassuming disposition peculiarly distinguish the child's nature ; the king's son is not ashamed to play with
the son of a beggar. This unassuming disposition is here the point
of comparison. Certainly it is exercised by children unconsciously,
while on the part of believers it is to be deliberately cherished. The
comparison therefore does not on all points hold good, which it
could not possibly do, for the reason, that earthly relations present
no perfect analogy to the spiritual nature which is the subject of
the comparison. Into such an unassuming frame does the Lord
now exhort that the disciples to turn their minds (στρέφεσθαι to change
their spiritual direction ; instead of aspiring to a high position, they
must descend to a humble one), then will they find entrance to the
heavenly kingdom. The passage is thus wholly parallel to the important verse, John iii. 3, for the γίνεσθαι ὡς παιδίον, become as a
child, is nothing else than the new birth, in which alone such as
unassuming child-like feeling can be implanted. By the resolutions
and efforts of the natural man it cannot be produced. As an evidence of this child-like feeling Christ brings prominently forward the
ταπεινοῦν ἑαυτόν, humbling one's self, in opposition to the ὑψοῦν ἑαυτόν,
exalting one's self; as the child, in whatever circumstances placed,
will unassumingly be content with a lowly position, so should also the
new-born saint, instead of climbing to high stations, descend to the
secure vale of humility. The expression "humbleth himself" retains
here its widest meaning, inasmuch as even in the regenerate, constant and positive effort is needful to keep down the ambitious
aspirings of the old man. The humbling may therefore be viewed as
a special and stronger expression for becoming a child, and the being
greater in the kingdom as contrasted with the mere entrance into it.

Ver. 5.—Matthew, who alone gives the preceding verses, shews himself here again exceedingly exact in detailing our Lord's discourses. According to Mark and Luke, who do not give these verses, it is not so easy to understand the presenting of the child, nay, it acquires with them a different meaning. They both speak directly of "the receiving of children," whence also Mark (ix. 36), can add ἐναγκαλισάμενος αὐτό, *taking it in his arms*, an act not in immediate accordance with the representation of Matthew; for since, with him, the child was simply a symbol of humility, it must in these circumstances have been a meaningless act to embrace him. (In Luke ii. 28, the term ἐναγκαλίζεσθαι = δέχεσθαι εἰς ἀγκάλας refers to *little* children, in whom alone the character of humility is purely developed. The verb προσκαλέσασθαι at Matth. xviii. 2, does not contradict this; it is only necessary that we do not understand it exactly as meaning sucklings.) It accords well, however, with the train of thought in Mark and Luke, which attaches to παιδίον mainly the idea of a beloved, a dear one. Still the question arises, how we shall trace here the general course of thought; for although Matthew primarily applies the presentation of the child to a different purpose, yet he also proceeds in v. 5 to the "receiving" (δέχεσθαι), and in v. 6 to its opposite, so that from this agreement of the three Evangelists, we must hold that these words were spoken on the occasion referred to. It certainly seems from the connexion here, most natural to consider the "receiving" as an act of unassuming self-humbling love, so that it connects itself with the declaration πρῶτος πάντων διάκονος, *the first, the servant of all* (Mark ix. 35). But with this view, the last clause at Luke ix. 48, *he that is least among you*, etc., little harmonizes, for it is there apparent that the disciples are themselves the *little ones* who are to be received, not the recipients. (Compare also Mark ix. 41, from which this plainly follows.) The connexion may therefore better be understood thus, " Be ye eager to become lowly, little-noticed as this child, for the little ones (the regenerate who have the true child's feeling) are very dear and precious to the Lord, so that he regards what is done to them as done to himself." According to this chain of ideas, then, that which Matthew relates must be held as having previously occurred; for it is this which contains the ground of Christ's attachment to them. Παιδίον = μικρός ver. 10, is then the symbol of the regenerate. (See on Matth. x. 42.) The only thing still remaining obscure is how the expression " he who receiveth a little child, receiveth me" should precisely in this discourse be used to denote God's fatherly love for his spiritual children. The simplest explanation is, that this form of description is occasioned by the preceding mention (made distinctly by Matth.) of entering into the kingdom of God. With this, as something future, stands closely connected the receiving, as that which is present, so that the meaning is—" He who thus humbles himself in true lowliness, is great in the kingdom of God ; nay even amidst the sufferings of the regenerate on earth, they are so precious to the Lord that he holds what is done to them as done to himself;" (as to the thought itself, compare Matth. x. 40, seq., where it already occurred in another connexion).

In Mark (ix. 38–41), and Luke (ix. 49, 50), there follows here a question by John with the answer of Jesus, which Matthew has omitted, as not beloning to the main scope of the discourse, but as rather interrupting it. The brevity with which Luke touches this intervening question of John, would have left it in many respects obscure, had not the more exact account of Mark enabled us to trace the connexion. For the preceding words of Jesus, in which he speaks of receiving the little ones, plainly refer to the relation in which the disciples stood to those around them. John, who might not have penetrated fully into the meaning of our Lord's words, selects a circumstance which had perhaps occurred at the time, and had particularly struck himself, and lays it before the Saviour. Some one, it would appear, who doubtless had seen our Lord's miracles, or those of the apostles, had himself made the attempt to heal in the name of Jesus. The disciples, in their selfish exclusiveness, saw in this an infringement on their spiritual jurisdiction, and inasmuch as he did not habitually attach himself to the company of Jesus, had interdicted him.* This the Saviour reproves, and refers his disciples to that comprehensive love and humility of the true children of God, who child-like receive and acknowledge all that is akin to themselves, under whatever form they find it. The individual referred to is thus viewed as one befriended by the benevolent Saviour of men, and from whom the disciples might expect support, it being at the same time implied that he would not be left without a blessing. Thus understood, this incident takes its place most fittingly in the context ; it is, as it were, an example of how the Lord does good to those who *favour* his disciples, even when these latter cannot understand aright the proofs of love. The sententious phrase in which Jesus expresses the doctrine which he wished on this occasion to teach his disciples, " he who is not against you is for you" (ὃς οὐκ ἔστι καθ' ὑμῶν ὑπὲρ ὑμῶν ἐστι), is parallel to the statement at Matth. xii. 30, " he that is not with me is against me" (ὁ μὴ ὢν μετ' ἐμοῦ κατ' ἐμοῦ ἐστι), which is found also at Luke xi. 23. Both are equally true of

---

* A narrative precisely similar is recorded at Numbers xi. 27, seq. When Elded and Medad prophesied in the camp, Joshua said to Moses, " My lord Moses, forbid them." But Moses replies, " Enviest thou for my sake ? would God all the Lord's people prophesied, and that the Lord would put his Spirit upon them!"

different characters and grades of vocation. He whose calling is to spiritual labour, is *against* the Lord and his cause, if he do not positively further them ; he whose vocation is of a lower grade, who may be placed in a state of spiritual dependence on others (as the people were ruled by the Pharisees), is *in favour of* God's cause, if he keep himself free from the generally prevailing hostile influences, and so continue susceptible of the Divine. It remains, however, a singular circumstance, that, even in Christ's own times, persons should have used his name for the working of miracles without attaching themselves to his followers ; it is a proof of the general notice which his miracles had attracted. At a later period, we find, in the history of Simon Magus (Acts viii.) and the seven sons of Sceva (xix. 13, seq.) something of the same kind. If, however, the apostles judge of these men in a way wholly different from what the Saviour does here, the cause of the difference must assuredly be sought in the *motive* from which such a use of the name of Jesus proceeded. It might, as in the case of the person here mentioned, flow from faith—perhaps an unconscious faith—in Christ's heavenly power, and was therefore to be borne with (although the declarations of Jesus respecting him certainly do not exclude the necessity of his being further instructed, and made to know that the special object of Christ's coming was not to impart the gift of working miracles, but to change the human heart); but on the other hand it might proceed from motives wholly impure, as with the sons of Sceva, and must in that case be unconditionally resisted. For, these men used the name of Jesus as a peculiarly powerful form of adjuration, just as they would other formulæ of their art, for their selfish objects. Thus, it is not the outward act itself, but rather the *feeling* from which it flows, that determines its being admissible or not.

Ver. 6.—The idea which follows of the σκανδαλίζειν ἕνα τῶν μικρῶν, *offending one of the little ones*, connects itself most appropriately with the *receiving*, of ver. 5. He merely expresses the opposite thought, so that the sense of these words is, " the little ones are so precious to the Lord, that whatever good is done them he looks on as done to himself, and rewards it ; whatever evil is inflicted on them, he most indignantly punishes." The peculiar form, however, in which this thought is brought out by Matthew, and more especially by Mark, does not seem to suit the context. We do not see in what connexion it stands with the strife among the apostles. This might render it probable that there are inserted here portions of discourses originally spoken in another connexion. (Comp. on Matth. v. 29, 30, where something similar occurs.) But at Matth xviii. 10, 14, we again find marked references to the antecedent *little ones*, and at Mark ix. 50, also the clause εἰρηνεύετε ἐν ἀλλήλοις, *be at peace among yourselves,* again points back to the strife among the disciples, from which the discourse took its rise. We must then prove that these words respecting the σκανδαλίζειν stand connected with the entire discourse. For, even granting that they had originally been spoken in other circumstances by the Lord, this much is clear, that both evangelists meant here to place them in a fitting connexion. It only remains, then, that we regard the sense of μικρός, *little,* as modified in such a way that the expression here forms the counterpart of μέγας, *great.* Usually the New Testament employs the term μικρός, *little, little one,* to denote *believers,* the *regenerate* in general (see more fully on this point at Matth. x. 42), but again we also find a distinction drawn between the great and the small in the kingdom of God (see at Matth. xi. 11, and v. 19). Applying this distinction here, the connexion of the passage may be taken in this way. The strife among the disciples as to their place in the kingdom of God might have given offence to the other believers, so that they were perplexed as to whether the truth dwelt within the circle where such things could occur. This led the Lord to declare his mind as to the guilt of those who gave offence, even to the weakest among the believers. The seventh verse, in Matth. however, seems to be in opposition to this view of the connexion, for the offences are there ascribed to the world. But in reference to this, we must observe, that the disciples, in so far as they gave offence to believers, did themselves belong to the world, and thus the Saviour here passes over from the particular to the general, just as at Matth. xvi. 23, he traces Peter's declaration at once to the origin of evil from whose influence he was not yet wholly free. With this, also, ver. 8, seq., well agrees, where he speaks of self-offence (ἑαυτὸν σκανδαλίζειν), man being thus presented as in a conflict between the new and the old principles of his nature.

As to the meaning of σκάνδαλον, the old form of the word σκανδάλητρον properly denotes *a trap* for ensnaring animals, then in general, *a noose, a snare, laying wait for.* In the New Testament it is transferred to spiritual things, and under σκάνδαλον everything is included which can hinder the development of spiritual life, or deter men from faith in the Divine = πρόσκομμα, in Hebrew מכשׁל, *a cord, a noose,* or מכשׁול *offence.* (On this account also in the New Testament, παγίς, θήρα, stand connected with σκάνδαλον, see Rom. xi. 9.) The verb σκανδαλίζειν consequently means *to give* offence, to prepare spiritual obstruction, σκανδαλίζεσθαι, *to take* offence. There is a peculiarity, however, in the meaning of σκανδαλίζειν in ver. 8, of this passage, according to which the σκανδαλίζων and the σκανδαλιζόμενος appear united in the same individual. This internal conflict in man himself is to be explained, as has been already said, from regeneration, through which the new man is brought into life who wrestles and struggles with the old man for dominion. The greatness of the guilt involved in giving spiritual offence, or in deterring the little ones from a life of faith, is depicted by the Saviour in a form palpable to the senses, inasmuch as he represents the sin of these delinquencies as greater than those crimes on which the heaviest political punishment is inflicted. (The συμφέρει αὐτῷ, *it were better for him*, expresses a heavier, namely, a spiritual and eternal punishment.—The sinking into the sea was not practised among the Jews, but was in use among other nations. See for example, Sueton., August. c. 68. Instead of the less usual expression μύλος ὀνικός in Matthew and Luke, Mark has λίθος μυλικός. Μύλος = μύλη denotes properly *the mill itself*, and in a secondary sense the *mill-stone*. The word ὄνος is commonly used of the lower mill-stone, which does not move. The adjective form, ὀνικός, is not in use as applied to it. The words μύλος ὀνικός therefore cannot well mean the lower and heavier mill-stone. We do better to adhere to the sense of *set in motion by asses*, as expressing the size of the stone. The ass mill-stone is contrasted with the stone of a mill driven by the hand of man.)

Ver. 7.—This thought again meets us at Luke xvii. 1, where we shall more closely consider it. Here it is only incidental, and unconnected with the rest of the discourse. (Κόσμος the counterpart of βασ. τ. Θ. See in regard to it more at length in the exposition of John i. 9.)

Ver. 8, 9.—After speaking of offence given to others, Jesus passes on to that inward offence which he who is born again may give to himself. The general meaning of the words is clear. The cutting off hand and foot, the plucking out of the eye, is intended to denote the denying ourselves of what is dearest and most indispensable to the outward life, when through sinful influences transmitted from without, it endangers the spiritual life. But here, as at Matth. ver. 29, 30, a difficulty is raised by the additional clause, It is better for thee to enter into life (sc., eternal) *lame, maimed, one-eyed* (χωλὸν, κυλλὸν, μονόφθαλμον).* For, I cannot persuade myself to regard this as a mere embellishment, which has no meaning of its own. The sense of the whole comparison rather seems to be this. The cutting off of hand or foot, can, as is self-evident, be only taken spiritually, since the outward act were meaningless (compare on Matth. xix. 12), unless the inward root of sin were destroyed. Hand, foot, eye, here appear to be used by the Saviour to denote mental powers and dispositions, and he counsels their restraint, their non-development, if their culture interferes with that of the higher elements of spiritual life. The unrestricted

---

* Compare as to μονόφθαλμος Lobeck's Phrynichus, p. 136. The pure Greek form is ἑτερόφθαλμος

development of all our faculties, the inferior as well as the more
elevated, is the highest attainment, yet he who finds by experience
that he cannot cultivate certain faculties—the artistic for example
—without injury to his holiest feelings, must renounce their cultivation, and first of all preserve by pains-taking fidelity, the central
principle of his soul, the life imparted by Christ, which in the manifold distraction of his powers can so easily be lost. Nor let the
sacrifice of some subordinate principle, be matter of painful regret.*
True, we must add, that this loss is only in appearance, for, in the
development of man's higher life, every lower principle which he had
sacrificed, is again restored with increase of power. But in the first
instance, he has the real experience of such a sacrifice, and it still
remains true that it is a higher and better thing to learn to cultivate
even the lower faculties in harmony with the higher. Where, however, that cannot be, we should choose the safer course. Mark gives
finally, a very lengthened version of this discourse, without, however,
adding anything to the thought. The simple πῦρ αἰώνιον, *everlasting fire*, of Matthew is in Mark paraphrased by γέεννα, πῦρ ἄσβεστον
ὅπου ὁ σκώληξ αὐτῶν οὐ τελευτᾷ καὶ τὸ πῦρ οὐ σβέννυται, *hell, un-
quenchable fire where their worm, etc.* The words are taken from
Isaiah lxvi. 24, whence they had already been quoted at Sir. vii. 19;
Judith xvi. 21. They depict the ἀπώλεια, *perdition*, by imagery
taken from death and putrefaction, inasmuch as life is contrasted
with eternal death. (See as to κρίσις αἰώνιος the remarks on Matth.
xii. 32.) The expression σκώληξ = תֹּלַעְתָּם denotes properly the worm
that devours the dead body (Ps. xxii. 7; Sir. x. 13); here standing
in parallelism with πῦρ, it must be understood as inflicting pain.
The seeming tautology in the passage τὸ πῦρ ἄσβεστον ὅπου τὸ πῦρ οὐ
σβέννυται disappears when we supply αὐτῶν to the πῦρ as in the case
of the antecedent σκώληξ, which stands so placed also in Isaiah.
For in that case the first expression is a general description of the
place of punishment, the second the special infliction of its agonies
on these guilty ones.

We have an interesting remark at the conclusion of these words
in Mark, ver. 49, 50, " For every one shall be salted with fire, and
every sacrifice shall be salted with salt" (πᾶς γὰρ πυρὶ ἁλισθήσεται καὶ
πᾶσα θυσία ἁλὶ ἁλισθήσεται). This thought closes very appropriately the
foregoing discourse, for it concentrates into one general principle, as
it were, what had previously been set forth. The salting with fire

* Thus also had Origen already spoken (Comm. in Matth., Tom. xiii. ed. de la Rue,
vol. iii. 603). Tholuck remarks (Comm. on Sermon on the Mount, p. 234), in opposition
to this that my exposition bears a modern character, inasmuch as the distinction of the
various mental faculties belongs to modern metaphysical philosophy. His objection appears to me ill-founded, for men have always perceived the distinction between different
powers of mind. What people ever wholly confounded memory with reason—the fancy
with the will ?

neither refers simply to the everlasting fire, nor merely to the exhortation to self-denial, but includes both, so that the πᾶς, *every one*, is
to be understood literally of the whole human race. The sense of the
expression therefore is this, because of the general sinfulness of the
race, every individual must be salted with fire, either on the one
hand by his entering of his own free will on a course of self-denial
and earnest purification from his iniquities, or on the other hand, by
his being carried against his will away to the place of punishment.
The fire appears here first as the cleansing, purifying element (so it
often does, for example, Malachi iii. 2; Sir. ii. 5),* and then, as that
which inflicts pain. But, for him who submits in earnest to the
pain which is necessarily associated with the overcoming of sin, it
works beneficially. (1 Pet. iv. 1.) The term ἁλίζεσθαι, *being salted*,
is well chosen to express the effect of fire, first, because of the succeeding quotation, in which salt is spoken of, and next, because it
harmonizes perfectly with the description of fire, the operation of
salt being closely allied to that of fire. From hence in the profound and appropriate symbolism of Scripture, salt derives its
peculiar meaning, especially as applied to sacrifices. According to
Lev. ii. 13, all sacrifices must be seasoned with salt. This passage
is here referred to, so that we might supply the words ὡς γέγραπται,
as it is written. The Old Testament practice, therefore, of
seasoning sacrifices with salt, is here regarded by our Lord in
its deeper meaning. As every sacrifice is, on the part of him
who offers it, a type of his inwardly devoting himself with all
that he is and has to the eternal source of his being, so the
salt was intended to shew that such a sacrifice could never be
well-pleasing to God without the pain of self-denial, and the
quickening influence of the Fire-Spirit from on high. The fire-
baptism (Matth. iii. 11) is just this act of purification in the saints
through the salt of self-denial, and even the Son of God himself
submitted to it, though he was sinless, in order that he might in
the fire of suffering, perfect and glorify the human nature which he
had assumed. We are then so to explain the grammatical connexion of the clauses as not to understand by the sacrifice being salted
with fire another and a different thing from the person's being salted
with salt: the one clause contains the sensible image and type of
the spiritual process indicated by the other. It is not, necessary,
however, on this account to give to the καί the meaning of *sicuti*,
quemadmodum; we have only to supply διὰ τοῦτο, so that the
sense should be, "and for this reason (as it stands written) must
every sacrifice be salted with salt." We have, therefore, in this passage, an authoritative explanation of the meaning of a sacrifice, and

---

* So I think, in the baptism of fire, Matth. iii.—[K.

of the ceremony of presenting them to the Lord sprinkled with salt.*
Among the manifold other explanations of this passage, we are
specially bound to reject as contrary to the use of the language, that
which takes ἀλίζεσθαι = נִמְלָח in the sense of being *annihilated* referring to Is. li. 6. For in the latter passage the word נִמְלָח has a meaning wholly unconnected with the term מֶלַח, *salt.* (Compare Gesen.
in Lex. sub. voc.)—It is still further difficult to connect ver. 50 with
the preceding context. For the discourse makes a transition to the
nature of salt in general, and brings forward the circumstance that
if it have lost its strength there is no means by which it may be
regained. The same thought occurred at Matth. v. 13 ; Luke xiv.
34 ; but in such a connexion that the disciples are themselves called
the salt of the earth, in so far, namely, as they are the seasoning,
quickening element in humanity. Here the import of the thoughts
is somewhat modified, but not essentially changed. For, in the
disciples themselves, a distinction is drawn between the natural life
by which they were allied to the world (Compare Matth. xviii. 17),
and the higher and heavenly principle which animated them. It is
here enjoined on them to preserve this last, and so gradually to pervade with salt from heaven all their faculties and dispositions of
mind. In the passage, Matth. v. 13, they are called the salt of the
earth in so far as they, compared with the great mass of men, were
prevailingly filled from above with the fiery influence. In both
passages, however, here as well as at Matth. v. 13, man's own faithfulness is represented as called for to guard the salt of the Spirit.
To *call forth* that higher life, is what man cannot do, it is a pure
gift of grace, but he can *stifle* it, or he can *protect* it as a mother
can, to a certain extent, secure the child that is under her heart from
harm and mischance, though she has not the power of calling it into
existence. In this exhortation, therefore, ἔχετε ἐν ἑαυτοῖς ἅλας, *have
salt in yourselves,* there lies an admonition to earnestness in self-
denial and perseverance, as the means by which the gift bestowed
may be preserved. And this admonition is sharpened by recalling
to their minds the impossibility of seasoning salt which has lost its
powers (ἐν τίνι αὐτὸ ἀρτύσετε). The closing words καὶ εἰρηνεύετε ἐν
ἀλλήλοις, *and be at peace with one another,* point back to the commencement of the discourse at Mark ix. 33. Perhaps the expression *have salt,* is intended to form a contrast to the *be at peace.*
The former seems to describe a sharp and caustic, the latter
a gentle mode of action ; both are to be united in the regener-

* Hamann has already said in allusion to this passage, "the anxiety which prevails in
the world is perhaps the only proof of our heterogeneous constitution. For were nothing
wanting to us we should act as the heathen, and the transcendental philosophers who
know nothing of God, and are enamoured of lovely nature. This impertinent disquietude,
this holy hypochondria, is the fire by which we are salted sacrifices. (Works, Part vi.; p.
194.)

ate ; in regard to the ungodliness that is in the world he must re-
prove and rebuke, and in so far he must, like Christ himself (Matth.
x. 34), bring in strife, but in regard to all that is congenial and
kindred in the children of God, gentleness must prevail. As therefore salt does not season salt, but only that which is unsalted, so the
living energy of the children of God should not be expended in con-
tests among themselves, but devoted to the awakening of life in the
world. The closeness with which the last verses in Mark connect
themselves both with the preceding context and with the commencement of the whole discourse, makes it to my mind improbable that
they originally stood in any other connexion, and here, therefore, we
have an instance in which Mark also contributes to the train of
thought something peculiarly his own.

Ver. 10.—While hitherto Matthew has had a parallel account in
Mark, he now pursues the discourse alone to the end of the chapter.
The connexion of thought between the first clause and the preceding context is simple, inasmuch as the καταφρονεῖν, despise, ver. 10,
refers back to the σκανδαλίζειν, offend, of ver. 6. It is not necessary
to remark, that in this case also the little ones are the regenerate,
and consequently anything like a special connexion between angels
and children, we are unable here to discover. A peculiar argument
is here employed by our Lord to enforce the exhortation against
despising the little ones. He brings forward their preciousness in
the view of his Father in heaven (who is also their Father, for believers bear within them the life of Christ, see ver. 5) in the remark
which he makes, "their angels continually see God's face." First,
then, the words βλέπειν τὸ πρόσωπον τοῦ πατρός, beholding the
face, etc., are by no means to be reduced to a mere oriental form
of speech : they rather describe simply the reality of the relation.
The degree of their nearness to God marks the degree of holiness in their nature, and the meaning would seem to be, that
the regenerate (even the most insignificant members of the kingdom
of God), as being representatives of the highest holiness on earth, are
also in the heavenly world (in which all the phenomena of earth
have their root) represented by the holiest beings. Any analogies
to this exhibited in political arrangements, are merely a more or less
intentional imitation of the original relation. (Compare 1 Kings
x. 8 ; Esther i. 14 ; Jerem. lii. 25.) The idea of angels who take
their stand in immediate proximity to the Father often meets us
amidst the teachings of Scripture (Dan. vii. 10 ; Rev. i. 4 ; iv. 4), but
in no passage elsewhere do we find that these angels particularly are
placed in such a connection with believers as is here indicated by
the words their angels. Although, however, in a certain sense this
passage stands alone, and is also not strictly of a didactic character,
yet we must not regard it as uttered in any accommodation to Jew-

ish myths. There was not here the slightest occasion for suggesting the idea unless it possessed an internal truth. That every individual had his angel, as inferred from the passage by the fathers of the church (Compare Schmidt de Angelis tutelaribus* in Illgen's Denkschrift, Leipzig 1817), it does not expressly state In Daniel, angels are spoken of as the representatives of whole nations (x. 20 ; xii. 1), and we may thus conceive a single angel as representing several persons. Yet on the other hand, Acts xii. 15 indicates a representation of individuals. Yet the passage bears necessarily a degree of obscurity, as it cannot be illustrated by a comparison with others. Often, finally, is the angelic world viewed in Scripture as standing connected with believers (Ps. xxxiv. 8 ; Ps. xci. 11 ; Heb. i. 14), since the development of the church appears as the central point of the whole (1 Peter i. 12).

Ver. 11–14.—In some MSS. (B. L. and others) verse 11 is wanting ; it might have been taken from Luke xix. 10, where he has also the following verses in connection with kindred topics. But first it is improbable that this verse from a passage of Luke's gospel, and that assuredly not parallel, should have been thrust in here ; and in the next place, it agrees too closely with Matthew's context to prevent our believing this much, at least, that Matthew himself inserted it in this passage, although we may doubt whether it was originally uttered in this precise connexion. For the Son of Man stands beside the angels as one exalted above them, and the fact that the little ones are the object of the mission of the Son of Man, is a new proof of their preciousness in the sight of God. The term ἀπολωλός, lost, plainly points to the following parable of the lost sheep, whose fuller exposition will find a place at Luke chap. xv. Here I only observe with reference to its connexion with the entire discourse, that the contrast between the strayed sheep and the ninety-nine which did not stray, would stand wholly isolated, unless, as was remarked above, we adhere to the distinction between the μικρός, little, and the μέγας, great, which runs through the discourse. The parable thus acquires in this passage a modified sense foreign to it in Luke, where it rather represents the just and the unjust in their relation to Divine grace.

Ver. 15–17.—It was mentioned in the general remarks on this chapter, that the following thoughts on forgiveness may also belong to the discourse as integral parts of it, if we assume that the strife among the disciples had led to offences, that Peter had been the person offended, and on this very account, therefore, the one exhorted to forgiveness. But although the following parable (ver. 22–35), accords well with this assumption, yet to my mind it is ren-

* Meyer gives an extract from this treatise in the Blatt. f. hoh. Wahrheit, Th. i. S 183, seq.

dered improbable by the connexion sustained by ver. 18, 19, to the
rest of the discourse. Had the disciples been themselves both
the offenders and the offended, these verses would hardly have
formed part of the exhortation, for they are better fitted to lift up
the disciples than to humble them. I can more easily suppose that
Matthew, as his manner is, has conjoined kindred elements with the
thoughts that form the basis of the discourse. In this instance he
wished to depict the character of the children of the kingdom in
their humility and meekness. After having, in what goes before,
warned believers against offending weaker brethren, the discourse
brings to view the opposite point of the contrast, and describes how
a believer should conduct himself if injury be inflicted upon him (ἐὰν
ὁ ἀδελφός σου ἁμαρτήσῃ εἰς σέ), and specially if it be done by a fellow
believer (ἀδελφός is here a brother Christian, a member of the kingdom of God). This instruction, however, is conceived in terms so
general, that it at once stands forth as a precept for the whole
church, and it rests on the spiritual character of the disciples of
Jesus and the everlasting presence of Christ in his church. This
makes it in the highest degree improbable that the words were
occasioned by a strife among the diciples themselves, otherwise ver.
18 must be held as meaning "if one of you exclude another from
the communion of God's kingdom, that exclusion is held as effectual
in the sight of God," an idea obviously untenable. The disciples
were not to exclude one another ; but they are here viewed as the
real and the pure germ of the church, which no power of evil should
overcome ; but if room was left for their being sinned against by
their brethren less enlightened than themselves by Christian principle, they must in that case act on the rule here laid down. Thus
the kingdom of heaven (ver. 23), by no means appears in this passage as a communion absolutely perfect (compare on Matth. xiii. 47),
but as one in which good exerts a predominating influence, repress-
ing, consequently, and restraining evil ; so that this passage once
more plainly shews that the Saviour intended to found an *external*
church, in which, as a kernel in its shell, the ideal kingdom of God
should be developed. The disciples appear as representatives of this
kernel of God's kingdom ; to them is entrusted the guiding and
ruling of this community ; they are the salt, and have to care for the
preservation of the whole body in the strength of him who is unceasingly amongst them. If they (through unfaithfulness) were to
lose their power, the kingdom of God would fall to pieces ; the sin
even of others should be repressed by them. It must, however,
here again be observed, that these injunctions of the Saviour do not
apply to the form of the outward church at all times (Compare as
to this on Matth. v. 39, seq.), but are valid only in reference to true

believers.* For, the external church has relapsed, since the fourth
century, into the Old Testament form, and to such as are not emancipated from the law, such precepts as the above have no meaning ;
against the injuries of the world a Christian has the protection of
the magistrates, and he errs if he believes that owing to this ordinance of Jesus he may not call in their aid.† This progressive
series of admonitions, first apart, then before certain witnesses, and
finally in presence of the church, presupposes a state of mind not
hardened against the power of the truth, even where no threat is
used to enforce it. The universal carrying out of it would as completely disorganise civil society, as if each man were to give his coat
to any one who had demanded of him his cloak. For the unawak-
ened, unconverted man it is wisdom to act on God's precept, " Eye
for eye, tooth for tooth" (Matthew v. 22). Fritzche's remark (on
the passage) is most correct, that it is better to place the interpunc-
tuation after αὐτοῦ than after μόνον. [?] The phrase μεταξύ σου καὶ
αὐτοῦ is perfectly sufficient by itself, and the μόνον ἐάν σου ἀκούσῃ is
fittingly conjoined into a distinct clause, since the idea of unity
stands here in contrast to the subsequent plurality. [Such a position of μόνον before ἐάν is not in accordance with Matthew's style.]
The leading principle of the whole line of conduct prescribed is
mildness, long-suffering, and an endeavour to give ascendancy to
Divine influences in the mind of a brother. The conversation,
therefore, does not deal merely with the isolated fact of the offence
given, but refers to the whole state of the offender's soul from which
that act proceeded. The point it concerned them to aim at, was to
change this frame of mind, and to this reference is made by the
term κερδαίνειν scil. εἰς ζωὴν αἰώνιον, gaining, viz., to eternal life.
Every sin, especially against a brother, is submission to the dominion of the sinful principle (1 John iii. 8), and this leads to perdition.
When, therefore, any one, by the gentle power of love, wins a
brother for the kingdom of love, he gains = saves him, of course by
the power of Christ working in him. Love, once repulsed, renews
its assault : the admonition is made more impressive and solemn by
the presence of others. The Saviour here refers to Deut. xix. 15.
(The ῥῆμα corresponds here to the Hebrew דָּבָר in the sense of causa,
a cause in law; στόμα is put for oral testimony, in which the depon-
ent is himself produced in evidence.) He here applies this Mosaic
ordinance in an elevated form, suited to more elevated relations.

---

* Better ; these precepts refer not to *Christianity and Christian states*, but only to
Christian church organization. But to the latter it is by no means essential that it consist exclusively of regenerated persons, but only that it have an organized system of discipline for offences.—[E.

† In this way must 1 Cor. vi. 1 be understood, in the exposition of which further
details will be given.

For it is by no means evidence *against* an erring brother that in the first instance is here spoken of, but simply an impressive mode of working on his mind. If this produced no impression on him, then the presence of witnesses certainly took the form of evidence against him, inasmuch as his case was laid before the whole church. This appears as the final attempt to call forth the influence of a Christian spirit in the brother who had erred and who clung to his error. The ἐκκλησία here, like קָהָל, is the assemblage of all the believers in one place, to which assembly the separate individual belongs as a member. If he also refuse to follow this most emphatic rebuke, then the only means of help, as well as the sole punishment, is to exclude him from the community. Where spiritual life has left a soul, the withdrawal of fellowship with kindred minds is often the surest means of rousing its slumbering aspirations. (The expressions ἐθνικός and τελώνης denote that sphere of life generally, which lies without the Christian circle.)

Ver. 18.—As to the thought contained in this verse, compare on ver. 16, 17. Here the only question is, how the Evangelist's words are to be understood, as connected with the context. Plainly, the *ye* must be held parallel with the *church* of the foregoing verse, so that the sure and binding nature of the church's decision is here affirmed. "What in such a case the church ordains, is no mere human decision, but since in the church divinity itself appears manifested on earth, its decisions also are of Divine validity."

Ver. 19, 20.—The connexion of the following verses with the preceding is simply this : the spiritual power of the church to bind and to loose depends on the efficient influence in it of the heavenly Father ; that influence, however, is independent of the extent of the congregation, or of locality (we might add, according to Matth. xxviii. 20, of *time*) ; God in Christ is universally present in his church. (The πάλιν ἀμήν gives no incongruous meaning ; the authority of manuscripts favours the omission of the ἀμήν.) The *church* is here contemplated in its narrowest possible limit (δύο ἤ τρεῖς) ; an individual cannot form a church, but any plurality of persons who bear within them the same principle of spiritual life, constitutes a κοινωνία τοῦ πνεύματος (1 John i. 3), and consequently a church. From the κοινωνία, *fellowship*, therefore, may proceed a συμφωνία (an harmonious agreement of will for some special end), and this the Father hears. To the expression "on earth" corresponds the "Father in heaven," so that the church appears united by the Spirit to the Father, who carries into effect its wishes. The general expression, περὶ παντὸς πράγματος, *concerning every thing*, is usually considered as restricted to whatever is fitted to advance the welfare of the church, or that belongs to the sphere of Christian life. This is certainly so far correct, that things spiritual form the

sole object of a believer's labours, an object in which for him everything else terminates, in so far as it is in itself good. But just
because everything does so terminate, must the "everything" be
taken in a literal sense, inasmuch as everything, in so far as it stands
connected with the wants of the church, may form the object of a
believer's prayers. The possibility of abusing this command, or
rather, this high permission, given by the Saviour to his own people,
is excluded by the fact, that it is only the Spirit of the Father in
Christ Jesus himself who creates and calls forth the spiritual fellowship, the agreement thence arising in the special case, and the
prayer itself. When, then, all this does not really exist, or is set
forth in mere deceptive show, the words of the Lord find no application ; but wherever it in reality is found, there his words are
eternally true. It is wholly independent of time and place ; wheresoever (οὗ scil. τόπου), the believers may be assembled together if
they meet in the name of Jesus (and pray in his name), there the
Lord is in the midst of them.* (And, according to Matth. xxviii.
20, there is no restriction of time; ἐγὼ μεθ' ὑμῶν εἰμὶ πάσας τὰς ἡμέρας.)
What defines the thought in these words is the expression εἰς τὸ
ἐμὸν ὄνομα, in my name. (The εἰς here is not to be confounded with
ἐν. In the formula εἰς ὄνομα, the name is, as it were, the point of
union, so that it corresponds to the German auf seinem Namen,
upon his name. In the formula ἐν ὀνόματι, the name is the uniting
power by means of which the conjunction is conceived of as effected
and maintained. Compare on Matth. xxviii. 19.) Ὄνομα, however,
= םֵשׁ, name (compare on Luke i. 35), denotes the person, the essential being, not indeed as incapable of being known, or as actually
unknown, but as manifested. The assembling, then, in the name
of Jesus, and the praying in his name, presuppose the life of the
spirit of Jesus in those so meeting together. It is no isolated act
which every one in all circumstances is able, by the self-determining
power of his own mind, to do ; it requires rather as a necessary condition, that man should be under the power of living Christian
principle. But, as even the believer has hours of spiritual darkness,
he may, from negligence and want of watchfulness, be present in
the assemblies of believers, not in the name of Jesus ; this, therefore, makes a watchful, self-conscious state of faith necessary ; for
the object to be aimed at in our advancement as Christians, is, that
we never be without prayer (Luke xviii. 1, seq.), never without the
name of Jesus, either when alone, or in the company of others.

---

* Interesting allusions to this truth, that the Divine is present in the human assemblies of those who seek it, are to be found among the Rabbins. Thus, in the Treatise
Pirke Aboth, iii. 2, it is said, duo si assident mensæ et colloquia habent de lege שְׁכִינָה
(the symbol of God as acting, of the Son, compare on John i. 1), quiescit super eos secundum Mal. iii. 16.

(Compare further as to prayer in the name of Jesus on John xiv. 13, 14 ; xvi. 24.) If, moreover, the Father is spoken of at ver. 19, and the Son is at ver. 20 represented as he who is present in the assembly (and consequently, as he who acts and who fulfils prayer), this is explained simply by the relation of the Father and the Son. For, in so far as the Father manifests himself only in the Son, and the Son performs only what the Father prompts (John viii. 28), the operation of Father and Son is one and the same agency of the living God. To assemble in the name of the Father, and to pray in him, apart from the Son, is an impossibility, it is merely to pray in one's own name, which is no prayer ; for, whosoever denieth the Son, hath not the Father. These last verses, finally, have again the elevated tone of John, and seem to have been spoken in moments of holiest exultation. The parable which follows, at once sinks again into a lower region, doubtless, however, for this reason, because Peter's question proved that he (and with him, certainly the other disciples also), was not yet prepared for the full understanding of the foregoing thought.

Ver. 21, 22.—If Peter in what follows speaks of forgiveness, there had yet been no express mention made of that subject by Jesus in the preceding discourse, but the whole precepts (ver. 15, seq.) as to the treatment of erring brethren, had proceeded necessarily on the supposition of forgiveness. The man who, in his own heart, gives way to anger, will continue to cherish a sense of the individual offence ; but the man who forgives will strive as a peacemaker (Matth. v. 9), to remove the ground of the sin from the heart of his brother. The imperfect moral culture of Peter, however, did not admit of his understanding even the fundamental idea of forgiveness. Mistaking the nature of pure love, which never can do otherwise than love, he conceives of some limit to forgiveness, being apprehensive, as is usual with natural men, that boundless forgiveness must be a thing impossible. (The ἑπτάκις, seven times, as also the following ἐβδομηκοντάκις ἑπτά, seventy times seven, contains merely the idea of the limited and the unlimited, expressed, according to the Jewish practice, by the number seven. Compare Gen. xxxiii. 3 ; 1 Kings xviii. 43.)

Ver. 23.—The Saviour, having perceived from Peter's question how far his discernment was here at fault, proceeds to explain to him in a parable the grounds on which a member of God's kingdom must ever stand ready to grant forgiveness ; as, only through forgiveness extended towards himself could he have obtained entrance into that kingdom. To every individual, even to such as took their stand on the footing of the law, this must have formed a decisive motive to forgiveness. It was only the law of recompense to which expression was thus given. While, therefore, the inquiry of Peter seemed to presuppose the *right* to act at one's own discretion in bestowing forgiveness or withholding it, the Saviour explains that nothing of this kind existed. He who was himself in debt for *his all* could advance a claim for *nothing*. (As to the formula ὡμοιώθη ἡ βασιλεία τῶν οὐρανῶν ἀνθρώπῳ (compare Matth. xiii. 24.—Λόγον συναίρειν, rationem conferre, *to take account*. The δοῦλοι are, as the summing up shews, the servants with whom the disciples are here compared).

Ver. 24–26.—The sum of 10,000 talents is very great. If it were the Hebrew talent (כִּכָּר = 3000 shekels, see Exodus xxxviii. 25, 26), it would amount to fifteen millions of dollars.* The magnitude of the sum, however, accords well, on the one hand, with the financial operations of a king; and on the other hand with the idea involved in the parable, namely, that the sinner's debt to God is too great for him to discharge. According to ancient custom, the family of the debtor was considered as belonging to the creditor. In the Old Testament, however, this custom is mitigated by the wise institution of the jubilee year, in which the debtor with his family must be set free. (Comp. Levit. xxv. 39, seq.) The wish of the debtor to see the payment postponed (μακροθυμεῖν, in construction with ἐπί, as well as with εἰς, means in the New Testament to exercise forbearance, to give a respite), and his hope of discharging the debt, are merely an expression of anxiety and care, but the thing is to be viewed as in itself impossible, and for this reason, the king compassionately forgives him the debt.

Ver. 27–30.—The severity of the debtor towards his own subordinates contrasts most strikingly with the mildness of the king. (As to σπλαγχνίζεσθαι see on Luke i. 78.—The verb ἀπολύειν, as denoting deliverance from personal confinement and slavery is distinguished from the remission of the debt.—Δάνειον, *borrowed money*, occurs only in this place.) The σύνδουλος, *fellow-servant*, is not to be conceived of as standing on the same footing with the first; the intention merely is to bring out the equally dependent relation of both to the king, in order to mark more prominently the severity of the debtor. On the same ground also, so small a sum (100 denarii = 12 dollars) is mentioned.

Thus, then, in that idea which the parable is intended to exhibit, this point stands prominently forth, that all indebtedness of man to man (σύνδουλος), is inconsiderable in comparison with his indebtedness to God; he can never therefore enforce it against man, while conscious of his heavier liabilities to God. [The debt of the fellow-servant is thus, as it were, transferred to God. The servant was infinitely more indebted to God, and yet all was forgiven him. He is therefore now (in another sense) accountable to God himself and that

* Taking the dollar at 75 cents, this would amount to 11,500,000 dollars.—[K.

for *all.* Also all demands which he had against others, it is not now for *him* but for *God* to enforce against them, the God to whom it is not too much to remit 10,000 talents !] This hard-hearted servant, whose feelings the graciousness of the king failed to soften, permits himself to inflict even bodily violence on his debtor, which the custom of antiquity allowed him to do. (The verb κρατεῖν is not pleonastic, it is the necessary antecedent of πνίγειν = ἄγχειν. In ver. 28, the reading εἴ τι ὀφείλεις is to be preferred to ὅ τι. This last plainly betrays its real nature as a correction of the εἴ τι, which is not to be understood as implying that the debt is in any way doubtful, but merely as a courteous mode of expression. The formula ἕως οὗ ἀποδῷ τὸ ὀφειλόμενον, reminds one of Matth. v. 26. As to its meaning in connexion with the idea of the parable, see on ver. 34.)

Ver. 31-33.—It is not undesignedly that sorrow and not anger is mentioned as the feeling of the rest of the servants, for, the former denotes the nobler emotion as cherished by men standing on the same footing with the offender (compare ver. 34), and by it are the rest of the servants contrasted with the single hard-hearted fellow-servant. If we suppose that Peter had been the offended party in their contention, and so corresponded to the creditor, while some one else was the debtor, and that immediately not forgiveness, but revenge sprung up in his heart, the parable certainly gains a very special application. But we have already called attention to the difficulties of this supposition. In our Lord's rebuke the *reception* of compassion is set forth as a motive for its *exercise* towards others, and precisely in this circumstance lies the whole point of the parable.

Ver. 34, 35.—Against the hard-heartedness, however, of the sinner, anger manifests itself on the part of the Lord. Where man cherishes compassionate sorrow for the sins of his fellow-men (λύπη, see ver. 31), wrath reveals itself on the part of God. For, in the case of man, conscience testifies that he has within him the roots of the same sin which he sees in his brother, but in God there is pure hatred of evil. The idea of the anger of God does not contradict his love (whose manifestation in mildness is χάρις, *grace*), but rather, the wrath of God is nothing else than the manifestation of himself as love, in opposition to evil. According to his righteousness, therefore, which gives to every one his due, and which naturally cannot be conceived of as dissociated from the essence of the Divine love, God does good in his grace to those akin to him, but inflicts woe in his wrath on those alienated from him. Since man, however, is not evil itself, but only in one or another respect admits it within him, God's anger is directed merely against the evil that is *in him.* In the Divine wrath, therefore, there is displayed only another form of God's sanctifying agency. When his operations *in mercy* are misunderstood or abused, as by this servant, his *punishments* come into action. The punishment is here explained as a παραδιδόναι τοῖς βασανισταῖς ἐν τῇ φυλακῇ, *delivering to the tormentors in prison.* The βασανισταί, *torturers,* are, according to the connexion, the guardians of the prison, who, also, were certainly employed to inflict torture. There were, however, no special racks or tortures provided for debtors. It is precisely this punishment which ver. 35 denounces against the hard-hearted, who refuse to forgive as they have been forgiven. The additional clause, ἀφιέναι ἀπὸ τῶν καρδιῶν, *forgive from the heart* (Ephes. vi. 6, ἐκ ψυχῆς), expresses more clearly the nature of true forgiveness, which is here intended to be put forward as a characteristic of the children of the kingdom. It is no mere *outward* act, but presupposes a state of mind which only true repentance can produce. Of this inner state the outward act of forgiveness, by word or deed, is merely the corresponding expression. (The words τὰ παρᾳπτώματα αὐτῶν I am disposed, with Fritzsche, to hold as genuine, in opposition to Griesbach and Schulz; for, as ver. 35 contains the application and short exposition of the parable, it is very much to the purpose to explain the δάνειον by the term παραπτώματα. The verb ἀφιέναι is also commonly conjoined with an object, comp. Matth. vi. 14, 15; Mark xi. 25, 26.) The formula παραδιδόναι εἰς φυλακήν, ἕως οὗ ἀποδῷ πᾶν τὸ ὀφειλόμενον, *deliver to prison, till he has paid all the debt,* still demands here our special consideration in its connexion with the creditor. Already at Matth. v. 26, we remarked that it · could not denote everlasting punishment; in the words ἕως οὗ it is implied obviously that a limit is fixed. For, should it be said that in any event the punishment must be viewed as an endless one, inasmuch as the debt could never possibly be liquidated, it is undoubtedly true, that the creature never can get free from his obligations to the Creator. But since, according to the representation in the parable, the hard-hearted servant is not devoid of repentance (he willingly admits his debt), he is also susceptible of the Divine forgiveness, and this cannot be conceived of as existing without manifesting itself.* The purport of the whole, then, clearly seems

---

* The translator may perhaps be allowed to say that this view is one to which he cannot assent. If the amount of repentance implied in the sinner's merely admitting that in point of fact he *is* a sinner, be sufficient to ensure ultimate salvation, few indeed can fail of reaching heaven. In that case broad were the way leading to life! But how the parable can fairly be so construed, it is impossible to see. The consignment of the servant to prison is done in the way of punishment, it is done in wrath (ὀργισθείς), and the period fixed for terminating that punishment is, confessedly, one which can never come. In the parable these points seem essential and distinctive. They ought not to be explained away, even though they land us in a doctrine so solemn as that of eternal punishments. The reader who wishes to investigate the truth of Scripture on this subject, may consult with advantage the "Miscellaneous Observations" of President Edwards— the more lengthened work by his son, Dr. Edwards, of Newhaven, entitled "The

to be this, that when love shews itself in a way so imperfect, that it is seen merely in the *receptive* form, not in the *communicative*, there is, in that case, no fitness for the kingdom of God. The man devoid of love is committed to the φυλακή, that the conviction of his real state may be brought home to him. Thus it is plain that it is not the standard of the law which is here applied (for according to law, it is not unrighteous to take violent measures in enforcing debt), but that of the Gospel. He who wishes, however, to be meted by this measure, must himself apply it to others. (Matth. vii. 2.) As the hard-hearted servant did not so act, the severity of the law fell on his own head. The φυλακή here is thus = ἅδης = שאול the general assembling-place of the dead who did not die in the Lord, but all of whom, it does by no means follow, shall on this account sink into eternal condemnation. (Compare more at length on Luke xvi. 19, seq.) According to 1 Peter iii. 19; Matth. xii. 32, there is plainly such a thing after death as deliverance from the φυλακή in behalf of some, and, according to the connexion of the parable, we must avail ourselves of that fact in explanation of the circumstances here presented to us. Absolute exclusion from the face of the Lord is made to depend on the entire want of active and receptive love, and so, on the want of faith, without which there can be no love in the soul. (See on Matth. ix. 2 ; xiii. 58.)

salvation of all men strictly examined, and the endless punishment of those who die impenitent, argued, etc.," and Fuller's Eight Letters to Vidler on the doctrine of Universal Salvation.—TR.

FOURTH PART.

OF CHRIST'S LAST JOURNEY TO JERUSALEM,

AND CERTAIN INCIDENTS WHICH TOOK PLACE THERE.

(Luke ix. 51—xxi. 38; Matth. xix. 1—xxv. 46; Mark x. 1—xiii. 37.)

FIRST SECTION.

REPORT OF THE JOURNEY BY LUKE.

(Luke ix. 51—xviii. 14.)

HITHERTO, we have been able to make the Gospel of Matthew the groundwork of our exposition, as it was easy, in the course of his narrative, to take up the little that was peculiar to Mark or Luke. In this fourth part, however, we find ourselves compelled, throughout the first section, to take Luke for our guide, as he records incidents and discourses of the Saviour which none of the other Evangelists touch. Since Luke, in recording this series of communications, which are peculiar to himself, proceeds on the fact of a journey to Jerusalem which seems to be described as the last; and since the Saviour on various occasions throughout this section is described as engaged in travelling (ix. 57; x. 38; xiii. 22; xvii. 11), it is not improbable that we are in it furnished with a *report of the journey*. Certainly, however, it is difficult to say *what* journey this report is intended to recount. For, to hold it as the last journey of Jesus from Galilee to Jerusalem, an opinion which one might adopt on comparing Luke xviii. 35; xix. 29, with Matth. xx. 17, 29; xxi. 1, would bring the account of Luke into direct contradiction with that of John.* For, according to the latter Evangelist, the Lord left Galilee to attend the feast of dedication (x. 22), and never returned to Galilee, but remained in Peræa. (John x. 40, where is found added the statement καὶ ἔμεινεν ἐκεῖ.)

---

* Against this hypothesis comp. my Krit. der Ev. Geschichte, § 31, 32. From ch. 10, Luke manifestly arranges his matter according to the *contents*, the subjects treated.—[E.

From Peræa the Saviour came back to Bethany in order to raise Lazarus (John xi). After this miracle, however, he went to Ephraim in the neighbourhood of the desert (John xi. 54), and stayed there with his disciples. It thus appears that, according to John, the journey of Jesus to the last passover did not begin exactly at Galilee ; there intervenes, it would rather seem, his stay at Jerusalem during the feast of dedication, and at Peræa and Ephraim in the interval. Luke, on the other hand, makes it appear as if Jesus went directly from Galilee to the passover. If, however, to escape these difficulties, we understand the account as applying to the journey from Ephraim to Jerusalem, our view would well harmonize with the passage Luke ix. 51, for the lifting up of the Lord is there expressly spoken of, which stands in direct connexion with his journey from Ephraim to the passover. But in that case the passage Luke x. 13, seq., which treats of the guilt of the cities, Chorazin and Bethsaida, is altogether removed from its proper connexion, for Jesus had left Galilee long before. Nor can Luke x. 38 be reconciled with this view, for, according to that passage, Jesus is already in Bethany, while at xvii. 11, he again appears on the boundaries of Samaria and Galilee, and not till Luke xix. 29 (compare Matth. xxi. 1 ; Mark xi. 1), makes his entry into Jerusalem. Besides, in that case Luke's narrative leaves too great a space in the life of Christ. Hence the chronological series of events must be at once and wholly abandoned, and the idea of our having in this section a journal of travel must be given up, unless its variations from John can be removed, who, undoubtedly, claims the preference in points of chronological or topographical exactness. This, however, seems to be effected most simply by the hypothesis of *Schleiermacher* (on the writings of Luke, p. 158, seq.), which regards the section as blending the narratives of two journeys.* This acute and learned man observes most correctly, that, not Luke xviii. 14, must be regarded as the conclusion of the section, but Luke xix. 48, which records the entry into Jerusalem.† With this, the account of the journey fittingly ends, while at Luke xviii. 14, no termination is to be found. This entire account, then, according to Schleiermacher's view, Luke inserted without change, and it

---

* Care should be taken that we are not tempted to confound this hypothesis with De Wette's view of this section, which he thus expresses: " We shall have to notice in this section an unchronological and unhistorical collection, which was occasioned probably by the circumstance that Luke found a good deal of gospel material which he could not elsewhere arrange into its place, and which, consequently, he here threw together.

† If nevertheless, in our exposition, we keep to Luke xviii. 14, as the conclusion of the section, this is done simply because our leading object is not criticism so much as the full understanding of the facts in themselves. To facilitate this, however, we must, after Luke xviii. 15, again take Matthew as our groundwork, because his Gospel, subsequently to that point, becomes richer in detail.

again owed its existence to some one who made use of two smaller
imperfect reports of two different journeys of Christ, and incorporated the one with the other, not knowing that between the two he
abode for a time at Jerusalem. The conjoining of the narratives
of these two journeys Schleiermacher does not ascribe to Luke himself, for this reason, that his practice is to insert into his narrative
the compositions of others unchanged. Now, although this last
opinion seems to me unsupported by proof, and Luke is rather to
be considered as having rewrought the materials presented to him
(it is by no means improbable that Luke rewrote certain portions,
even though he did insert into his work others unchanged, e. g.,
the family histories [ch. i. ii.] as holy relics), yet on the whole,
this view is satisfactory. For, according to it, Luke can be completely reconciled with the more precise account of John. The
circumstance that at Luke x. 38, Jesus is already at Bethany, while
at xvii. 11, he is again on the borders of Galilee and Samaria, is
easily explained, if the former passage be referred to the time of
his presence in Jerusalem at the feast of dedication, the latter to
his presence at Ephraim (John xi. 54). The expressions used by
John regarding the Lord's stay at Ephraim (διέτριβε μετὰ τῶν μαθητῶν
αὐτοῦ) allow very well the idea that short excursions were made from
that point, or that he had gone out of the direct road in travelling
up to Jerusalem at the last passover. This being presupposed, the
only difficulty that remains in the section, is, that nothing should
be said of Christ's coming to Jerusalem, and his stay there. What
is recorded in Luke x. 25, seq.; xiii. 1, seq., *might* certainly have
happened in Jerusalem, but there is no distinct intimation to that
effect. This *argumentum a silentio*, however, is the less calculated to
overturn the entire hypothesis, because the circumstance admits an
easy explanation from the general want of topographical references.
The feast journeys are entirely omitted in Luke, as also in Matthew
and Mark, and consequently it is not surprising that he does not
give his readers fuller information as to the minuter incidents after
the last journey from Galilee.* It is enough that on matters of
fact there is not the slightest contradiction between the account of
John and that of Luke.

Finally, with respect to the *mode of treatment*, Luke's peculiar
way of rendering the *discourses* of Jesus, is in this section very
manifestly displayed. (Compare the Introduction, § 6.) With
great delicacy and truth he gives the nicer shades of the dialogue. True, this accuracy belongs primarily to the original author
of the report which Luke made use of ; but the Evangelist shews

---

* The same thing applies to Matthew and Mark, who speak in terms quite as general
of Christ's last journey to Jerusalem. (Comp. on Matth. xix. 1, and xxi. 1.)

his appreciation of such accounts, by not defacing their peculiarities ; and besides, in the Acts of the Apostles, Luke displays in his own writing a similar skill.

§ 1. JAMES AND JOHN ARE INCENSED AGAINST THE SAMARITANS.

(Luke ix. 51–56.)

The words with which Luke's lengthened account opens, can only be understood as applying to the Saviour's last journey, which ended in his being offered on the cross and exalted in the resurrection. The expression ἀνάληψις, receiving up (the substantive is found only in this passage, the verb, on the contrary, is often used, of Christ's exaltation, to the Father's right hand, Acts i. 2, 22 ; 1 Tim. iii. 16), denotes here Christ's elevation to the Father, which necessarily presupposes his humiliation. That it is not his being lifted up on the cross which primarily we are to understand, is shewn by the expression ἡμέραι τῆς ἀναλήψεως, in which the whole process of his exaltation, from the resurrection to the ascension, is included. (Only figuratively, according to the analogy of John xii. 32, 33, could the expression refer to the crucifixion.) The period of this exaltation is regarded as fixed by a higher necessity, and the past as a space extending to that point, and requiring to be filled up. (Whenever the words πληροῦσθαι or συμπληροῦσθαι [the two expressions are used synonymously] are applied to time, we must always thus assume that some definite period has been fixed, either by human [Acts ii. 1] or Divine [Gal. iv. 4], determination.) But it may be a question how far this fixed period can be said to have already come on the occasion of Christ's departure from Galilee, when, according to John, so much was to intervene before the passover. The expression employed, ἐν τῷ συμπληροῦσθαι τὰς ἡμέρας τῆς ἀναλήψεως, when the days were accomplished in which he should be received up, seems more applicable to the journey of Jesus from Ephraim to Jerusalem (John xi. 54), than when he was leaving Galilee for the feast of dedication. But, looking simply with the eye of a Galilean, and such we must suppose the narrator to have been, it is easy to explain how the Saviour's 'last departure from Galilee must stand in direct connexion with his end, and all that intervenes be passed over in silence. In his view the scene of all Christ's mighty labours shifted between Galilee and Jerusalem ; and so soon, therefore, as he had finally left the former place, his work, in the view of the writer, seemed finished. The formula πρόσωπον στηρίζειν, corresponds to the Hebrew הֵשִׂים פָּנִים לָתֵת לְבִלְתִּי, Jerem. xxi. 10. The LXX. indeed so translate it. Gesenius [in Lex. sub.

voc. פָּנִים] compares with it the phrase at Ezek. iv. 3, אֶל פָּנֶיהָ הֲכִין which, however, the LXX. translate ἑτοιμάζειν πρόσωπον.

Ver. 52, 53.—In order to prepare a lodging, and provide the necessary supplies, the Saviour sent messengers forward to a Samaritan village, but the inhabitants turned them away.—Σαμαρείτης, Samaritan, in the Hebrew שֹׁמְרֹנִי (from שֹׁמְרוֹן, the capital of the district), denotes, as is well known, an inhabitant of that province of Palestine, in which, after the Babylonian exile, there arose a mixed population formed from the Jews left behind, and the foreign tribes transplanted thither. (2 Kings xvii. 24.) They arrayed themselves against the Jews who returned from the exile, and at a later period they set up on Mount Gerizim a peculiar form of worship modelled on that at Jerusalem. The opposition continued down to the time of Christ and after it (John iv. 9, οὐ συγχρῶνται Ἰουδαῖοι Σαμαρείταις), although, as was natural, it did not shew itself alike vehemently in all individuals (John iv. 30), nor at all times. At festival seasons, when the religious life among the Jews and Samaritans was in its fullest vigour, their hostility was most powerfully developed, the more especially that a leading point of difference between them was the place of Divine worship. Hence, in this instance, it is mentioned as the ground of their unfriendliness ; ὅτι τὸ πρόσωπον αὐτοῦ ἦν πορευόμενον εἰς Ἱερουσαλήμ, because his face was turned toward Jerusalem. (In regard to this use of πρόσωπον compare 2 Sam. xvii. 11, פָּנֶיךָ הֹלְכִים בַּקְרָב. The term δέχεσθαι includes, as at Matth x. 14, and the parallel passages, all the friendly services of hospitality in its widest sense.)

Ver. 54.—That James and John, who were here introduced as speaking, are the two brethren, the sons of Zebedee, is in the highest degree probable, even though Mark iii. 17, as will be immediately shewn, cannot be adduced in proof of the fact. In their fiery zeal against the churlishness of the Samaritans, they are inclined to bring down on them a destructive judgment, and only await the command of their Lord (θέλεις) to be themselves the instruments of carrying such a judgment into effect. A bold faith reveals itself in these words, and a powerful conviction of the Lord's majesty, and of the relation in which they stood to him. Thus far their frame of mind betrays nothing censurable. But the form in which it was manifested bore altogether an Old Testament type. On noticing, therefore, the expression of disapprobation in the look of Jesus, they sought to ground their declaration on an example from the Old Testament, appealing to what is related in the history of Elias (2 Kings i. 10, 12). (The omission of the words ὡς καὶ Ἠλίας ἐποίησε in some MSS. is assuredly a false reading. The following words plainly contrast the disciples with Elias, the Old Testament with the New.)

Ver. 55, 56.—As Jesus saw that this fiery zeal of his disciples was not a mere outburst of feeling, but arose from their confounding the relation of the economy of the Old Testament with the New, he in a few words guides them to a right view of the point. After his lengthened intercourse with them, he could take for granted that the distinction between the two economies was not only clearly known to them, but familiar to their habits of thought.* The simple mention of it was sufficient to recall them to the conviction that the compassionate love of the Gospel had been forgotten by them, in the justice of the law. The "Spirit," therefore, in these words of the Lord, is to be understood in its usual sense ; for between *you* and Elias there is a contrast in respect of the principle that animates the two. This principle is the "Spirit." Both principles were pure and Divine, but the heavenly element in its progress through humanity, presents its perfect form in the spirit of the Gospel, whose essence is grace and mercy, which were personified in the Saviour (John i. 17). Elias, therefore, does nothing wrong when he commands fire to fall from heaven ; as a messenger of God, he exercised justice. But Jesus did *better,* inasmuch as he exercised mercy, which he had come to render supreme amidst the human race. The disciples therefore sinned only in so far as they who ought to have received into their hearts the perfect spirit of forgiving love, allowed themselves still to be swayed by the Old Testament spirit of avenging justice. As *they* were aware of the distinction, and had access to the spirit of pure love, they sinned in that very act which on the part of Elias was right. (At Heb. xii. 24, the same contrast is denoted by Christ and Abel. Abel's blood demands *vengeance,* as representing justice, the blood of Jesus pleads for *forgiveness,* for in him dwelleth grace.) Many are of opinion that it was in consequence of this occurrence, that the sons of Zebedee received the name of Βοανεργές (Mark iii. 17). As regards, first, the etymological explanation of the expression, it has already been rightly given by Mark, inasmuch as he adds ὅ ἐστιν υἱοὶ Βροντῆς = בְּנֵי רֶגֶשׁ. (The βοανε, βανε is probably the Galilean form for βενε; רָגַשׁ, however, and the kindred רָגַשׁ in the sense of to *quake,* to *tremble,* to *roar,* expresses with great propriety the idea of thunder.) The only thing remaining obscure is, what this name *refers to.* The older Christian interpreters found the resemblance in the majestic and

---

* The most numerous and best MSS. (particularly A, B, C, E, G, H, L, S, and others, see the New Testament of Griesbach—Shulz on this passage), even omit the words of the textus receptus, καὶ εἶπεν οὐκ οἴδατε οἵου πνεύματός ἐστε ὑμεῖς, as given by the Cod. D. and others. In any case, the longer recension of the words of Jesus, ὁ γὰρ υἱὸς τοῦ ἀνθρώπου οὐκ ἦλθε ψυχὰς ἀνθρώπων ἀπολέσαι, ἀλλὰ σῶσαι, is an unauthentic addition, and even the shorter form of it is not beyond suspicion. The supplementary clause, however, corresponds perfectly with the whole connexion, and the origin of the gloss is easily explained, inasmuch as the ἐπετίμησεν seemed to call for a closer definition.

lofty impression made by thunder, so that the name, sons of thunder, was used not in the way of blame but of *praise*, as expressing
the strength of that holy zeal which animated the sons of Zebedee.
More recent interpreters, however, frequently refer it to the fact
before us, and understand it in the way of *censure*, and as intended
to characterize a false and merely natural zeal. (See further details
in the learned treatise by *Gurlitt* in Ullmann's *Studien*, vol. ii., part
iv., p. 715, seq.) Were it proved that the name referred to this
passage, the latter explanation would undoubtedly recommend itself
as the more probable, for the term ἐπιτιμᾶν, *rebuke*, in Christ's discourse, is easily reconciled with any name of praise, as the disciples
could then have been merely *reminded* of the name (already on a former occasion bestowed ön them) so that the connexion would stand
thus, " know ye not that ye ought to be led by another spirit, that
as ye are the sons of zeal ?" But, granting even this to be the
true connexion, it seems to yield no thought that suits the context,
for there is nothing contradictory between the name of the disciples
and their conduct, inasmuch as they shewed no want of zeal but of
mildness. And yet such a contrast is assuredly required by the
connexion. Moreover, on other grounds, it seems to me improbable,
that the name sons of thunder is to be associated with the occurrence here recorded. For, *in the first place*, it is unexampled in
Bible history, and stands opposed to the idea of the new name, that
a second designation should be given to any one in the way of
punishment. In this way, his sin would be, as it were, immortalized.
Secondly, the position of the name in Mark iii. 17, is against the
supposition of its involving censure. It stands entirely parallel to
the name Peter which was given to Simon, and it is therefore
hardly credible that the first name is one of praise, marking the
spiritual character of the first apostle, and the second an epithet of
censure. And it is the less credible when we consider that the three
apostles first named at Mark iii. 17, and furnished with surnames,
are precisely those who stood nearest to the Lord. We hence regard the fathers as entirely right in recognizing in the name " sons
of thunder," a description of the spiritual character of the two sons
of Zebedee. Thus the bestowal of these names acquires in the case
of the apostles the same significancy which the new names (Abraham
for Abram, Israel for Jacob) have in the Old Testament. They
characterize the new men, and are, as it were, symbols of the new
nature. (Is. lxii. 2 ; lxv. 15 ; Rev. ii. 17.) How far the name sons
of thunder agreed with the personal dispositions of James and John,
cannot be shewn in regard to the former, for no detailed account of
him is given. In reference to John, however, it may seem doubtful
how far the name is appropriately chosen, as it has been usual to
regard him as of a weak nature. But as we have often remarked,

to attribute weakness to John is wholly to mistake his nature. His whole writings shew that with all its passive gentleness, his character combined active energy, and sternness even to severity against evil ;* it was this which the surname in question denoted, and thus the union of energy with humility in Peter, of decision and severity with gentleness in James and John, formed the basis of their new nature.†

§ 2. OF FOLLOWING JESUS.

(Luke ix. 57–62 ; Matth. viii. 19–22.)

The short passage which here follows, flowing directly from the contemplation of the immediate circumstances, appears to hold its place most appropriately in the narrative of a journey. Some one (according to Matthew he was no less than a γραμματεύς, scribe) who had been powerfully attracted by the Saviour, expressed on the way a wish to accompany him, and Jesus sets before his view the difficulties attending his life and labours. In Matthew a portion of this passage stands amidst a collection of the miracles of Jesus, and consequently in a less appropriate connexion. Nay, in the account of Matthew there is wanting that very point which, with Luke, stands prominently forth as the connecting link with the preceding narrative. For, as the sufferings which his enemies were preparing for the Saviour had been there described, so the following history states how it stood between Jesus and those friends whose affections his appearance and his words attracted. One portion of them pressed most hastily forward, but a single word as to the difficulties caused them to withdraw ; another portion of them were called by the Lord himself, but their anxiety on the subject of the world deterred them from at once embracing the call. In Luke, then, we are not to overlook the contrast between " Some one said to him," and "Jesus said to another," ver. 59, which mark the several positions of Christ's different friends.

* Let John's first epistle especially be read. It is full of Divine βροντή as well in its descriptions of the true spirit as of the false (comp. iv. 1, seq). He who considers the Apocalypse to have been written by John will not fail to trace in it also the character of spiritual power. [John's relation to Christ is femininely passive; filled by him, it is that of manly energy against everything anti-Christian. Smiting and crushing, like a genuine son of thunder, he turns the force of a heaven-descended fire against the principles of ungodliness.]

† A doubt as to this view may be raised by the circumstance that the name Sons of Thunder never elsewhere again occurs. Had it been intended as the designation of their new nature, one may suppose that like the name Peter it would have been generally used. As it was, however, bestowed on two persons at once, it could not like the name Peter come into general use, and this sufficiently explains its being passed over in silence.

Ver. 57, 58.—The address ἀκολουθήσω σοι ὅπου ἂν ἀπέρχῃ, *I will follow thee wherever thou goest*, plainly implies a certain consciousness already of the difficulties involved in being the companion of Jesus. The "wherever thou goest" cannot refer merely to the change of locality, but denotes dangers, for example those attending the journeys of Jesus to the feasts, in which every one acquainted with the circumstances (and that this well-disposed scribe was acquainted with them we must believe), must have seen peril both for the Saviour and those about him. The words then are akin to the exclamation of Thomas, ἄγωμεν καὶ ἡμεῖς ἵνα ἀποθάνωμεν μετ᾽ αὐτοῦ (John xi. 16), and with Peter's declaration, Matth. xxvi. 35, inasmuch as both these declarations, like that of the scribe before us, came from the natural man, who, failing to weigh the greatness of the self-denial required, quickly starts upon the path, but soon falls. According to the connexion, the term "follow" refers primarily to an external companionship, but it also involves at the same time a spiritual following, *i. e.*, the choice of that path of life which Christ opened, a walk in righteousness and truth, and consequently a contest undertaken with unrighteousness and falsehood. The Lord acknowledging, indeed, the good intentions of the supplicant, but perceiving his weakness, sets before him in the strongest terms the difficulty of following him. The want of necessaries, which are provided by the Creator even for the lower animals, of personal property and the shelter of a roof, must be encountered in following the Son of man. (Φωλεός occurs only in this passage. Hesychius explains it as τόπος οὗ τὰ θηρία κοιμᾶται.—Κατασκήνωσις = מִשְׁכָּן.) The proper sense of οὐκ ἔχειν ποῦ τὴν κεφαλὴν κλίνειν, *not having where to lay his head*, is that of the entire renunciation of everything which man can call his own, which was exhibited even externally in the life of the Saviour, but which is to be spiritually repeated in the life of all his followers, as we are taught at 1 Cor. vii. 29, seq. Although it is not expressly recorded what effect this admonition of Jesus produced, yet from the following narratives we may infer that probably it had deterred the scribe. The remarks of the two persons whom Jesus asked to follow him lead us to conjecture that they could not as yet resolve to abandon *everything* in order to embrace Christ, for the necessity of so doing is brought forward as the main idea of the short narrative. (See on Matth. xix. 27.)

Ver. 59, 60.—As in the preceding case, the scribe had volunteered to follow the Saviour, Jesus in this instance himself gives the invitation to do so. While the former, however, was deterred by difficulties, the latter were apparently held back by sacred duties. The truth of greatest prominence to be drawn from the following narrative, and to which most importance should be given, is this, that not merely sins and crimes (which call first for forgiveness through that repentance and faith which the following of Christ presupposes) but even legal righteousness, nay, regard to the noblest duties of earthly relationship, may keep men back from following Jesus. Burying one's father and taking leave of one's household must be held, when viewed in an earthly light, to denote even noble and tender duties. (The verb ἀποτάξασθαι, ver. 61, is in the sense of to take leave. The relatives are to be considered as at a distance, so that he means to stipulate for a journey home.) We have here, therefore, a commentary of fact on Matth. x. 37. In obeying the command of Christ all other duties are absorbed ; not that they are thus depreciated in importance or neglected, but that every act of man assumes its just relation to the ultimate ends alike of the individual, and the entire body. From this point of view the Saviour can ask the son to abandon to others even the last duties to a deceased father ; the favourable moment for giving to his whole course of life a nobler direction must be seized at once. This man having already become a believer, must now decide on consecrating his life to the preaching of God's word (διάγγελλε τὴν βασιλείαν τοῦ θεοῦ). The expression, let the dead bury their own dead (ἄφες τοὺς νεκροὺς θάψαι τοὺς ἑαυτῶν νεκρούς), has here assuredly no reference to the Jewish opinion that he who touched the dead became polluted. Jesus merely wished to bring immediately to a decision the man whom he had called to follow him, and induce him to give up for his sake everything in itself lawful, nay, even that which was considered necessary. Just as little ought the " dead" to be referred to the grave-diggers, a view which enfeebles the whole sense of the passage. The Saviour rather regards the call given as a call to eternal life, and demands that the person called should unconditionally resolve in favour of it, and that he should leave everything of an external nature (even such acts of piety towards a deceased father after the flesh) to those who were as yet wholly occupied with externals, instead of which occupations he should yield obedience to the call of his heavenly Father. Thus the word νεκρός, dead, must in one of these instances be understood as used figuratively of those who have not yet been awakened from the death of natural life (Rom. vii. 8, seq). The dead who are to be buried, are of course those naturally deceased ; but the language " bury their own dead" unquestionably intimates that the deceased were in a condition in no respect essentially different from that of the living who were to bury them.

Ver. 61, 62.—To the last, who like the others presents himself as a follower, the Saviour replies with the statement of a general principle which rebukes his declaration, and conveys the idea that an unconditional determination was necessary for having part in the kingdom of God. The χεῖρα ἐπιβάλλειν ἐπ' ἄροτρον, putting the hand *to the plough,* united with the βλέπειν εἰς τὰ ὀπίσω, *looking back,* denote figuratively, a state of indecision, irresolution. (Gen. xix. 26.)   In opposition to this we are to look on the entire determination of the will as a necessary requisite to labouring in the kingdom of God (εὔθετος, *well-ordered, fitting, suitable.*   See Luke xiv. 35), which lays claim to all the powers of man. This sentence, however, as well as the preceding ἄφες τοὺς νεκρούς κ. τ. λ. contains a truth of permanent importance for all times and circumstances of the church; for never can any one be a disciple of Christ save he who renounces all that he has (Luke xiv. 33), and strives to love God with all his powers (Mark xii. 30) ; since Christ's call to follow him is the call of God, and man must serve no master *beside* God (Luke xvi. 13).

§ 3. THE SENDING FORTH OF THE SEVENTY DISCIPLES, WITH THE ADDRESS OF JESUS TO THEM.

(Luke x. 1–24; [Matth. xi. 20–27.])

The sending out of the seventy disciples stands in immediate connexion with the special object of Luke's gospel. Matthew and Mark, who wrote merely for Jews, record only the mission of the *twelve;* Luke, for the sake of the heathen, [?] narrates the sending forth of the *seventy,* and in the following discourse omits all those ideas based on the exclusive character of Judaism, which are mentioned at Matt. x. 5, seq. (Compare Eisenmenger's entd. Judenthum, Part ii., p. 3, seq., respecting the notion of the Jews that there were seventy distinct nations on the earth.) The passage, Num. xi. 16 seq., regarding the seventy elders to whom Moses imparted of his spirit, may be compared as parallel. To this corresponded the Sanhedrim of seventy assessors with the president (נָשִׂיא) who represented Moses. From the idea that the members of the Sanhedrim were seventy-two in number (*i. e.,* twice six times six, or six times twelve), arose the reading ἑβδομήκοντα δύο, which is supported certainly by some good MSS. (as B. D.) but must yield in authority to the common one. Strikingly, however, as this fact agrees with the general scope of the gospel of Luke, it seems little in harmony with that narrative of the Saviour's journey of which it forms a part. This sending forth of the disciples in the midst of a journey seems scarcely natural. [?]   It would seem, therefore, that in the information thus given, a passage from some earlier period had been inserted into the account of their last journey. Perhaps the Saviour, shortly before his final departure from Galilee, having given up all hope of Chorazin, Bethsaida and Capernaum, sent forth once more the seventy messengers into some other region. This harmonizes alike with the mention of the fall of these cities (x. 13–15), and with the remarkable declaration (ver. 18) which expresses the confident assurance of the triumph of his cause notwithstanding all opposition and unbelief. The μετὰ ταῦτα, *after this* (ver. 1), however, cannot be taken strictly in its chronological meaning, but must be understood generally somewhat in the sense of *moreover* (Schleiermacher on Luke, p. 169). The address of the Lord to his departing disciples as given by Luke, closely resembles that in Matthew (chap. x.), except that in the latter it is more extended and complete. Similar circumstances assuredly led most naturally to similar ideas, but in the exact agreement of the clauses, transfers and transpositions are not improbable. The mention of the unbelieving cities, however, stands in appropriate connexion with the context in Luke, while it stands only very loosely in its place at Matth. xi. 20–24. For, if the Lord had closed his preaching in Galilee, and knew that he should never more set foot within it, this would give, as nothing else would, its full meaning to the reproof in which he rebukes the unbelief of those who so long had listened to him and seen his works.

Ver. 1.—The word ἀνέδειξε, *appointed*, points to a specific act of election, such as, according to Matth. x. 1, seq., took place in the case of the twelve, to a formal ἀνάδειξις (Luke i. 80). The verb ἀναδείκνυμι is to be understood in the sense of " to appoint," with the accessory idea of a solemn and public setting-forth of the dignity bestowed. (Compare 2 Macc. ix. 23, 25 ; x. 11 ; xiv. 12 ; 3 Esr. ii. 3.) The disciples were moreover sent out two and two (ἀνὰ δύο), that they might mutually support each other, and might, in the places Jesus intended to visit, prepare men's minds beforehand for his coming.

Ver. 2.—Luke here places at the outset of the discourse of Jesus, the same thought which at Matth. ix. 37, 38, precedes the choosing of the twelve ; though certainly the connexion in Matthew is more loose, inasmuch as the words with him, primarily refer to the sight of the people without leaders or teachers. At the foundation of the expression θερισμός, *harvest*, lies obviously the comparison of the Divine word to seed, and mankind to the field. (Compare Matth. xiii. 4, seq.) According to this the Old Testament period is to be considered as the time during which the Divine Word had been in operation, whose great result was that lively sense of the need of atonement which shewed itself among the people. This is viewed in relation to the past as a harvest, but as compared with what was to follow, it appears as merely the given possibility of a new and nobler growth, whose harvest was to be expected in the end of the day at the coming of the Son of man in his glory. The apostles and all the labourers, in the first instance, stand forth simply as witnesses of the harvest ; but in another respect, in so far, namely, as they have themselves received the quickening~principles of the Gospel, they appear as those who are called to disseminate it more widely abroad, and indeed this is referred to by the admonition δεήθητε τοῦ κυρίου κ. τ. λ. The fervent prayer of those who have themselves already been received into the kingdom of God, and who labour in the spirit of it, is the means of procuring its ever wider extension, by the stirring up of living labourers for it. The very sending out of the seventy was of itself an answer to the prayer, which, on the occasion of sending forth the twelve, Jesus urged his disciples to offer.

Ver. 3, 4.—According to Luke, the discourse, immediately after the command to go forth, begins with the mention of threatening dangers. Matth. x. 16 mentions them later in the discourse, where see more particularly. This remark, respecting the relation of believers to the world, seems to be contradicted by what follows, μὴ βαστάζετε κ. τ. λ. For, while the allusion to the wolves seems to awaken fear and anxiety, the subsequent admonition to go forth without the preparations suggested by human foresight, bespeaks believing confidence. But this contrast is the very thing here intended. "Without considering such danger, go forth free from care, everything shall be provided for you." (As to particulars, compare my remarks on Matth. x. 9, 10.—Βαλάντιον = צרור [Job xiv. 17] in translating which it is used by the LXX., is allied to πήρα, crumena.) The μηδένα κατὰ τὴν ὁδὸν ἀσπάσησθε still remains obscure, even though we seek an explanation in the oriental practice of saluting each other by tedious forms of courtesy, and so causing detention, for, the injunction—ye must not linger[*]—agrees neither with what goes before, nor what follows. It is better to understand ἀσπάζεσθαι as meaning to salute, to receive, or welcome as a friend, with the secondary sense of seeking for favour. In this way the expression stands on the same footing with those which precede it, which all denote preparations for the journey, measures of human foresight.

Ver. 5, 6.—As to the conduct which Jesus exhorts his messengers to pursue towards those with whom they sojourn, compare Matth. x. 13. The Spirit seeks what is akin to itself, and where that is wanting finds no abode. The expression given by Luke, son of peace, in some respects conveys a meaning peculiarly its own, in others it is a clearer and closer statement than that of Matthew, who merely speaks of the house as worthy or not worthy. According to Luke, those minds disposed to receive the Gospel must be distinguished from those in the same house who were resolved to

---

[*] Compare the parallel passage 2 Kings iv. 29, where Elisha enjoins on Gehazi the greatest haste, and says כִּי תִמְצָא־אִישׁ לֹא תְבָרְכֶנּוּ וְכִי יְבָרֶכְךָ אִישׁ לֹא תַעֲנֶנּוּ.

reject it. To the former the blessing of God's kingdom is promised, to the latter not.

Ver. 7.—The exhortation, that in the house where they had taken up their quarters, they should content themselves with what the occupants had to give (τὰ παρ' αὐτῶν), is connected in Luke so closely with the μὴ μεταβαίνετε ἐξ οἰκίας εἰς οἰκίαν, go not from house to house, that the latter idea is more completely modified by it, than is the case at Matth. x. 11, where this connexion is wanting. It seems, according to the representation of Luke, that our Lord intended to warn them against leaving the cottages of the poor, and seeking instead the dwellings of the rich. The labourer in the field of God, receives his hire (Matthew has τροφή x. 10), i. e., his bodily nourishment, and the supply of his necessities. The seeking for more than this, cometh of evil.

Ver. 8–11.—In Luke, the cures, and the preaching of the kingdom of God, appear in the light of spiritual rewards for bodily services. In Matthew the same ideas are brought forward in another connexion. (Compare Matth. x. 8.) As to their conduct towards those who resisted them, compare Matth. x. 14. ('Απομάσσεσθαι is found only here. It corresponds to the ἐκτινάσσειν in Matthew.) As to the former the nearness of the kingdom of God is a message of joy, so it is to these a message of terror, implying for the one the possibility, for the other the impossibility of their entering it.

Ver. 12–15.—The woe which the Lord utters against such an unbelieving city, is most appropriately followed by a curse on the places which had been the witnesses of his greatest glory. The words seem to have been originally uttered in this connexion, viz., at the close of the labours of Jesus in Galilee, although Matthew (xi. 20–24) has inserted them not unfittingly into his context. (As respects the exposition, see the details in Matthew, ut supra.)

Ver. 16.—According to Luke, the address of Jesus to the seventy concludes with the general idea, that he, the Saviour, recognized such living union with his children, that what was done to them was done to him. (Compare on Matth. x. 40, where the same thought, but only as conceived under a single aspect, is expressed.)

Ver. 17.—The circumstance that in the following passage the return of the disciples is anticipated, goes to prove the correctness of the opinion that it is impossible in this section of Luke to keep the chronological thread. The discourses of Jesus connected with this return, form a well compacted whole, so that here again the account of Luke bears a more original character than that of Matthew. First the evangelist makes the disciples on their return express to Jesus their child-like joy for the deeds which in his name they had been able to perform. (The *casting out devils* is one of the many miracles which they did. This might appear to them of special importance, as it presupposed a control over the mighty kingdom of evil.) Most deeply is this representation drawn from the life. A secret joy seizes a man when he finds that he acts with an energy more than human, for example, that through him the spiritually dead are awakened. In this joy there is the implied testimony that man is called to act with power from on high, but there lies in it also a temptation so dangerous, that the Saviour, though he acknowledges the joy as right and well-founded, yet warns them at the same time against giving themselves up to it without watchfulness, and exhorts them to keep fully in view the foundation of that real joy which can never lead astray.

Ver. 18.—Singularly remarkable is the declaration of the Lord, which, in Luke, follows immediately after the expression of joy on the part of the disciples. Inasmuch as he makes a transition from the δαιμόνια to Satan himself, without any occasion for it, and in the circle of his immediate disciples, we must say that here is an additional passage (compare on Matth. xiii. 39) leading us to infer that the Saviour himself teaches the existence of a prince of darkness, and that this doctrine is by no means to be looked on as a Jewish superstition. Here would have been the place, even on the supposition of Christ's accommodating himself to the views of the multitude, in which to point out the unfounded and ruinous nature of such a belief, and to advise (in accordance with the views of some) that the use of the idea by way of accommodation, be restricted to cases of necessity. But in the expression itself, "I beheld Satan," etc., the "beheld" (θεωρεῖν) is, of course, not to be understood of bodily sight, but of spiritual contemplation, for the object seen was itself spiritual. The nature of spiritual vision, however, involves the conception of the future as present. We may, in explanation, compare the parallel passage, John viii. 56, where Jesus says of Abraham, "he saw my day" (εἶδε τὴν ἡμέραν τὴν ἐμήν). As here in prophetic vision Messiah and the whole Messianic future is represented as present in spirit to Abraham, so the Saviour in this passage says that he beheld as a present event the annihilation of the dominion of evil. The preterite tense ἐθεώρουν, I was beholding, therefore, must be referred not merely to the period during which the seventy were absent, but to past time in general, so that the meaning would be—for a long time have I seen in spirit the power of evil as vanquished. For, the cures wrought by the disciples, are obviously to be considered not as the causes, but as the effects of the overthrow. Because the power of evil was broken by the Saviour's appearance in the midst of mankind, and through him the energies of a higher life were imparted to the disciples, therefore could they do such deeds. It was impossible, however, for the deeds of the disciples to effect that which was the object of Christ's entire mission and ministry. But being the *results* of the overthrow of evil, their actions were at the same time the *evidences* of that great victory, and thus far was their joy well-grounded, and the transition made by Christ from their deeds to the overthrow of Satan himself, sufficiently accounted for. The figurative expression, " fall from heaven" (πίπτειν ἐκ τοῦ οὐρανοῦ), is probably chosen after the remarkable passage, Is. xiv. 12, in which the king of Babylon (as the type of the prince of darkness) is represented as by proud effort scaling the heavens, that he might set his throne above the stars of God, but cast headlong from his self-chosen exaltation. The LXX. translate it πῶς ἐξέπεσεν ἐκ τοῦ οὐρανοῦ ὁ ἑωσφόρος. (Compare as to this the expositors of Isaiah.) The addition ὡς ἀστραπήν, as *lightning*, depicts (as at Zech. ix. 14), the swiftness of the fall. The whole passage consequently expresses the same thought as in John xii. 31, ὁ ἄρχων τοῦ κόσμου τούτου ἐκβληθήσεται ἔξω, the prince of this world shall be cast out (according to another reading it is even κάτω βληθήσεται, to which consequently ὑψωθῆναι of the Saviour forms an appropriate contrast), namely this, that in Christ and with Christ, evil is seen as overcome, and good is displayed in all its glory. We may compare also on this point the peculiar representation given in the Revelation of John, where, however, the casting out of Satan (xii. 7, seq.) is distinguished from the complete chaining up of his power (xx. 2, seq).

Ver. 19.—This verse mentions exemption from all liability to personal injury, as a new *result* of the victory thus won by truth— of that victory which our Lord, in the spirit of prophecy, beheld as actually wrought out. As the Saviour's power sets the captive free, so does it preserve his people from the assaults of hostile force during their subsequent progress. Serpents and scorpions ("Οφεις καὶ σκορπίοι) are mentioned, as being amongst animals the representatives of the kingdom of evil, as in them poison is collected, and inflicts, on contact, physical injury. (Compare Ps. xci. 13.) The expression originates in that profound view of natural life pervading all Scripture (compare further on Rom. viii. 19, seq.) according to which the disorders of sin in the spiritual world express themselves also in the physical. What follows καὶ ἐπὶ πᾶσαν δύναμιν (אֵב‎ στρα‑ τιά) τοῦ ἐχθροῦ, fills up the first expression, and extends it so as to comprehend *every* form of assault from the world of evil. The mightier power of Jesus gives security against the influence of these in every shape. Such passages as Mark xvi. 17, 18 ; Acts xxviii. 5 ; shew that here we are by no means to exclude all reference to what is external. But this reference stands connected in general with the continuance of the Charismata as outward manifestations of the Spirit of Christ. After these Charismata have ceased, the *spiritual* application of the words alone becomes prominent.

('Aδικεῖν stands as = βλάπτειν, as at Rev. vii. 2, 3. Compare Mark xvi. 18.)

Ver. 20.—To these words, which acknowledge as well-founded the triumphant declarations of the disciples (ver. 17), there is now subjoined a warning. In their connexion, therefore the words, "rejoice not," etc. (μὴ χαίρετε—χαίρετε δέ), are not to be understood as an absolute prohibition of joy over the power of the Spirit in them, but only as forbidding them to make even this matter of supreme and exclusive rejoicing. For, in case the believer makes the workings of God's Spirit through himself his sole, or even leading object of attention and joy, he is in danger of withdrawing his view from the *source* of this higher life, and no sooner does he cease to draw from that fountain, than life dries up, and self-indulgence, vanity, pride, spring up in his soul. Hence, the Saviour here brings forward as the true and abiding object of a Christian's regard and joy, the fact that their names are written in heaven (ὅτι τὰ ὀνόματα ὑμῶν ἐγράφη ἐν τοῖς οὐρανοῖς). At the foundation of this language lies the figure of the book of life, in which the names of believers are inscribed, a figure already often used in the Old Testament (Exod. xxxii. 32 ; Ps. lxix. 28 ; cxxxix. 16). The inscribing is conceived of as the act of God (ἐγράφη ὑπὸ τοῦ Θεοῦ), so that the election of grace by which the saints are chosen, and which they have themselves certainly to make sure (2 Pet. i. 10), is thereby denoted. Hence, in contrast with human agency authoritatively gifted with higher powers, there is placed a Divine agency acting upon man ; the former is a very doubtful object of joy, for by means of it self-pleasing and vanity easily insinuate themselves, inasmuch as the will is seldom delivered from self. Divine grace on the other hand, and its manifestation, the calling of man, is clearly the object of holiest joy, for God's will is as pure as it is unchangeable, and in his election of grace therefore, of which he can never repent (Rom. xi. 29), lies the ground of all salvation and all blessedness to mankind. Even therefore, if he cannot perform any great spiritual deeds (2 Cor. xii. 9), this remains as the joy of the believer, which, as being personally his own, he can never be deprived of, that he lets his soul satisfy itself in the grace of God.

Ver. 21, 22.—With singular appropriateness there is here added this expression of *holy* joy on the part of our Lord, which stands in strong contrast with the joy of *sense* (ver. 17) as felt by the disciples. The latter exulted over the external splendour of the work ; the Saviour drew his delight from its hidden glory, from this, namely, that God's true wisdom was revealed by the Father, not to the prudent and wise ones of the world, but to the νήπιοι, *babes ;* in the new creation, blossoming unnoticed in the hidden circle of his friends, he had his quiet and humble joy. Rightly, then, did the

Divine consciousness repose in this lowliness and self-humiliation. Conscious of his dignity as God, he recognized himself as at once the *organ* and the *object* of every true revelation of God. (For the more minute details compare on Matth. xi. 25–27, where the same words occur, but in a more loose connexion.)

Ver. 23, 24.—These verses were already explained more in detail at Matth. xiii. 16, 17, where they stand in a wholly different connexion. Here, the leading idea of the two verses, that superabundant grace had been manifested towards them (the disciples), stands intimately connected with the preceding, to wit, that *they* were the chosen ones to whom the Lord revealed more than to the saints of the Old Testament. Only, in this connexion the στραφεὶς πρὸς τοὺς μαθητὰς κατ' ἰδίαν εἶπε, *turning to his disciples he said apart*, occasions some obscurity. The στραφείς may easily be understood as referring back to ver. 21, where the Saviour in his discourse addresses himself to God, but the κατ' ἰδίαν, *apart*, remains a difficulty, inasmuch as the whole preceding discourse had already been spoken in the most private circle of his disciples. As the common text, however, has the words " he turned and said to his disciples" before ver. 22, the κατ' ἰδίαν may best admit of being explained thus. While the discourse was going on, some hearers had gathered around him (as the following 25th verse seq., immediately shews); on their account Jesus spake the last words in a low tone to those more immediately about him, uttering the rest aloud in the hearing of all. In this case, the reading of the common text (ver. 22) would be the correct one, and this view should be at once adopted for this further reason, that the omission of the clause may easily be explained from the parallel words of the following verse, but the addition less easily. Whether, however, the words are found here or in Matthew in their original connexion, or whether the Saviour, as in the case of such a declaration may well be conceived, more than once gave utterance to them, it is in this case hard to decide.

§ 4. PARABLE OF THE TENDER-HEARTED SAMARITAN.

(Luke x. 25–37.)

A lawyer comes up to Jesus on the road, in order to hold conversation with the celebrated prophet. His purpose does not seem to have been strictly bad ; it was rather curiosity which led him to try how Jesus would express himself. The Saviour's way of dealing with him, does not permit us to suppose that he was a Sadducee who put the question, one who himself believed in no eternal life, and who was now only asking in irony after the way to Utopia.

He seems rather to have held the views common among the Pharisees, and only to have been desirous of discovering what more or
better knowledge than his own, Jesus possessed. The ἐκπειράζειν,
trying, therefore, here has no connexion with the laying of snares for
Christ, to make him politically suspected—an attempt which,
according to the gospel history, the Pharisees frequently permitted
themselves to make (compare Matth. xxii. 15, seq). This narrative
rather is parallel to Matth. xxii. 35, seq. An enquiry respecting
eternal life was not suited to a design that was simply wicked.
With admirable wisdom does our Lord on the present occasion treat
this blind lawyer. Entrammelled in his Rabbinical narrowness and
formalism, he asks some outward rule by which to set bounds to
the duties of love, and secure exemption from its universal exercise. Instead of giving him such a wished-for rule, the Saviour
relates a narrative, in which nothing whatever is said of the
object of love—the immediate object of the lawyer's question
—but of those who exercise it. Priest and Levite, members of
the same order with the enquirer, and persons on whom the observance of the law was especially incumbent, pass heartlessly by,
reckoning that the sufferer might probably be no neighbour. The
Samaritan, whom they deemed a heretic, exercised the law of love.*
In every point from which it can be viewed, reproving, rebuking,
demanding repentance, this parable must have arrested the ques-
tioner. He must have felt that not merely was his question false,
but the whole state of mind from which it could have proceeded.
To the man who was asking after a law for the exercise of love, it
must have become obvious that he himself neither possessed nor
knew it, inasmuch as its single law is this, that it is a law to itself.
Love loves, and asks not when, how, where; it is the primordial, innermost life, which ignores the whole world of reflections and prudential rules, and blesses even its enemy. Into this world of pure love
which the heart of Jesus contained (for whosoever exercises it has it
only through him), he opens a glimpse for the benefit of the lawyer
hardened in his legal subtleties, and by this means alone could he
be helped out of his heartless state. Thus Jesus exercised towards
even him that very love, of which he was teaching him the knowledge ; he blessed the man who was trying him.

Ver. 25–27.—Νομικός and νομοδιδάσκαλος, were terms applied to
that tribe of scribes (γραμματεῖς = סוֹפְרִים) who occupied themselves
with the (casuistical) interpretation of the law. Luke employs for
the most part the term νομικός as more intelligible to his readers
(Luke vii. 30 ; xi. 45, 46, 52 ; xiv. 3), while the Hebraizing Mat-

---

* According to the view which refers this Gospel especially to the heathen, this putting forward of one not a Jew as the model of pure love, possessed something peculiarly
attractive.

thew uses γραμματεῖς = סוֹפְרִים. It is the more generic term, while Φαρισαῖοι denotes a particular party among the νομικοί. A Sadducee might also be a νομικός. (Compare on Matth. xxii. 35.) The question as to eternal life, being the final object of all theological enquiry, is put forward by the lawyer, under the conviction that, in replying to it, Jesus must bring out whatever was peculiar in his opinions. (The formula κληρονομεῖν ζωὴν αἰώνιον, or βασιλείαν τοῦ θεοῦ [1 Cor. vi. 9, 10; xv. 50] has without doubt, its foundation in the comparison of the land of Canaan as a sensible type of eternity, and of rest in it, with eternal life. The expression κληρονομεῖν τὴν γῆν at Matth. v. 5, refers to this.) The Saviour, however, refers him to the old well-known word of God, saying, as it were, what thou askest has lain from of old expressed in the revealed word ; take it thence for yourself. The lawyer now brings forward most correctly the passages of Deut. vi. 5, in connexion with Numb. xix. 18 (which passages are in a similar way conjoined by another law-yer at Mark xii. 33), hence it only remained for him to translate into living act the contents of these deep words, which, rightly understood, involve the whole New Testament. That this had not as yet been done by him, the course of the conversation shews. Further, a remarkable feature in the citations of this passage, both here and elsewhere in the Gospels, is their deviation alike from the Hebrew text and from the LXX. In Hebrew there stand the ex-pressions לֵבָב, נֶפֶשׁ, מְאֹד. The LXX. translate these, διάνοια, ψυχή, δύναμις. In the quotations of the evangelists, however, the words run thus :

Luke x. 27.　　καρδία, ψυχή, ἰσχύς, διάνοια.
Mark xii. 30.　　καρδία, ψυχή, διάνοια, ἰσχύς.
Mark xii. 33.　　καρδία, σύνεσις, ψυχή, ἰσχύς,
Matth. xxii. 37.　καρδία, ψυχή, διάνοια.

This constant variation of the Gospel quotations from the LXX. in the rendering of לֵבָב and מְאֹד leads almost to the conjecture that the evangelists either followed another reading, or that this version of it had been taken by one of them from another. For, it is inconceivable that this deviation should have taken the same form in the three evangelists, if they had written independently of each other. To me it seems most probable, that in this instance the common agreement originated with Luke, and passed over from him to Mark and the Greek Matthew. (As to the meaning of the synonyms in the passage, compare my Program on Trichotomy in the Opusc. Theol. p. 143, seq., and on Matth. xxii. 37.) The exalted idea, however, of loving God with all our powers, and loving him also *wholly* with them all, embraces at once the whole, both of religion and morality.* For, the addition "and thy neighbour as thyself," is at bottom only an unfolding of the contents of the first commandment, as Matth. xxii. 37, seq., shews. In love to God, which, on the part of the creature, can only take the form of receptive love, there lies the love of his will, and consequently the implied love of one's neighbour. To draw, however, from the command thus to love God, the inference, that man must therefore be able to do it in his own strength, would be wholly out of place. Since only that which is Divine knoweth God (compare on Matth. xi. 27), so only that which is Divine can love God ; and when God commands us therefore to love God, it involves for the creature an injunction to receive the Spirit of God, in whom alone he can be loved. This Spirit, however, the New Testament imparts, and consequently this command of the Old Testament (as indeed the whole law) for its fulfilment, presupposes the Gospel. This same Spirit, who teaches us to love God, wholly and entirely with all our faculties, alone enables us also rightly to love our neighbour. As pure love to God loves God more than it does self apart from God, so it also loves God more than our neighbour apart from God ; but self and our brother being looked at as in God, and God in them, true self-love and genuine brotherly love are then at one with the love of God. Hence does the Lord say that the *second* commandment is like unto the *first* (Matth. xxii. 39), for this reason, that it is *the same thing* with it. Love to one's neighbour, if it be genuine love, that is, if the creature be loved not merely as a creature (for in that lies the distinctive character of natural love), is nothing less than love to God. This is also shewn by the following parable.

Ver. 28, 29.—The answer of the lawyer was in itself satisfactory to the Saviour, but he directly urged him to follow out the command into action, remarking that life lay in the practical fulfilling of it. But it was precisely this that brought to light his inward perverseness ; his knowledge wanted the will which was inclined to carry it out into life, and this want of moral power again obscured his discernment. He asks, feeling himself struck—who then was his neighbour ? a question which in his own mind he would have been able himself to answer, if he had sought to exercise perfect love. (Δικαιόω has no peculiar meaning here ; it merely refers, through the word ἑαυτόν, to the person wishing to justify himself.) Because of his want of experience, Jesus transfers him into the midst of the realities of life, and makes him behold love actually loving. (The term ὑπολαμβάνειν = ἀποκρίνεσθαι, excipere, is in the New Testament found only here. It occurs frequently in the LXX.; Job ii. 4 ; iv. 1.)

* As to this and the following thoughts, compare the fuller discussion on the passage Matth. xxii. 37, seq.

Ver. 30–33.—The traveller whom the robbers assaulted is perhaps to be conceived of as a Jew ; for in that case it would on the one hand be more striking that the priest and Levite refused him their help, and on the other hand that the Samaritan gave him assistance when he might so easily have availed himself of a sophistical excuse. (᾿Αντιπαρέρχεσθαι is not different from παρέρχεσθαι. It is found in the New Testament only here. Συγκυρία also occurs only here in the New Testament. It denotes an accident. Among profane writers also this form of the word rarely occurs ; συγκύρησις is more usual.)

Ver. 34, 35.—Most carefully is the compassionate treatment which the despised Samaritan bestows on the suffering stranger, delineated. From the impulse of love he does even more than was incumbent. (Wine and oil, well-known means of cure in the East. The πανδοχεῖον is the Caravanserai of the nearest place, that at Jericho, perhaps, in the neighbourhood of which Jesus might then be staying.) It is a fine trait, that he cares also for the subsequent wants of the sick man, and promises to repay the outlay.

Ver. 36, 37.—The enquiry had now reversed its character. The lawyer asked, ver. 29, who was the neighbour to whom support should be given. Jesus enquires who was the neighbour—was it the man who exercised or who refused to exercise love ? Even here, however, lay the great doctrine, that love is not determined by its object, but has inherently in itself its own standard. Pure love loves even an enemy, as here the Samaritan does the sufferer who is a stranger, and one who from difference of creed might have appeared hostile. The acknowledgment, therefore, that true love dwelt in him, involved an answer to the question, and thus it only remained to impress upon his mind the admonition ποίει ὁμοίως, do likewise. It was an obvious suggestion to trace in the compassionate conduct of the Samaritan a figurative representation of the Saviour's work. The wounds of the sick (Is. i. 6), which they who sat on Moses' seat left undressed, he whom they reviled as a Samaritan (John viii. 48) bound up with oil and wine.

§ 5. MARY AND MARTHA.

(Luke x. 38–42.)

The following little narrative presents to us Jesus in Bethany, in the neighbourhood of Jerusalem (John xi. 1). That Martha and Mary are to be sought for nowhere else than in Bethany, is certain from Gospel history ; in this passage Martha is described as possessing a house of her own in the village. Whether she was a widow, or lived unmarried with her sister and Lazarus cannot be determined. [Her sister Mary appears from John xii. 1, comp. with Matth. xxvi. 6; Mark xiv. 3, to have been married to Simon, and from John xii. 2—where Lazarus is among the invited guests—to have had a separate household.] The evangelists are remarkably sparing in their historic notices of the persons mentioned by them. They confine themselves to what is barely necessary, and devote themselves rather to the delineation of their spiritual life. Hence the account of the two sisters here given, marks them, though in few touches, so strikingly and clearly, that they are often chosen as exemplars of the peculiarities of two distinct religious tendencies. We find in Martha the type of a life busily devoted to externals; in Mary, the type of quiet devotion to religion as the one thing needful. To a certain extent both elements should be combined in each believer, but it is not to be overlooked that there are different vocations, and many are better fitted for busy outward labour than a life of contemplation, although the most active must in the depths of his soul be devoted to the Lord, and the man of contemplation must consecrate his energies to the advancement of God's kingdom. Hence, even the Saviour's rebuke to Martha (ver. 41) is no absolute censure, and is rather occasioned by her own antecedent remark (which shews that she had mistaken her own position as well as Mary's) than called forth by her conduct itself. Martha serves, as it were, only as a foil to the figure of Mary, in whom appears a mind wholly and undividedly given up to Divine influence. She is another example of the complete fulfilment of the command " Thou shalt love the Lord thy God with all thy heart," (x. 27). The Samaritan practised it actively, Mary passively.

Ver. 38–40.—Probably Jesus had enjoyed opportunities of becoming acquainted with the family at Bethany in his former yearly journeys to the festivals. Mary seats herself confidingly at his feet to listen to the words of her Lord; Martha busies herself to provide the best possible outward entertainment for the beloved guest. (We are to view the sitting at the feet (παρακαθίζειν παρὰ τοὺς πόδας) as denoting merely Mary's staying beside Jesus, and certainly in an attitude fitted to catch his instructive and life-awakening words.) Martha was zealous meanwhile about externals, which certainly were necessary in part, but with self-gratification she gave herself up entirely to them. Περισπᾶσθαι, distrahi, in the New Testament occurs only here, in the Old Testament frequently; also the substantive περισπασμός = יִנְיָן, Eccles. i. 13; ii. 23, 26. (Διακονία, service, includes here all domestic services in which Martha lost herself with needless bustle.) From this satisfaction in her own occupations arose the reproving speech directed against her sister; perhaps conscience was aroused, and testified that Mary had more of Jesus than she. But as her craving for heavenly enjoyments was not sufficiently strong and pure, she suffered herself to be fettered by external activities, which in reality were more agreeable to her, and out of this state of mind arose her speech. Jealous of Mary, she wished her to be as she herself was. (The verb συνανπλαμβάνεσθαι, to *support*, to *help*, occurs again only at Rom. viii. 26.)

Ver. 41, 42.—The address of Jesus to Martha refers less to household activity in itself (for that must be cared for) than to the •state of mind in which she went about it, and the comparison she instituted in this respect between herself and Mary. He rebukes first the μεριμνᾶν, *being careful*, and τυρβάζειν, *being troubled* (the word occurs only here in the New Testament, it corresponds to the Latin *turbare*), that is, her restless spirit of action, as moved by the impulses of creature-affection ; and he next contrasted the *many things* with the *one thing*, along with the intimation that for the sake of the former she was losing the latter, while yet this latter, not the former (compare on Matth. iii. 14, 15), was of essential necessity* (χρεία). It is one of the peculiarities of the Saviour's discourses, that they often in few words say all that is necessary to bring everlasting truth, in some special view of it, home to all times and circumstances. Standing at the very heart and centre of the spiritual world, he without violence entwined the minutest and least important circumstances of the present with the loftiest eternal verities. In the efforts of the two sisters the Lord brings the nothingness of all love and care for the creature, into close comparison with care for what is everlasting. The one thing must so be laid hold of by the soul, that no striving after anything else may similarly rouse it ; and having begun with one thing it will be able to deal not merely with many things, but with all things else—not in such a way, however, that these shall have the ascendancy and take captive the mind's life, but that it shall itself bear sway and bring every act into harmony with the highest end of life. This pure and holy effort after the one and the Eternal portion, had Mary chosen. The expressions μέρις, *part*, *allotment*, and ἐξελέξατο, *chose*, mutually determine each other's meaning. The former points to the election of grace, the latter to man's free determination to embrace it. By the combination of the two (2 Pet. i. 10) spiritual life is rendered complete, inasmuch as the individual thus lays hold of the gift as his own, and in doing so places it beyond the reach of

* The clause ἑνὸς δέ ἐστι χρεία is wanting in Cod. D. Other MSS. read ὀλίγων or ὀλίγων ἢ ἑνός. On these readings J. D. Michaelis founds his translation—one dish is enough for us. Certainly the reading ὀλίγων seems to be grounded on some such idea. The common text, however, is sufficiently established by critical authorities, and the reference of the passage to a dish of food is altogether excluded, as well by the δέ as also by the subsequent expression ἀγαθὴ μέρις.

loss. Without the free decision of his will to embrace it, a man may lose his calling (Matth. xxv. 29). For Martha, the thought thus expressed includes also this warning, to care for the one thing first, and in that way to make her calling (which certainly was a different one from that of Mary) equally firm and imperishable.

§ 6. DIRECTIONS RESPECTING PRAYER.

(Luke xi. 1–13.)

The indefinite ἐν τόπῳ τινί, *in a certain place*, shews [that Luke is far from having in view a narrative of a journey, and with this a series of events regularly succeeding each other in time and place] ; he may, therefore, have been often guided in his arrangement more by the connexion of the matter than by local association.

Ver. 1–4.—As to the detailed exposition of the Lord's prayer compare Matth. vi. 9–13. It only remains for us to speak here of the particular form it bears in the text of Luke, for it is not to be doubted that the text in this Gospel has been interpolated from the more lengthened recension of Matthew. First, in the address, the words ἡμῶν ὁ ἐν τοῖς οὐρανοῖς are undoubtedly genuine in Matthew, but like the entire petition γενηθήτω τὸ θέλημά σου κ. τ. λ., which is the firmly established reading of Matthew, they are in Luke of questionable authority. The same thing applies also to the concluding words ἀλλὰ ῥῦσαι ἡμᾶς κ. τ. λ. It is true that by these omissions the prayer is in no respect rendered specifically different, for the γενηθήτω κ. τ. λ. is merely a further carrying out of the ἐλθέτω σου ἡ βασιλεία, in the same way that the ἀλλὰ ῥῦσαι κ. τ. λ. contains a filling up of the antecedent idea μὴ εἰσενέγκῃς ἡμᾶς εἰς πειρασμόν. But the beautiful harmony which the prayer exhibits as given by Matthew is wanting in the shorter recension of Luke, for the first half of it (compare on Matth. vi. 9), comprising only two clauses, is disproportionately curtailed. The recension of Matthew should therefore be considered as the original form of the prayer, for what is peculiar to him cannot possibly be a mere amplification originating in later traditions ; that of Luke on the other hand as an abbreviated form, inasmuch as he deals in a similar way with several of those passages which Matthew has included in the Sermon on the Mount. (Compare the beginning of the Sermon on the Mount.)

Ver. 5–8.—To the prayer thus given, there are fittingly subjoined admonitions as to the use of it. Especially is persevering earnestness of supplication urgently enjoined. In the first verses this is done in the form of a parable, in the last (9–13) by figurative expressions. The latter verses have already been explained at Matth. vii. 7, seq. ; the parable of the benighted traveller who by continued entreaty prevails with his neighbour and causes him to fulfil his desire, is peculiar to Luke. It has no difficulties beyond the single circumstance, that as appears from this comparison, the *impure* motives (the ἀναίδεια) as well of the suppliant as of him who suffered himself to be persuaded, form the point of comparison for illustrating the most exalted relations. (Of the same nature is Luke xviii. 1, seq., which passage also treats of prayer, and in it God is compared to an unjust judge.) But first as respects the importunity (ἀναίδεια) of the suppliant, it is not to be overlooked that he is here pleading not for himself but for his guest ; his pressing importunate petitions acquire thus a nobler motive ; he entreats bread that he may not be compelled to violate the holy rites of hospitality. From the man who yields to the prayer, we cannot indeed dissociate an unworthy motive ; the nobler one of love is expressly excluded, and he grants what is asked, only that he may get rid of the suppliant—and yet this is applied to God. Here, however, we must have recourse to that usage in regard to parables (compare on Matth. ix. 16), which makes the comparison express not merely the positive objective truth, but modifies it to meet the subjective position of him for whose understanding and instruction it is designed. Here the Saviour places himself on the level of the man who knows from experience that God often delays long the fulfilment of prayer, delineating him directly as unrighteous (see on Luke xviii. 1), in doing which he merely sets forth fully the impression as felt in such circumstances by a petitioner weak in the faith, and he adds the requisite exhortations according to this impression. Thus do the parables constantly appear as having proceeded from the liveliest conception of man's circumstances, and a truthful expression of spiritual relations adapting themselves immediately to our earthly condition. How far the interpretation of individual traits in the parable (for example here the midnight as denoting the time of deepest internal darkness and need) should be carried, must certainly remain somewhat uncertain. In the parables of Jesus, however, which proceed upon powers of conception so rich, it should on the whole be maintained as a rule that no single trait is lightly to be overlooked, unless in adhering to it, we do obvious violence to the similitude as a whole.